LOCAL NETWORK EQUIPMENT

Harvey A. Freeman / Kenneth J. Thurber

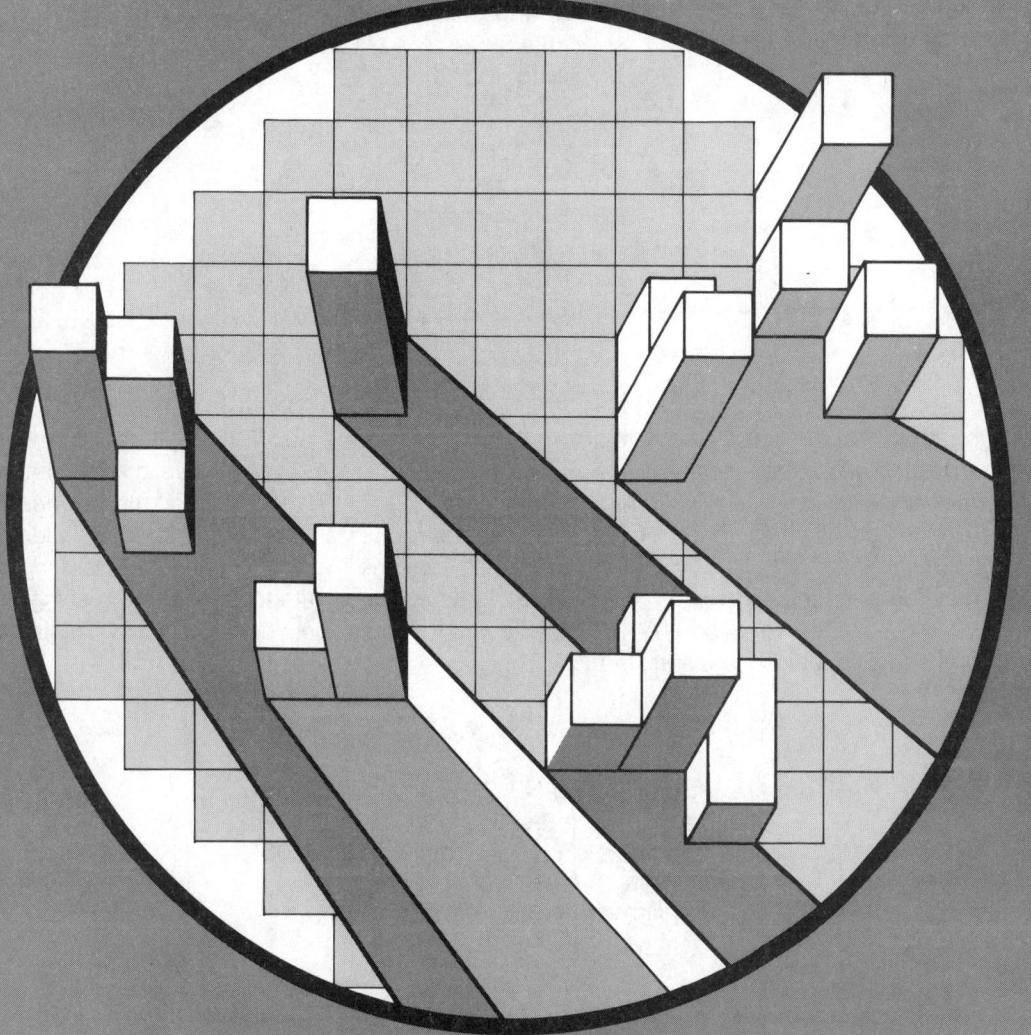

IEEE CATALOG NUMBER EHO228-7
LIBRARY OF CONGRESS NUMBER 85-60466
IEEE COMPUTER SOCIETY ORDER NUMBER 605
ISBN 0-8186-0605-3

 IEEE COMPUTER SOCIETY COMPUTER SOCIETY PRESS   THE INSTITUTE OF ELECTRICAL AND ELECTRONICS ENGINEERS, INC.

Published by IEEE Computer Society Press
1109 Spring Street
Suite 300
Silver Spring, MD 20910

IEEE Catalog Number EHO228-7
Library of Congress Number 85-60466
IEEE Computer Society Order Number 605
ISBN 0-8186-0605-3 (Paper)
ISBN 0-8186-4605-5 (Microfiche)

Order from: IEEE Computer Society   IEEE Service Center
             Post Office Box 80452   445 Hoes Lane
             Worldway Postal Center   Piscataway, NJ 08854
             Los Angeles, CA 90080

THE INSTITUTE OF ELECTRICAL AND ELECTRONICS ENGINEERS, INC.

Acknowledgment

We wish to acknowledge the help of Margaret Brown, C.G. Stockton, and Chuan-lin Wu of the Computer Society, and Michael Petry of Architecture Technology and Washington University, St. Louis. Without their help, this tutorial would not exist.

Preface

Since our first tutorial text on local networks was published in the summer of 1980, the local network field has grown from a handful of commercially available networks to more than 200 today. The installed base of local networks has grown at least an order of magnitude in value to an estimated $500 million today. By the end of the decade, another order of magnitude growth is expected.

The growth and acceptance of local networks is due in large part to manufacturers building and installing systems that truly work, and that efficiently and effectively support such tasks as word processing, electronic mail, message switching, distributed processing, voice and data integration, and the like. Although much has now been written on the theory behind local networks, until now a large part of the practical side has been overlooked.

This tutorial is offered as a means of learning more about the products and systems that are being used today or will be used in the near future. The articles describe the various companies' experiences in building their products, in supporting the many applications for local networks, and in dealing with the theoretical issues of local networks in practical terms.

In 1980, there were many people who did not quite believe in the concept of local networks. With the recent entry of AT&T into this field with a number of offerings, and with IBM's local network cabling scheme for its forthcoming token ring local network, there are few people left today who are not aware of the benefits of local networks and the fact that local networks are a viable concept that will soon encompass everything from the home to the office to the factory. This book includes articles describing both of these organizations' local network thrusts.

Articles by authors from the various companies are interspersed with descriptions of certain products that we prepared ourselves. In the hectic rush to the marketplace, not every company takes the time for or encourages the publication of articles about its productions. In those cases where the product was felt to be significant for one reason or another, we have taken the time to describe it. Our choice for inclusion was based on the number of systems sold, the features, the ability to survive the onslaught of AT&T and IBM, and the like.

Finally, what will exist in the next three to five years will be based on the current activities of the various standards organizations. Chip manufacturers are looking to these groups for direction, just as the network manufacturers look to the chip people for components with which to implement their ideas. We have included a brief overview of these standards activities to afford the reader an opportunity to project what the local network equipment will look like in the future. We also have included articles on local network chips to show what the local networks will look like in the near term.

Our first tutorial book *Local Computer Networks* was considered a significant step in the continued exploration and development of local computer networks. We feel that this book will be significant in consolidating the gains in this area and showing the way to practical future systems.

Inasmuch as this book emphasizes the practical, i.e., commercial local network products, it assumes that the reader has some knowledge of the theory, terms, and issues involved. If this is not the case, the reader should refer to *Local Network Technology,* a tutorial by William Stallings that was published by the IEEE Computer Society Press in December 1983. For more information on the commercial products, especially those that are not mentioned in this text, the reader should consult the *LOCALNetter Designer's Handbook* published annually and sold by Architecture Technology Corporation, Minneapolis, Minnesota.

Harvey A. Freeman
Kenneth J. Thurber
January 1985

Table of Contents

Section 1: Introduction

The purpose of this tutorial is to present a look at the area of local computer networks from the viewpoint of the people who make the products that are available on the market today. Since more than 300 commercially available local area networks have been identified (as of the time of this publication), we have been forced to present only a limited number of them in this book. Those included are products which we feel, based upon our experience as researchers, designers, consultants, and publishers in the field, have had, or will have, the greatest impact on the field.

As the field matures, some companies will prosper while others will be bought or even shut down. In order to offer the reader of this tutorial as complete a guide as possible to the vendors in this field, we have included, as an Appendix, a listing of all of the local network vendors that we have identified as of January 1985.

The book is organized into six sections. The first section is a general introduction to local area networks. This is followed by four sections which present the networks that are commercially available today. In most cases, these articles are written by the people who designed the products. For those products for which there were no suitable articles available, we included a short summary of the product. The final section presents a sampling of the important controller chips around which local networks are being designed.

The first section gives a general introduction to the field of Local Area Networks, discussing what they are, what they are becoming, and how they are put to use. The first article is a basic survey of LAN technology. It presents some fundamental concepts needed to understand LANs and it discusses a few of the critical issues concerning networks that have yet to be resolved. In particular, the characteristics of bus and ring topologies are reviewed, and the performance of two media-access control techniques, CSMA/CD and token passing, are compared.

The second article deals with the progress that is being made in the standardization of local networks. It describes the International Standards Organization's Open System Interconnect Reference Model (ISO OSI/RM) and the various "official" and *de facto* organizations contributing to the standardization of local networks. In particular, the standard proposed by IEEE 802 is unusual because it is not a single standard, but rather several different sets of standards, thereby allowing individual manufacturers to choose which set to follow. This article concludes with the current (as of January 1985) status of these groups' efforts.

The final article in this section addresses many of the system design issues in local networks. The specifics of network components, both hardware and software, are discussed, and the general trends of the industry today are summarized.

EHO228-7/85/0000/0001$01.00 © 1985 IEEE

1

Local-Area Communication Networks—An Overview *

K. Kümmerle
M. Reiser
IBM Zurich Research Laboratory

ABSTRACT   Local-area communication networks represent a new field of activity. In this paper we first describe three scenarios for the use of these networks, and then discuss various technical approaches. Particular emphasis is put on bus and ring systems with various media-access control mechanisms. Specifically, we compare the delay-throughput characteristic of two access methods, carrier-sense multiple access with collision detection and token passing, and discuss some significant differences of bus and ring systems concerning wiring, media, transmission, and reliability.

1. Introduction

In the sixties and early seventies, major activities in networking were focused on private and public data networks using either circuit and packet-switching technology or integrating both switching methods into a single network. In this time frame, manufacturers of main frames defined and implemented network architectures, e.g., [1,2,3,4,5,6], the International Organization for Standardization (ISO) started work on the reference model of the Open-System Interconnect (OSI) Architecture [7], and the X-series of interfaces [8] was recommended by the International Telegraph and Telephone Consultative Committee (CCITT).

Local-area communication networks represent a comparatively new field of activity which can be viewed as an extension to data networks for making high-speed packet-switching services available to the in-house domain. Currently, much research and development work is being pursued in this field, both at universities and in industry. The term local refers to communication on the users premises, i.e., within a building or among a cluster of buildings.

A typical example of a system widely used today for local data communication between hosts and display terminals is depicted in Figure 1. Sets of terminals are attached to control units which are tightly coupled to a processor via input/output (I/O) channels. The necessary terminal control functions are provided in the control unit and shared among a set of terminals. This leads to low attachment costs.

Today, we are witnessing an explosive growth of terminals. Many establishments forecast a density approaching one per workplace by the end of the decade. Also, multisystem data processing (DP) centers will proliferate, even in medium-sized or small establishments. In this environment, the system structure of Figure 1 becomes a serious impediment to management and growth of the system because:

1. Control units must be physically close to the host computers (within 200 feet typically). Making room available in the specially secured and conditioned DP center may be costly.

2. The star topology requires an individual coaxial cable to be strung to each terminal.

---

*Part of this paper, including figures 1-13 and 16, was presented at the NTG/GI Fachtagung, Ulm, 1982, and published in the NTG-Fachberichte Band 80: Struktur und Betrieb von Rechensystemen, 1982, © Copyright 1982 by VDE-VERLAG GmbH, Berlin 12.

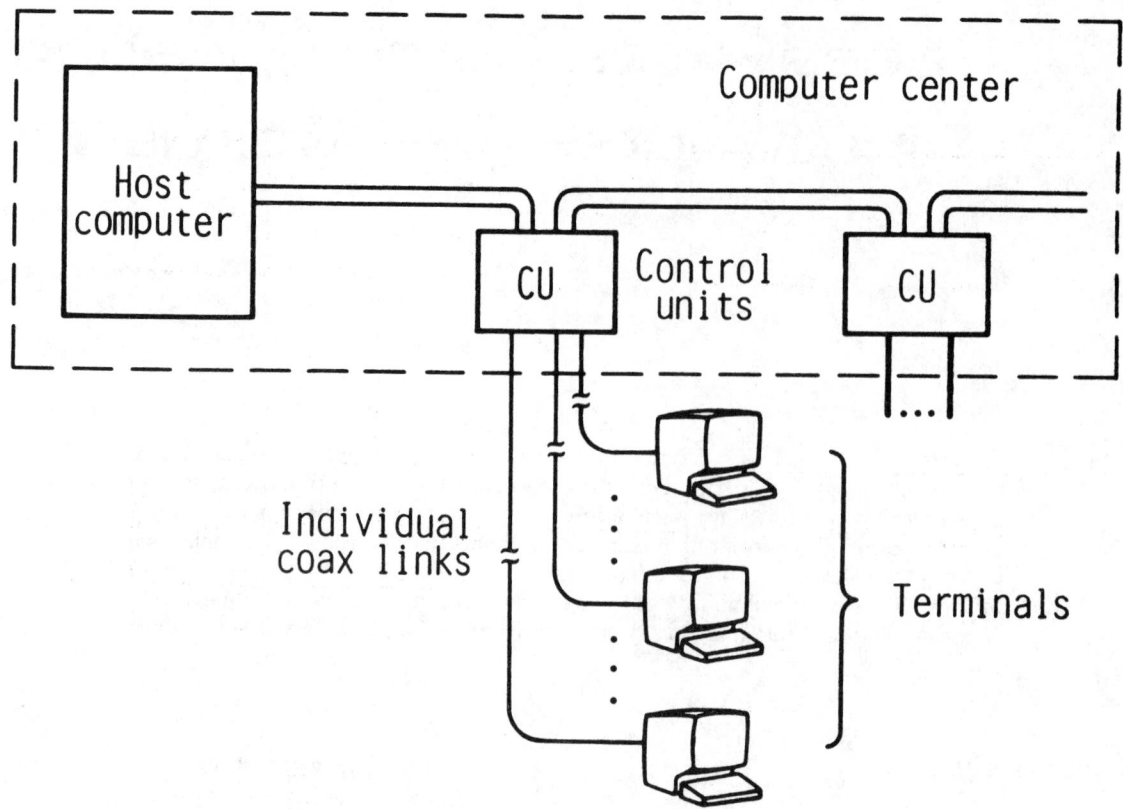

Figure 1. Star System for Local Data Communication.
© Copyright 1982 by VDE-VERLAG GmbH, Berlin 12.

This is expensive in terms of labor, and may lead to serious crowding of cable ducts in some buildings.

3. Terminals are bound to one data host. Thus, switching the terminal among hosts providing different services requires physical attachment to more than one control unit. Consequently, more than one wire is required per terminal, a fact which aggravates Problems 1 and 2 above.

In contrast to the local communication system of Figure 1 (called a local cluster), tele-processing (TP) networks [1,2,3,4,5,6] do allow remote placement of terminal controllers, called *cluster controllers*, sharing of links and flexible switching among applications residing in different data hosts. However, TP networks do not provide the same local-cluster bandwidth; hence, the response times seen by a remotely attached terminal may not be adequate. Figure 2 portrays the structure of a *TP network*. *Communication controllers*, which attach to data hosts, provide a meshed network and switch-addressed data frames (packet or message switching).

Long-haul or TP networks can be characterized by the following technical facts which, as we shall see later, give them different characteristics compared to local-area networks. First, communication lines represent an expensive commodity, and therefore we have the design objective to optimize utilization of the transmission capacity. Second, the data rate of TP lines is in the range of 2400 bits per second (bps) to 56 thousand bps (Kbps). This means that the speed of the processors in the communication and cluster controllers is high compared to the rate with which data frames arrive over the transmission lines. Thus, processors in network switching nodes have time to perform functions which ensure error-free transmission and message integrity. These functions are performed in each switching node in the path between end points, i.e., hop-by-hop.

The entire DP system, irrespective of whether we have a network topology according to Figures 1 or 2, has a structure as shown in Figure 3. Communication between terminal and host computer is provided by the front-end network, whereas communication between

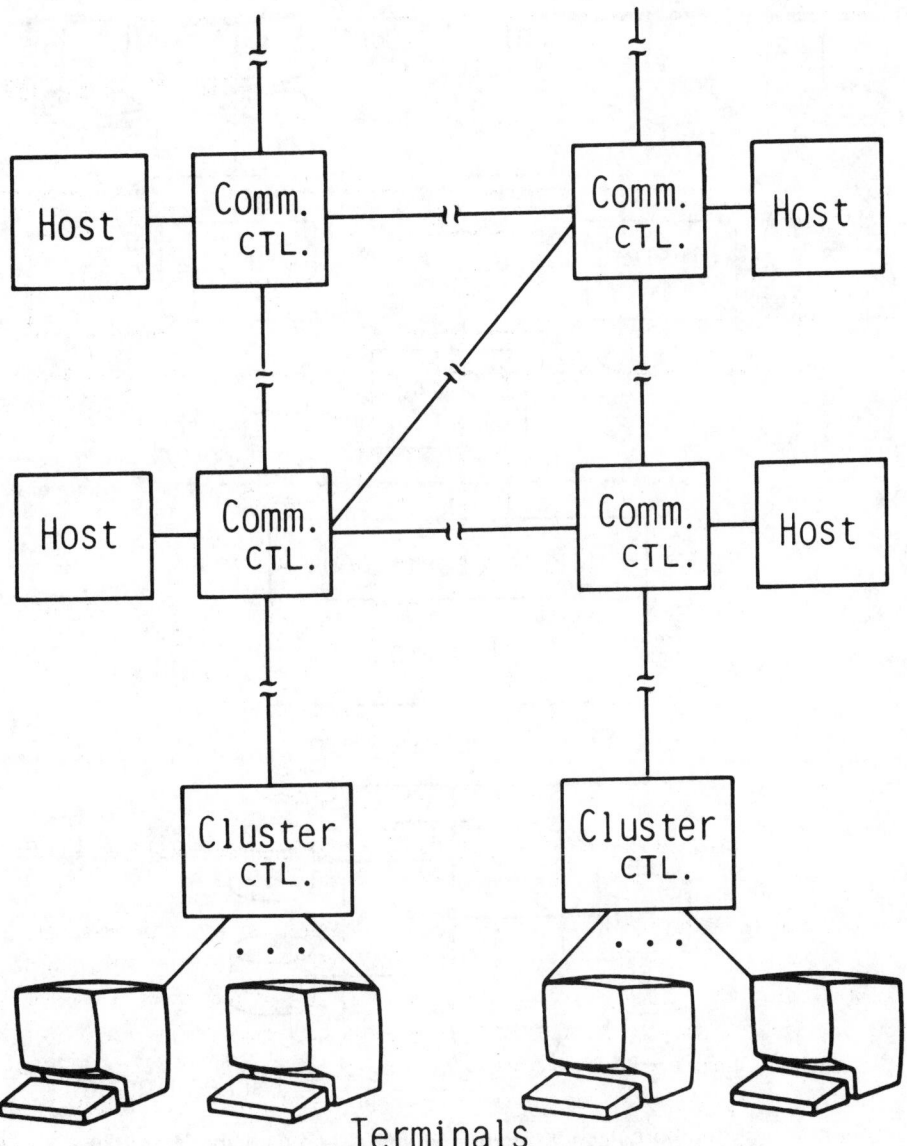

Figure 2. Meshed Teleprocessing Network.
© Copyright 1982 by VDE-VERLAG GmbH, Berlin 12.

the host computer and its associated mass storage devices takes place through the back-end network which in current installations degenerates to an I/O channel.

Unlike in the TP environment, transmission lines in the local domain do not represent an expensive commodity, and data rates in the range of 1–10 million bps (Mbps) are available at low costs. The implication is that processors are no longer fast compared to rates with which data frames arrive over transmission lines. The consequence is that functions executed *hop-by-hop* in teleprocessing networks should be moved to the end points and executed *end-to-end*.

The availability of low-cost Large Scale Integration/Very Large Scale Integration (LSI/VLSI) components is another driving force leading to system designs that will differ from Figure 1, because:

1. Network adapters can be provided at reasonably low cost, i.e., the cost advantage of using shared-logic controllers diminishes.
2. Workstations/personal computers will have substantial amounts of processing capacity as a result of powerful microprocessors. However, it is unreasonable to expect the availability of sufficient mass storage, files, or high-quality and powerful printers, e.g.,

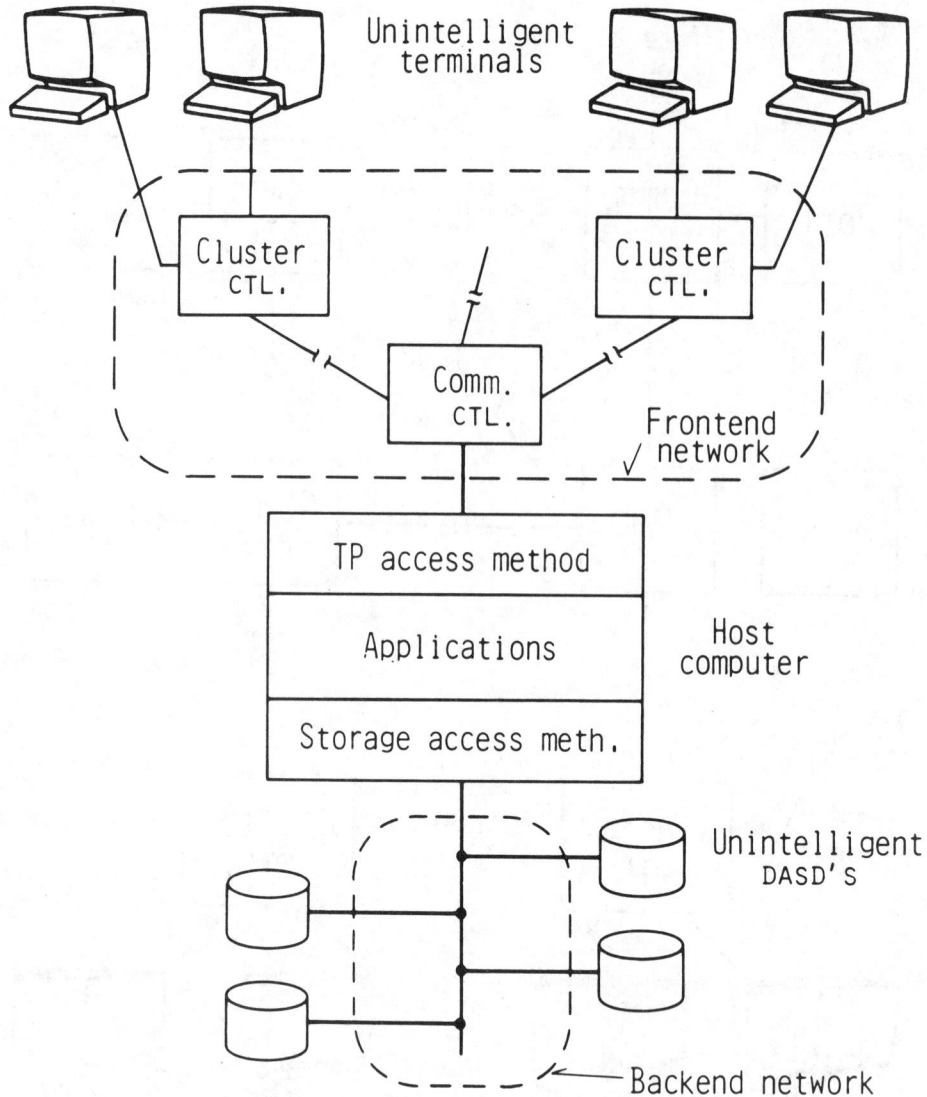

Figure 3. Current System Structure: Frontend and Backend Networks.
© Copyright 1982 by VDE-VERLAG GmbH, Berlin 12.

laser printers, for each workstation for cost reasons. In the case of cost-effective hard disks which could be afforded for each workstation, one might like to have them geographically separated from the workstation since they are noisy.

Under the term *local-area networks*, we understand high-speed shared-media transmission systems that address the problems outlined above. In section 2, three scenarios will be discussed of how local-area networks can be used. Section 3 shows various possibilities of technical approaches. It also contains a description of several access methods for systems with either bus or ring topology. Finally, in section 4, we provide some arguments for a system comparison.

2. Local-Area Network-Usage Scenarios

The intent of this section is to illustrate how local-area networks are already being used or might be used in the future. In the subsequent considerations, we deliberately do not address the question of whether these scenarios physically use the same or separate networks. It should be noted, however, that all scenarios represent a departure from the systems outlined in the previous section.

2.1 Terminal-to-Host Communication: Frontend Network. A first possibility to use a local-area network is for terminal-to-host communication. In this case, depicted in Figure 4, the most important function provided by the network is allowing terminals to select a host

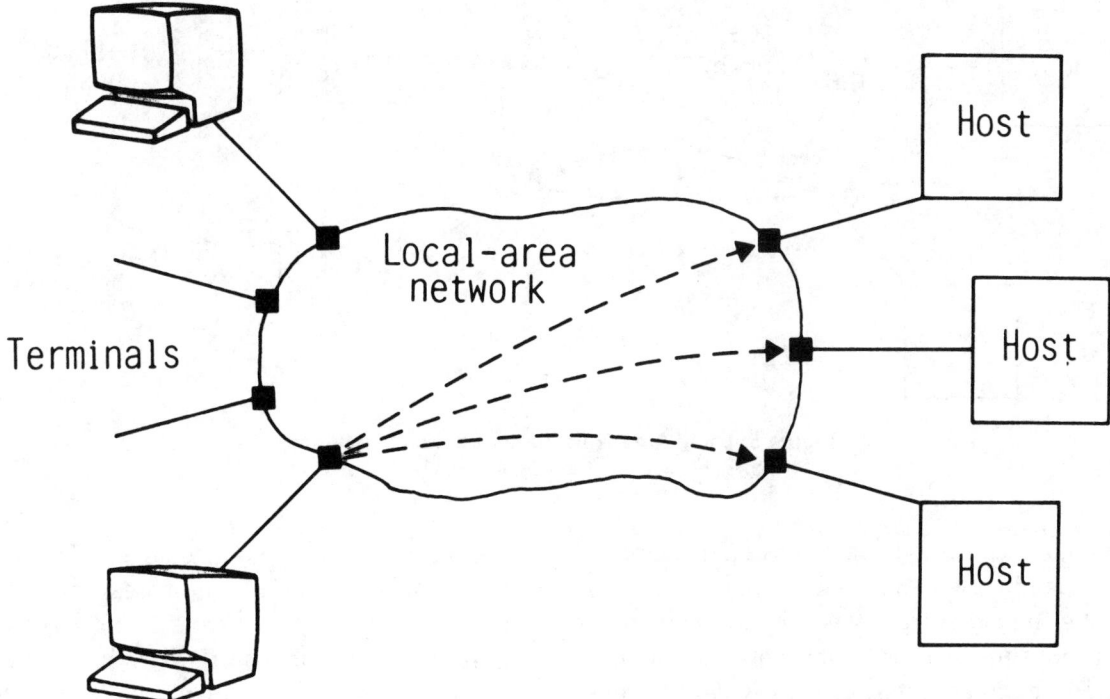

**Figure 4. Local-Area Network for Terminal-to-Host Communication:
Frontend Network.**

machine, i.e., a capability generally not available in systems according to Figure 1. Furthermore, the local network solves the problems of crowded cable ducts by providing shared transmission resources, and of congesting the DP machine room with cluster controllers, by allowing the sharing of them through the network. It should be pointed out that in this scenario, emphasis is on system flexibility rather than on exploitation of the high-speed communication facility. In this sense, the scenario of Figure 4 can also be viewed as the migration of current equipment and applications to a new network whose full functions can only be exploited by new equipment and new applications.

There is a problem that needs careful consideration: Should a terminal be attached directly to the network through a control unit which it shares with other terminals? Apart from cost considerations, the answer will also be determined by whether one has the concept of a general wall plug in mind associated with the capability to readily move stations from office to office, i.e., to dynamically change the configuration during operation of the system.

2.2 Backend Network. Today, *direct-access storage devices* (DASD) are slaved to their processor (Figure 3), and are tightly coupled to the I/O channels. Given a local-area network of adequate bandwith, processors can be connected dynamically through serial I/O channels with their DASD's through the network as shown in Figure 5. This implies some intelligence at the DASD for network-access purposes and for the execution of protection mechanisms. Besides the communication between processors and DASD's, a backend network can also carry channel-to-channel traffic. The systems described in [9,10] are examples of local-area networks supporting the latter.

2.3 Client-Server Network. The two preceding scenarios are generalizations of today's system structures. The *client-server network* [11] shown in Figure 6 represents the scenario currently being discussed most frequently, particularly in the context of office communication. The stations attached to the network are assumed to be intelligent workstations, i.e., driven by suitably powerful microprocessors. Compared with the configuration described

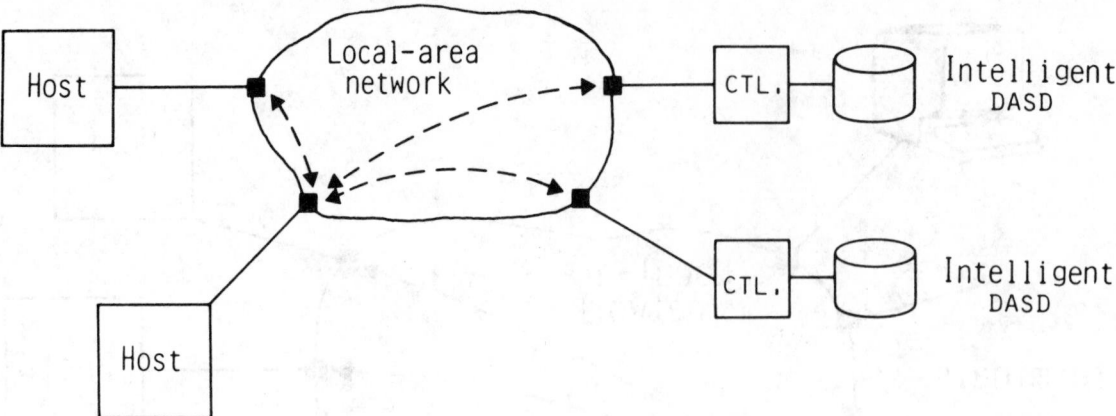

Figure 5. Local-Area Network as Backend Network.
© Copyright 1982 by VDE-VERLAG GmbH, Berlin 12.

in Figure 1, the attachment costs per station—as already mentioned—will only be slightly higher and be fully justified by the additional functions made available through the network.

These workstations, called *clients*, communicate through the network with support functions, called *servers*, which can be implemented in a centralized or distributed way. Some examples of servers follow. For many workstations, it will not be cost-justified to have a private data base. In this case, they will have to share the file system with other workstations. The key element of the file system is the file server which provides the two basic functions of reliably storing information on behalf of clients, and of allowing the sharing of data among clients. The transport of information between workstation and file server is achieved through a file-transfer protocol. Compared with the structure of current systems, Figure 3, this scenario has new features. Previously, the station had its application resident in the host computer where it was executed in a time-sharing mode, and the host computer communicated with the unintelligent direct-access storage devices. Now, these functions are split. Application processing is performed in the intelligent workstation, and the intelligence in the host computer, required for controlling and communicating with the DASD's, got moved to the file server. The scenario shown in Figure 6, in this sense, represents a step away from the world of time-sharing, potentially just as significant as the step from batch processing to time-sharing. We should like to point out, however, that in our opinion, this new scenario will not decrease the importance of the big data-processing machines which will manage networks and data bases of ever-increasing size.

Similarly, workstations will share high-quality printers, e.g., laser printers, which are attached to the local-area network via a printer server. Communication takes place only between workstation and printer server, most likely using the same file-transfer protocol. The printer server then has files printed on behalf of workstations. Other examples of servers are an electronic-mail server which allows workstations to exchange mail, and a name server with whom all stations have to register when they join the network. The name server allocates addresses to stations which register, and resolves names into addresses upon request.

We conclude the discussion of the client-server network with another functional capability it can support (Figure 6). We assume that there are workstations with a common architecture; but for cost reasons they are optionally equipped with different amounts of random access memory (RAM), diskettes and/or hard disks. Based on their actual configuration, they will depend on a central processing facility which will: (1) download the appropriate software packages into the workstation through the network, or in other words customize the workstation, and (2) perform functions on behalf of the workstation.

Networks for process-control applications [12] or for use in the production-floor environment also fall into the category of local-area networks. Their special requirements and characteristics are beyond the scope of this paper.

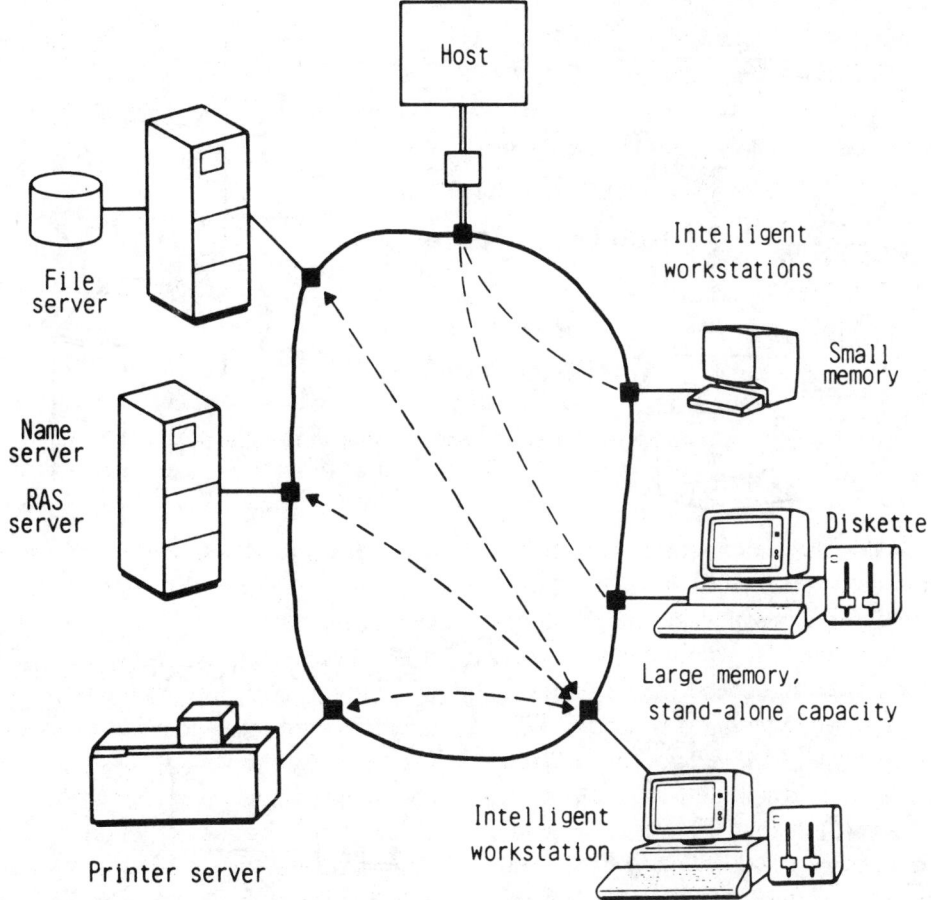

Figure 6. Local-Area Network Supporting Client-Server Architecture.

3. Approaches and Classification

3.1 Technical Approaches. In this section, we shall briefly discuss possible approaches to local-area communication without making an attempt to predict which one will prevail in the future.

The most widely used local communication system is the *private automatic branch exchange* (PABX). Most of the PABX's installed today are optimized for real-time voice and use analog technology. The advent of *computer-controlled private branch exchanges* (CBX), implemented in digital technology and providing standard 64 Kbps Pulse Code Modulation (PCM) channels paves the way for one approach to local-area networks [13].

CBX's employ centralized switching with central control; the switching technology is circuit switching, and from a topological point of view, they represent star systems. Thus, with a suitably dimensioned CBX, both local data-switching and transmission needs of a class of terminals can be satisfied. A channel is set up

and then held between two communicating devices for the entire duration of a session. In the long run, CBX's may represent the interesting perspective of extending the Integrated Services Digital Networks (ISDN) [14], currently being defined and studied for the public domain, into the local area.

System proposals not based on CBX's but also using centralized switches are discussed in [15] and [16]. These switches use packet-switching technology instead of circuit switching, and therefore have the capability to handle bursty traffic.

The disadvantage of any centralized approach is the entry cost for small installations because of the use of centralized switching and control facilities. The alternative to centralized switching/control is to use a *distributed control structure* to regulate access to the transmission system. Topologies which inherently provide broadcasting, such as busses and rings, lend themselves readily to implement distributed access control, see Figure 7 and [17,18,19,20,21,22,23,24,25,26]. For both

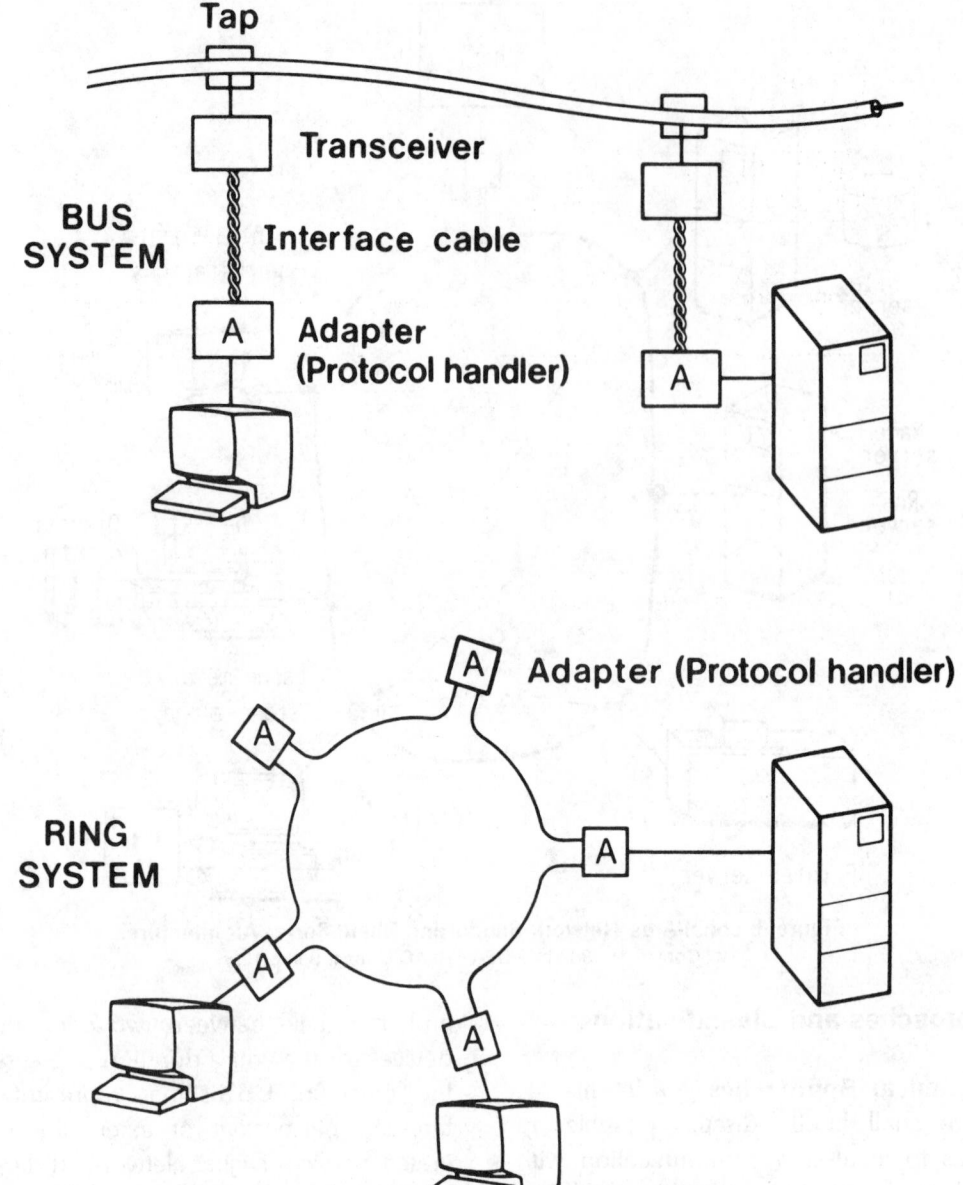

Figure 7. Bus and Ring Networks.
© Copyright 1982 by VDE-VERLAG GmbH, Berlin 12.

topologies, the functions provided in the set of network adapters through which stations are attached represent this distributed access-control system. It should be noted that all adapters are peer partners and that there does not exist a master adapter or a master station controlling access of the others.

This approach has important architectural consequences which become clear when we compare a multipoint system currently used for TP applications with data-link control procedures such as High-Level Data Link Control (HDLC) or Synchronous Data Link Control (SDLC) [27,28] and a bus or ring system for local-area networks as being standardized by Project 802 [29] of the Institute of Electrical and Electronics Engineers (IEEE) and by the European Computer Manufacturers Association (ECMA) [30]. These differences are represented in Figure 8. In a multipoint system, the primary station has to poll the secondary stations before they can transmit a frame to the primary. From an architectural point of view, this means that access to the transmission system is controlled with commands and responses of the elements of procedure of HDLC or SDLC. In local-area networks, on the other hand, the current data-link layer, level 2 in the

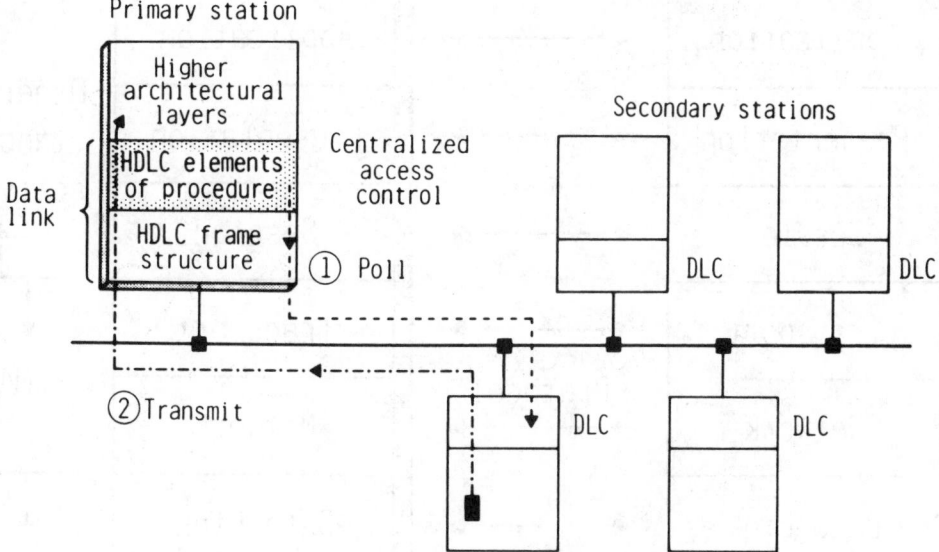

Primary-to-secondary communication: One to many

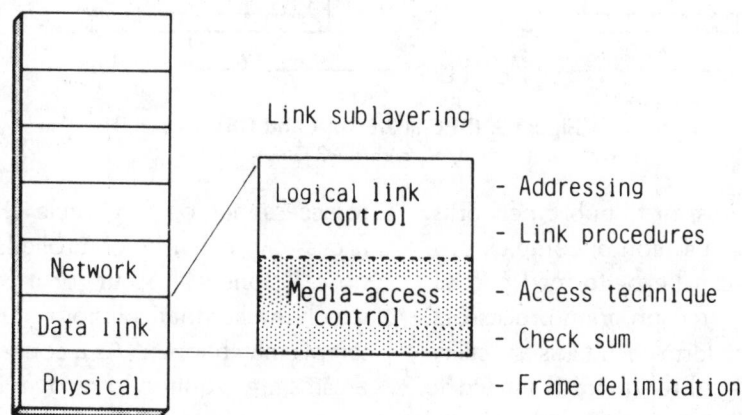

Peer-to-peer communication: Any to any (IEEE 802 Project/ECMA)

Figure 8. Primary-to-Secondary versus Peer-to-Peer Communication.
© Copyright 1982 by VDE-VERLAG GmbH, Berlin 12.

ISO reference model [7], is split into two independent sublayers: media-access control and logical-link control. Media-access control is part of the distributed control structure mentioned above and determines when a station may transmit. It also allows peer-to-peer communication among all stations attached to the network and not only between primary and secondaries as before. The logical-link control layer can contain any data-link control procedure and is no longer responsible for controlling access to the transmission medium.

The IEEE and ECMA standard activities on local-area networks in relationship to the complete ISO reference model are shown in Figure 9.

A single bus or ring system will not be able to serve establishments with a large number of attachments. Therefore, the capability to interconnect the bus or ring systems, called *subsystems* in this context, is an important requirement (Figure 10). Subsystems are interconnected through elements called *bridges* [31,32]. An important feature of a bridge is that it only performs a simple routing function and message buffering, but does not execute higher-level protocols (e.g., retransmission of erroneous frames, delivery in sequence sent, etc.).

Thus, the bridge is simple enough to be implemented directly in low-cost hardware and to carry traffic at the full network speed of several Mbps. Access to other local-area net-

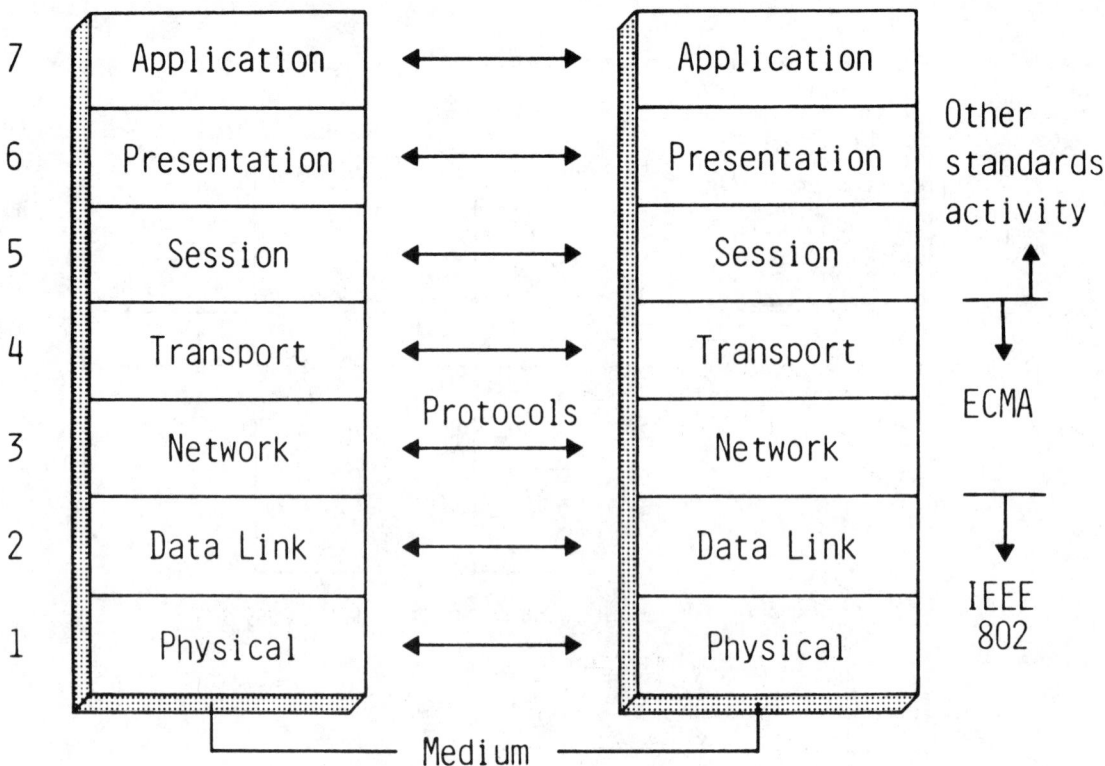

Figure 9. IEEE 802/ECMA and OSI.
© Copyright 1982 by VDE-VERLAG GmbH, Berlin 12.

works, to TP networks, or to public networks, however, requires translation of complex protocols. Such tasks can be performed cost effectively only with stored-program processors. Controllers which perform such tasks are called *gateways* [33]. Their throughput is limited to approximately 1 Mbps when current standard microprocessors are employed.

If the network grows beyond two subsystems, bridges will be interconnected through a *high-level network*. Depending on traffic patterns, the high-level network may be of the same variety as the subsystems, or it may have to carry several times the subsystem traffic and thus require different technology and/or topology.

In the remaining part of this article, we shall confine the discussion to bus and ring systems with distributed access control.

3.2 Classification of Local-Area Networks.

This section provides a classification of subsystems and a brief discussion of several access-control mechanisms. An obvious differentiation is according to topology where we distinguish between bus and ring systems (Figure 7). Within these categories, we can distinguish according

to access method (see Table 1). Basically, the access can either be controlled, in which case no collisions will occur, or it can be random, which implies that collisions of transmission attempts may happen. As a consequence, mechanisms are required to recover from collisions.

Table 1. Classification According to Access Method

BUS	*Controlled Access*
	—Token
	—Multilevel Multiple Access (MLMA)
	Random Access
	—Carrier-Sense Multiple Access with Collision Detection (CSMA/CD)
RING	*Controlled Access*
	—Token
	—Slotted
	—Buffer/Register Insertion

• **Token Ring:** The data flow in a ring system is unidirectional, and stations are ordered sequentially. In a token ring [18,19,29], a data structure which basically consists of a delimiter signal and a free indicator, called the token, circulates continuously when no

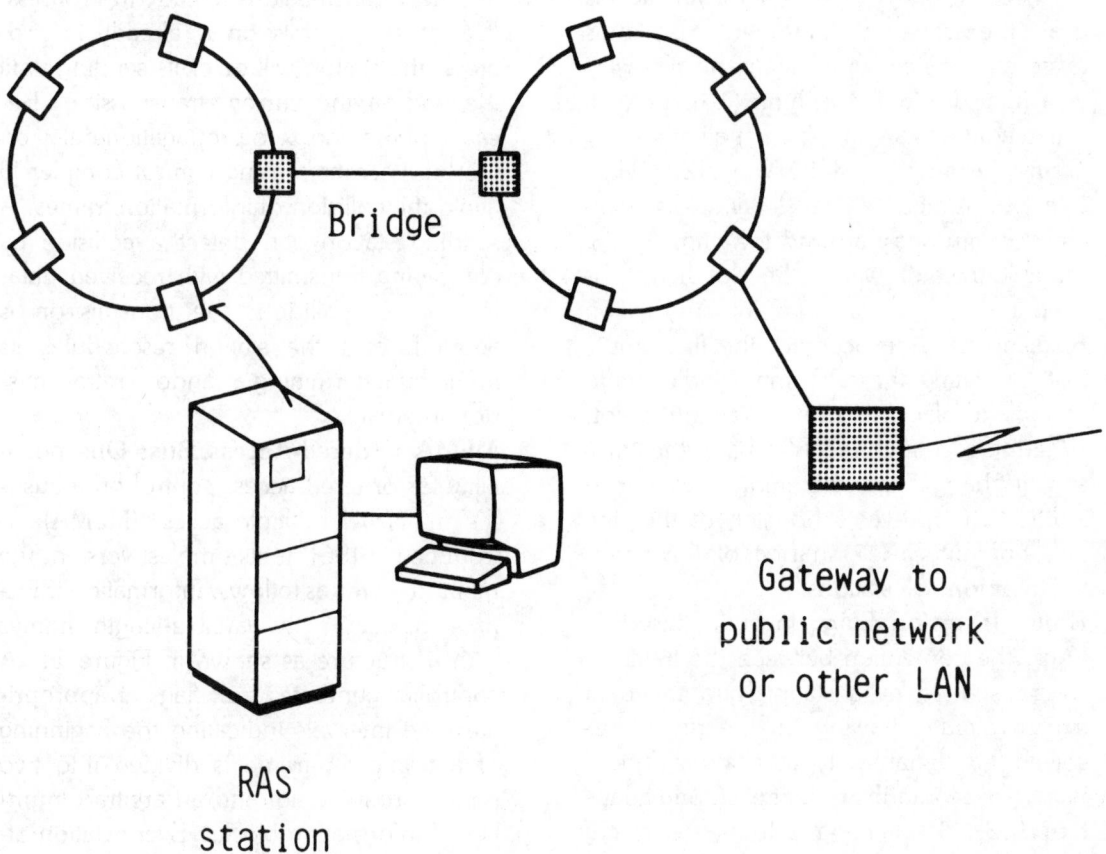

Figure 10. Bridges and Gateways.
© Copyright 1982 by VDE-VERLAG GmbH, Berlin 12.

traffic is offered for transmission. If a station requests to send, its adapter will wait for the delimiter signal and check whether the token is free. If this is not the case, then the transmission attempt will have to be deferred. Otherwise, the station sets the token to busy, and data transmission commences. The frame which can be of arbitrary length passes all adapters. The destination recognizes its address as part of the frame, and copies the information into its receive buffer. When the frame returns to the sending station, it gets erased from the ring. The sending-station adapter also has the re-

sponsibility of issuing a new free token and passing it along the ring.

Obviously, the ring must be properly initialized, i.e., the first delimiter signal and free token have to be generated, and its integrity maintained at all times. As shown in [19], ring initialization and recovery from errors can be solved by introducing a monitor function which is available in each ring adapter. At any given point in time, only one monitor function is active and protects the circulating token against loss, permanent busy condition, or duplication. The monitor functions in other adapters are passive and supervise the health of the active monitor function. In case of a monitor failure, the passive monitor functions activate themselves, compete for the role of the active monitor, and after the contention has been resolved, one monitor function is again the active one. Another possibility is to perform token supervision and recovery in a fully distributed fashion [18], i.e., all active adapters are involved at all times.

- **Slotted Ring:** In a slotted ring [20,21], a constant number of fixed-length slots circulates continuously around the ring. A full/empty indicator within the slot header is used to signal the state of a slot. Any station ready to transmit occupies the first empty slot by setting the full/empty indicator to "full," and places its information in the slot. When the sender receives back the busy slot, it changes the full/empty indicator to "free." This prevents hogging of the ring and guarantees fair sharing of the bandwidth among all stations.

- **Buffer Insertion Ring:** In buffer insertion rings, the contention between the traffic to be transmitted by a station and the data stream already flowing on the ring is resolved by dynamically inserting sufficient buffer space into the ring at each ring adapter [10,22,23]. In contrast to the token ring where the sender is responsible for removal of the frame it transmitted, this function is performed by the receiver.

With regard to the point in time when a station is allowed to transmit one of its pending messages, we can distinguish between two operational modes: station priority and ring priority [34].

In the case of station priority, a station having a transmit request pending is allowed to transmit its information blocks immediately, when there is no block in transit at that moment. Otherwise, it must defer its transmission until the end of the transit block being currently transmitted. With ring priority, a station cannot begin transmission of one of its information blocks prior to the state when the insertion buffer is empty, i.e., all traffic already on the ring has passed the station.

- **CSMA Collision Detection Bus:** The best-known random-access scheme for bus systems is carrier-sense multiple access with collision detection (CSMA/CD) as described in [17,35]. Under a CSMA protocol, every station ready to send must listen before transmitting an information frame in order to detect transmissions already in progress. If another transmission is already in progress, the station will defer its sending until the end of the current transmission. Because of the non-zero propagation delay on the bus, carrier sensing cannot completely avoid the collision of information frames. A sending station can detect a collision by comparing transmitted with received data. In case of collision, the transmission is aborted, and the station reschedules its frame by determining a random retransmission interval.

- **MLMA Ordered-Access Bus:** One possibility for ordered-access control on a bus is the multilevel multiple access (MLMA) introduced in [36]. In its simplest version, the method works as follows. Information transmission occurs in variable-length frames with a structure as shown in Figure 11. A controller generates start flags at appropriate time intervals indicating the beginning of a frame. A frame is divided into two parts: a request slot and an arbitrary number of information blocks. Every station attached to the bus owns one bit within the request slot. By setting its bit, a station indicates a request for transmission within this frame. At the end of the request cycle, all stations know which other stations are going to transmit within this frame. The actual transmission sequence is determined by a priority assignment known to all stations.

- **Token Bus:** Another controlled-access scheme on a bus uses a permission token in a similar way to that described for a ring system. This scheme is currently being studied by the IEEE 802 group [29]. Token access on a bus means that the station ready to transmit and which received the free token can send an information frame. At the end of the transmission, the station frees the token and passes an addressed token to the next station which should have an opportunity to transmit. It is important to note that in contrast to a token-ring system, the token has to be addressed since a bus sys-

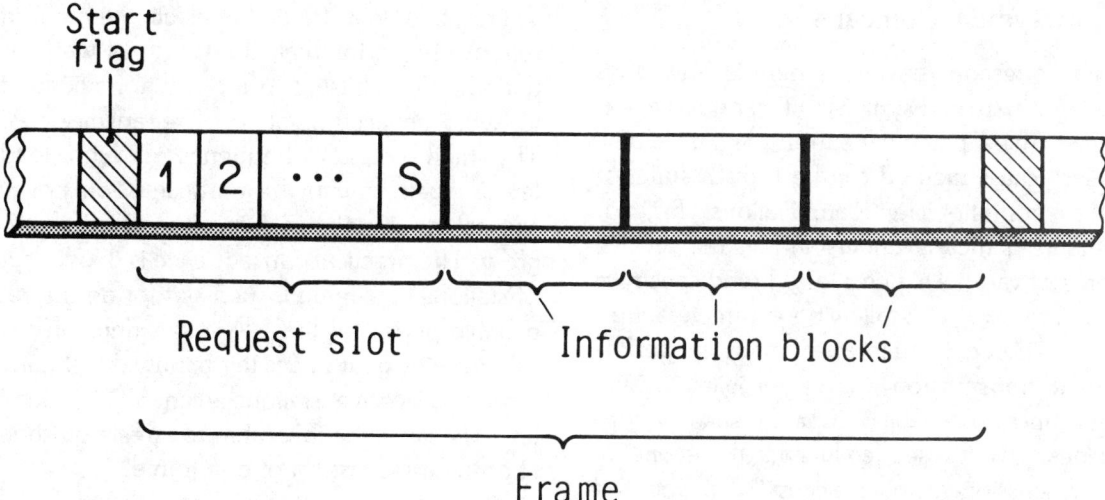

Figure 11. Frame Structure of MLMA Bus ([41]).
© Copyright 1982 by VDE-VERLAG GmbH, Berlin 12.

tem does not provide sequential ordering of the stations attached.

In addition to topology and access method, we can classify subsystems according to the transmission technique. We can differentiate between baseband and broadband systems. In a baseband system, data is transmitted as electrical pulses without prior modulation of a radio frequency carrier. In a broadband system, the available frequency spectrum is subdivided into different frequency bands where frequency multiplexing techniques are required to separate the bands. References [24, 25,37] provide examples of such a system. Figure 12 schematically shows the principle. The bands can be used independently of one another, e.g., one band for CSMA/CD or token access, a band for voice, and other bands for video. The economic viability of these systems is determined by the modem cost incurred on top of the cost for implementing the access scheme.

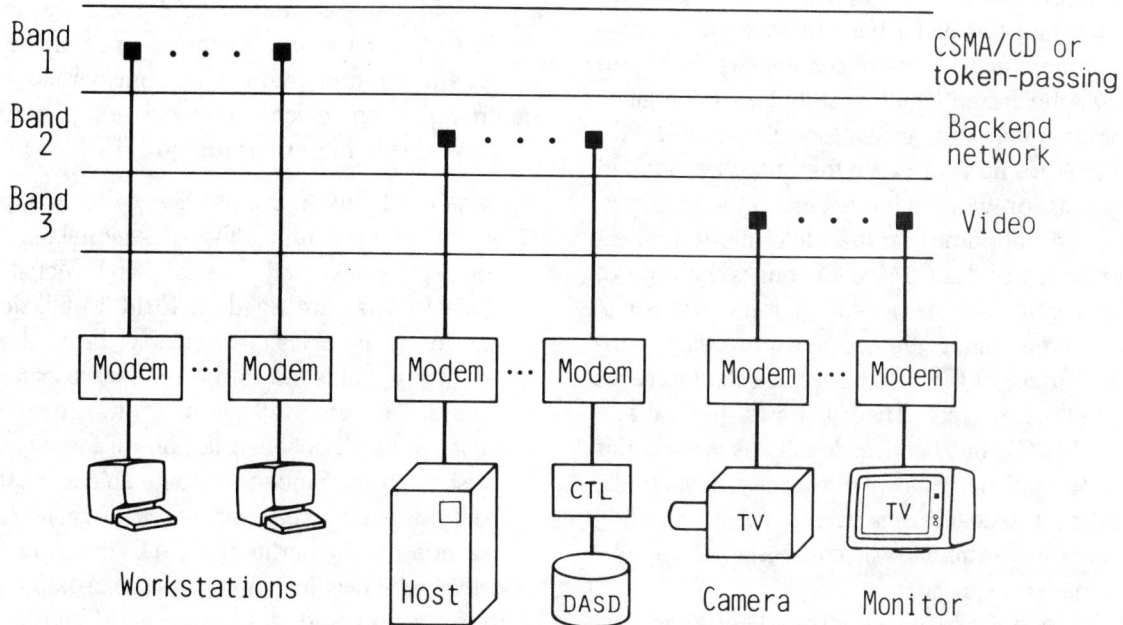

Figure 12. Principle of Broadband System.
© Copyright 1982 by VDE-VERLAG GmbH, Berlin 12.

4. Subsystem Comparison

The question that arises here is how does one compare subsystems? It cannot be expected that a particular subsystem with a particular access method can be proven superior for all conditions and applications. Instead, comparing means understanding the relative merits of various systems for a broad spectrum of parameters. The following parameters must be considered in such a comparison: performance, transmission, wiring, reliability, availability, and serviceability. For the sake of conciseness, we subsequently limit the scope of our discussion to token access on a ring and CSMA/CD on a bus.

4.1 Protocol Performance.

Two performance aspects are of primary interest: the delay-throughput characteristic of the media-access control schemes, and system behavior when the load approaches the saturation point. There exists a large body of performance analyses of ring and bus systems; some examples are given in [38,39,40]. In the following, we use some of the results reported in [41]. Figures 13a, b, and c show the delay-throughput relation of token ring and CSMA/CD bus for two data rates: 1 Mbps and 10 Mbps. The general conclusions we can draw from these results are: (1) at a data rate of 1 Mbps, both systems perform equally well; (2) if the data rate is increased to 10 Mpbs, the token ring has better performance characteristics over a wide range of parameters. In Figure 13a, the frame-length distribution is negative exponential with an average value of 1,000 bits. A frame represents the entity transmitted by a station when it has access to the medium. The critical parameter that determines the performance of the CSMA/CD bus is the ratio of propagation delay to mean frame transmission time. Since the propagation delay is independent of the data rate, this ratio increases with the data rate. Theory shows, [41], that a CSMA/CD bus behaves ideally as long as this ratio is sufficiently low. If, for reasonable traffic loads, it exceeds 2-5 percent, the increasing collision frequency will cause significant performance degradation.

If on a CSMA/CD bus, collision occurs, transmission will be aborted, and the station will reschedule its frame by selecting a random retransmission interval, the length of which is dynamically adjusted to the actual traffic load to avoid an accumulation of retransmissions. The high collision frequency at high load levels together with the retransmission policy causes the variation of the transfer delay to grow. The practical consequence is the danger of stations becoming locked-out for an unpredictable period of time. A token ring, on the other hand, guarantees fair bandwidth sharing among all active stations even at high load levels because the token has to be relinquished after the transmission of one frame.

The general validity of the conclusions drawn above is supported by Figures 13b and c. In Figure 13b, all parameters are the same as before except for the length of the cable, which is now 10 km instead of 2 km. The curve for the CSMA/CD bus at 10 Mbps illustrates the impact of the propagation delay, and confirms the importance of the ratio propagation delay and average frame transmission time. As a practical consequence, all CSMA/CD systems being discussed specify a maximum distance which is less than 10 km. Finally, Figure 13c further demonstrates the robustness of the results. There, the frame-length distribution has a coefficient of variation of 2.

4.2 Electrical Characteristics.

A large volume of literature exists on the protocol aspect of local-area networks, particularly on performance. However, in choosing a particular system for implementation, considerations stemming from electrical engineering may play an equally important role [42,43].

- **Baseband Bus Systems:** Bus systems rely on a shared medium with bi-directional taps. For high transmission rates (> 1 Mbps), coaxial cables are needed. Field-installable taps for such cables are available. From the tap, the signal is fed to the sender/receiver circuits. To avoid reflections on the coaxial cable, the stub between tap and transceiver must be short. Since the main cable is most likely installed in cable ducts or in ceilings, the adapter is partitioned into the *transceiver* which is in close physical proximity to the main cable and the *protocol handler* which is most likely located in the attaching

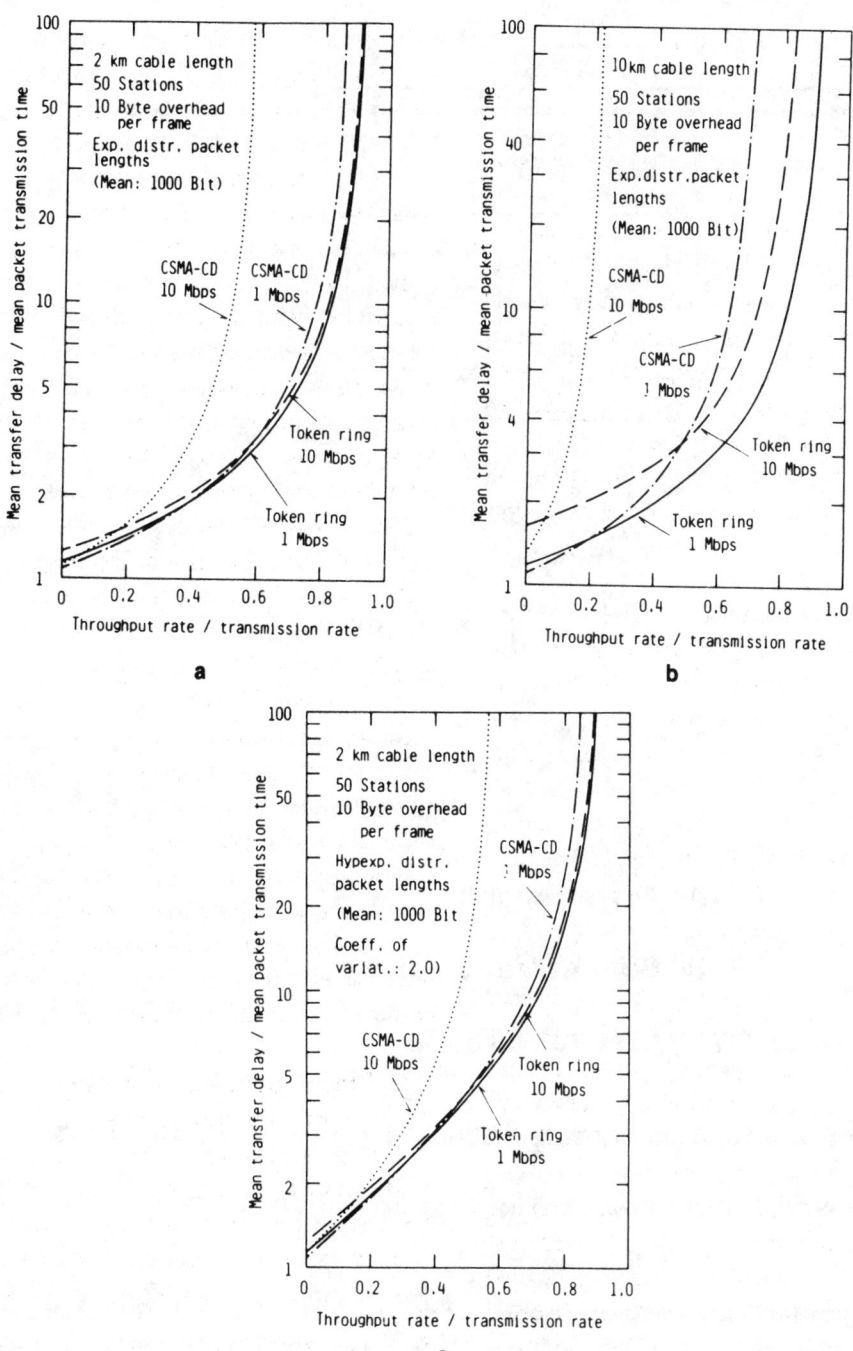

Figure 13. Delay-Throughput Characteristic for Token Ring and CSMA/CD Bus.
© Copyright 1982 by VDE-VERLAG GmbH, Berlin 12.

station. Transceiver and station are connected via an *extension cable* which consists of multiple twisted pairs for power, data, and controls (*see* Figures 7 and 14).

When there is no traffic on the system, the bus is without energy. A data frame starts at an arbitrary point in time with a synchronization preamble during which all transceivers lock to the transmission. The majority of systems for which data was published use Manchester or differential Man-

chester coding. IEEE 802 and ECMA [29, 30] also propose these coding schemes.

For its reliable operation, the CSMA/CD protocol requires that a transceiver must be capable of detecting the weakest other transmitter during its own transmissions, and of distinguishing the signals from the other transmitter from the echoes of its own transmitter. Furthermore, for its efficient operation, collisions have to be detected at the earliest possible moment to abort transmis-

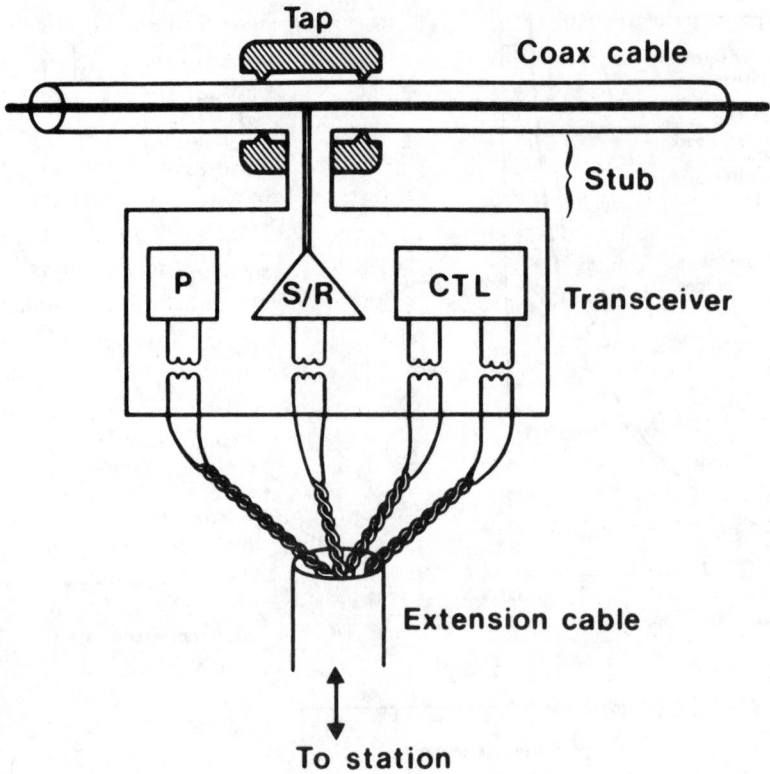

Tap

Coax cable

Stub

P

S/R

CTL

Transceiver

Extension cable

To station

P: Power supply

S/R: Sender/receiver circuits

CTL: Control circuits

Transformer signals indicate galvanic separation

which can also be achieved differently.

Figure 14. Schematic Diagram of Transceiver in a Baseband CSMA/CD System.

sion. Even the best collision-detection circuits developed so far limit the allowable attenuation to a value significantly smaller than for a point-to-point transmission without collisions. Consequences are the need to use high-quality cable and a limitation of the distance which can be covered by a single segment between repeaters.

As shown in Figure 14, the transceiver circuits are galvanically coupled with the coaxial cable. To avoid ground-loop problems, the entire transceiver must be carefully isolated from the attaching station. In

Figure 14, this is schematically indicated by the transformer symbols. In practice, other devices such as electro-optical couplers can be used. The galvanic coupling of the transceiver to the coaxial cable causes reliability exposures which require additional protective components. A short circuit in one transceiver, for example, would bring the network down. Circuits requiring multi-component failures to short the cable have been proposed. An additional consequence of the galvanic coupling is that a segment can only be grounded at one point.

The number of stations, which can be attached, is limited by the residual reflections caused by the taps. To keep the noise from reflections low, the placement of taps must be controlled. A typical 10 Mbps system [29,30] allows segments with a length of 500 m and requires a minimum distance between taps of 2.5 m. Also, the number of transceivers per segment should be less than 100.

From the above discussion, we conclude:

1. A baseband bus system is engineered around one single grade of coaxial cable. Mixing of media in one system is not possible, and at present, suitable taps for optical-fiber cables are not available.

2. If CSMA/CD is employed, the distance will be limited by the collision-detection circuitry.

3. The transceivers must be located at the coaxial cable and electronically insulated from the station. They contain a significant analog engineering component which has to be carefully designed. This, together with the transceiver packaging, adds significantly to its cost.

- **Token-Ring System:** A ring network consists of a closed sequence of individual point-to-point links. For its efficient operation, the token protocol requires minimal delay per station, and the ability to change a single bit, e.g., the token, "on-the-fly." To achieve minimum delay, the individual links are synchronized to a temporary master clock as discussed in [19,43]. In such a design, station delays of half-a-bit time can be achieved, except for the station providing the clock. In this station, an elastic buffer of a few bits is used to equalize the accumulated timing jitter. Other approaches to coordinate the clock are mentioned in [42]. Since the ring consists of point-to-point segments, mixing of different media (including optical fibers) in one system is easily achieved.

The engineering of optimized sender and receiver circuits for point-to-point links is well understood. Because reflections are controlled, high attenuations can be accepted, and hence long distances reached. One problem, however, requires careful study: the design of the clock extraction circuits. The solution described in [43] uses a phase-locked loop (PLL) in each repeater which tracks the next active repeater upstream. The number of stations that can be inserted into one ring subsystem is limited by the accumulation of the timing errors in the PLL circuits (called jitter). The PLL needs to be optimized to minimize accumulation of jitter. Such an optimized PLL design is discussed in [43], and an analysis shows that up to 300-400 stations can be attached to a single ring [44].

When a new station is inserted into the ring, it needs to synchronize its receiver to the clock extracted from the incoming signal. When this has been performed, the receiver downstream from the newly inserted station loses energy. To resynchronize the whole ring quickly, it is necessary to avoid full resynchronization of all links downstream from the station which observed loss of energy. The solution proposed in [43] uses the following principle: The frequency of the local oscillator of the sender in the repeater which detected loss of energy is frozen to its momentary value. When the newly inserted station starts to transmit a properly synchronized signal, then all that needs to be done is to equalize a phase difference between the new signal and the frozen oscillator. The control action can be performed quickly, and resynchronization times as short as 20 μsec/station have been observed in an experimental token-ring network [43].

The attachment of a station to the ring is schematically shown in Figure 15. Sender and receiver circuits, together with the protocol handler can be packaged on the same card, which is located in, and powered from, the station. This is a significant advantage with respect to the LSI/VLSI integration and low-cost packaging. Direct current-free (DC-free) coupling of in- and out-bound links and balanced transmission, e.g., via transformers, makes the system immune to ground-loop problems. The station is switched into the ring via electromechanical (or electronic) relays. To reduce cable length between repeaters (and also to increase reliability), it is desirable to locate the

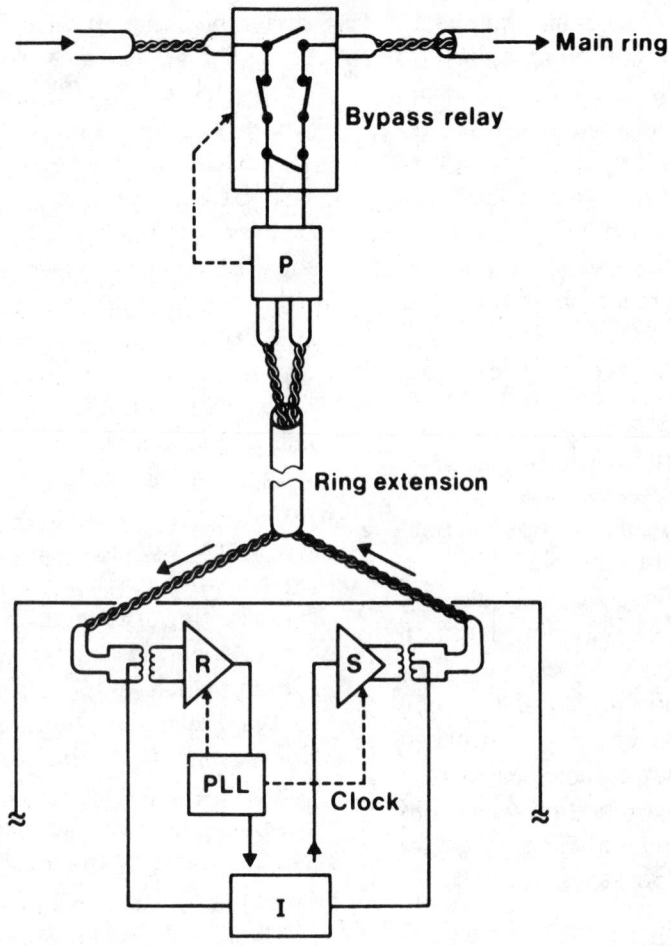

P: Phantom circuit to power bypass relays

R: Receiver circuits

S: Sender circuits

I: Insert control

Figure 15. Schematic Diagram of Station Attachment to a Token Ring.

relays remotely in distribution panels [18,19]. The number of wire pairs in the extension cable can be limited to two by powering the relays from the attaching station via phantom circuits. In Figure 15, the media portrayed is shielded twisted-pair cable. Such cables are attractive because of low cost and electrical symmetry which minimizes electromagnetic interference (EMI) problems. It is also easy to install because of its flexibility. One should note, however, that other media such as coaxial cables or even optical fibers can also be used, and that different media can coexist.

In summary, we conclude:

1. The ring system consists of synchronous point-to-point links which tolerate high attenuation (hence, long distance) and allow mixing of media in one system.

2. The ring system is open for the introduction of optical-fiber links.

3. Transceiver and protocol handler are packaged together and located in the station. The analog engineering com-

ponent in a ring system is small. The solutions to the ring engineering problems can all be implemented in digital technology, and therefore can benefit from technological improvements in LSI/VLSI.

4.3 Reliability, Serviceability and Installation Characteristics.

High reliability, paired with high availability, is a key requirement for a local-area network. Automated fault isolation and serviceability by non-technical personnel will be key requirements from the point of view of the vendors. Ease of installation and the ability to wire buildings in a planned and systematic manner, and to provide wall plugs inexpensively in a large number of offices will be important from the user's point of view. All these requirements are well addressed by the established voice-switching industry (PABX). The new local-area network technologies will still have to prove their worth in all those aspects. Subsequently, we shall limit our discussion to a few basic considerations.

- **Baseband Bus:** Some reliability aspects of the transceivers have been previously discussed. The system is insensitive to power failures or to damage to the extension cable. However, if the main coaxial cable is mutilated or otherwise shorted, e.g., through a malfunctioning transceiver or a tap not properly installed, transmission on the afflicted segment will break down because of the reflections which occur at the point of failure. *Time-domain reflectometry* (TDR) has been proposed to locate such faults. In TDR, the time between sending of a pulse and arrival of its echo is correlated to the distance of the problem point on the cable. However, even with the addition of TDR circuits to each adapter, the problem of correlating linear distance measured on the cable (which is strung through ducts and ceilings) with a location in a building is not solved, in practice.

Since the transceiver cost is a large fraction of the total network cost, an incremental installation of the system is favored over a systematic pre-wiring which includes wall plugs in all offices.

- **Token Ring:** A reliable ring protocol was already described [19]. But ring systems must also be made robust with respect to repeater failure and cable breakage. To a great extent, this can be achieved by using *distribution panels* with by-pass relays (Figure 16), [43]. A main ring cable linking distribution panels is installed in conduits or ceilings. *Wall outlets* are connected to the distribution panels through *extension wires* or local lobes. If the relays, which are activated by phantom circuits, remain unpowered, the local lobe will not be inserted into the ring. Thus, power failure of the station or breakage of the extension wire will automatically remove the station from the active ring which will resume proper operation after a short resynchronization interval.

A failure of the main ring cable, however, will bring the system down. Such a failure is detected by the next adapter downstream from the breakage. Since communication in the sequence of downstream links is unaffected, the adapter which detects the failure can be programmed to send a message to a *network supervisor* which can easily locate the faulty link.

If the station providing the (temporary) clock is removed, e.g., through power-off, loss of power or extension-cable breakage, a new clock must be provided. This can be achieved through the convention that the adapter which serves at a given moment as monitor function [19] also provides the clock. Thus, the automatic monitor switch-over protocol also backs up the clock.

One can test a station before it is inserted through a *wrap-around circuit* (Figure 15). In such a test, the station sender is connected to its receiver through the extension cable. Only if proper operation of both the adapter and the extension cable are diagnosed, will permission for relay activation and station insertion be granted.

In its simplest form, the distribution panels are passive boxes which house the relays. Thus, the cost of the wall plug is primarily determined by the cost of cable and relay. If desired, prewiring of a building is possible at low cost, and rings can be configured later, as needed, at the distribution panels.

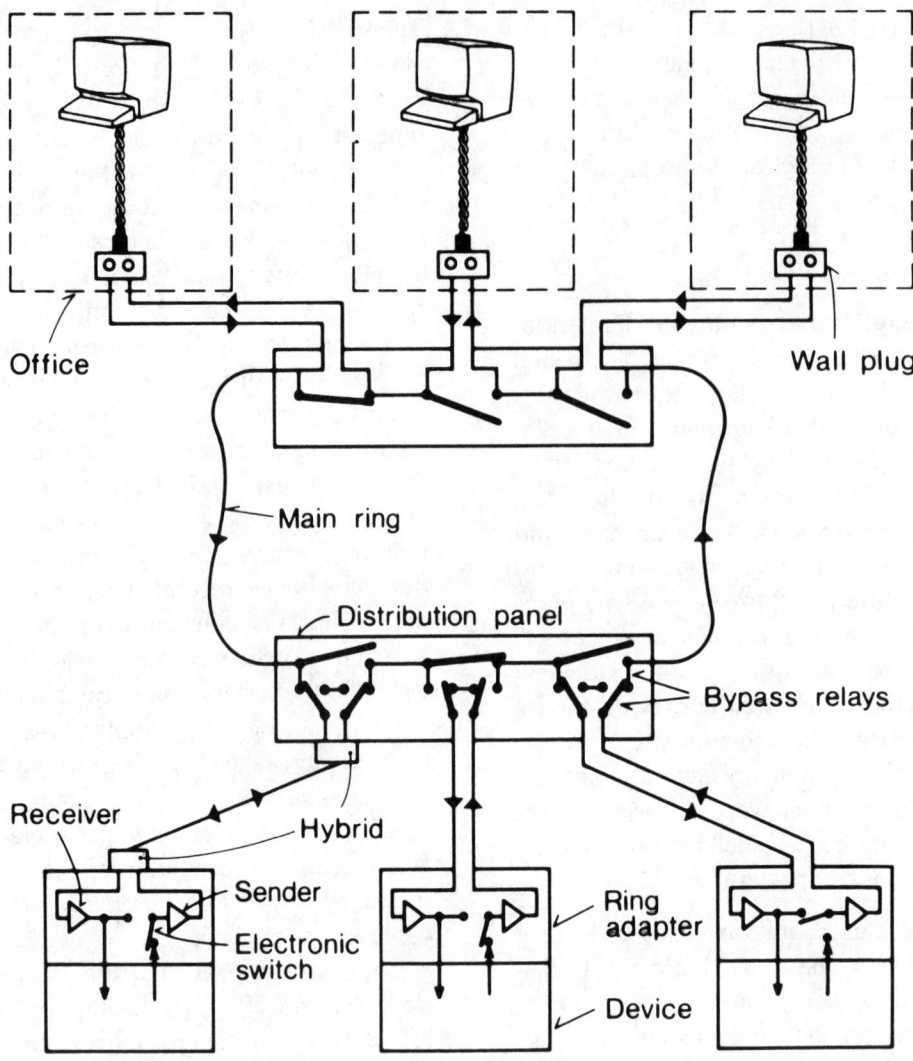

Figure 16. Ring with Distribution Panels.
© Copyright 1982 by VDE-VERLAG GmbH, Berlin 12.

At the expense of adding a power supply and a microprocessor to the distribution box, further reliability of the main ring can be achieved through back-up cables automatically activated to bypass a breakage.

5. Summary

Local-area networks are a new technology expected to play an important role in future establishments. The field is under intense study, and a large number of vendors offers early systems. All technologies discussed in this paper have their adherents and are being tried in practice.

With respect to transmission, most systems employ baseband, but there are a number of broadband systems either available or announced. Faced with such diversity, the user community seems to be reacting cautiously. Standardization efforts reflect the technical activity and are currently led by the IEEE Project 802 and by ECMA. Not awaiting final standards, major semiconductor houses have announced local-area network LSI components.

In particular, we have highlighted the following key ideas:

1. Computer-controlled private branch exchanges and ring and bus systems with various access methods represent feasible approaches to solve the problem of local-area communication.

2. The most likely application scenarios will encompass terminal-to-host communication, channel-to-channel and processor-to-DASD communication, and the case where intelligent workstations operate in a

distributed processing environment and access-shared resources through the network via servers.

3. Ring and bus systems can employ a broad spectrum of access methods; the particular choice will have a significant impact on performance. The comparison of token ring and CSMA/CD bus shows that for data rates of 1 Mbps, they have the same delay-throughput characteristic, whereas for data rates of 10 Mbps, the token ring clearly shows the better performance over a wide range of parameters.

4. Significant differences of ring and bus systems are in the areas of wiring and of providing centralized maintenance and reconfiguration facilities. The ring has a considerable amount of flexibility to mix media and to migrate to newly emerging transmission technologies, because of the point-to-point nature of its transmission system. Bus systems do not have this flexibility. Also, since rings do not require transceivers located adjacent to the transmission medium, prewiring of buildings and the installation of wall plugs in all offices can be cost justified. Furthermore, the use of distribution panels in ring systems provides points for centralized maintenance and reconfiguration.

Today, there is scant information on how different local-area network products perform on user premises. It will be such experience rather than scientific and engineering analysis which will eventually resolve the contention for the one (or few) predominant local-area network technology.

Acknowledgments

The authors gratefully acknowledge useful discussion with W. Bux, P. Janson, and H. R. Müller, during the preparation of the paper, and their help in reviewing the manuscript.

References

1. "System Network Architecture," General Information, 1975, IBM Publication GA 27-3102.

2. Conant, G. E. and Wecker, S. "DNA—An Architecture for Heterogeneous Computer Networks," *Proc. ICCC 1976*, Toronto, Canada, pp. 618-625.

3. McGovern, J. P. "DCA—A Distributed Communications Architecture," *Proc. ICCC 1978*, Kyoto, Japan, pp. 347-367.

4. Booth, G. M. "Honeywell's Distributed Systems Environment," *Proc. ICCC 1978*, Kyoto, Japan, pp. 347-351.

5. Naemura, K. "Network Architecture Developments in Japan," *Proc. ICCC 1978*, Kyoto, Japan, pp. 501-506.

6. Feldmann, J., Jilek, P., and Nowak, R. "Das Datenfernverarbeitungssystem TRANSDATA von Siemens," Telecom Report 1, 1978, pp. 70-77.

7. "ISO Reference Model of Open-Systems Interconnection," ISO/TC 97/SC 16, DP 7498, 1980.

8. CCITT Orange Book, Vol. VIII. 2, Public Data Networks, 1977.

9. Thornton, J. E. "Overview of Hyperchannel," *Proc. COMPCON*, 1979, San Francisco, pp. 262-265.

10. "Local Communication Controller Description," 1981, IBM Publication GA 34-0142.

11. Israel, J. E., Mitchel, J. G., and Sturgis, H. "Separating Data from Function in a Distributed File System," *Proc. Workshop on Operating Systems*, 1978, Paris, pp. 17-22.

12. Sloman, M. S. and Prince, S. "Local Network Architecture for Process Control," *Proc. IFIP WG 6.4 International Workshop on Local Networks*, 1980, Zurich, pp. 407-427.

13. van Kampen, H. "Local-Area Networks and the Intelligent PABX," *Proc. Conference on Local Networks and Distributed Office Systems*, Online, 1981, London, pp. 175-184.

14. Becker, D. and Schmidt, P. "Zur Integration von Fernmeldediensten in digitalen Netzen. Parts 1 and 2," Nachrichtentechnische Zeitschrift, 1981, pp. 288-292 and pp. 366-370.

15. Fraser, A. G. "Datakit—A Modular Network for Synchronous and Asynchronous Traffic," *Proc. ICC 1979*, June 1979, Boston, pp. 20.1.1-20.1.3.

16. Rothauser, E. H., Janson, P. and Müller, H. R. "Meshed Star Networks for Local Communication Systems," *Proc. IFIP WG 6.4 International Workshop on Local Networks*, 1980, Zurich, pp. 25-41.

17. Metcalfe, R. M. and Boggs, D. R. "Ethernet Distributed Packet Switching for Local Computer Networks," *Communications of the ACM*, Vol. 19, 1976, pp. 395-404.

18. Saltzer, J. H. and Pogran, K. "A Star-Shaped Ring Network with High Maintainability," *Proc. Local Area Communications Network Symposium*, Mitre Corp., 1979, pp. 179-190.

19. Bux, W., Closs, F., Janson, P., Kümmerle, K. and Müller, H. R. "A Reliable Token-Ring System for Local-Area Communication," *National Telecommunication Conference*, 1981, New Orleans, pp. A2.2.1-A.2.2.6.

20. Penney, B. K. and Baghdadi, A. A. "Survey of Computer Communication Loop Networks. Parts 1 and 2," *Computer Communications*, Vol. 2, 1979, pp. 165-180 and pp. 224-241.

21. Hopper, A. "Data Ring at Computer Laboratory, University of Cambridge. Computer Science and Technology: Local Area Networking," Washington, DC: National Bureau of Standards, NBS Special Publication 500-31, 1977, pp. 11-16.

22. Reames, C. C. and Liu, M. T. "A Loop Network for Simultaneous Transmission of Variable Length Messages," *Proc. 2nd Annual Symposium on Computer Architecture*, 1975, Houston, pp. 7-12.

23. Hafner, E. R., Nenandal, Z. and Tschanz, M. "A Digital Loop Communications System," *IEEE Trans. Commun.*, Vol. COM-22, 1974, pp. 877-881.

24. Hopkins, G. T. "Recent Developments on the MITRENET," *Proc. Conference on Local Networks and Distributed Office Systems*, Online, 1981, London, pp. 97-105.

25. Biba, K. J. "Packet Communication Networks for Broadband Coaxial Cable," *Proc. Conference on Local Networks and Distributed Office Systems*, Online, 1981, London, pp. 611-625.

26. Tada, M., Kiyono, M., Takumi, K. and Hatta, H. "N 6670 DATALINK—A Homogeneous Optical Loop Network," *Proc. ICC 1982*, Philadelphia, pp. 6C.3.1-6C.3.5.

27. "Data Communication—High Level Data Link-Control Procedures—Elements of Procedures (Independent Numbering)," Int. Standard ISO 4335.

28. "IBM Synchronous Data Link Control," General Information, 1975, IBM Publication GA 27-3093.

29. IEEE Project 802, Local Network Standard, Draft C, May 1982.

30. Standard ECMA-80-81-82, Local Area Networks: Coaxial Cable System—Physical Layer—Link Layer, September 1982.

31. Boggs, D. R., Shoch, J. F., Taft, E. and Metcalfe, R. M. "PUP: An Internetwork Architecture," Xerox Palo Alto Research Center, Techn. Report CSL-79-10, 1979.

32. Bux, W., Closs, F., Janson, P., Kümmerle, K., Müller, H. R. and Rothauser, E. H. "A Local-Area Communication Network Based on a Reliable Token-Ring System," *Proc. Symposium on Local Computer Networks*, 1982, Florence, pp. 69-82.

33. Elden, W. L. "Gateways for Interconnecting Local-Area and Long Haul Networks," *Proc. Conference on Local Networks and Distributed Office Systems*, Online, 1981, London, pp. 391-406.

34. Bux, W., Schlatter, M. "An Approximate Method for the Performance Analysis of Buffer Insertion Rings," to appear in *IEEE Trans. Commun.*, Vol. COM-30, 1982.

35. Clark, D. D., Pogran, K. T. and Reed, D. P. "An Introduction to Local-Area Networks," *Proc. IEEE*, Vol. 66, 1978, pp. 1497-1517.

36. Rothauser, E. H. and Wild, D. "MLMA: A Collision-Free Multi-access Method," *Proc. IFIP Congress 77*, 1977, Amsterdam, pp. 431-436.

37. Meisner, N. B. "Time-Division Digital Bus Techniques Implemented on Coaxial Cable," *Proc. Computer Network Symposium*, 1977, Gaithersburg, National Bureau of Standards, pp. 112-117.

38. Konheim, A. G. and Meister, B. "Waiting Lines and Times in a System with Polling," *J. ACM*, Vol. 21, 1974, pp. 470-490.

39. Lam, S. S. "A Carrier Sense Multiple Access Protocol for Local Networks," *Computer Networks*, Vol. 4, 1980, pp. 21-32.

40. Tobagi, F. A. and Hunt, V. B. "Performance Analysis of Carrier Sense Multiple Access with Collision Detection," Technical Report 173, Computer Systems Laboratory, Stanford University, Stanford, CA, 1979.

41. Bux, W. "Local-Area Subnetworks: A Performance Comparison," *IEEE Trans. Commun.*, Vol. COM-29, 1981, pp. 1465-1473.

42. Saltzer, J. H. and Clark, D. D. "Why a Ring?," *Proc. 7th Data Communications Symposium*, 1981, Mexico City, pp. 211-217.

43. Müller, H. R., Keller, H. and Meyr, H. "Transmission in a Synchronous Token Ring," *Proc. International Conference on Local Computer Networks*, April 1982, Florence, pp. 125-147.

44. Keller, H., Meyr, H., Müller, H. R. and Popken, L. "Synchronization Failures in a Chain of Repeaters," to appear in *Proc. Globecom 82*, 1982, Miami.

About the Authors

Karl Kümmerle received the M.S. and Ph.D. degrees in electrical engineering from Stuttgart University, Stuttgart, West Germany, in 1963 and 1969, respectively. From 1963 to 1969 he was Research Assistant with the Institute for Switching Techniques and Data Processing at Stuttgart University, where he was engaged primarily in investigations in the field of telephone traffic theory and mathematical statistics. From 1970 to 1972 he was Research Associate of the National Research Council at the Computation Laboratory of NASA's Marshall Space Flight Center. There he worked in the field of computer performance evaluation. In 1972 he joined the IBM Zurich Research Laboratory and has worked in the field of data communication networks. His current interest is in local area networks, where he is manager of a research project.

Martin Reiser was born in Switzerland in 1943 and received his education from the Swiss Federal Institute of Technology (ETH) where he obtained his Ph.D. in 1971. One year later, he switched from the IBM Zurich Research Laboratory, Switzerland to the IBM Thomas J. Watson Research Center in Yorktown Heights, NY, where he joined the Performance Evaluation group. He specialized in the numerical solution of queueing networks, and made contributions to the theory of multichain networks and their numerical solution. Together with J. Buzen and H. Kobayashi, M. Reiser laid the foundation for today's fast algorithms in queueing networks and created one of the first modeling software packages, known as QNET 4. M. Reiser is author and co-author of numerous publications in the field. After spending about one year at the IBM Research Laboratory in San José, CA, he returned to Yorktown Heights where he was soon appointed manager of Performance Evaluation. He led efforts in analysis, hierarchial modeling, and system measurement. In late 1977, he started a new group in the area of Computer Communication Network Modeling and Architecture. This activity led to a new assignment in 1978 as senior manager of Communications and Computer Science back at the IBM Zurich Research Laboratory, a position he still holds. M. Reiser's latest technical interests are in mean value analysis, a theory he co-founded with S. S. Lavenberg and which he applied to computer networks. M. Reiser is a member of ACM, IFIP WG.7.3, and IFIP WG.6.4.

Local Network Standards

Introduction to the ISO Reference Model

A computer communication protocol is a set of conventions, defined and agreed upon before communication begins, which is designed to facilitate communication between distinct computer processes. A protocol is necessary for the orderly exchange of information between computer processes.

Most of the terminology associated with communication protocols is derived from the Reference Model for Open Systems Interconnection (OSI/RM) produced by the International Standards Organization (ISO).

Typically, protocol consists of three separate but related parts:

1. *Syntax*: The syntax of a protocol relates to the physical structure of the information to be transmitted between processes. Depending upon the level at which a protocol operates, syntactic specifications describe items such as electrical signal levels or the position of various information fields (i.e., addresses, control information, user data) within the blocks of information exchanged between the communicating processes.

2. *Timing*: Protocol timing includes issues such as the actual bit rates associated with communication, the minimum time interval allowed between the transmission of blocks of data, and speed matching between processes which handle communicated information at different rates.

3. *Semantics*: The semantics of a protocol interpret the data communicated between processes. For example, certain protocols may define specific message types or information fields within messages which control future communication, i.e., a message may be communicated from one process to another indicating that an error was detected in a previously received block of data, and that the block of data should be retransmitted.

To facilitate discussion of computer communication protocols, the International Standards Organization (ISO) has produced an abstract model of computer communications, called the Open Systems Interconnection Reference Model. The Reference Model was originally produced to describe communications in the long-haul network environment, but it is applicable to local networks as well. The model provides a conceptual framework within which the features and facilities of a system can be discussed. It was not intended to provide detailed guidelines and design rules for system implementors and users.

A basic understanding of the ISO Reference Model is vital to an understanding of the issues involved in selecting and using standard computer communication protocols. Additionally, because most of the terminology currently being used in the literature with regard to protocols and standards is derived from the ISO model, a discussion of the model is included in this tutorial.

The key concept of the ISO model is the protocol layer. A layer is a level of abstraction within the process of computer communication. Two interfaces are associated with any layer; for example, associated with layer N are the interfaces to the next higher-level layer (layer N + 1) and the next lower level layer (layer N-1). One may assume that layer N provides a well-defined class of services and an interface to layer N + 1. Layer N is in turn implemented using services provided through the interface to layer N-1 and subsequent lower layers within the model. There is not a strict ordering among the layers in the sense that abstractions at higher levels may not require the use of all abstractions at lower levels. Furthermore, the classification of layers may depend upon one's viewpoint. A particular view of the system may cause certain layers to be transparent, or what might be a complete structure of layers may depend upon one's viewpoint. A particular view of the system may cause certain layers to be viewed (from higher layers) as simply a single layer and its interface. Layers are only allowed to interact through layer interfaces. Communication takes place within the model between peer levels, that is, between layers which exist at the same level on distinct network hosts.

The basic concept of layering and modular design has been highly touted (if not always practiced) in software design circles for many years. Some of the reasons to view and design the system as a hierarchy of layered services are the following:

1. Any facilities necessary to implement the functionality of a given layer can be made invisible to all other layers, thereby enforcing modularity.

2. Complex systems can be broken down into understandable subsystems.

3. The system can evolve in a simple fashion because the facilities that implement a layer can be changed without impact on other layers, so long as the interface remains the same.

4. Services offered at a particular level may share or multiplex the services of lower levels.

5. Alternative implementations which preserve the functionality and interfaces of a layer may be co-existent with the system.

6. Layers can be extended, simplified, or deleted at any time, based upon the need for services provided by that layer.

7. Each layer may be analyzed and tested independently of all other layers; thus, the system may be developed in a series of independent operations and verified layer-by-layer for correct operation.

Overview of Model

The ISO Reference Model is designed as a hierarchy of seven distinct protocol layers:

1. Physical
2. Link
3. Network
4. Transport
5. Session
6. Presentation
7. Application

The structure of the model is illustrated in the Figure where communication between peer levels is indicated by dashed lines. Each of these layers is discussed below in turn.

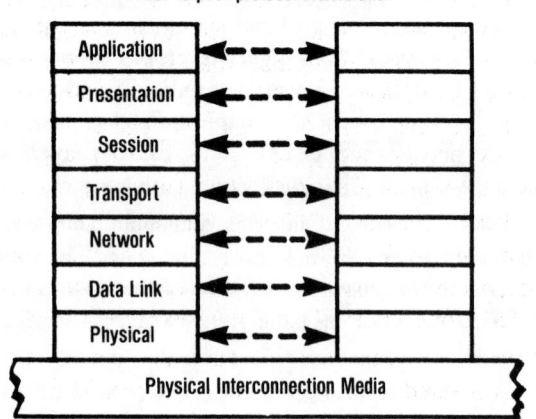

Peer to peer protocol interrelation

Figure: ISO Seven-Layer Reference Model

- *Physical Layer*: The physical protocol layer is concerned with electrical and mechanical specifications, i.e., signal levels and connectors. The function performed by the physical layer is the transmission/reception of an unstructured stream of bits over the network communication media.

  Examples of physical layer protocols include the common RS-232, RS-449, and CCITTs X.21, as well as the proprietary connection strategies employed by a variety of manufacturers to allow connection to their baseband and broadband local networks.

- *Link Layer*: The function performed by the link protocol layer (also called the data link layer) is the transmission/reception of a structured stream of bits over the network media. Whereas the physical layer provides for the transmission of a raw bit stream, the data link layer provides the ability to sub-divide this bit stream into structured blocks of information commonly called frames or packets. Frames are typically delimited by reserved bit patterns, reserved character sequences, or through the inclusion of an explicit bit or byte count within the frame.

  Data link protocols usually include some means of error detection, typically based upon a simple checksum included at the end of the frame.

  Examples of data link protocols include HDLC, SDLC, ADDCP, BiSync, and Ethernet's CSMA/CD protocol.

- *Network Layer*: The function of the network layer is to facilitate the transmission/reception of a packet from a source node to a destination node within the network. In traditional point-to-point store-and-forward networks, packets are typically passed from source to destination through a series of intermediate nodes, and, hence, some strategy for routing a packet to its eventual destination must exist. This strategy is implemented within the network layer.

  Typically, within the local network's sphere, packet routing is not required due to the inherent "broadcast" nature of the network. Hence, in many local networks, the network layer is small or even totally empty.

  An example of a network layer protocol is CCITT's X.25 protocol, DARPA's Internet Protocol, and Xerox's Internet Datagram Protocol.

- *Transport Layer*: The function of the transport layer is to provide for reliable end-to-end or host-to-host communication over the network. Two differing strategies have evolved to support this reliable communication, virtual circuits and datagrams. Datagrams are self-contained messages which include explicit source and destination addressing information, and which are delivered reliably under the control of transport layer protocols. Virtual circuits allow logical (or physical) connections to be established between source and destination and provide for a reliable data stream to be passed over the "circuit" from end-to-end.

  Virtual circuit based transport services have been the most widely used to date, and, thus, much of the machinery contained within the transport layer allows for the opening and closing of communication links or "calls" between machines. Some observers feel that the dominance of virtual circuit protocols is a reflection of the difficulty involved in efficiently implementing a reliable datagram service on the long-haul store-and-forward networks which were the impetus for the creation of the ISO Reference Model, rather than any inherent advantage which they have over datagram protocols. It will typically be easier to implement a reliable datagram service within the constrained environment of the local network, and since the overhead associated with connection establishment is not present in datagram protocols, the growth of local network technology may promote renewed interest in reliable datagram-based protocols within the transport layer.

Examples of well-defined transport layer protocols are Xerox's Internet Transport Protocols, DARPA's Transmission Control Protocol, and the NBS Transport Protocol.

- *Session Layer*: The function of the session layer is the management of end-to-end communication between processes running on network hosts. Typically, the session layer provides facilities to map logical process or port names (character strings) into network address information meaningful to the transport layer. The session layer manages interprocess communication within the network by opening, closing, and sending data over transport layer virtual circuits, or by sending transport layer datagrams, or both, depending upon the facilities which are available at the transport layer.

Currently DARPA's File Transfer Protocol and ISO's Session Layer Protocol are the most widely identified session layer protocols.

- *The Presentation Layer*: The function of the presentation layer is the tranformation of data to be sent to or received from the session layer. For example, one might wish to use a text compression algorithm in order to minimize the amount of data to be sent through the network. Text would be compressed within the presentation of the transmitting host and expanded again in the presentation layer of the receiving host. Similarly, data encryption algorithms might be implemented at the presentation layer.

Examples of presentation layer protocols include Xerox's Courier Protocol and DARPA's TELNET.

- *The Application Layer*: The function of the application layer is to provide a variety of application-specific protocols to application layer protocols, and might include services to facilitate funds transfer, information retrieval, electronic mail, text editing, and remote job entry. The variety of services provided at the application layer is theoretically limited only by the variety of possible application programs to be run in the network environment. However, only a limited number of standard application layer protocols exist today. These include Xerox's Clearinghouse Protocol and the ANSI X3V1 Electronic Mail and Messaging Protocols.

Standards Activities

There are many development activities that contribute to the local network standards process. Some of these are elected or nominated groups whose efforts are subscribed to by governments, organizations, companies, and the like. Others are the efforts of particular manufacturers who, by virtue of being first in the marketplace, superior approaches, wide-spread publicity, etc., developed what are *de facto* standards. Though not "officially" accepted, their implementation and wide-spread use eventually result in some type of "official" recognition.

In general, in the standards area, there are thousands of participants in hundreds of technical committees, subcommittees, study groups, working parties, working groups, task groups, etc. It is beyond the scope of this report to deal with each one. Rather the official groups—ISO, NBS, the Department of Defense, and IEEE 802—and the *de facto* standardization groups—General Motors and Xerox—that will have the most influence on the local network market are covered by this description.

The groups involved with the standardization of local networks are listed in the Figure.

Most of the "official" standards that have emerged to date involve only the first two layers of the OSI model. The heated debates such as broadband versus baseband, coaxial cable versus twisted pairs, Carrier Sense Multiple Access with Collision Detection versus Token Ring, Ethernet versus LocalNet, etc., have all revolved around issues restricted to the physical and data link layers. Only the *de facto* Xerox Network Systems protocols currently exist to address the complete range of network services up through the application layer. The ISO's effort is the most comprehensive undertaking to develop standards that cover the complete range, but this organization's work will not result in standard protocols for every level for at least another four years.

Unfortunately, the protocol standardization efforts of the groups covered here, despite being executed under the administration of hopefully "objective" professional organizations, often are entangled by economic and political overtones. Occasional rivalry between different standards organizations themselves sometimes further complicate an already difficult situation. The trend, however, is toward standardization, no matter how painful the process may appear to some observers and participants. In the long term, economic issues will be the prime mover, forcing the acceptance of standardization for local networks and networks in general.

The following groups are included in this discussion:

- *IEEE 802*: At the IEEE 802 (the Local Networks Standards Committee) meeting in San Diego, October 29 through November 2, 1984, more than 220 people

Organization	Affilliation	Representation	Influence
ANSI (American National Standards Institute)	Voluntary	Manufacturers, organizations, users, and common carriers	U.S. representative for ISO
DoD (Department of Defense)	Government agency	Government/military	All vendors dealing with the military. Developed TCP/IP
ECMA (European Computer Manufacturers Association)	Computer suppliers selling in Europe	Trade organization of suppliers	Contributes to ISO and also issues own standards
General Motors	Public corporation	Manufacturers and users	Purchaser of very large quantities of equipment
IEEE (The Institute of Electrical and Electronics Engineers, Inc.)	Professional society	Dues-paying individuals	Contributes to ANSI and issues own standards such as 802 local networks standards
ISO (International Standards Organization)	Voluntary	Standards bodies in participating nations. U.S. representative is ANSI	Responsible for OSI model
NBS (National Bureau of Standards)	Government agency	Government agencies, and network users	Issues Federal Information Processing Standards (FIPS) for equipment sold to Fed. Government; DoD is exempted
Xerox Corporation	Public corporation	None. Followed by other companies	Being first attracts a large following

Figure: Groups Involved with Local Network Standards

participated in the Committee's work. Although some people felt that 802's work was completed, this large attendance indicates that there is still a great deal more to do. With the basics defined, expansion to cover different media, signaling techniques, metropolitan area networks, etc., are receiving much more attention.

The 802.1 Local Network Standards Overview Document is still out for balloting with results due by the next meeting in February 1985. The 802.1 group also reported substantial progress on preparing the network management document that it is currently developing. In another effort, members of this subcommittee are examining what others are doing about internetworking for incorporation into its documents at a later date.

The 802.2 Link Level Subcommittee is working on specifying a Type 3 service to add to its specification. This type of service is somewhere between a datagram and a full connection service. It is a way to receive acknowledgments without needing higher-level proto-cols, as in a pure datagram service. This kind of service would be very useful in the process control industry and in various transaction environments.

The 802.3 CSMA/CD document on Cheapernet, a lower-cost local network approach, has been sent for ballot to the members of the IEEE Computer Society's Technical Committee on Computer Communication. This is really an addendum to the 802.3 Standard, to allow RG58 ohm coax cable to be used instead of the thicker cable now specified. The network would still operate at 10 Mbps, but over shorter distances and with fewer connections. The result of this different cable scheme would be to reduce costs, especially where individual networks or subnetworks can be formed that in turn connect to a Standard 802.3 cable as a back-bone.

The 802.3 group also is studying other proposals for reducing the cost of a CSMA/CD network. One pro-posal by Sytek and Intel is to incorporate a 2-Mbps

CSMA/CD operation over a broadband system (a la IBM's PC Network). Another proposal, put forth by AT&T, is called STAR LAN and runs at 1-Mbps on existing twisted pair. This 802.3 effort is strictly in the study phase now.

Another 802.3 effort is making progress in developing an AUI-compatible broadband model. This will allow a baseband transceiver to be replaced by a broadband modem to run 10-Mbps CSMA/CD on broadband.

The 802.4 Token Bus group currently is defining 10- and 20-Mbps broadband schemes. Also in progress is work on further defining a 10-Mbps token bus baseband phase coherent coding scheme.

The 802.5 Token Ring specification has been approved as an IEEE Standard, and, as such, has been presented to ISO. At the same time, a British presentation of a slotted ring (a la Logica VTS Polynet) was made to ISO. ISO will now have to sort out these competing methods.

In the Metropolitan Area Network Subcommittee, 802.6, Burroughs made a presentation on a 100-Mbps fiber optic ring for city-wide use. This appeared similar to X3T9.5's work on a 100-Mbps computer room fiber optic network scheme, so perhaps some joint developments are possible. In any case, no short-term results are expected in the way of an 802.6 Standard.

The 802.7 Broadband Advisory Group is currently putting together a broadband wiring procedures guide. Recommendations will be included covering types of cables, numbers of taps, and the like.

The 802.8 Fiber Optic Advisory Group is looking for areas in which to advise the other groups on the use of fiber optics. One possibility is its use as a fiber optic inter-repeater link.

- *ISO*: The ISO Technical Committee 97, Information Processing Systems, Subcommittee 6, Telecommunications and Information Exchange between Systems (ISO/TC 97/SC 6), held its annual meeting in Washington, DC, at the end of October 1984. At this meeting, it was reported that the effort to develop OSI service definition standards that follow the basic reference model was progressing. These service definitions specify further the layer services, and the interactions with the adjacent layer above that are needed for performing the layer's functions. Standards for the network-, transport-, and session-layer service definitions have been completed and approved while work continues on the other four layers.

Currently, the local network specifications developed by IEEE 802—802.2 (Logical Link Control), 802.3 (CSMA/CD), and 802.4 (Token Bus)—are out on a six month ballot for approval as international standards. The SC 6 meeting in October agreed to add 802.5 (Token Ring) and the United Kingdom's proposal for a Slotted Ring for ballot approval.

Two ISO Draft Proposals were recently submitted for connection-oriented presentation service and protocol (Layer 6). The connection-oriented presentation service definition defines the service primitives and interactions by which the connection-oriented presentation service is provided by the presentation layer to users of the application. The connection-oriented presentation protocol specification specifies the formats of the presentation protocol data units (PPDUs), the sequences of PPDUs exchanged between presentation entities, and the way in which the presentation entities use the session service to provide the connection-oriented presentation service.

- *GM MAP*: The GM MAP Task Force is continuing to develop its specification and its implementation. Currently, the MAP work is concentrating on ISO layers 6 and 7 and is based on working drafts from the various standards groups. The interim MAP specifications for file transfer, messaging, virtual terminals, directory service, and network management are unique because no international standards exist. GM is developing software that will be a mix of GM-specific and standard protocol based on pilot GM needs and the approval process of standards group.

Along with GM's efforts, a GM MAP user group has been formed. The last meeting of the MAP Users Group was held in Gaithersburg, Maryland, at the National Bureau of Standards on January 14-15, 1985. The meeting dealt with such topics as conformance/testing issues, GM current MAP activities, MAP/Standards Groups interaction, and standards affecting MAP.

- *NBS*: NBS continues to play a major role in solidifying the ISO transport specification. Its aggressive efforts are a significant factor in the acceptance it has been receiving despite the competition from the existing TCP and XNS transport layer de facto standards. By sponsoring workshops such as that for the MAP Users Group and demonstrations such as that at the 1984 NCC, NBS is dramatically demonstrating the power of standardization and its effects.

At a recent meeting of the NBS Workshop on OSI, a special interest group was formed to study connection-oriented network service. This group will study the possibility of providing connection-oriented internetworking in the next demonstrations on OSI protocols that are jointly sponsored by NBS and industry. This demonstration, scheduled for 1985, will also include internetworking capabilities. Intitially, only the NBS connectionless internetwork protocol was planned, but significant interest in a connection-oriented approach may add this to the demonstration.

- *ANSI*: The American National Standards Institute is currently conducting a 60-day public review of the IEEE 802 specifications. These are the same ones currently being considered by ISO.

- *ECMA*: The European Computer Manufacturers Association has maintained a close liaison with the IEEE 802. In June 1983, ECMA approved a token ring technique, but subsequent changes by IEEE 802.5 has resulted in ECMA incorporating the new provisions into a revision of its standard so that full alignment with IEEE 802 specifications will be maintained.

ECMA's process of approving standards at semi-annual meetings, as opposed to lengthy letter ballots, leads to early establishment specification. Thus, the need for revisions, expansions, and enhancements, which are reflected in subsequent ECMA document editions, continues to exist.

- *Xerox*: In 1984, Xerox was busy enhancing its product line and demonstrating the effectiveness of its XNS protocols, one of the de facto industry standards.

In 1984, Xerox introduced its new network services for the IBM PC, PC XT, or fully IBM-compatible personal computers using MS-DOS 2.0 or 2.1. The IBM and COMPAQ personal computers (using 3Com interface boards!) on the network, like all the Xerox workstations on the Ethernet, had full access to network services for electronic printing, electronic filing, electronic mail, and mainframe access. By using Xerox's internet protocols, all of these workstations could access machines, not just on the particular Ethernet to which they were connected, but on remote Ethernets as well.

Xerox introduced a remote batch service that was designed to provide multi-vendor document interchange. It supports IBM 2770/2780/3780 communication protocols as well as flexible document format conversion. Using this service, information created on IBM mainframes can be sent to Xerox network systems for integration and enhancement. Information created on Xerox systems can be sent to mainframes for processing or archiving. The remote batch service also supports document interchange with other mainframes, word processors, and workstations that support the IBM protocols and formats. The service is available to all equipment on the Xerox internetwork through the Xerox filing protocol.

While the various standards organizations are still drafting proposals for higher-level protocols, Xerox has defined and is now offering products based on its own definitions. The addition of capabilities to communicate with IBM and DEC products, to print on different types of printers from different manufacturers' computers, and the like, illustrates the scope of Xerox's efforts. By publishing the specifications to these higher-level protocols, Xerox has attracted and will continue to attract a large following of manufacturers and, in turn, users that have made Xerox Network Systems (XNS) a *de facto* standard. By the time the "official" standards are finalized and published by ISO and NBS, one may just find so many followers and customers of XNS that it is the "practical" standard. In any case, these new Xerox products (and many more to come over the next year), as well as additions and enchancements to its XNS protocols will make Xerox a significant force in the local network standards area.

Overview of Local Computer Network Design Issues

All of the articles in this tutorial describe commercially available or soon-to-be available local networks. This article touches upon the many system design issues confronting the purchaser of these networks and summarizes the overall design problems common to all these considerations. Because the requirements of any purchasing organization place different weights on the parameters involved in selection, no attempt is made here to rank issues by their degree of importance. The top priority of one organization may not even be a consideration of another organization.

The design and operational issues in a local area network (LAN) are similar to many of the issues that arise within the context of multiprocessors, multiple computer systems, distributed systems, and computer network systems in general. However, in the case of local networks, these issues may be grouped and summarized in a different format. We discuss here network components—both hardware and software—and configurations of these components: network operation, performance, and user-oriented concerns.

Network Entities

A number of factors must be considered in determining the components needed in a network and the characteristics required of those components. One of the primary considerations in component selection is heterogeneity, i.e., the question of whether or not products of different manufacturers can be interconnected, and whether or not different processors and/or peripherals from the same manufacturer can be used.

LAN systems vary in their approach to this issue. Some, such as 3Com's EtherSeries, use de facto standards and widely available and compatible homogeneous processors (IBM PCs and compatibles); others, such as the Apollo Domain employ only the company's own specially designed family of homogeneous processors. In most cases, however, heterogeneity is common: Net/One, LocalNet, PLAN 4000, HYPERchannel, and several others all incorporate processors ranging from micros and minis to large mainframe computers.

Mode of connection to the network is a significant design issue because of the variety of performance-compatible devices available. AMD, Fujitsu, Intel, and others offer special purpose VLSI communication interface chips which allow the use of existing protocols; e.g., Intel is offering an Ethernet chip. Some networks, such as ARCnet, have designed their interfaces so that they were candidates for implementation in LSI or VLSI (the ARCnet chip is produced by Standard Microsystems and is designated the COM 9026);

others, such as Net/One, use off-the-shelf microprocessors such as the Z80 or Intel 80186 in their interface units.

While most of the hardware entities in a local network are already available, the same is not true of the software components. A network operating system may be required that can perform the critical functions—such as resource sharing, security, and scheduling—within the constraints of the selected network architecture. In an attempt to make these network functions attainable, manufacturers are developing various network operating systems. NETEX from Network Systems is an attempt to address this problem, as is the operating system furnished by CDC in its loosely coupled network (CDC LAN). In the PC LAN area, this is changing with the introduction of products like the Novell NetWare OS and Microsoft MS-Net.

Network Architectures

Organization and configuration of the various components are the foremost concerns in network architecture design. Shared memories, buses, rings, stars, trees, and meshes are all possible and have been implemented, in one form or another, in at least one of the identified LAN systems. Some networks, such as HYPERchannel and CDC's LCN, have implemented multiple links for efficiency and reliability. ProNet is available as a ring or a star-shaped ring. A number of manufacturers are using token buses, and IBM will offer a star-shaped ring.

Another key design issue is that of distribution of network components, i.e., whether they should be centralized (or clustered) or distributed within the network locale (as destined by the definition of an LAN). Once again, examples of both arrangements can be found in existing systems. If the components are to be distributed, the maximum allowable interconnect distances and the limits on interconnectability must be considered. Many of the networks are limited to interconnect distances of less than 5,000 feet; some broadband systems claim distances of up to 50 miles.

Network interconnection is yet another issue which concerns designers. Many manufacturers are in the process of developing, or have developed, gateways and bridges to allow local network interconnection to other LANs, or to global networks. An important consideration here is whether or not the gateways between networks for the local-to-local network interconnection differ from those for the local-to-global application. A local network may itself be used as a gateway between different networks. Bridge Communications and Ungermann-Bass appear firmly established as the leading companies building gateway products.

Flexibility of the installed LAN configuration must also be considered. Most LANs do offer considerable flexibility to add nodes, execute tasks at nodes other than the user's, and modify the software of the network; however, on some networks this job is performed by reprogramming PROMS. More and more companies are offering implementations of various levels of the OSI/ISO Reference Model protocols in read/write memory.

Network architecture depends to a large extent on the bandwidth required or achievable. Type of communication medium is a factor here; coaxial cable, twisted-pair, fiber-optic, microwave, VHF/UHF, and laser links may all be available. Rates are usually lower in networks using twisted-pair than in those using coaxial cable. NEC's 6770 achieves rates of 32 Mbps using fiber-optic cables. Combinations are also possible; the ARCnet network, for example, may include infrared and twisted-pair media in addition to coax.

Major trade-offs must be considered when choosing from the competing technologies of PBX, broadband, and baseband. This choice, however, is highly dependent on the user's desire to integrate voice and data on the same system. Because there is a wide variety of system design choices available in each area, the most important decision factor is the degree of integration desired. Fourth generation PBXs are about to appear that are themselves designed around broadband (the CXC Rose) and baseband (the Ztel PNX) technology.

Network Operation

The primary network operation issue is the method of network control over such items as load, stations on the network, resource allocations, and the like. Despite the paramount importance of control methodology, very little control equipment, as such, is currently available. Experts have yet to agree on whether centralized or distributed control is more desirable. Control centered in a network operating system may be one solution.

Because most LANs have the ability to share resources, contention disputes must be resolved. Some networks— e.g., the LAN—allow only one user at a time to transmit a request; others have various retransmission schemes if contention is detected. Ethernet coordinates transmission through statistical arbitration and generates random retransmission intervals in case of contention, while HYPERchannel assigns unique retry intervals on the basis of some previously established (and changeable) priority scheme.

One issue often overlooked by LAN designers is that of efficiency in jobs or processes. Most set up a standard scheduling algorjDPm at each node and use contention avoidance techniques to resolve problems.

Access control and other security features should be provided. Password systems, as in the PLAN 4000 file server, are the usual control implementations. Localnet 20 offers a secure network interface based upon a DES encryption system. Although some security features may be unnecessary due to the locality of the network, provision may be made for them to allow for future interconnection between local computer networks.

Another operational control issue to address is the strategy to be used for routing in the local network. Point-to-point and broadcast transmissions are both widely used.

The protocols or procedures used in implementing these aspects of control are very important and differ from those used in geographically distributed networks. Local networks usually have a higher bandwidth, less transmission delay, greater reliability, and, in addition, have usually been optimized for a particular application. Therefore, the design and construction of LAN protocols may be unique to the particular network and may be greatly influenced by the intended applications. Ethernet uses its own link protocol, while HYPERchannel uses a variation of IBM's SDLC.

One final network architecture issue is that of reliability and tolerance to faults. Almost all LAN designs address this issue. NEC 6770 uses a redundant path, while proNet provides a wire center. IBM clearly believes that its announced corporate strategy of a single token system is the best choice.

Performance

In terms of operational efficiency, network performance and measurement of that performance are both important concerns. Throughput and response time are two measures of network effectiveness. Most LANs are combinations in that high throughput, low delay, and high reliability all may have been design goals.

Network tuning based on performance data should become commonplace. Data transmission bottlenecks, inefficient resource utilization, and other problems can be detected through hardware and software instrumentation. Statistics and other performance data can be collected at each node and transmitted to one node for evaluation.

In the various stages of LAN design and implementation, a performance model would be quite valuable. Developing and validating this model, however, remains a major task. Little in the way of products has appeared in this area. The current state-of-the-art is exhibited by the Excelan Nutcracker, an Ethernet performance measurement tool.

User

User-oriented issues fall into two categories, cost and ease of use—two sometimes mutually exclusive considerations. In fact, local networks will soon disappear if they are not cost effective. Cost considerations must include the impact on existing systems, total development costs, recurring costs, maintenance costs, manufacturers' support, and development and implementation time.

Ease of use is an important consideration often overlooked in network design. If little thought is given to human factors, more people—more highly skilled people—will be needed to operate the system, thus driving up the cost of the network. Factors pertaining to ease of use include the ease of meeting password and security requirements, ease of obtaining the status of the network, and ease of locating unknown resources and data. In addition, simplicity of commands and user operations, the time spent waiting, the ease of establishing an accounting system and charging users, and the ease of access to the network must be considered.

Conclusion: The Future

Currently most manufacturers are dealing at or below level 4 of the ISO model. In the future, these manufacturers may well be expected to try raising the levels covered by their systems. Continue to expect to see more significant OS and VLSI chip offerings implementing more levels of protocols at a significantly lower cost.

Examples of particular design issues can be found in the articles found throughout this tutorial.

Section 2: Bus and Star Type Baseband Networks

The papers in this section describe examples of bus and star type baseband networks. The bus topology has long been the favored topology in the United States because of the advantages in reliability and flexiblility that many United States manufacturers believe this topology has over-ring and star-type networks. With the arrival of fiber optics into the networking field the star topology has made a comeback. This is because the present fiber optic technology cannot yet cost effectively produce the splitters and joiners that would be needed for a bus topology fiber optic network.

With these topologies, a wide range of network transmission rates are available. Included in this section are examples of low speed (less than 1 Mbps), medium speed (1-10 Mbps), and high speed (greater than 20 Mbps) networks.

The leading article in this section is one authored by the developers of Ethernet, which today is one of the basic models for local area networks. Originally developed at the Xerox Research Center in Palo Alto (1972) and later updated in a cooperative effort involving DEC, Intel, and Xerox (1980), it is a system designed to connect computers that are located within .1 to 10 kilometers of each other.

Communication occurs at 10 Mbps over a 50 ohm coaxial cable using a packet switched, distributed control algorithm known as Carrier Sense Multiple Access with Collision Detection (CSMA/CD). Since Ethernet was one of the first and most successful networks available, it has had a great influence on subsequent products, including the spawning of a slew of "Ethernet-like" networks and being the basis upon which the IEEE 802.3 CSMA/CD bus structure standard was developed.

Ungermann-Bass' Net/One, which is described in the next paper, was initially a 4 Mbps, heterogeneous system. When the Ethernet specification was published in 1980, Ungermann-Bass quickly revised their network to meet the specifications, coming out with a commercially available 10-Mbps Ethernet before Xerox. An extremely flexible system, the Net/One has grown to include both personal computer and broadband connections to the orginal baseband network. With more than 600 systems installed, Net/One is well established in the computer networking market.

With the advent of personal computers, there has been a great deal of interest in connecting these small computers with larger computers to give them the power of computer systems while keeping the advantages of the personal computer. 3Com provided the first connection to Ethernet for the IBM PC. It consists of a single board which plugs into the PC bus and associated server software. Connection to Ethernet is via an on-board BNC connector with no other external transceivers needed.

Bridge Communications is a company that specializes in developing products which enable Ethernet systems to communicate with each other or with various other networks and devices. In its article, its communication and gateway servers and the software that runs them are discussed in detail.

The next article examines one of the possible ways to test and debug these Ethernet networks. Excelan's Nutcracker is a comprehensive development and management system for Ethernet or IEEE 802.3-based systems. The Nutcracker is a tool capable of performing functions analogous to a logic analyzer at the network packet level, generating any type of packet, and accumulating and analyzing statistics from the general network traffic or from the output of filters which allow only specified packets through.

The use of fiber optic as the transmission medium in an Ethernet environment presents some special problems. Among these are the problems with detecting collisions in the CSMA/CD protocol and the problems with trying to emulate the bus structure in a star topology system. Seicor FiberLAN offers a fiber optic system which deals with these problems, and its solutions are discussed in the article.

The system discussed next, HYPERchannel, is the oldest of the local area networks. It was designed for use with the large mainframes and minicomputers located in computer centers. It operates at 50 Mbps, a speed comparable to computer channel speeds. It has proved to be a flexible system, interfacing to a large number of different computers.

In the following article, the founders of Network Systems, Jim Thornton and Gary Christensen, discuss the two methods by which HYPERchannel networks can be interconnected. Through the use of link adapters, it is possible to connect networks over short-haul terrestrial distances, or over long-haul and satellite links. With the link adapters comes Netex, a software system which provides the access method for the interconnection. Netex conforms to the ISO reference model for data communications.

Omninet, the next product discussed, is one of the earliest local area networks developed for use with microcomputers. It operates with a CSMA access scheme at 1 Mbps. Its most impressive feature is its ability to connect a large variety of incompatible micros, including Apples, IBM PCs, and others. This flexiblity has been widely appreciated in the market with 5000 networks already installed.

While all of the previous networks use some form of contention, Datapoint's ARCnet was the first network to use a token-passing access method. Datapoint computers interface to the network bus through Resource Interface Modules

(RIM). Hubs connect as many as 10 RIMs in a star-shaped configuration. Hubs, in turn, can be interconnected to cover as many as 4 miles in extent. These modules handle all network considerations, allowing the processors to function normally. Presently there are more than 6000 ARCnets installed around the world.

Nestar's Plan 4000 also uses a token passing scheme. Unlike ARCnet, though, it is geared toward connecting personal computers, in particular Apples and IBM PCs. In developing their product, Nestar applied Datapoint's technology via a Standard Microsystems chip (the COM 9020) to construct interface boards which plug directly into the expansion slots of IBM and Apple personal computers. The Plan 4000 was designed using the ISO reference model, and in addition to using token-passing protocol for the physical and datalink layers, it uses Xerox Network System for the network and transport layers and Nestar server software for the higher layers.

Datakit, AT&T Network Systems' (the regulated AT&T entity) entry into the data communications market, was announced in 1983 with about 50 systems installed by the summer of 1984. Datakit is a hierarchical network which uses twisted-pair wire for its transmission medium. This wiring scheme allows the use of in-place wiring, which is in direct competition with the extensive wiring concept that IBM has planned for its network.

AT&T Information Systems' (the unregulated entity) new LAN scheme, the Information Systems Network (ISN) is based on the architecture of the previously described Datakit Virtual Circuit Switch. The ISN adds a time-slotted transmission bus to the Datakit node, allowing the contention bus to be solely concerned with providing efficient and fair allocation of the transmission bus. ISN uses twisted-pair wire for its transmission medium. This wiring scheme allows the use of in-place wiring also. In 1984, AT&T approached the IEEE 802.3 committee in an effort to standardize their new network. Under the name Starlan, there appears to be considerable sentiment within 802.3 to approve this approach as yet another standard.

Evolution of the Ethernet Local Computer Network

As it evolved from a research prototype to the specification of a multi-company standard, Ethernet compelled designers to consider numerous trade-offs among alternative implementations and design strategies.

John F. Shoch, Yogen K. Dalal, and David D. Redell, Xerox
Ronald C. Crane, 3Com

Reprinted from *Computer,* August 1982, pages 10-27. Copyright © 1982 by
The Institute of Electrical and Electronics Engineers, Inc.

With the continuing decline in the cost of computing, we have witnessed a dramatic increase in the number of independent computer systems used for scientific computing, business, process control, word processing, and personal computing. These machines do not compute in isolation, and with their proliferation comes a need for suitable communication networks—particularly local computer networks that can interconnect locally distributed computing systems. While there is no single definition of a local computer network, there is a broad set of requirements:

- relatively high data rates (typically 1 to 10M bits per second);
- geographic distance spanning about one kilometer (typically within a building or a small set of buildings);
- ability to support several hundred independent devices;
- simplicity, or the ability "to provide the simplest possible mechanisms that have the required functionality and performance";[1]
- good error characteristics, good reliability, and minimal dependence upon any centralized components or control;
- efficient use of shared resources, particularly the communications network itself;
- stability under high load;
- fair access to the system by all devices;
- easy installation of a small system, with graceful growth as the system evolves;
- ease of reconfiguration and maintenance; and
- low cost.

One of the more successful designs for a system of this kind is the Ethernet local computer network.[2,3] Ethernet installations have been in use for many years. They support hundreds of stations and meet the requirements listed above.

In general terms, Ethernet is a multi-access, packet-switched communications system for carrying digital data among locally distributed computing systems. The shared communications channel in an Ethernet is a passive broadcast medium with no central control; packet address recognition in each station is used to take packets from the channel. Access to the channel by stations wishing to transmit is coordinated in a distributed fashion by the stations themselves, using a statistical arbitration scheme.

The Ethernet strategy can be used on many different broadcast media, but our major focus has been on the use of coaxial cable as the shared transmission medium. The Experimental Ethernet system was developed at the Xerox Palo Alto Research Center starting in 1972. Since then, numerous other organizations have developed and built "Ethernet-like" local networks.[4] More recently, a cooperative effort involving Digital Equipment Corporation, Intel, and Xerox has produced an updated version of the Ethernet design, generally known as the Ethernet Specification.[5]

One of the primary goals of the Ethernet Specification is compatibility—providing enough information for different manufacturers to build widely differing machines in such a way that they can directly communicate with one another. It might be tempting to view the Specification as simply a design handbook that will allow designers to develop their own Ethernet-like network, perhaps cus-

EHO228-7/85/0000/0037$01.00 © 1982 IEEE

tomized for some specific requirements or local constraints. But this would miss the major point: Successful interconnection of heterogeneous machines requires equipment that precisely matches a single specification.

Meeting the Specification is only one of the necessary conditions for intermachine communication at all levels of the network architecture. There are many levels of protocol, such as transport, name binding, and file transfer, that must also be agreed upon and implemented in order to provide useful services.[6-8] This is analogous to the telephone system: The common low-level specifications for telephony make it possible to dial from the US to France, but this is not of much use if the caller speaks only English while the person who answers the phone speaks only French. Specification of these additional protocols is an important area for further work.

The design of any local network must be considered in the context of a distributed system architecture. Although the Ethernet Specification does not directly address issues of high-level network architecture, we view the local network as one component in an *internetwork* system, providing communication services to many diverse devices connected to different networks.[6,9] The services provided by the Ethernet are influenced by these broader architectural considerations.

As we highlight important design considerations and trace the evolution of the Ethernet from research prototype to multicompany standard, we use the term Experimental Ethernet for the former and Ethernet or Ethernet Specification for the latter. The term Ethernet is also used to describe design principles common to both systems.

General description of Ethernet-class systems

Theory of operation. The general Ethernet approach uses a shared communications channel managed with a distributed control policy known as *carrier sense multiple access with collision detection*, or CSMA/CD. With this approach, there is no central controller managing access to the channel, and there is no preallocation of time slots or frequency bands. A station wishing to transmit is said to "contend" for use of the common shared communications channel (sometimes called the Ether) until it "acquires" the channel; once the channel is acquired the station uses it to transmit a packet.

To acquire the channel, stations check whether the network is busy (that is, use *carrier sense*) and defer transmission of their packet until the Ether is quiet (no other transmissions occurring). When quiet is detected, the deferring station immediately begins to transmit. During transmission, the transmitting station listens for a collision (other transmitters attempting to use the channel simultaneously). In a correctly functioning system, collisions occur only within a short time interval following the start of transmission, since after this interval all stations will detect carrier and defer transmission. This time interval is called the *collision window* or the *collision interval* and is a function of the end-to-end propagation delay. If no collisions occur during this time, a transmitter has ac-

quired the Ether and continues transmission of the packet. If a station detects collision, the transmission of the rest of the packet is immediately aborted. To ensure that all parties to the collision have properly detected it, any station that detects a collision invokes a *collision consensus enforcement procedure* that briefly jams the channel. Each transmitter involved in the collision then schedules its packet for retransmission at some later time.

To minimize repeated collisions, each station involved in a collision tries to retransmit at a different time by scheduling the retransmission to take place after a random delay period. In order to achieve channel stability under overload conditions, a controlled retransmission strategy is used whereby the mean of the random retransmission delay is increased as a function of the channel load. An estimate of the channel load can be derived by monitoring the number of collisions experienced by any one packet. This has been shown to be the optimal strategy among the options available for decentralized decision and control problems of this class.[10]

Stations accept packets addressed to them and discard any that are found to be in error. Deference reduces the probability of collision, and collision detection allows the timely retransmission of a packet. It is impossible, however, to guarantee that all packets transmitted will be delivered successfully. For example, if a receiver is not enabled, an error-free packet addressed to it will not be delivered; higher levels of protocol must detect these situations and retransmit.

Under very high load, short periods of time on the channel may be lost due to collisions, but the collision resolution procedure operates quickly.[2,11-13] Channel utilization under these conditions will remain high, particularly if packets are large with respect to the collision interval. One of the fundamental parameters of any Ethernet implementation is the length of this collision interval, which is based on the round-trip propagation time between the farthest two points in the system.

Basic components. The CSMA/CD access procedure can use any broadcast multi-access channel, including radio, twisted pair, coaxial cable, diffuse infrared, and fiber optics.[14] Figure 1 illustrates a typical Ethernet system using coaxial cable. There are four components.

Station. A station makes use of the communication system and is the basic addressable device connected to an Ethernet; in general, it is a computer. We do not expect that "simple" terminals will be connected directly to an Ethernet. Terminals can be connected to some form of terminal controller, however, which provides access to the network. In the future, as the level of sophistication in terminals increases, many terminals will support direct connection to the network. Furthermore, specialized I/O devices, such as magnetic tapes or disk drives, may incorporate sufficient computing resources to function as stations on the network.

Within the station there is some interface between the operating system environment and the Ethernet controller. The nature of this interface (often in software) depends upon the particular implementation of the controller functions in the station.

Controller. A controller for a station is really the set of functions and algorithms needed to manage access to the channel. These include signaling conventions, encoding and decoding, serial-to-parallel conversion, address recognition, error detection, buffering, the basic CSMA/CD channel management, and packetization. These functions can be grouped into two logically independent sections of each controller: the transmitter and the receiver.

The controller functions are generally implemented using a combination of hardware, microcode, and software, depending on the nature of the station. It would be possible, for example, for a very capable station to have a minimal hardware connection to the transmission system and perform most of these functions in software. Alternatively, a station might implement all the controller functions in hardware, or perhaps in a controller-specific microprocessor. Most controller implementations fall somewhere in between. With the continuing advances in LSI development, many of these functions will be packaged in a single chip, and several semiconductor manufacturers have already announced plans to build Ethernet controllers. The precise boundary between functions performed on the chip and those in the station is implementation-dependent, but the nature of that interface is of great importance. As many of the functions as possible should be moved into the chip, provided that this preserves all of the flexibility needed in the construction and use of system interfaces and higher level software.

The description of the controller in this article is functional in nature and indicates how the controller must behave independent of particular implementations. There is some flexibility in implementing a correct controller, and we will make several recommendations concerning efficient operation of the system.

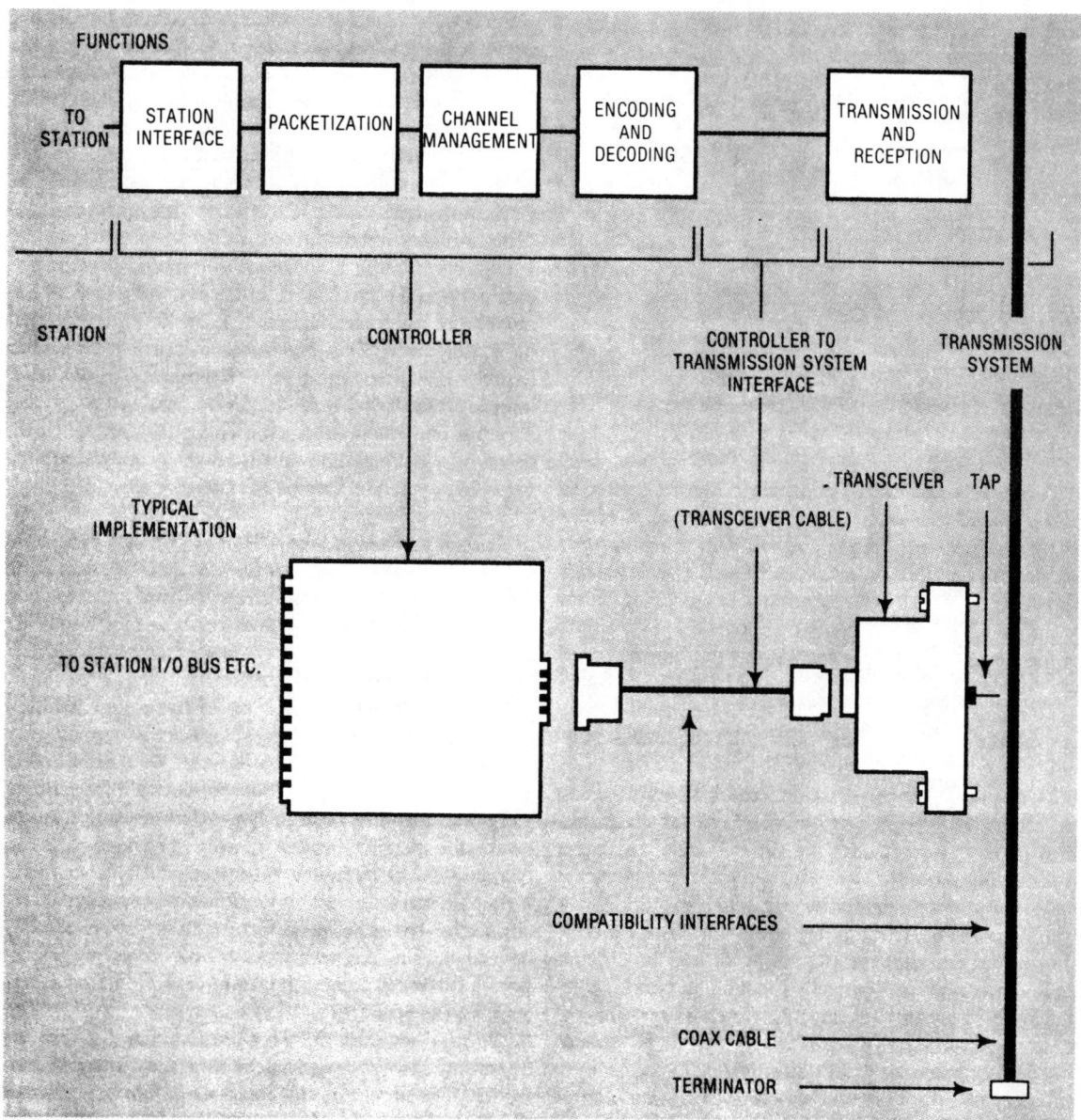

Figure 1. A general Ethernet implementation.

Transmission system. The transmission system includes all the components used to establish a communications path among the controllers. In general, this includes a suitable broadcast transmission medium, the appropriate transmitting and receiving devices—transceivers—and, optionally, repeaters to extend the range of the medium. The protocol for managing access to the transmission system is implemented in the controller; the transmission system does not attempt to interpret any of the bits transmitted on the channel.

The broadcast transmission medium contains those components that provide a physical communication path. In the case of coaxial cable, this includes the cable plus any essential hardware—connectors, terminators, and taps.

Transceivers contain the necessary electronics to transmit and receive signals on the channel and recognize the presence of a signal when another station transmits. They also recognize a collision that takes place when two or more stations transmit simultaneously.

Repeaters are used to extend the length of the transmission system beyond the physical limits imposed by the transmission medium. A repeater uses two transceivers to connect to two different Ethernet segments and combines them into one logical channel, amplifying and regenerating signals as they pass through in either direction.[15] Repeaters are transparent to the rest of the system, and stations on different segments can still collide. Thus, the repeater must propagate a collision detected on one segment through to the other segment, and it must do so without becoming unstable. A repeater makes an Ethernet channel longer and as a result increases the maximum propagation delay of the system, meaning delay through the repeater and propagation delay through the additional segments. To avoid multipath interference in an Ethernet installation, there must be only one path between any two stations through the network. (The higher level internetwork architecture can support alternate paths between stations through different communications channels.)

Controller-to-transmission-system interface. One of the major interfaces in an Ethernet system is the point at which the controller in a station connects to the transmission system. The controller does much of the work in managing the communications process, so this is a fairly simple interface. It includes paths for data going to and from the transmission system. The data received can be used by the controller to sense carrier, but the transmission system normally includes a medium-specific mechanism for detecting collisions on the channel; this must also be communicated through the interface to the controller. It is possible to power a transceiver from a separate power source, but power is usually taken from the controller interface. In most transmission systems, the connection from the controller is made to a transceiver, and this interface is called the transceiver cable interface.

Two generations of Ethernet designs. The Experimental Ethernet circa 1972 confirmed the feasibility of the design, and dozens of installations have been in regular use since then. A typical installation supports hundreds of stations and a wide-ranging set of applications: file transfer, mail distribution, document printing, terminal access to timesharing systems, data-base access, copying disks, multimachine programs, and more. Stations include the Alto workstation,[16] the Dorado (an internal research machine),[17] the Digital Equipment PDP-11, and the Data General Nova. The system has been the subject of extensive performance measurements confirming its predicted behavior.[12,13]

Based upon that experience, a second-generation system was designed at Xerox in the late 1970's. That effort subsequently led to the joint development of the Ethernet Specification. Stations built by Xerox for this network include the Xerox 860, the Xerox 8000 Network System Processor, and the Xerox 1100 Scientific Information Processor (the "Dolphin").

The two systems are very similar: they both use coaxial cable, Manchester signal encoding, and CSMA/CD with dynamic control. Some changes were made based on experience with the experimental system or in an effort to enhance the characteristics of the network. Some of the differences between the systems are summarized in Table 1.

An "Ethernet Technical Summary," which brings together the important features of Version 1 of the joint specification on two pages, is included for reference (pp. 14-15). (In building a compatible device or component, the full Ethernet Specification[5] remains the controlling document. In describing the Ethernet Specification, this article corresponds to Version 1.0; Version 2.0, including extensions and some minor revisions, will be completed later this year.)

Figure 2 is a photograph of some typical components from the Experimental Ethernet, including a transceiver and tap, transceiver cable, and an Alto controller board. Figure 3 is a photograph of similar components based on the Ethernet Specification. Note that both controller boards have been implemented with standard MSI circuits.

Transmission system design

A number of design issues and trade-offs emerged in the development of the Ethernet transmission system, and several lessons were learned from that experience.

Coaxial cable subsystem. In addition to having favorable signaling characteristics and the ability to handle multimegabit transmission rates, a single coaxial

**Table 1.
Comparison of Ethernet systems.**

	Experimental Ethernet	Ethernet Specification
Data rate	2.94M bps	10M bps
Maximum end-to-end length	1 km	2.5 km
Maximum segment length	1 km	500 m
Encoding	Manchester	Manchester
Coax cable impedance	75 ohms	50 ohms
Coax cable signal levels	0 to +3V	0 to −2V
Transceiver cable connectors	25- and 15-pin D series	15-pin D series
Length of preamble	1 bit	64 bits
Length of CRC	16 bits	32 bits
Length of address fields	8 bits	48 bits

Ethernet 1.0 Technical Summary

Packet Format

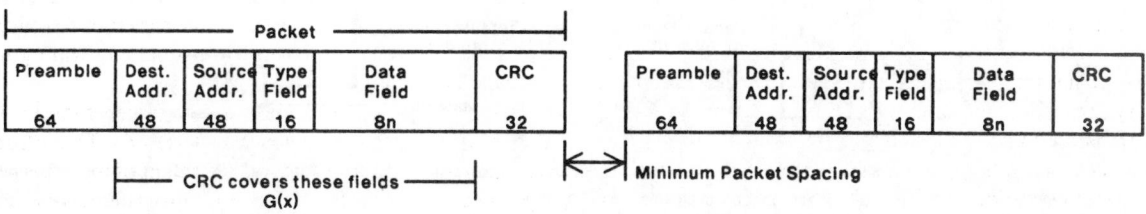

Stations must be able to transmit and receive packets on the common coaxial cable with the indicated packet format and spacing. Each packet should be viewed as a sequence of 8-bit bytes; the least significant bit of each byte (starting with the preamble) is transmitted first.

Maximum Packet Size: 1526 bytes (8 byte preamble + 14 byte header + 1500 data bytes + 4 byte CRC)

Minimum Packet Size: 72 bytes (8 byte preamble + 14 byte header + 46 data bytes + 4 byte CRC)

Preamble: This 64-bit synchronization pattern contains alternating 1's and 0's, ending with two consecutive 1's. The preamble is: 10101010 10101010 10101010 10101010 10101010 10101010 10101010 10101011.

Destination Address: This 48-bit field specifies the station(s) to which the packet is being transmitted. Each station examines this field to determine whether it should accept the packet. The first bit transmitted indicates the type of address. If it is a 0, the field contains the unique address of the one destination station. If it is a 1, the field specifies a logical group of recipients; a special case is the broadcast (all stations) address, which is all 1's.

Source Address: This 48-bit field contains the unique address of the station that is transmitting the packet.

Type Field: This 16-bit field is used to identify the higher-level protocol type associated with the packet. It determines how the data field is interpreted.

Data Field: This field contains an integral number of bytes ranging from 46 to 1500. (The minimum ensures that valid packets will be distinguishable from collision fragments.)

Packet Check Sequence: This 32-bit field contains a redundancy check (CRC) code, defined by the generating polynomial:

$$G(x) = x^{32} + x^{26} + x^{23} + x^{22} + x^{16} + x^{12} + x^{11} + x^{10} + x^8 + x^7 + x^5 + x^4 + x^2 + x + 1$$

The CRC covers the address (destination/source), type, and data fields. The first transmitted bit of the destination field is the high-order term of the message polynomial to be divided by $G(x)$ producing remainder $R(x)$. The high-order term of $R(x)$ is the first transmitted bit of the Packet Check Sequence field. The algorithm uses a linear feedback register which is initially preset to all 1's. After the last data bit is transmitted, the contents of this register (the remainder) are inverted and transmitted as the CRC field. After receiving a good packet, the receiver's shift register contains 11000111 00000100 11011101 01111011 (x^{31}, ... ,x^0).

Minimum Packet Spacing: This spacing is 9.6 usec, the minimum time that must elapse after one transmission before another transmission may begin.

Round-trip Delay: The maximum end-to-end, round-trip delay for a bit is 51.2 usec.

Collision Filtering: Any received bit sequence smaller than the minimum valid packet (with minimum data field) is discarded as a collision fragment.

Control Procedure

The control procedure defines how and when a station may transmit packets into the common cable. The key purpose is fair resolution of occasional contention among transmitting stations.

Defer: A station must not transmit into the coaxial cable when carrier is present or within the minimum packet spacing time after carrier has ended.

Transmit: A station may transmit if it is not deferring. It may continue to transmit until either the end of the packet is reached or a collision is detected.

Abort: If a collision is detected, transmission of the packet must terminate, and a *jam* (4-6 bytes of arbitrary data) is transmitted to ensure that all other participants in the collision also recognize its occurrence.

Retransmit: After a station has detected a collision and aborted, it must wait for a random *retransmission delay*, defer as usual, and then attempt to retransmit the packet. The random time interval is computed using the backoff algorithm (below). After 16 transmission attempts, a higher level (e.g. software) decision is made to determine whether to continue or abandon the effort.

Backoff: Retransmission delays are computed using the *Truncated Binary Exponential Backoff* algorithm, with the aim of fairly resolving contention among up to 1024 stations. The delay (the number of time units) before the nth attempt is a uniformly distributed random number from [0 to 2^n-1] for $0 < n \leq 10$ ($n = 0$ is the original attempt). For attempts 11-15, the interval is *truncated* and remains at [0 to 1023]. The unit of time for the retransmission delay is 512 bit times (51.2 usec).

Channel Encoding

Manchester encoding is used on the coaxial cable. It has a 50% duty cycle, and insures a transition in the middle of every bit cell ("data transition"). The first half of the bit cell contains the complement of the bit value, and the second half contains the true value of the bit.

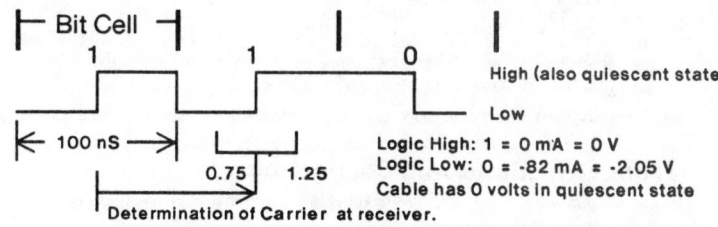

Data Rate

Data rate is 10 M bits/sec = 100 nsec bit cell $\pm$ 0.01%.

Carrier

The presence of data transitions indicates that carrier is present. If a transition is not seen between 0.75 and 1.25 bit times since the center of the last bit cell, then carrier has been lost, indicating the end of a packet. For purposes of deferring, carrier means any activity on the cable, independent of being properly formed. Specifically, it is any activity on either receive or collision detect signals in the last 160 nsec.

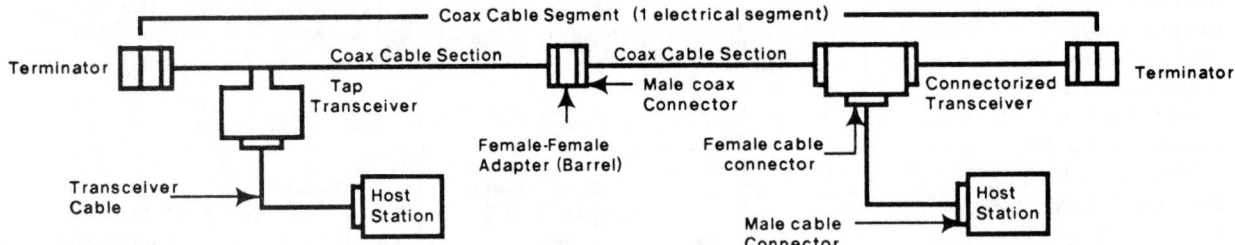

Coax Cable

Impedance: 50 ohms ± 2 ohms (Mil Std. C17-E). This impedance variation includes batch-to-batch variations. Periodic variations in impedance of up to ± 3 ohms are permitted along a single piece of cable.

Cable Loss: The maximum loss from one end of a cable segment to the other end is 8.5 db at 10 MHz (equivalent to ~500 meters of low loss cable).

Shielding: The physical channel hardware must operate in an ambient field of 2 volts per meter from 10 KHz to 30 MHz and 5 V/meter from 30 MHz to 1 GHz. The shield has a transfer impedance of less than 1 milliohm per meter over the frequency range of 0.1 MHz to 20 MHz (exact value is a function of frequency).

Ground Connections: The coax cable shield shall not be connected to any building or AC ground along its length. If for safety reasons a ground connection of the shield is necessary, it must be in only one place.

Physical Dimensions: This specifies the dimensions of a cable which can be used with the *standard tap*. Other cables may also be used, if they are not to be used with a tap-type transceiver (such as use with connectorized transceivers, or as a section between sections to which standard taps are connected).

Center Conductor:	0.0855" diameter solid tinned copper
Core Material:	Foam polyethylene or foam teflon FEP
Core O.D.:	0.242 " minimum
Shield:	0.326" maximum shield O.D. (>90% coverage for outer braid shield)
Jacket:	PVC or teflon FEP
Jacket O.D.:	0.405"

Coax Connectors and Terminators

Coax cables must be terminated with male N-series connectors, and cable sections will be joined with female-female adapters. Connector shells shall be insulated such that the coax shield is protected from contact to building grounds. A sleeve or boot is acceptable. Cable segments should be terminated with a female N-series connector (can be made up of a barrel connector and a male terminator) having an impedance of 50 ohms ± 1%. and able to dissipate 1 watt. The outside surface of the terminator should also be insulated.

Transceiver

CONNECTION RULES

Up to 100 transceivers may be placed on a cable segment no closer together than 2.5 meters. Following this placement rule reduces to a very low (but not zero) probability the chance that objectionable standing waves will result.

COAX CABLE INTERFACE

Input Impedance: The resistive component of the impedance must be greater then 50 Kohms. The total capacitance must be less than 4 picofarads.

Nominal Transmit Level: The important parameter is average DC level with 50% duty cycle waveform input. It must be -1.025 V (41 mA) nominal with a range of -0.9 V to -1.2 V (36 to 48 mA). The peak-to-peak AC waveform must be centered on the average DC level and its value can range from 1.4 V P-P to twice the average DC level. The voltage must never go positive on the coax. The quiescent state of the coax is logic high (0 V). Voltage measurements are made on the coax near the transceiver with the shield as reference. Positive current is current flowing out of the center conductor of the coax.

Rise and Fall Time: 25 nSec ± 5 nSec with a maximum of 1 nSec difference between rise time and fall time in a given unit. The intent is that dV/dt should not significantly exceed that present in a 10 MHz sine wave of same peak-to-peak amplitude.

Signal Symmetry: Asymmetry on output should not exceed 2 nSec for a 50-50 square wave input to either transmit or receive section of transceiver.

TRANSCEIVER CABLE INTERFACE

Signal Pairs: Both transceiver and station shall drive and present at the receiving end a 78 ohm balanced load. The differential signal voltage shall be 0.7 volts nominal peak with a common mode voltage between 0 and +5 volts using power return as reference. (This amounts to shifted ECL levels operating between Gnd and +5 volts. A 10116 with suitable pulldown resistor may be used). The quiescent state of a line corresponds to logic high, which occurs when the + line is more positive than the - line of a pair.

Collision Signal: The active state of this line is a 10 MHz waveform and its quiescent state is logic high. It is active if the transceiver is transmitting and another transmission is detected, or if two or more other stations are transmitting, independent of the state of the local transmit signal.

Power: +11.4 volts to +16 volts DC at controller. Maximum current available to transceiver is 0.5 ampere. Actual voltage at transceiver is determined by the interface cable resistance (max 4 ohms loop resistance) and current drain.

ISOLATION

The impedance between the coax connection and the transceiver cable connection must exceed 250 Kohms at 60 Hz and withstand 250 VRMS at 60 Hz.

Transceiver Cable and Connectors

Maximum signal loss = 3 db @ 10 MHz. (equivalent to ~50 meters of either 20 or 22 AWG twisted pair).

Transceiver Cable Connector Pin Assignment

1.	Shield*		
2.	Collision +	9.	Collision -
3.	Transmit +	10.	Transmit -
4.	Reserved	11.	Reserved
5.	Receive +	12.	Receive -
6.	Power Return	13.	+ Power
7.	Reserved	14.	Reserved
8.	Reserved	15.	Reserved

*Shield must be terminated to connector shell.

Male 15 pin D-Series connector with lock posts.

4 pair # 20 AWG or 22 AWG
78 ohm differential impedance
1 overall shield Insulating jacket
4 ohms max loop resistance for power pair

Female 15 pin D-Series connector with slide lock assembly.

cable can support communication among many different stations. The mechanical aspects of coaxial cable make it feasible to tap in at any point without severing the cable or producing excessive RF leakage; such considerations relating to installation, maintenance, and reconfigurability are important aspects in any local network design.

There are reflections and attenuation in a cable, however, and these combine to impose some limits on the system design. Engineering the shared channel entails trade-offs involving the data rate on the cable, the length of the cable, electrical characteristics of the transceiver, and the number of stations. For example, it is possible to operate at very high data rates over short distances, but the rate must be reduced to support a greater maximum length. Also, if each transceiver introduces significant reflections, it may be necessary to limit the placement and possibly the number of transceivers.

The characteristics of the coaxial cable fix the maximum data rate, but the actual clock is generated in the controller. Thus, the station interface and controller must be designed to match the data rates used over the cable. Selection of coaxial cable as the transmission medium has no other direct impact on either the station or the controller.

Cable. The Experimental Ethernet used 75-ohm, RG-11-type foam cable. The Ethernet Specification uses a 50-ohm, solid-center-conductor, double-shield, foam dielectric cable in order to provide some reduction in the magnitude of reflections from insertion capacitance (introduced by tapping into the cable) and to provide better immunity against environmental electromagnetic noise. Belden Number 9880 Ethernet Coax meets the Ethernet Specification.

Terminators and connectors. A small terminator is attached to the cable at each end to provide a termination impedance for the cable equal to its characteristic impedance, thereby eliminating reflection from the ends of the cable. For convenience, the cable can be divided into a number of sections using simple connectors between sections to produce one electrically continuous segment.

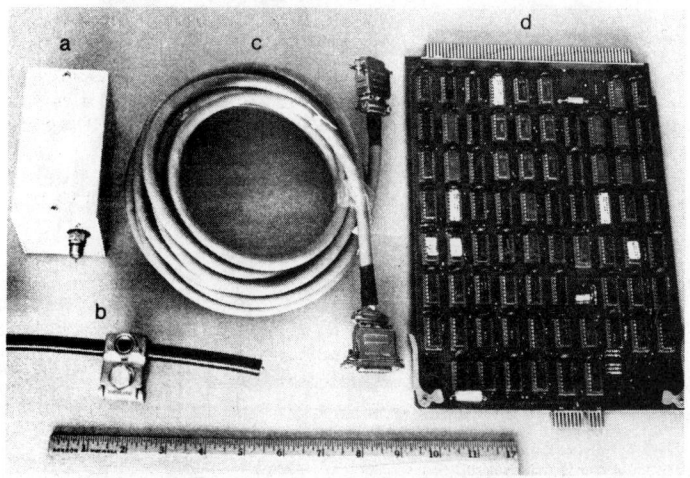

Figure 2. Experimental Ethernet components: (a) transceiver and tap, (b) tap-block, (c) transceiver cable, and (d) Alto controller board.

Segment length and the use of repeaters. The Experimental Ethernet was designed to accommodate a maximum end-to-end length of 1 km, implemented as a single electrically continuous segment. Active repeaters could be used with that system to create complex topologies that would cover a wider area in a building (or complex of buildings) within the end-to-end length limit. With the use of those repeaters, however, the maximum end-to-end length between any two stations was still meant to be approximately 1 km. Thus, the segment length and the maximum end-to-end length were the same, and repeaters were used to provide additional flexibility.

In developing the Ethernet Specification, the strong desire to support a 10M-bps data rate—with reasonable transceiver cost—led to a maximum segment length of 500 meters. We expect that this length will be sufficient to support many installations and applications with a single Ethernet segment. In some cases, however, we recognized a requirement for greater maximum end-to-end length in one network. In these cases, repeaters may now be used not just for additional flexibility but also to extend the overall length of an Ethernet. The Ethernet Specification permits the concatenation of up to three segments; the maximum end-to-end delay between two stations measured as a distance is 2.5 km, including the delay through repeaters containing a point-to-point link.[5]

Taps. Transceivers can connect to a coax cable with the use of a *pressure tap,* borrowed from CATV technology. Such a tap allows connection to the cable without cutting it to insert a connector and avoids the need to interrupt network service while installing a new station. One design uses a tap-block that is clamped on the cable and uses a special tool to penetrate the outer jacket and shield. The tool is removed and the separate tap is screwed into the block. Another design has the tap and tap-block integrated into one unit, with the tap puncturing the cable to make contact with the center conductor as the tap-block is being clamped on.

Alternatively, the cable can be cut and connectors fastened to each piece of cable. This unfortunately disrupts the network during the installation process. After the connectors are installed at the break in the cable, a T-connector can be inserted in between and then connected to a transceiver. Another option, a connectorized transceiver, has two connectors built into it for direct attachment to the cable ends without a T-connector.

Experimental Ethernet installations have used pressure taps where the tap and tap-block are separate, as illustrated in Figure 2. Installations conforming to the Ethernet Specification have used all the options. Figure 3 illustrates a connectorized transceiver and a pressure tap with separate tap and tap-block.

Transceiver. The transceiver couples the station to the cable and is the most important part of the transmission system.

The controller-to-transmission-system interface is very simple, and functionally it has not changed between the two Ethernet designs. It performs four functions: (1) transferring transmit data from the controller to the transmission system, (2) transferring receive data from the transmission system to the controller, (3) indicating to the controller that a collision is taking place, and (4) providing power to the transmission system.

It is important that the two ground references in the system—the common coaxial cable shield and the local ground associated with each station—not be tied together, since one local ground typically may differ from another local ground by several volts. Connection of several local grounds to the common cable could cause a large current to flow through the cable's shield, introducing noise and creating a potential safety hazard. For this reason, the cable shield should be grounded in only one place.

It is the transceiver that provides this ground isolation between signals from the controller and signals on the cable. Several isolation techniques are possible: transformer isolation, optical isolation, and capacitive isolation. Transformer isolation provides both power and signal isolation; it has low differential impedance for signals and power, and a high common-mode impedance for isolation. It is also relatively inexpensive to implement. Optical isolators that preserve tight signal symmetry at a competitive price are not readily available. Capacitive coupling is inexpensive and preserves signal symmetry but has poor common-mode rejection. For these reasons transformer isolation is used in Ethernet Specification transceivers. In addition, the mechanical design and installation of the transceiver must preserve this isolation. For example, cable shield connections should not come in contact with a building ground (e.g., a cable tray, conduit, or ceiling hanger).

The transceiver provides a high-impedance connection to the cable in both the power-on and power-off states. In addition, it should protect the network from possible internal circuit failures that could cause it to disrupt the network as a whole. It is also important for the transceiver to withstand transient voltages on the coax between the center conductor and shield. While such voltages should not occur if the coax shield is grounded in only one place, such isolation may not exist during installation.[1]

Negative transmit levels were selected for the Ethernet Specification to permit use of fast and more easily integrated NPN transistors for the output current source. A current source output was chosen over the voltage source used in the Experimental Ethernet to facilitate collision detection.

The key factor affecting the maximum number of transceivers on a segment in the Ethernet Specification is the input bias current for the transceivers. With easily achievable bias currents and collision threshold tolerances, the maximum number was conservatively set at 100 per segment. If the only factors taken into consideration were signal attenuation and reflections, then the number would have been larger.

Controller design

The transmitter and receiver sections of the controller perform signal conversion, encoding and decoding, serial-to-parallel conversion, address recognition, error detection, CSMA/CD channel management, buffering,

and packetization. Postponing for now a discussion of buffering and packetization, we will first deal with the various functions that the controller needs to perform and then show how they are coordinated into an effective CSMA/CD channel management policy.

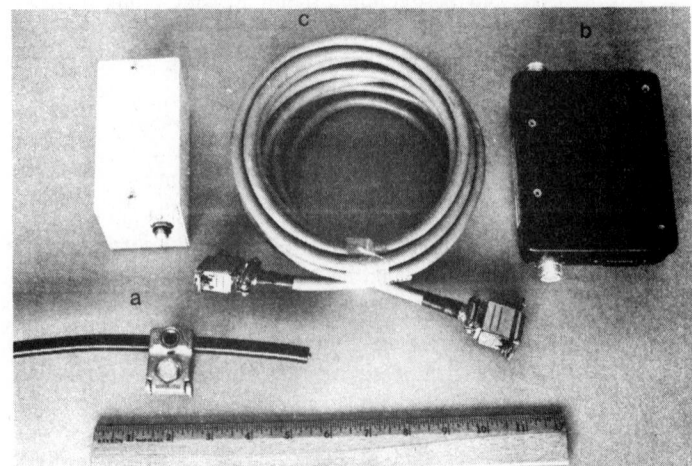

Figure 3. Ethernet Specification components: (a) transceiver, tap, and tap-block, (b) connectorized transceiver, (c) transceiver cable, (d) Dolphin controller board, and (e) Xerox 8000 controller board.

Signaling, data rate, and framing. The transmitter generates the serial bit stream inserted into the transmission system. Clock and data are combined into one signal using a suitable encoding scheme. Because of its simplicity, Manchester encoding was used in the Experimental Ethernet. In Manchester encoding, each bit cell has two parts: the first half of the cell is the complement of the bit value and the second half *is* the bit value. Thus, there is always a transition in the middle of every bit cell, and this is used by the receiver to extract the data.

For the Ethernet Specification, MFM encoding (used in double-density disk recording) was considered, but it was rejected because decoding was more sensitive to phase distortions from the transmission system and required more components to implement. Compensation is not as easy as in the disk situation because a station must receive signals from both nearby and distant stations. Thus, Manchester encoding is retained in the Ethernet Specification.

In the Experimental Ethernet, any data rate in the range of 1M to 5M bps might have been chosen. The particular rate of 2.94M bps was convenient for working with the first Altos. For the Ethernet Specification, we wanted a data rate as high as possible; very high data rates, however, limit the effective length of the system and require more precise electronics. The data rate of 10M bps represents a trade-off among these considerations.

Packet framing on the Ethernet is simple. The presence of a packet is indicated by the presence of carrier, or transitions. In addition, all packets begin with a known pattern of bits called the *preamble*. This is used by the receiver to establish bit synchronization and then to locate the first bit of the packet. The preamble is inserted by the controller at the sending station and stripped off by the controller at the receiving station. Packets may be of variable length, and absence of carrier marks the end of a packet. Hence, there is no need to have framing flags and ''bit stuffing'' in the packet as in other data-link protocols such as SDLC or HDLC.

The Experimental Ethernet used a one-bit preamble. While this worked very well, we have, on rare occasions, seen some receivers that could not synchronize with this very short preamble.[18] The Ethernet Specification uses a 64-bit preamble to ensure synchronization of phase-lock loop receivers often used at the higher data rate. It is necessary to specify 64 bits to allow for (1) worst-case tolerances on phase-lock loop components, (2) maximum times to reach steady-state conditions through transceivers, and (3) loss of preamble bits owing to squelch on input and output within the transceivers. Note that the presence of repeaters can add up to four extra transceivers between a source and destination.

Additional conventions can be imposed upon the frame structure. Requiring that all packets be a multiple of some particular byte or word size simplifies controller design and provides an additional consistency check. All packets on the Experimental Ethernet are viewed as a sequence of 16-bit words with the most significant bit of each word transmitted first. The Ethernet Specification requires all packets to be an integral number of eight-bit bytes (exclusive of the preamble, of course) with the least significant bit of each byte transmitted first. The order in which the bytes of an Ethernet packet are stored in the memory

of a particular station is part of the controller-to-station interface.

Encoding and decoding. The transmitter is responsible for taking a serial bit stream from the station and encoding it into the Manchester format. The receiver is responsible for decoding an incoming signal and converting it into a serial bit stream for the station. The process of encoding is fairly straightforward, but decoding is more dif-

---

> **During transmission a controller must recognize that another station is also transmitting.**

---

ficult and is realized in a *phase decoder*. The known preamble pattern can be used to help initialize the phase decoder, which can employ any of several techniques including an analog timing circuit, a phase-locked loop, or a digital phase decoder (which rapidly samples the input and performs a pattern match). The particular decoding technique selected can be a function of the data rate, since some decoder designs may not run as fast as others. Some phase decoding techniques—particularly the digital one—have the added advantage of being able to recognize certain phase violations as collisions on the transmission medium. This is one way to implement collision detection, although it does not work with all transmission systems.

The phase decoders used by stations on the Experimental Ethernet included an analog timing circuit in the form of a delay line on the PDP-11, an analog timing circuit in the form of a simple one-shot-based timer on the Alto, and a digital decoder on the Dorado. All stations built by Xerox for the Ethernet Specification use phase-locked loops.

Carrier sense. Recognizing packets passing by is one of the important requirements of the Ethernet access procedure. Although transmission is baseband, we have borrowed the term ''sensing carrier'' from radio terminology to describe the detection of signals on the channel. Carrier sense is used for two purposes: (1) in the receiver to delimit the beginning and end of the packet, and (2) in the transmitter to tell when it is permissible to send. With the use of Manchester phase encoding, carrier is conveniently indicated by the presence of transitions on the channel. Thus, the basic phase decoding mechanism can produce a signal indicating the presence of carrier independent of the data being extracted. The Ethernet Specification requires a slightly subtle carrier sense technique owing to the possibility of a saturated collision.

Collision detection. The ability to detect collisions and shut down the transmitter promptly is an important feature in minimizing the channel time lost to collisions. The general requirement is that during transmission a controller must recognize that another station is also transmitting. There are two approaches:

(1) *Collision detection in the transmission system.* It is usually possible for the transmission system itself to recognize a collision. This allows any medium-dependent technique to be used and is usually implemented by comparing the injected signal with the received signal. Comparing the transmitted and received signals is best done in the transceiver where there is a known relationship between the two signals. It is the controller, however, which needs to know that a collision is taking place.

(2) *Collision detection in the controller.* Alternatively, the controller itself can recognize a collision by comparing the transmitted signal with the received signal, or the receiver section can attempt to unilaterally recognize collisions, since they often appear as phase violations.

Both generations of Ethernet detect collisions within the transceiver and generate the collision signal in the controller-to-transmission-system interface. Where feasible, this can be supplemented with a collision detection facility in the controller. Collision detection may not be absolutely foolproof. Some transmission schemes can recognize all collisions, but other combinations of transmission scheme and collision detection may not provide 100-percent recognition. For example, the Experimental Ethernet system functions, in principle, as a wired OR. It is remotely possible for one station to transmit while another station sends a packet whose waveform, at the first station, exactly matches the signal sent by the first station; thus, no collision is recognized there. Unfortunately, the intended recipient might be located between the two stations, and the two signals would indeed interfere.

There is another possible scenario in which collision detection breaks down. One station begins transmitting and its signal propagates down the channel. Another station still senses the channel idle, begins to transmit, gets out a bit or two, and then detects a collision. If the colliding station shuts down immediately, it leaves a very small collision moving through the channel. In some approaches (e.g., DC threshold collision detection) this may be attenuated and simply not make it back to the transmitting station to trigger its collision detection circuitry.

The probability of such occurrences is small. Actual measurements in the Experimental Ethernet system indicate that the collision detection mechanism works very well. Yet it is important to remember that an Ethernet system delivers packets only with high probability—not certainty.

To help ensure proper detection of collisions, each transmitter adopts a *collision consensus enforcement* procedure. This makes sure that all other parties to the collision will recognize that a collision has taken place. In spite of its lengthy name, this is a simple procedure. After detecting a collision, a controller transmits a *jam* that every operating transmitter should detect as a collision. In the Experimental Ethernet the jam is a phase violation, while in the Ethernet Specification it is the transmission of four to six bytes of random data.

Another possible collision scenario arises in the context of the Ethernet Specification. It is possible for a collision to involve so many participants that a transceiver is incapable of injecting any more current into the cable. During such a collision, one cannot guarantee that the waveform on the cable will exhibit any transitions. (In the extreme case, it simply sits at a constant DC level equal to the saturation voltage.) This is called a *saturated collision.* In this situation, the simple notion of sensing carrier by detecting transitions would not work anymore. In particular, a station that deferred only when seeing transitions would think the Ether was idle and jump right in, becoming another participant in the collision. Of course, it would immediately detect the collision and back off, but in the extreme case (everyone wanting to transmit), such jumping-in could theoretically cause the saturated collision to snowball and go on for a very long time. While we recognized that this form of instability was highly unlikely to occur in practice, we included a simple enhancement to the carrier sense mechanism in the Ethernet Specification to prevent the problem.

We have focused on collision detection by the transmitter of a packet and have seen that the transmitter may depend on a collision detect signal generated unilaterally by its receiving phase decoder. Can this receiver-based collision detection be used just by a receiver (that is, a station that is not trying to transmit)? A receiver with this capability could immediately abort an input operation and could even generate a jam signal to help ensure that the collision came to a prompt termination. With a reasonable transmitter-based collision detection scheme, however, the collision is recognized by the transmitters and the damaged packet would come to an end very shortly. Receiver-based collision detection could provide an early warning of a collision for use by the receiver, but this is not a necessary function and we have not used it in either generation of Ethernet design.

CRC generation and checking. The transmitter generates a cyclic redundancy check, or CRC, of each transmitted packet and appends it to a packet before transmission. The receiver checks the CRC on packets it receives and strips it off before giving the packet to the station. If the CRC is incorrect, there are two options: either discard the packet or deliver the damaged packet with an appropriate status indicating a CRC error.

While most CRC algorithms are quite good, they are not infallible. There is a small probability that undetected errors may slip through. More importantly, the CRC only protects a packet from the point at which the CRC is generated to the point at which it is checked. Thus, the CRC cannot protect a packet from damage that occurs in parts of the controller, as, for example, in a FIFO in the parallel path to the memory of a station (the DMA), or in the memory itself. If error detection at a higher level is required, then an end-to-end software checksum can be added to the protocol architecture.

In measuring the Experimental Ethernet system, we have seen packets whose CRC was reported as correct but whose software checksum was incorrect.[18] These did not necessarily represent an undetected Ethernet error; they usually resulted from an external malfunction such as a broken interface, a bad CRC checker, or even an incorrect software checksum algorithm.

Selection of the CRC algorithm is guided by several concerns. It should have sufficient strength to properly detect virtually all packet errors. Unfortunately, only a limited set of CRC algorithms are currently implemented in LSI chips. The Experimental Ethernet used a 16-bit CRC, taking advantage of a single-chip CRC generator/checker. The Ethernet Specification provides better error detection by using a 32-bit CRC.[19,20] This function will be easily implemented in an Ethernet chip.

Addressing. The packet format includes both a source and destination address. A local network design can adopt either of two basic addressing structures: *network-specific* station addresses or *unique* station addresses.[21] In the first case, stations are assigned network addresses that must be unique on *their* network but may be the same as the address held by a station on another network. Such addresses are sometimes called *network relative* addresses, since they depend upon the particular network to which the station is attached. In the second case, each station is assigned an address that is unique over all space and time. Such addresses are also known as absolute or universal addresses, drawn from a flat address space.

To permit internetwork communication, the network-specific address of a station must usually be combined with a unique network number in order to produce an unambiguous address at the next level of protocol. On the other hand, there is no need to combine an absolute station address with a unique network number to produce an unambiguous address. However, it is possible that internetwork systems based on flat (internetwork and local network) absolute addresses will include a unique network number at the internetwork layer as a "very strong hint" for the routing machinery.

If network-specific addressing is adopted, Ethernet address fields need only be large enough to accommodate the maximum number of stations that will be connected to one local network. In addition, there must be a suitable administrative procedure for assigning addresses to stations. Some installations will have more than one Ethernet, and if a station is moved from one network to another it may be necessary to change its network-specific address, since its former address may be in use on the new network. This was the approach used on the Experimental Ethernet, with an eight-bit field for the source and the destination addresses.

We anticipate that there will be a large number of stations and many local networks in an internetwork. Thus, the management of network-specific station addresses can represent a severe problem. The use of a flat address space provides for reliable and manageable operation as a system grows, as machines move, and as the overall topology changes. A flat internet address space requires that the address space be large enough to ensure uniqueness while providing adequate room for growth. It is most convenient if the local network can directly support these fairly large address fields.

For these reasons the Ethernet Specification uses 48-bit addresses.[22] Note that these are station addresses and are not associated with a particular network interface or controller. In particular, we believe that higher level routing and addressing procedures are simplified if a station connected to multiple networks has only one identity which is unique over all networks. The address should not be hardwired into a particular interface or controller but should be able to be set from the station. It may be very useful, however, to allow a station to read a unique station identifier from the controller. The station can then choose whether to return this identifier to the controller as its address.

In addition to single-station addressing, several enhanced addressing modes are also desirable. *Multicast* addressing is a mechanism by which packets may be targeted to more than one destination. This kind of service is particularly valuable in certain kinds of distributed applications, for instance the access and update of distributed data bases, teleconferencing, and the distributed algorithms that are used to manage the network and the internetwork. We believe that multicast should be supported by allowing the destination address to specify either a physical or logical address. A logical address is known as a *multicast ID. Broadcast* is a special case of multicast in which a packet is intended for all active stations. Both generations of Ethernet support broadcast, while only the Ethernet Specification directly supports multicast.

Stations supporting multicast must recognize multicast IDs of interest. Because of the anticipated growth in the use of multicast service, serious consideration should be given to aspects of the station and controller design that reduce the system load required to filter unwanted multicast packets. Broadcast should be used with discretion, since all nodes incur the overhead of processing every broadcast packet.

Controllers capable of accepting packets regardless of destination address provide *promiscuous* address recognition. On such stations one can develop software to observe all of the channel's traffic, construct traffic matrices, perform load analysis, (potentially) perform fault isolation, and debug protocol implementations. While such a station is able to read packets not addressed to it, we expect that sensitive data will be encrypted by higher levels of software.

CSMA/CD channel management

A major portion of the controller is devoted to Ethernet channel management. These conventions specify procedures by which packets are transmitted and received on the multi-access channel.

Transmitter. The transmitter is invoked when the station has a packet to send. If a collision occurs, the controller enforces the collision with a suitable jam, shuts down the transmitter, and schedules a retransmission.

Retransmission policies have two conflicting goals: (1) scheduling a retransmission quickly to get the packet out and maintain use of the channel, and (2) voluntarily backing off to reduce the station's load on a busy channel. Both generations of Ethernet use the *binary exponential back-off algorithm* described below. After some maximum number of collisions the transmitter gives up and reports a suitable error back to the station; both generations of Ethernet give up after 15 collisions.

The binary exponential back-off algorithm is used to calculate the delay before retransmission. After a collision takes place the objective is to obtain delay periods that will reschedule each station at times quantized in steps at least as large as a collision interval. This time quantization is called the *retransmission slot time*. To guarantee quick use of the channel, this slot time should be short; yet to avoid collisions it should be larger than a collision interval. Therefore, the slot time is usually set to be a little longer than the round-trip time of the channel. The real-time delay is the product of some retransmission delay (a positive integer) and the retransmission slot time.

Collisions on the channel can produce collision fragments, which can be eliminated with a fragment filter in the controller.

To minimize the probability of repeated collisions, each retransmission delay is selected as a random number from a particular retransmission interval between zero and some upper limit. In order to control the channel and keep it stable under high load, the interval is doubled with each successive collision, thus extending the range of possible retransmission delays. This algorithm has very short retransmission delays at the beginning but will back off quickly, preventing the channel from becoming overloaded. After some number of back-offs, the retransmission interval becomes large. To avoid undue delays and slow response to improved channel characteristics, the doubling can be stopped at some point, with additional retransmissions still being drawn from this interval, before the transmission is finally aborted. This is referred to as *truncated binary exponential back-off*.

The truncated binary exponential back-off algorithm approximates the ideal algorithm where the probability of transmission of a packet is $1/Q$, with Q representing the number of stations attempting to transmit.[23] The retransmission interval is truncated when Q becomes equal to the maximum number of stations.

In the Experimental Ethernet, the very first transmission attempt proceeds with no delay (i.e., the retransmission interval is [0-0]). The retransmission interval is doubled after each of the first eight transmission attempts. Thus, the retransmission delays should be uniformly distributed between 0 and $2^{min(\text{retransmission attempt, 8})} - 1$. After the first transmission attempt, the next eight intervals will be [0-1], [0-3], [0-7], [0-15], [0-31], [0-63], [0-127], and [0-255]. The retransmission interval remains at [0-255] on any subsequent attempt, as the maximum number of stations is 256. The Ethernet Specification has the same algorithm with ten intervals, since the network permits up to 1024 stations; the maximum interval is therefore [0-1023]. The back-off algorithm restarts with a zero retransmission interval for the transmission of every new packet.

This particular algorithm was chosen because it has the proper basic behavior and because it allows a very simple implementation. The algorithm is now supported by empirical data verifying the stability of the system under heavy load.[12,13] Additional attempts to explore more

sophisticated algorithms resulted in negligible performance improvement.

Receiver. The receiver section of the controller is activated when the carrier appears on the channel. The receiver processes the incoming bit stream in the following manner:

The remaining preamble is first removed. If the bit stream ends before the preamble completes, it is assumed to be the result of a short collision, and the receiver is restarted.

The receiver next determines whether the packet is addressed to it. The controller will accept a packet in any of the following circumstances:

(1) The destination address matches the specific address of the station.
(2) The destination address has the distinguished broadcast destination.
(3) The destination address is a multicast group of which the station is a member.
(4) The station has set the controller in promiscuous mode and receives all packets.

Some controller designs might choose to receive the entire packet before invoking the address recognition procedure. This is feasible but consumes both memory and processing resources in the controller. More typically, address recognition takes place at a fairly low level in the controller, and if the packet is not to be accepted the controller can ignore the rest of it.

Assuming that the address is recognized, the receiver now accepts the entire packet. Before the packet is actually delivered to the station, the CRC is verified and other consistency checks are performed. For example, the packet should end on an appropriate byte or word boundary and be of appropriate minimum length; a minimum packet would have to include at least a destination and source address, a packet type, and a CRC. Collisions on the channel, however, can produce short, damaged packets called collision fragments. It is generally unnecessary to report these errors to the station, since they can be eliminated with a fragment filter in the controller. It is important, however, for the receiver to be restarted promptly after a collision fragment is received, since the sender of the packet may be about to retransmit.

Packet length. One important goal of the Ethernet is data transparency. In principle, this means that the data field of a packet can contain any bit pattern and be of any length, from zero to arbitrarily large. In practice, while it is easy to allow any bit pattern to appear in the data field, there are some practical considerations that suggest imposing upper and lower bounds on its length.

At one extreme, an empty packet (one with a zero-length data field) would consist of just a preamble, source and destination addresses, a type field, and a CRC. The Experimental Ethernet permitted empty packets. However, in some situations it is desirable to enforce a minimum overall packet size by mandating a minimum-length data field, as in the Ethernet Specification. Higher level protocols wishing to transmit shorter packets must then pad out the data field to reach the minimum.

At the other extreme, one could imagine sending many thousands or even millions of bytes in a single packet. There are, however, several factors that tend to limit packet size, including (1) the desire to limit the size of the buffers in the station for sending and receiving packets, (2) similar considerations concerning the packet buffers that are sometimes built into the Ethernet controller itself, and (3) the need to avoid tying up the channel and increasing average channel latency for other stations. Buffer management tends to be the dominant consideration. The maximum requirement for buffers in the station is usually a parameter of higher level software determined by the overall network architecture; it is typically on the order of 500 to 2000 bytes. The size of any packet buffers in the controller, on the other hand, is usually a design parameter of the controller hardware and thus represents a more rigid limitation. To insure compatibility among buffered controllers, the Ethernet Specification mandates a maximum packet length of 1526 bytes (1500 data bytes plus overhead).

Note that the upper and lower bounds on packet length are of more than passing interest, since observed distributions are typically quite bimodal. Packets tend to be either very short (control packets or packets carrying a small amount of data) or maximum length (usually some form of bulk data transfer).[12,13]

The efficiency of an Ethernet system is largely dependent on the size of the packets being sent and can be very high when large packets are used. Measurements have shown total utilization as high as 98 percent. A small quantum of channel capacity is lost whenever there is a collision, but the carrier sense and collision detection mechanisms combine to minimize this loss. Carrier sense reduces the likelihood of a collision, since the acquisition effect renders a given transmission immune to collisions once it has continued for longer than a collision interval. Collision detection limits the duration of a collision to a single collision interval. If packets are long compared with the collision interval, then the network is vulnerable to collisions only a small fraction of the time and total utilization will remain high. If the average packet size is reduced, however, both carrier sense and collision detection become less effective. Ultimately, as the packet size approaches the collision interval, system performance degrades to that of a straight CSMA channel without collision detection. This condition only occurs under a heavy load consisting predominantly of very small packets; with a typical mix of applications this is not a practical problem.

If the packet size is reduced still further until it is less than the collision interval, some new problems appear. Of course, if an empty packet is already longer than the collision interval, as in the Experimental Ethernet, this case cannot arise. As the channel length and/or the data rate are increased, however, the length (in bits) of the collision interval also increases. When it becomes larger than an empty packet, one must decide whether stations are allowed to send tiny packets that are smaller than the collision interval. If so, two more problems arise, one affecting the transmitter and one the receiver.

The transmitter's problem is that it can complete the entire transmission of a tiny packet before network acquisition has occurred. If the packet subsequently experiences a collision farther down the channel, it is too late for the transmitter to detect the collision and promptly schedule a retransmission. In this situation, the probability of a collision has not increased, nor has any additional channel capacity been sacrificed; the problem is simply that the transmitter will occasionally fail to recognize and handle a collision. To deal with such failures, the sender of tiny packets must rely on retransmissions invoked by a higher level protocol and thus suffer reduced throughput and increased delay. This occasional performance reduction is generally not a serious problem, however. Note that only the sender of tiny packets encounters this behavior; there is no unusual impact on other stations sending larger packets.

While occasional collisions should be viewed as a normal part of the CSMA/CD access procedure, line errors should not. One would therefore like to accumulate information about the two classes of events separately.

The receiver's problem with tiny packets concerns its ability to recognize collision fragments by their small size and discard them. If the receiver can assume that packets smaller than the collision interval are collision fragments, it can use this to implement a simple and inexpensive fragment filter. It is important for the receiver to discard collision fragments, both to reduce the processing load at the station and to ensure that it is ready to receive the impending retransmission from the transmitter involved in the collision. The fragment filter approach is automatically valid in a network in which there are no tiny packets, such as the Experimental Ethernet. If tiny packets can occur, however, the receiver cannot reliably distinguish them from collision fragments purely on the basis of size. This means that at least the longer collision fragments must be rejected on the basis of some other error detection mechanism such as the CRC check or a byte or word alignment check. One disadvantage of this approach is that it increases the load on the CRC mechanism, which, while strong, is not infallible. Another problem is that the CRC error condition will now be indicating two kinds of faults: long collisions and genuine line errors. While occasional collisions should be viewed as a normal part of the CSMA/CD access procedure, line errors should not. One would therefore like to accumulate information about the two classes of events separately.

The problems caused by tiny packets are not insurmountable, but they do increase the attractiveness of simply legislating the problem out of existence by forbidding the sending of packets smaller than the collision interval. Thus, in a network whose collision interval is longer than an empty packet, the alternatives are

(1) *Allow tiny packets.* In this case, the transmitter will sometimes fail to detect collisions, requiring retransmis-

sion at a higher level and impacting performance. The receiver can use a partial fragment filter to discard collision fragments shorter than an empty packet, but longer collision fragments will make it through this filter and must be rejected on the basis of other error checks, such as the CRC check, with the resultant jumbling of the error statistics.

(2) *Forbid tiny packets*. In this case, the transmitter can always detect a collision and perform prompt retransmission. The receiver can use a fragment filter to automatically discard all packets shorter than the collision interval. The disadvantage is the imposition of a minimum packet size.

Unlike the Experimental Ethernet, the Ethernet Specification defines a collision interval longer than an empty packet and must therefore choose between these alternatives. The choice is to forbid tiny packets by requiring a minimum data field size of 46 bytes. Since we expect that Ethernet packets will typically contain internetwork packet headers and other overhead, this is not viewed as a significant disadvantage.

Controller-to-station interface design

The properties of the controller-to-station interface can dramatically affect the reliability and efficiency of systems based on Ethernet.

Turning the controller on and off. A well-designed controller must be able to (1) keep the receiver on in order to catch back-to-back packets (those separated by some minimum packet spacing), and (2) receive packets a station transmits to itself. We will now look in detail at these requirements and the techniques for satisfying them.

Keeping the receiver on. The most frequent cause of a lost packet has nothing to do with collision or bad CRCs. Packets are usually missed simply because the receiver was not listening. The Ethernet is an asynchronous device that can present a packet at any time, and it is important that higher level software keep the receiver enabled.

The problem is even more subtle, however, for even when operating normally there can be periods during which the receiver is not listening. There may, for instance, be turnaround times between certain operations when the receiver is left turned off. For example, a receive-to-receive turnaround takes place after one packet is received and before the receiver is again enabled. If the design of the interface, controller, or station software keeps the receiver off for too long, arriving packets can be lost during this turnaround. This occurs most frequently in servers on a network, which may be receiving packets from several sources in rapid succession. If back-to-back packets come down the wire, the second one will be lost in the receive-to-receive turnaround time. The same problem can occur within a normal workstation, for example, if a desired packet immediately follows a broadcast packet; the workstation gets the broadcast but misses the packet specifically addressed to it. Higher level protocol software will presumably recover from these situations, but the performance penalty may be severe.

Similarly, there may be a transmit-to-receive turnaround time when the receiver is deaf. This is determined by how long it takes to enable the receiver after sending a packet. If, for example, a workstation with a slow transmit-to-receive turnaround sends a packet to a well-tuned server, the answer may come back before the receiver is enabled again. No amount of retransmission by higher levels will ever solve this problem!

It is important to minimize the length of any turnaround times when the receiver might be off. There can also be receive-to-transmit and transmit-to-transmit turnaround times, but their impact on performance is not as critical.

Sending to itself. A good diagnostic tool for a network interface is the ability of a station to send packets to itself. While an internal loop-back in the controller provides a partial test, actual transmission and simultaneous reception provide more complete verification.

The Ethernet channel is, in some sense, half duplex: there is normally only one station transmitting at a time. There is a temptation, therefore, to also make the controller half duplex—that is, unable to send and receive at the same time. If possible, however, the design of the interface, controller, and station software should allow a station to send packets to itself.

Recommendations. The Ethernet Specification includes one specific requirement that helps to solve the first of these problems: There must be a minimal interpacket spacing on the cable of 9.6 microseconds. This requirement applies to a transmitter getting ready to send a packet and does not necessarily mean that all receivers conforming to the Specification must receive two adjacent packets. This requirement at least makes it possible to build a controller that can receive adjacent packets on the cable.

Satisfying the two requirements described earlier involves the use of two related features in the design of a controller: full-duplex interfaces and back-to-back receivers. A full-duplex interface allows the receiver and the transmitter to be started independently. A back-to-back receiver has facilities to automatically restart the receiver upon completion of a reception. Limited back-to-back reception can be done with two buffers; the first catches a packet and then the second catches the next without requiring the receiver to wait. Generalized back-to-back reception can be accomplished by using chained I/O commands; the receiver is driven by a list of free input buffers, taking one when needed. These two notions can be combined to build any of the following four interfaces: (1) half-duplex interface, (2) full-duplex interface, (3) half-duplex interface with back-to-back receive, and (4) full-duplex interface with back-to-back receive.

The Experimental Ethernet controller for the Alto is half duplex, runs only in a transmit or receive mode, and must be explicitly started in each mode. The need to explicitly start the receiver (there is no automatic hardware turnaround) means that there may be lengthy turnaround times in which packets may be missed. This approach allows sharing certain components, like the CRC function and the FIFO.

Experimental Ethernet controllers built for the PDP-11 and the Nova are full-duplex interfaces. The transmit-to-receive turnaround has been minimized, but there is no provision for back-to-back packets.

The Ethernet controller for the Xerox 8000 processor is a half-duplex interface with back-to-back receive. Although it cannot send to itself, the transmit-to-receive turnaround delay has been avoided by having the hardware automatically revert to the receive state when a transmission is completed.

The Experimental Ethernet and Ethernet Specification controllers for the Dolphin are full-duplex interfaces with back-to-back receivers. They are the ultimate in interface organization.

Our experience shows that any one of the four alternatives will work. However, we strongly recommend that all interface and controller designs support full-duplex operation and provide for reception of back-to-back packets (chained I/O).

The controller-to-station interface defines the manner in which data received from the cable is stored in memory and, conversely, how data stored in memory is transmitted on the cable.

Buffering. Depending upon the particular data rate of the channel and the characteristics of the station, the controller may have to provide suitable buffering of packets. If the station can keep up with the data rate of the channel, only a small FIFO may be needed to deal with station latency. If the station cannot sustain the channel data rate, it may be necessary to include a full-packet buffer as part of the controller. For this reason, full compatibility across different stations necessitates the specification of a maximum packet length.

If a single-packet buffer is provided in the controller (a buffer that has no marker mechanism to distinguish boundaries between packets), it will generally be impossible to catch back-to-back packets, and in such cases it is preferable to have at least two input buffers.

Packets in memory. The controller-to-station interface defines the manner in which data received from the cable is stored in memory and, conversely, how data stored in memory is transmitted on the cable. There are many ways in which this parallel-to-serial transformation can be defined.[24] The Ethernet Specification defines a packet on the cable to be a sequence of eight-bit bytes, with the least significant bit of each byte transmitted first. Higher level protocols will in most cases, however, define data types that are multiples of eight bits. The parallel-to-serial transformations will be influenced by the programming conventions of the station and by the higher level protocols. Stations with different parallel-to-serial transformations that use the same higher level protocol must make sure that all data types are viewed consistently.

Type field. An Ethernet packet can encapsulate many kinds of client-defined packets. Thus, the packet format includes only a data field, two addresses, and a type field. The type field identifies the special client-level protocol that will interpret the data encapsulated within the packet. The type field is never processed by the Ethernet system itself but can be thought of as an escape, providing a consistent way to specify the interpretation of the rest of the packet.

Low-level system services such as diagnostics, bootstrap, loading, or specialized network management functions can take advantage of the identification provided by this field. In fact, it is possible to use the type field to identify all the different packets in a protocol architecture. In general, however, we recommend that the Ethernet packet encapsulate higher level internetwork packets. Internetwork router stations might concurrently support a number of different internetwork protocols, and the use of the type field allows the internetwork router to encapsulate different kinds of internetwork packets for a local network transmission.[25] The use of a type field in the Ethernet packet is an instance of a principle we apply to all layers in a protocol architecture. A type field is used at each level of the hierarchy to identify the protocol used at the next higher level; it is the bridge between adjacent levels. This results in an architecture that defines a layered tree of protocols.

The Experimental Ethernet design uses a 16-bit type field. This has proved to be a very useful feature and has been carried over into the Ethernet Specification.

Summary and conclusions

We have highlighted a number of important considerations that affect the design of an Ethernet local computer network and have traced the evolution of the system from a research prototype to a multicompany standard by discussing strategies and trade-offs between alternative implementations.

The Ethernet is intended primarily for use in such areas as office automation, distributed data processing, terminal access, and other situations requiring economical connection to a local communication medium carrying bursts of traffic at high peak data rates. Experience with the Experimental Ethernet in building distributed systems that support electronic mail, distributed filing, calendar systems, and other applications has confirmed many of our design goals and decisions.[26-29]

Questions sometimes arise concerning the ways in which the Ethernet design addresses (or chooses not to address) the following considerations: reliability, addressing, priority, encryption, and compatibility. It is important to note that some functions are better left out of the Ethernet itself for implementation at higher levels in the architecture.

All systems should be reliable, and network-based systems are no exception. We believe that reliability must be addressed at each level in the protocol hierarchy; each level should provide only what it can guarantee at a reasonable price. Our model for internetworking is one in which reliability and sequencing are performed using end-to-end transport protocols. Thus, the Ethernet provides a "best effort" datagram service. The Ethernet has been designed to have very good error characteristics, and, without promising to deliver all packets, it will deliver a very large percentage of offered packets without error. It includes error detection procedures but provides no error correction.

We expect internetworks to be very large. Many of the problems in managing them can be simplified by using absolute station addresses that are directly supported within the local network. Thus, address fields in the Ethernet Specification seem to be very generous—well beyond the number of stations that might connect to one local network but meant to efficiently support large internetwork systems.

Our experience indicates that for practically all applications falling into the category "loosely coupled distributed system," the average utilization of the communications network is low. The Ethernet has been designed to have excess bandwidth, not all of which must be utilized. Systems should be engineered to run with a sustained load of no more than 50 percent. As a consequence, the network will generally provide high throughput of data with low delay, and there are no priority levels associated with particular packets. Designers of individual devices, network servers, and higher level protocols are free to develop priority schemes for accessing particular resources.

Protection, security, and access control are all system-wide functions that require a comprehensive strategy. The Ethernet system itself is not designed to provide encryption or other mechanisms for security, since these techniques by themselves do not provide the kind of protection most users require. Security in the form of encryption, where required, is the responsibility of the end-user processes.

Higher level protocols raise their own issues of compatibility over and above those addressed by the Ethernet and other link-level facilities. While the compatibility provided by the Ethernet does not guarantee solutions to higher level compatibility problems, it does provide a context within which such problems can be addressed by avoiding low-level incompatibilities that would make direct communication impossible. We expect to see standards for higher level protocols emerge during the next few years.

Within an overall distributed systems architecture, the two generations of Ethernet systems have proven to be very effective local computer networks. ∎

Acknowledgments

Many people have contributed to the success and evolution of the Ethernet local computer network. Bob Metcalfe and David Boggs built the Experimental Ethernet at the Xerox Palo Alto Research Center, and Tat Lam built and supplied the many transceivers. Since then, Ed Taft, Hal Murray, Will Crowther, Roy Ogus, Bob Garner, Ed Markowski, Bob Printis, Bob Belleville, Bill Gunning, and Juan Bulnes have contributed to the design and implementation of the Ethernet. Cooperation among Digital Equipment Corporation, Intel, and Xerox also produced many important contributions to the Ethernet Specification.

References

1. R. C. Crane and E. A. Taft, "Practical Considerations in Ethernet Local Network Design," *Proc. 13th Hawaii Int'l Conf. Systems Sciences,* Jan. 1980, pp. 166-174.

2. R. M. Metcalfe and D. R. Boggs, "Ethernet; Distributed Packet Switching for Local Computer Networks," *Comm. ACM,* 19:7, July 1976, pp. 395-404.

3. R. M. Metcalfe, D. R. Boggs, C. P. Thacker, and B. W. Lampson, "Multipoint Data Communication System with Collision Detection," US Patent No. 4,063,220, Dec. 13, 1977.

4. J. F. Shoch, *"An Annotated Bibliography on Local Computer Networks"* (3rd ed.), Xerox Parc Technical Report SSL-80-2, and IFIP Working Group 6.4 Working Paper 80-12, Apr. 1980.

5. *The Ethernet, A Local Area Network: Data Link Layer and Physical Layer Specifications,* Version 1.0, Digital Equipment Corporation, Intel, Xerox, Sept. 30, 1980.

6. D. R. Boggs, J. F. Shoch, E. A. Taft, and R. M. Metcalfe, "PUP: An Internetwork Architecture," *IEEE Trans. Comm.,* Apr. 1980, pp. 612-624.

7. H. Zimmermann, "OSI Reference Model—The ISO Model of Architecture for Open Systems Interconnection," *IEEE Trans. Comm.,* Apr. 1980, pp. 425-432.

8. Y. K. Dalal, "The Information Outlet: A New Tool for Office Organization," *Proc. On-line Conf. Local Networks and Distributed Office Systems,* London, May 1981, pp. 11-19.

9. V. G. Cerf and P. K. Kirstein, "Issues in Packet-Network Interconnection," *Proc. IEEE,* Vol. 66, No. 11, Nov. 1978, pp. 1386-1408.

10. F. C. Shoute, "Decentralized Control in Computer Communication," Technical Report No. 667, Division of Engineering and Applied Physics, Harvard University, Apr. 1977.

11. R. M. Metcalfe, "Packet Communication," Thesis Harvard University, Project MAC Report MAC TR-114, Massachusetts Institute of Technology, Dec. 1973.

12. J. F. Shoch and J. A. Hupp, "Performance of an Ethernet Local Network—A Preliminary Report," *Local Area Comm. Network Symp.,* Boston, May 1979, pp. 113-125. Revised version *Proc. Compcon Spring 80,* San Francisco, pp. 318-322.

13. J. F. Shoch and J. A. Hupp, "Measured Performance of an Ethernet Local Network," *Comm. ACM,* Vol. 23, No. 12, Dec. 1980, pp. 711-721.

14. E. G. Rawson and R. M. Metcalfe, "Fibernet: Multimode Optical Fibers for Local Computer Networks," *IEEE Trans. Comm.,* July 1978, pp. 983-990.

15. D. R. Boggs and R. M. Metcalfe, Communications network repeater, US Patent No. 4,099,024, July 4, 1978.

16. C. P. Thacker et al., "Alto: A Personal Computer," Xerox Palo Alto Research Center Technical Report CSL-79-11, Aug. 1979.

17. "The Dorado: A High-Performance Personal Computer," Three Reports, Xerox Palo Alto Research Center, CSL-81-1, Jan. 1981.

18. J. F. Shoch, *Local Computer Networks,* McGraw-Hill, in press.

19. J. L. Hammond, J. E. Brown, and S. S. Liu, "Development of a Transmission Error Model and an Error Control Model," Technical Report RADC-TR-75-138, Rome Air Development Center, 1975.

20. R. Bittel, "On Frame Check Sequence (FCS) Generation and Checking," ANSI working paper X3-S34-77-43, 1977.

21. J. F. Shoch, "Internetwork Naming, Addressing, and Routing," *Proc. Compcon Fall 78,* pp. 430-437.

22. Y. K. Dalal and R. S. Printis, "48-bit Internet and Ethernet Host Numbers," *Proc. Seventh Data Comm. Symp.,* Oct. 1981.

23. R. M. Metcalfe, "Steady-State Analysis of a Slotted and Controlled Aloha System with Blocking," *Proc. Sixth Hawaii Conf. System Sciences,* Jan. 1973. Reprinted in *Sigcom Review,* Jan. 1975.

24. D. Cohen, "On Holy Wars and a Plea for Peace," *Computer,* Vol. 14, No. 10, Oct. 1981, pp. 48-54.

25. J. F. Shoch, D. Cohen, and E. A. Taft, "Mutual Encapsulation of Internetwork Protocols," *Computer Networks,* Vol. 5, No. 4, July 1981, pp. 287-301.

26. A. D. Birrell et al., "Grapevine: An Exercise in Distributed Computing," *Comm. ACM,* Vol. 25, No. 4, Apr. 1982, pp. 260-274.

27. H. Sturgis, J. Mitchell, and J. Israel, "Issues in the Design and Use of a Distributed File System," *ACM Operating Systems Rev.,* Vol. 14, No. 3, July 1980, pp. 55-69.

28. D. K. Gifford, "Violet, an Experimental Decentralized System," Xerox Palo Alto Research Center, CSL-79-12, Sept. 1979.

29. J. F. Shoch and J. A. Hupp, "Notes on the 'Worm' Programs—Some Early Experiences with a Distributed Computation," *Comm. ACM,* Vol. 25, No. 3, Mar. 1982, pp. 172-180.

John F. Shoch is deputy general manager for office systems in the Office Products Division of Xerox Corporation. From 1980 to 1982, he served as assistant to the president of Xerox and director of the corporate policy committee. He joined the research staff at the Xerox Palo Alto Research Center in 1971. His research interests have included local computer networks (such as the Ethernet), internetwork protocols, packet radio, and other aspects of distributed systems. In addition, he has taught at Stanford University, is a member of the ACM and the IEEE, and serves as vice-chairman (US) of IFIP Working Group 6.4 on local computer networks. Shoch received the BA degree in political science and the MS and PhD degrees in computer science from Stanford University.

Yogen K. Dalal is manager of services and architecture for office systems in the Office Products Division of Xerox Corporation. He has been with the company in Palo Alto since 1977. His research interests include local computer networks, internetwork protocols, distributed systems architecture, broadcast protocols, and operating systems. He is a member of the ACM and the IEEE. He received the B. Tech. degree in electrical engineering from the Indian Institute of Technology, Bombay, in 1972, and the MS and PhD degrees in electrical engineering and computer science from Stanford University in 1973 and 1977, respectively.

David D. Redell is a staff scientist in the Office Products Division of Xerox Corporation. He was previously on the faculty of the Massachusetts Institute of Technology. His research interests include computer networks, distributed systems, information security, and computer architecture. He received his BA, MS, and PhD degrees in computer science from the University of California at Berkeley.

Ronald C. Crane, a founder of 3Com Corporation in Mountain View, California, now heads advanced engineering for the firm. From 1977 to 1980 he served as a technical staff member and subsequently a consultant to Xerox's Office Products Division in Palo Alto where he was a principal designer of the Digital, Intel, Xerox Ethernet system. His research interests have included adaptive topology packet networks, digital broadcasting systems (Digicast), and baseband transmission systems. He is a member of the ACM and IEEE. He received the BS degree in electrical engineering from the Massachusetts Institute of Technology in 1972 and the MS degree in electrical engineering from Stanford University in 1974.

INTERCONNECTION SERVICES OF NET/ONE

John M. Davidson
Net/One Architect

Ungermann-Bass, Inc.
2560 Mission College Boulevard
Santa Clara, California 95050

ABSTRACT

This paper presents a discussion of the interconnection services provided by Net/One, a local area network communication system produced commercially by Ungermann-Bass, Inc. Net/One was designed especially to provide communication among user devices which are attached to the network. The services are provided by the networking software; they include a virtual circuit service, used for logically connecting two devices so they may exchange bytes with one another, and a datagram service, used by intelligent packet-oriented hosts to communicate simultaneously with any number of other such hosts. The paper provides an overview of these services as seen by the user of Net/One. In addition, it offers some discussion on hybrid variants of these services and the additional capabilities they provide for interconnection of user equipment.

INTRODUCTION

There is a simplistic point of view that says the universe of user computing equipment is divided into two camps--the intelligent devices and the non-intelligent, or dumb, devices. Net/One [1,2,5] is a local area network which provides communication services for both kinds of devices; it does so with two distinct kinds of services, the virtual circuit service and the datagram service. The virtual circuit service provides the means for a dumb device to reliably exchange byte streams with another dumb device anywhere in the network. (Of course, intelligent devices can take advantage of the virtual circuit service too; in fact any device which is, or which can talk to, a dumb device can be accommodated.) The datagram service provides the means for an intelligent device to exchange packets with any collection of other intelligent devices anywhere in the network.

The following sections present the characteristics of these services as seen from a user's (or the device's) point of view, and then elaborate on those aspects of the services which can

This paper was originally presented at Electro 81.

be modified to provide communications for an entire spectrum of devices in a not-so-simplistic universe.

NET/ONE HARDWARE BASE

Net/One is a local communications network which was designed to utilize a wide range of communication media. In its first embodiment a linear bus technology similar to the experimental Ethernet described in [3] is utilized. The current implementation consists of a single coaxial cable and an arbitrary number (from 2 to 200) of Network Interface Units (NIUs) placed at arbitrary locations along the cable [see 1]. The NIUs are packet switching computers which employ specially designed hardware and software to provide user devices with communication services. The NIUs transmit information on the shared coaxial cable at 4 Mbps or at 10 Mbps (according to the Ethernet Standard [6]), depending on which of two current data rate options is selected. General purpose NIUs may be scaled to provide from 4 to 16 serial (RS-232C) ports and from 2 to 8 parallel ports for the attachment of user devices. Other physical interfaces, such as IEEE-488, are also available now, while some, such as RS-449, will be added in the near future. Individual Net/One segments may be joined in an internetworking arrangement similar to that described in [4] by the use of gateway processors. All Net/One protocols employ Internet Headers to allow for whatever future extensions prove necessary.

The basic means by which the NIUs gain access to the shared coaxial cable is through the use of a Carrier Sense Multiple Access scheme using Collision Detection (CSMA/CD) as described in [3]. In this scheme NIUs listen before transmitting to insure the channel is free, and listen during their own transmissions to insure no other NIU is also transmitting. A collision occurs if two or more NIUs transmit at once; on detecting a collision the colliding stations reschedule their transmissions for another attempt at some future time.

THE VIRTUAL CIRCUIT SERVICE

The virtual circuit service derives its name from the physical circuit switching systems and services that it emulates. The most familiar of these services is the worldwide telephone system, which uses switched, physical communication links to enable point-to-point communications between two telephone instruments anywhere in the world.

The virtual circuit service, by contrast, provides a circuit-like service without the need for physical switching of communication links. Within Net/One, circuits are implemented by software that switches packets of data on the shared broadcast communications medium (the coaxial cable). The software generates, transmits and receives packets on a per-circuit basis, keeping separate the data of the individual circuits.

Net/One virtual circuits are used to carry data between any two user devices in the network, irrespective of their physical placement. In order to emulate circuit switching services, Net/One ensures that the data on each circuit arrive in the proper order, without error, and without duplication. Virtual circuits have many advantages over physical circuits. For example, they can allow for the resolution of speed mismatch between the data-generating and data-consuming end points; they can provide for data retransmissions in case of transient communication errors; and they can easily allow for transformation of the information that traverses the circuits.

As stated, virtual circuits in Net/One are used to connect two devices (such as a terminal and a host computer I/O port) for the purpose of data exchange. The circuits are implemented by software, and although the devices are the ultimate end points of any circuit, the logical end points seen by the virtual circuit service are processes within the respective NIUs. Processes are simply asynchronous software tasks which cooperatively share the processor as dictated by an underlying multi-tasking kernel. Since these software processes control the devices at the source and destination sites, the effect as far as the user is concerned is still just as though the devices were the end points. This parallels the telephone system once again: while the communicating end points in the phone system are generally humans, all circuits are in fact established between two telephone instruments--the parallel to the software processes.

Using software-controlled processes as the end points for virtual circuits provides enormous flexibility in the types of service that can be provided for any particular connection. For example, process end points can be individually tailored to accept or reject connection attempts so that various types of

access control can be placed on a particular device.

Finally, the use of processes allows devices to establish circuits to network "services" as well as to other devices, so that as the capabilities of Net/One grow the means for accessing these new services is readily available to all existing users of the virtual circuit service.

METHODS OF ESTABLISHING VIRTUAL CIRCUITS

Net/One provides three separate ways for circuits to be established. The first is for an attached device to directly command that a circuit be established to some other device. To provide this capability, Net/One offers a software process that implements the functions of a command interpreter. Devices which are served by this process can issue it commands directing it to open a connection to whatever remote device they want. Interactive terminals are usually served by the command interpreter process so their users can switch their conversations among a number of different destination devices throughout the day. However, computers too may be served by the command interpreter process so that programs can command connection to one or another network device (e.g., one or another printer) as they desire. Note that a given device needs the command interpreter process only for placing an "outgoing call". If the device wants to receive "incoming calls", it can issue a command to the interpreter telling it to listen for a connection attempt. The device can of course resurrect the command interpreter services any time it wants by simply issuing another command. The analogy here is again just like the telephone system---you can make an outgoing call whenever you want, but you can only receive incoming calls once you've hung up your phone.

Virtual circuits established by a device's interaction with a command interpreter are referred to as "session-oriented" virtual circuits, because the circuit exists precisely for the duration of the desired interaction with the remote device.

The second type of circuit is the "bound circuit". This circuit is established not by a user's command, but by the actions of a process created at system initialization time. Table entries in each NIU define which circuits should be created when the NIU is initialized. The initialization process attempts to create these circuits and persists at regular intervals until the circuit is completed. Bound circuits provide for a static or permanent virtual circuit service. They are in effect a "wire replacement". The circuits are permanent, of course, only when the table entries in the NIU remain unchanged. Tools for changing the table entries associated with each NIU are provided to the network administrator through a convenient utility program.

An interesting variation on the bound "permanent" circuit is the bound "initial" circuit. An initial circuit is created by an initialization procedure just like a permanent circuit, but may be broken once it has served its purpose. Initial circuits are used generally to provide default connections for users who only seldom need to establish connec-

tions to other devices.

The third type of virtual circuit is one which is dynamically created by the network administrator. Facilities are provided in the administrator's NIU to allow two arbitrary remote devices to be connected or disconnected as required by simple commands from the administrator. Such connections are called "administrative circuits" to distinguish them from bound or session-oriented circuits. Of course, it is not the circuits that differ, but the means of creating them, since once established they are all the same. Phrases such as "device-specified", "process-specified", or "administrator-specified" circuits would serve just as well to distinguish them. Note that administrative circuits are extremely powerful because the "administrator" can actually be a computer. Thus a sophisticated mechanism for reconfiguring network circuits and services can easily be implemented.

DATA FLOW ON VIRTUAL CIRCUITS

Circuits can be established between two devices attached to a single NIU, or between two devices attached to different NIUs. The circuit established when both devices are attached to the same NIU is termed an "internal" circuit. Internal circuits provide all the same services associated with their external counterparts but do not require the use of any networking protocols.

Circuits that connect a device attached to one NIU to a device attached to a different NIU are called "external" circuits, or in general just "circuits". The Net/One Virtual Circuit Protocol (VCP) is employed to carry data between the processes that serve as the end points of an external virtual circuit. VCP is a state-of-the-art, packet-oriented communications protocol that provides sequencing, retransmission, flow control, and error control to create the virtual circuit service. It has been developed expressly for use in stand alone networks or in internetworking environments comprised of many individual Net/One local networks. The protocol allows for many packets to be in transit at once on a given connection, and has a sliding acknowledgment window that allows packet acknowledgments to be grouped whenever possible. The flow control algorithms ensure both minimal delay for interactive traffic and maximum channel efficiency for sustained data bursts.

DEVICE FLOW CONTROL

VCP is the protocol used to carry data reliably between the process end points of a virtual circuit. The flow control algorithms of VCP automatically govern the rate at which either process can send data to the other. However, because the ultimate source and destination of these data are usually the devices to which the processes attach, the provision of flow control between the two processes is not always sufficient to ensure a complete device-to-device flow control capability. This is true because data can be lost unless the source process can keep the source device from overrunning it with data. This requires some form of flow control between the source device and the source process in those cases where device data bursts

can exceed the buffering capacity of the virtual circuit.

Net/One allows the use of several industry standard flow control techniques. An example is the XON/XOFF character strategy which a receiving party may use to turn on and off the other party's transmissions. As the receiver's buffers become full, it sends an XOFF character to its counterpart to tell it to suspend transmission. When space again becomes available, it sends an XON. Many devices currently employ this kind of simple flow control mechanism to keep from being overrun by other data generating devices. Other types of flow control involve the manipulation of various RS-232C signals (RTS/CTS or DSR/DTR), and these too are supported by the NIU.

TECHNIQUES FOR CLOSING VIRTUAL CIRCUITS

There are three ways in which virtual circuits can be terminated: voluntarily, when either end decides to disconnect; involuntarily, when the net administrator commands a disconnect; and involuntarily, when the connection becomes inoperative.

A circuit may be voluntarily terminated whenever the device at either end of the circuit issues a "disconnect sequence" to its NIU. A disconnect sequence is an arbitrary string of one to four characters which may be defined differently for each device and which is reserved by the device explicitly for telling its NIU to close its virtual circuit. The use of a disconnect sequence is mandated for compatability with existing devices. Ideally, one would like some out-of-band signal or special "disconnect" key to be provided on interactive devices so that users could unambiguously indicate their desire to close the connection, but such special functions (aside from artifacts like the "break" key, which is supported, incidentally) are not generally available on user devices. (Interestingly, the character sequences associated with the special function keys available on many CRTs may be defined as disconnect sequences in order to give the effect of a disconnect key. Devices may also employ certain of the RS-232C control signals to indicate their desire to disconnect.)

Devices using the command interpreter process may redefine their disconnect sequences on a per-session basis so that different sequences may be used for different connections. While the sequence is generally used only to request a disconnect, techniques are also provided for actually sending the characters of a disconnect sequence through the circuit when they occur as real data.

Circuit termination is also modeled after the telephone system. When one party to a circuit issues a disconnect sequence, the other party's process will be told he has "hung up". The "hang up" indication is a signal to this other process that it should release its side of the connection as well.

The second way in which circuits may be terminated is by a special command from the network administrator. This has the effect of making each party think the other has hung up, forcing each to itself hang up thus disolving the circuit.

Finally, circuits will be terminated when either NIU involved in a connection "disappears". This may be due to an error condition, reinitialization of an NIU (power-down or manual or remote reset), or a relocating or reloading of an NIU. Note that session or administrative circuits are closed for good, while permanent circuits will be re-established as soon as both NIUs are functional again.

NAME SERVICE

Each device (and each process-oriented service) in Net/One may be given a name and optionally a collection of aliases. These names are used in connection establishment. Connection end points are specified by name in both user commands (for session-oriented circuits) and administrator commands (for administrative circuits). Names and aliases may be arbitrary strings of ASCII characters (e.g., "UNIX PORT", "John's terminal", "2nd floor printer", ...). If two or more devices are assigned the same name (e.g., "UNIX"), then a connection request specifying this name as an endpoint will result in a connection to whichever one of the named devices is first determined to be available. Such a "rotoring" capability is useful when equivalent services are available through a number of distinct NIU ports as is the case for access to a time-sharing host, say. Devices can be given both rotored names and unique names. Whenever a rotored name is employed to establish a connection, a special unique name is reported to the initiating device (user or administrator) in the event it later on wants to re-establish its connection to precisely the same port. On an individual Net/One segment, name service is completely distributed. Name lookup employs a broadcast protocol and each NIU maintains only a portion of the total name data base--normally only the names of the devices which are attached to it specifically.

THE DATAGRAM SERVICE

In addition to providing the virtual circuit service for devices which can send and receive bytes, Net/One also provides a datagram service for intelligent devices (hosts) which know how to send and receive packets. (The term "datagram" was chosen instead of "packet" in part to relate this service to a similar service offered in public networks; in addition, the host provides only addressing information to the NIU, and not the routing information which is present in all Net/One packets. The NIU never knows whether the host thinks of its outputs as packets or datagrams, of course.) It is assumed that these hosts can implement their own protocols on top of the datagram service-- including virtual circuit strategies of their own if they like--for talking among themselves. Examples of packet switching hosts which might easily take advantage of this service are ARPANET hosts (running TCP/IP) and DECNET hosts running DECNET protocols. The goal of the datagram service is to appear to hosts exactly like a shared broadcast medium (such as the cable) with the following simplifications: host datagrams are not subject to collisions; host data rates do not need to be identical; hosts can employ conventional serial or parallel interfaces to send and receive

their packets.

The datagram service requires the host to follow a simple datagram protocol, SDP. SDP requires the host to append a Net/One Internet Header to the front of any packet it cares to send. The header contains addressing information which is used by the NIU in selecting a route for the packet to traverse. The addressing information allows the host to invoke broadcast, multicast, or point-to-point routing strategies for its packets. When given special privileges, SDP hosts are permitted to send packets to NIUs--in order to participate in Net/One protocols-- as well as to other hosts.

SDP does not guarantee reliable delivery of host packets-- just as a real cable does not guarantee error-free delivery of NIU packets. But in the normal course of events, the only errors which can affect reliable delivery of packets are real transmission errors and a deficiency of receive buffers at a destination host or NIU. Collisions are of course resolved by the NIU hardware just as for any other type of packet being gated onto the net. The problem of receive buffers is real and must be taken into account in any system design.

SDP is available to hosts via RS-232C, 8-, 16-, and 32-bit parallel, and IEEE 488 interfaces; a shared memory interface is also possible for processors which can be tied to the NIU's internal bus. Since serial and parallel devices are commonly managed by existing host operating systems, and thus available to host application programs, the use of packet protocols is easily made available to user applications; no major modifications to the existing operating systems are required. For example, a BASIC application program running on a microcomputer-based development system can send packets into or through the net via its host's RS-232C port and can contribute to any desired form of distributed operation it desires, including net management, measurement, administration, etc.

SDP is implemented by two processes within the NIU. One, the SDP packet mover, forwards the user's packets between the host and the cable. The other, the SDP controller, maintains a data base which reflects the operation of the packet moving process. The data base includes statistics on the operation of the packet mover, and parameters which are used to control its operation. User hosts are permitted to send SDP datagrams to any controller process for the purpose of reading or (interpretively) writing the database. This service is used primarily for statistics collection in support of host monitoring and measurement programs, but a wide variety of other services are planned for the future.

It is interesting to note that while the channel presented to the user actually operates on a CSMA/CD network, the SDP service might conceivably be tailored to emulate other techniques for access control, including CSMA variants or even token passing. (Token passing is one access technique currently under study in the IEEE Local Network Standards Committee. In a token passing scheme, a station is only allowed to transmit when it holds a special permission-granting (software) token. When done transmitting, the station passes the token on to some other station in the net. The token is passed from station to station according to whatever access policy is dictated for network administration.) Such a capability—provided by emulating these protocols in software—is not expected to be of interest to most SDP customers, and thus is not planned as a product offering. It is mentioned here to encourage speculation by the local networking research community on the utility of this kind of experimental laboratory for modeling and measuring the performance of these different access methods.

HYBRID SERVICES

What about the user who wants to have both virtual circuit and datagram services available from a single serial (or parallel) port? This is a common request for systems which can't afford to continually reserve one of their ports (many systems have only one port) for a given service.

In this arena there are four possibilities which depend on both the default mode of operation of the host (and net) and on the instigator of the change in service.

1. A host in VC mode wants to switch to SDP mode.

2. A host in SDP mode wants to switch to VC mode.

3. The net has SDP packets for a host currently in VC mode.

4. The net has an incoming call for a host currently in SDP mode.

We examine the case where a small host has been programmed to be the manager of a collection of user resources. At various times throughout the day, it will want to interact with these resources to oversee them in their tasks. It must talk to the dumb devices by use of VCs and to the intelligent devices by the use of datagrams, and thus must switch between the two types of service. While it is obviously a host-dependent issue as to when it wants to switch, the means for it to switch are provided in the network by a very simple mechanism: a version of the SDP packet mover which is accessed by a virtual circuit. (Here the value of using processes in the support of virtual _ circuits becomes apparent.) The host always employs the virtual circuit service. When it wants to converse with a dumb device, it does so by use of a direct connection. When it wants to converse with an intelligent device, it does so by opening a virtual circuit to the SDP packet mover. It then employs the SDP service precisely as if it were attached directly to the packet mover, being careful to use an escape sequence if the disconnect sequence is ever embedded in an outgoing packet. When it's finished with SDP for the moment, it can disconnect from the packet mover and return to its normal virtual circuit handling.

When the situation is reversed (a device on the network wants to change some target host's operation from VC to SDP, or vice versa), the mechanisms will be a little different. There are many options here, most of them host-dependent requiring a specially-tailored version of the packet mover which knows how to start and stop the SDP service on the host. Since the details are host-dependent, specific examples are left for some other paper. Note that variations of these special processes can be envisioned which help ameliorate the distinction between dumb and intelligent devices. In fact, variants can even be envisioned which create within the net a message switching service by hybridization of the circuit switching and packet switching services discussed in this paper, thus bringing full circle the range of interconnection services provided by Net/One.

REFERENCES

(1) Charlie Bass, Joseph S. Kennedy, John M. Davidson, "Local Network Gives New Flexibility to Distributed Processing", Electronics, Sept. 25, 1980, pp. 114-122.

(2) John M. Davidson, "Local Network Technologies for the Office", ELECTRO '81 proceedings, New York City, April 1981.

(3) Robert M. Metcalfe and David R. Boggs, "Ethernet: Distributed packet switching for local computer networks", CACM, 19:7, July 1976, pp. 395-404.

(4) David R. Boggs, John F. Shoch, Edward A. Taft, and Robert M. Metcalfe, "Pup: An Internetwork Architecture", IEEE Transactions on Communications, April 1980.

(5) Tod Snook, Cary D. Wyman, Richard J. Broberg, Fred P. Sammartino, Douglas R. Bourn, Allen B. Goodrich, Stephen B. Jackson, "Net/One Programmer's Reference Manual", Ungermann-Bass Technical Report S81-1, in preparation.

(6) "The Ethernet, A Local Area Network: Data Link Layer and Physical Layer Specifications", Version 1.0, September 30, 1980. Available from Intel, Digital Equipment, and Xerox Corporations.

Controller/transceiver board drives Ethernet into PC domain

BOB METCALFE, 3Com Corp.

*Outfitted with a compact circuit board,
IBM PCs can be part of a high-speed LAN at reasonable cost*

Until very recently, the cost of connecting microcomputers to the Ethernet local network was prohibitive to both personal-computer makers and users. But the introduction of VLSI controller chips, refinements in Ethernet transceivers and space-efficient board design have brought Ethernet connection within the realm of the second-generation, 16-bit-based microcomputer. By putting the transceiver on the controller board and using VLSI data-link controllers, it is possible to provide a complete local-network connection, including software, for less than $1000 per station.

Initially aimed at IBM Corp.'s Personal Computer, 3Com Corp.'s EtherSeries provides the Ethernet physical and data-link control layers at board level and supplies networking software for such applications as file and printer sharing and electronic mail. The product's levels of networking service allow flexibility of configuration and implementation by both OEMs and nonprogramming end users.

Shaving component size and cost

To meet the goals of providing low-cost Ethernet connection required eliminating some high-level controller functions not necessary in a microcomputer local network, shrinking the controller circuitry and redesigning the transceiver to fit on a controller board. The combined power consumption of the controller and transceiver was reduced by a factor of four, and 104 sq. in. of components were squeezed onto a 52-sq.-in. PC board.

3Com worked closely with Seeq Technology Inc. in designing and testing a suitable Ethernet controller chip. Like most other chips being developed by semiconductor manufacturers, Seeq's meets the required OSI level two requirements, but it has fewer added functions, which lowers production costs (see "Transmission control chip," p. 180). Because this

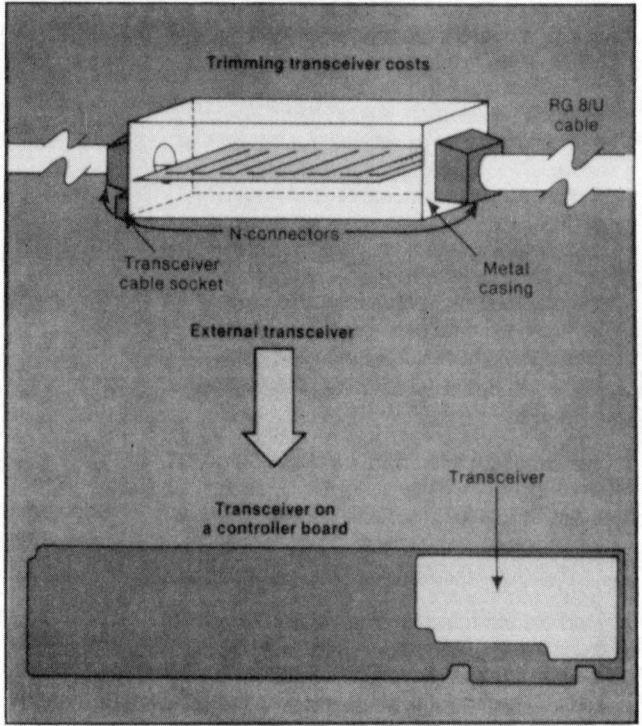

Fig. 1. Until EtherSeries, Ethernet transceivers were separately **housed circuits** *connected directly to the network cable and interfaced to the station using a transceiver cable containing four twisted pairs. Now, the transceiver can be located on the board next to the controller chips. A redesigned circuit also yields fewer parts, lowering the cost of the transceiver and its cable. Future VLSI of the transceiver function will facilitate implementation and eventually, with volume production, reduce board costs.*

controller incorporated much of the circuitry found on board-level controllers, the board size could be reduced, and other Ethernet functions could be built on the same smaller board. This favorably affected the economics of board manufacturing: the layout was less complex, boards were less costly, parts count fell

64

drastically, and statistical reliability increased.

The transceiver also needed cost trimming. Until EtherSeries, Ethernet transceivers were housed in separate enclosures containing the transceiver circuitry, a tap or a pair of N-connectors and a transceiver cable socket. With redesign, it was possible to put the transceiver circuit on the same PC board as the controller chip and its support circuits. This immediately eliminated the cost of the separate enclosures, the transceiver cable connector, the transceiver cable and the power regulator (Fig. 1). The EtherSeries controller is connected directly to the transceiver through copper connections on their common board.

In putting the transceiver on the board, parts location becomes even more critical than for a separate-

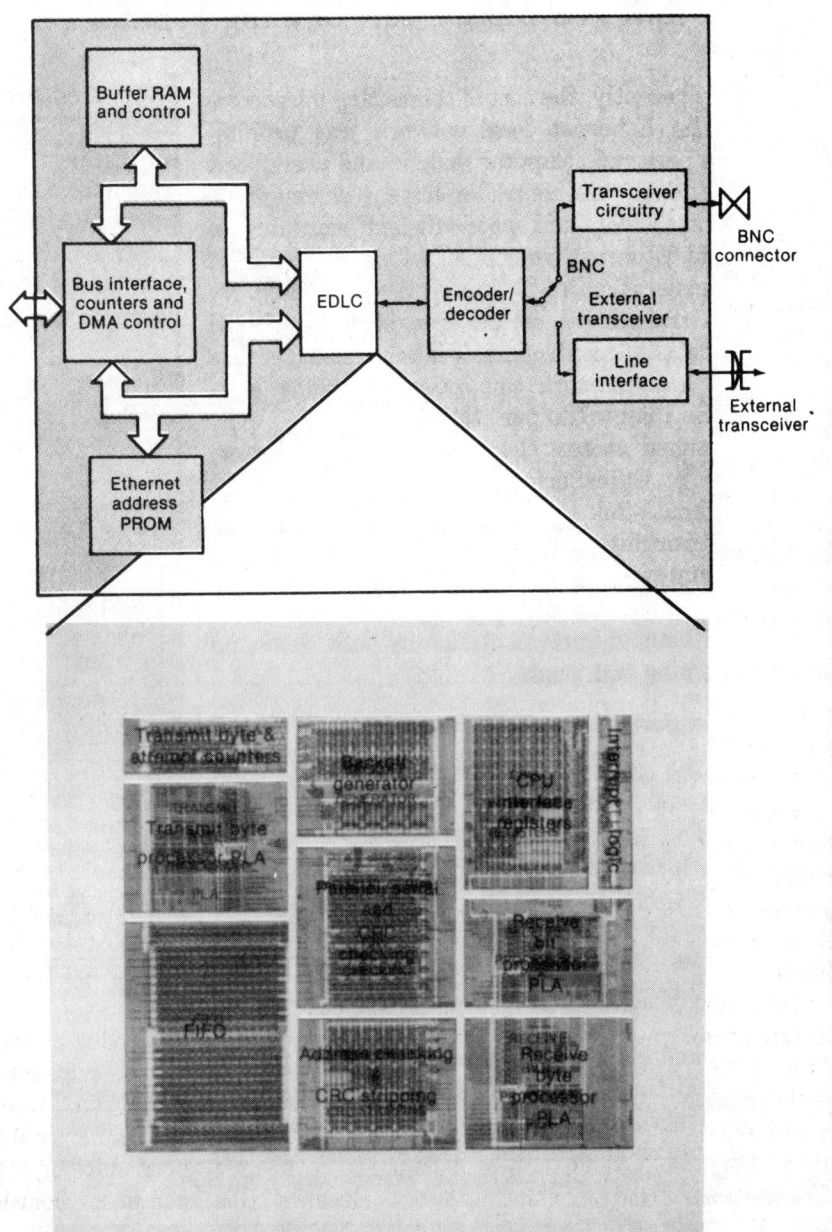

TRANSMISSION CONTROL CHIP

At the heart of 3com's EtherSeries is Seeq Technology Inc.'s 8001 Ethernet data-link controller chip. The 8001 provides the minimum CSMA/CD functions according to Ethernet specifications, allowing system integrators to supply the higher level functions such as buffer management, DMA control and address hashing.

Developed with the help of a silicon compiler, the 8001 silicon structures are arranged in a logical functional order. The chip contains (from lower left, counterclockwise) two FIFO buffers, an address-checking and CRC-stripping section, the receive-byte processor program-logic array, the receive-bit processor program-logic array, the CPU interface registers, the back-off generator, the transmit-byte and attempt counters and the transmit-byte processor program-logic array. In the center is the parallel/serial and CRC-checking circuitry.

On 3com's EtherLink board, the Seeq chip is coupled to a serial interface subsystem on one side and a 2K-byte packet buffer on the other. Packets intended for transmission are transferred via DMA over the PC system bus to the on-board transmit FIFO. The controller performs framing of the packet to include the prescribed preamble and CRC information. (The address fields, type field and data field are prepared in external memory before initiating transmission and pass transparently through the EDLC chip.)

If the network has been quiet for at least 9.6 μsec. and the back-off time requirements are satisfied, the packet data are serialized and shifted to the transceiver for transmission. If collision occurs, the controller halts the transmission by sending a jam pattern and signaling the CPU to begin the back-off algorithm. Transmission is reinitiated when the initial bytes of the frame information field are reloaded into the EDLC transmit FIFO.

ly housed transceiver. Now, standard logic circuits and buses with 5V square-wave pulses coexist in close proximity with precision analog circuits designed to respond to millivolt levels. This called for the combined talents of analog and digital engineers to ensure conformity to both FCC regulations and Ethernet specifications.

Because EtherSeries' on-board transceiver allows direct or indirect Ethernet connection, users have a choice of cabling. Ethernet uses a 50-ohm coaxial cable, which is available in more than one diameter and price. Therefore, users can take advantage of lower cost, thinner cable for shorter distances.

The main differences between a thick, 50-ohm cable and a thin one are flexibility and attenuation. Thinner cable is easier to bend around corners and, consequently, easier to bring to a workstation cabinet rather than to install in walls and ceilings and bring a transceiver to it. Thinner cable has a higher attenuation factor, though, which means that signal levels reach limiting values over shorter distances than with thicker cables.

EtherSeries permits two connection methods (Fig. 2). The on-board transceiver has a BNC connector located at the rear of the IBM PC to which a BNC "tee" connector and the thinner RG 58 A/U coaxial cable can be

connected. This coaxial cable, in turn, can be directly connected to the thicker RG 8/U type, using a standard adapter. Users can alternately connect the PC to an external transceiver that is connected to RG 8/U-type cable. The use of thinner cable in no way interferes with the 10M-bps Ethernet-specified data-transfer rate. EtherSeries supports as much as 350m. of thin coaxial cable.

Implementation

EtherSeries has several levels of networking services. The fundamental connection of the IBM PC to Ethernet is implemented by EtherLink. Higher level local-network services (those providing network-through application-level protocols) are handled through EtherShare, EtherDisk, EtherPrint and EtherMail. The hardware and software can be combined to build configurations ranging from a backbone local network to a complete networking system (Fig. 3). Consequently, OEMs can purchase the hardware and possibly system software, but add value to their products by supplying application software. On the other side, professional nonprogramming users can buy the whole package to take advantage of application programs that require little or no training, an option that will become even more attractive as 16-bit-based personal computers infiltrate high-level management in business.

IBM PCs equipped with EtherLink become network stations retaining all their personal-computer charac-

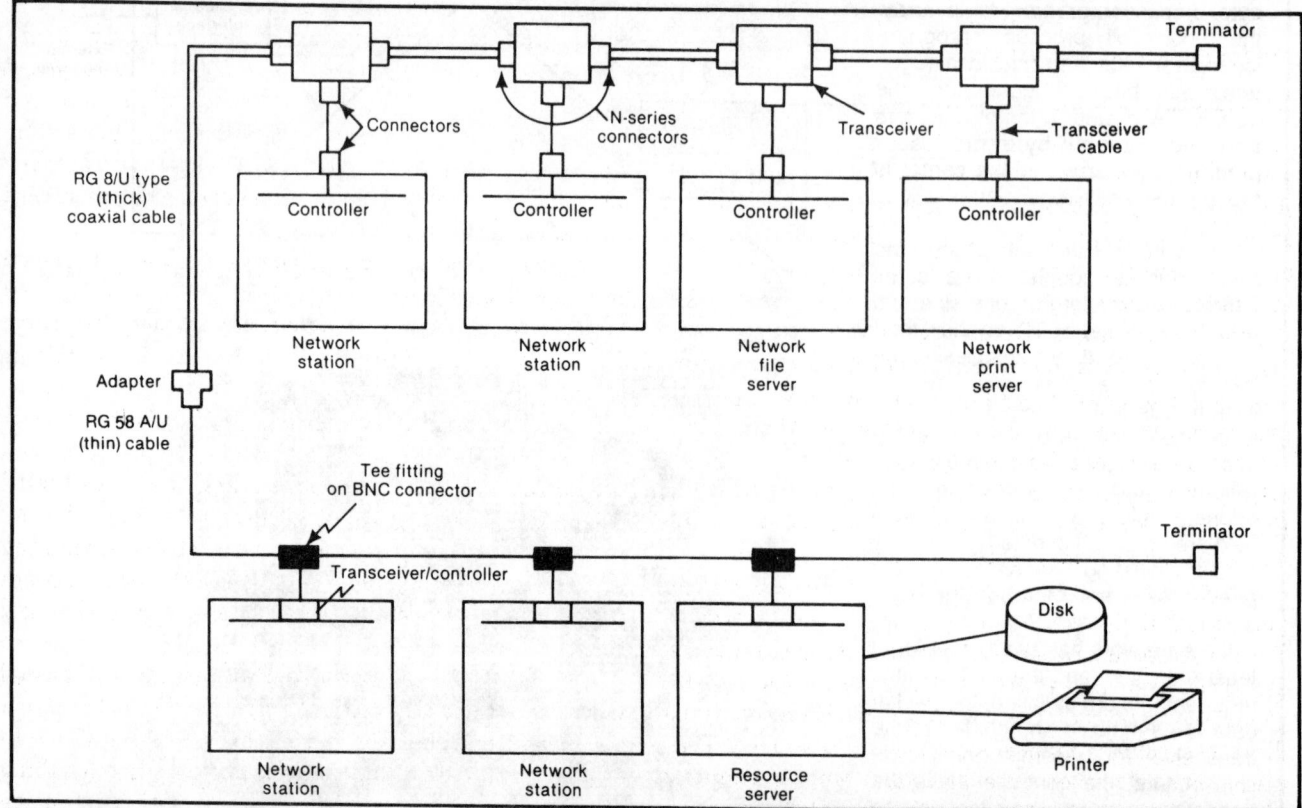

Fig. 2. Cable and connector costs can be lowered by using thin RG 58 A/U instead of thick RG 8/U coaxial cable. Thick cable requires an external transceiver and cabling from the controller board to the transceiver; thin cable connects directly to Ethernet's "tee" connector. There is no performance penalty in thinner cable, although its attenuation factor does limit distance. Thin and thick cables can be connected through an adapter.

66

teristics and gaining access to networked resources such as expensive peripherals. EtherLink consists of an Ethernet controller/transceiver board that plugs into the PC's backplane, a software diskette and a user's manual. The EtherLink software package includes two applications: remote disk access from one PC to any other connected to the network and printer sharing. All disk requests, including those of IBM DOS, are automatically and transparently routed across the network so that file transfer is achieved through the IBM DOS copy command. A PC with a printer can be shared by other PCs that are attached to the network but do not have their own printer. In both cases, the PC with the printer or disk to be shared effectively becomes a resource server.

Higher level services

Extended disk- and printer-sharing capabilities, as well as other higher level services such as electronic mail, are available through EtherShare, a network resource server. The basic EtherShare is a 16-bit

---

An important feature of EtherSeries is its levels of service that can provide complete networking services or a network backbone.

---

computer with 10M-byte hard-disk drive (Fig. 4). Accompanying software packages—EtherDisk, Ether-Print and EtherMail—are menu-driven for simplicity and offer a HELP command that explains all commands and procedures.

EtherShare with EtherDisk allows all common programs and data to be stored on disk and accessed by any PC, eliminating separate diskettes of common programs at every PC. Data files constructed at a user's PC station also can be stored on the disk, permitting others to access them via the network. In addition, EtherShare provides standard disk backup on flexible diskettes or optional tape backup.

At 10M bits per sec., data can be transferred from disk to PC at nearly the disk's raw data-transfer rate. This provides users with a "virtual" connection to the disk that seems to users as if the disk were directly connected to the PC. The user interface is one of virtual diskettes, called volumes, mounted and unmounted on a user's virtual drive. The software emulates the PC diskette drive such that, once a virtual diskette has been mounted, all standard IBM DOS functions work as usual.

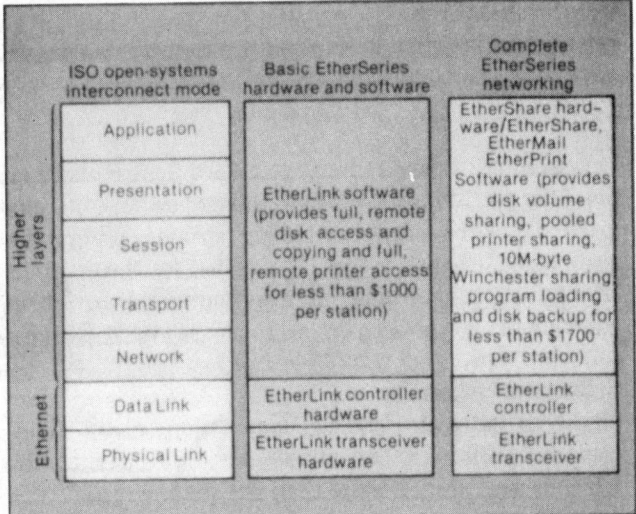

Fig. 3. EtherSeries provides all levels of the ISO's open-systems-interconnection model. *Because of EtherSeries' modularity, users can add or subtract services at the higher levels to suit their networking needs.*

Two programs support the EtherDisk software. One is for creating and manipulating volumes in the EtherShare, and one is for managing users assigned to the EtherShare. When volumes are created through the VOL CREATE command, they are defined as "public" or "private." Public volumes are available to all users listed in the EtherShare directory and are limited to read-only operations. Private volumes can be accessed only by their creator and are available for read/write operations. Both public and private volumes can be protected by a password. Volume parameters, such as name, size and password, can be changed by a volume's owner using the VOL MODIFY command. The physical act of inserting a diskette into a user's PC is emulated by the VOL MOUNT command; diskette removal is done with VOL UNMOUNT. VOL DIR displays summary information about volumes, and VOL ERASE deletes a virtual diskette from the EtherDisk.

User management comands include USER ADD, which adds a new user to the EtherDisk directory, and USER ERASE, which removes a user from the directory, thereby preventing that user's access to any public or private files.

Any user can list the other users in the EtherDisk directory by the USER DIR command. When a PC station is to be shared by two or more users, the USER LOGIN permits user changeover without rebooting the PC station. USER LOGOUT enables a user who is leaving the station to protect his files. USER MODIFY permits users to add, change or remove their access password at any time.

An EtherShare equipped with a printer and loaded with the optional EtherPrint software will behave as a spooling printer server, permitting the PC stations to off-load print data at high speeds and continue handling other tasks. This is an advantage in a text-intensive environment, such as an office, in which a high-performance PC can be severely restrained by the difference between its bus transfer rate and lower printer speed. The EtherShare/EtherPrint duo performs queuing and buffering so that the printer operates at its highest rate without causing the PCs to

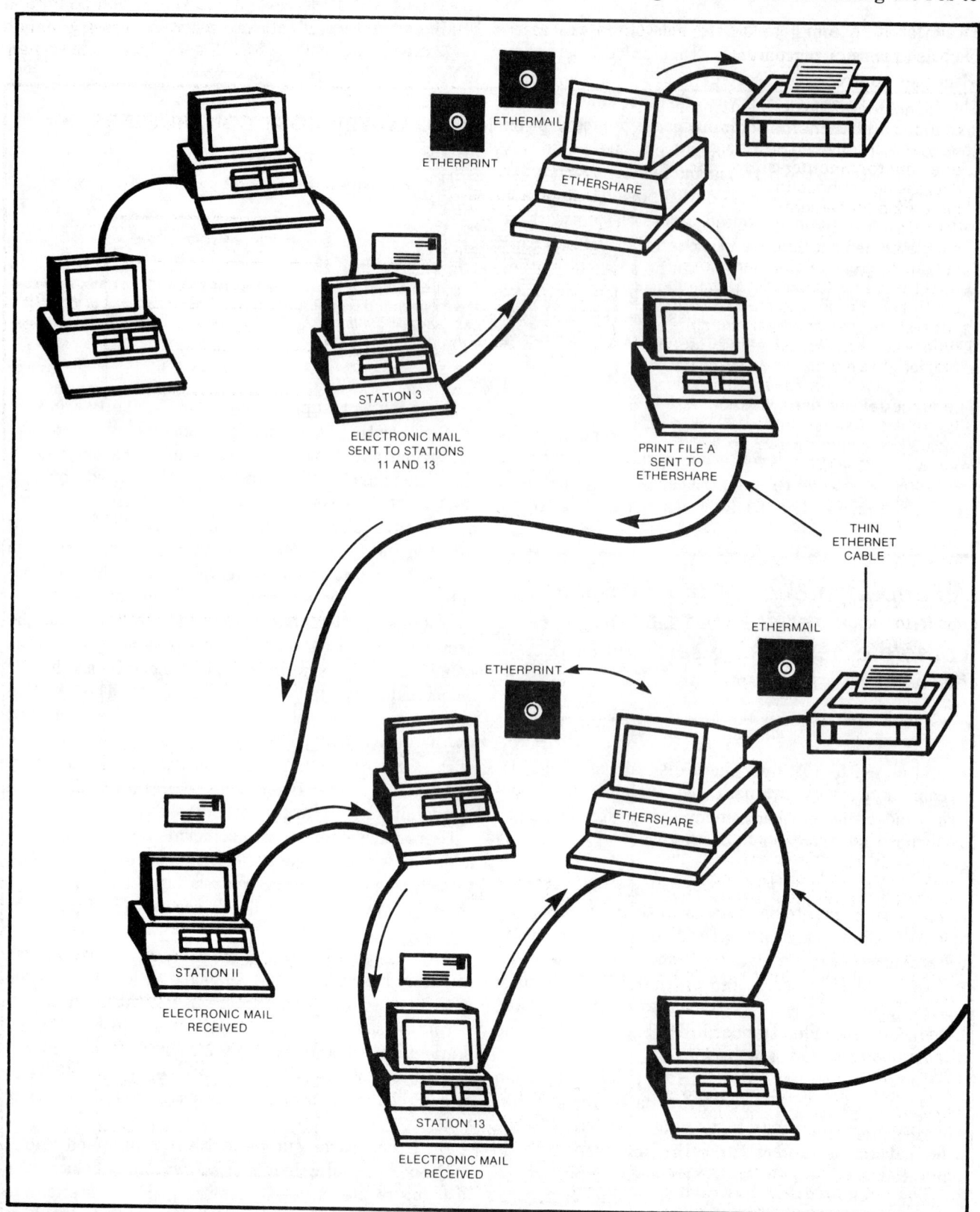

Fig. 4. EtherShare is a network resource server that can also be used as a spooled printer (print server) when equipped with a letter-quality or high speed printer. The standard EtherShare provides disk sharing, disk backup and networked program loading and optionally supports tape backup. When loaded with EtherMail software, EtherShare provides a simple yet comprehensive electronic-mail capability. EtherPrint software plus an add-on printer permits EtherShare to provide shared spooling printer service. EtherShare is also used for running EtherSeries application software.

LOCAL NETWORKS

wait for it to complete its service. Users can access spooled printers concurrently.

An EtherShare loaded with optional EtherMail software becomes a post office for receiving and distributing electronic mail among PC network users. The EtherMail software supports a very simple message-creation process using a simple text editor and taking advantage of soft-key controls, screen prompts and mnemonic commands. Users can obtain new

Technology advancements have reduced the Ethernet-computer interface from multiple boards to one microcomputer-sized card, decreasing connection costs by more than 30 percent.

Following the 1980 joint announcement of Ethernet specifications by Digital Equipment Corp., Intel Corp. and Xerox Corp., the first controllers brought to market were subsystems designed using microprocessor and/or SSI and MSI bipolar (TTL) logic chips. To implement these controllers usually required two or more boards, and the costs ranged from $3000 to $3500, not including transceivers or software.

Within a year, more controllers were announced using off-the-shelf programmable-array-logic chips. Aimed at the moderate ranges of Ethernet network applications, these newer controllers lowered the costs of connection by more than half to about $1500, including compatible transceivers. Nevertheless, that level of integration still imposed size, cost and power constraints, barring Ethernet's entry into the personal-computer fold.

Through the new LSI and VLSI controller chips, 3com Corp. finally scaled down the board size, power requirements and cost to fit the personal-computer market. These chips, being produced by semiconductor manufacturers such as Intel, American Micro Devices, Inc., Mostek Corp., Fujitsu, Seeq Technology Inc., National Semiconductor Corp. and Zilog, Inc., provide the basic Ethernet data-link protocol, although they vary considerably in price and added functions.

To squeeze more on a board, 3com incorporated Seeq's EDLC 8001, which packs the controller circuitry onto one chip that occupies only one portion of a microcomputer board. This allowed room on the board for other Ethernet functions, including the transceiver.

Ethernet connection boards will shrink even more in size and price when the encoder/decoder and transceiver chips arrive.

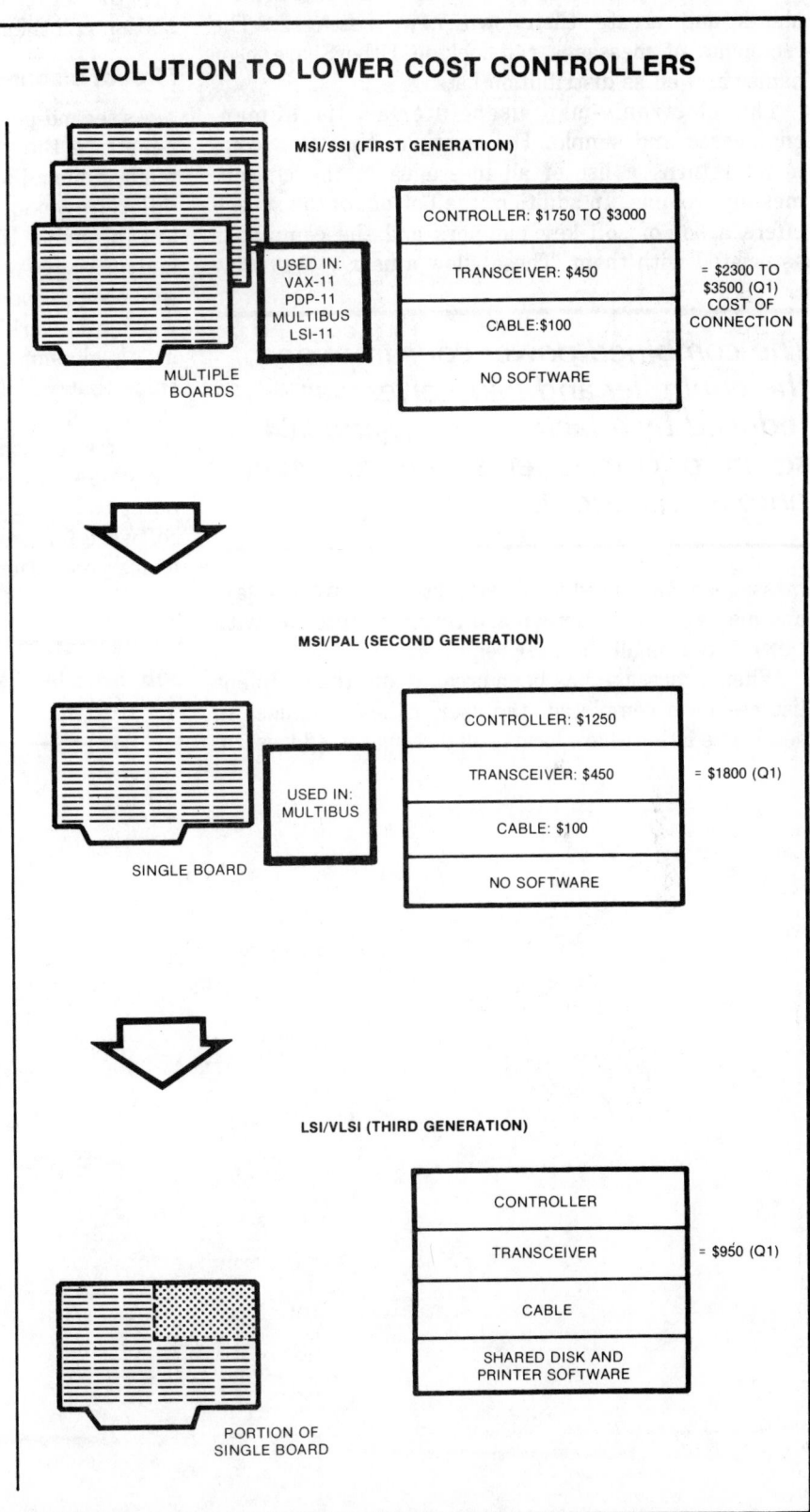

EVOLUTION TO LOWER COST CONTROLLERS

MSI/SSI (FIRST GENERATION)

MULTIPLE BOARDS

USED IN:
VAX-11
PDP-11
MULTIBUS
LSI-11

CONTROLLER: $1750 TO $3000	
TRANSCEIVER: $450	= $2300 TO $3500 (Q1) COST OF CONNECTION
CABLE: $100	
NO SOFTWARE	

MSI/PAL (SECOND GENERATION)

SINGLE BOARD

USED IN:
MULTIBUS

CONTROLLER: $1250	
TRANSCEIVER: $450	= $1800 (Q1)
CABLE: $100	
NO SOFTWARE	

LSI/VLSI (THIRD GENERATION)

PORTION OF SINGLE BOARD

CONTROLLER	
TRANSCEIVER	= $950 (Q1)
CABLE	
SHARED DISK AND PRINTER SOFTWARE	

messages addressed to them, display the messages, delete them, forward them to others and add attachments and create their own new messages. The recipients of messages can include EtherShare user names as well as distribution lists.

The electronic-mail user interface is human-engineered and simple. For example, the MAIL command returns a list of all messages in the current message volume. In addition, the bottom of the screen offers a list of soft-key numbers and the commands associated with them. These allow a user to GET new

---

The combined power consumption of the controller and transceiver was reduced by a factor of four, and 104 sq. in. of components were squeezed onto a 52-sq.-in. board.

---

messages transferred to his PC station, SHOW (display) any message on the screen and return to IBM DOS with DONE if that is all the user requires.

When a message has been created and the recipient list has been completed, the user makes a request to send. The EtherShare locates all destination addresses.

Next follows an "OK-to-send?" query. If the user types "Y," the server begins distributing the mail, and the PC station can then go on to other processing tasks.

First of a series

As second-generation personal computers continue to penetrate the professional nonprogramming user domain, demand will increase for the interconnection of different vendors' machines. Connecting these computers to enable them to share information, peripherals and messages will be made easier as VLSI-chip technology becomes more sophisticated.

3Com is working with semiconductor manufacturers in developing the encoder/decoder and transceiver chips that will further reduce the size of the boards. Plans include expanding the EtherSeries line with products for connecting the Apple Computer, Inc. (in early 1983), and Digital Equipment Corp. microcomputer (within a year and a half), as well as application software for providing services such as voice mail and forms generation. ☐

Bob Metcalfe is chairman of 3Com Corp., Mountain View, Calif.

AN ARCHITECTURE FOR HIGH PERFORMANCE PROTOCOL IMPLEMENTATIONS

Valerie Lasker, Monte Lien, Eric Benhamou

Bridge Communications, Inc.
10440 Bubb Road
Cupertino, CA 95014

ABSTRACT

Developing a high performance communications computer without compromising on modularity or expandability presents some complex design challenges. This paper discusses the architectural choices made and the implementation techniques used to meet these requirements in the context of Bridge Communications' ESPL. It also describes the tools and experiments used to measure performance, and discusses some of the key results achieved.

As local area networks develop, reaching the office, the factory, and data processing environments, the need for high-performance network servers such as communications servers, gateway servers, printing and filing servers is becoming more apparent. The population of network users is rapidly growing, expressing demands for network resources of increasingly higher throughput, and a greater diversity of sophisticated network services. While justified by genuine needs and applications, these demands pressure network system designers to reconcile the goal of high performance with a concern for modularity in order to easily expand network service offerings with a minimum of development and support overhead.

This paper discusses the architectural choices made and the implementation techniques employed to meet these requirements in the context of Bridge Communications' Ethernet Systems Product Line (ESPL). The paper does not attempt to present a comparative analysis of alternative implementation techniques (see [Ref 2, 6]). Within the context of the ESPL, it defines the major system development goals and presents an overview of the product line architecture and development environment. The discussion then focuses on the software components and system charac-teristics that most significantly contribute to high performance. This discussion is followed by a brief description of the tools and experiments used to measure performance in the Bridge ESPL implementation.

System Architecture

The following paragraphs provide an overview of the main architectural goals and characteristics of the ESPL communications systems. A detailed discussion of the actual network services the systems provide is beyond the scope of this paper and may be found in [Ref 2, 3].

The system architecture of the ESPL is guided by three major goals:

o   High performance
o   Modularity
o   Expandability

The requirement for high performance comes from the server nature of all the ESPL products. As servers, the products receive, process and generate far more packet traffic than individual workstations. The network interfaces must posess good real-time processing characteristics, while the main processor needs large amounts of buffer memory as well as raw processing power in order to efficiently process packets of information through multiple layers of communications protocols.

Modularity is desirable for several reasons: first of all, the complexity of high-performance communication system implementation dictates the use of structured programming methods, which naturally promote the technique of modular decomposition and the discipline of well-specified module interfaces. In addition, the concept of modular communication software is essential to the ability to easily offer new network services by recombining or building upon existing modules. Good decoupling between modules also ensures that enhancements made by OEM

Reprinted from *The Proceedings of INFOCOM 84*, 1984, pages 156-164.
Copyright © 1984 by The Institute of Electrical and Electronics Engineers, Inc.

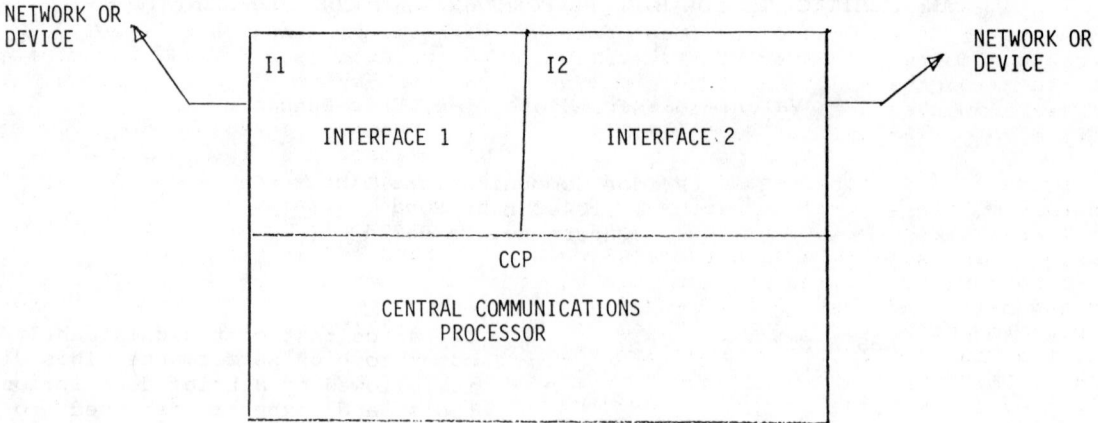

FIGURE 1:   BASIC MODULES

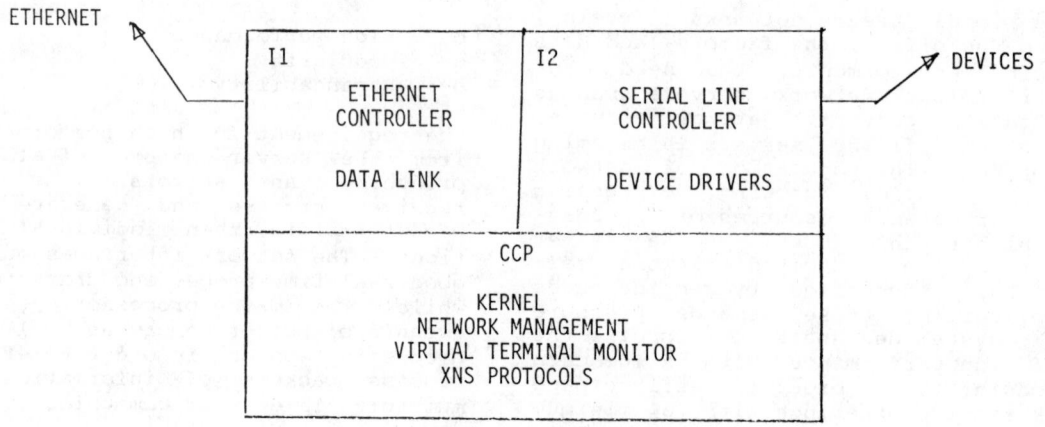

FIGURE 2:   CS/1

customers have localized impact on the communication software.

Along the same line, expandability must be designed into the products, from both hardware and software points of view, in order to allow the addition of new boards or software modules and provide additional or more specialized network services.

ESPL systems are constructed around a standard Multibus (TM) backbone, with several free backplane slots for system expansion. The systems use multiple 68000 microprocessors to provide the processing power and memory addressability needed for high performance. Every ESPL system is structured in three logical modules: the Central Communications Processor (CCP) module and two external interface modules (I1 and I2).

The CCP module consists of the Main CPU board (MCPU), which contains a 10 MHz 68000 microprocessor and up to 384 KB of local memory. This memory is used as code and local data space, so that no opcode fetch operation requires Multibus access. The kernel, the communication protocols and any application or protocol translation software execute on the MCPU. The MCPU is a Multibus master and can access Multibus memory.

The I1 module consists of a high-performance Ethernet (or IEEE 802) Interface. It contains a 68000 microprocessor for execution of the Ethernet data link code and a large shared buffer (128 KB) which is used as a packet buffer area for the various protocol layers. The shared memory also provides the common address space used for interprocessor communication. The Ethernet Interface contains a sophisticated chaining DMA, capable of performing scatter/gather operations on incoming or outgoing Ethernet frames. This function, combined with the features of the Kernel buffer manager, eliminates the need for copying packet buffers as they are passed through the protocol layers.

The second interface (I2) varies with each product of the ESPL family. For the CS/1-A communications server, I2 consists of a multiport, intelligent, asynchronous serial interface and serial I/O driver. For the CS/1-BSC communications server, I2 consists of a multiport, intelligent, byte-synchronous serial interface and serial I/O driver. For the CS/1-V Versatec printer server, I2 consists of a printer controller and printer driver. For the GS/1 X.25 gateway, I2 consists of a bit-synchronous serial interface and the X.25 protocols (see [Ref 3] for an overview of the ESPL family).

Figure 1 illustrates the basic set of modules. Figure 2 shows the modules as they are implemented in the CS/1-A.

The salient features of the hardware architecture that most directly contribute to the high performance characteristics of the ESPL systems are as follows:

1. The high speed of the 68000 microprocessor of the CCP module, combined with the large local memory accessed with no wait states, directly affects packet processing above the data link and I/O driver levels.

2. The high performance Ethernet controller can sustain very heavy Ethernet traffic and receive multiple back-to-back frames as well as other critical packet sequences, with no loss of data.

3. The large receive buffer area allows the system to cope with long bursts of Ethernet packets and minimizes the need for higher level retransmissions.

4. The chaining DMA eliminates expensive copy operations. The packet is never moved from shared memory. It is processed directly by the CCP and I2 processors with minimum overhead in interprocessor synchronization.

Development Environment

All ESPL software is developed in the "C" programming language, because of its efficiency compared to other structured high-level languages, its ease of use in low level driver programs, and its growing popularity as a system language.

The development system is a VAX minicomputer running the UNIX operating system with a cross-development package for the 68000 processor. UNIX is gaining increasing popularity as a standard operating system. It provides the necessary tools for large, structured development efforts, allows shared file access among engineers and projects, enables file version control (through the Source Code Control System program) and facilitates module-sharing between different members of the ESPL family.

The Bridge Kernel

The Bridge Kernel manages the processes that run on the MCPU. It is designed to be an efficient kernel in an environment of well-behaved system processes, and is tailored to the needs of protocol processing.

The kernel provides the following facilities:

o   process management
o   interprocess communication
o   memory management
o   buffer management
o   timers
o   interrupt handling

Process Management

All processes share a single address space
with no memory protection, and all run in
supervisor mode on the 68000. Processes
can be dynamically created and deleted.
There are different process priorities,
and process scheduling is round-robin
within each priority, with pre-emption if
a higher-priority process becomes ready.
Since the processes are known to yield
control of the CPU when they are done,
Bridge chose not to add the overhead of
time-slicing.

In most implementations using the "C" programming language, every process has its
own stack, and each stack is large enough
to handle the worst-case nesting depth the
process might need. A typical stack size
is 1K on the 68000. In environments such
as the CS/1, where there is one process
per connection per protocol layer, stacks
can consume very large amounts of memory.
Therefore, the Bridge kernel optionally
allows a process to share a stack with all
others of the same priority. Shared-stack
processes must obey certain rules: they
are invoked by the kernel to process a
message, and must return to the kernel
after processing that message (i.e., they
cannot block internally). Note that this
is precisely how a protocol process
modelled as a finite-state machine would
operate.

InterProcess Communications

Processes communicate with each other by
sending messages to mailboxes. Processes
can have multiple mailboxes, but they are
created with a single, default mailbox.
To reduce overhead, no copying is done by
the interprocess communication primitives.
When a process sends a message, the specified message block is queued at the destination mailbox and the destination process
automatically becomes the owner of the
message.

A mailbox can be either enabled or disabled for message reception. A message
will be delivered to the owner of a mailbox whenever there is a message queued on
an enabled mailbox and the owner issues
one of the kernel's "receive" primitives.

Mailboxes have a depth (which may be
infinite) specifying the number of messages that can be queued. The "send message" primitive returns a "mailbox full"
error when the mailbox depth is exceeded.

The kernel provides primitives for asynchronously notifying a sender process that
a mailbox becomes non full. The finite
mailbox depth is the key to the interlayer
backpressuring mechanism used in the ESPL.
The section on Flow Control describes the
way in which these mechanisms are used by
the protocol processes.

Memory Management

Available memory is divided into lists of
different, fixed-size blocks. There are
two sets of lists: one for private memory
on the MCPU and one for shared memory on
the Multibus. Memory blocks used internally within each process and for message
blocks are obtained from private memory,
because private memory has a faster access
time. The buffer management primitives
described in the next section always use
shared memory.

When a process requests a block of "n"
bytes of memory, the allocation primitive
dequeues and returns the first block on
the list that is size at least "n" bytes
long. A call to the memory deallocation
primitive queues the returned block at the
front of the list from which it was taken.

This algorithm was chosen for its efficiency. No searching is done on either
allocation or deallocation and no garbage
collection is ever needed. The number of
blocks of each size, and the sizes themselves, are tuneable, so that little
memory is wasted.

Buffer Management

All memory for protocol packets is
obtained from the buffer management primitives, which are built on top of the
kernel's basic memory management primitives. Buffer management allows protocol
processes to manipulate packets without
ever physically copying any data. This is
very important because data copying is one
of the most time-consuming operations in
protocol processing. For example, the time
to copy a 512-byte packet on a 10 MHz
68000 processor approaches 350
microseconds, plus the time needed to
acquire a free buffer from the kernel
(approximately 300 microseconds on the
ESPL kernel). The combined delays of a
single packet copy operation would account
for 15 to 20 percent of the average packet
processing time.

Typical protocol operations are as follows: As a packet moves down the ISO
layers [Ref 4], each layer treats the
header and data from the layer above as
pure data, and prefixes its own header to
the data. The packet transmitted onto the
physical network is a collection of potentially discontiguous data segments. As a

packet moves up the ISO layers, each layer strips off its own header, and passes up the remaining data. Reliable protocol layers must retain a copy of the data in order to initiate retransmission. Also, packets may need to be split or recombined depending on the maximum packet size restrictions of each layer.

In the kernel's buffer management scheme, a data buffer is represented by either a single buffer descriptor (BD) or a linked list of buffer descriptors. A buffer descriptor is a block of memory which points to a buffer segment.

The buffer allocation primitive obtains a buffer segment and buffer descriptor from available memory and returns a pointer to the BD. There are primitives which add and delete data from the front and rear of a buffer, either by altering pointers and lengths, or by adding and deleting buffer segments. There are also primitives for splitting and combining buffers. Buffers may be logically copied (i.e. the BDs are replicated but not the actual data). The kernel keeps track of how many logical copies are outstanding at one time.

Timers

The MCPU has a clock that is used as an interval timer. A process schedules an alarm by passing an alarm message block to the kernel's "set alarm" primitive. This message is sent back to the process's default mailbox after the specified interval has elapsed. Alarm messages are treated as normal IPC messages, so it is easy for a process to wait until a message arrives or a timeout occurs.

The kernel also provides a primitive for stopping an alarm. Since protocol processes tend to stop alarms before they time out (e.g. alarms on retransmissions) the code is optimized to make stopping alarms very efficient [Ref 6].

Interrupt Processing

Standard interrupt routines on the MCPU include the clock and the agents for the I1 and I2 modules. Communication between the MCPU and the I/O modules is accomplished by queueing packets in shared memory and having each processor interrupt the other when there is work to be done. The kernel provides the facilities for trapping interrupts, stopping the currently running process and calling the appropriate interrupt handler. An agent such as the Ethernet data link agent is not a process but rather a combination of an interrupt routine for packet reception and a transmit subroutine which is called directly by the process sending the packet. The receive routines use the "send message" primitive to pass incoming packets up to waiting protocol processes.

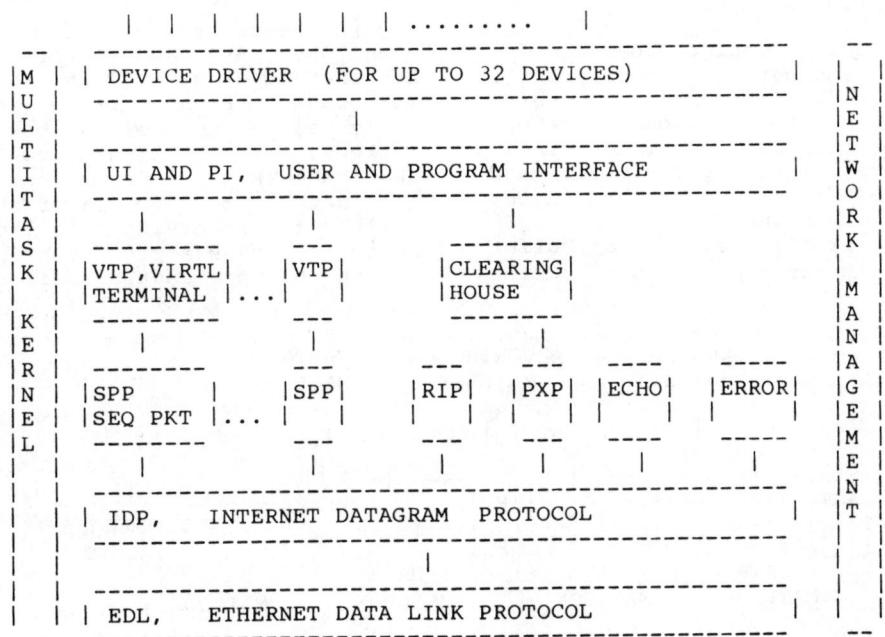

FIGURE 3. CS/1 PROCESS MAPPING

Process Mapping

The CS/1 process mapping is shown in Figure 3. In the CS/1, for modularity reasons, there is a different process or set of processes for each protocol layer. The datagram-oriented protocols, such as the Internet Datagram Protocol (IDP), the XNS [Ref 5] network layer protocol, are implemented as a single process. The connection-oriented protocols, such as Virtual Terminal Protocol (VTP) and the Sequenced Packet Protocol (SPP), the XNS transport layer protocol, are implemented as a set of processes, consisting of a "parent" process plus one "child" process per connection. The child processes are dynamic and are created by the parent at connection establishment time. Having one child process per connection is preferable to having one process for all connections because it allows the kernel to make all the multiplexing/de-multiplexing and scheduling decisions. It also simplifies the per-connection code. The cost of these child processes is very little, since they are shared-stack processes, and also share the same code.

Packets arriving on the Ethernet are processed by the I1 module, which handles the data link layer, and then passed via interrupt to the Ethernet agent on the MCPU. Here the packets are sent on to the network process, the transport process, the terminal process, and then through the serial agent to the I2 module, which handles the asynchronous lines.

No data is physically copied anywhere in the CS/1. The Ethernet agent supplies the data link driver with a list of shared memory buffers available for packet reception. Short packets are read into single buffer segments; longer packets are read into multiple segments. The agent receives each incoming packet as a data buffer composed of a linked list of buffer descriptors. It sends on the data buffer

to the network process in a "received data" message. Each of the layers use the buffer management primitives to strip off their headers before passing the remaining data in a message to the next layer. The serial driver transmits its data from the same shared memory locations into which the data buffer was received from the Ethernet, and is capable of transmitting linked buffer segments.

Processing in the reverse direction, from the serial lines to the Ethernet, is very similar. In this direction, each of the protocol layers use the buffer management primitives to prefix their headers onto the data before passing it in a message to the next layer. The data link driver is capable of transmitting a data packet composed of many linked buffer segments.

The SPP connection process makes a logical copy of each data buffer for retransmission. The first copy is freed when the Ethernet agent completes transmission of the data buffer. The second copy is freed when SPP receives the acknowledgement that the data buffer has arrived.

Process scheduling is done in such a way as to minimize the amount of time that a packet spends in the CS/1 and therefore achieve a lower average delay for each packet (Refer to [Ref 2] for a more detailed discussion on scheduling issues).

Flow Control Between Protocol Layers

Figure 4 shows the data flow among the SIO agent, VT, SPP, and IDP processes and the Ethernet agent as well as the associated mailboxes. Each protocol process typically has one control mailbox (its default mailbox) for receiving timeouts and notification messages, one mailbox for receiving data from the layer above, and one mailbox for receiving data from the layer below. For example, each SPP connection process has one control mailbox, one mail-

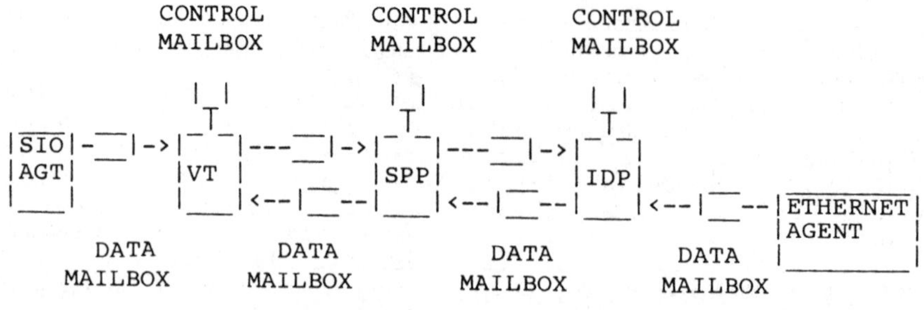

```
    CONTROL         CONTROL         CONTROL
    MAILBOX         MAILBOX         MAILBOX

       |_|             |_|             |_|
        T               T               T
|SIO|-__|->|__ _|->|__ _|->|__ _|
|AGT|     |VT |---|   |SPP|---|   |IDP|
|___|     |   |<--|___|   |<--|___|   |<--|__ --|ETHERNET|
          |___|           |___|           |___|   |AGENT   |
                                                  |_____|
     DATA          DATA            DATA          DATA
    MAILBOX       MAILBOX         MAILBOX       MAILBOX
```

FIGURE 4. CS/1 DATA FLOW AND MAILBOX

box for receiving data from the Ethernet via the network layer process, IDP, and one mailbox for receiving data from the serial lines via the terminal process, VT. The default mailboxes have infinite depth and are never disabled. The data mailboxes have a small depth (such as two messages).

Processing data buffers is very efficient in the normal, non-flow-controlled case. Each layer sends data buffers to the data mailbox belonging to the adjacent layer, and all data mailboxes are enabled for message reception. There are no explicit acknowledgements between processes. The sending process relinquishes ownership of the data in the "send" primitive.

A process disables one of its data mailboxes whenever it cannot accept any more data from its client. For example, SPP connection processes can only send the number of packets in their send window (typically 3) to the other side before receiving acknowledgements for them. When an SPP connection process transmits the last packet in its send window, it disables the data mailbox used by the terminal process, VT, to pass data to SPP.

When a protocol process issues a "send message" call to a data mailbox and receives the return code "mailbox full", the process enters a flow-controlled state and disables the data mailbox from its client. That client's data mailbox will eventually fill up, causing that process to flow-control and disable the data mailbox from its client, and so on. Thus, flow control propagates up and down the protocol layers by backpressure. At the highest layer, when the serial line agent discovers that the terminal process's data mailbox is full, it issues an "XOFF" to the line.

When the congestion clears (for example, when SPP can again send packets to the other side) the process exits from the flow-controlled state and enables the data mailbox from its client. When a message is read from this data mailbox, making that mailbox no longer full, the kernel sends an asynchronous notification back to the sender that causes it to exit flow control state. This in turn causes the state change to propagate to the client layer. At the top layer, the serial agent eventually issues an "XON" and data flow is normal once again.

The use of an efficient backpressuring and depressuring mechanism that eliminates polling overhead provides a quicker propagation of flow control state changes through the protocol layers. This results in a lower average delay per packet and dramatically improves the overall responsiveness of the system.

Performance Measurement Tools and Methodology

The ESPL product development is carried out in well defined phases:

o Top level system design
o Unit design and implementation
o Hierarchical integration
o Final test

The concern for performance must be present from the very early stages of the development work. Performance must also be constantly monitored during all the development phases through measurement tools, and results must be fed back into the system implementation process to eliminate or minimize bottlenecks as they are identified. In the course of the hierarchical integration phase in particular, every integration level is succeeded by performance measurements and enhancements before the next level of integration is started.

The performance optimization of the ESPL is based upon a queuing model analysis and a critical path analysis. In addition, measurement tools are developed at both the module level and the system level and provide information on packet throughput, packet delay, and buffer utilization in order to validate the queuing model and adjust the critical path logic.

The following paragraphs describe in more detail the critical path optimization of the CS/1, the queuing model, the performance tools, and a few measurements.

Critical Path Optimizations for the CS/1

This section summarizes some of the optimizations that were made after the initial implementation of the CS/1 software to improve performance on the critical path, ie. - the path of data flowing from the Ethernet to the serial line and vice versa.

The key source of optimization was to minimize system overhead along the critical path of a data packet. All the places where kernel calls are invoked were carefully reviewed and parameter passing methods improved as necessary. In addition, in the case of memory management calls, standard streamlining techniques were employed to ensure that storage blocks and buffers in particular were reused as much as possible and that allocation and deallocation calls were made only when strictly necessary (typically one pair of calls per packet).

For large segments, it is better to link and manage buffer descriptors than to either perform expensive copy operations or always waste the memory needed for maximum size packets. This linking overhead is not justifiable, however, for small segments. Since the size of each protocol header in the serial line to Ethernet data path is fixed and known, another optimization that was made is to always receive data from the serial lines into data buffers that have enough room at the front for all these headers. The serial agent uses the buffer management primitives to get large enough data buffers, and then leaves enough room for the headers before passing them to the serial line module for reception of incoming data.

Queueing Model Analysis

All ESPL servers are modeled as multiple two-stage m/m/l queues [Ref 7]. Input from the Ethernet and the SIO lines to the MCPU forms the first stage, and the input from the MCPU to the Ethernet and the SIO lines forms the second stage. The packet length distribution is assumed to follow the Ethernet measurement by Shoch and Hupp [Ref 1] (80 percent of packets are minimum size and 20 percent of packets are maximum size), yielding an average packet size of 112 bytes. The throughput, average service time, delay through the server, and the probability of running out of buffers are derived as functions of traffic loading and total number of allocated buffers in the system. The total number of buffers, the buffer sizes (and consequently, the total memory requirement), and the maximum number of SIO lines supported are determined from the queueing model analysis.

Kernel Measurement Tools

Two sets of measurement tools are provided in the kernel. The first set of tools measures the timing of kernel calls involved in the critical path of packet processing. The second set of kernel tools provide a means for other processes to perform measurements. These measurements include:

o   CPU time spent on each process and interrupt routine
o   execution flow sequence
o   process memory usage
o   queue depth of process mailboxes
o   number of busy processes
o   stack size
o   scheduling algorithm efficiency
o   timer interrupt overhead
o   context switch occurrences

Measurement Tools in Protocol Processes

All protocol processes also provide built-in tools to support performance measurement. The measurements include:

o   SIO parity error and buffer overflow counts per port

o   VT call setup, transmission and reception byte counts

o   SPP per session transmission, retransmission, reception packet counts and round trip delay

o   IDP transmission, receiving, internet, and intranet packet counts

o   Ethernet Data Link transmission, retransmission, and reception packet counts; alignment, CRC, packet-too-short, packet-too-long, collision error counts, and interpacket arrival intervals

A packet generator process supplies input traffic in many test and measurement configurations. This process is implemented as a client of the VT protocol. It is capable of regulating the packet generation rate when the VT connection is in a flow-controlled state. The parameters used to control the test include input packet rate, input packet size, the length of the testing period, and a choice of unidirectional or bidirectional traffic generation.

Performance Measurement Procedures

The measurement procedures include both field and laboratory procedures.

The field procedures provide on-line measurement of the system's CPU and buffer utilization, byte and packet throughputs, error rates and other statistics, and are used by the customer to optimize network configuration and to plan network growth.

The field measurement procedure provides five network management reports, with detailed measurements for four different intervals (ranging from the busiest 4-second sample and busiest single minute of the day to 1-hour and 24-hour intervals) plus a per-port cross section combining all these intervals.

The laboratory procedures are used in the product development phase to fine tune the system performance. These procedures measure detailed performance of major functions in the protocol layers, the kernel and the driver that are critical to system

performance. As an example, two packet generators (PG#1 and PG#2) and a CS/1 are connected to the same Ethernet, as shown in Figure 5. Two packet generators ensure that enough traffic can be generated to saturate the tested CS/1.

Connections are established from both

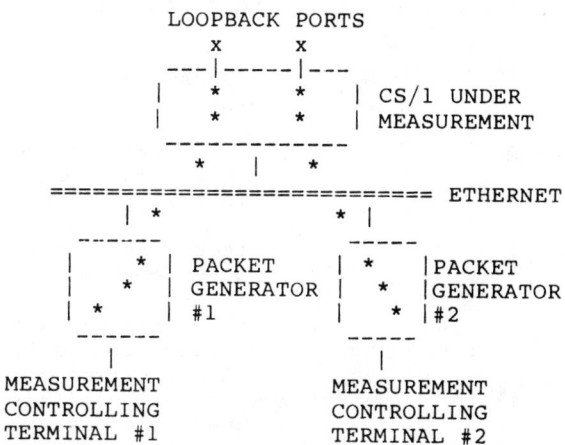

```
    LOOPBACK PORTS
        x    x
   ---|-----|---
   |   *    *   | CS/1 UNDER
   |   *    *   | MEASUREMENT
   -------------
        *  |  *
=============================== ETHERNET
   |  *        *  |
  ------        -----
  |    *  | PACKET   |  *  |PACKET
  |   *   | GENERATOR|  *  |GENERATOR
  | *     | #1       |    *|#2
  ------            -----
     |                |
MEASUREMENT        MEASUREMENT
CONTROLLING        CONTROLLING
TERMINAL #1        TERMINAL #2
```

FIGURE 5. CS/1 MEASUREMENT CONFIGURATION

packet generators to loopback ports on the CS/1, causing all packets to be remotely looped back through the CS/1 under test. Both packet generators perform time stamping on all packets transmitted and record packet delay. The CS/1 collects and computes the processing time spent at every protocol layer. By varying the traffic load from the packet generators, the CS/1 throughput, delay, and processing times in each protocol layer are measured.

The resulting measurements indicate that the average time to process a packet is 0.65 ms for the Ethernet Agent, 1.0 ms for IDP, 1.47 ms for SPP, 0.87 ms for VT, and 0.87 ms for the SIO Agent. The throughput of the physical layer, data link layer, and the IDP protocol is 606 packets per second. The throughput of all layers up to SPP is 352 packets per second, the throughput of all layers up to VT is 250 packets per second, and the CS/1's overall throughput is 205 packets per second. A more detail description of the measurement has been presented in [Ref. 8].

In file transfer applications, the typical packet contains the maximum size of 576 bytes allowed by the XNS protocols. This corresponds to a maximum CS/1 throughput of approximately 1 Mbps. In this case, the performance bottleneck is often the data throughput achieved on the access line into the CS/1.

In interactive terminal applications, the typical packet originated from a terminal contains but a very small number of characters (1 to 10). Measurements for this type of traffic on an actual network indicate that a CS/1 serving 32 terminals rarely exceeds a load of 100 packets/sec, which is less than half of its capacity.

In extreme cases however, when all packets are single-character and when character echo is done remotely, the packet processing of the MCPU becomes the performance bottleneck.

The average delay through the CS/1 for a traffic load of 205 packets per second is 49 ms.

Conclusion

Robust and sophisticated communication are known to consume large amounts of CPU and memory resources. However, the performance achieved with a system architecture tailored for communications processing can be dramatically higher than with general purpose architectures of comparable raw processing power. The CS/1, for example, is four to five times faster at packet processing than a VAX 11-750 in a UNIX or VMS environment. This level of performance proves to be more than sufficient for switching the traffic of 32 users, even in the case of highly responsive, screen-oriented applications. It also enables CS/1 systems to be used as front-end processors for larger hosts and main frames. The modularity of the architecture allows these characteristics to carry over to the entire family of ESPL products.

References

[1]. J. Shoch and J. Hupp, "Measured Performance of an Ethernet Local Network", Communications of ACM, December, 1980.

[2]. E. Benhamou, J. Estrin, "Applications and Architectural Requirements of Multilevel Internetworking Gateways", Computer Magazine, November 1983.

[3]. "Ethernet System Product Line Overview", Bridge Communications, August 1983.

[4]. H. Zimmermann, "OSI Reference Model - The ISO Model of Architecture for Open Systems Interconnection", IEEE Transactions on Communications, 28, 4, April 1980

[5]. Internetwork Transport Protocols, XSIS 028112, Xerox Corporation, 1981

[6]. D. Clark, "Modularity and Efficiency in Protocol Implementation", MIT Lab for Computer Science, Computer Systems and Communications Group, RFC 817, July 1982

[7]. L. Kleinrock, "Queueing Systems Volume 1 Theory", John Wiley & Sons, 1975.

[8]. M.D. Lien, "Experience in Implementing XNS Protocols", Mini/Micro West 1983 Computer Conference, San Francisco, November 8-11, 1983.

IMPLEMENTATION OF STANDARD LAN PROTOCOLS--
TOOLS FOR DEVELOPMENT AND VERIFICATION

Dr. Inder M. Singh

Excelan, Inc.
2180 Fortune Drive
San Jose, California 95131

Abstract

Recent progress in the standardization process for Local Area Networks highlights activity in the implementation area. There is a strong need for tools to facilitate development, debugging, and verification of compliance with the standards. This paper discusses the issues involved in developing such tools. The Excelan Nutcracker[TM], a comprehensive development and management system for Ethernet and IEEE 802.3 based LAN systems, is used to illustrate these issues.

The Need For Tools

The emergence of widely accepted standards is essential for the technology of Local Area Networks (LANs) to come into widespread use. Very significant progress has been made recently in this area with the work of the IEEE 802 committee and ECMA. The International Standards Organization is making steady progress in developing standards for the higher layer protocols, which are just as important for inter-operability as the physical and link level LAN standards.

For the standards to be effective, it is of course essential that they not only exist, but that they be widely accepted and used in actual product implementations. This requires tools for development, debugging and testing. Since inter-operability is the goal of standardization, it is especially important to have tools to facilitate verification to assure compliance with the standards as well. This need for tools for development, debugging, testing and verification of standard protocols exists at all seven levels of the Open Systems Interconnect model.[1]

The Excelan Nutcracker

In this paper, we use the Nutcracker[TM], a product from Excelan, to illustrate the issues involved in developing these kinds of tools. The Nutcracker is a very comprehensive system for developing, testing, monitoring and managing baseband CSMA/CD Local Area Network systems that comply with the Ethernet or IEEE 802.3 specifications. It operates at the link level (level 2 of the ISO model) and directly addresses all of the above areas for the link level. In addition, it provides a powerful, general-purpose tool with which the user can address these issues for implementations of standard protocols for the higher-level layers of a LAN built upon an Ethernet[2] or IEEE 802.3[3] link level.

We next provide a brief overview of the Nutcracker, followed by a discussion of the major issues involved in developing tools for standard LAN protocols and how these issues are addressed by the Nutcracker.

The Nutcracker[4] consists of specially enhanced and instrumented LAN hardware integrated into a computer workstation consisting of a CRT console, 20 Mbytes of winchester and 600 Kbytes of floppy disk storage, and a printer, controlled by a 8086 CPU with approximately 1 Mbyte of memory.

The Nutcracker software manages these resources to present a conceptual view of the system consisting of four major functional subsystems: the Acceptor, the Tracer, the Injector and the Statistician. Figure 1 illustrates these elements and the general flow of data through the Nutcracker.

Reprinted from *The Proceedings of COMPCON Spring '84*, 1984, pages 261-265. Copyright © 1984 by The Institute of Electrical and Electronics Engineers, Inc.

Environment

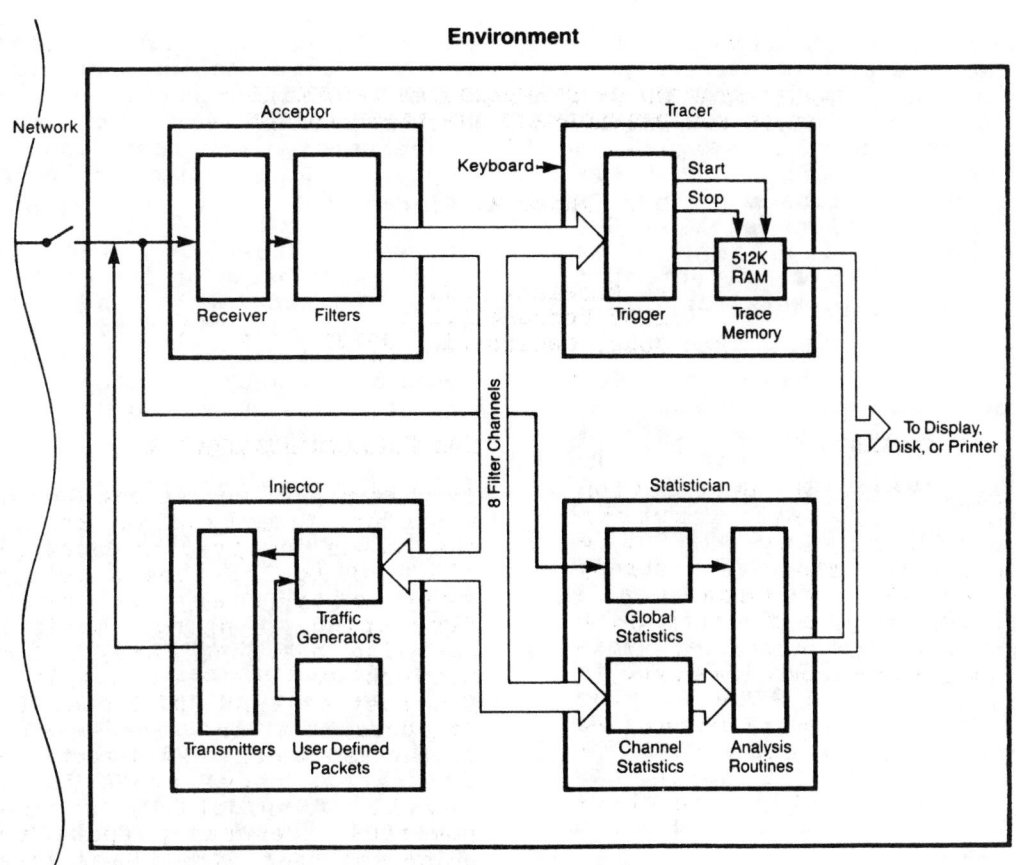

[figure 1 - Nutcracker block diagram]

The Acceptor subsystem. The Acceptor, consisting of the receiver and the filters, forms the front-end of the Nutcracker. The receiver is concerned with receiving packets; it can be directed to reject or accept packets with errors and specification violations such as CRC errors, illegal preambles, etc. and to apply time stamps to incoming packets. The filters generate substreams of incoming packets for further analysis. Each packet entering the Nutcracker is matched simultaneously against eight user-specified patterns to generate packet substreams on eight channels. Each filter examines the first 128 bytes of all packets, which typically contain the protocol headers for all the protocol layers as well as other significant control fields. The match conditions which can be specified for any byte position include don't care, exact match, above, below or within a range of values, match any of a set of values, etc. Filtering is accomplished by hardware in real time at 10 Mbps and is independent of traffic load.

The Tracer subsystem. The Tracer is functionally analogous to a logic analyzer operating at the level of network data packets instead of logic signals. A trigger is activated by a user-specified set of events involving combinations of hits on the filters (or N hits on filter X OR M hits on filter Y) and absolute or relative time events (e.g. 20 msec after 5 hits on filter 3). The trigger can be set up to initiate or terminate tracing (capture) of packets, or user-specified fields within the packets, from one or more of the filter channels of the Acceptor. The trace data can be buffered in a RAM trace buffer of 512 Kbytes and written to the 20 Mbyte disk. Traces can be named, stored, displayed and printed.

The Injector subsystem. Traffic generators within the injector subsystem allow user-defined packets to be transmitted on the network in controlled ways. The traffic generators interpret user-written scripts that can consist of sequences of user-specified packets, packets that are functions of incoming packets from the filter channels, inter-packet delay functions, and control constructs such as conditionals and nested loops. Multiple traffic generators can be active concurrently to emulate multiple network nodes with different characteristics. The outputs of the generators can be assigned to different user-specified transmitters which can introduce deliberate errors or specification violations such as CRC errors and forced collisions. The Transmitters can also be directed to time-stamp out-going packets for timing analysis.

The Statistician subsystem. The statistician accumulates and analyzes statistics from the general network traffic or from the outputs of the filters. Counts or frequency distributions can be developed and presented in table, graph or histogram formats to help in characterizing and tuning of the network system. Hardware counters capture the data which is post-processed by the Statistician software to guarantee accurate statistics independent of network traffic or other concurrent activities within the Nutcracker.

Requirements for LAN Protocol Development Tools

We next discuss some of the key issues that face the designer of LAN development and debugging tools and examine the manner in which these issues are addressed by the Nutcracker.

Observability

The ability to observe the behavior of the implementation of a protocol is the most basic requirement of such a tool. There already exist tools, such as software debuggers and in-circuit emulator (ICE) development tools to monitor the internal behavior of a single node. What is needed in a LAN environment is the ability to observe the interaction of multiple entities in the network when they are active simultaneously. This is best accomplished by monitoring the data traffic on the LAN, which in most LANs is a logical bus, i.e., all network data can be observed at a single point.

It is particularly important that this function of capturing and analyzing data on the network operate successfully even under conditions of peak network activity; for it is under these circumstances that the pathological conditions are most likely to occur and must be seen. The high speeds involved in LANs, with 10 Mbits/sec. being the most widely used speed at this time,

makes this a significant challenge. In the Nutcracker Acceptor subsystem, this is achieved by powerful controller hardware, consisting of several independent microcoded state machines, supported by generous buffering of the received data.

The Tracer subsystem, described above, can capture data for extended periods of time, if necessary, and under heavy network loads, including periods of network saturation. The flexible trigger mechanisms aid in ensuring that the data of interest can be captured.

Selecting Data Substreams

Another aspect of observability that is particularly relevant in the LAN environment is the ability to select, out of all the data that flows across the net, a substream that is of particular interest. Even between a pair of nodes, there may be multiple "conversations" going on between different communicating entities. In the Excelan Nutcracker, this is accomplished by the Filters in the Acceptor subsystem. The Filters employ special pattern-matching hardware that compare the first 128 bytes of any packet against 8 user-specified patterns in real time. The first 128 bytes will typically contain all the protocol header fields and other control fields of interest. The Nutcracker provides a rich repertoire of functions based on these fields to make it easier to isolate and home in on the data of interest.

Testing Against a Known Good Side

An important part of the process of testing a protocol implementation and verifying its conformance to the standard specification consists of sending it a series of increasingly complex data patterns that excercise various parts of the logic, and observing the responses. In the absence of suitable tools such as the Nutcracker, one typically goes through a process of building a series of ad-hoc test harnesses and tools for this purpose. This not only takes time and energy that is better spent developing the protocol itself, but it creates the additional task of debugging the test tools as well. In order to have a high degree of confidence in the compliance verification process, this process needs to be comprehensive and dependable.

The Injector subsystem, described above, with its script-driven traffic generators, facilitates this process of controlled generation of test patterns to excercise the target implementation.

Handling the Boundary Conditions

In debugging any complex system, it is very important to test the behavior of the system around the boundary conditions. One wants to determine if the system can deal with stimuli that are just within the specifications, as well as ensure that it can handle violations of the specifications in a reasonable, deterministic manner. While communicating with another system that has bugs and behaves in unexpected ways in violation of the specification, the system should not crash nor should it continue to operate without flagging the error condition and thereby generate undesirable conditions in other parts of the system. It is also important that the development tools be able to detect violations of the specification by the target system and be able to handle them in a reasonable manner.

The Nutcracker transmitters can introduce deliberate violations of the IEEE 802.3 specifications under user direction, such as illegal packet length, illegal preambles, CRC errors and forced collisions. The Nutcracker Receiver checks for these specification violations and flags them. In addition, it can be directed to receive data even in the presence of these violations, to facilitate further analysis.

For protocols above the link layer, the user can generate specification violations using the comprehensive script generation and traffic generation facilities. The Acceptor Filters and the Triggering facilites of the Trigger/Trace subsystem can be used for the detection of many specification violations. Potential future enhancements include canned facilities for specific standard higher-layer protocols, similar to the built-in features for the IEEE 802.3 link layer protocol.

Homing in on That Elusive Bug

After a protocol implementation has undergone a basic systematic checkout process, there remains the task of testing it in a "real-life" system environment in networks of different sizes and complexity, and under a variety of workloads. Problems that do show up at this level are often particularly difficult to catch, reproduce and analyze.

The Nutcracker provides a rich repertoire of functions to aid in the process of homing in on these elusive problems. The Tracer subsystem enables the user to capture data for analysis over long periods of time, with the ability to display, store or print the data or to post-process it. The Filters in the Acceptor subsystem make it possible to qualify the data stream in various ways to aid in narrowing down the scope of the analysis. The Trigger/Trace subsystem provides a powerful facility similar to a logic analyzer, except that it operates on network packet fields rather than on voltage waveforms. The user can define events of interest that are related to the problems being analyzed. The events can be defined in terms of hits on specific filters, absolute or relative time, and logical functions of these. The events defined in this manner can be used to start or terminate the tracing process, and one can analyze the trace data leading up to or following the triggering event.

Performance Issues

Tuning the implementation of the protocols to get acceptable performance is an important but complex part of the development process. Unexpected delays and other timing anomalies could also point out design or implementation bugs. The Nutcracker Statistician's facilities for reporting a variety of important performance related parameters, combined with the emulation capabilities provided by the Injector subsystem are powerful aids in this area, along with the time stamping function provided by the receivers and the transmitters.

Summary and Future Directions

In this paper, we discussed the need for tools to help in the implementation of standard Local Area Network Protocols. The Excelan Nutcracker was used to illustrate the key issues involved in designing such tools.

Future Extensions of this work include greater and more direct support of the standard protocols for the layers above the link layer. As other link level standards, such as IEEE 802.4 token bus and IEEE 802.5 token ring protocols, and other physical level technologies such as broadband and fiber optics move further along the process of standardization, there is a clear need for similar tools for these kinds of LANs to gain widespread acceptance.

References

[1] International Standards Organization, "Reference Model of Open Systems Interconnection", ISO/TC97/SC16,Draft International Standard ISO/DIS/7498, 1982

[2] DEC, Intel and Xerox, "The Ethernet, A Local Area Network, Data Link Layer and Physical Layer Specifications", Version 2.0, November 1982

[3] IEEE Computer Society,"Draft IEEE Standard 802.3 CSMA/CD Access Method and Physical Layer Specifications", Revision D, December 1982

[4] Excelan, Inc., "The Excelan Nutcracker LAN System Analyzer/Simulator for Ethernet", Preliminary Product Description, September 1, 1983

[5] Randall Rustin, ed., "Debugging Techniques in Large Systems", 1971, Prentice-Hall

Transceiver Design and Implementation Experience in an Ethernet-Compatible Fiber Optic Local Area Network

R.P. Kelley, J.R. Jones, V.J. Bhatt, P.W. Pate

Siecor FiberLAN, P.O. Box 12726, Research Triangle Park, North Carolina 27709
(919) 544-3791

ABSTRACT

The use of fiber optic transmission in telephony-type trunking applications is well established and is now widely used. Fiber optic transmission has recently emerged as a promising medium for local area networks (LAN's). This paper outlines the system design requirements involved in designing an optical fiber transmission system to be used in an Ethernet-compatible (CSMA/CD) local area network. The operational specifications for the transceiver and a multiple-access cable network are presented and the design implementation is shown. The problem of detecting a collision between two simultaneous transmissions in fiber optic bus systems is discussed. A novel approach to providing reliable collision detection in such a network is described.

INTRODUCTION

Fiber optics communications technology, initially developed for use in long-distance telephony networks, is now being increasingly considered for use in local area networks as well. This paper discusses the use of fiber-optic technology within the framework of an existing local area network standard: Ethernet. The Ethernet standard was chosen because of the greater percentage of installed networks of this kind, as well as the number of existing products that are compatible with such networks. Accordingly, a development effort was undertaken to design a fiber optic transmission subsystem for Ethernet that would replace the coaxial cable and coax transceivers of the conventional Ethernet transmission subsystem, using a passive transmissive star coupler, fiber optic cables, and a fiber optic transceiver.

This fiber optic transmission subsystem is functionally the same as a metallic Ethernet, and appears identical to an Ethernet subsystem at the station-to-transceiver connection. This transmission subsystem complies with section 7 (Physical Layer Specification) of the Ethernet specificaton (version 2.0) except that the coaxial cable will be replaced with a fiber optic cable. The detection of a collision between two transmitters presents special problems and is discussed in a separate section of this paper.

SYSTEM DESIGN REQUIREMENTS

A typical fiber optic Ethernet transmission system is shown in figure 1. The stations send the data to be placed on the network to the fiber optic transceivers. In the transceiver, the electrical signal is converted to an optical signal for transmission on the optical fiber. The data then travels to the star coupler. The star coupler is a transmissive type that takes any optical signal on the incoming port and transmits it to all fibers on the outgoing ports. This is the system component that actually implements the multiple access and broadcast functions on which Ethernet is based.

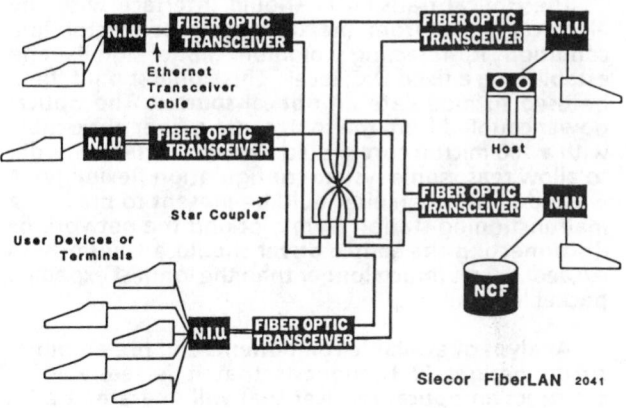

Figure 1. Typical Fiber Optic Ethernet System

The design requirements for the fiber optic transmission subsystem are summarized below. Emphasis is placed on transceiver requirements. Following that, a description of a transceiver implemented to meet these requirements is given.

The design requirements for the electrical side of the transceiver are largely determined by the Ethernet specifications for the transceiver-to-transceiver cable interface (section 7.4.2) [1]. The transceiver interfaces to a station through the standard Ethernet transceiver cable with a DASM-15 connector. The station is to be presented with transmit, receive, and collision-detect

Reprinted from *The Proceedings of INFOCOM 84*, 1984, pages 2-7. Copyright © 1984 by The Institute of Electrical and Electronics Engineers, Inc.

signals identical to those it would see if it were connected to a coaxial Ethernet transceiver. The balanced termination impedance should be 78 ohms ± 1%, and the common mode impedance should be 18.5 ohms or more. The signal level is to be + 5 volt ECL levels of about 700 mV_{p-p} (AC coupled). The transceiver should operate over a common mode voltage range of 0 to + 5 volts. The event of a collision is to be indicated to the Station by the presence of a 10 MHz signal on the collision pair, per Ethernet specification. The station supplies power to the transceiver at any voltage in the range of + 11.4 to + 15.75 volts. The maximum current required should not exceed 500 mA. The required isolation impedance and the breakdown voltage, which is specified by Ethernet to be equal to or better than 250K Ohms and 250 V_{rms} respectively, should not present a problem since the fiber optic cable is not electrically conductive.

The fiber optic transceivers should contain the optical drivers and receivers necesssary to perform the electrical/optical signal conversion for transmission over the optical cable system. It also should contain circuitry that examines the received signal for evidence that another transmitter is active. If this is the case, the transceiver is to inform the station of the data collision so that it may take the prescribed action. A reliable means of collision detection is imperative.

The optical transmitter should interface with the electrical signal from the transceiver connector and condition it, rejecting common mode signals and establishing a fixed D.C. level. This signal should then be used to modulate an optical source. The optical power coupled from the source into a fiber optic cable with a 100 micron core should exceed -15 dBm in order to allow reasonable system configuration flexibility. A watchdog timer circuit should be present to prevent a malfunctioning station from blocking the network by disconnecting the source driver should a transmission exceed 250 ms (much longer than the longest expected packet length).

Analysis of available components and pre-amplifier circuit designs [2,3] suggests that it is feasiable to construct an optical receiver that will operate at a bit error rate (BER) of 10^{-9} or better with a minimum optical power level of -40 dBm and a dynamic range of 20 dB. This can be accomplished by using a PIN photodiode and transimpedance amplifier. The combined performance of the transmitter and receiver should allow at least 25 dB of system gain to be allocated to losses in the optical cable subsystem.

The received data from the optical receiver is to be sent to the station through Ethernet-compatible line drivers.

Another transceiver requirement is that any data that is transmitted by the transceiver should be looped back through the optical media (full-duplex transceiver) in a manner similar to that of a coaxial cable transceiver. This loop back allows each station to constantly check the transceiver, fiber optic cable, transmissive star coupler, and optical connectors for proper operation.

The optical cable subsystem should be implemented to minimize excess loss and allow a reasonable number of nodes and a reasonable cable length between nodes. For example, the system should be capable of up to 64 nodes with a 500 meter node-to-node spacing.

TRANSCEIVER DESIGN

A block diagram of the transceiver developed to meet the above requirements is shown in figure 2. The transceiver can be divided into seven parts: the transceiver cable receiver, the source driver, the optical receiver, the comparator circuit, the collision detection circuit, the transceiver-cable driver, and the power supplies. Of these seven parts, five will be discussed in this section. The collision detection circuit requires a general discussion of the problem of detecting two optical signals simultaneously, thus it is covered in a separate section. The design of the power supplies used in the transceiver is not discussed because they are general purpose modules, purchased "off the shelf"

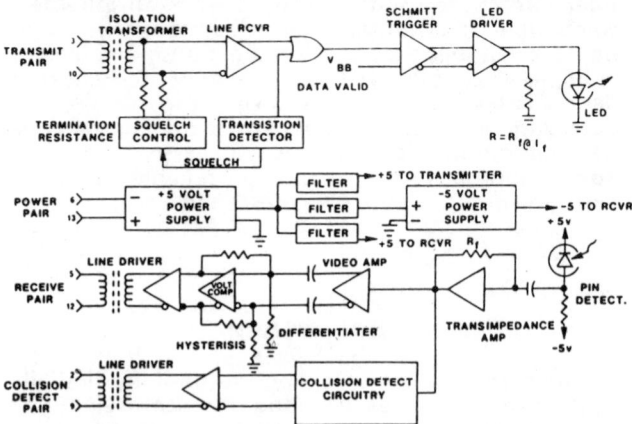

Figure 2. Transceiver Block Diagram

The transceiver cable receiver circuit interfaces to the cable through a 1:1 transformer for isolation and to increase the rejection of common mode signals. The transition detector keeps the output of the cable receiver squelched unless the magnitude of the received signal exceeds 175 mV. In the presence of signal transitions on the transceiver cable in excess of 175 mV, the transition-detect circuit drops the "data-valid line" low, allowing the signal from the line receiver to drive the optical source driver. The transition-detect circuit will assert the data-valid signal within two bit-times of the received signal, and will release the data-valid signal within 2 microseconds of the last received data bit. The watchdog timer is started when the data-valid signal is asserted. In the event that a transmission should continue longer than about 250 milliseconds, the watchdog timer disables the LED driver and prevents a malfunctioning station from tying up the network. ECL (10,000 series) is used throughout the Ethernet cable receiver circuit.

The conditioned signal from the transceiver cable receiver circuit is used to drive the optical source driver circuit. This is a balanced driver, that is, current either flows through the LED's forward resistance at the drive-current level or through a load resistor. This approach minimizes the noise generated by the LED modulation.

The optical receiver circuit uses a PIN photodiode to convert the optical signals into electrical currents. The resulting weak electrical signal is fed into a FET-input transimpedance amplifier that has a gain equal to R_F in ohms. The output signal from the transimpedance amplifier is further amplified by a video amplifier. Since the transimpedance amplifier has a large amount of gain, it is completely enclosed in a shield.

The electrical signal from the optical receiver circuit goes through a differentiator into a voltage comparator. The voltage comparator is driven differentially to reduce its sensitivity to common mode amplitude changes and to increase its dynamic range. The voltage comparator is also provided with a small amount of hysteresis to increase its noise immunity. The output of the voltage comparator circuit is 5 volts, differentially driven, for any input signal greater than 50 mV. The output of the comparator is translated to ECL levels and amplified by the ECL line receiver. The output of the ECL line receiver is transformer-coupled to the transceiver cable in order to meet the A.C. coupling requirements of the Ethernet specification.

As implemented, the transceiver has an output power of -10 dBm (coupled into a 100 micron core fiber) and a receiver sensitivity of -36 dBm (for a 10^{-9} BER), thus meeting the 25 dB system gain requirement. A 20 dB dynamic range has been achieved. Component selection and circuit "tweaking" allows the receiver to achieve -40 dBm sensitivity.

COLLISION DETECTION PROBLEM

When optical fibers are used in networks which have a contention-based access protocol such as Ethernet, there must be some provision for detecting the collision of two signals. A collision is the result of two (or more) network stations attempting to broadcast at the same time, and must be detected and reported back to those stations so that they can take the appropriate action to retransmit the data, otherwise network throughput will be affected. Collision detection is handled in a straight-forward manner on a coaxial media network: the transmitters place some D.C. information (such as a voltage level) on the media along with the data traffic. The transmitters monitor the media as they transmit, watching for a change in the D.C. information, which indicates that another transmitter is accessing the media. This scheme will work only if the media's attenuation doesn't differ appreciably in the various paths between transceivers, and provided the D.C. information is transmitted at the same level in the different transmitters. That is the case in the coax medium. As a result, collision detection in coax Ethernets is highly reliable.

With an optical fiber medium, however, the signal levels of colliding signals will vary due to: 1) varying system cable lengths and loss characteristics, 2) the use of optical light sources that can vary by as much as 3 dB, and 3) the port-to-port variations of the star coupler (up to 3 dB). The accumulated difference can be 10 dB or more.

To illustrate the problem of detecting collisions in this manner, the following analysis is given. If we use power equation (1) and assume a 100K transimpedance front end, we can obtain the fractional voltage variation (the fraction that the output voltage will vary due to the summing of the two optical signals) as a function of the difference between two optical signals.

$$\frac{V_1 + V_2}{V_1} = \frac{\log^{-1}\left(\dfrac{dBm_1}{10}\right) + \log^{-1}\left(\dfrac{dBm_2}{10}\right)}{\log^{-1}\left(\dfrac{dBm_1}{10}\right)} \quad (1)$$

If the two colliding optical signals are nearly the same (or within 2 to 3 dB of each other), the fractional voltage variation is substantial. As the difference increases, however, the variation is correspondingly less and becomes difficult to detect. It would be impractical to require that all optical signals in a system be balanced to within 3 dB of each other. Therefore, collision detection schemes based on this approach were not pursued. Other approaches have been reported and are discussed below.

Rawson, Schmidt, et. al. describe a method of detecting the collisions using an active star scheme [4]. In this scheme, the cental node is composed of several optical transceivers, with their electrical outputs connected to a metalic Ethernet backplane bus. Collisions are detected on the backplane bus in the conventional manner of sensing the D.C. voltage rise due to two stations transmitting at the same time. The detection of a collision on the backplane bus is signalled to the stations by a low frequency jam signal transmitted over the fiber optic link. This method can detect collisions easily, and the design of the transceivers is fairly simple. However, a major disadvantage of detecting collisions this way is that the star contains the active circuitry responsible for the network communications and represents a single-point failure mechanism.

Collisions can also be detected in the time domain, as suggested by Bhatt [5] and Moustakas and Witte [6]. In this scheme, the star contains only passive components, thus providing higher reliability than the active star approach. The collisions are deteced by the transceivers, based on the transceiver's a priori knowledge of how long it takes the optical signal it transmits to loop through the star and return. If the transceiver detects a signal before the signal it sent out was due to return, it is obvious that this signal is from another transmitter, and it declares a collision. The other transceivers are notified via a special jam signal. This approach circumvents the problem of resolving collisions between packets of different amplitudes. The main drawback of this approach to collision detection is the fact that if two colliding packets arrive at a transceiver within the resolution time of the receiver (typically the bit cell time interval), the collision will not be detected. Calculations indicate that the probability of missing a collision is roughly 2%

or higher depending on network size and the number of colliding terminals.

COLLISION DETECTION SCHEME

After critically examining various collision detection schemes and their respective limitations, we have developed a novel approach. This scheme has been tested and proven to be successful in detecting collisions (with a very high probability of success) between packets of a wide range of amplitude.

In a fiber optic CSMA/CD type network, the "bus" is emulated by a star coupler. A signal, upon reaching the star coupler, is divided equally and broadcast to all stations on the network. Due to the nature of such an implementation, two optical signals cannot collide before reaching the star; the collision takes place inside the star coupler. Our method of detecting collisions recognizes this and works as follows (refer to Figure 3 for a block diagram of the key elements of the collision detection approach):

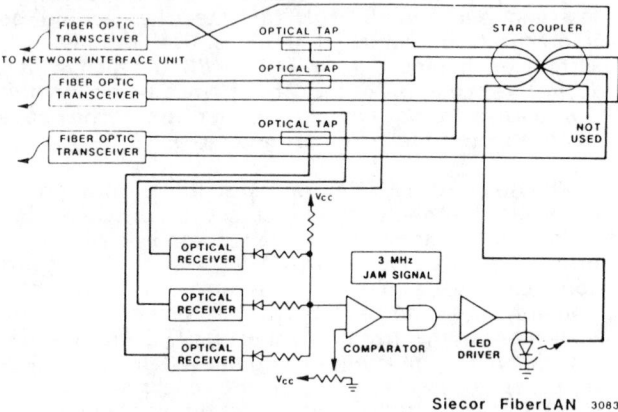

Siecor FiberLAN 3083

Figure 3. Block Diagram of Collision Detection Scheme

The incoming fiber cables are connected to the star coupler through "taps". A tap is a passive fiber-optic device that allows the input light to be split into two outputs. One of these outputs is connected to the star coupler while the other output is branched off to the collision detection circuit, which is physically located near the star coupler. Each incoming cable is individually tapped. The amount of light tapped is only a small fraction (10%, for example) of the incoming light, allowing most of the optical power to go through into the star coupler.

The output arm of each tap is connected to an individual optical receiver which is a part of the central node collision detection circuit. The receiver's sole function is to detect the presence or absence of a signal, not to recover data.

When more than one central receiver detects a signal, a collision has taken place. The central node then transmits a jam signal to all of the transceivers. The transceivers contain circuitry that allows detection of the jam signal (a 3 MHz square wave). That signal is sufficiently different from the 10 Mbits/second data signal that the jam signal detection is easily accomplished using the amplitude-based methods

described earlier. Furthermore, the jam signal is, by design, higher in amplitude than the data signal by at least 3 dB, ensuring ease of detection.

A primary benefit of this system is that it completely bypasses the problem of resolving collisions by observing distortions in the amplitude domain caused by colliding signals as described earlier. Even when a very strong signal is colliding with a weak signal, the collision can be detected successfully. This is so because each signal accessing the channel is individually detected and the determination of a collision condition is based on the number of signals present in the channel at any time, not their respective amplitudes.

Another advantage of this collision detect system is that it is independent of some network-specific features. For example, the detection of collision is possible for networks using a different bit rate or a different signalling code (e.g. another version of Manchester coding). This advantage makes the central collision detect system highly versatile.

Unlike other systems with an active central node, this system does not have a critical single point of failure in the signal path. In the event of a failure of active components at the central node, this system simply returns to the passive mode. The signals continue to propagate through the passive star coupler, and the network becomes a CSMA-type network. Self-diagnostic circuitry can be implemented in the central collision detection circuitry to allow reporting of failed components. Furthermore, if the colliding signals are within 4 dB of each other, the jam signal detection circuitry in the transceivers will operate as a "back-up" collision detection circuit since it operates as an amplitude-domain-based collision detection circuit. The actual design of this circuit is discussed below.

COLLISION DETECTION DESIGN

The design of the central collision detection scheme involves three parts: the design of the central node optical receivers and the logic to detect that more than one transmitter is active, the design of the jam signal transmitter, and the design of a versatile collision detection circuit in the transceiver that will detect collisions either by examining the optical signal for artifacts of a collision, or by detecting the central node's jam signal.

The receivers used in the central node are very similar to those used in the transceiver except that their output is a DC voltage level that goes to zero when a signal is present on that line. This level is connected to the collision bus via a diode and a resistor. When one or more lines go low, a voltage divider is formed. A comparator is set to a level between the voltages formed when one line is low (no collision) and the voltage formed when two lines are low (collision). Resistor values were chosen to maximize the difference between the no collision and collision voltage levels. The comparator output goes high when there is a collision, and this level is ANDed with a 3MHz jam signal. This jam signal is transmitted by a LED back into one of the inputs on the star coupler so that it is broadcast to all stations.

In this method, we are only looking for the presence or absence of a signal, and no other information. Thus, the receiver gain is set high enough to detect the smallest possible signal, with no conern given to distortion. The current implementation of the optical receiver is more sensitive than the receiver located in the transceiver so that this will not limit system performance.

Redundant jam signal transmitters are used to increase the reliability of the collision detection system. The system will continue to operate if one transmitter or LED fails. Furthermore, the use of two LED's ensures that the jam signal will always be at a much higher power level than the data signals.

In the transceiver, the optical data signals are examined in the amplitude domain at a level just above the noise threshold of the receiver. Refer to the block diagram of the optical receiver (figure 4). The optical signal is converted into weak electrical currents in the photodiode, amplified in the transimpedance amplifier, and fed into a video amp. At the output of this video amp, the electrical signal is a good representation of the stronger optical signal. The signal from the video amplifier is fed into a voltage comparator to reshape the edges and provide a signal that can be interfaced to the digital circuitry.

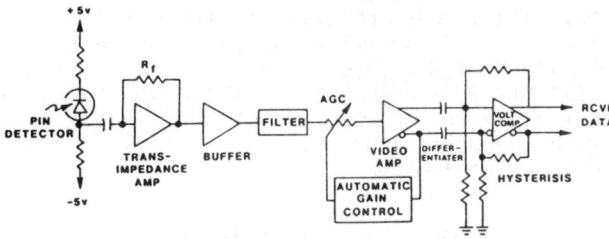

Figure 4. Optical Receiver Block Diagram

In order to detect collisions an additional circuit is added to the receiver circuitry shown above (figure 5).

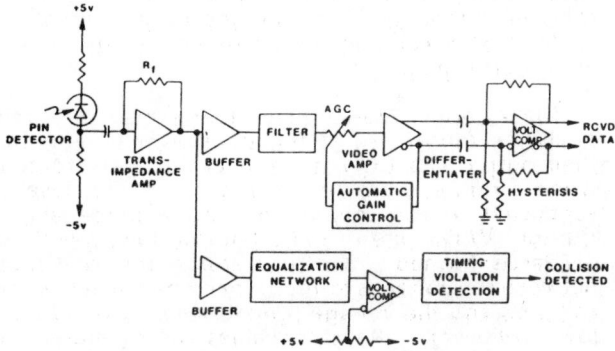

Figure 5. Collision Detection Circuit Block Diagram

This additional circuitry splits off a portion of the signal before the AGC, and amplifies it separately. This signal is equalized to improve its response and is then sent to a voltage comparator where the decision level is set just above the expected level of the noise floor. The output of this voltage comparator is a waveform, that while not useful for recovering data, contains artifacts of the colliding signal (figure 6). This signal is then examined for timing violations. A timing violation is defined as a pulse whose ON-time exceeds the maximum ON-time of properly formed Manchester-encoded pulses. This is equal to 100 ns for an Ethernet-specified 10 Mbps data stream consisting of alternate ones' and zero's. Detected timing violations will activate the collision detect signal which is supplied to the station.

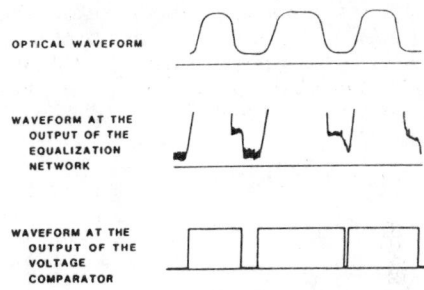

Figure 6. Waveforms Resulting From A Collision

SUMMARY

The fiber optic Ethernet transmission system described above was built and successfully tested. The transceiver electrical interface met Ethernet specifications (section 7.4.2) [1]. Transceivers were connected to a fiber optic network consisting of several transceivers and a star coupler. The transceiver electrical interfaces were connected to standard Ethernet network interface units. This network was then exercised and found to perform at an error rate better than 10^{-9}.

The transceivers are now installed in a "beta" site and field testing is underway.

REFERENCES

[1] __, THE ETHERNET A Local Area Network, Data Link Layer and Physical Layer Specifications, Version 2.0. Digital, Intel, Xerox, (November 1982).

[2] Smith, R.G. and Personick, S.D., "Receiver Design for Optical Fiber Communication Systems", Topics in Applied Physics, Springer-Verlang (vol. 39, 1982), pp 89-160.

[3] Jones, J.R., lecture notes from lecture #15 and #16 presented at North Carolina State University, (1983).

[4] Rawson, E.G., Schmidt, R.V., et. al., "Fibernet II ; An Active Star Configured Fiber Optic Local Computer Network with Data Collision Sensing", OFC'82, (April 1982).

[5] Bhatt, V.J., "A Time-Domain Collision Detection Scheme for Fiber Optic Local Area Networks", unpublished work, (August, 1982).

[6] Moustakas, S. and Witte, H., "Passive Optical Star Bus with Collision Detection for Local Area Networks", IOOC'83, (June 1983).

OVERVIEW OF HYPERchannel[TM]

James E. Thornton

Network Systems Corporation
Brooklyn Center, Minnesota 55430

ABSTRACT

The HYPERchannel product family of Network Systems Corporation represents the first commercially available local computer network architecture. This paper is a review of the objectives, history and perspective of this new architecture.

Conceptual Objectives

The founders of Network Systems Corporation approached computer system architecture from the direction of the very large scale computer and the large computer center. Problems within these large computer centers were viewed as an opportunity to provide new systems and new technology for their solution. Most large computer centers have begun to encounter problems arising from the need to support local and remote terminal access in ever growing numbers. Considerable effort has been expended in servicing the terminal network; however, until HYPERchannel very little has been done to enhance the operation of the central site.

The central site node in a terminal network has grown by adding host computers and storage units to the point that their local interconnection is the main system performance bottleneck. Standard computer data channels and I/O control systems do not allow flexibility in responding to this interconnect bottleneck. These channels, after all, were designed for stand alone computer I/O. Distance limitations on standard channels force very restrictive crowding of the physical space in a computer center. Sharing of resources is a rarity even though the desire to do so is strong.

One solution to the central site problems is the creation of a local high speed communication network. This network would augment, not replace, conventional channels and other equipment. The major objectives of this network were:

- **extension of interconnect distance to 1000 feet minimum** -- this facilitates a floor space area relief in excess of 750,000 square feet.

- **interface to any standard channel** -- in order to accomplish this, the network must be format independent except at its interfaces. This objective did not contemplate data format conversion.

- **elimination of single points of failure** -- for high reliability and availability, all units connected to the local network should be allowed equal access without master/slave relationship and without dependency on each other.

- **network operation at computer channel speeds** -- this objective was aimed at the file transfer function or for computer to computer traffic.

- **speed decoupling by use of buffer memory** -- judicious use of buffer memories within the network could allow units with different data rates to communicate, each at its own rate.

- **ready attachment of new technology** -- new memory technology may be more effective by network connection than by direct computer channel connection.

- **unpredictable and uncoordinated access** -- units interfaced to the local high speed communications network are assumed to require unplanned use of the network.

- **maximum practical utilization of network capacity** -- the network should be sophisticated and intelligent enough to supply high bandwidth and fast response.

Reprinted from *The Proceedings of COMPCON S'84*, 1984, pages 262-265. Copyright © 1984 by The Institute of Electrical and Electronics Engineers, Inc.

HYPERchannel -- A Local Network

There are a number of significant differences between a long-haul terminal network utilizing the telephone system and the requirements of a local network. Table 1 outlines some of these differences.

TABLE 1

LONG-HAUL NETWORKS	SHORT-HAUL NETWORKS
Many Miles	Under One Mile
Low Speed	High Speed
- thousands of bits/second	- millions of bits per second
Slow Response	Fast Response
- milli-seconds	- micro-seconds
Short Records	Long Block Transfers
- one print line	- one disk sector
Many Record Protocol	Single Block Protocol

Integrated circuit technology had reached the point that a serial coax bus could be used as the basis for the HYPER-channel local network. This choice allowed acceptable values for the bus bandwidth and distance as well as the number of drops, or connections, attached to it.

With the serial coax bus as a basis, a local network is configured as shown in Figure 1. Access to the bus is made by interfacing a computer data channel to the HYPERchannel Adapter, labeled A.

Some characteristics of interest in this new system architecture include:

- multidrop access to the serial bus -- passive connection to the bus is regarded as the simplest and most reliable method.

- broadcast with positive response -- the bus is a broadcast medium in which all units receive the transmitted signal, with the proper receiver responding immediately.

- demand allocation of the bus -- any unit may transmit, unless carrier is already present, leaving a brief period for possible collision of two simultaneous transmits. Collisions are detected and resolved by a unique contention algorithm.

- alternate paths by adding separate buses -- this allows added capacity and availability and the possibility of interesting subnetworks.

- network partitioning for fault isolation -- each adapter applies an access code, independent of the adapter address, directly to the transmitted frame. This code is checked by hardware and can be used to partition groups of units without physically removing them from a bus.

- convert to any parallel interface -- every transmission on the bus is a serial bit string, thereby allowing the assembly and disassembly to any parallel interface. Adapter types are all alike except for the external interface.

The local network as characterized above is best described as a site data channel which differentiates it from a computer data channel and also from a digital phone network.

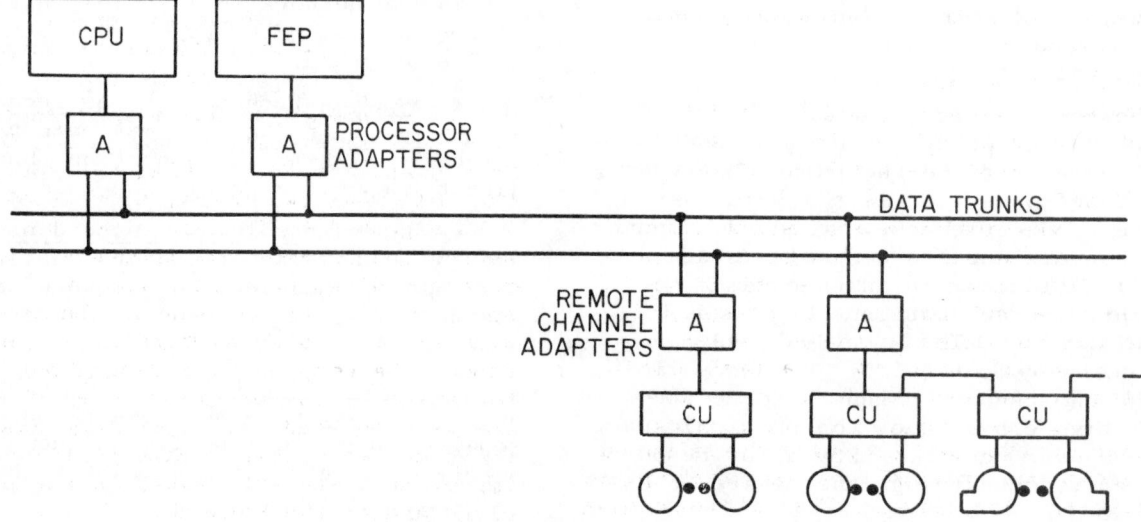

Figure 1

One of the major objectives of the HYPERchannel architecture was to off-load the local network communication function from the host CPU. This doesn't mean that the network is totally hidden from the CPU since this would be self-defeating and would prevent future evolution. The approach taken was to define and implement the "bottom" two layers of a multi-layer protocol environment. To do this required intelligence and memory in each adapter.

In Figure 2, an adapter is shown in block diagram form. The microprocessor executes from read-only-memory and maintains control over the box.

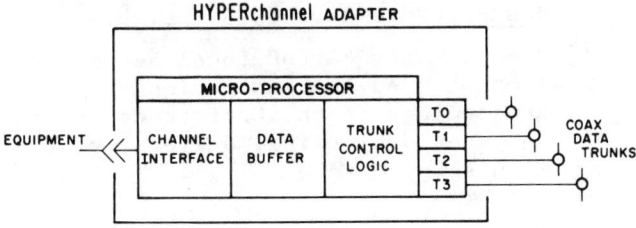

Figure 2

The interfaces are initiated and monitored by the microprocessor, but because of the speeds involved, the interfaces themselves transfer using independent hardware.

The adapter contains high speed buffer memory of one kilobytes of control and four kilobytes of data expandable to eight kilobytes. This memory has an aggregate bandwidth of 100 megabits per second. As a result, one bus interface and the external interface can be transferring data up to a maximum of 50 megabits per second each simultaneously.

Each bus interface contains complete transmitting and receiving hardware such that a busy response can be returned to a sender even though the adapter is in use or reserved.

The link-level protocol which directly controls the bus is the lowest level protocol. The intent of this protocol is to provide open and immediate accessibility to the bus for lightly loaded conditions and to gradually convert to a priority ordering of the bus as the loading approaches maximum capacity. This protocol is timer derived and is fully distributed throughout the network with no single point of failure. Adapters utilize it to resolve contention and to retransmit to obtain a share of the bus capacity[1][2].

The next level of protocol is executed in the adapter's microprocessor. Network messages are submitted by host CPUs for transmission in the form of a short message proper optionally followed by an arbitrary amount of associated data. A reservation technique is used to insure complete successful transmission of the message. Since the associated data can be an arbitrary amount of data, the reservation algorithm also constitutes a flow control for that data.

Higher level protocols execute in the host CPUs and coexist with other operating system elements and access methods. To date most implementations have been application-independent, and standard protocols appear to be developing for HYPERchannel.

Some History and Status

Following the founding of Network Systems Corporation in 1974, the concept of the HYPERchannel product family was developed and first published in 1975[3]. The goal of the Company had been, and continues to be, the development of products which address the storage management problems of the large computer centers. The network component as perceived by the Company founders was a necessary first stage. The decision in 1975 to utilize a microprocessor-based adapter design significantly enhanced the role of the network and has provided the flexibility now seen to be so valuable for computer center evolution.

Other dates of importance are:

Jul 1976 -- demonstration of prototype
Oct 1976 -- field installation of prototype
Apr 1977 -- shipment of first production units
Dec 1978 -- over 250 units installed in over 25 sites

First prototype units entered field test in a site containing Control Data 7600 computers[4]. During the course of the following two years, that local network expanded to include other host computers and numerous peripherals, including magnetic disk, magnetic tape, unit record and fast display terminals. In connection with the fast display terminals, they exceeded the response and throughput characteristics of the previous local displays and were located some 1500 feet away from the computer center. This performance improvement was attributed to new displays and to the network.

Computers interfaced to date include IBM, CDC, UNIVAC, DEC, Data General, SEL, Modcomp and Interdata with a number of others scheduled in 1979. Obviously, our Company did not own any of these computers, and we are grateful to our customers at these early pioneering sites for their cooperation in completing the interface developments.

Since most of the sites were installed in 1978, there has been only limited measurement of performance. As field experience is being gained HYPERchannel is proving to be everything we hoped.

Computer Room of the '80s -- A Concluding Perspective

The traditional families of computers since the early '70s have attempted to be all things to all users. In view of the growing demand, the concept of dedicating applications to the machines that run them best could really have arrived. It may be possible to identify machines that are superior to others in one language, while inferior in another. It will undoubtedly be true that specialized computers will be built for which it would be unreasonable to require all the traditional general purpose trappings.

The computer room of the '80s will become a computer complex. Computers will diffuse into the building or building complex. The current distance limitations will be eliminated, allowing for the physical placement and configuration to be more logical.

Large scale computers will coexist with minicomputers and special purpose boxes. Control over the computer complex will become a visible function centered in a "war room" for the purpose of overall maintenance, configuration management and security. Computer center directors are being challenged now by their management to operate "an acre and a half or so of big machines" unattended, 24 hours a day, with on-line diagnostics, in which a person can come through once a day and take care of any problems. In view of the high probability that there will be multiple vendors represented in the center, this is a tall order indeed.

The fact remains, however, that hardware and firmware technology have now reached the point in which many of these problems can be solved and objectives met. One of the new alternatives to systems architecture is the local computer network --- HYPERchannel ---.

References

[1] Christensen, G.S., "Data Trunk Contention in a HYPERchannel[TM] Network," Proceedings of the Conference on Local Computer Networking, University of Minnesota, October, 1977.

[2] Christensen, G.S., Franta, W.R., "Design and Analysis of the Access Protocol for HYPERchannel[TM] Networks," Proceedings of the 3rd USA-JAPAN Computer Conference, Section 4-4-1 - 4-4-8, October, 1978.

[3] Thornton, J.E., Christensen, G.S., and Jones, P.D., "A New Approach to Network Storage Management," Computer Design, November, 1975, pg. 81-85.

[4] Green, M.I., "A DoD Local Network - A Structured Implementation," Proceedings of the Conference on Local Computer Networking, University of Minnesota, October, 1977.

This 50M-bps local area network uses special hardware and software protocols to accommodate the unique problems inherent in high-speed data circuits, especially those in satellites.

Hyperchannel Network Links

James E. Thornton and Gary S. Christensen
Network Systems Corporation

Reprinted from *Computer*, September 1983, pages 50-54. Copyright © 1983 by The Institute of Electrical and Electronics Engineers, Inc.

Network Systems' Hyperchannel* is a 50M-bps local area network that includes both hardware and software components. In the local area, Hyperchannel uses a baseband, multidrop coaxial cable (coax), and various adapter models provide a matching data channel or DMA interface to a wide range of mainframes, mainframe peripheral subsystems, and minicomputers. Link adapters, interface external communications facilities such as Bell T1 (1.5M bps) to T2, microwave to T3 (44.7M bps), fiberoptics to T3, and satellite circuits to T2C (6M bps).

The link adapters connect two remotely located Hyperchannel local areas and use a private protocol. The Netex* host software modules support these links in the network environment and use a continuous protocol to support the relatively high-speed and delay relationships encountered with high-speed data circuits, especially those in satellites.

Hyperchannel is currently installed in over 175 large computing centers with multiple mainframes and numerous peripherals. Applications are either computer-to-computer network communications between processors from the same or different manufacturers, or network attachment of IBM or IBM-plug-compatible peripheral subsystems to IBM and non-IBM mainframes. Peripheral subsystems include tape drives, printers, and terminals.

*Hyperchannel and Netex are trademarks of Network Systems Corporation.

Performance characteristics

The Hyperchannel coaxial data trunk uses multidrop connections, equivalent to coaxial T-connectors (Figure 1). Network adapters interface various manufacturers' processor and peripheral control units (Figure 2). The coaxial trunk contains no active elements, and the failure of an adapter does not affect the operation of the trunk. The trunk operates at a fixed data rate of 50M bps, and data, transmitted at baseband frequency, are phase-modulation-encoded, providing self-clocking. Data are transmitted in communication frames, allowing digital-data transmission and providing checkword error protection.

With inexpensive, physically small, coaxial cable, communication distances of 1000 feet are operational. An installation of 3000 feet has been implemented with a higher quality, larger cable. Since the coaxial cable is shared by the attached adapters on a contention basis, there is no single point of failure of a master control element, there is no sensitivity to configuration, demand multiplexing is provided on the coaxial trunk, and "any-to-any" communications are possible. A sophisticated carrier sense multiple access contention scheme is used to allow very high trunk use and eliminate usage loss at high demand levels.

Each network adapter is attached to a maximum of four coaxial data trunks, operating one trunk at a time (Figure 3). The multiple trunks provide backup and

EHO228-7/85/0000/0095$01.00 © 1983 IEEE

allow additional traffic. The network adapters contain 4K or 8K bytes of data buffering. Data transfer among equipment via Hyperchannel takes place in three independent phases—data channel to adapter buffer, adapter buffer to adapter buffer, and adapter buffer to data channel. The network adapters transmit half the contents of the data buffer at a time on the coaxial data trunk and use an alternative buffer technique to allow a

continuous data stream of unlimited length to be transmitted by the adapter. Adapters share the coaxial trunk on a burst basis, with the burst containing 2K or 4K bytes. Since the data source and destination rates are normally lower than the trunk rate, each adapter does not have to acquire the trunk in real time. Consequently, simultaneous data movements can share the coaxial trunk with the CSMA contention scheme. A micropro-

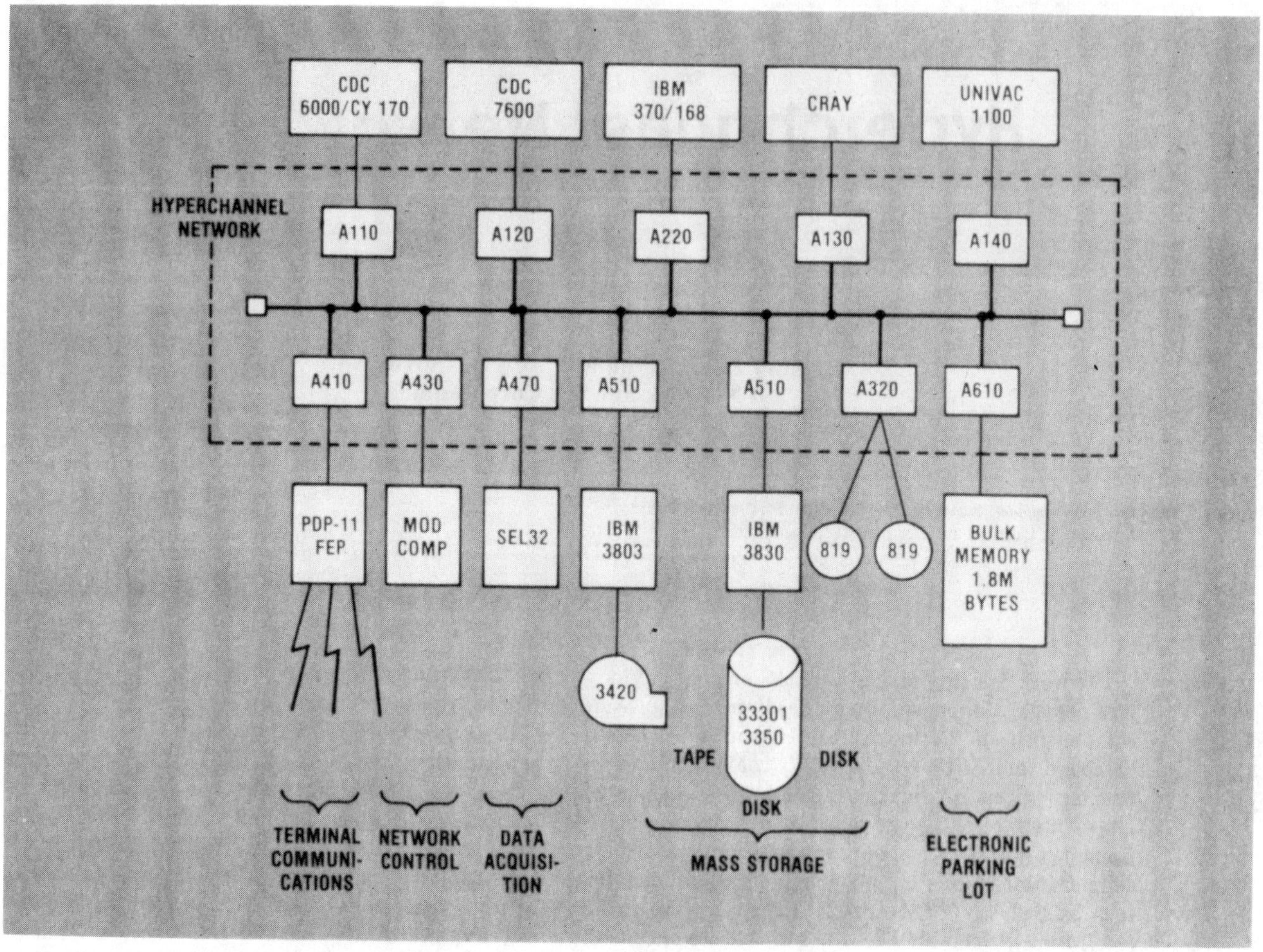

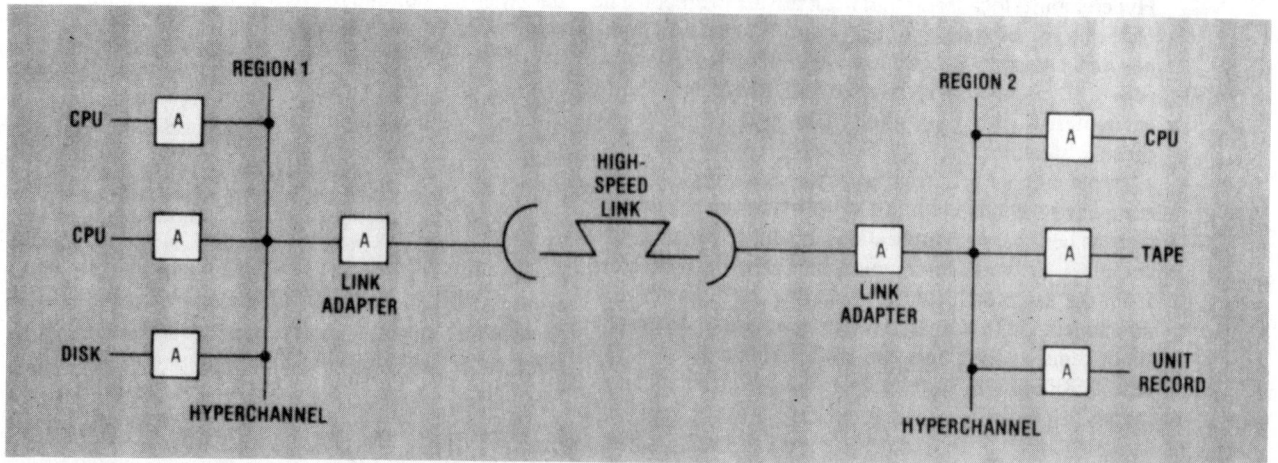

Figure 1. A sample Hyperchannel configuration.

Figure 2. The network's link-adapter scheme.

September 1983

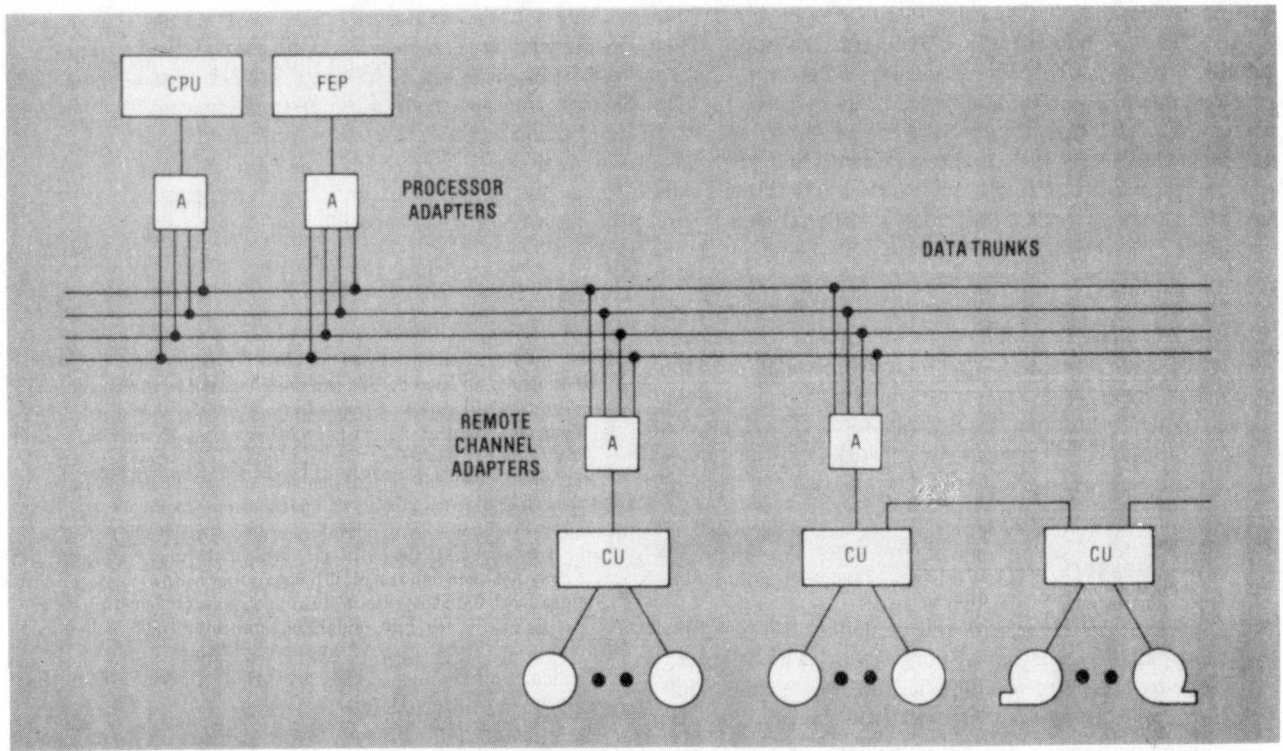

Figure 3. Hyperchannel coaxial data trunks and connections.

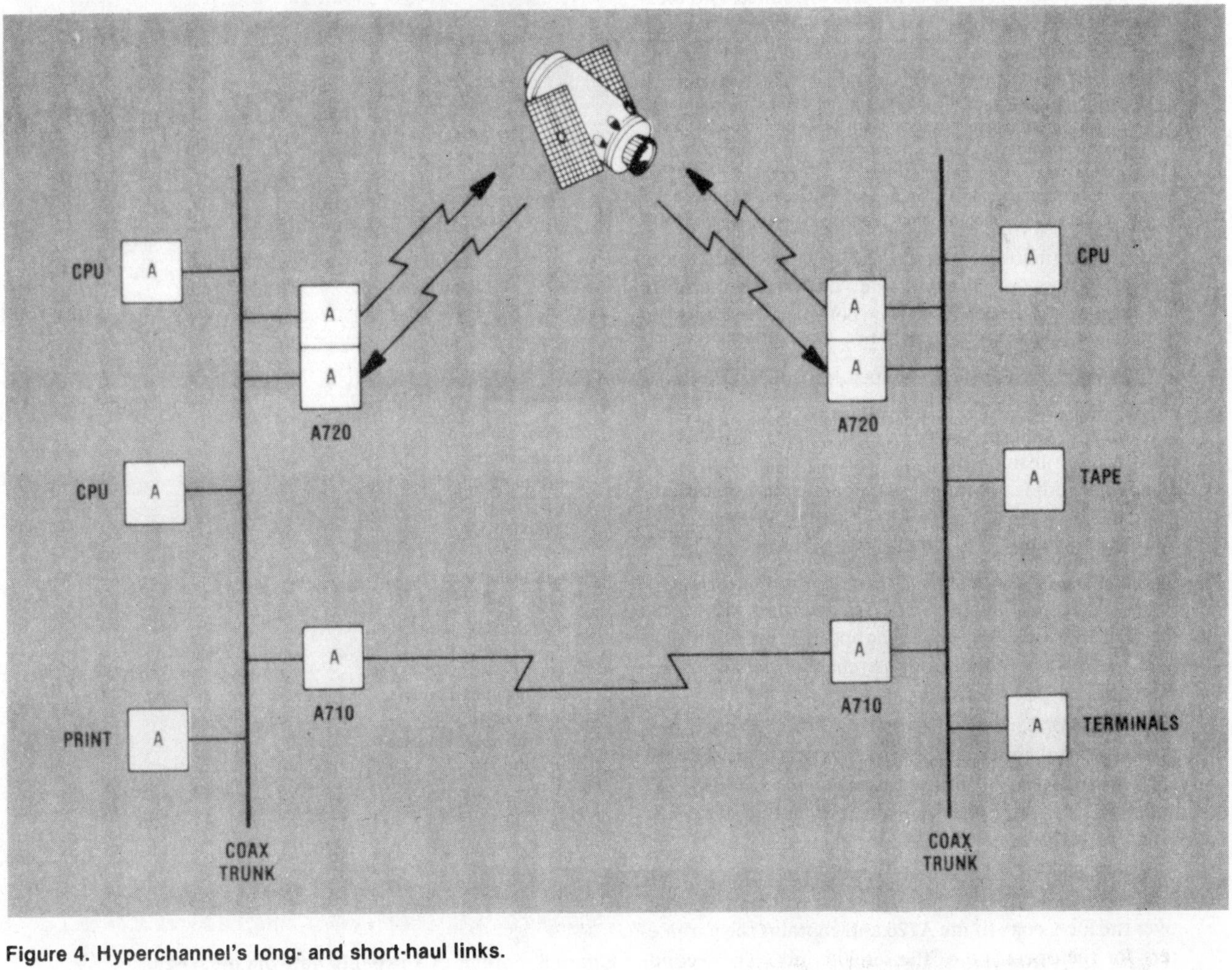

Figure 4. Hyperchannel's long- and short-haul links.

cessor in the network adapter provides for extended functions, including the retransmission of blocks in error.

The network is addressed using an eight-bit destination address, which is also included on each frame the adapter transmits on the coaxial bus. Frames are "broadcast" on the bus, and the adapter with the corresponding address accepts the data and responds.

The adapter that drives peripherals also executes IBM-type channel programs against the attached devices. The channel programs are delivered to the adapter via the network, and responses and data are returned via the network. The device adapter functions as a block multiplexer channel, executing detail-timing locally, to allow for the full-speed operation of the network periperals, even though they are far away from the initiating mainframe.

Link adapters

There are two categories of link adapters: (1) A710 for short-haul terrestrial applications in which a half-duplex, block-by-block protocol satisfies the requirements, and (2) A720 for long-haul terrestrial and satellite links, in which full-duplex and continuous-block protocols are required.

The link adapters are used in pairs to connect two local Hyperchannel networks (Figure 4). Data frames on a local network coax, which are directed to the remote network coax, are picked up by or directed to the local link adapter. The local link adapter transmits the frame to the remote link adapter, which in turn transmits it on the remote network coax for receipt by the remote network port.

The A710 short-haul link adapter will respond to a range of destination addresses on the connected remote network coax. Addressing of the A710 link is therefore transparent, and all adapters in both networks use the same adapter address range of 256.

The A710 uses a block-by-block transmission and acknowledgment scheme. The block size is 2K or 4K bytes, the normal network frame. Missing frames or frames in error are retransmitted. The A710s operate the link circuit as half duplex, with only one data transmission taking place at a time. Link faults, such as an inoperative link, can be reported to the initiator of a transmission or to any local network address such as a control center.

The A720 link adapter requires that data frames be directed to it, which is done by appending an additional header onto the standard Hyperchannel network message (Figure 5).

The network message for local A710 connected networks uses only one message header. Nine bytes are used for network control information and the network TO and FROM addresses, and the remaining bytes are available for user parameters.

The A720 routed message header contains the same control and address information, directing the frames over the local coax to the A720 and contains the parameters for the operation of the satellite link. The second,

embedded header, is used by the remote A720 to route the frames to the destination on the remote network coax.

This configuration provides for an extended address range and for more control of transmission on the two coax trunks and the satellite link.

Each A720 consists of two adapters at each end, which operate the satellite link as dual simplex; the transmit and receive circuits operate independently. The receiving A720 adapter detects missing frames and frames in error, reporting the error but not participating in the specific retransmission protocols. Errors may be optionally reported to the initiator of the message or to the message receiver. When an error is detected, the stream of frames making up a network message can be stopped.

This approach to satellite links was taken for two reasons. First, the wide range of applications expected on the link makes it very difficult to pick a single error-handling protocol that would provide efficient error handling for that many applications. Second, the error rate expected on the links is low, so the satellite link adapter allows the error-handling protocol to be tuned to the application. Because errors are not frequent, error handling by the host machine is effective.

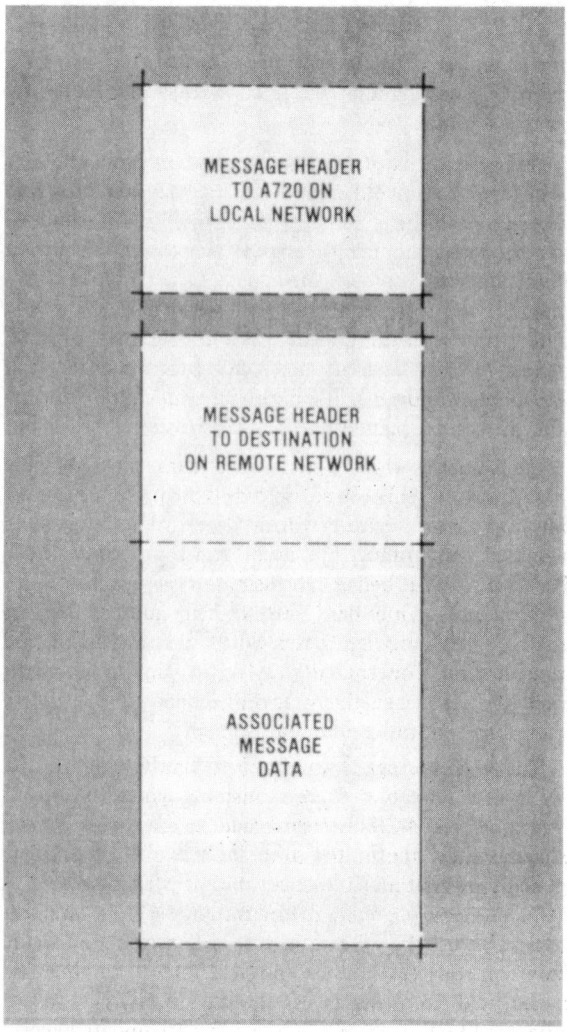

Figure 5. Format of a satellite network message.

Netex

Netex software provides a universal access method for computer systems interconnected by a Hyperchannel network. Netex allows application programs in separate hosts to communicate with each other without regard to the actual network configuration. There are a number of versions of Netex, each tailored to a specific manufacturer's instruction set and operating system. Computers from different manufacturers can communicate via Netex if each has the proper version of this software.

Netex has been designed to conform to the International Standards Organization's open systems architecture reference model for data communications. As a result, Netex has service calls at the session and transport levels. The high-level language interface allows high-level language programs (for example, Fortran, Cobol, or PL1) to be moved from one host to another without changing the call logic.

Netex uses a continuous-transmission protocol to maintain the very high data rates available with Hyperchannel, while ensuring that no data are lost and that error retransmission does not use excessive transmission capacity. In this protocol, Netex transfers and acknowledges data independently. Thus, several blocks of data can be transmitted before waiting for an acknowledgment. Similarly, an application can issue several write requests before reading an acknowledgment from the remote application.

Netex uses a record-numbering technique that allows it to efficiently recover from the worst possible error or lost message conditions. Netex gives each record transmitted two sequence numbers: a logical record number and a physical record number. The logical record number is sequential with respect to the user's transmission of the data. Any retransmitted records will have their original logical record. Because each transmitted record has a logical record number, the receiving application ensures that the records remain in the proper order.

Each record, whether it is being transmitted for the first time or is being retransmitted, is also given a unique physical record number. Physical record numbers are assigned sequentially for each transport connection. Thus, a record being retransmitted is given a new physical record number. The physical number is then used by the receiving Netex when acknowledging the transmission. Consequently, a record can be acknowleged (ACK) or negatively acknowledged (NAK) more than once, without creating a problem.

The ACK message is stand-alone; that is, every ACK, by itself, is capable of reestablishing synchronization. Any number of ACK messages could be lost, but when one is successfully transmitted over the network, it contains enough information to resynchronize the transmitter.

The acknowledgment field contains: (1) The highest logical record that the transport will accept (used for flow control), (2) the last physical record number received, and (3) a history of the last 16 physical record numbers (ACK or NAK). These items are updated every time a message is received.

A message containing an ACK field is not necessarily sent after every message is received. If the transmitter has enough buffers, the receiver will gather acknowledgments until enough arrive to justify a stand-alone acknowledgment or until a time out expires, or the receiving application writes something.

Because the histories of the last sixteen physical records are returned in every ACK message, skipping an ACK transmission presents no problems. The succeeding ACK message will cover the records previously processed.

Network Systems' Hyperchannel provides a data channel speed communications capability within local areas and across communications links. Various models of network adapters and various versions of the Netex software provide for communications among computers from different manufacturers. The network reports errors to the communicating computers, and the errors are handled by the host software to better match a wide range of application requirements in long propagation delay links such as those in a satellite circuit.

The Netex software provides standard application level interfaces to users. It uses a continuous-transmission protocol and a dual-block numbering scheme to ensure that no data are lost and to provide for maximum utilization of any link type.■

James E. Thornton is chairman of the board and chief executive officer for Network Systems Corporation, as well as one of its founders. He was formerly vice-president of the Computing Development Laboratories at Control Data Corporation, where he helped design the CDC 1604, CDC 6400, and CDC 6600, and headed the laboratory that developed the CDC Star-100 and other computer products. Thornton has also worked for Electronics Research Associates and the Univac Division of Sperry Rand. He holds several design patents and has written *Design of a Computer, the Control Data 6600*. He has been chairman of an advisory committee of the National Academy of Sciences and a member of the National Science Foundation panel.

Gary S. Christensen is a founder of Network Systems Corporation, where he is now vice-president of development and principal architect of the company's products, including high-speed data communications units that interconnect large-scale computers and minicomputers. Previously, he was manager of the Advanced Communications Laboratory for Control Data Corporation. In this position, he directed the development of the storage and peripheral subsystems for the CDC Star-100, the 7600, and earlier CDC computing systems.

Christensen received a BSEE from Iowa State University in 1959 and served as an engineering officer in the US Navy.

CORVUS OMNINET AND ITS POSITION IN A HIERARCHICAL NETWORK

by Bruce T. Eisenhard
Corvus Systems, Inc.
San Jose, CA 95131

It has become apparent that no single network can satisfy all the needs of the computing community. Each style of network optimizes one of the parameters of cost, speed, number of users or distance. The optimum solution to networking will rely on a variety of different networks connected together in a hierarchy.

OMNINET is a good candidate for the low-cost yet moderate performance network to be used to connect a variety of personal and mini-computers. This paper will describe OMNINET and its position in a multi-typed network hierarchy.

INTRODUCTION

A good deal of thought and energy has been expended on finding a solution to the problem of interconnecting the huge array of incompatible information processing devices which one finds in the modern office. So far, however, only a very few companies have attempted to go after the all-encompassing-network market. A universal network would interface to all electronic office equipment including telephones, microcomputers, mainframes, and peripherals, and would carry point to point communications for every combination of devices on the system. The main difficulty here is that, because of the vast array of different kinds of signals which must be carried, interface devices would be more expensive than some of the devices to be interconnected.

Once one realizes that the idea of interfacing directly to all individual devices is inherently costly, it becomes clear that there is a superior solution. If small, low-cost networks can be developed which link like devices, then one higher level network can link these smaller networks also at relatively low cost. Point to point communications involving devices located on a single low level network will then not involve the high level network at all. Only when a device on one network wishes to communicate with a device on another network will the high level network be utilized. Isolation of the traffic load on various networks within the hierarchy would mean better performance than a single universal network could provide. Device interfaces to small local networks could be reasonably inexpensive and costs of the network interfaces to the high level network would be shared among all the devices.

To achieve greater distances, all networks require more expensive transceivers, but these costs can be minimized since only the higher levels of the hierarchy need to cover large distances. These higher levels would provide large bandwidth trunk services over metropolitan or local areas. Specialized small area nets would provide services to different categories of devices but would exchange information through gateways or bridges to the broadband trunks.

Thus we would expect that a network hierarchy provides us with a superior solution compared to some universal network. A network hierarchy should be less expensive and perform better than any single network can. Nevertheless, it behooves us to examine more closely the pros and cons of the network hierarchy as a solution to actual user needs before making any final decision.

NETWORK NEEDS

The number of possible network applications in a business environment is currently large and will probably grow as both manufacturing and office work become increasingly automated. However, it is clear that any network which aspires to satisfy all the demands of a modern business must provide certain basic services.

Voice communication has long been a staple of the office community; an intra-office phone system is a requirement for the running of any business. Office PBXes are a relatively mature technology, no LAN will replace them, but LANs may serve as trunks for these systems in the future. The earliest telephone networks were constructed in a star pattern with a PBX at the center of the star and individual telephones at the extremities. Concentrators now are used so that one line from the concentrator runs to the PBX rather than one from each telephone. When concentrators share a single common bus with the main plant PBX the amount of wiring is reduced further. This arrangement is very similar to what we will propose for a hierarchical network structure.

A second application of networking in the business world is in the area of process control. Computer communications with plant service systems such as lighting, heating, and security, allow automated control of these facilities. In addition, the automation of manufacturing allows for the possibility of computer controlled production. Networks could allow microprocessors or mainframes to communicate with and thus control production lines. Such communication requires a data transmission rate of approximately 10,000 baud.

In the past, terminal traffic to mainframes was probably the most important requirement of an office computer network. The network serves to connect a large number of distant terminals to a single mainframe computer. This type of communication should also proceed at 10,000 baud.

Interconnection of personal computers is a relatively new requirement stemming from the development of software and small machines suited for the office. Such things as electronic mail and more importantly, peripheral sharing, are requirements of these networks. This type of communication should proceed at speeds of about 1 megabit, using networks such as Corvus OMNINET. We will discuss OMNINET and its position in a network hierarchy later on.

Interconnection of mainframes has so far been more important than interconnection of personal computers simply because mainframes have been in existence longer. Nevertheless, communication between mainframes will remain important for file transfers and interprocess communication. Networks which connect mainframes must provide a data transmission bandwidth of at least 10 Mbits.

Finally, it is possible that offices will wish to communicate video signals from point to point. Such communication would require analog signal bandwidths of 10Mhz.

Reprinted from *The Proceedings of INFOCOM 83*, 1983, pages 247-253.
Copyright © 1983 by The Institute of Electrical and Electronics Engineers, Inc.

HIERARCHICAL NETWORKS

Given the many varied demands on a universal office network, how well would a network hierarchy satisfy these demands? It is immediately clear that in order for a single network to carry signals from all of the above sources, a network trunk with a large bandwidth is necessary. The best way to implement a network hierarchy would therefore be to use a broadband network at the highest level of the structure. The division of the large bandwidth into many channels would enable the trunk to carry all the information required while current implementations would allow distances of up to 50km.

There would, unfortunately, be high set up costs with such a network; Interfaces to lower level networks would probably cost in the range of $500 apiece. Nevertheless, the total cost of a network hierarchy would still be below that of any single super-network. We conclude that a network hierarchy with a broadband network at the highest level is capable of satisfying all the needs of the business community at lower cost and with better performance. In fact, a network hierarchy offers the complete range of services from voice to video.

There are other advantages to a network hierarchy. Within a particular business, we can define a "community of interest" as a department or sector within the business which is responsible for a particular aspect of the overall business operation. Such communities of interest most frequently need to exchange information between the individual members of the community and only rarely need to have contact with other communities. Thus the ideal networking system to deal with these communities would be one which links together each community on its own network free from interference from others but which also allows occasional communication with devices on other networks. The network hierarchy does exactly this.

To understand how a network hierarchy might function in a moderate to large size business we present this example of a company with several individual departments responsible for finance, personnel, service, research and development, and marketing respectively. Each of these is a community of interest because they need most frequently to communicate only among themselves. Additionally, individual departments may have particular reasons for not wanting other departments to share their network. Personnel might wish to be isolated for security reasons as it is much easier for someone to break security when they are located on the same network. R&D and service might both wish to be isolated because their testing operations might cause network breakdowns which would not be tolerated by the other departments. And yet, in spite of these needs for isolation, communication between communities is often necessary. In fact, if we assume that the only printers or possibly the best printers, are located on one of the networks, it is evident that users will frequently demand inter-network communication. Examples include file transfer and sharing of high performance printers and other peripherals.

Bridges or gateways between individual community networks solve these problems. Furthermore, as the company grows, the network expands modularly. Eventually, though, it makes more sense to bridge or gate each individual network to a broadband trunk which allows communication between every possible network pair. Ultimately, the hierarchy network is the solution. (Fig 1)

CORVUS OMNINET

There are many positions which Corvus OMNINET can occupy in a network hierarchy. OMNINET currently handles networking of personal computers and supports both peripheral sharing and direct communication applications such as electronic mail. It is therefore a good candidate for linking communities of interest which do not require the computing facilities of a mainframe. Additionally, OMNINET can and will move into new areas of networking in order to satisfy other business needs. OMNINET can easily function as a process control network. It is well equipped to establish links between data gathering equipment and robots on the production line, and small computers which control the production operations. Finally, it could provide for terminal service to mainframes, allowing a large number of distant terminals to access a single computer.

As its name implies, OMNINET is a system for interconnecting any and all personal computers within a certain area into an efficient communications network. Once this network is established users at different work sites working on the personal computers of various different manufacturers can communicate not only with each other but also with multiple shared peripherals such as disk drives and printers. The network itself will support up to 64 host computers but links can be established through the network to other OMNINET systems or to the larger computer networks of other manufacturers to allow communication with quite distant users and devices operating in very different environments.

The OMNINET package provides the services of the bottom four layers of the ISO seven layer network model. Corvus Systems provides its own high level networking software for a host computer on OMNINET. This package, called Constellation, allows single user operating systems such as UCSD Pascal, CP/M, MS/DOS and others to share mass storage, printers and other peripherals on the OMNINET system. Constellation is only one of many possible ways in which to use OMNINET, and various software vendors are developing network software packages such as electronic mail and teaching tools.

OMNINET is a CSMA system using RS-422 (twisted pair) wire and transceivers. The reasons for choosing twisted pair as the communications medium for OMNINET are several. First is the low cost per foot of cable. The second reason is that a nontechnical person can install an OMNINET interface with pliers and a screwdriver; the experience is similar to hooking up hi-fi speakers.

Connections to the OMNINET trunk cable are made through devices called transporters. Every host device on the network be it a computer, a disk drive, or a printer, has its own transporter to handle communication with other devices. (fig 2)

All transporters on the network perform exactly the same functions and no master network controller is required. All network management is handled by the individual transporters. In order to reduce the software burden placed on the host computer, the transporter performs many of the high level network tasks which are usually the host's responsibility. Generation and reception of message acknowledgements, message retransmission when messages are not acknowledged, and detection of duplicate messages are all handled automatically by the OMNINET transporter. A host computer communicates by issuing a simple command to its transporter, and it is not disturbed again until messages have been successfully sent or received.

A host computer issues a command to its transporter by first formatting a command vector in memory and then sending the address of that vector to the transporter. The transporter interprets the command vector and executes the command. There are seven commands which are currently implemented on OMNINET, the two most common of which are the send message command and the setup receive command. Only one message may be sent at a time, but up to four messages may be received without intervention from the host. These four sockets are activated by a unique setup receive command vector and as a result operate completely independently. In addition, all messages for a socket are split into a user data portion and a user control portion and each is given its own host memory buffer region by the setup receive command for that socket. Thus, a message destined for a given socket can be routed by the host to any desired place in memory and the user data and user control portions of the message can be sent to separate locations.

ADVANTAGES OF OMNINET

In its current implementation, OMNINET has many qualities which make it a good choice for a small area network for microcomputers. First, is its diversity; all the popular personal business computers have been interfaced to OMNINET by

Corvus Systems. Corvus also supplies a variety of peripherals directly connectable to OMNINET that can then be shared by all nodes on the net. These peripherals include Winchester disks, printers, modems, and archival tape stores.

As of March 1983, there will be 5,000 OMNINET installations with 30,000 nodes. OMNINET is a high performance network which transmits data at speeds which match those of the computers it serves. The amount of overhead in the host computer is reduced as the transporter filters all messages and performs network housekeeping chores. The host machine is only interrupted when a message has been sent or received successfully. OMNINET transfers data at 1 megabaud and has minimal line overhead providing useful bandwidths approaching 880 kbits. (fig 3)

The modular nature of the OMNINET transporter means that the creation of an interface for a new computer requires the addition of only a few glue parts. More importantly, OMNINET support software requirements are minimal as the interface includes a microcomputer that handles the network responsibilities to the transport layer of the ISO model. The amount of driver software required to use OMNINET is normally about 1 kbyte. (fig 4)

Corvus began to license OMNINET about one year ago. The modularity of hardware and software make it possible to bring up an OMNINET system in man-months rather than the man-years required for a new net or one that does not provide as high a level of network support. Corvus supplies both hardware and software support for its licensees. Already a number of vendors have adopted it as a standard. A wider range of network products and services can be expected to be available as a result of the license program.

A major advantage of OMNINET is its low cost. OMNINET transporters retail at $500. Licensee costs are proportionately less, depending on quantity and specific types of hardware and software. Our goal is to considerably reduce costs, both retail and licensee, in the next two years. Meanwhile, twisted pair cable retails at about 15 to 20 cents per foot, and tap boxes retail at about $10.

OMNINET STRUCTURE AND OPERATION

We turn now to a brief discussion of OMNINET command mechanisms and transfer protocols. We also present an overview of the hardware interface between a host and its transporter.

COMMAND MECHANISM

Host devices on the network initiate commands by sending a 24 bit address to the transporter in the form of 3 bytes. At this address is the command vector which contains a command code, a result record address and other command dependent information. When the command is completed, the transporter will signal the host by altering the result record. On host computers that support interrupts, an interrupt will occur after the result record has been modified.

The commands supported by the transporter are:

Initialize ----------- initialize transporter (this automatically occurs at power on).
Send Message -- send a message to a specified node or broadcast a message
Setup Receive -- prepare to receive a message
End Receive ----- stop receiving messages
Who Am I --------- return node ID number
Echo ---------------- check for the existence of a specified node (this command does not affect any state of the specified node)
Peek/Poke ------- set transporter parameters (# retries, etc.)

The values for the Return Codes which result from the various commands are shown in the table below:

00--Command was successfully completed.
00-3F--Node identification number.
01-7F--Transmit retry count.
80--Transmit failure (no acknowledgement after maximum number of retries).

81--Transmitted message user data portion was too long for receiver's buffer.
82--Message was sent to an uninitialized socket.
83--Transmitted message user control portion size did not equal receiver's control buffer size.
84--Bad socket number in command (must be 80, 90, A0 or B0).
85--Receive socket in use; a valid buffer is attached.
86--Bad node number in command (must be 0-7F or FF).
C0--Received an ACK for an Echo command.
FE--Receive socket setup.

The unit of transfer, as seen from the host level, is a single message which is transmitted directly from the originating host to the receiving host. The transporter creates a network packet from the host data by adding a certain amount of overhead information and converting the resultant packet into a synchronous serial bit stream, which "travels" along the network bus to all other nodes.

The transporter to which the packet is directed (the addressing information is contained within the message packet) strips off the packet overhead, converts the serial data stream back to bytes, and transfers the message data to the receiving host. Note that transfer is direct from one host memory to the other via simultaneous DMA. Network collision avoidance, error detection, error recovery, and duplicate packet detection are all handled by transporters in a manner which is completely transparent to the hosts.

A message consists of two portions, both of which are variable length and may be null. The portions are called the user data portion and the user control portion. Thus a message destined for a given socket can be routed by the host to any desired place in memory and the user data and user control portions of the message can be sent to separate buffers increasing system performance.

There are four sockets which may be activated for receiving a message. Each socket will accept messages destined for that host and that socket number only.

HARDWARE INTERFACE

All of the lines in the host-transporter interface are TTL compatible and have the characteristics described below. (fig 5)

Address lines

There are 24 address lines through which the transporter selects which byte of host memory it is writing to or reading from during a DMA cycle. When the host computer is driving the address lines (no DMA cycle in progress), the transporter ignores them.

Data Lines

There are 8 bi-directional DATA lines which are used for reading and writing data from and to the host memory.

DMA Control

Three lines are provided for control of DMA transfers to and from host memory.

DMA REQUEST line from the transporter.
DMA GRANT line from the host.
DMA DIRECTION line from the transporter. The transporter drives this line high or low depending on whether it is reading or writing.

Command Control

READY line from the transporter.
STROBE line from the host.

Interrupt

A low going pulse on the interrupt line is generated by the transporter whenever a command is either accepted or completed. The interrupt is intended to indicate to the host that it should check the return code.

BUFFERED AND UNBUFFERED TRANSPORTERS

In most cases, the transmission of a message by a transporter requires that the data to be sent be retrieved out of host memory from the location pointed to in the Send

Message command vector. By the same token the reception of a message usually requires that the transporter write the data which it is receiving to the location in host memory specified in the Setup Receive command. Both of these operations take place through DMA but there are some microprocessors which for one of a number of reasons may not be able to support DMA. It may be that it is impossible for the microprocessor to relinquish control of its memory address bus or that host memory is too slow to keep up with a continuous stream of direct memory accesses at the rate of incoming or outgoing messages. Whatever the reason, in these systems the normal DMA Transporter must be modified to accommodate the microprocessor. The Buffered Transporter is the result.

The Buffered Transporter simply adds a certain amount of fast random access memory (RAM), usually about 4k, to the DMA Transporter. The host is allowed access to this memory and places all message and command data in it. The transporter, meanwhile, treats this memory as if it were host core memory and transfers data in and out of it utilizing normal DMA procedures. Host addressing of the buffer is performed via a counter which is automatically incremented after each byte read or byte write.

The hardware interface lines to control a buffered transporter are listed below (all TTL compatible).

Data Lines

There are 8 bi-directional DATA lines which are used for reading and writing data from and to the buffer memory.

Buffer Control

Five lines are provided for control of transfers to and from the buffer.

Read/write lines determine data bus direction.

Enable signal validates control line state.

2 Select lines control the buffer memory operation:
—set buffer address pointer
—read/write buffer memory
—read transporter status
—write command vector address to transporter

Interrupt

A low going pulse on the interrupt line is generated by the transporter whenever a command is either accepted or completed. The interrupt is intended to indicate to the host that it should check the return code.

PACKET TRANSMISSION

When a transporter has a packet to transmit, the line is checked for the idle state. If there are no line transitions during the check period (10 usec nominal), then the transporter forces a transition on the line, the first zero of the first flag byte, and continues to transmit the packet. If the transporter cannot transmit either because the line is not idle or because another transporter starts transmitting during the check period, the transporter which is waiting to transmit calculates a random delay factor which, when multiplied by a scale factor, yields a delay count. This delay count is then decremented only during line idle periods and when the count reaches zero the transporter attempts to acquire the line again. This process is repeated until either the transporter acquires the line or the number of retries have exceeded an internal retry limit.

The random delay mechanism eliminates the problem of several transporters all attempting to acquire the line at once as soon as it becomes available.

Once the transmitting transporter has acquired the line, the packet is sent with no further attempt to detect collision with another transporter. Nevertheless, no collision will occur as all other transporters waiting to transmit will sense that the line is busy.

The receiving transporter makes a number of checks as the packet is received. If no errors are discovered, the transporter accepts the packet and sends off an ACK packet to the sending transporter.

Once the message packet has been sent, the transmitting transporter waits for an ACK or NAK packet to be returned by the receiving transporter. If no such packet is received within 50 usec., the transmitting transporter makes an attempt to reacquire the line and retransmit the message.

As soon as an ACK or NAK packet is received, the transaction is considered to have been completed and the host will be informed of the transaction status.

To guard against duplicate message packets being received (when an ACK is sent by the receiver, but not seen by the transmitter) there is special avoidance logic which utilizes two packet header fields as well as long-term memory in both the transmitting and receiving transporters.

The crucial fields in the packet header are the retry count field and the transaction parity field. The retry count is always zero on the first transmission attempt for any packet and is then incremented on each retry. The transaction parity is a single bit and basically alternates in value between zero and one for each new (non-retry) packet being transmitted.

Each transporter contains a table of parity bits, one bit for each possible transporter on the network (itself plus 63 others). During normal operation, taking two transporters A and B as an example, the Ath bit in B's table and the Bth bit in A's table will be equal in value. This fact will be used in the manner explained below to prevent duplicate packets from being received.

The transmitting transporter (A transmitting to B) will include the complement of the Bth bit of its table in all packets. If the packet is ACKed, the transporter will then complement the Bth bit in the table; otherwise the Bth bit is left unmodified.

The receiving transporter (B receiving from A) updates its Ath table entry from the PARITY bit in the packet whenever it ACKs a packet. The receiving transporter also examines the parity bit in a packet whenever the retry count is unequal to zero; in that case, if the parity bit is equal to the Ath bit of its table, a duplicate has just been received (transporter A missed the ACK) and the receiver sends another ACK and throws the packet away.

Note that in a NAK situation neither the transmitting nor receiving transporter updates its internal table, thus retaining mutual synchronization.

The duplicate avoidance scheme requires that all parity tables be synchronized prior to the beginning of message transfers. A synchronizing packet from transporter A tells all other transporters in the network to set the Ath bit of their parity tables to zero. This packet is sent many times on initialization to assure synchronization. Initialization occurs on power-up and on hardware resets.

All active transporters have the ability at any time during normal network operation, to receive synchronizing packets from transporters being initialized. Transporters update their parity tables on the basis of the information they receive through synchronization packets but they do not respond with ACK packets.

LINE PROTOCOL

The Advanced Data Link Controller (ADLC), an MC6854 chip which communicates directly with the line drivers, ensures that all packets transmitted will have the same general format shown below:

Packet Information

User Message

Leading Flags	Header	User Control	User Data	CRC	Trailing Flags

User Message Packet:

Destination Address	
Source Address	
Validation = A5	
Destination Socket	
Retry Count	
Parity Bit	
User Data Length	msb
	1sb
User Control Length	
Packet I.D.	msb
	1sb

Destination Address—The OMNINET node number of the intended receiver. 0-63 are legal node numbers, with a value of 255 (FF hex) indicating a "broadcast" message. All transporters receive messages addressed to destination 255 but none acknowledges such a message.

Source Address—The OMNINET node number of the message originator. 0-63 are legal node numbers.

Validation Byte—A constant A5 hexadecimal (165 decimal).

Destination Socket Number—The transporter socket number within the receiver. Hexadecimal 80, 90, A0 or B0 are the legal values.

Retry Count—Contains the number of times this message has been retransmitted. In the very first transmission of a message, the value is zero.

Parity Bit—Contains 00 or 01. This is the parity bit used for duplicate packet detection discussed earlier.

User Data Length—The length, in 8-bit bytes, of the user data portion of the message. Possible values range from 0 to 2047.

User Control Length—The length, in 8-bit bytes, of the user control portion of the message. Possible values range from 0 to 255.

Packet I.D.—A 16-bit number which uniquely identifies any message when used in conjunction with the source host number.

User Message

The user message can be up to 2302 bytes long, and consists of two portions.

User Control Portion—0 to 255 bytes as specified by the user control length byte in the packet header. The data in this portion of the message are not examined by the transporter.

User Data Portion—0 to 2047 bytes as specified by the user data length bytes in the packet header. The data in this portion of the message are not examined by the transporter.

Acknowledgement Packet Format

The acknowledgement packet is the vehicle by which a receiving transporter sends a positive or negative acknowledgement to a transmitting transporter after a message packet (or echo packet) has been received. If a message has been received without difficulty and without detectable errors, a positive acknowledgement (ACK) is sent. If errors were detected or if for some other reason the packet could not be received, a negative acknowledgement (NAK) is sent.

50
ACK/NAK Code
Validation = A5
(reserved)

Note that the acknowledgement packet contains no destination address yet is intended for only one host. This is possible because the acknowledgement packet is sent immediately after the message packet is received. No bus idle time is allowed between message and acknowledgement so there is no possibility that another transporter could have sent a message and thus also be expecting an acknowledgement.

Sync Packet Format

The sync packet is the vehicle by which a transporter makes its presence known to all of the other transporters in the network. It has the effect of initializing all of the transporters' transaction parity tables as explained earlier.

60
Source Address
Validation = A5
8 bytes (Reserved for future use.)

Echo Packet Format

The echo packet is the vehicle by which one host may verify the presence of another node without disturbing the host attached to that node. If it is functioning properly, the receiving transporter will acknowledge reception of the packet but will not inform its host that anything happened.

Destination Address
Source Address
Validation = A5
Socket Number=00
7 bytes (Reserved for future use.)

HIERARCHICAL NET

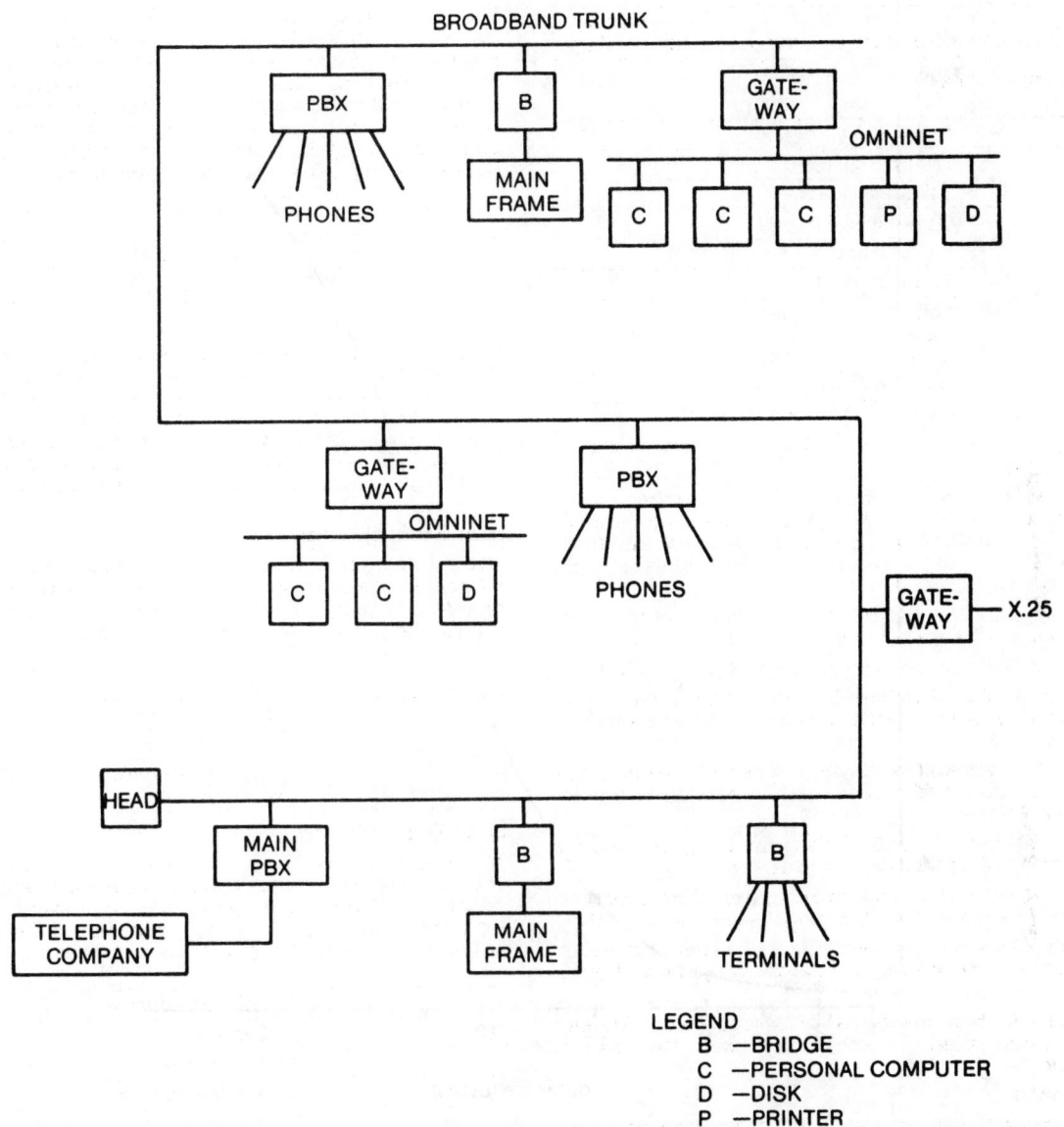

FIGURE 1

OMNINET STATION TO STATION THROUGHPUT VS. PACKET SIZE

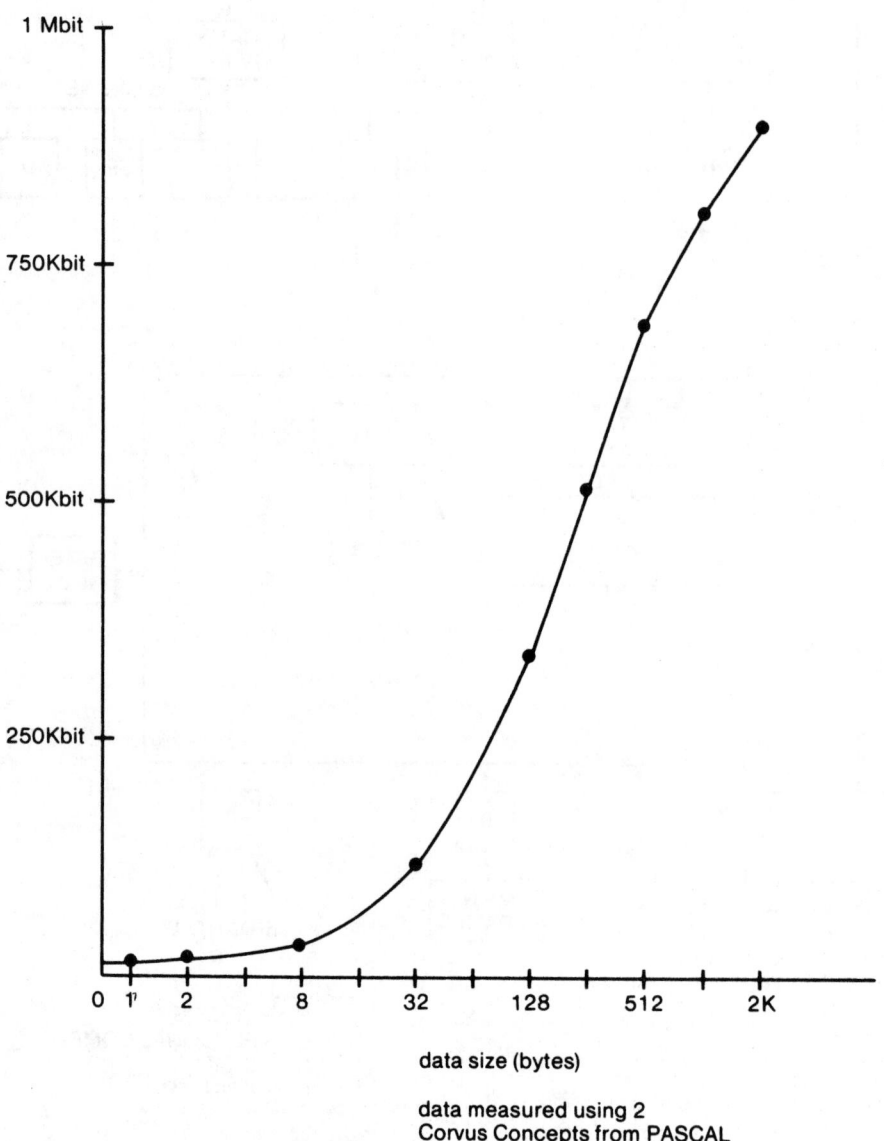

data size (bytes)

data measured using 2
Corvus Concepts from PASCAL

FIGURE 2

Reprinted from *The Proceedings of INFOCOM 83*, 1983, pages 512-517.
Copyright © 1983 by The Institute of Electrical and Electronics Engineers,
Inc.

ARCNET
Design and Implementation of a Local
Network

Ted Rohling

DATAPOINT CORPORATION
San Antonio, Texas

Abstract

ARCNET, a baseband local area
network developed by Datapoint, uses a
token-passing scheme to control access to
the network by up to 255 processors or
processor-based peripherals.

Processors interface to the network
through intelligent devices called
Resource Interface Modules which handle
all networking considerations without
involvement by the processors. The RIMs
are connected to each other through
junction boxes which filter and amplify
the signal and see that every RIM hears
the transmissions of every other RIM.

When a RIM receives control of the
network, it is allowed to send a packet
of up to 253 bytes, and then must pass
control to the next RIM.

ARCNET: Design and Implementation of a
Local Network

Local area networks are now the
"hottest item" in the information
processing field. Thurber and Freeman in
the December 1981 issue of Data
Communications identified over 60 vendors
of local area networks or their
components. Datapoint entered the local
area network arena in 1977 with a product
called ARC® , the Attached Resource
Computer®. The network hardware coupled
with Datapoint's Disk Operating System
and/or Resource Management System is now
installed at more than 4,000 sites
worldwide.

Datapoint's decision to enter the local
area network field was a business
necessity. Historically Datapoint's
products consisted of small, desk-top
computers which were used in dispersed
data processing activities. Each small
computer had it's own storage media,
diskette or hard disk. As organizations
grew, a number of computers were
installed at each site. The users at
these sites needed a way to communicate
efficiently between computers so that new
computers could share the expensive disk
resources of previously installed
computers. So, in 1976 Datapoint's
Research and Development group went to
work on the prototypes of what is today
called ARCNET™ .

ACCESS METHOD

The initial investigative work on the
Resource Interface Module, or RIM,
network interface was targeted toward a
scheme known today as Carrier Sense
Multiple Access. The first prototype
worked successfully but contained a
factor that was not readily acceptable to
the development team. The random backoff
was the stumbling block. The designers
did not want to include any random
factors in a network where performance is
a requirement.

The second prototype system was based
on a contention free, self-polling
scheme, known today as token passing.
Each node in the network has a unique
address. As the token came to the next
sequential node in the network, that
station sent data if it had any, or
simply passed the token to the next node
in the sequence if it did not. If the
sending node heard any activity on the
network, such as a new node joining the
network, it gave up control, waited the
maximum amount of time required for the
signal to pass through the system, and
then repeated the attempt to pass control
to the next sequential node.

Several optimizations were made to
ARCNET before its completion. Each node
was made to remember the address of the
node next in the sequence so that less
time was spent waiting for responses from
non-existent node addresses. Hardware
modifications included a packet
acknowledgement to reduce the number of
packet exchanges as well as the time
required if the acknowledgements were

EHO228-7/85/0000/0107$01.00 © 1983 IEEE

generated by software.

A FREE BUFFER ENQUIRY request was added to the protocol so that a complete packet would not be sent to a node that did not have the buffer space to store it.

Through the use of the token passing scheme, ARCNET insures the user an even chance with all other users on the bus. Once a user sends a packet, all other users get a chance to transmit before the first user gets a second attempt.

MEDIA

ARCNET today is implemented utilizing a baseband system and coaxial cable. The primary advantages of the baseband system are simplicity and low cost. One disadvantage of a baseband system is the inability to easily tap on to the bus to add additional stations. These taps typically cause signal reflections which, if severe enough, can swamp the transmissions of the nodes on the network. Datapoint solved the reflection problem by introducing a special device known as a "hub."

The function of the hub in the network will be described later.

Broadband systems at the time ARCNET was being developed were too expensive for the common user to implement. Datapoint did, however, realize the importance of the broadband capability of carrying multiple communications modes over the same cable. ARCNET was designed to fit into the frequency allocation of a television channel so that at a later date it could be included in the broadband family.

ARCNET

The ARCNET protocol allows up to 255 network nodes to communicate on a token bus at a speed of 2.5 million bits per second. The network media in use today is RG62/A or RG62/B coaxial cable connected to the RIMs and hubs by BNC connectors. ARCNET itself encompases Layer 1, Physical Link, and Layer 2, Data Link, in the ISO-OSI Data Communications Network Model.

TOPOLOGY

ARCNET is a free-form tree or a collection of stars. Each RIM is connected via coax to a port on an ARCNET hub. The hub is the center of each of the stars. The reflection problems that commonly occur in baseband networks are handled by the hub. Signals are passed from the RIM to the hub through a series of transformer coupling and matching

filter circuits. The hub then amplifies the signal and retransmits it to all of the ports. The ports on the hub act as an ideal tap. They are "ideal" since they suppress reflections and have no insertion or tap loss. The ports on a hub may be connected to another hub, a RIM on an ARCNET node, an unterminated length of coax, or nothing at all.

Installation and growth of an ARCNET is simplified by the use of the hub. The coaxial cable is fanned out from the hub to the various nodes in the network. Since there are no taps to be placed on the bus itself, the cable can be run through the same conduit and raceways as the telephone system. There are no critical connection points that have to be observed and the hubs can be placed in almost any location that has the necessary 115v power supply. Adding on to the network is as simple as plugging a new length of coax into the hub and then into the RIM of the new node. In order to install the network between floors, a single coax is typically run from a hub on one floor to a hub on another floor. The same is true from building to building.

There are few physical limitations on coaxial cable length. Each coax can be no longer than 2000 feet from RIM to hub or hub to hub, with a maximum length of coax in the network of up to four miles. The four-mile limitation will be explained later. Datapoint also supplies an infrared light tranceiver known as LIGHTLINK® which allows ARCNET to extend up to 1 mile across free space at the network data rate of 2.5 million bits per second.

Internode distance is limited to 31 microseconds. This limitation is part of the timing factors involved in the protocol of ARCNET. If you extrapolate 31 microseconds into physical distance, considering the effect of the hubs and the cabling, you arrive at the four mile cable length limit.

SIGNALING

ARCNET is a serial, asynchronous communication system utilizing 11-unit start-stop operation at a data rate of 2.5 million bits per second. Two 100ns wide positive pulses in succession followed by the identically shaped negative pulses indicate a mark, and a space is indicated by no energy transmission at all. The result is essentially no intersymbol interference in the system.

The idle status of the bus is signified by the spacing condition, no signal being transmitted by any node. When a transmission begins it is started with an alert burst made up of six mark signals. Each eight-bit character transmitted is proceeded by two marks and one space.

NETWORK TRAFFIC

Each node in the system has a unique identification from 1 to 255. ID Ø is used by the network to indicate a broadcast message to all nodes on the network. The RIM will only accept messages that contain it's own ID or ID Ø for broadcast messages. In this way it is not possible for nodes on the network to eavesdrop on the transmissions of other nodes. The token is passed from a node to the next node with a higher ID in sequence.

Each node determines the next node in the sequence during a system reconfiguration. A system reconfiguration takes place when no token is circulating through the network, when a new node enters the network or when a token is lost. When operating properly the network will never experience a delay of over 78us between transmissions.

When a node determines that a token is not passing because of over 78us idle time, it begins the system reconfiguration sequence. To avoid collisions of the reconfiguration sequence, each node sets the NEXT ID (NID) to the value of it's own ID. It then sets a time-out value equal to 146us times 255 minus its own ID. If the node sees the timeout expire without any line activity, the node attempts to pass the token. Because of the time-out formula, the time-out expires first for the node that has the highest ID in the system.

TOKEN PASSING

Token passing is initiated by sending an INVITATION TO TRANSMIT packet. The INVITATION TO TRANSMIT packet consists of an alert burst followed by an EOT and two repeated Desitination ID (DID) characters which are the current NID of the node.

| Alert Burst | EOT | DID | DID |

The transmitting node will wait for a response for 74us. If there is no response the Next ID will be incremented by one and the token pass request tried again. If it hears any activity during the timeout period, it will release control of the line. During the SYSTEM RECONFIGURATION phase, INVITATIONS TO TRANSMIT will be sent to every possible ID in the network. In this fashion each node will have determined the Next ID. No time will be wasted sending INVITATIONS

TO TRANSMIT to node ID's that are not active on the network.

The time required to do a SYSTEM RECONFIGURATION is a function of the number of nodes on the system and the value of the highest ID, but usually falls between 24 and 61us.

ADDING A NODE

Since ARCNET can recover from a lost token by doing a SYSTEM RECONFIGURATION, the easiest way for a new node to enter the network is by destroying the token. When a node is turned on or has not received a token in 840ms it issues a RECONFIGURATION BURST. A RECONFIGURE BURST consists of a set of eight marks and one space, sent 765 times. This burst is sufficient to destroy the token and terminate the line activity. Since the RECONFIGURE BURST is longer than any other packet it will interfere with the next INVITATION TO TRANSMIT. It also provides line activity so that the node transmitting the INVITATION TO TRANSMIT drops control of the line, no node has control and the SYSTEM RECONFIURATION sequence begins.

REMOVING A NODE FROM THE NETWORK.

If a node is turned off or unplugged from the network a SYSTEM RECONFIGURATION is not required. The node which has the disconnected node's ID as its NID will attempt to pass the token with an INVITATION TO TRANSMIT, receive no response, increment its NID and search for the next ID on the bus until it receives a response.

ERROR DETECTION

ARCNET contains error checking procedures. Each transmission received is checked to see that it has the following:

o At least one mark and exactly one space preceding each character;

o An EOT, ENQ, SOH, ACK or NAK following the Alert Burst;

o Proper CRC (for data packets only);

o Proper number of characters (1, 3, or 8 to 26Ø);

o At least nine space intervals following the last character.

MESSAGE FORMATS

The INVITATION TO TRANSMIT message has already been detailed above. The other message formats available are as follows:

o FREE BUFFER ENQUIRY -- An Alert
Burst followed by an ENQ and two
DID characters. Used to ask a
node if it has the buffer space
available to accept a packet.

| Alert Burst | ENQ | DID | DID |

o PACKETS -- An Alert Burst
followed by from 8 to 260
characters consisting of an SOH,
a Source ID (SID), two DID
characters, a count of characters
in the packet, 1 to 253
characters including a system
code and data bytes and two CRC
characters. Used to move data
between nodes.

| Alert Burst | SOH | SID | DID | COUNT | ...

1 to 253 bytes
...|System Code and Data Bytes | CRC | CRC |

o ACKNOWLEDGEMENTS -- An Alert
Burst followed by one character,
an ACK. Used to acknowledge
successful receipt of PACKETS or
as an affirmative response to
FREE BUFFER ENQUIRIES.

| Alert Burst | ACK |

o NEGATIVE ACKNOWLEDGEMENTS -- An
Alert Burst followed by one
character, a NAK. Used to provide
a negative response to a FREE
BUFFER ENQUIRY.

| Alert Burst | NAK |

The symbols ACK, NAK, SOH, EOT and ENQ
are used to represent the ASCII code
representations typically used in data
communications protocols.

NETWORK OPERATION

In order to better understand the
ARCNET protocol, it is necessary to
review the interaction between the RIM
and the processor it is servicing. The
RIM typically services the processor
through a status register, a command
register and some number of 256 byte
memory buffers. The processor is unaware
of the actual operation of the network,
only that a resource is available to send
and receive messages from one location to
another.

MESSAGE TRANSMISSION -- PROCESSOR ACTION

To transmit a message, the processor
places the destination ID, the length of
the packet in characters and the data
into a memory buffer. As an added
convention for layer 3 of the ISO-OSI
model, the first byte of each data packet
is considered a system code. This allows
multiple systems with entirely different
data packet formats to exist and be
serviced on the same ARCNET network. The
processor must then signal the RIM that
the packet is ready to transmit. To do
this it interrogates the status register
and checks the value of two bits, the
Transmitter Available (TA) bit and the
Transmitted Message Acknowledged (TMA)
bit. If TA is true the processor issues
the write command to the RIM. The RIM
sets the TA bit to false, indicating that
the transmitter is busy. Once the
transmit sequence is completed the TA bit
again becomes true and another packet can
be sent to the RIM. When the RIM receives
an acknowledgement to the transmitted
packet the TMA bit is set to true. Only
at this time can the processor be sure
that the packet was sent successfully.

MESSAGE TRANSMISSION -- RIM ACTION

When the RIM receives an INVITATION TO
TRANSMIT (the "token"), it checks to see
if the TA is false, that is, a packet is
waiting to be transmitted. If TA is true
the token is passed to the NID. If TA is
false the RIM checks the Destination ID
(DID) of the packet for a 000. If it is a
000 it is a broadcast packet and is
transmitted immediately. If it is not a
broadcast packet, then the RIM sends a
FREE BUFFER ENQUIRY to the DID node. If
the DID node responds with an ACK the
packet is then sent. If the DID node
responds with a NAK, indicating no
buffers are available to receive the
packet, then the token is passed to the
NID and the RIM will resend a FREE BUFFER
ENQUIRY on the next pass of the token.

Upon completion of sending the PACKET
the RIM waits 74us for a response. If the
response is ACK then it sets TMA true and
the TA true. The RIM just sets TA to true
and passes the token to the NID if it
times-out following the transmission --
packets are never NAK'ed. Retransmission
of the non-acknowledged PACKET is the
responsibility of the program running in
the processor.

MESSAGE RECEPTION -- PROCESSOR ACTION

In order for a processor to receive a
message, it must issue a command to the
RIM to enable reception of a message into
a particular buffer. Optionally, the
ability to receive broadcast messages can
be enabled. The status bit Receiver
Inhibited (RI) is set to false when the
command is issued and is not set to true
until a packet is received.

MESSAGE RECEPTION - RIM ACTION

When a RIM receives a FREE BUFFER

ENQUIRY from another RIM attempting to
transmit, it checks the status of the RI
bit. If RI is set to true, indicating
that the receiver is inhibited from
receiving, then the RIM responds with a
NAK. Otherwise it sends an ACK and waits
for the PACKET.

When the RIM receives the SOH
indicating the start of a PACKET it first
writes the Source ID into the receive
buffer and then checks the first DID. If
the DID byte is 000 indicating a
broadcast message, the RIM verifies that
broadcast reception has been enabled. If
not, the packet is ignored. If the DID
byte is the same as the RIM's ID or 000
with broadcast receive enabled, the RIM
places the rest of the packet in the
receive buffer. If the packet fails the
length check or the CRC check the RIM
ignores it. If it was a broadcast packet
the RIM sets RI to true. If the packet
was a normal data packet it sends an ACK
and then sets RI to true.

The RIM performs the bulk of the
verification and validation of the
messages in the transfer from RIM to RIM.
The application in the processor is
responsible for retransmission of
non-acknowledged packets and for keeping
track of the movement of data from
processor to RIM and from RIM to
processor.

NETWORK PERFORMANCE

In a token passing network the most
interesting aspect in performance is the
amount of time a node has to wait before
it can transmit again. Other than
infrequent error corrections and
retransmission, there are two factors
that are involved in determining the wait
time: the time for a simple token pass
and the time for a message transmission
followed by a token pass.

In ARCNET the simple token pass takes
about 28us, ignoring propagation delay.
The amount of time required to transmit a
message is 141us plus 4.4us per
character, again ignoring propagation
delay. The complete round trip time for a
token, if each node were transmitting a
message, would be 28us per node plus
113us per message plus 4.4us per byte.
For example, in a system with 10 nodes
and each node sending messages no longer
than 100 bytes, the complete token trip
would take 280us with no message
transmission and not longer than 5810us
if all 10 nodes send 100 byte messages.
If only one node is sending messages it
can send one every 833us a rate of 1200
messages a second. If all 10 nodes are
sending messages each one can send one
every 5810us, a rate of 172 messages per
second per node.

At the Datapoint Research and
Development Department in San Antonio,
Tx., there is an ARCNET installation with
anywhere from 150 to 200 nodes active at
any one time. This network supports two
totally independent operating systems,
links five separate buildings, and is
being used for program development, word
processing, print spooling, electronic
mail, laser printing, color business
graphics and other applications. The
traffic load on this network rarely falls
below 400 messages per second, yet less
than 2% of the nodes on the network send
a message on the average token trip. The
time required for the token trip stays
very near the no-traffic level. Peak
activity near the value of three times
the no-traffic rate are very rare.

SOFTWARE IMPLEMENTATION.

In 1977 Datapoint announced the
Attached Resource Computer (ARC) as a
network product utilizing it's Disk
Operating System as the foundation. Under
DOS the capabilities of ARCNET were those
of the current range of products from
other networking vendors. File processors
(file servers) were offered to make disk
data available to the other processors in
the network. Special processors with no
disks attached were developed and brought
into the product line to take advantage
of the ARC capabilities at a lower cost
to the user. Print unspoolers (printer
servers) were also introduced to make the
expensive printer resources available to
the entire network. All of this was done
with existing equipment technology. After
the minor software modification necessary
to use the ARC, Datapoint fitted it's
existing hardware and software offerings
to ARCNET networking capabilities. The
concept of the Integrated Electronic
Office™ was introduced. The local area
network with inexpensive processors all
working together sharing the same
resources is the ideal place to implement
such a function. Datapoint responded with
word processing software, IEOS, and an
Electronic Message System. Our normal
communications capabilities for batch and
on-line communication continued to be a
mainstay in the ARCNET environment.
Additionally, communications servers were
added to the network providing gateways
into the communications networks of major
mainframe vendors.

In 1980, Datapoint announced and
delivered it's Resource Management
System™. The ideas of file servers and
print servers went away. The disks,
printers and communications devices
became resources which were available to
users anywhere in the network. A
processor was no longer dedicated to a
single task such as providing file
resources. It could at the same time

drive other peripherals and perform on-line or batch processing tasks. New processors were added to the product line, still utilizing the same ARCNET capabilities, but giving the user a new dimension of flexibility not experienced before. File handling capabilities were enhanced through a File Management System and the first batch job control system for a local network was introduced, allowing execution of batch jobs on nodes with idle processing power.

CONCLUSION

Until recently Datapoint has held the ARCNET protocol as proprietary information. With the completion of agreements with Tandy Corporation and Standard Micorsystems, the decision was made to provide this information to the general public. We feel this is justified because of the acceptance of our products in the marketplace. Continued improvement is one of Datapoint's major goals. In the five years since Datapoint has been shipping ARCNET systems we have changed the ARCNET interface itself. Originally the RIM was a 900 cubic inch "shoebox" utilizing MSI TTL. Today it is a 35 square inch board designed around custom MOS LSI chips. Processors and peripherals are available that have the ARCNET coax connector as the only I/O device.

Datapoint is extremely proud of its record in the local area network market. Our future developments will provide even more links in the future.

Reprinted from *IEEE Journal on Selected Areas in Communications*, November 1983, pages 857-868. Copyright © 1983 by The Institute of Electrical and Electronics Engineers, Inc.

Experiences with a Layered Approach to Local Area Network Design

GARY M. ELLIS, MEMBER, IEEE, SAM DILLON, SKIP STRITTER, MEMBER, IEEE, AND JERRY WHITNELL

Abstract —The Nestar Plan 4000 network was designed using the ISO Open Systems Interconnection model. The Xerox Network Systems Internet Transport Protocols (XNS) were chosen for the network and transport layers, a token-passing protocol (Arcnet) for the physical and datalink layers, and existing Nestar server software for the highest layers.

The physical and datalink layers are supported by a VLSI chip and their implementation was straightforward. In spite of their detailed specification, implementing the network and transport layers presented some unanticipated challenges. This paper discusses details of our experience in implementing the network with emphasis on the problems encountered and how they were solved.

I. INTRODUCTION

THE International Standards Organization (ISO) has defined the "Open Systems Interconnection—Basic Reference Model" [1] as a guideline for structuring the architecture of local area networks. The model is characterized by a "layered" approach in which the architecture is divided into seven independent layers, each of which builds on the function provided by lower layers and adds function of its own. The OSI model itself is not a standard, but rather a guide to network design. The use of a conceptual framework or "model" is useful in software engineering because it helps understanding of complex systems such as networks. Our reasons for using the layered approach include, in addition, the potential for compatibility with other networks and the possibility of interchangeability of different implementations of individual layers.

Manuscript received April 15, 1983; revised August 19, 1983.
The authors are with Nestar Systems, Inc., Palo Alto, CA 94303.

This paper presents a case study of how Nestar Systems, Inc., Palo Alto, CA, developed a new network [2] using this model. This network will typically be used to provide an underlying data-sharing, service-sharing, and interstation communication environment for application systems that run on personal computers. These applications range from individualized programs such as word processors to network-wide systems such as a medical records database or a foreign exchange trading package. Our purpose is not to present new knowledge in the field of local area networks, but rather to explain the reasoning behind our choices of existing technologies and to detail our experiences in the implementation of the network. The primary design goal was the need to replace our aging Cluster/One technology [3] with a faster network in time to meet changing market needs.

II. THE STRATEGY

A. Overall Design Goals

The user stations environment supported by the new network was to consist of relatively low cost personal computers, therefore the cost per station to connect to the network had to be low also. When the project was started in June 1982, the cost of a workstation was roughly $2000–$3000. It was desired that the cost per connection be about 25 percent of this. An order of magnitude increase in maximum data throughput (from 250 kbits/s to 2.5 Mbits/s) over the previous generation [3] was desired, although we were aware that other considerations would prevent the user from seeing the full ten times speed improvement. In addition, the forecasted marketing window limited the amount of time available for the implementation. We had approximately five months to produce a working prototype plus two to three additional months to finish, tune, and reliably manufacture the system.

Our existing network supported a single type of personal computer. This allowed a relatively high-reliability design in which the file server was hosted on one of the same computers. If the file server processor failed, another workstation could easily take its place. Since the new network was planned to support several types of personal computers, a decision was made to move away from hosting the file server on a workstation. Our experience to date has been that almost all of our networks are sold to users who purchase the workstations at the same time. As such, individual networks usually consist of a single type of computer, and for marketing reasons, would require the file server to run on the same type of machine. This would have led to supporting a large body of software in a number of different machine environments. For this reason, and the goal of higher computing performance, we chose to design proprietary file server hardware based on a commercially available 68000 processor board.

B. Choices For the Levels

We decided on the layered approach for several reasons. Ease of parallel development, maintainability, and ability to easily interface to other networks are all strong points which are inherent in a modular approach. A side effect of this decision was that it allowed us to choose implementations for groups of layers that are relatively independent of each other, yet have advantages that a more homogeneous approach would not have. A major drawback that we considered was that layering the software could seriously degrade performance. The limited interfaces that are a goal in modular programming can lead to more data copying and procedure calls than a monolithic approach.

We chose to use Datapoint's Arcnet technology [4] for the physical and datalink layers (levels 1 and 2), the Xerox Network Systems Internet Transport Protocols (XNS) [5] for the network and transport layers (levels 3 and 4), and existing Nestar server software for the upper layers (levels 5-7) (see Fig. 1).

C. Motivation for Arcnet Physical and Datalink Protocols

The decision as to which technology to use at the data-link level involved a number of tradeoffs. Besides the obvious ones of speed and class of service (token-passing versus CSMA/CD, baseband versus broadband), these factors included the availability of a standard, the cost and time required for implementation, the availability of parts, the amount of circuit board space required, and the ease of installation and maintenance. We chose baseband over broadband because of our relatively simple requirements —there was no requirement for voice or video transmission in the desired system. The difficulty in installing and tuning a broadband system would have added an undesirable level of complexity. Also, the lack of VLSI implementa-

Layer	Purpose	Nestar Implementation	
Application	The program that the user runs		
Presentation	Library routines provided by operating system	client station software	server station software
Session	Users interface to the network		
Transport	Maintains virtual connections between user processes. Divides messages into packets	Xerox Network Systems Internet Transport Protocol	
Network	Maps global (Ethernet) address into local network address. Performs gateway function for packets bound for other networks		
Datalink	Receives packets from other stations on local network. Makes best effort to send packets to stations on local network	ARCNET	
Physical	Cable and electrical interface		

Fig. 1. ISO model of Plan 4000 network.

tion would have greatly increased the cost of the interface.

The choice of Arcnet was made for several reasons. The first was the overall cost of connecting a station to the network. In late 1982, an Arcnet chip set was being shipped in sample quantities, but there were no VLSI Ethernet parts available. This meant that we could produce an Arcnet interface for 30–50 percent of the cost of an Ethernet interface. Having been installed in over 4000 installations and in use for six years, Arcnet possessed a maturity of use that we felt was lacking in Ethernet. Datapoint had decided to make the formerly proprietary technology freely available and was willing to share technical information with us. This was an important factor in minimizing implementation time. Finally, there are some technical advantages (detailed in Table I) that Arcnet has over Ethernet.

We felt that these advantages were more important than the (theoretical) four times speed advantage of Ethernet (10 Mbits/s compared to 2.5 Mbits/s for Arcnet). Our experience indicates that the lower speed does not restrict the actual throughput achieved in a working network. As discussed in a later section, other issues limit end-to-end effective throughput to substantially less than the theoretical potential in this and other networks.

D. Motivation for Xerox Internet Transport Protocols

For the next two layers of the protocol (network and transport), the Xerox XNS protocols were chosen. Initially, there were three choices for levels 3 and 4. We could use XNS, DARPA TCP/IP [6], [7], or we could design our own. Other standards, such as those of the National Bureau of Standards (NBS) or X.25, were either unavailable at the time the decisions were made, or judged to be inappropriate for local area networks.

TABLE I
ARCNET VERSUS ETHERNET COMPARISON

	ARCNET	**Ethernet**
Physical topology	Unrooted tree of cable segments	Cable segments connected by repeaters (max 2 between stations)
Maximum cable segment length	610 meters	500 meters
Maximum distance between stations	6700 meters	1500 meters
Packet collision avoidance	No collisions—only token holder xmits	Collisions detected by transmitter listening to itself
Acknowledged packet delivery	Yes	No
Datalink flow control	Yes	No

We quickly rejected the option of designing our own protocols because of the time constraint. We had an average of 12 engineers and programmers and five months to do the job. Subtracting some time for management and other nondevelopment activities, there were 40–45 man months available for both the software and hardware development efforts. In order to meet schedules, we felt that a well-defined protocol that was already debugged and in use was required. It was also felt that some commercial acceptance of the selected protocols would help in marketing the new product.

The TCP/IP protocol, used mainly for ARPAnet, was originally designed for data transfer over low speed serial communication lines such as the telephone. As such, the protocol is not well suited to the interactive applications we intended to run on the new Nestar network. Also, there were essentially no major commercial environments supporting TCP/IP. This meant that a large amount of protocol translation software would be required to interface with other vendors' products.

Because of Xerox's early entry into the field, and the fact that their protocol is very well specified and in the public domain, we felt that XNS would become a de facto standard for internetwork communication. It has the advantage that it is independent both of the layers below it (how a packet is transmitted from one node to another) and the layers above it (how a client process wishes to use the network). This allowed us to keep most of our existing upper level server software. It also gave the option of adding support for other low level transmission protocols (e.g., Ethernet layers 1 and 2) without changing upper level software. The published specification allows other suppliers to write applications which use the protocol. A significant number of other vendors (more than 30 in mid 1982) had announced corporate support for Ethernet for their local networks and although we are using token passing rather than CSMA/CD, using the Ethernet Internet protocols would make it relatively easy to produce gateways to those networks.

E. Motivation for Nestar High Levels

It was necessary that the change to a new network technology be invisible to existing user application software because providing an upgrade path for existing customers was a primary goal. On the user station side of the connection this meant that everything from the interface of the session layer software up had to be identical to that in the current network. There were consequently no major design alternatives to choose from in the user station higher level software—it was necessary only to change the session layer software to interface to the new transport layer below it.

The situation with the file server however, was somewhat different. New higher performance server hardware based on the 68000 and 256 kbytes of memory was being developed, and the possibility existed of rewriting a large part of the existing software to take advantage of it. The file server software was originally written for a lower performance noninterrupt driven computer and operating system. A faster network and a somewhat higher cost file server (which probably meant less servers per network) made it desirable to squeeze as much power as possible out of the new file server. This would have meant changing the presently single-threaded code into a number of concurrent tasks. The major disadvantage to this alternative was the need to find (or possibly develop) a suitable real-time operating system for the new software to run under. The time constraint for implementation (five months) made this an almost impossible task.

The chosen alternative, using the present software relatively unmodified, was more attractive for several reasons. A single-tasking operating system (and Pascal compiler) already existed for the new hardware which was very similar to the language/operating system environment of the previous server. A port of the software could be made relatively easily. The only additional software needed was a new session layer to interface to the new transport layer. The existing software had been operating in the field for about three years, so it was reliable and its behavior was well understood. This allowed us to concentrate the greatest part of our development resources on producing new network protocol software.

F. Advantages to the Layered Approach

Implementations of the different layers were assigned to different programmers. This concurrent development continued until the final debugging stages. As a measure of the independence of the software development efforts, support for one user station was written at a sister company in the United Kingdom. Only after both user station and file server software were essentially complete did the two attempt to communicate over the network. Four people working less than a month managed to repair most bugs. Having two completely separate groups implement the protocols in entirely different ways (one used Pascal, one used assembly language) proved to be a good method of validating the protocols and the documents defining them.

The modular approach also allows changing any layer of the network software without modifying the others. This is a great advantage for future gateway or bridge implementations. For example, to create a Plan 4000/Ethernet gateway would only require creating Ethernet levels 1 and 2 for the gating computer. Similarly, by replacing levels 3 and 4 we could create a gate to the higher levels of Datapoint's Arcnet software. It also allows the freedom to

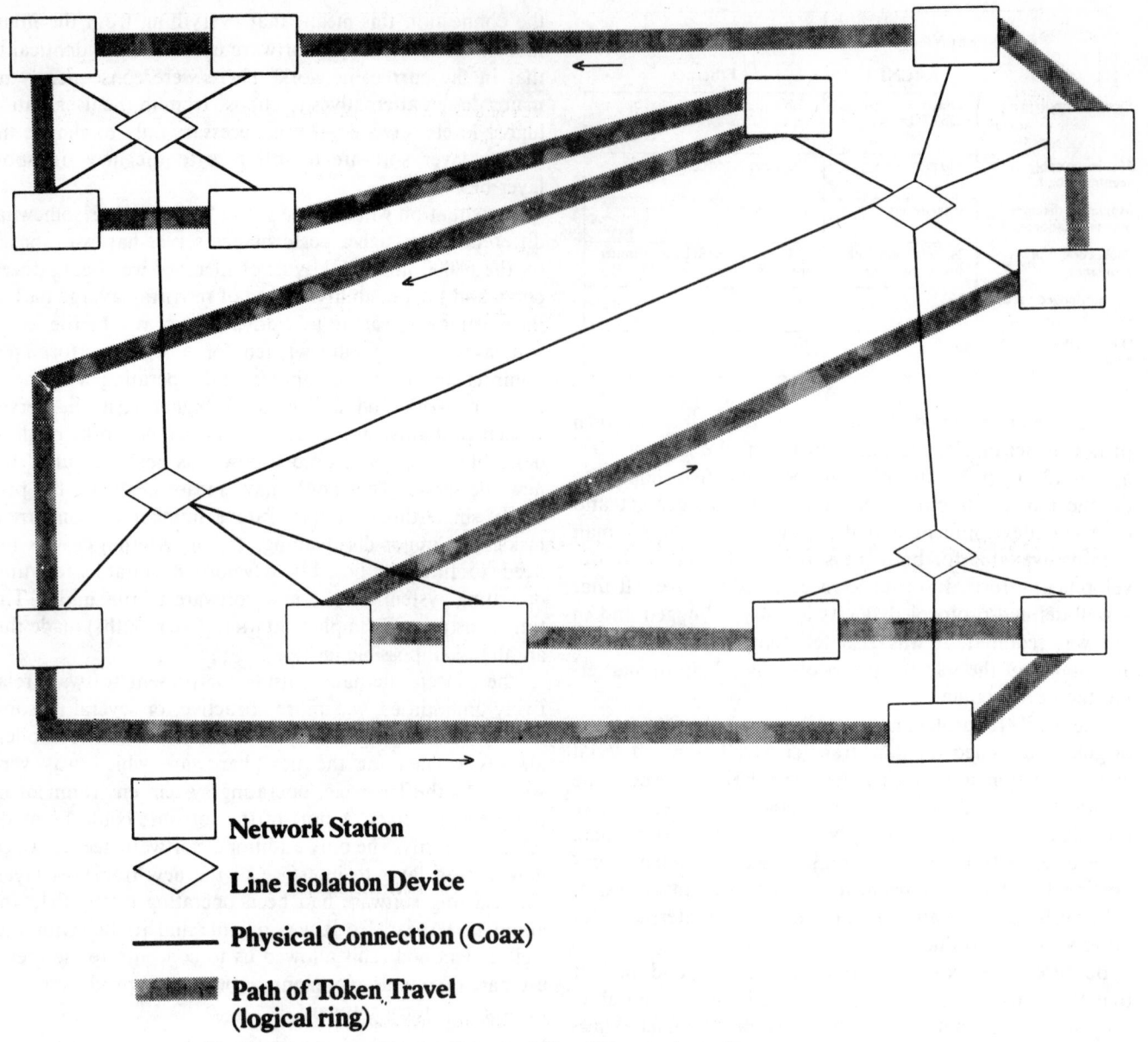

Network Station

Line Isolation Device

Physical Connection (Coax)

Path of Token Travel (logical ring)

Fig. 2. Example of Plan 4000 network topology.

adopt a different physical layer for the network. We could move to a fiber optic network by only redesigning the transmission/reception hardware of level 1 and not modifying any software.

III. SUMMARY OF THE CHARACTERISTICS OF THE CHOSEN LAYERS

A. The Physical and Datalink Layers

The first two layers (physical and datalink) are Datapoint's Arcnet. Physically, Arcnet is an unrooted tree structure (Fig. 2) with up to 255 stations allowed. New stations may be connected to the network at any point through a length of coaxial cable. The only constraints are that there must be no loops in the structure and the distance between any two nodes must not exceed 6700 m. Details of how Arcnet works are given in Appendix A and [4].

The datalink layer software provides a clean interface to the network protocol chip (called the RIM chip, Standard

Microsystems 9026; see Appendix A for more detail) and other hardware. It supplies its client (the network layer) with the ability to send a packet to any station on the network, to send to all stations on the network, to determine if a packet has been received and if so, what station it was from. All details of token management and packet transmission are handled transparently by the network protocol chip.

B. The Network and Transport Layers

The network and transport layers are based on the Xerox XNS standard, which defines the internetworking protocols used by Xerox with Ethernet. (They are not, strictly speaking, part of the Ethernet standard [8], [9], which defines only the physical and datalink layers.) (See Appendix B for a description of the entry points for Nestar's implementation of levels 3 and 4.) The network layer implements the translation from Ethernet addresses (which are used at the higher levels) to Arcnet addresses

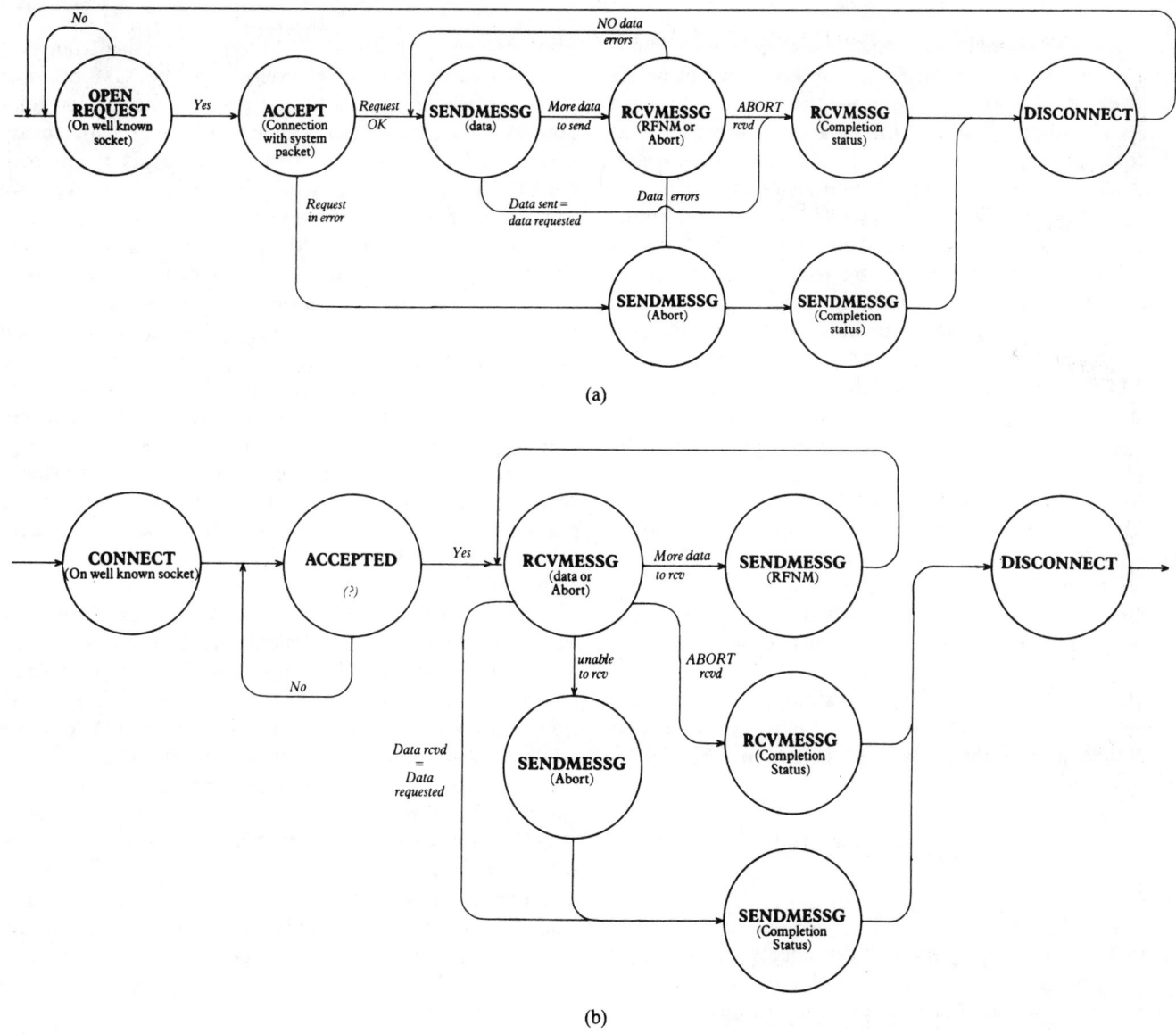

Fig. 3. (a) File server disk read transaction. (b) Client disk read transaction.

(for the low levels). It decides whether the station is on the local net, or on one which is connected by a gateway or bridge, and routes the message appropriately. Finally, it implements the concept of "sockets" (virtual ports into a machine). Our initial implementation was required to access only the attached local network, so most of the internet routing function was left out. Using the Arcnet address as one byte of the Ethernet host address allows a simple Ethernet to Arcnet address mapping in the isolated network case.

The transport layer provides reliable and safe conversations between sockets. It allows its client (the session layer) to connect to another station on the network, to send and receive arbitrarily long messages and then disconnect, knowing that all the messages will get to the destination in the order they are sent, without any losses, as long as the destination machine is available.

C. The Session, Presentation, and Application Layers

The Nestar software at the upper levels provides the ability to request services from or exchange data with other stations. The file server accepts I/O requests over the network and emulates local disks for the workstation on its hard disk. The file server also supports commands directly from the workstation to create, delete, or rename virtual volumes on the server's disk and to provide synchronization services. Other servers exist which can print files from any file server on the network, transfer files between file servers, and provide communication with mainframe computers.

The file server and its clients communicate at the session layer through transactions which are produced through the use of transport layer services. Fig. 3 shows a disk read transaction from the perspectives of both a server [Fig. 3(a)] and a client [Fig. 3(b)]. In the diagrams, the bubbles represent transport layer entry points. The conditions on control flow (arrows) can be either the value of an associated bubble (if it represents a Pascal function) or the value of a session layer variable. A "RFNM" (request for next message) is a special session layer message that a receiver uses to notify a sender of the amount of buffer space available for a data message. That buffer space is allocated by the application layer and its size is simply passed to the sender by the session layer. An "abort" is a zero (data) length message that one side's session layer uses to notify the other of its inability to continue the transaction. Since there are no data associated with an abort, it can be sent at any time without the necessity to allocate buffer space. Whenever one end of a connection sends an abort, our protocol requires that end to send a completion status message indicating the reason for the abort. In the case of a normal termination (indicated by received-data-length = requested-data-length) the receiver sends a completion status message to the sender to indicate that the transaction has been successfully finished. Note that the transport layer acknowledgment protocol is not sufficient to mark end-of-transaction because nonnetwork related problems, such as a disk error, could require the transaction to be retried.

The session layer message types referred to above are actually defined by a field in the transport layer header. This method of definition is part of the Xerox XNS specification. One of the parameters returned by the transport layer from a RCVMESSG call is that message type. (In an analogous fashion, the session layer supplies a message-type parameter to the transport layer in a SENDMESSG call.) This is essentially a performance enhancing part of the XNS protocol that gives one layer a quick indication of the contents of the data passed to it by the next lower layer.

IV. IMPLEMENTATION EXPERIENCE AND PROBLEMS

A. Design and Coding

Despite the fact that the services provided by each of the layers in the ISO model are well documented in the Xerox XNS specification, the interfaces and entry points are not defined. This was both a help and a hinderance. We were not forced to emulate an inappropriate design or implement an interface that was not really suitable for our needs. On the other hand, we had much more design work to do. Also, because there is no published or standard interface, our code will not interface to other implementations of specific layers without being modified. It is not clear whether the lack of interface definition allows enough freedom so that separate implementations could be truly incompatible, as opposed to merely stylistically different. Appendix B details our choice of interface.

In addition to the interface, certain details of how each layer should provide its services are not defined in the specification. For instance, the usage of certain control bits in headers, such as when acknowledgments should be requested, became clear only after we had had some experience with data transfer between stations on the network. Our initial understanding of the function of the Send Acknowledgment bit in the transport layer header was to request an immediate ACK of the last received packet. The implementations in both the file server and the user station, had the transport layer setting Send Acknowledgment on every message boundary. This had the effect of causing a system packet to be sent by the receiver after every message. (A system packet is used by the transport layer to communicate protocol information to another transport layer—it carries no higher level data.) The XNS protocol allows acknowledgments to be "piggy-backed" on regular user-data packets so that system packets are not always necessary for this function. In our attempts to improve performance by limiting the number of system packets, we experimented with not setting Send Acknowledgment at the same time as End of Message. This led to deadlock situations where the sender of a message required an ACK before sending the next message, and the receiver was waiting until its next send to piggy-back the ACK. It soon became apparent that the real meaning of the Send Acknowledgment bit is "I need an acknowledgment before I will send any more data—send it in the most efficient manner possible." The solution was to change the transport layer code to record the fact of the acknowledge request, and if it is determined at a later time that a piggy-backed ACK is not possible (i.e., the session layer makes two RECVMESSG calls in a row), then send a system packet.

One of the technical advantages that Arcnet has over Ethernet is the packet acknowledgment protocol performed automatically by the RIM chip. Other physical and data-link protocols, such as Ethernet, give best-effort packet transmission only. A design decision was made to avoid reliance on this automatic acknowledgment by higher levels of the protocol—each layer uses only its own reliability checks. This way if we produce an Ethernet low level interface (or some other best-effort-only lower level), we will not have to rewrite level 3 and above to make up for nonguaranteed service from lower levels. Performance studies done after the installation showed that checksum failures occur on only 1/10 of 1 percent of all transmitted packets, so the cost of not using the acknowledgment protocol is small.

The limited interfaces that are a part of a modular design proved helpful several times. The file server transport layer code was heavily modified during the integration testing with the user stations. After the first release of the product, the datalink layer was rewritten to enhance performance. The transport layer code on some of the supported computers was completely rewritten several times, either to improve performance or to conserve memory space on very small computers. None of these modifications led to any code changes in other layers on the same computer, or in any layers in other machines.

No insurmountable problems were experienced while porting the file server application layer software to the new environment. Since memory address space was restricted to 64 kbytes in the Cluster/One file server, a fair amount of nonstandard Pascal had been added to the software during its life which had to be cleaned up for the new environment. Some of the utilities that were supplied with the new operating system had bugs that occasionally slowed progress. In spite of this, however, it took five people only three months to produce an operating file server on the new network. An additional 14 man months produced network integration for three different user station computers running a total of six different operating systems.

B. Verification

One major problem was the lack of verification tools. We found that making the protocols work was not difficult. A more subtle question is how to monitor the network to see what is really going on and be sure that it is doing what is intended in the most efficient manner. As others have reported [10], the very design of the network, with elaborate mechanisms for recovery from errors and lost packets, can interfere with finding subtle problems. For example, an error which results in generating many duplicate packets may be hidden because the receiving end (by design) discards the duplicates. We found several instances of such errors, which were not causing network failure, but were degrading network performance.

We built a special hardware network monitor from a specially modified network interface dubbed the "sniffer." It accepts every packet that goes over the net regardless of destination address, which is something not ordinarily permitted by the RIM hardware. We developed filtering software that allows us to keep only the packets we want in a large circular buffer holding about 2000 packets. This allowed us to manually verify network transactions and proved invaluable in debugging the protocols.

The interactions of various timeout parameters in the system, both intraserver and between servers and clients, have proved to be the most complex part to understand and tune. One example involves how long the datalink layer continues to attempt transmitting a packet and how long the transport layer attempts to pass a packet to the network layer for transmission. The latter operation may fail because of a lack of an available transmit buffer in the physical layer. Originally, the datalink and transport layers in the file server were implemented by different programmers and there was little coordination of timeout values between the layers. (In fact, our lack of understanding of the way the network functioned as a system would have made such coordination of little value anyway.) The datalink timeout was set to several seconds, with the idea that a less powerful user station might take a relatively long time to empty its receive RIM buffers. The transport "send-packet" timeout however, was about 1/5 as long. The overall effect of this was that the datalink was attempting to service a packet for about five times longer than the transport layer was. Aside from being a tremendous waste of datalink resources, it was causing a great deal of transport error recovery code to be executed whenever a user station failed to complete a transaction (a common occurrence in an environment where a user can abort a program at will).

Using the "sniffer" to observe the interstation network behavior, we discovered two problems. One was that since the network code in the user stations was designed to keep the RIM buffers empty as much as possible (either through interrupts, or a tight polling loop during a network transaction), it was highly likely that an unavailable buffer condition meant that the client was in an error state, and would be unable to complete the transaction anyway. As the file server is a resource to be shared among many users, it could not afford to wait too long for a client to fulfill its protocol duties. The datalink timeout could therefore be safely set to a much shorter time—less than a second. The other change made was to adjust the transport "send packet" timeout to slightly more than the datalink timeout. This ensures that transport layer will always be able to send a packet through the lower layers.

Another open question is how to verify that our implementation of the published protocols really conforms to the specification. The proof will have to wait until we have an opportunity to interconnect our network with others which claim to conform to the same specifications. We have no automatic way (like the NBS testbed) to verify either the design or the implementation.

C. Performance

The implementation of a network following the ISO model has each layer (starting with 7, the application) passing data and some form of control information to the layer below. Each layer does whatever housekeeping is necessary before passing (possibly translated) data and control information to the next layer down. At the transport layer, the message is broken into packets and encapsulated with header information that uniquely identifies that packet to the corresponding layer in the receiving machine. This is usually done by prepending a header to the packet. The software in the receiving machine passes the packet back up through the layers. Each level strips off the header and sends up only the data that were given to the corresponding layer in the source machine.

A layered system like this, when implemented naively, can be very inefficient if the data are copied each time a layer encapsulates or decapsulates information from neighboring layers. Our software and hardware has been designed to avoid unnecessary data movement. For example, messages containing information to be written to disk by the file server are processed by levels 1–5 but the disk data are moved only once, from the network buffer to the file server's disk controller buffer.

As in most real systems, a few "cheats" were made. To prevent performance degradation, pointers to data are passed through the levels, rather than copying data several times. Also, certain levels are allowed access to data "belonging" to other levels. As an example, the transport layer looks at the length field of the network level header as a quick check of whether the incoming packet was large enough to contain a full level 4 header. This could be considered a violation of the separation of layers since truly separate layers would not share memory, except through interface parameters.

Another attempt at reducing the number of system packets transmitted led to allowing the session layer to be aware of the existence of transport layer acknowledgments, something that should be transparent to a client of the transport layer. Since the session layer knew the direction of traffic flow in a transaction, it was able to determine whether or not a piggy-backed acknowledgment was possible and could inform the transport layer with each call to SENDMESSG, whether or not the send ack bit in the transport header should be set. Our later discovery of the correct way for the transport layer to respond to the send acknowledgment bit obviates the need for this "cheat."

We have also found that the data transfer rate between applications on the network is largely independent of the raw bit rate of the physical layer. In general, local area networks are able to transfer data at an effective bandwidth of 20–50 kbits/s (see, for instance, [11]). The Plan 4000 moves about 32 kbits/s during an average virtual disk data transfer (from a file server disk across the network into the user station application). The greatest constraints on throughput seem to be the efficiencies of the various network software layers, along with the ability of the server to respond quickly to incoming service requests. The implication is that a 10 Mbyte/s medium, though four times as fast as that of Plan 4000, would not give a factor of four improvement in throughput.

V. Summary

We have implemented a new local area network following the ISO Open Systems Interconnection model, using Datapoint's Arcnet for the data transmission levels, Xerox Internet protocols for the network and transport levels, and existing Nestar server software and application programs for the highest levels. Using a layered approach to network design, both during the design and implementation phases, and in subsequent stages of network "tuning," allowed the implementation to occur in a relatively short period of time for a project of this magnitude. It also gave us the ability to choose an optimum implementation for each layer, based on its individual merits, rather than on its membership in a particular technology. We found that although the Xerox XNS internet protocols were well specified, certain subtle aspects were only understood after its implementation.

Appendix A
Description of Arcnet Protocols

Logically, Arcnet appears to the user (the datalink layer) as a token-passing ring. One token is passed between stations and only the station that has the token may transmit. When a station receives the token, if it has nothing to transmit it passes the token on to the next station in the "ring." If it has something to transmit to a particular station on the network (rather than a "broadcast" packet which is sent to all stations on the network) a "free-buffer enquiry" handshake is used to ensure that the receiver has sufficient buffer space for the packet. If it does, or the packet is for broadcast, it is transmitted at this point. The receiver will return an acknowledgment if the packet is received correctly. The datalink layer is informed of the success or failure of the packet transmission and the token is passed on.

To connect to the network, each station has one or more network interface cards (NIC). A VLSI circuit, called a resource interface module (RIM), implements the Arcnet protocol. The part was designed by Datapoint using their experience with the discrete RIM's used in most of their existing installations. The RIM manages a 2 kbyte RAM buffer in which up to four packages may be stored (either to be sent or that have been received). The RIM is also given a station id (a number from 1 to 255), which must be unique on the net, which it uses to identify itself to other stations, to implement the logical ring, and to identify messages intended for it that come from other stations.

All the algorithms associated with token passing and packet transmission are handled by the RIM. Lost or destroyed tokens are automatically regenerated by a distributed algorithm. Reconfiguration, as workstations join the network, is done transparently and efficiently. When a new station joins the network it is not part of the logical ring and does not receive the token. After 840 ms it times out and sends a reconfigure burst which destroys the token. All other stations on the network detect the loss of the token and start a timeout based on station number. The timeout value is $(146 \ \mu s) (255-\text{station number})$, so that the highest station number on the net will timeout first. If any network activity is detected during the timeout period, then some other station has timed out and will generate a new token. If the timeout expires at a station, then that station creates a new token and sends it to the next higher address (mod 256). If there is no response in 74.7 μs, the station increments the target station number and tries again until a station accepts the token. The original station remembers that address as the next station number in the logical ring. The second station continues the operation, looking for the next higher station on the net. This is continued until all 255 possible id's have been tried ("0" is used for a broadcast packet, so it is not in the set of legal station numbers). The time required to reconfigure the network depends on the number of nodes, the propagation delay between nodes, and the highest station number on the net. It falls in the range of 24–61 ms. Other than the destruction of the token there are no packet collisions, even during reconfiguration.

When a station is powered off there will be no response to the token holder's attempt to pass the token. Rather than cause a reconfiguration, the token holder will timeout on passing the token and send the token to successively higher numbered stations until the next station in the ring is found. That station number is recorded internally as the logical "next" station to which the token is to be passed.

There is network flow control at the datalink level through the free-buffer enquiry and acknowledgment protocols. These prevent wasted cable bandwidth on collisions and lost packets when the target station is not listening, is not there, or does not have buffer space. Unlike Ethernet, the protocol is efficient when efficiency is important—during periods of heavy traffic [12]. Also, damaged packets are detected immediately using the CRC, and a negative acknowledgment (NAK) is sent back to the sender. The sender does not have to wait for a software timeout to determine whether retransmission is required.

Network interface cards are connected to the network through RG62 coaxial cable (the same as used for IBM 3270 display units). Rather than having all stations tap into one cable (as in common-wire networks like Ethernet), each station connects through a port on a line isolation device (LID). The LID provides an electrically-ideal connection to the rest of the network, reducing or eliminating problems caused by a physical tap into the cable. In addition, it suppresses reflections from unterminated lines, allowing any station to be detached from the network either at the station or the LID. LID's are available with 4–16 ports and may be cascaded (up to ten LID's in the path between any two stations).

The LID also helps isolate hardware faults. Shorts or opens in a cable affect only stations that must transmit through that cable segment, leaving the rest of the network operational. There is a light for each station on the LID that is lit when the station is circulating the token normally. Failing units are easily detected by observing the lights and each can be disconnected at a few central points (the LID's). This eliminates the need for crawling around in the ceiling or visiting each office. In addition, the network is transformer isolated which limits ground-loop problems.

The raw transmission speed is 2.5 Mbits/s. Passing the token through an idle station takes 31 μs, and transmitting a packet takes 129.6 μs plus 4.4 μs/byte of data. A 256 byte packet then, takes 1256 μs, giving an effective throughput of 204 000 bytes/s (or 1.63 Mbits/s).

APPENDIX B
PASCAL DESCRIPTION OF NETWORK AND TRANSPORT LAYER ENTRY POINTS

```
{*** NETWORK LAYER ***}
TYPE

        address         =       ↑byte;
        netid           =       fourbytes;
        hostid          =       sixbytes;
        socketno        =       twobytes;
        socketaddr      =       record

                (network    :       netid;
                 host       :       hostid;
                 socket     :       socketno);

        end;

        connectno       =       twobytes;   {Level 4 types}
        headerptr       =       ↑headdesc;
        headdesc        =       packed record

            {*** Level 3 (network) header ***}

                chksum      :       twobytes;       {Checksum of packet (−1 = not used)}
                length3     :       integer;        {Length of packet.}
                notused     :       nibble;
                hopcount    :       nibble;         {How many stations to pass through}
                ptype       :       byte;           {Packet type (SPP, etc.)}
                destin      :       socketaddr;     {Ethernet address of receiver}
                source      :       socketaddr;     {Ethernet address of sender}

            {*** Level 4 (transport) header ***}

                control     :       byte;           {Control bits}
                packettype  :       byte;           {what type of level 4 packet}
                srcid       :       connectno;      {Sender's connection number}
                destid      :       connectno;      {Receiver's connection number}
                sequence    :       integer;        {Sequence number for this packet}
                ackno       :       integer;        {Seq num of last packet received}
                allocno     :       integer;        {Seq num of packet we can accept to}

        end;

FUNCTION listen (socket  :  socketno)  :  boolean;
    {Condition level 3 to accept incoming packets on this socket (May be a well known socket or may be allocated)}

FUNCTION allosocket (VAR socket  :  socketno; migrate  :  boolean)  :  boolean;
    {Allocate a floating socket and return the number of the socket in 'socket', with allosocket returning TRUE. If
```

allosocket returns FALSE, then there are none available. If a socket is allocated, a listen is started automatically. If migrate is TRUE, socket should be set to unmigrated socket (for consistency check) and packet socketno will be changed to the new socket.}

FUNCTION freesocket (socket : socketno) : boolean;
{Free the specified socket. If not allocated, returns false. Freeing a well known socket simply stops any listener set up for it.}

FUNCTION rcvready (VAR hdr : headerptr) : boolean;
{Return false if no packet is waiting (hdr is nil). Return TRUE if a packet is waiting, with hdr pointing to the header in the RIM buffer.}

PROCEDURE rcvblockmove (socket : socketno;
                    offset : integer;
                    bufadr : address;
                    length : integer);
{Move a block of data from the current packet for socket "socket" to the buffer pointed to by "bufadr". Start move at 'offset' bytes and move 'length' bytes.}

PROCEDURE rcvrelease (socket : socketno);
{Release the current packet and listen for another.}

FUNCTION sendpkt (socket : socketno;
              hdr : headerptr;
              data : address;
              datalen : integer) : boolean;
{Send a packet through socket 'socket'. 'Hdr' is a pointer to the level 3/level 4 header with the level 4 and the level 3 destin and ptype fields filled in. Data points to the level 5 data to be sent, with datalen the number of bytes of level 5 data to send. Level 3 copies all of the data to the appropriate buffer and sends it out. If sendpkt returns false, no buffer is available}

{*** TRANSPORT LAYER ***}
TYPE

    transfer_status = ({replies to send/rcv functions}
            tf_ok,   {stable state}
            tf_unknown,   {transaction/connection ID unknown}
            tf_in_prog,   {status OK but unfinished}
            tf_nosockets,   {no free sockets}
            tf_hostfail,   {conn abend due to host loss}
            tf_overflow,   {input buffer overflow}
            tf_error   {some sort of protocol error}
           );

FUNCTION newlistener (socket : integer) : boolean;
{Initializes for reception on socket "socket." Return TRUE if socket was free.}

FUNCTION openreceived (socket : integer;
                  VAR conid : integer;
                  VAR caller : socketaddr) : boolean;
{Checks for incoming connection on "socket." If there is one, return TRUE, allocate and return a conid, and the caller's socketaddr. If the connect packet was also a data packet, do not move it anywhere yet.}

FUNCTION connect (destination: socketaddr;
                msgtype: byte;
                msgptr: address;
                msglen: integer;
           VAR conid: integer;
           VAR status: transfer_status) : boolean;
{Send an open-connection packet, which is also the first packet of the specified message if msglen $> = 0$. Return the connection id to be used for subsequent identification of this connection. Transmission of the message proceeds asynchronously as for sendmsg. The connection is not necessarily known to be established until a packet is received from the destination.}

FUNCTION accept (conid : integer) : transfer_status;
  {Accept the new connection by sending a system packet which contains an ack for the opening packet and migrates the socket to a newly allocated socket. This call is optional, and should be used when the connect packet is not a complete message, or the first sendmessg for this connection will not be for awhile yet.}

FUNCTION accepted (conid: integer;
                     VAR status: transfer_status): : boolean;
  {This is an inquiry procedure which indicates whether a previous connect has yet been accepted by the destination. Another equivalent indication of an accepted connection is receipt of a message from the destination.
  This function may be used to get early indication of successful connection, since it will be TRUE after the first packet has been received.}

FUNCTION rcvprepare (conid: integer;
                     bufaddr: address;
                     bufsize: integer) : transfer_status;
  {Supplies the buffer to be used for the next incoming message. Once a buffer has been supplied, calls to any level 4 routines are free to add to the message as the packets are received. If a previously received message has not yet been acknowledged, send a system packet acknowledging it.}

FUNCTION rcvmessg (conid: integer;
                    VAR msgtype: byte;
                    VAR msglen: integer;
                    VAR status: transfer_status
) : boolean;
  {Check if a complete message has been received in the supplied message buffer. If so, return TRUE, and return the message type and actual length. Record the number of the highest packet which must now be acknowledged.
  If an outgoing message has not been completely sent, this call (as well as all others) will continue the progression of outgoing packets as data-link-level resources are available.}

FUNCTION acknow (conid: integer) : transfer_status;
  {If a previously received message has not yet been acknowledged, send a system packet with an ack.}

PROCEDURE sendmessg (conid: integer;
                      msgtype: byte;
                      msgptr: address;
                      msglen: integer;
                      requestack: boolean;
                  VAR status: transfer_status);
  {If any previous outgoing message is not completely sent and acknowledged, then complete the message and wait for an acknowledgment. This is the only condition under which these subset level 4 routines block the caller. If the caller wants to be nonblocked, he can guarantee that the previous message has been sent and acknowledged by calling l4_status.
  Start sending the specified message. Send a piggy back acknowledgment for all received packets in all outgoing packets. Remember the parameter information so that the message can be resent if necessary. If ACKREQUEST is TRUE, set the ACK_REQ bit on the last packet of the message.
  The first message sent after an "openreceived" is equivalent to the "accept" procedure of the full level 4, and causes the socket to change to a newly allocated socket, thus freeing the listening socket for new connections.
  The buffer may not be reused by the caller until the message has been sent and acknowledged. This can be guaranteed to have happened by any of the following:
    1. repeat until L4_status = tf_ok
    2. sendmessg for the next message
    3. disconnect}

FUNCTION l4_status (conid : integer) : transfer_status;
  {Return the status of the connection and last outgoing message. This can be used as the "idling" procedure to pass periodic control to level 4 while waiting for a message to be sent. If the message has been sent but not acknowledged after a suitable delay, it will be retransmitted by level 4.}

FUNCTION disconnect (conid : integer; abort : boolean) : transfer_status;
  {Terminate the connection. If there is an unacknowledged outgoing message, and "abort" is FALSE, wait for the ACK and retry as necessary. If unacknowledged packets have been received, send a system packet acknowledging everything received.}

ACKNOWLEDGMENT

The authors wish to thank H. Saal, L. Shustek and the referees for their constructive criticism of drafts of this paper. Thanks also go to J. Thagard for doing the artwork.

REFERENCES

[1] H. Zimmermann, "OSI reference model—The ISO model of architecture for open system interconnection," *IEEE Trans. Commun.*, vol. COM-28, pp. 425–432, Apr. 1980.

[2] W. P. Pearson *et al.*, "3-in-1 local network links personal computers," *Electronics*, Dec. 29, 1982.

[3] E. P. Stritter and L. J. Shustek, "Local network links personal computers in a multi-user, multi-function system," *Electronics*, June 16, 1981.

[4] J. A. Murphy, "Token-passing protocol boosts throughput in local networks," *Electronics*, Sept. 8, 1982.

[5] *Internet Transport Protocols*, Tech. Manual, Xerox Corp., Dec. 1981.

[6] *DOD Standard Transmission Control Protocol*, U. S. Dep. Commerce, Nat. Tech. Inform. Service, Publ. AD-A082 609.

[7] *DOD Standard Internet Control Protocol*, U. S. Dep. Commerce, Nat. Tech. Inform. Service, Publ. AD-A079 730.

[8] The Ethernet: A Local Area Network, *Data Link Layer and Physical Layer Specifications*, Version 1.0, Tech. Manual, DEC-Intel-Xerox, Sept. 1980.

[9] R. M. Metcalfe and D. R. Boggs, "Ethernet: Distributed packet switching for local computer networks," *Commun. ACM*, vol. 19, pp. 395–404, July 1976.

[10] J. F. Schoch and J. A. Hupp, "Measured performance of an Ethernet local network," Palo Alto Res. Center, Xerox Corp., Feb. 1980.

[11] J. G. Mitchell and J. Dion, "A comparison of two network-based file servers," *Commun. ACM*, vol. 25, pp. 233–245, Apr. 1982.

[12] C. K. Miller and D. M. Thompson, "Making a case for token passing in local networks," *Data Commun.*, pp. 79–88, Mar. 1983.

Sam Dillon was born in Ft. Hood, TX, on December 3, 1955. He received the B.S. degree in biochemistry from the University of California at Riverside, Riverside, CA, in June 1978.

In September 1978 he joined the Burroughs Corporation and worked in production of mainframe peripherals. In 1979 he moved to the Research and Development Group, Magnuson Computer Systems, to work on the design of a cache memory for a 4300 compatible CPU. In February 1980 he joined the Software Development Group, Advanced Micro Computers, first writing diagnostics and then porting the Thoth operating system to the Z8000. Currently, he is with Nestar Systems, Inc., Palo Alto, CA, where he has worked on network protocols, network device drivers for workstations, system backup software, and porting network utility software between different workstations.

Skip Stritter (M'77) received the B.A. degree in mathematics from Dartmouth College, Hanover, NH, in 1968, and the M.S. and Ph.D. degrees in computer science from Stanford University, Stanford CA, in 1969 and 1967, respectively.

He worked at Motorola on microprocessor architecture, as a Professor of Computer Science, University of Texas, Austin, TX, and as a member of the Technical Staff, Bell Laboratories. He now directs new product development at Nestar Systems, Inc., Palo Alto, CA. He has contributed to the design and managed the implementation of the local area network described in this paper.

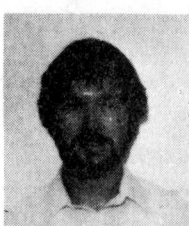

Gary M. Ellis (S'72–M'77) received the B.S. degree in electrical engineering from the University of Washington, Seattle, in 1977.

He worked on in-flight software verification at the Boeing Company and operating system implementation at Advanced Micro Computers. He has been with Nestar Systems, Inc., Palo Alto, CA, since January 1982 where he has been involved in networking protocols and file server design and implementation.

Jerry Whitnell received the B.S. degree in computer science from the University of California at Santa Barbara, Santa Barbara, CA.

He joined Nestar Systems, Inc., Palo Alto, CA, in May 1982 to work on the Plan 4000 network. His interests include programming languages, software tools, computer architecture, and local area networks.

Mr. Whitnell is a member of the IEEE Computer Society.

A CENTRALIZED-BUS ARCHITECTURE FOR LOCAL AREA NETWORKS

A. S. Acampora   M. G. Hluchyj   C. D. Tsao

American Bell
Holmdel, New Jersey 07733

ABSTRACT

A Local Area Network architecture based upon a centrally located short bus is described. This architecture enjoys several distinct advantages relative to bus architectures of a distributed nature. Among these are (1) the ability to operate the short bus at high data rates and traffic loads, independent of the geographical separation among interconnected devices, (2) a simple media access protocol that permits the integration of widely disparate traffic types, including real-time synchronous data and voice, and (3) centralized administration and maintenance. The bus contention mechanism results in a flexible distributed scheduling of packets that not only provides low contention delay under heavy traffic load conditions, but also permits the integration of circuit- and packet- switching features on a common bus. Traffic is collected by a system of geographically distributed remote concentrators that interconnect with the centrally located short bus by means of high capacity point-to-point links such as optical fibers. With its modular construction, the centralized-bus architecture provides necessary flexibility to serve new needs and take advantage of new technologies.

1. INTRODUCTION

Local Area Networks (LANs) are data communication networks limited in geographic scope to a building or campus of buildings. Such networks are intended to provide high-bandwidth communication (typically between 1 Mb/s and 100 Mb/s) over inexpensive transmission media with low error rates. A principal application for LANs is that of providing the communications backbone for future office and factory automation.

Over the past decade, numerous architectures for LANs have been proposed. Two such architectures are the distributed bus and ring, with each having many variations [1,2]. We use the adjective "distributed" when referring to these architectures to indicate that the media access electronics in each case are distributed throughout the network. Specifically, as illustrated in Figures 1 and 2, near each device (e.g., terminal, computer) to be connected to the network is an interface (BIU for Bus Interface Unit and RIU for Ring Interface Unit) that sits between the device and the transmission medium. It is the function of this unit to interface between the communication protocols associated with the device and those associated with the network.

In this paper, we describe a different LAN architecture based upon a centrally located short bus as shown in Figure 3. This architecture is an extension of the DATAKIT™ Packet Switch invented by A. G. Fraser [3]. Here, the BIUs are single circuit cards physically housed within a common cabinet, and the bus consists of backplane wiring that terminates each BIU. Access lines radiate out from the central hub to the devices connected to the network. The

---

DATAKIT is a trademark of AT&T.

short-bus architecture enjoys a fundamental advantage relative to distributed approaches in that the propagation delay along the length of the bus is smaller than the transmission time of a single bit, even at data rates of tens of megabits per second. This feature can be exploited to provide simplicity and efficiency in accessing the transmission medium.

Much effort has gone into the design of media access protocols for distributed bus and ring architectures. The two most popular are CSMA/CD (Carrier Sense Multiple Access with Collision Detection) for the bus and Token Passing for the ring [1,2]. Many investigators have analyzed and compared the performance of these two schemes (see, e.g., [4,5]). For CSMA/CD one finds that the efficiency degrades with an increase in bus length or transmission rate, or a decrease in message size. Token Passing shows a reduction in performance as the ring latency increases, which occurs as more RIUs are added to the transmission medium. The throughput-delay performance of both media access schemes are often compared with that achieved by "perfect scheduling." Perfect scheduling, where both collisions and channel idles during busy periods are eliminated, represents a desired but generally unattainable level of performance in a distributed system. Its performance is a lower bound on the throughput-delay performance of any media access protocol for distributed bus and ring architectures. One of the remarkable features of a centralized short-bus architecture is that perfect scheduling of message transmissions is possible using a very simple media access protocol. Moreover, we shall see that with an overhead cost of as little as three bits per packet, one can implement a flexible distributed scheduling of the transmission medium which includes multiple priority classes, round-robin-like scheduling within each priority class, and even integrated circuit- and packet-switching. With these features, efficient integration and servicing of disparate traffic types (including real-time synchronous data and voice) are readily achieved.

With its interface units and high-bandwidth transmission medium maintained in a common cabinet, the centralized architecture enjoys several other advantages relative to a distributed architecture. A common location for all electronics permits ease of monitoring and servicing of the various network components. This implies that when a failure occurs, the time required to locate and replace the defective component can be greatly reduced. Also, since the high-bandwidth transmission medium has merely to span a distance proportional to the cabinet size, it is less susceptible to electromagnetic interference or accidental severing. Note that the data rate on any access line between the central hub and an attached device need not be any higher than that required by the device. Moreover, severing or interfering with any access line affects only the service provided to the attached device. Concerning privacy, since the interface units and shared transmission medium are housed in a common cabinet, no device has direct access to the communication channel. This makes it difficult for any device to eavesdrop on other conversations.

Reprinted from *The Proceedings of the IEEE International Conference on Communication*, 1983, pages 932-938. Copyright © 1983 by The Institute of Electrical and Electronics Engineers, Inc.

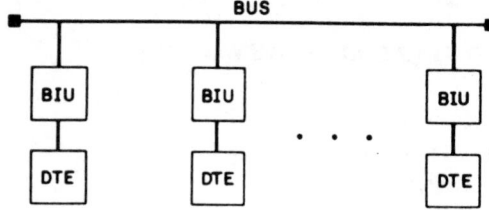

Figure 1. Distributed Bus

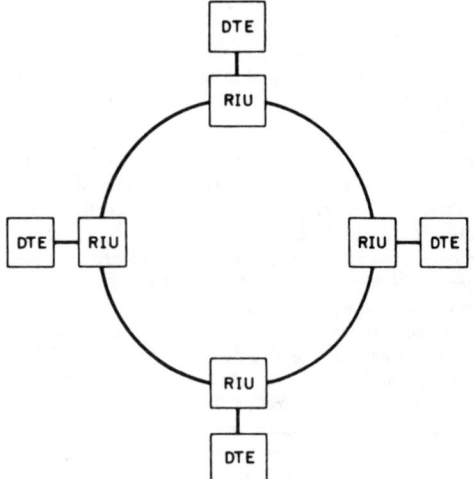

Figure 2. Distributed Ring

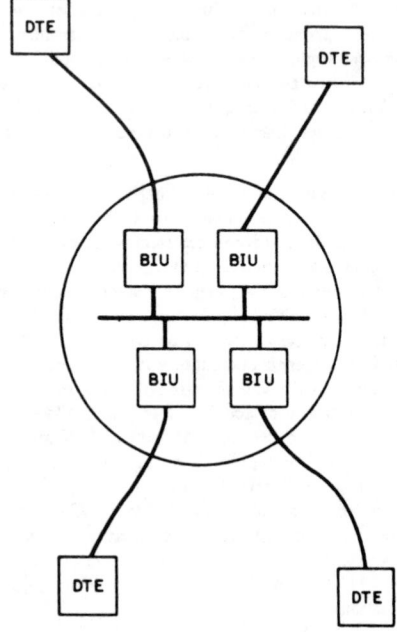

Figure 3. Centralized Bus

The same attributes of modularity and reliability associated with a distributed architecture can also be achieved with a well designed centralized architecture. To add additional devices, one simply adds additional access lines (if they are not already part of the building wiring) and the appropriate BIUs. As with the distributed bus, the BIUs are designed such that the failure of any one does not affect communication among the others. In practice, of course, all architectures exhibit failure modes capable of causing a network-wide service disruption. Good engineering design will ensure that such failures are sufficiently infrequent.

We begin in Section 2 with a brief description of the DATAKIT Packet Switch and how we propose to extend it for an LAN environment. In Section 3 we describe the bus access protocol and present representative examples of delay versus load. In Section 4 we extend the basic architecture to that of a rooted tree by including remotely located data concentrators with high-speed optical fiber links to the central node. This greatly reduces the amount of building wiring required and extends the range of LAN service. Such fiber links can also connect host computers with the central node. A common fiber protocol, implemented by the remote concentrators and/or host computers, permits use of a single BIU design at the central hub.

2. FUNDAMENTALS OF THE CENTRALIZED-BUS ARCHITECTURE

The centralized-bus architecture that we propose for configuring Local Area Networks has its origins with the DATAKIT Packet Switch invented by A. G. Fraser [3]. A modified version of the DATAKIT Packet Switch forms what we refer to as a *node* in our LAN architecture. For consistency we shall refer to the DATAKIT Packet Switch as a DATAKIT node. The physical and functional characteristics of a DATAKIT node are shown in Figures 4 and 5, respectively. Physically it consists of a cabinet into which one plugs interface modules (i.e., BIUs), each a separate circuit card. The interface modules are fundamental to the building-block philosophy of the DATAKIT Packet Switch. Certain modules are used for connecting terminals (say through RS232 ports) to the node, others interface to host computers, and still others exist for trunking between DATAKIT nodes. All have a common interface to the backplane so that they may be interchanged at will. All data enters and exits a node via the interface modules.

In addition to interface modules at a node, there exists a clock module and a switch module, along with two data buses - the contention bus and broadcast bus - that reside on the backplane. Data incoming to an interface module from a device is divided into fixed-length packets which then enter a queue (FIFO) for eventual transport on the time-slotted contention bus. The header of each packet transmitted on the contention bus contains a source address consist-

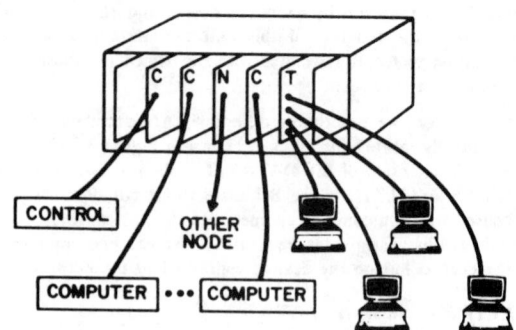

Figure 4. Physical View of a DATAKIT Node

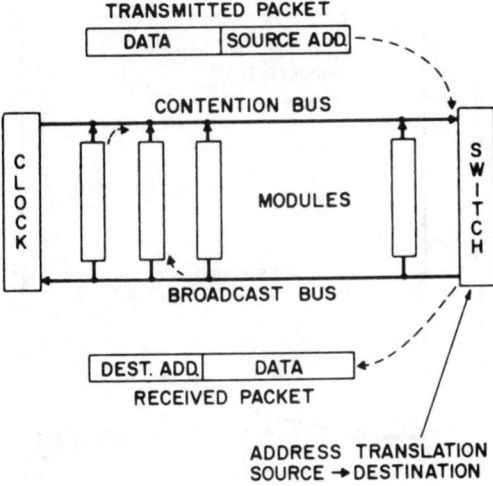

Figure 5. Functional View of a DATAKIT Node

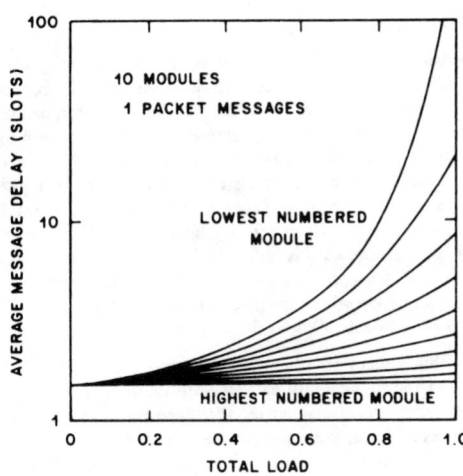

Figure 6. DATAKIT Fixed Priority Delay Performance

ing of a module number followed by a channel number. As shown in Figure 5, each transmitted packet is removed from the contention bus by the switch module which translates the source module and channel numbers to the destination module and channel numbers. The specific translation is established by a prior call set-up procedure. The packet is then retransmitted on the broadcast bus where it is received by the specified destination module. The destination channel number indicates to which of the conversations passing through the module the packet belongs. In this way, a virtual circuit transport mechanism is implemented. There is a processor at the node that handles call set-up and take-down along with necessary maintenance and administration functions. Finally, the clock module generates timing signals that are distributed to all modules via additional buses on the backplane not shown in Figure 5.

There are two fundamental properties associated with the contention bus that allow packet transmissions to be perfectly scheduled. First, the bus is "short" in the sense that the end-to-end propagation delay is less than the time to transmit one bit. Second, each module can simultaneously transmit and receive with the bus functioning as a logical OR.[1] Hence, before the end of a bit transmission (where all modules are bit synchronized), each module will observe the state of the bus to be the logical OR of all transmitted bits. This leads to the following simple mechanism for resolving contention on the bus. At the start of each time-slot (i.e., the synchronized beginning of a packet transmission on the bus), each module with a buffered packet begins transmitting its module number (most significant bit first) while simultaneously reading the bus. After each bit, if what a module transmitted differs from what is on the bus, it stops contending. More specifically, if a module transmits a 0 and receives a 1, it refrains from transmitting any additional bits during the current time-slot. In effect, it yields the bus to those modules with higher module numbers. Hence, at the end of the module number transmission, the contending module with the highest module number wins the contention and continues to transmit the remainder of its packet without interference. One may view the contention process as a simple binary tree search, similar to one proposed by Hayes [6] in a polling context. Mark [7] proposed a similar contention scheme using a separate channel to resolve bus contention.

---

1. This characteristic is present in open collector bus drivers where the conducting state (0 volts = logical 1) has dominance over the nonconducting state (+3 volts = logical 0).

There are two important points to note here. First, since it is necessary in any packet-switching architecture to include unique address information in the transmitted packets, the module number does not represent any additional overhead to the contention process. Second, although perfect scheduling is achieved, contention based only on the module number results in an unfair allocation of the bus. As shown in Figure 6 (using results derived in [8]), under heavy loading, packets from high numbered modules incur considerably smaller delay than those from low numbered modules. In the next section we show how to avoid this unfairness, and yet take advantage of the priority structure, without requiring that module numbers change with time.

The architecture that we propose for Local Area Networks differs from that of the DATAKIT Packet Switch in two ways. First, by appending additional contention bits before the module number we obtain a more flexible scheduling of the bus. Second, to solve the local distribution problem, we add concentrators to each node forming a tree topology rooted at the node. (Using trunk modules, nodes within the network may be connected in an unconstrained topology.) These two modifications are discussed in the next two sections.

3. FLEXIBLE DISTRIBUTED SCHEDULING OF THE CONTENTION BUS

To obtain a more flexible scheduling of packets on the contention bus, we append additional bits to the beginning of each packet. We refer to these as priority bits and refer to their assigned value as a priority code. Unlike the module number, priority codes can change with time and two or more modules may use the same priority code simultaneously. The bus contention occurs over both the priority code and module number. Thus, after the priority code transmission, only those contending modules using the highest priority code continue to contend using their module numbers.

It is apparent that one can form different priority classes through use of the priority codes. In fact, the selection of a priority code can be traffic dependent. For example, network control messages could use a higher priority code than interactive data messages which in turn could use a higher priority code than long file transfers. It is also possible, however, to use the priority bits to achieve a fair round-robin-like scheduling within a priority class. Moreover, one can use the priority bits to integrate circuit- and packet-switched services on the shared bus. We first describe these two techniques separately, and then indicate how they can be efficiently combined.

Group Contention

Suppose that all modules belong to the same priority class, and that we wish to have a fair scheduling of the bus within this class. Without changing module numbers, this can be accomplished with one priority bit. The technique, referred to as group contention, was devised by A. G. Fraser [9] and works as follows. When a module first contends for the bus, its priority bit is set at 0. If it loses contention because another contending module had this bit set at 1, it continues to contend with its priority bit set at 0. If it loses contention and the winner had this bit set at 0, it contends in the next, and all subsequent slots until it wins, with its priority bit set at 1. Whenever a module wins contention, its priority bit is reset, if necessary, to 0 before contending again.

With this contention scheme, cycles appear on the bus for which all slots but the first contain packets with the priority bit equal to 1. In effect, each module is given the opportunity to transmit one packet in each cycle, with the proviso that a packet newly arriving to an interface module must wait until the next cycle before it can be transmitted. Hence, with group contention, a more equitable sharing of the bus is achieved. This is illustrated in Figure 7 (using results derived in [10] and the same parameters as in Figure 6), where upper and lower bounds on the average delay for the lowest and highest numbered modules, respectively, are plotted.

By appending additional priority bits to the beginning of each packet, multiple priority classes can be formed with separate group contention algorithms operating within each class. Figure 8 shows the average delay performance for each of three priority classes. Note that the bus can be operated at a higher total load by assigning priorities to each traffic type according to its delay requirement.

Integrated Circuit- and Packet-Switching

With or without group contention, access to the bus is asynchronous: contention may cause packets from the same device to be delayed varying amounts before transmission. Certain applications in a LAN environment, however, require real-time synchronous transmission of data where both the bandwidth and delay are fixed, PCM voice, for example, requires such a service. Although packet-switching is quite effective for asynchronous traffic, synchronous service is typically provided using circuit-switching techniques. To take advantage of the benefits of resource sharing, there is considerable interest in integrating these two services [11,12,13]. We now show how this can be accomplished using the priority bits.

We define a frame interval, containing an integral number of time-slots, such that periodic access to a given slot position in each frame constitutes a synchronous circuit. We propose two simple distributed schemes for establishing and maintaining a synchronous circuit on the contention bus. The first uses one priority bit, the second uses two.

In the first scheme, the single priority bit is always at 0 for asynchronous traffic. A module wishing to establish a synchronous circuit first contends for the bus with its priority bit set at 0. As illustrated in Figure 9, when it eventually wins contention, it transmits its first packet and then continues the transmission in the same slot one frame later. Here, and until the completion of its transmission, the priority bit is set at 1. To relinquish its synchronous circuit, the module simply stops transmitting.

Note that with this scheme, the module is guaranteed that its "captured" slot is available every frame. This follows since the priority bit set at 1 prevents any asynchronous or new synchronous transmissions (contending with priority bit set at 0) from accessing the slot, and any ongoing synchronous transmission in that slot would have prevented the module from capturing the slot initially.

With the second scheme, we are able to make available slots unused in a synchronous circuit for asynchronous traffic. Slots may be unused because the actual synchronous transmission rate may be

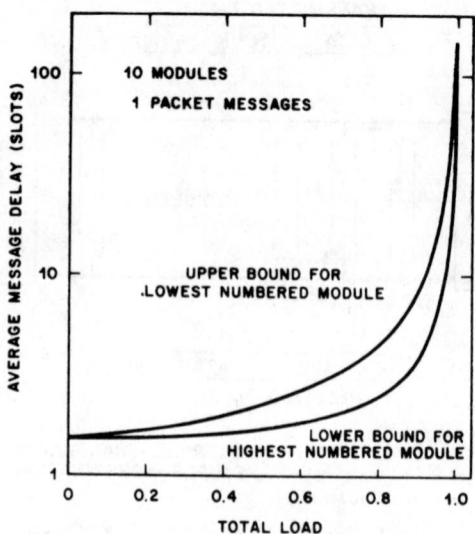

Figure 7. Bounds on Group Contention Delay Performance

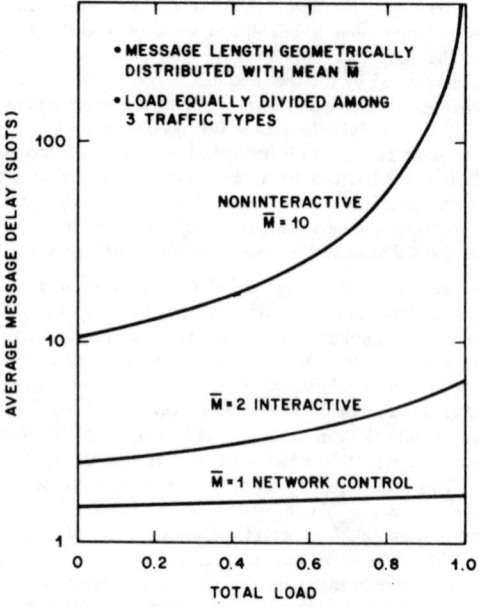

Figure 8. Delay Performance for Mixed Traffic Types

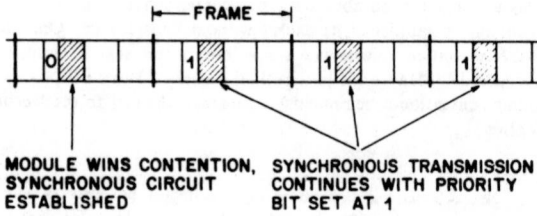

Figure 9. Simple Integrated Circuit- and Packet-Switching

less than the frame rate. In addition, the synchronous circuit may be established for the duration of a conversation, but only used intermittently by the attached device (e.g. with voice, the circuit may be unused during silence periods). The mechanism that we propose to make this unused capacity available for asynchronous traffic in no way interferes with synchronous transmissions. In fact, a module holding a synchronous circuit has instantaneous control over which of the slots comprising its circuit it frees for asynchronous traffic.

In the second scheme, two priority bits are used as follows. When a module wishes to establish a synchronous circuit, it proceeds as before with its two priority bits set at 00. After eventually winning a slot, this slot is available for its use in the next frame and every frame thereafter until the module chooses to relinquish it. When the module wishes to use the slot, it sets its two priority bits to 11. When it does not need the slot in a given frame, but prefers to keep the synchronous circuit for later use, it sets the priority bits to 01 and contends for the slot only during the two priority bits. Finally, asynchronous transmissions have the priority bits set at 10. Note that the priority code 11 prevents any other module from accessing the captured slot. The priority code 01 allows asynchronous packets (with priority code 10) to use the slot, but prevents new synchronous transmissions (with priority code 00) from capturing the slot. This is illustrated in Figure 10.

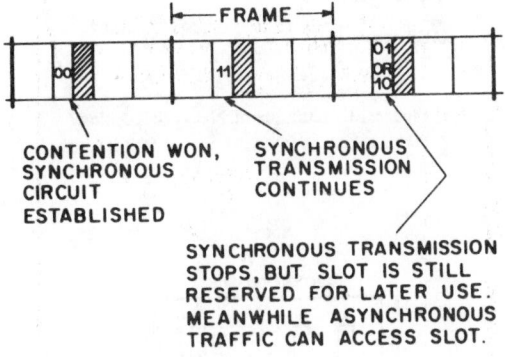

Figure 10. Integrated Circuit- and Packet- Switching with Efficient Use of Slots

Priority Code Assignment

We now wish to assign priority codes to accommodate the second scheme for integrating synchronous and asynchronous traffic, along with multiple priority classes for asynchronous traffic and group contention within a priority class. Figure 11 gives such a priority code assignment using only three priority bits. Here synchronous transmission assumes the highest priority code and synchronous contention (for establishing a synchronous circuit) and synchronous reservation (for freeing unused slots to asynchronous traffic) occupy the two lowest priority codes. The five remaining priority codes are used by the asynchronous traffic to form three priority classes. The lower two classes use two priority codes each, where the two most significant bits define the priority class and the least significant bit is varied according to Fraser's group contention scheme. In general, if n priority bits are used, there will be $2^n - 3$ priority codes for asynchronous traffic; where a group contention priority class requires the use of two codes.

PRIORITY CODES	FUNCTION
111	SYNCHRONOUS TRANSMISSION
110	NETWORK CONTROL
101	INTERACTIVE TRAFFIC
100	INTERACTIVE TRAFFIC
011	NONINTERACTIVE TRAFFIC
010	NONINTERACTIVE TRAFFIC
001	SYNCHRONOUS RESERVATION
000	SYNCHRONOUS CONTENTION

(ASYNCHRONOUS TRAFFIC: 110, 101, 100, 011, 010)

Figure 11. A Priority Code Assignment

4. LOCAL DISTRIBUTION AND INTERNETWORKING

Local Distribution

A Local Area Network may provide communications among a very large number of devices. Due to physical space limitations at the node, and for economic reasons, it may be prohibitive that every device be connected to the node by a dedicated access line. Under these conditions we propose the use of remote *concentrators*, as shown in Figure 12, to permit sharing of an interface module at a node among several devices. Each remote concentrator is connected to the node by a high-speed point-to-point link, such as an optical fiber. For inherently high-speed devices, such as host computers, a separate fiber might be deployed from the node for exclusive use by that device. The overall topology of the centralized-bus LAN has now become hierarchical. Devices are leaves located at the bottom of a rooted tree, concentrators are represented by intermediate branching points, and the root is the node containing the switching function.

The architecture of the concentrator is very similar to that of the node. The concentrator contains an assembly of modules, each one a separate circuit card. The same interface modules that previously resided at a node, can, in fact, be used in the concentrator. Each such module operates the same access protocol, as described in Section 3, to transmit fixed-length packets on a time-slotted contention bus. A simplified "switch" module directs all traffic from devices connected to the concentrator to an interface module located at the node. The switch residing at the node provides the necessary routing function, according to the module and channel numbers accompanying each packet. In this way, no address translation switch or call control processor is required at the concentrator, which functions only as a statistical multiplexor.

As already mentioned, optical fiber is an excellent candidate for use as the transmission link between each concentrator and the node. It offers significant size and weight advantages relative to wire

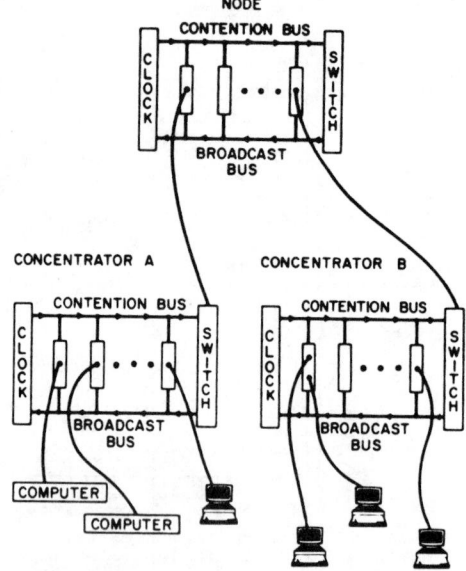

Figure 12. Interconnections between Concentrators and Node

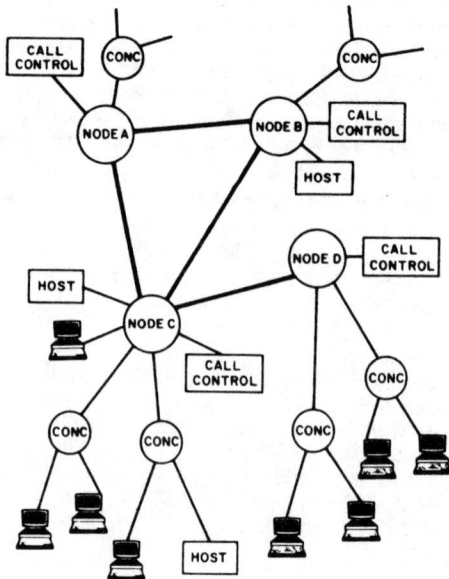

CONC: CONCENTRATOR

 : TERMINAL

Figure 13. Example of Network Topology

(twisted pair) and coaxial cable, and is also immune from interference. Its high-bandwidth can be exploited to permit packet assembly and disassembly to be done remotely at the concentrator, thereby reducing the complexity at the node. The fiber terminates at the remote concentrator which serves several devices, thereby permitting a single fiber to be shared among these devices. By implementing a common protocol on all fibers, all modules at the node with a fiber interface become identical. The concentrators and direct fiber-connected hosts assume the responsibility for implementing the common fiber protocol. Use of a common fiber protocol also facilitates node-to-node internetworking to be described next.

Internetworking

It may be desirable to allow interconnection of nodes, either to handle traffic growth or to accommodate a very large number of devices in a Local Area Network environment. This can be achieved by linking trunk modules located at different nodes, forming a network as indicated in Figure 13. For connecting two nodes on the same premises, two high-speed trunk modules (one at each node) are connected by an optical fiber employing the common fiber protocol. Low-speed trunk modules operating at say 56 kb/s can be used for connecting nodes located at different sites over DDS lines. In either case, devices communicate over trunk modules through end-to-end virtual circuits that are established at call set-up by the call control processors along the virtual circuit paths. This virtual circuit approach simplifies the necessary control logic in each trunk module. Note also that a relatively small packet size may be used, thus permitting the pipelining of data to reduce end-to-end transport delay in the internetworking environment.

A Local Area Network is often only one part of a more global communication system. Devices may need to communicate with remote devices through a private or public long-haul network. This is accomplished by designing a gateway, which might take the form of a module located at a node as illustrated in Figure 14. The gateway is shared among all devices that reside on the same LAN, and performs necessary protocol translations, address mapping, and speed matching between the LAN and long-haul network.

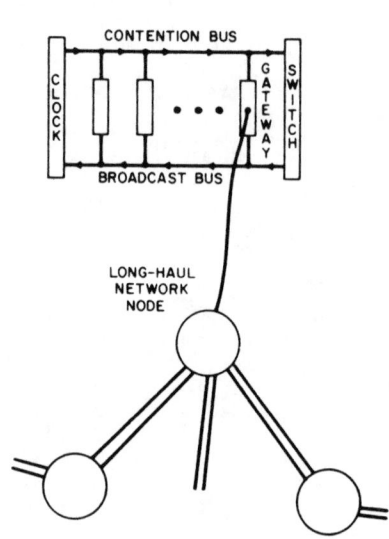

Figure 14. Interconnection between a Node and Long-Haul Network

130

5. CONCLUSIONS

We have described the architecture of a centralized-bus Local Area Network having several distinct advantages over other LAN architectures of a distributed nature. Its short-bus construction permits a flexible distributed scheduling of the shared transmission medium which includes (1) multiple priority classes, (2) round-robin-like scheduling within each priority class, and (3) the integration of circuit- and packet-switching services. With these features one can satisfy the individual delay requirements of widely varying traffic types, and yet at the same time increase the usable bus capacity.

Other advantages associated with the architecture include (1) a central location for maintenance and administration, (2) difficult direct access to the shared transmission medium resulting in greater privacy of communication, and (3) modular construction which provides necessary flexibility to serve new needs and take advantage of new technologies. In addition, without changing the attached devices, access lines, concentrators, or fibers, one can upgrade the bus data rate at the node and thus increase the capacity of the system. This may be done, for example, by using a parallel, rather than a serial, bus for data transport and a separate serial bus for contention. Here, contention for a given time-slot occurs during the previous time-slot on the separate centention bus.

The use of remote concentrators simplifies the building wiring and allows a larger number of devices to access a single node. With the use of trunk modules, both intrapremises and interpremises nodes can be interconnected providing a simple mechanism for network growth. Finally, gateways may be used to establish connections with long-haul networks, thus achieving an overall communications capability.

REFERENCES

[1] D. D. Clark, K. T. Pogran, D. P. Reed, "An Introduction to Local Area Networks," *Proc. IEEE*, vol. 66, pp. 1497-1517, Nov. 1978.

[2] C. Tropper, *Local Computer Network Technologies*, Academic Press, NY, 1981.

[3] A. G. Fraser, "Datakit - A Modular Network for Synchronous and Asynchronous Traffic," *Proc. ICC*, pp. 20.2.1 - 20.1.3, June 1979.

[4] W. Bux, "Local-Area Subnetworks: A Performance Comparison," *IEEE Trans. on Comm.*, vol. COM-29, pp. 1465-1473, Oct. 1981.

[5] E. Arthurs et al., Traffic Handling Characteristics Committee Report, IEEE Project 802 on Local Area Network Standards, Working Draft - June 1982.

[6] J. F. Hayes, "An Adaptive Technique for Local Distribution," *IEEE Trans. on Comm.*, vol. COM-26, pp. 1178-1186, August 1978.

[7] J. W. Mark, "Distributed Scheduling Conflict-Free Multiple Access for Local Area Communication Networks," *IEEE Trans. on Comm.*, vol. COM-28, pp. 1968-1976, Dec. 1980.

[8] M. G. Hluchyj, C. D. Tsao, R. R. Boorstyn, "Performance Analysis of a Preemptive Priority Queue with Applications to Packet Communication Systems," *submitted to the BSTJ.*

[9] A. G. Fraser, private communication.

[10] M. G. Hluchyj, C. D. Tsao, "Analysis of a Synchronous Gated Polling System," (in preparation).

[11] G. J. Coviello, P. A. Vena, "Integration of Circuit/Packet Switching by a SENET (Slotted Envelope Network) Concept, "*NTC Conf. Rec.*, pp. 42-12 - 42-17, Nov. 1975.

[12] M. J. Ross, A. C. Tabbot, J. A. Waite, "Design Approaches and Performance Criteria for Integrated Voice/Data Switching," *Proc. IEEE*, vol. 65, pp. 1283-1295, Sept. 1977.

[13] H. Rudin, "Studies on the Integration of Circuit and Packet Switching," *ICC Conf. Proc.*, pp. 20.2.1 - 20.2.7, June 1978.

A New Local Area Network Architecture Using a Centralized Bus

Anthony S. Acampora
Michael G. Hluchyj

Combining the advantages of bus, ring, and star architectures for LAN devices

August 1984—Vol. 22, No. 8
IEEE Communications Magazine

LOCAL AREA NETWORKS are currently enjoying tremendous popularity as a means for providing wideband interconnection and communications among data terminals, host computers, and other types of digital equipment located throughout a single building or a campus of buildings. Such networks are typically based on bus, ring, or star architectures, each of which manifests its own set of advantages and disadvantages. In this paper, an architectural approach is described that draws upon and integrates the advantages found separately in these three different architectures, while avoiding the major disadvantages found in any one. This new architecture employs a centrally located short bus that provides an extremely efficient packet-switching service to the devices attached to the network. Bandwidth on the short bus is dynamically allocated in response to instantaneous demands by means of a highly efficient but flexible priority-based bus contention scheme. The approach permits multiple priority classes with fair allocation of bandwidth within each class, along with a capability for integrated circuit and packet switching. The architecture can also make use of existing twisted-pair building wiring, and at the same time take advantage of emerging optical-fiber technology. In addition, the architecture provides a means to expand the network beyond a local area, resulting in a wide-area network capability.

Introduction

In recent years, many different architectures have emerged for Local Area Networks (LAN's) based on star, bus, and ring topologies [1]. Arguments abound concerning the superiority of one LAN architecture over another, but in fact, on close examination, each has its own set of advantages and disadvantages.

Star topologies, as applied to LAN's, are typically implemented around a digital PBX core. A digital PBX enjoys the advantage of superior network management features, where centralization eases fault detection and isolation and permits careful system configuration and performance tracking by an administrator. Also, centralization makes for a more secure system, and although it can be cumbersome at the switch itself, the twisted-pair building wiring is uniform and backed by years of installation and maintenance experience.

On the negative side, the circuit-switched architecture of traditional digital PBX's does not permit high-speed statistical multiplexing of data; the end devices are often limited to a single 64-kb/s digital pipe through the switch. Not only is this circuit-switched connection poorly matched to the demands of bursty data traffic, with switch ports unnecessarily tied up for long periods with little or no interactive traffic, but the limited data rate is not conducive to high-speed host-to-host communications. Furthermore, the lack of statistical multiplexing hinders the trend toward multiple virtual connections between devices, and does not make efficient use of generally expensive leased trunking facilities between locations.

Distributed-bus and ring LAN architectures avoid the major pitfalls of a traditional circuit-switched PBX by providing shared, packet-switched access to a single high-speed data channel. The distributed nature of these architectures also allows for simple modular growth. In addition, some contend that distributed architectures are inherently more reliable.

EHO228-7/85/0000/0132$01.00 © 1984 IEEE

This, however, is arguable since even with these architectures there exist failure modes capable of bringing down the entire network; these are often more difficult and time consuming to isolate than with a centralized architecture.

In the literature, most LAN comparisons are made between distributed-bus and ring architectures and their respective media-access techniques [2,3]. Beyond questionable security, arguments against distributed-bus architectures center on the CSMA/CD media-access scheme and its limitations: cable length, bus transmission rate, packet size vs. efficiency trade-off (see the section entitled "Bus Contention"), instability at high utilizations, and nondeterministic delays. Furthermore, it has been argued that a distributed bus cannot make use of current optical-fiber technology. Arguments against token-passing rings center on the protocol complexity to protect against lost tokens, and hardware complexity to protect against broken rings and failed ring interface units. It is also argued that, when devices are added to or removed from a distributed bus, no disruption in service is experienced, in contrast to rings. Finally, with both architectures, the associated protocols are geared for one network located on one premises; interconnection of networks for either on-premises growth or interpremises communications requires gateways.

In what follows, we describe a new LAN architecture—based on a centrally located short bus—that combines the advantages of the digital PBX, distributed-bus, and ring architectures while avoiding their disadvantages. Like the digital PBX, the centralized nature of this new LAN architecture allows for secure communications with a rich set of network management features for fault detection and isolation, and system configuration and performance tracking. However, as with distributed-bus and ring architectures, it avoids the major drawbacks of a circuit-switched PBX by providing shared, packet-switched access to a single high-speed data channel—the short bus.

Unlike distributed-bus and ring architectures, the media-access scheme, which takes advantage of the small propagation delay on the bus, is both simple and efficient. It achieves a perfect scheduling of packet transmissions wherein there are neither destructive collisions nor periods when the bus is idle with packets awaiting transmission. Moreover, this desirable characteristic is robust with respect to the geographical separation among the attached devices, the bus transmission rate, and the selected packet size. In particular, a small packet size, say under 200 bits, can be selected to provide a high degree of pipelining through the system. In addition, the scheduling of packet transmission is flexible, permitting multiple priority classes, round-robin-like scheduling within a priority class, and even integrated circuit and packet switching. With these features, efficient integration and servicing of disparate traffic types are readily achieved.

Two other areas in which the centralized-bus architecture has important advantages over other LAN architectures are building distribution and networking. The building distribution allows for the use of twisted-pair wiring from an office to a satellite closet, while avoiding wire congestion at the central location through the use of a fiber-optic backbone. Besides its small size and light weight, fiber also enjoys the advantages of high bandwidth, high noise immunity, and security from tapping. Finally, as we describe in the next section, the basic building block in the centralized-bus

architecture is a node containing a fast hardware packet switch designed specifically for use with virtual circuits. As such, nodes can be interconnected via simple interfaces, to both permit on-premises growth and provide metropolitan and nationwide networking without the need for complex gateways.

Basic Network Architecture

The shared transmission medium in the centralized-bus architecture is a short bus, consisting of backplane wiring in a cabinet, with the bus interface units (referred to as interface modules) residing in the cabinet on separate circuit cards (as shown in Fig. 1). The short-bus backplane and interface modules form the basic building blocks of the LAN, from which concentrators and network nodes are constructed.

As illustrated in Fig. 2, the concentrators, nodes, and attached devices (such as terminals, workstations, hosts, and printers) are interconnected using point-to-point transmission media. The nodes may be interconnected in a flexible mesh topology, using optical fiber for on-premises connections and leased or private transmission facilities for interpremises connections. As Fig. 2 further shows, each node taken alone is the root of a tree—the attached devices form the leaves and the concentrators form the branch points. Fiber again would be used for connecting the concentrators to the node and also for attaching devices, such as host computers, that require a high-speed multiplexed data link to the network. Terminal and workstation connections to a node or concentrator may be made with twisted-pair wiring.

The architecture of the node has its origins in the DATAKIT[1] Packet Switch invented by A. G. Fraser [4]. All data enters and exits a node via the interface modules which all have a common interface to the backplane. Each interface module contains bus contention logic and packet buffers, along with any functionality associated with the particular interface (for example, an asynchronous terminal interface module would have a packet assembly and disassembly function). As Fig. 3 shows, a node also contains a clock module, a switch module, and a common control processor, along with the three data busses that reside on the backplane—the transmit, broadcast, and contention busses.

---

[1]DATAKIT is a trademark of AT&T.

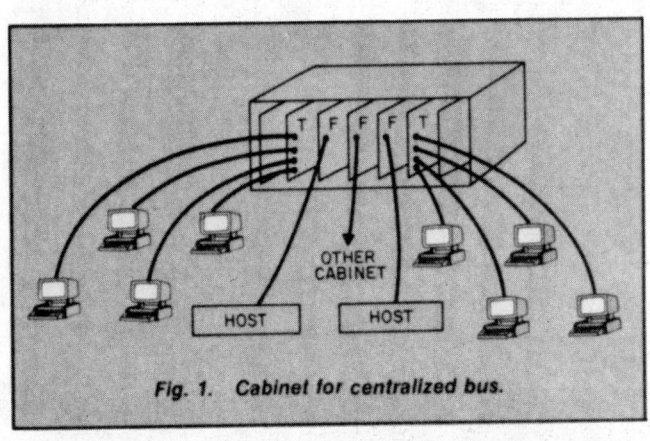

Fig. 1. Cabinet for centralized bus.

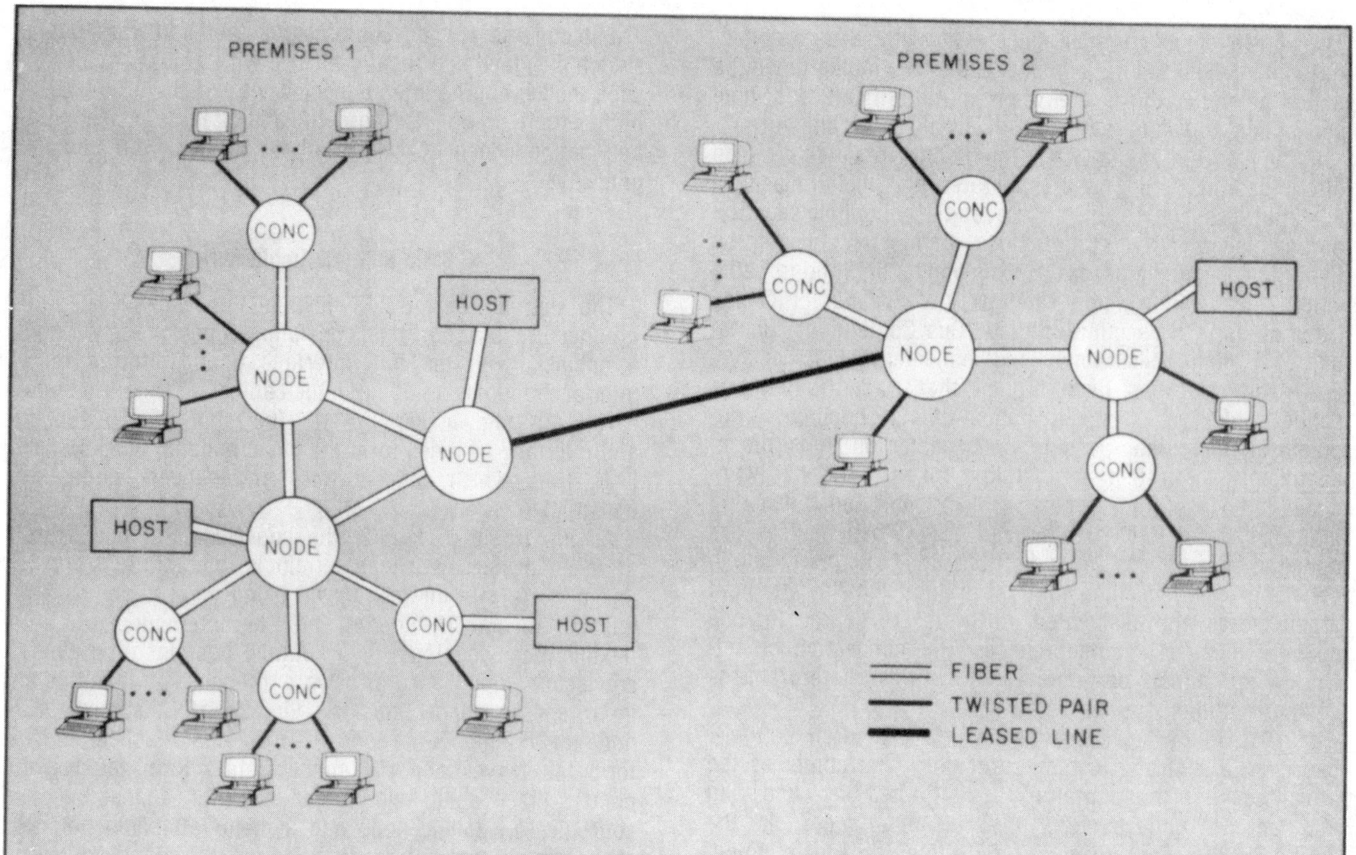

Fig. 2.   Network structure.

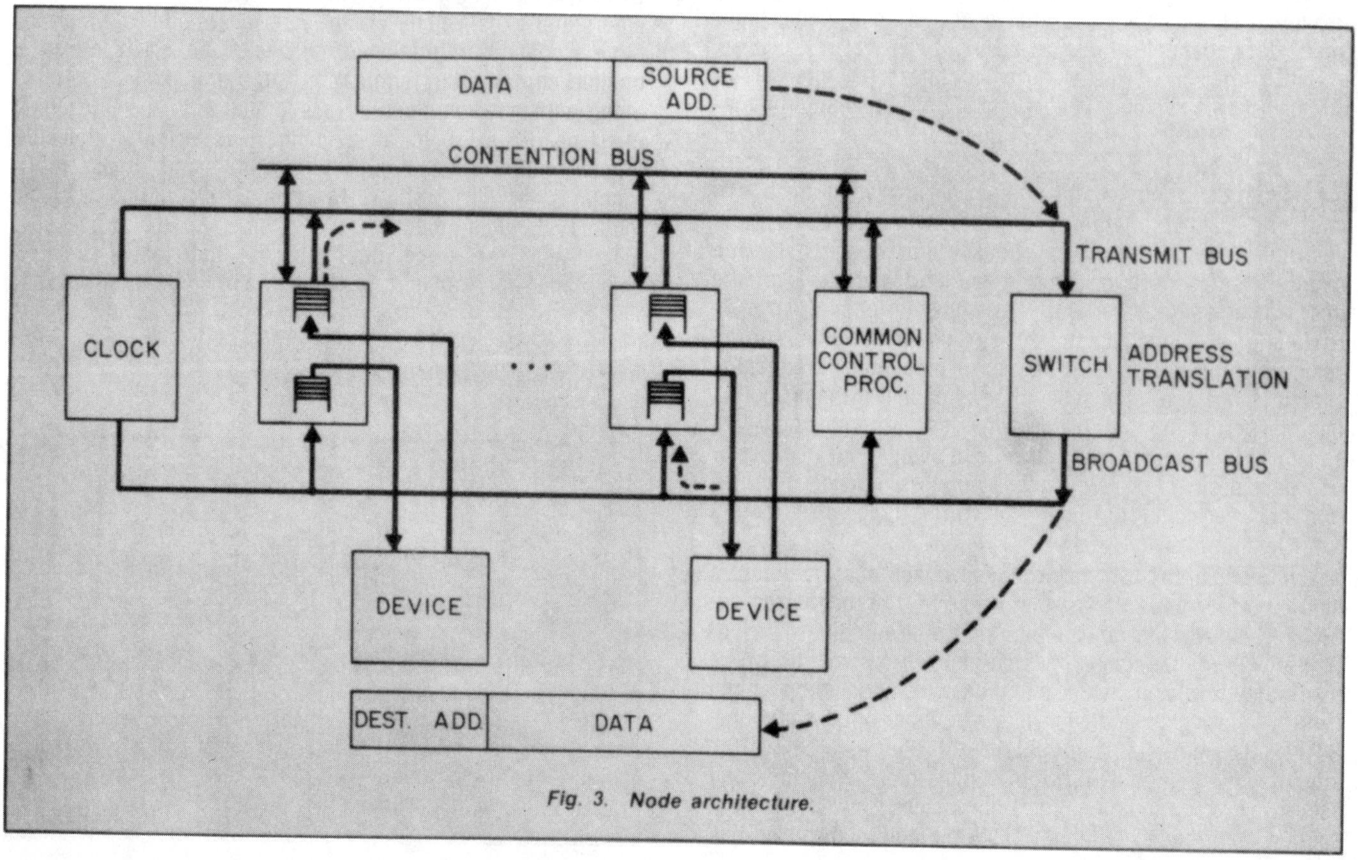

FIBER
TWISTED PAIR
LEASED LINE

Fig. 3.   Node architecture.

As we describe later, the contention bus is used by the interface modules to gain access to the time-slotted transmit bus. The transmit bus and broadcast bus are used for sending and receiving packets, respectively. The header of each packet placed on the transmit bus by an interface module contains a source address consisting of a module number followed by a channel number. The module number uniquely identifies the transmitting interface module, and the channel number is used to distinguish among the different conversations passing through that module. As Fig. 3 shows, each packet placed on the transmit bus is removed by the switch module, which translates the source module and channel numbers to the destination module and channel numbers. The specific translation is established by a prior call-set-up procedure. The packet is then retransmitted on the broadcast bus where it is received by the specified destination module. In this way, a virtual circuit transport mechanism is implemented, wherein the common control processor at the node handles call step-up and take-down along with necessary maintenance and administration functions.

A packet passing through two or more nodes first has its source module and channel numbers translated, by the switch module at the first node, to those of a trunk interface module, also located at the first node. After receiving the packet, this trunk module strips the module number and, retaining the channel number information, transports the packet over the trunk to a trunk interface module located at the second node. Here, the packet contends for access to the transmit bus of the second node, and is transmitted with the new trunk module number and the same channel number used over the trunk. The switch module at the second node translates this address to the destination address at the second node, which may be that of the end device or, if the packet is destined for another node, that of another internode trunk module. The proper address translation at each node along the path is established during the call-set-up procedure. Note that, although we are discussing the centralized-bus architecture in the context of LAN's, the nodes and trunk interface modules can be used to construct wide-area networks with an arbitrary mesh topology.

The last major component of the centralized-bus architecture is the concentrator. Although a concentrator cabinet may be smaller than that of a node, both may share a common backplane design, thus permitting the same interface modules to be used in either the concentrator or node. Unlike the node, however, the concentrator would not contain a switch module or a common control processor (CCP). All packets placed on the concentrator transmit bus are forwarded, via optical fiber, to a fiber interface module at the node. (Contention for the concentrator's transmit bus is resolved via the same mechanism applied at the node.) Likewise, all packets coming from the node are placed on the concentrator broadcast bus to be received by the destination interface module. In this way, neither switching nor call control processing is done at the concentrator, which functions only as a statistical multiplexor.

Having described the basic components of the centralized-bus architecture, the remainder of the paper will focus on four important aspects: bus contention, networking, building distribution, and network management. The centralized-bus architecture finds its major strengths in these four areas.

Bus Contention

Often emphasized when comparing packet-switching LAN architectures are the performance and complexity of the associated media access schemes. The simplicity, efficiency, and flexibility of the bus contention scheme emerge as clear advantages of the centralized-bus architecture. In this section we describe the contention scheme, compare its performance with other access schemes, and describe its inherent flexibility.

Short-Bus Contention Scheme

Access to the transmit bus in both the node and concentrator is governed by a bus contention scheme operating on a separate serial contention bus. As shown in Fig. 4, both the transmit bus and contention bus use the same slot timing (generated by the clock module) and operate in parallel; contention for a given time slot on the transmit bus occurs in the previous time slot on the contention bus. A contention code is transmitted in each access time slot on the contention bus; this consists of a priority code followed by the module number for the "winning" module. This module has won the sole right to transmit one fixed-length packet onto the transmit bus in the next time slot. Messages arriving to a module of length greater than this fixed-length packet are decomposed into a sequence of fixed-length packets; all such packets independently contend, in sequence, for access to the transmit bus. The contention process, which occurs at the beginning of each time slot, is such that the module having the highest contention code wins contention and transmits its packet in the next time on the transmit bus. Although the module number is fixed and unique to each interface module on the backplane, the priority code can change with time, allowing a flexible distributed scheduling of packet transmissions.

The contention mechanism itself relies on two properties of the contention bus. First, the bus is short in the sense that the end-to-end propagation delay is less than the time to transmit one bit. Second, each module can simultaneously transmit and receive with the (open collector) contention bus

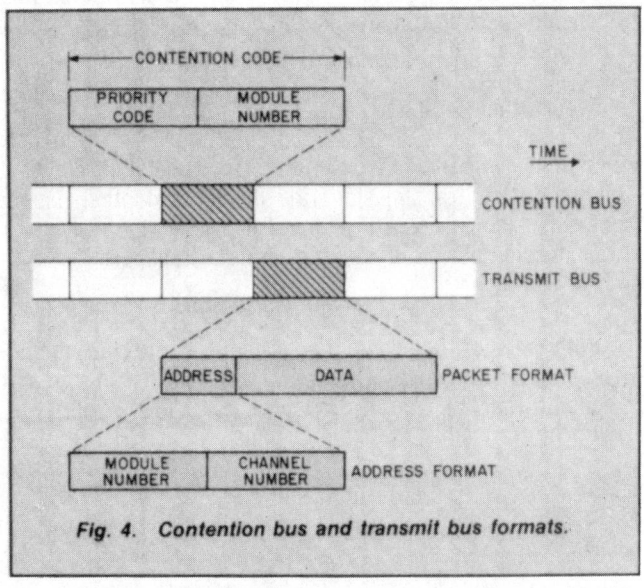

Fig. 4. *Contention bus and transmit bus formats.*

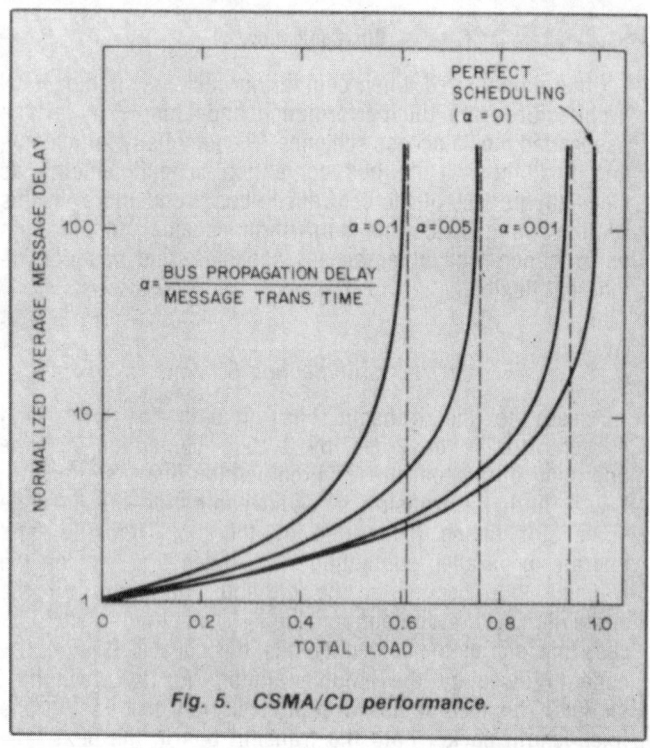

Fig. 5. CSMA/CD performance.

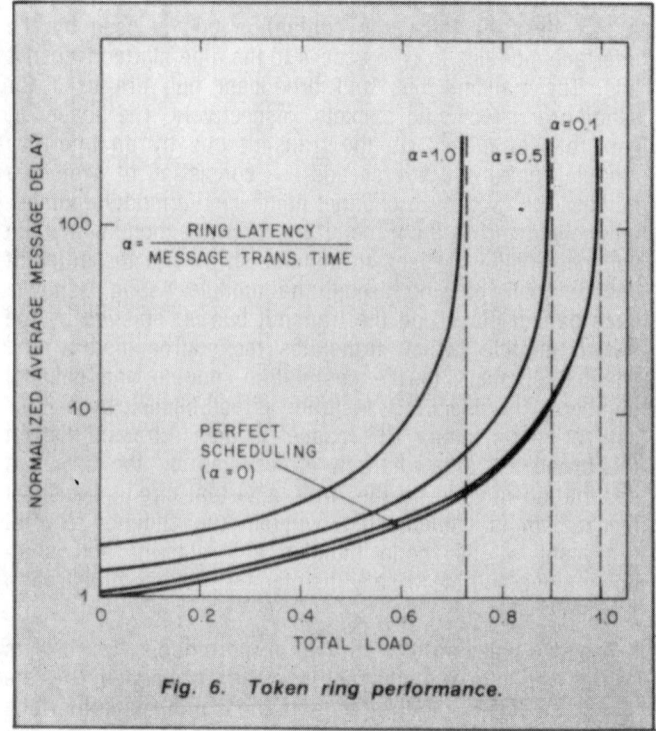

Fig. 6. Token ring performance.

functioning as a logical OR. Hence, before the end of a bit transmission on the contention bus, each module observes the state of the bus to be the logical OR of all transmitted bits. This leads to the following simple scheme for resolving contention. At the start of each time slot, each contending module begins transmitting its contention code on the contention bus. If what a module transmits differs from what is read off the bus after each bit, it stops contending. That is, if a module transmits a 0 and reads a 1, it drops out of contention and waits for the next time slot before contending again. Hence, by the end of the time slot, the contending module with the highest contention code wins contention and then transmits, without interference, its packet in the next time slot on the transmit bus.

One may view the contention process as a simple binary tree search, similar to one proposed by Hayes [5]. Mark [6] proposed a similar contention scheme for a distributed bus. It should also be noted that the contention process could take place at the beginning of each time slot on the transmit bus [7], eliminating the need for a separate contention bus. However, the use of a separate contention bus decouples the contention process, and its restriction on the bit transmission time, with that of packet transmission; this allows a higher packet transmission rate than would otherwise be possible. In particular, a parallel rather than a serial transmission bus could be used for data transport.

Performance Comparisons

With the short-bus contention scheme, an interface module contends continuously whenever it has a packet to transmit; modules that lose contention back off without interfering with the transmission of the eventual winner. Hence, aside from a small delay of between 1 and 2 slot times[2]

[2]Note that at 10 Mb/s, a 200-bit packet size corresponds to a slot time of only 20 μs.

(corresponding to the time waiting for the start of the next time slot and contention for access to the transmit bus), packet transmissions are perfectly scheduled, avoiding both collisions and bus idle periods when there are packets awaiting transmission. This is to be contrasted with popular media-access schemes, such as CSMA/CD and token passing for distributed-bus and ring architectures, respectively [1]. Figures 5 and 6 show what have now become well-known delay vs. load performance results for CSMA/CD and token passing (single-token system). Here, the average delay is normalized with respect to the mean message-transmission time, and the total load is the fraction of bus capacity utilized in the successful transmission of messages. The CSMA/CD performance curves in Fig. 5 were obtained from results derived in [8] under the assumptions of Poisson message arrivals and exponentially distributed message lengths. The token passing performance curves in Fig. 6 were obtained under the same assumptions from results derived in [9].

For CSMA/CD, the parameter α in Fig. 5 corresponds to the ratio of the bus end-to-end propagation delay and the mean time to transmit a message. Note from Fig. 5 that the delay vs. load performance for CSMA/CD degrades from that of perfect scheduling as α increases from zero. An increase in α results from an increase in the bus length or transmission rate, or a decrease in the mean message size. For a system with a 2-km cable length and a mean message length of 1000 bits, the three values of α—0.01, 0.05, and 0.1—in Fig. 5 correspond respectively to a bus transmission rate of 1, 5, and 10 Mb/s. Note that as α increases, the fraction of usable bandwidth provided by the bus diminishes, that is, the delay experienced approaches infinity at smaller normalized offered loads. This trade-off between bus length, transmission rate, and message length is a fundamental limitation of CSMA/CD systems arising from finite speed-of-light considerations.

With token-ring architectures, the media-access efficiency decreases as the ring latency increases. The ring latency is the delay in transmitting a bit completely around the ring, which includes both the ring propagation delay and the processing delay at each ring interface unit. Figure 6 shows the degradation in performance for a single token system as α (now the ratio of the ring latency and the mean message transmission time) increases. Note that α increases with an increase in the ring length, transmission rate, number of interface units, or processing delay per interface unit; or with a decrease in the mean message size. For a system with 50 interface units, a 2-km cable length, and a mean message length of 1000 bits, the three values of α—0.1, 0.5, and 1.0—in Fig. 6 correspond respectively to a transmission rate and per-interface-unit processing delay of 5 Mb/s and 1 bit, 10 Mb/s and 8 bits, and 20 Mb/s and 16 bits. Again, we note that the usable bandwidth decreases as α increases.

From these comparison results, we conclude that the perfect scheduling performance for the short-bus contention scheme is superior to that of CSMA/CD and token passing. In particular, its performance is robust with respect to the bus transmission rate, geographical separation and number of attached devices, and selected packet size. The ability to use small packets, in fact, becomes important when considering the pipelining performance of a system.

Pipelining Considerations

The performance results shown thus far have ignored the effects of the access line speed. Implicit in the results is an assumption that each message generated by a device arrives instantly to its respective network interface unit. For LAN's, the speed of the shared transmission media (bus or ring) is typically much greater than the access line speed, particu-larly when considering that most terminals connected to LAN's today operate at less than 20 kb/s. Figure 7 illustrates the reduction in transport delay, under these conditions, that is possible by dividing messages into small packets and pipelining them on a high-speed bus. It is assumed that the line speeds for both transmitting and receiving devices are equal but less than the bus transmission rate, and that there is no other traffic on the bus (that is, the bus contention delay is zero). The "excess delay" indicated in each case is that delay in excess of the situation where the two devices are directly connected. The excess delay for the pipelined case is simply the time to receive one packet of data over the access line plus the time to transmit the packet on the bus. For the nonpipelined case, the excess delay consists of the entire line delay for the message plus the time to transmit the message on the bus. Hence, the excess delay for the pipelined case is proportional to the packet size, while the excess delay for the nonpipelined case is proportional to the message size.

There is, of course, a limit on how small a packet size one can select. With a fixed overhead per packet, as one reduces the packet size there results an increase in the percentage of overhead. However, the use of virtual circuits reduces the address overhead for each packet, so that even a small packet, containing say 16 data bytes, can maintain a per-packet addressing overhead of under 10%.

The advantage of the centralized-bus architecture and its ability to pipeline traffic becomes clear by considering a specific example. Suppose that a large number of sources are attached, by means of 64-kb/s access lines, to an LAN bus operating at 10 Mb/s. Furthermore, assume that each source generates exponentially distributed messages of mean length $\overline{M}$ according to a Poisson process; the LAN traffic load is increased by increasing the message arrival rate. Two cases are compared with the results shown in Fig.

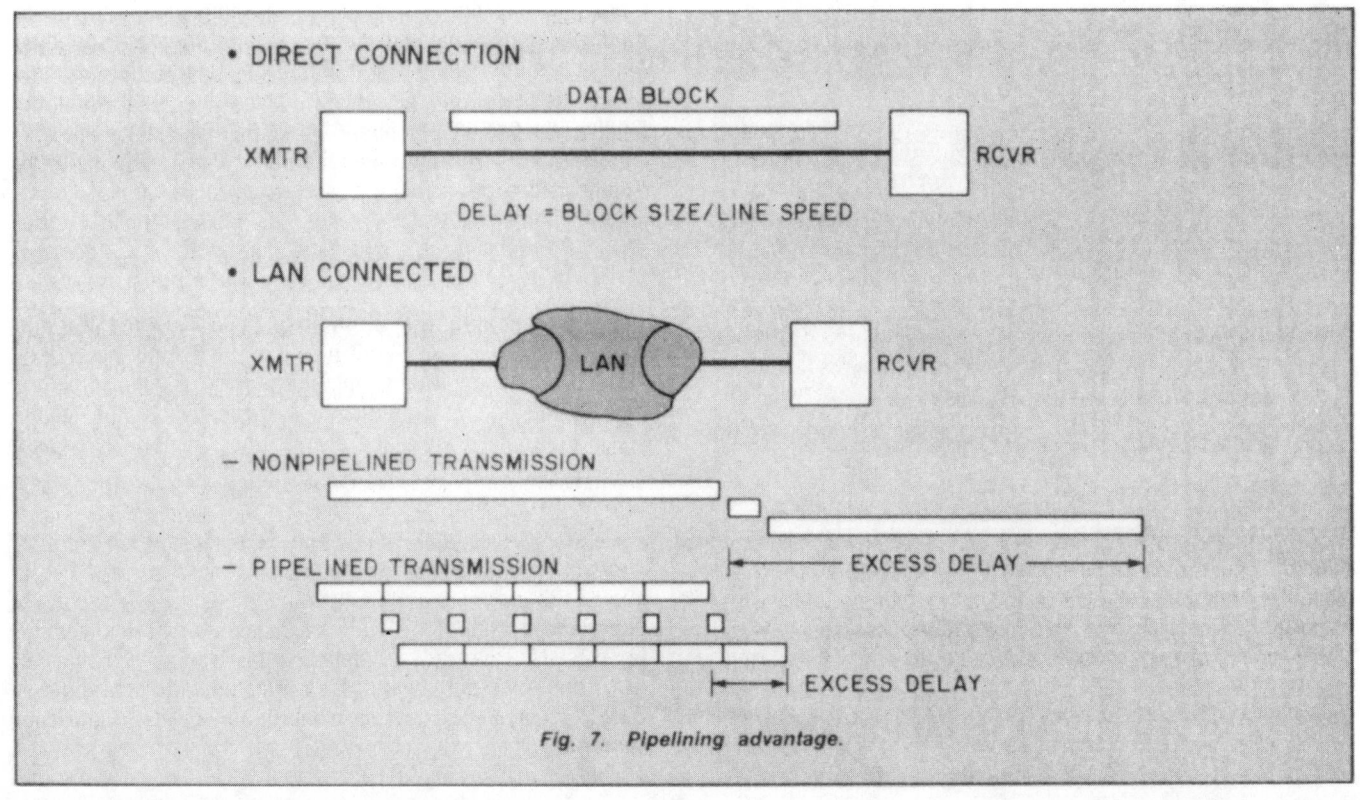

Fig. 7. Pipelining advantage.

8. For the first case, the mean message length M is 1000 bytes, and the LAN is a short bus with a packet size of 16 bytes. For the second case, the LAN is a 2-km distributed bus using the CSMA/CD contention protocol and, to bring out all relevant points, mean message lengths of 16 bytes and 100 bytes are considered, along with the 1000-byte mean message length assumed for the short-bus LAN. The short-bus performance curve in Fig. 8 was obtained through an approximate analysis based on the $M/M/m$ queuing model (where the number of servers $m = 10 \cdot 10^6/64 \cdot 10^3 \simeq 156$) [10]. The CSMA/CD curves were obtained by adding a message line delay to the results derived in [8]. In both cases, any per-message or per-packet overhead was ignored.

We note from Fig. 8 that, as a result of pipelining, the average excess delay for the short bus is about 2 ms (this is the time it takes for 16 bytes to arrive over the 64-kb/s access line) for traffic loads as high as 80%. In this regime, the bus-contention delay is negligible in comparison to the 2-ms packetization delay. Above 80% load, however, the contention delay overshadows the packetization delay and so the average excess delay grows rapidly with increasing load. Note that one can view the 10-Mb/s bus as providing 156 time slots every 2 ms; each time slot contains 16 bytes, and access to one time slot every 2 ms provides a 64-kb/s channel. Hence, up to 156 simultaneous messages can be pipelined through the short bus with the bus contention delay upper bounded by 2 ms. Only when the number of simultaneous messages arriving at the bus exceeds 156 can transmission delays grow beyond 2 ms.

For the 2-km distributed bus, several effects are noted. First, for a mean message length of 1000 bytes, good bus utilization efficiency is achieved since α (the ratio of the bus end-to-end propagation delay and the mean message transmission time on the bus) is small. However, the average excess delay for light loads is about 125 ms. To reduce this excess delay, suppose that sources are restricted to transmit messages with mean lengths of 100 bytes rather than 1000 bytes. Then the delay at light loading falls to about 12.5 ms, but the distributed-bus LAN becomes unstable at traffic loads greater than 55%. Similarly, if the mean message length is limited to 16 bytes to provide an excess delay of 2 ms at light loading (comparable to the short bus), then the distributed-bus LAN becomes unstable for offered loads greater than 17%. Thus, we see that a distributed bus with CSMA/CD cannot simultaneously provide low-excess delay and high-bandwidth utilization efficiency. By contrast, the short-bus contention scheme provides a lower bound on excess delay as compared to any distributed-bus parameter set.

The pipelining advantage becomes even more dramatic when one considers networking among LAN nodes by means of off-premises transmission facilities. Here, because bandwidth is generally much more expensive, the transmission rates of off-premises communications links might be 2 or 3 orders of magnitude lower than typical LAN rates. Under these conditions, the pipelining advantage is enjoyed along each link on a path from source to destination. Specifically, suppose that a particular network connection involves K nodes, as shown in Fig. 9. For simplicity, suppose that the access lines connecting the end devices, as well as all internode trunks, operate at a data rate of R b/s. Without pipelining, the entire message is assembled at each node input port before placing the message on the corresponding high-speed bus, and at each output port before the message is sent over a trunk or device access line. Following the single-node discussion, and ignoring any message overhead, it follows that, without pipelining, the excess delay incurred at light loading is

$$D_{excess} = K[M/R + M/S]$$

where S is the data rate on the high-speed bus and M is the length of the message. With pipelining, it is only necessary that single packets from a long message be assembled before placing the packet onto the high-speed bus or the lower-speed internode trunks and access lines. Hence, the excess

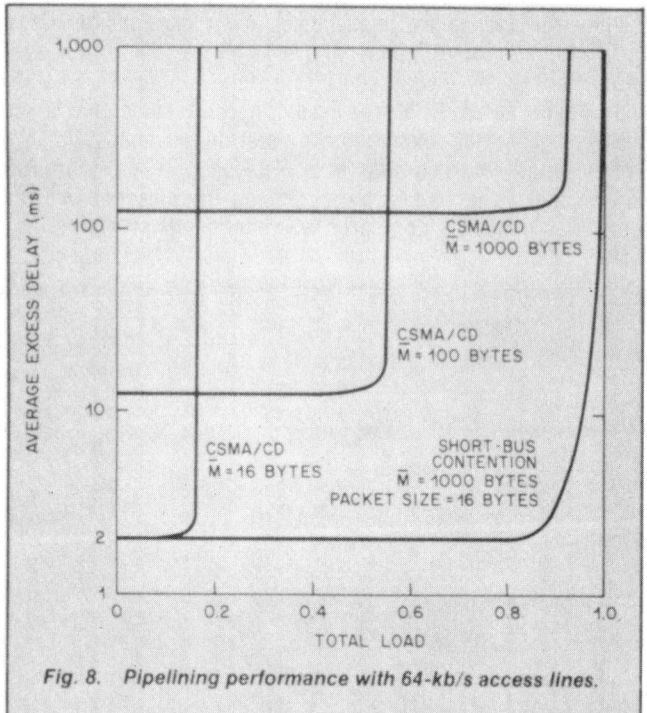

Fig. 8.   Pipelining performance with 64-kb/s access lines.

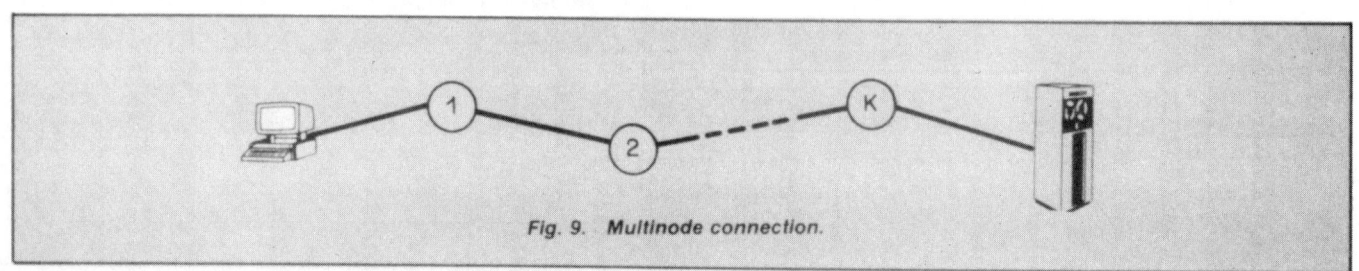

Fig. 9.   Multinode connection.

delay with pipelining is independent of the message length and is given by

$$D_{\text{excess}} = K[P/R + P/S]$$

where P is the packet size and, again, any packet overhead is ignored.

A simple numerical example is instructive. Suppose that a particular path in the network passes through three nodes, and R = 64 kb/s. Let the bus speed S be 10 Mb/s and the message length M be 1000 bytes; and, for pipelining, let the packet size be 16 bytes. Then, at light loading, the excess delay without pipelining is 377 ms; with pipelining, the excess delay is only 6 ms. Improvement of almost two orders of magnitude is noted with pipelining.

The concept of dividing messages into small units before transmission in a data-communications network is not new. The advantages of such an approach have long been recognized and, in fact, have resulted in the acceptance of packet-switching over message-switching techniques. The point to be made here, however, is that the media-access efficiency of the short-bus contention scheme is, unlike that in CSMA/CD and token passing, insensitive to the selected packet size. Hence, one has the flexibility to select a small packet size without incurring a loss of media-access efficiency, and thereby enjoy a small end-to-end delay by virtue of message pipelining.

Flexible Distributed Scheduling

Along with perfect scheduling of packet transmissions and its associated performance advantages, the bus contention mechanism also provides considerable flexibility in the way packets are scheduled. As described earlier, the contention code used by an interface module is composed of two parts: a priority code followed by the module number. The module number ensures that no two interface modules ever contend using the same contention code. Basing contention on the module number only, however, would result in an unfair allocation of the bus. Under heavy loading, packets from lower-numbered modules would incur a larger delay than those from higher-numbered modules. This could be avoided by having the module number itself change with time [11], but this requires a certain amount of coordination among the interface modules to ensure that no two ever use the same number. Preceding the fixed module number with a priority code, which can change with time, avoids this problem and in fact permits much flexibility in scheduling packet transmissions on the bus.

One may, for example, make use of the priority code to assign different types of traffic to different priority classes. Network control messages could use a higher priority code than interactive data messages, which in turn could use a higher priority code than long file transfers. In addition, by using two consecutive priority codes (say differing in the least-significant bit) for each priority class, one can achieve a fair round-robin-like scheduling within the priority class. This technique, which is based on an algorithm that has been around for some time [12], has modules switching from the lower priority code to the higher to ensure a fair sharing within the priority class. Specifically, a module first contends using the lower of the two priority codes. If the module loses contention because either: 1) a module in a higher priority class won, or 2) a module in its own priority class won using the higher priority code, it continues to contend using the lower priority code. If the module loses contention and the winner was in its priority class using the lower priority code, the module contends in the next time slot and all subsequent time slots, until it wins, using the higher priority code. Whenever a module wins contention, it begins its next contention using the lower priority code.

For each priority class using this scheme, variable-length cycles appear on the contention bus for which all time slots won by the priority class (except the first in the cycle) have the priority code set at the higher value. In effect, each module in the priority class is given the opportunity to transmit one packet in each cycle, with the proviso that a packet newly arriving to an interface module must wait until the next cycle before it can be transmitted.

Another use of the priority code, described in [7] and illustrated in Fig. 10, guarantees a module access to a time slot on a periodic basis, much like circuit-switched TDMA. With this technique, a module first contends with a low-priority code and then, after winning a time slot, contends periodically using a higher priority code. A variation on this technique allows a module holding such a synchronous circuit to relinquish unused slots to asynchronous traffic.

Hence, we see that the perfect scheduling performance of the short-bus contention scheme is further enhanced by its great scheduling flexibility. This flexible scheduling is made possible by the inherent priority structure in the contention mechanism.

Networking

An important feature of the centralized-bus architecture is its ability to conveniently support internode networking to accommodate both on-premises growth and interpremises

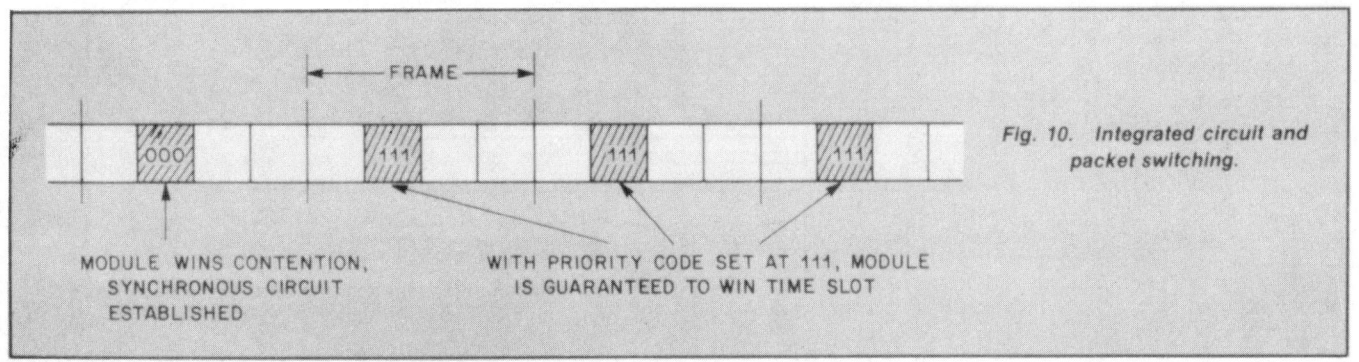

Fig. 10. Integrated circuit and packet switching.

MODULE WINS CONTENTION, SYNCHRONOUS CIRCUIT ESTABLISHED

WITH PRIORITY CODE SET AT 111, MODULE IS GUARANTEED TO WIN TIME SLOT communications. As Fig. 2 shows, nodes can be interconnected in an arbitrary mesh topology using bidirectional, point-to-point transmission facilities carrying statistically multiplexed traffic between nodes. For on-premises growth, optical fiber can be used for node interconnection; for interpremises communications, use may be made of leased (for example, DDS or T1) or private (for example, microwave) transmission facilities. In both cases, two nodes are interconnected simply by inserting, into the backplane of each, a trunk module that interfaces to one end of the communications link. The trunk modules themselves need not contain much intelligence since their main functions involve bus contention, packet buffering, and interfacing to the internode transmission facility. The real intelligence for internode networking resides in the CCP located at each node.

The CCP's communicate with each other over the internode trunks to establish end-to-end virtual circuits through the network. A device (such as a terminal) originating a call to another device (such as a host computer) first communicates its request to the CCP located at its node. The CCP determines whether the called device resides at its node; if it does not, it proceeds to select, according to a routing algorithm, an outgoing trunk to another node to communicate the request. This next CCP in turn determines whether the called device resides at its node and, if not, selects an outgoing trunk to another node to communicate the request. This process repeats until arriving at the node at which the called device resides. Then, assuming the destination device accepts the call, the process works its way backwards to the originating device, across the established path, with the appropriate address translations written into the switch module memory at each node. Once established, this path through the network remains fixed for the duration of the call, thus maintaining the proper sequence of packets delivered to the destination.

The virtual circuit service provided for both single and multinode configurations in the centralized-bus architecture makes for a highly effective data-transport capability. By using the same basic building blocks to construct both local-area and wide-area networks, one eliminates the need for complex gateways required in other architectures for network growth. Also, since full source-destination addressing is not required in each packet, addressing overhead can be kept to a minimum. Coupled with the bus contention efficiency, this permits the use of short packets to achieve a high degree of message pipelining, as discussed in the previous section. Finally, if desired, a permanent virtual circuit connection can be established between devices to remove the need for call set-up, while still using bandwidth only when there is data to transmit.

Building Distribution and Network Management

Important components of any LAN are its building distribution system and its network management features and services. Coaxial cable (both broadband and baseband), optical fiber, and twisted-pair wiring are all prominent candidates for an LAN transmission medium. The centralized-bus architecture conveniently exploits the latter two in a manner consistent with conventional building wiring for voice transmission. Referring to Fig. 11, we note that conventional voice wiring consists of two types of cabling: riser cables (between floors) and lateral cables (horizontal at each floor). The lateral cables terminate in remote apparatus and satellite equipment closets, from which emanate the individual twisted-pair cables running to each telephone.

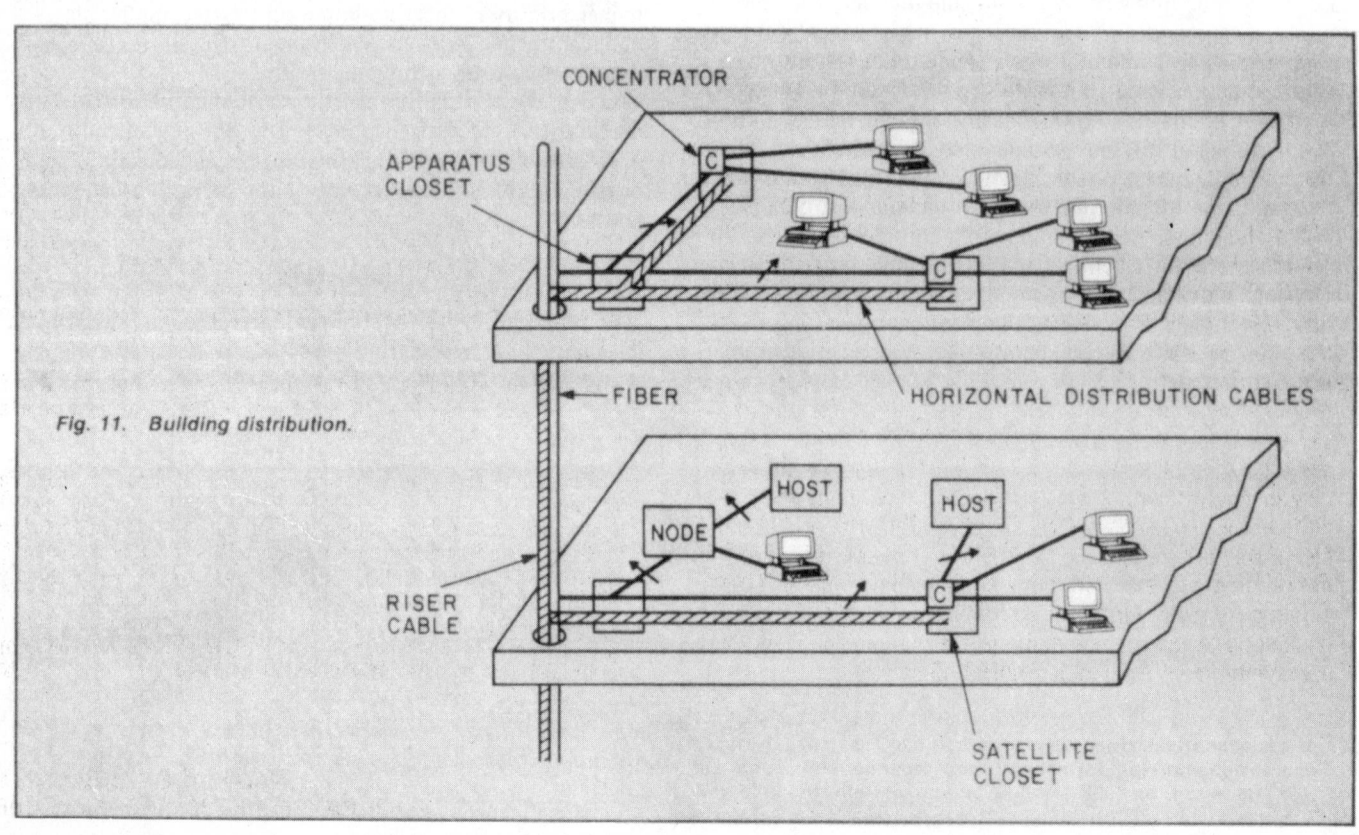

Fig. 11. Building distribution.

Appropriate cross-connect panels are housed in the apparatus and satellite closets.

The centralized-bus architecture permits the superposition of LAN transmission media onto such a topology. Using relatively short-length (new or existing) twisted-pair wiring, devices can be attached via cross-connect panels to concentrators located in satellite closets. Each concentrator is then connected to a node via a dedicated optical-fiber pair that shares wiring ducts and risers with existing cabling. The small-diameter, high-bandwidth, and light-weight advantages of fiber are exploited to reduce or eliminate the physical congestion problems prevalent in the wiring conduits of many existing buildings. In addition, the fiber links do not interfere with voiceband signals, and are themselves immune to electrical interference. Wideband devices (host computers, for example) requiring bandwidth in excess of that allowable on twisted-pair wiring would be allocated dedicated fibers to a concentrator or back to the node.

With the interface modules and common equipment residing in a relatively small number of locations on a premises, network management in the centralized-bus architecture is made easier. Nodes and concentrators located in computer rooms and satellite closets permit ease of monitoring and servicing of the various network components, and yet can be made secure from access by unauthorized personnel. The CCP could, in addition, play an important role in network management by periodically polling the interface modules for status. The status responses from the modules can be used to monitor the health, performance, and configuration of the network. The CCP might even have an attached, dedicated console for maintenance and administration functions. Finally, the interface modules can be designed so that the removal or, in many cases, malfunctioning of one does not interfere with the operation of the network.

Conclusions

We have described a new LAN architecture that has applications for both on-premises and interpremises data communications. This architecture combines the advantages of digital PBX, distributed-bus, and ring architectures to provide a low-delay, end-to-end virtual circuit connection service to the attached devices. The basic building blocks of the architecture, contained in both the concentrators and packet-switching nodes, are a short-bus backplane, and interface modules for attaching user devices to the network and interconnecting network components. The associated bus contention scheme, taking advantage of the short propagation delay on the bus, eliminates performance problems associated with other LAN architectures and at the same time provides considerable flexibility for scheduling packet transmissions; multiple priority groups, round-robin-like scheduling within a priority group, and even integrated circuit and packet switching are permitted. The architecture can also make use of a twisted-pair/optical-fiber building distribution system that both complements and enhances existing building wiring. In addition, its overall architecture is conducive to maintenance and administration services commonly found only in centralized networks.

References

[1] C. David Tsao, "A local area network architecture overview," *IEEE Communications Magazine*, vol. 22, no. 8, p. 7, Aug. 1984.

[2] J. H. Saltzer, K. T. Pogran, and D. D. Clark, "Why a ring?," *Comput. Networks*, vol. 7, pp. 223–231, 1983.

[3] W. Bux, "Local-area subnetworks: a performance comparison," *IEEE Trans. Commun.*, COM-29, pp. 1465–1473, Oct. 1981.

[4] A. G. Fraser, "Datakit—a modular network for synchronous and asynchronous traffic," *Proc. ICC*, pp. 20.1.1-20.1.3, June 1979.

[5] J. F. Hayes, "An adaptive technique for local distribution," *IEEE Trans. Commun.*, COM-26, pp. 1178–1186, Aug. 1978.

[6] J. W. Mark, "Distributed scheduling conflict-free multiple access for local area communication networks," *IEEE Trans. Commun.*, COM-28, pp. 1968–1976, Dec. 1980.

[7] A. S. Acampora, M. G. Hluchyj, and C. David Tsao, "A centralized-bus architecture for local area networks," *Proc. ICC*, pp. 932–938, June 1983.

[8] S. S. Lam, "A carrier sense multiple access protocol for local networks," *Comput. Networks*, vol. 4, pp. 21–32, 1980.

[9] O. Hashida, "Analysis of multiqueue," *Review of the Elect. Comm. Lab.*, Nippon Telegraph and Telephone Public Corp., vol. 20, 1972.

[10] L. Kleinrock, *Queueing Systems, Vol. 1: Theory*, New York, NY: John Wiley & Sons, 1975.

[11] A. K. Mok and S. A. Ward, "Distributed broadcast channel access," *Comput. Networks*, vol. 3, pp. 327–335, 1979.

[12] R. C. Chen, "Bus Communication Systems," Ph.D. Thesis, Computer Science Dept., Carnegie-Mellon University, Pittsburgh, PA, Jan. 1974.

Anthony S. Acampora was born in Brooklyn, NY on December 20, 1946. He received the B.S.E.E., M.S.E.E., and Ph.D. degrees from the Polytechnic Institute of Brooklyn in 1968, 1970, and 1973, respectively. From 1968 through 1981 he was a member of the technical staff at Bell Laboratories, initially working in the fields of high-power microwave transmitters and radar system studies, and signal processing. From 1974 to 1981 he was involved in high-capacity digital satellite systems research, including modulation and coding theory, time division multiple access methods, and efficient frequency reuse techniques.

In 1981, he became supervisor of the Data Theory Group at Bell Laboratories, working in the field of computer communications and LAN's. In January 1983 he transferred with his group to AT&T Information Systems to continue work on LAN's. In November 1983 he was appointed head of the Radio Communications Research Department at AT&T Bell Laboratories, where his current responsibilities include management of research in the areas of antennas, microwave and millimeter wavelength propagation, terrestrial radio and satellite communication systems, and multiuser radio communications.

Dr. Acampora is a member of Eta Kappa Nu, Sigma Xi, and of the IEEE, and serves as editor for Satellite and Space Communications of the *IEEE Transactions on Communications*.

Michael G. Hluchyj was born in Erie, PA on October 23, 1954. He received the B.S.E.E. degree in 1976 from the University of Massachusetts at Amherst; and the S.M., E.E., and Ph.D. degrees in Electrical Engineering from the Massachusetts Institute of Technology in 1978, 1978, and 1981, respectively. In 1981 he joined the technical staff at Bell Laboratories and in 1983 transferred to AT&T Information Systems. Dr. Hluchyj's work at Bell Laboratories and AT&T Information Systems has centered around the architectural design and performance analysis of LAN's. ∎

Section 3: Ring Type Baseband Networks

While the bus topology for local networks is favored in the United States, in Europe, the most popular topology has been a ring-shaped one. All the networks described in this section are of this type. Recently there has been a resurging interest in ring topology, spurred mainly by IBM's indications that this is the type of network it will use for its products. The efforts to improve the reliablity of ring networks seems to have produced significant advancements, with ring-shaped networks now challenging bus networks in reliablity.

In the first article, Apollo Computer's DOMAIN network is described. The DOMAIN is an integrated distributed system with entirely self-contained workstations. Each machine runs a complete set of standard software providing itself with all the facilities it needs, including file storage and name resolution. However, the DOMAIN will support the use of servers which provide network services like file handling. The choice of which configuration to use is determined by the particular situation in which the network is to be used. The network itself is geared mainly toward scientific-type applications. Its architecture allows the easy implementaion of CAD and CAE.

Proteon's proNET is an example of a star-shaped ring, which is one of the advanced forms of the basic ring topology. Proteon has developed a wire center for each node on the ring that improves the reliability of the ring by passively providing a bypass circuit if any malfunction in its area of the ring occurs. One of the advantages of the ring topology is that fiber optic is easily employed as a transmission medium, since no splitting or joining of the medium is required. Proteon can, therefore, offer fiber optic cabling as an option to coaxial cable.

The next article summarizes what is known about IBM's long-awaited token-ring network. It describes the architecture and system performance of a prototype token-ring local network that was implemented at the IBM Zurich Research Laboratory. The final IBM product, which IBM announced (in 1984) would be released in 1986 or 1987, should not be too different from this prototype.

What IBM did release in 1984 was a cabling system so that prospective token ring customers could wire their buildings in anticipation of the network. The next article briefly describes the IBM Cabling System, which permits traditional types of connections to be made between devices with a common cable consisting of twisted pairs of copper conductors. The cabling system connects wall outlets in offices to wiring closets. Called a star-wired system, the cable fans out from each closet to special outlets. The outlets are installed in the walls to connect to data devices and, optionally, telephones. Most currently available IBM products, including workstations and small and intermediate computers, can be plugged into the outlets.

The integration of fiber optics into local area networks is beginning to become a force in the market, as NEC's C&C Optonet demonstrates. The Optonet is offered with fiber optic cable as the only available transmission medium, making it a true fiber optic network. It was designed primarily for high speed computer-to-computer communication. To date it has been marketed mainly in the Japanese market but it is beginning to be seen in the United States also. This network is used with NEC Telephone's NEAX 2400 PBX to supply a high-speed, local data network to this switch.

The local area network SILK uses the not-so-well-known "buffer insertion" access method. This technique, Hasler claims, gives a better throughput rate than conventional token-passing and has a more constant throughput rate under varying traffic loads than does either token or CSMA access methods. So far Hasler has not found a spot in the United States market place, and their system is being used mainly in Europe.

The article by Hopper and Williamson in this section describes a ring local network based on the empty slot principle. Data are transmitted using minipackets containing two bytes of data at a rate of 10 Mbps. The paper covers the design process, decisions, and trade-offs made in implementing an integrated system which incorporates both analog and digital components. A number of companies, including Logica VTS in London with its Polynet and Racal-Milgo in the United States with its Planet, offer commercial implementations of the Cambridge University ring local network.

The Architecture of an Integrated Local Network

PAUL J. LEACH, MEMBER, IEEE, PAUL H. LEVINE, BRYAN P. DOUROS, JAMES A. HAMILTON, MEMBER, IEEE, DAVID L. NELSON, AND BERNARD L. STUMPF, MEMBER, IEEE

Reprinted form *IEEE Journal on Selected Areas in Communications*, November 1983, pages 842-857. Copyright © 1983 by The Institute of Electrical and Electronics Engineers, Inc.

Abstract —The DOMAIN system is an architecture for networks of personal workstations and servers which creates an integrated distributed computing environment. Its distinctive features include: a network-wide file system of objects addressed by unique identifiers (UID's); the abstraction of a single level store for transparently accessing all objects, regardless of their location in the network; and a network-wide hierarchical name space. The implementations of these facilities exhibit several interesting approaches to layering the system software. In addition to network transparent data access, interprocess communication is provided as a basis for constructing distributed applications; as a result, we have some experience to guide the choice between these two alternative implementation techniques.

Networks utilizing this architecture have been operational for almost three years; some experience with it and lessons derived from that experience are presented, as are some performance data.

I. INTRODUCTION

THIS paper presents the architecture of the Apollo DOMAIN system, an integrated local network of powerful personal workstations and server computers [1], [19]; both are called *nodes*. A DOMAIN system is intended to provide a substrate on which to build and execute complex professional, engineering, and scientific applications [20]. We decided that such a substrate would require three major features

1) a processor with significant computational power and a large virtual address space,

2) a high-speed local area network, and

3) a high resolution graphics display subsystem.

These three features would interact to support the system objectives as follows.

The high computational power of a personal node, plus its support of a large virtual address space, would allow tools that traditionally ran on mainframes or super-mini-computers to easily be ported to the professional's personal node, and to be executed with a performance often even exceeding that attained when sharing the larger machine with many other users.

The high computational power of a personal node, plus its display subsystem, would allow the creation of a human interface to maximize user productivity. In particular, allocating the display into multiple windows would allow multiple concurrent processes, each possessing its own window(s), to be controlled by the user simultaneously.

Manuscript received May 1, 1983; revised August 11, 1983.
The authors are with Apollo Computer, Inc., Chelmsford, MA 01824.

The network, plus a network-wide distributed file system, would allow the professional to share programs, data, and expensive peripherals, and to cooperate via electronic mail with colleagues in much the same manner as on larger shared machines, but without the attendant disadvantage of sharing processing power.

We will focus almost entirely on the networking and distributed systems aspects of the DOMAIN architecture.

A. Architectural Overview

The Eden project [14] and the LOCUS system [22] are two other distributed systems which were designed at about the same time as DOMAIN and which share many of DOMAIN's design goals. Both of them describe themselves as "integrated," but in two senses: one is related to the system's architecture, the other to its structure. These two aspects also apply to DOMAIN.

The DOMAIN architecture creates what the Eden project calls an "integrated distributed" environment: each node possesses a high degree of autonomy, but there are system-provided mechanisms and user-selectable policies that permit a high degree of cooperation and sharing when so desired. In the DOMAIN system, cooperation and sharing are facilitated by being able to name and access all objects in the same way regardless of their location in the network. Thus, all users and applications programs have the same view of the system, so that they see it as a single integrated whole, not a collection of individual nodes. Even so, it is still a distributed system, not a loosely coupled multiprocessor: for example, our emphasis on autonomy, and the expectation of partial failures, led to the design criterion that suitably configured machines must always be able to run even when disconnected from the network; other examples occur below. (Also, the focus primarily on personal workstations, which resulted in a greater emphasis on cooperation and, hence, less on autonomy, distinguishes us from [30].)

The system structure also conforms to the LOCUS "integrated model of distributed systems": each machine runs a complete (but highly configurable) set of standard software, which (potentially) provides it with all the facilities it normally needs—file storage, name resolution, and so forth. In contrast are "server model" distributed systems, wherein network-wide services are provided by designated machines ("servers") which run special purpose software tailored to

145

providing some single service or small number of services (e.g., Grapevine [2], WFS [31], and DFS [29]).

We have observed another aspect of the integrated-model–server-model distinction. Systems based on the integrated model have also stressed a network transparent data access model of computation, and so applications in an integrated environment typically use that model. Likewise, systems based on the server model have also stressed a message-based model of computation, and so applications in a server environment use that model.

The DOMAIN system, although it falls mainly in the integrated model category, nevertheless supports applications built on the other model. In addition to network transparent data access, interprocess communication is provided as a basis for constructing distributed applications; as a result, we have some experience to guide the choice between these two alternative implementation techniques. Our experience has led us to conclude that each model has a set of circumstances under which it is the appropriate choice, and to identify some criteria to making such a choice.

Thus, even though DOMAIN is an integrated distributed system, it has server nodes; however, they are created by configuring the standard software—a "file server" node, say, is made by configuring a machine to run several large disks; and they usually exist not for reasons of system structure, but for reasons like sharing expensive peripherals or large disks.

B. Architectural Features

The key to the integrated distributed environment is a distributed *object storage system* (OSS): a flat space of objects (storage containers) addressed by unique identifiers (UID's). Objects are typed, protected, abstract information containers: associated with each object is the UID of a type descriptor, the UID of an access control list object, a disk storage descriptor, and some other attributes. Object types include: alphanumeric text, record structured data, IPC mailboxes, DBMS objects, executable modules, directories, access control lists, serial I/O ports, magnetic tape drives, and display bit maps. (UID's are also used to identify persons, projects, organizations, and subsystems for protection purposes.) The distributed OSS makes the objects on each node accessible throughout the network (if the objects' owners so choose).

A unique aspect of the DOMAIN system is its network-wide single level store (SLS). (Multics [21] and the IBM System/38 [6] are examples of a single level store for centralized systems.) Programs access all objects by presenting their UID's and asking for them to be "mapped" into the program's address space (see [23] on the desirability of mapping in distributed systems); subsequently, they are accessed with ordinary machine instructions, utilizing virtual memory demand paging. A key component of SLS is the concurrency control mechanism, which manages the simultaneous caching of objects' pages in the primary memories of many nodes.

The purpose of the single level store is not to create network-wide shared memory semantics akin to those of a closely coupled multiprocessor; instead, it is a form of lazy evaluation: only required portions of objects are actually retrieved from disk or over the network. Another purpose is to provide a uniform, *network transparent* way to access objects: the mapping operation is independent of whether the UID is for a remote or local object. As long as programs make the worst case assumption that their objects are not local and, hence, that operations on them are subject to communication failures, they need not be aware of their location. (See [22] on the desirability of network transparency.)

Text string names for objects are created by a collection of directory objects managed by a *naming server*, which implements a hierarchical name space much like that of Multics or UNIX™ [24]. The result is a uniform, network-wide name space, in which objects have a unique canonical text string name as well as a UID. The name space supports convenient sharing, which would be severely hampered without the ability to uniformly name the objects to be shared among the sharing parties.

There are many interesting examples of layering in the implementation of the DOMAIN system. The layering of remote services on their local-only counterparts occurs in the OSS, the SLS, and in MBX, the system high-level IPC facility. The naming server and MBX illustrate how naming is layered on more primitive system services. Finally, a technique was used that removed most of concurrency management from the SLS implementation into a lock manager in a layer above it.

C. Organization

The rest of this paper is organized as follows. Section II is an overview of the DOMAIN system as a whole, including a brief description of those aspects not directly related to distributed computing. Section III presents information on the network hardware, focusing on features specifically tailored to support an integrated distributed environment. Section IV discusses low level interprocess communication. Section V describes the distributed OSS; Section VI describes the implementation of the single level store. Section VII presents some further topics and lessons learned from our operational experience; Section VIII presents some performance data for other designers and implementors to contrast with their systems. Finally, Section IX offers some conclusions.

II. DOMAIN System Environment

A DOMAIN system consists of a collection of powerful personal workstations and server computers (generically, nodes) interconnected by a high-speed local network.

Users interact with their personal nodes via a display subsystem, which includes a high resolution raster graphics display, a keyboard and a locating device (mouse, touch pad, or tablet). A typical display has 800 by 1024 pixels, and *bit BLT* (bit block transfer) hardware to move arbitrary rectangular areas at high speed. Server nodes have no display, and are controlled over the network.

A. CPU

There are several models of both types of nodes: a typical one has a "tick" time [12] of 1.25 μs and can have up to 3.5 Mbytes of main memory. Most personal nodes have 33 Mbytes of disk storage and a 1 Mbyte floppy disk, but no disk storage is required for a node to operate. Server nodes configured as file servers can have 300–600 Mbytes or more of disk storage; those configured as peripheral servers can have printers, magnetic tape drives, plotters, and so forth.

All nodes have dynamic address translation (DAT) hardware which supports up to 128 processes, with each process able to address up to 16 Mbytes of demand paged virtual memory (which is a limit of the VLSI CPU currently in use). The DAT hardware uses a reverse mapping scheme, similar to that used in the IBM System/38 [10]; it is a large, hardware hash table keyed by virtual address, with the physical address given by the hash table slot number in which a translation entry is stored. The DAT also maintains used and modified statistics on a per page basis for the use of page replacement software, and per page access protections controlling read, write, and execute access.

B. Network Controller

The network is a 12 Mbit/s baseband token passing ring (other ring implementations are described in [8], [33]). Each node's ring controller provides the node with a unique node ID, which is assigned at the factory and contained in the controller's microcode PROM's. The maximum packet size supported by the controller is 2048 bytes.

Network reliability is primarily achieved by bypassing each node's ring repeater with a relay which closes upon node crash or power failure. Network maintainability is enhanced by using a "star-shaped ring" configuration for the network [25], and by developing "quick-disconnect" hardware for attaching nodes to the ring so they can easily be removed if they fail and easily be reconnected after they are repaired. Also, if the token is destroyed (due to entry or exit of nodes from the ring), software timeouts will detect the condition and will recover by forcing a packet transmission, thereby reinserting a token on the ring.

The ring controller has a broadcast capability, which is used for topology determination, for booting nodes without local disks, and for freeing resources held on other nodes when rebooting after a crash. In the future, it will probably also be used for contacting routing servers in (local) internet environments.

Closed loop clock coordination is accomplished using phase locked loops to track a self-clocking, biphase encoded waveform; the per node transceive delay is 1.5 bit times.

C. Role of the Network in the Architecture

In the DOMAIN architecture, the local area network occupies the place usually accorded the backplane interconnect bus in other architectures: it is the system integration point, and the primary architectural feature held con-

stant across new hardware implementations. Thus, the above hardware description of a node's CPU, DAT, disks, and so forth, should all be regarded as transitory, and not at all critical to the fundamental architecture. The architecture was designed so that at a given point in time and for a given cost/performance goal, we can choose the best implementation of nodes using then-current technology. This freedom is attained because the architecture specifies only what nodes see through the network, and therefore does not constrain the implementation of the nodes themselves. (The architecture does not even constrain the choice of the network medium very much: above the device driver level, software only sees a logical view of the network as a message delivery system, and only the message contents matter.)

III. Network Hardware

Our network requirements included high transmission speed, decentralized control, fault tolerance, and support for efficient fault locating. We chose a token passing ring because it met all these requirements, and because we were more familiar with implementing rings than contention networks; as discussed above, the choice is not architecturally significant. (See [27] for a discussion of token passing versus contention for arbitrating network access. Saltzer's conclusion was that contention possessed no major inherent advantages over token passing.)

Our ring design incorporates a number of interesting special features. We should stress that individually none of these features may be especially significant; but taken all together they indicate the outcome of starting with the explicit goal of building an integrated local networking system, and applying it to all problems encountered. The ring offered opportunities to enhance performance by providing "free" hardware level information on the status of message delivery, and opportunities for enhanced failure diagnosis and recovery features. Also, we created several other hardware features, which are not ring specific, to enhance the performance of communication protocols.

A. Ring Specific Features

Receivers on the ring can modify packets as they are received to provide the transmitter with hardware level information on the status of message delivery. This information is contained in two "acknowledgment" fields: the *early ACK* and the *ACK byte*. In the packet, the early ACK comes after the destination address; the ACK byte comes at the very end. This information is used in various ways to increase the efficiency of message transmission.

The COPY bit in the ACK byte tells the transmitter that the destination node received the packet correctly. Some of our protocols, particularly the network paging protocol, are designed so that this acknowledgment relieves the receiving node of the responsibility of an explicit (and much more expensive) software originated acknowledge.

The *wait acknowledge* (WACK) bit in the ACK byte signals the transmitter that a destination node saw the packet and found nothing wrong with it, but was temporarily unable to receive it on this pass. The most common reason for a WACK is that the destination node temporarily has no receive pending, because it had just received a packet and not yet issued another receive request to the controller.

Combining the information from the COPY and WACK bits allows requestors to more intelligently select timeout values: a WACK indicates the use of a short timeout (the condition is transient); a COPY indicates the use of a timeout somewhat longer than the expected time to complete the operation requested (the transmitter can assume that the message has been received and that the requested operation is being performed). If neither is seen, then giving up quickly is indicated (the node is either crashed or nonexistent, and persistence is unlikely to be rewarded).

The "intend to copy" (ICOPY) bit in the early ACK is set by a receiver if it will attempt to receive the packet; so, when a transmitter sees the early ACK come back without the ICOPY bit set, it can abort transmission, thus conserving ring bandwidth. (When we were designing the ring controller, we thought that a network transparent style of system might load the network enough to make this feature useful; our load experience to date (see Section VIII) seems to indicate that we were wrong.)

B. Other Special Features

The following features are independent of the token passing arbitration mechanism, and could be used with any LAN.

The ring hardware offers special support for the transmission of pages. It allows single packets to be split in two variable length pieces called the *header* section and the *data* section. Each section can be transmitted from and received into separate buffers, even though the receiver may not know the actual length of either section when the receive operation is initiated. (It is the support for variable length sections that distinguishes this from normal scatter/gather features. The implementation is via a separate DMA channel for each section; the transmitter inserts a hardware mark to separate the sections, which tells the receiver to switch channels.) The header contains hardware and link level protocol information plus some client message data; the data portion is optional and contains just client data (see Figs. 1 and 2).

Although generally useful, header/data separation was specifically designed for the lowest level network paging protocol. Here, a paging request packet must carry the description of the page being requested and the actual page itself. The hardware supported header/data separation allows variable length protocol fields and page descriptors while still allowing virtual memory pages to be transferred to and from page-aligned physical memory buffers. As a result, the network paging protocol never copies page data; instead, it transmits pages from wherever they appear in the physical memory of the sending node and receives the page data into page-aligned buffers in the requesting node. Thus, newly received pages are accessed via simple manipulation of pointers instead of requiring data copies.

Network efficiency considerations also led to the mem-

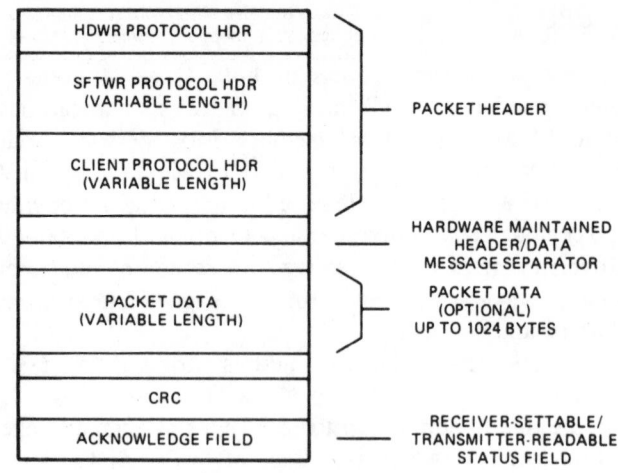

Fig. 1. Ring packet format.

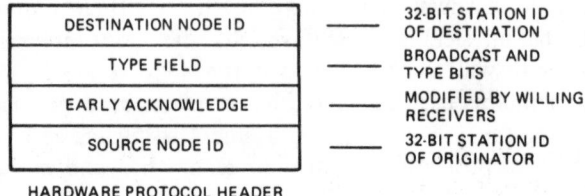

HARDWARE PROTOCOL HEADER

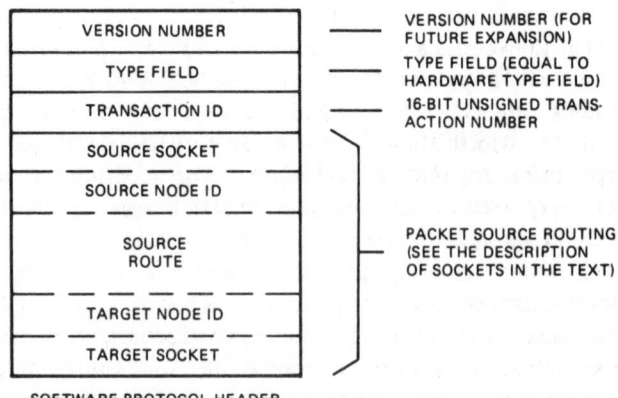

SOFTWARE PROTOCOL HEADER

Fig. 2. Ring packet header fields.

ory subsystem of the node being designed to be able to keep up with the network data rate under normal circumstances. This was done so that the controller would not have to internally buffer a whole message during transmission or reception, since buffering would at least triple the message transmission delay. Our goal was to have low enough per message software overheads that the extra hardware delay would be significant. We accomplished that goal: internal buffering would increase current message costs by 40 percent, and future software overheads, with more optimized software and faster processors, will only decrease. (See Section VIII.)

Another hardware supported feature is the packet *type field* and a corresponding ring controller *type mask* register (see Fig. 3). It has a dual purpose: to create a simple multicast capability, and for message classification. Normally, a node only receives a packet if its node ID and the destination node ID in the packet match; but if the *broadcast* bit is set in the type mask register, this check is

| BRDCST | HWDIAG | THANKS | PLEASE | PAGING | USER | SWDIAG | UNUSED |

Where:

BRDCST — Broadcast If this bit is set, the hardware forces the node ID in the destination field to match the node ID of this node.

HWDIAG — This bit has been reserved for hardware diagnostics.

THANKS — DOMAIN makes a distinction between messages that are requesting service and messages that are replies to service requests. A message whose type field has the THANKS bit set is a reply to a request.

PLEASE — A message whose TYPE field has the PLEASE bit set is a request for service. A node that wishes to refuse service to all requestors (an option supported by DOMAIN) can do so by not setting the PLEASE bit in its hardware type mask register.

PAGING — All paging packets have the PAGING bit set.

USER — All packets that were sent from the user-space socket interface have the USER bit set in their type fields.

SWDIAG — DOMAIN sends packets marked with the SWDIAG bit to determine network health, or to help announce a problem.

UNUSED — The UNUSED bit is currently unused.

Fig. 3. Type field description.

bypassed. In addition, it will not receive a packet unless at least one pair of bits in the same bit position of the type field and the type mask register are both set. Thus, if the broadcast bit is set, the type matching facility provides a form of multicast addressing [4]. This view of the type field allows messages to be sent to a class of nodes. Without the broadcast indicator, this facility provides a way to group packets into classes, using the type field to carry the packet's classification. Then, by appropriately setting the type mask register, a node can cheaply refuse certain classes of packets—the ring controller will reject all packets without the right type bits.

Currently, we combine both of these views in our use of the packet type field. The "please," "thanks," and "paging" bits indicate message classes. For example, a node may refuse to service requests from other nodes, while reserving the right to issue requests, by removing the "please" bit from its type mask register. The "hwdiag," "swdiag," and "user" bits, on the other hand, are used in conjunction with broadcast to communicate with *all* nodes that have expressed an interest in those types of message.

C. Network Management

An integrated local network, by promoting cooperation among users, will thereby promote dependence on the network. So, it will probably also intrinsically need higher reliability than a network whose goal is only to connect autonomous machines. Accordingly, two ring features were designed to help diagnose and repair failures: broken and noisy link detection, and topology determination.

Broken link detection uses the property of biphase encoding that the receiver component of a node's ring repeater can detect the absence of a coherent signal from its upstream neighbor. In such a case, the downstream node can conclude that the link is broken—recall that if the upstream node had crashed or if its power had failed, its relay would have closed, thus bypassing it in the ring altogether. When a node decides that a cable is broken, it broadcasts a failure report message; even though the cable is broken, the broadcast can still be received by all other active nodes on the network, since they are between the detecting node and the break. To avoid false reports the detecting node tries to measure the persistence of the failure; but within minutes of a cable being cut, every active node can tell which node is immediately downstream of the failure. (The same broadcast reporting technique is used in newer hardware which can detect *noisy links*: links over which data errors occur with greater than average frequency; they may indicate cable or repeater trouble and should be brought to the attention of the network administration.)

Determining the network topology means more than determining the obvious fact that the network is topologically a circle; it also means determining the order in which the nodes are joined to form that circle. Topology determination depends on two features of the network controller: the broadcast capability and the receiver modified ACK field carried with every packet. Its operation is most easily illustrated by means of an example. In a four node network of nodes A, B, C, and D, suppose that A wants to determine the topology. A broadcasts an "A wants topology" request which is received by B, C, and D. However, B sees the ACK field in its original state while C and D see that a receiving node has already modified the ACK field. B now knows that it is immediately downstream from A and can report this fact to A. B now rebroadcasts an "A wants topology"; this time C realizes that it is immediately downstream of B, and so on. In a network of n nodes, the algorithm requires the transmission of 2n messages (each node broadcasts once and sends one message to node A) and terminates when node A receives a topology request broadcast whose ACK byte is unmodified.

With a broken link report and a network topology map, link failures can be isolated to the nodes at either end of the link. To recover from a link failure, the star-shaped ring configuration is used to switch out the loop containing the failure and restore operation to the rest of the network;

the precise failure site is located and repaired, and the loop is reconnected to the network. Currently this reconfiguration is manual, but it can be automated by having a node listening to broken link and noisy link reports and controlling the loop switches.

IV. Low Level IPC: Sockets

The *socket* abstraction is the low level IPC mechanism; it provides an unreliable datagram delivery service. A socket is a queue of network packets, in the form of header/data pairs, between the network and the process to which the incoming packets are directed. They are identified by small integers which are only unique within a single node; thus, at this level, IPC messages are addressed to (node ID, socket ID) pairs.

There are two classes of sockets: *well-known* and *reply*. The well-known sockets are statically assigned to the standard system services available in every node; the socket ID for a given service is same on all nodes, and is known to all potential clients of the service. These services currently include the network paging server, the remote file server, the node status inquiry server, the diskless node boot server, and the high level IPC server, and might eventually include a (local) internet routing server and an authentication server.

Reply sockets are dynamically allocated to receive replies to requests for remote system services. Service requests include a return address composed of the sending node's ID and the ID of a reply socket. When a client's transaction with the server is complete, its reply socket is returned to the free socket pool.

A. Protocols; Lost and Duplicate Packets

The high speed and hardware reliability of local networks suggests a different approach to protocols than that usually taken for long haul networks: problems of error recovery, flow control, congestion control, and so forth, are not as significant in the local network context [18]. We use what the LOCUS project [22] called *problem oriented* protocols: each remote operation implements a protocol tailored to its needs. Thus, both the message format and the technique used to assure reliable completion are operation specific; however, some general observations can be made. The message format for a remote operation is usually straightforward—just the concatenated parameters of the operation. Reliability is usually attained by one of the following three techniques.

Operations that are idempotent (i.e., for which repeated applications have the same effect as a single application) use a *connectionless* protocol [31] and retry often enough to achieve the desired level of reliability. The protocol is said to be connectionless because it keeps no information about previous requests, which is also why it is simple and cheap. Because it is connectionless, it cannot reject duplicate requests; but the idempotence of the operation means that duplicate messages will cause no problems. Most operations are either naturally idempotent, or were designed to

be so, in order to be able to use a connectionless protocol.

Operations which are not idempotent (i.e., which have side effects), but which naturally have some state associated with them, can often be made idempotent using a transaction ID. Each time a client sends a new request (not a retry) to perform an operation, it chooses a new transaction ID. If an operation was performed once with a particular transaction ID, the receipt of a second request with the same ID should be rejected. File locking is an example: along with the lock state can be stored the transaction ID of the operation which set the lock. Since a duplicate request will be rejected (a duplicate lock request will have a transaction ID matching that of an existing lock; a duplicate unlock request will find no lock to unlock), retries can again be used to achieve the desired level of reliability. Note that this technique is cheap because the operation's database provided a natural place to put the connection state instead of requiring the communications substrate to keep it.

Some operations inevitably require that updates to databases of both the client and server be synchronized. For these operations, an RRA (request, reply, acknowledge) type of protocol [28] is needed. Our protocol uses the basic RRA idea, but is modified so that the automatic ring hardware acknowledge suffices to replace an explicit software acknowledge. Such replacement requires that the server be sure that the reply will be acted upon if the hardware acknowledge is positive. For this to be true, the server must know that the client is still waiting for the reply, and that the reply will not be discarded for lack of buffer space. To assure the first part, the client supplies the server a deadline, beyond which the client will not wait for a reply; as long as the server meets the deadline, it can be sure the client is awaiting the reply. (Rings, and LAN's in general, allow tight enough bounds on packet lifetimes for this approach, similar in some respects to the delta-T protocols of [5], to work.) To assure the second part, each client must supply the buffer pool enough buffers to service all its outstanding requests; thus, if a client is awaiting a reply, there is guaranteed to be a buffer into which to receive it.

The above paragraphs dealt with lost and duplicate requests; replies also have a similar problem. In addition, because reply sockets are reused over time, it is possible for a reply to an "old" request to be delivered to a socket that has been reallocated. (This can happen if a request is timed out.) To detect duplicated or delayed reply packets, transaction ID's are again used; a client requesting an operation always creates and sends a transaction ID for the operation. The transaction ID of a reply should always be the same as the transaction ID of the original request that prompted it; if a client is waiting for a reply to a previously requested operation and receives a reply with the "wrong" transaction ID, it can discard the reply.

B. Discussion

The protocols we used are cheap because they are end-to-end protocols [26]. They do not rely on the communications substrate (the socket mechanism) to provide any service guarantees; instead, each remote operation individually implements the least mechanism required by its reliability semantics. The net result is cheap because the semantics are themselves uncomplicated, and because the socket mechanism can be made extremely fast since it does not guarantee anything.

We should mention that our low level remote operations were not designed to act like atomic transactions in the face of node crashes or extended network failure; had this been a requirement, the protocols would undoubtedly have been more complicated and less efficient. However, even then, the end-to-end argument would apply, and say that such protocols must be implemented by the operations that required those semantics, and indeed could not be done by the communications substrate. (Guaranteed delivery alone is not sufficient for such protocols; they usually cannot send a reply until some information is committed to stable storage.) Fortunately, the simpler semantics are all that are required by a large number of useful applications; after all, much software has been written for systems that make few guarantees about failure atomicity.

We should emphasize that none of the above arguments rely on our use of a ring. With one exception, all of the ring related optimizations we made are actually optimization "hints," in the sense that protocols do not depend on them, and instead rely on replies and timeouts for their correct operation. For example, the WACK bit (see Section III-A) is used to do a quick automatic retransmission; but if a hardware failure caused a WACK to be lost, the only effect would be that the retry would be delayed until a timeout occurred. The exception is the optimized RRA protocol discussed above; however, it could be changed to expect an explicit reply if there were no ring acknowledgment, thus making the ring acknowledgment a true hint.

V. OBJECT STORAGE SYSTEM

The OSS is the DOMAIN counterpart of distributed file systems such as WFS [31] and DFS [29]. The purpose of the OSS is to provide permanent storage for objects, and to allow objects to be identified by and operated on using UID's, independent of their location in the network. At the level we will discuss here, an object is just a data container: an array of uninterpreted data bytes, or more precisely, an array of pages (1024 byte units into which objects are divided). Other attributes such as an object's length, type descriptor, and access control list are not used here, but are simply stored for the use of higher levels.

A. Identifying Objects

UID's of objects are bit strings (64 bits long); they are made unique by concatenating the unique ID of the node generating the UID and a time stamp from the node's timer. (The system does not use a global clock.) UID's are also location independent: the node ID in an object's UID cannot be considered as anything more than a hint about the current location of the object. (More detail on the use and implementation of UID's is presented in [15].)

At any point in time, the permanent storage for an object is always entirely at only one node; also, the system never attempts to transparently move it to a different node. So, for every object there is always one distinguished node which is its "home," and which serves as the locus of operations on the object.

Above the OSS level, only UID's are used to address objects; any operation requests whose UID's address remote objects are sent to the objects' home nodes to be performed. The operations provided by the OSS include: creating, deleting, extending, and truncating an object; reading or writing a page of an object; getting and setting attributes of an object such as the access control list UID, type UID, and length; and locating the home node of an object. Of these, we will focus on how pages are accessed and mostly omit the others, which use similar techniques.

B. Access to Local Objects

The object storage system implementation is in two layers. The first layer provides access to local objects: i.e., those objects stored on disks which are attached to the node accessing them. This layer primarily consists of disk and memory resident data structures used to translate object references to disk block addresses, where an object reference is a pair consisting of the object's UID and a page number within the object. Each disk block holds one page plus a header, which includes the UID and page number of the object containing the page, and a time stamp indicating when the page was last written.

The object-reference-to-disk-block translation is accomplished using the volume table of contents (VTOC). The VTOC for a volume contains an entry for each object on the volume; an object's VTOC entry contains the object's attributes and the root of its *file map*, which translates page numbers within an object to disk block addresses. (VTOC entries are very similar to UNIX *inodes* [32].) The VTOC is organized as an associative lookup table keyed by object UID, which permits rapid location of an object's VTOC entry given its UID. (Using a large direct mapped hash table with chained overflow buckets and avoiding high utilization, the average lookup time is just over one disk access.) The memory resident structure is basically just a cache over the disk resident one.

C. Access to Remote Objects

The second layer provides access to objects independent of location. If the object is local, it uses the local access mechanism just described; otherwise it uses the remote access mechanism, which is built using an object locating service, sockets, *remote paging server* and *remote file server* processes, and the local object access mechanism.

The locating service finds the ID of the node on which an object resides, given the object's UID. This is the fundamental distributed algorithm in the system: no global state information is kept about object locations. Instead, a heuristic search is used to locate an object. Complete details are in [15], including design considerations and the evolutionary history of the algorithm. To summarize briefly, the current algorithm relies heavily on hints about object location. One source is the node ID in the object's UID; another is the *hint file*. Any time a software component can make a good guess about the location of an object, it can store that guess in the hint file for later use; one particularly good source of hints is the naming server, which guesses that objects are colocated with the directory in which they are catalogued. If all hints fail to locate the object, then the requesting node's local disk is searched for the object. The algorithm works because, although it is possible for objects to do so, they rarely move from the node where they were created; and if they do, then the naming server's hint will nearly always be correct. A last resort, which would be completely sufficient, would be to accept user input into the hint file; this has not yet been implemented, as it has not really been needed.

Each node has a paging server process that handles all remotely originating requests to read or write pages of objects on that node. (A file server process is similar, except it handles nonpaging operation; we will not discuss it further.) The paging server has a socket assigned to it, with a well-known ID, upon which it receives requests; it uses the local access mechanism to fulfill those requests. Remote paging operations are requested via (**UID, page number**) pairs only, never by disk address, and other remote operations only via UID's; thus, a node never depends on any other node for the integrity of its object store. (This is one of the reasons the system is truly a collection of autonomous nodes—to which are added mechanisms permitting a high degree of cooperation—as distinguished from, say, a locally dispersed, loosely coupled multiprocessing system.)

VI. Single Level Store Implementation

The single level store concept means that all memory references are logically references directly to objects. This is in contrast to a multilevel store, which typically has a "primary" store and one (or more) "secondary" store(s); only the primary store is directly accessible by programs, so they have to do explicit "I/O" operations to copy an object's from secondary to primary store before the data can be accessed. To make the distinction between primary and secondary store transparent, a single level store has to manage main memory as a cache over the object store: fetching objects (or portions of objects) from permanent store into main memory as needed, and eventually writing back modified objects (or portions thereof) to the permanent store. SLS is thus a form of virtual memory, since all referenced information need not (indeed, could not) be in main memory at any one time.

Our implementation of SLS has many aspects in common with implementations of SLS for a centralized system: main memory is divided into page frames, each page frame holds one object page, main memory is managed as a write-back cache, and DAT hardware allows references to encached pages at main memory speeds. If an instruction references a page of an object which is not in main memory, the DAT hardware causes a page fault, and supplies the faulting virtual address and the ID of the

faulting process to software. The page fault handler finds a frame for the page, reads the page into the frame, updates the DAT related information to show that the page is main memory resident, and restarts the instruction. In our system, there is a per process table, the *mapped segment table* (MST), which translates a virtual address to a (**UID, page number**) pair; fetching the page is then just a request to the OSS, even if the page belongs to a remote object (see Fig. 4).

What distinguishes our implementation from a centralized one is the necessity of dealing with multiple main memory caches, in fact, one for each node in the network. This leads to the problem of synchronizing the caches in some way: of finding and fetching the most up-to-date copy of an object's page on a page fault, and of avoiding the use of "stale" pages (ones that are still in a node's cache, but have been more recently modified by another node). The objective of synchronization is to give programs a consistent view of the current version of an object in the face of (potentially) many updaters. A second objective is that the synchronization algorithm should be quite simple and need only a small database, as it would be part of the SLS implementation and, hence, be permanently resident in main memory.

These objectives appeared, for practical purposes, to be mutually exclusive, so our SLS implementation does *not* guarantee consistency or the use of the current version. Instead, the implementation *does* provide operations and information from which a higher level can build a mechanism that makes the stronger guarantees. In addition, the higher level can use the virtual memory provided by SLS, and thereby be in large measure freed of the constraints mentioned earlier, the size of it and its database. The system provides a readers/writers locking mechanism at the higher level; however, other clients are free to construct their own synchronization mechanism at this level if they do not wish to use ours.

A. Concurrency Control

We say that the lower level implements *concurrency control*, and that it detects a *concurrency violation* when an attempt is made to use more than one version of an object. To detect concurrency violations, a time stamp based version number scheme is used wherein an object's version number is its *date-time modified* (DTM) attribute. (See [11] for a survey of distributed concurrency techniques.) Every object has a DTM with 8 ms resolution associated with it, which records the time the object was last modified.

The DTM of an object is maintained at its home node. When an object is modified by locally originating memory writes, the page modified bits in the DAT hardware record that fact; periodically, the modified bits are scanned and cause the object's DTM to be updated. If an object is modified by a remote node, eventually the object's modified pages are sent back to the home node; the paging server updates an object's DTM in response to remotely originating OSS requests to write its pages.

Every node also remembers the DTM for all remote objects whose pages it has encached in its main memory.

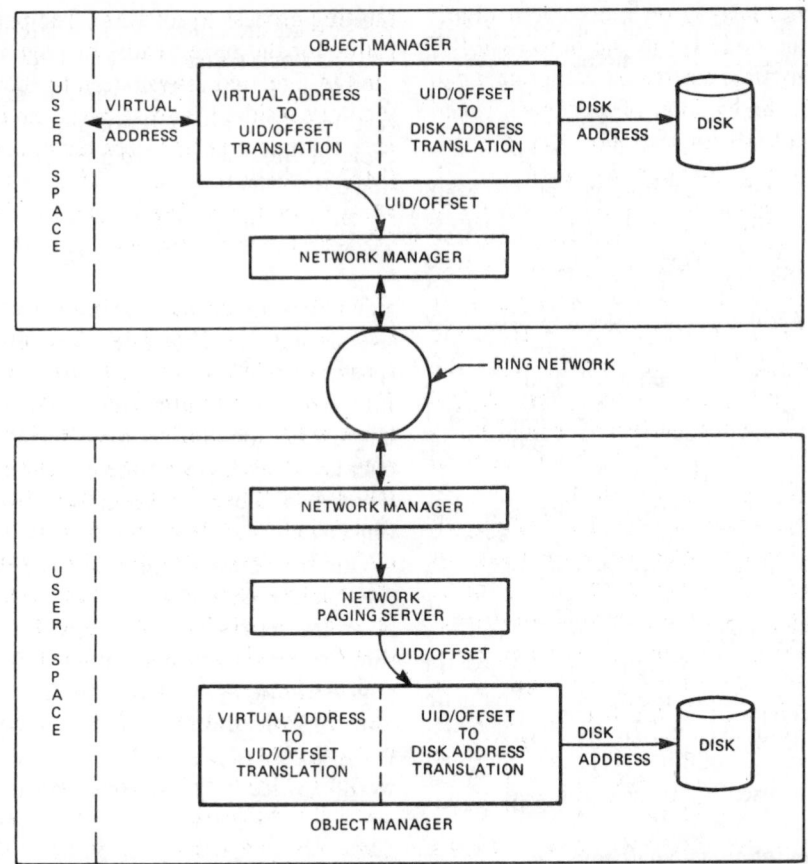

Fig. 4. DOMAIN virtual memory system. A user process causes a page fault. The faulting virtual address is translated into the unique identifier (UID) and page offset of the object behind that address. If the object resides on a physically local disk, the *local path* is taken. The UID/offset pair is translated into a physical disk address. When the object is remote, the UID/offset pair is passed via network page-in request to the *paging server* running on the object's home node. The paging server pushes the UID/offset pair through the same path the faulting process uses for local objects, gets the data page, and returns it to the faulting process in a page-in reply.

Every time an object's page is read from another node, its DTM is returned with it. If it is the only page of the object encached in this node, its DTM is remembered. If not, the returned DTM must match the remembered DTM for the object; otherwise a read concurrency violation has occurred. Every time a page of an object is written back to its home node, the current DTM is sent with the write request and an updated DTM is returned. The home node will only accept the page if it comes from the current version of the object—i.e., the request's DTM must match the home node's DTM for the object; otherwise a write concurrency violation has occurred.

A page write updates both the home node's and the requesting node's DTM for the object. It is easy to see that neither side can do the update until it is sure that both sides have the new DTM; otherwise further writes would cause a concurrency violation. Thus, the update has to be synchronized. The modified RRA protocol described above is used for this purpose; its use here in the SLS implementation was the primary motivation for the emphasis on its efficiency.

There are several operations exported by concurrency control for the use of higher level synchronization mechanisms. A *conditional flush* operation expunges from the cache all pages of an object that are not from the current version of the object. A DTM inquiry operation returns the DTM of the current version of an object. A *purification*

operation sends copies of all modified pages of an object back to the home node of the object (but leaves the pages encached for possible later use). A force write operation causes a page to be written to permanent store on its home node; its purpose is to be a minimally sufficient toe hold with which to implement more complex atomic operations.

There are several properties of this form of concurrency control to note.

1) Concurrency violations can only occur in multinode situations: if an object is used by only one node, that node is the only source of version number changes, and will, hence, always see a consistent view of the current version.

2) Even in multinode situations, concurrency violations will not occur if an object is used read-only: all nodes will have the same version number and see the same version.

3) If no concurrency violations occur, then all users of an object saw a consistent view of the object. However, even then, some could have seen an out-of-date version, and if multiple objects are used this means there is no guarantee of interobject consistency.

4) An object must be read before being written; thus, if two nodes read from the same version of an object, then each write the object, the first writer will update the version number, causing the second writer to get a concurrency violation. However, if the nodes' read–write pairs can be serialized, no violations will happen.

Note that the first two properties are what lets a higher

level use SLS: it can use SLS for its code and data as long as its writable data is only used on one node.

B. Locking: Guaranteeing Consistency

For clients whose semantics require more than the weak guarantees made by SLS, an object locking mechanism is available which can provide stronger guarantees. Locking an object makes sure that no other node can use it in an incompatible way (a way which might cause a concurrency violation). There are several types of lock request: read, write, and read with intent to write later [7], and requests to change one type of lock to another. There are several supported lock modes, with differing lock compatibilities. For the simple case readers/writers locks are used [9], which allow many readers or one writer (or a reader that intends to write later) for a whole object. A *co-writers* (colocated writers) lock mode is also provided, which makes no restrictions on the number of readers and writers; it allows the use of shared memory semantics, but only among processes located at the same node. (Guardians [16] employ this same notion, but at the level of linguistic support for distributed computation.) In all modes, when an object is locked, its version number (DTM) is returned to the client, which can be used to optimize some computations.

The locking implementation is analogous to that for concurrency control. Every node keeps a lock database, which records all of the objects, local or remote, that it has locked, and all of its objects that other nodes have locked. Lock and unlock requests for local objects just update the local lock database. Lock and unlock requests for remote objects are always sent to the home node of the object involved, and both the requesting node and the home node update their databases. A request to lock a remote object that is granted returns the current version number (DTM) of the object, which is used in a conditional flush operation, thereby removing stale pages of the object from the requesting nodes main memory. A request to unlock a remote object first purifies the object (forces modified pages back to the home node), then does the actual unlock. Locks are either granted immediately or refused; processes never wait for locks to become available, so there is no possibility of deadlock (but indefinite postponement is, of course, possible). This kind of locking is not meant for distributed database types of transactions, or for providing atomicity in the face of node failures, but for human time span locking uses such as file editing. For this same reason, locks are not timed out, since realistic timeouts would be unreasonably long.

As an example of the operation of our mechanism, let us use an application originally used to describe DFS [29]. (One of DFS's design goals is to support client caching of data.) The application involves a large, infrequently updated, distributed database; its task is to maintain a display terminal showing some subset of the database, and ensure that the information is current. Using SLS and locking, the application would repeatedly execute the following steps.

1) Obtain read locks for all objects being displayed.

2) Read the objects and update the display.
3) Unlock the read locks.

Notice that the SLS will automatically cache the data read in step 1, and will not normally have to reread it each cycle; it will only discard and reread an object's data if the object has changed.

C. Discussion

This approach to layering of concurrency management has several desirable attributes. First is that it allows the (presumably) more complicated and larger higher level protocol to use the services of SLS. Second is its flexibility: because the operations to manage the cache are exported, clients can implement their own schemes, any number of which can coexist as long as they manage disjoint sets of objects.

One restriction that it would be desirable to relax is that the concurrency granularity of the current implementation is at the level of entire objects. However, note that the same technique, but with a version number (DTM) per page, would allow page level concurrency control. We already store the DTM with each page on backing store; thus, keeping one DTM per main memory page frame would suffice for this extension.

VII. OTHER TOPICS AND LESSONS

A. Naming Objects

For users, UID's are not a very convenient means to refer to objects; for them, text string names are preferable. However, like UID's, they should be uniform throughout the network, so that the name of an object does not change from node to node. In DOMAIN, text string names for objects are provided by a directory subsystem layered on top of the single level store. The name space is a hierarchical tree, like Multics [21] or UNIX [24], with directories at the nodes and other objects at the leaves. A directory is just an object, with its own UID, containing primarily a simple set of associations between *component names* (strings) and UID's. (A symbolic link facility, like that of Multics, is the other major user of directories.) A single component name is *resolved* in the context of a particular directory by finding its associated UID (if any). The *absolute path name* of an object is an ordered list of component names. All but (possibly) the last are names of directories, which, when resolved starting from a network-wide distinguished "root" directory, lead to the UID of the object. Thus, an absolute path name, like a UID, is valid throughout the entire network, and denotes just one object. (There are other forms of path name besides the absolute form; these *relative* path names are mainly for convenience, since absolute path names are potentially very long in a large network with large numbers of objects. They are all expressible as the concatenation of some absolute path name prefix to the relative path name itself.)

Most distributed naming servers (e.g., Grapevine's [2]) are implemented as processes which communicate via some form of IPC, and we had initially intended to do so as well.

However, in order to minimize mechanism, and to exercise our single level store concept as much as possible, we decided to implement directories, even remote ones, as objects accessed using SLS instead of message passing.

The most important consequence we have observed is the efficiency of the SLS implementation. The usual overhead to resolve one component name in a remote directory using our SLS is three message pairs (requests and replies): one to lock the directory, one to read the directory page (perhaps unneeded if the page is already cached), and one to unlock the directory. On the other hand, a pure message based protocol would take only one message pair. As a result, we have reconsidered our initial decision, and the current version of the naming server uses message passing.

B. MBX: Higher Level IPC

The system offers a higher level IPC facility than sockets, called MBX (for mailbox). MBX offers a full-duplex virtual circuit service; messages are sent to and read from MBX objects, which are identified by UID and named in the network-wide name space. An MBX object is the storage container in which IPC messages are queued awaiting delivery.

The MBX facility is based on a server/client model of IPC. A server creates a mailbox, specifying how many *channels* (simultaneous client connections) the mailbox is to support, and supplying a full pathname by which the mailbox should be known. Once the mailbox is thus instantiated, clients of that server may form virtual circuits with the server by supplying the mailbox's pathname (which is immediately translated to its UID by the system naming server), and additional server instances can join the original one to help service requests.

The MBX mechanism supports both intra- and internode IPC. Local interprocess message exchange is implemented by sharing the MBX object. Both the server and its local client processes map the same MBX object into their address space and perform MBX operations directly. (This mechanism uses the colocated writers lock mode discussed in the section on object concurrency.) The remote IPC mechanism depends on an MBX *helper* process that acts on behalf of a server's remote clients. The helper owns a network socket with a well-known ID, and exchanges messages with remote clients via the socket mechanism. The MBX helper then passes the client data on to the server via the local MBX (shared memory) mechanism. The MBX remote protocol provides screening of duplicate and out-of-order packets as added value to the socket level's datagram service.

The MBX facility is another example of layering in the system: the layering of the remote facility on the local one, similar to the layering of the remote OSS on the local one; and the layering of naming. MBX uses three layers of names: text string names, UID's, and socket ID's. The top layer allows servers to "advertise" by creating a name for their MBX object, and putting it in the network-wide name space. The next layer allows the independent creation of new services without the need to coordinate the allocation and use of well-known socket ID's; thus, only the most basic services need to use the last layer.

C. Diskless Nodes

The architecture made it relatively easy to implement *diskless nodes* (nodes which could run without a local disk): once a diskless node is successfully running the operating system, it has full access to the distributed file system. Therefore, the only extra support needed for diskless nodes was a bootstrapping mechanism.

When a diskless node first powers up, it runs software stored in nonvolatile memory, which sends a broadcast packet addressed to the well-known socket ID of the diskless node bootstrap service. Nodes willing to act as partners for diskless nodes run a process which monitors this socket and which keeps a file containing a list of the nodes it is willing to bootstrap. (Not all nodes may wish to be partners, since it requires a significant resource committment; hence, they must be explicitly configured to relinquish their autonomy in this regard.) Partner nodes supply an OS environment to the diskless nodes they boot: an OS paging file to act as backing store for the operating system, hooks into the network name space, and a directory to store the names of node-specific objects.

Eventually, one or more servers reply to the diskless node's request; one is selected as the diskless node's partner. A copy of the operating system image is sent to the diskless node, followed by the UID's of the pieces of the OS environment. No further extraordinary diskless node support is needed: diskless nodes make requests for remote objects (which for them also include their OS environment objects) that are indistinguishable from those of nodes with disks.

D. Limiting Remote Use of Resources

The first implementation of the virtual memory system made no distinction between the paging demands of local processes and those of the paging server acting on behalf of remote processes. The local user, therefore, constantly competed with remote paging clients for use of his local physical memory, who would steal pages from his process' working sets; the resulting pressure would send the local user's paging rate skyrocketing. (The remote user, however, got little benefit, because only infrequently used pages were in the local node's memory.)

A later version allowed a local user to restrict the number of physical memory pages available to the paging server. Experiments showed that limiting the size of the pool to a small fraction of the total available physical memory (say 5 percent) dramatically reduced the working set pressure from remote users, yet left remote users generally with little or no degradation in performance.

The other major kind of competition, that over the use of the disk, seems an inherent consequence of the ability to share objects on the disk. However, the type bits in the ring controller hardware are used to allow a node to easily refuse all requests for service, while still being able receive replies to its own requests. Thus, if a user so desires, he can use the network's facilities without making any of his own available.

E. Network Management

Good network maintenance and troubleshooting facilities are essential to the success of a large local network. For us, the star-shaped ring organization has been crucial to managing our network. As of this writing, the network at Apollo corporate headquarters contains a total of over 170 nodes of which more than 160 are typically active at any one time. There are nodes belonging to every organization of the company on the same ring, including research and development, finance, marketing, customer service, and manufacturing. Network maintenance would be much more difficult without the ability to make the nearly continual network changes that are inherent in a large network (moving old nodes, adding new nodes, and adding new network subloops) in a nondisruptive fashion.

F. IPC Versus SLS

There can only be two fundamentally different ways to do computations in a distributed environment, where a computation and its data are not physically colocated: move the computation to the data, or move the data to the computation. (Combinations of the two are, of course, possible.) The first alternative corresponds to a message passing model of distributed computing, the second to a network transparent data access model. The former model leads to applications that are based on some sort of IPC facility, the latter to applications based on a facility such as our SLS. Which is the preferable model for constructing distributed applications? All through our implementation, we have tried to push the network single level store concept to the limit, after almost three years of experience, we have some general observations to offer on those limits.

Even though our implementation specifically focused on the efficiency of network paging, we have seen cases where IPC can be more efficient: the naming server was an example. Network transparent access to data can also complicate the problem of object encoding and abstraction. An example is our network registry: it uses a very simple object replication technique to store a small database, which is used to identify network users for access control purposes. The database has a moderately complex internal data structure, and although it has a "manager" which abstracts away from representational details, there is one instance of the manager per node. There is, therefore, network-wide knowledge of that internal structure; hence, it is hard to change the structure since it involves synchronizing the installation of a new version of the manager on each node. In contrast, if instances of the manager only ran at the nodes storing the registry, and all other nodes used IPC to communicate with the manager, the new version problem would be considerably simplified. Here, the lesson is that the use of the client–server model is required for information hiding to be effective in a distributed environment; data abstraction alone is not enough.

Despite these examples, we believe there are many cases where an application will have a set of demands that will cause SLS to be preferred to IPC as an implementation tool. Three criteria that the application must meet to make SLS preferable are the following.

1) There is a significant amount of data and simple synchronization requirements, so the synchronization overhead is small.

2) Data structure semantics are very close to the representation, so confining knowledge of the representation to only a few nodes is not necessary. (Examples where this could be true are text files, which are often logically arrays of bytes, both conceptually and representationally; and executable program formats, which are defined mostly by the CPU's instruction set.)

3) The computation must not need to be trusted (for protection purposes) by other nodes; trust cannot be achieved because, with current techniques (such as Needham and Schroeder [17]), trust depends upon the computation being moved to the (security related) data. (For example, we know of no way to implement a trusted authentication server without using IPC.)

When these criteria hold, then the limitations of SLS noted earlier do not apply. In such cases, an SLS-based application gets the following advantages.

1) It gets a simple model of access to data, and one which is the same for both local and remote objects. Hence, new applications are easier to write, and many applications that run on centralized systems can easily be ported to our distributed environment.

2) It automatically gains the caching, the automatic read ahead of data, and the "lazy evaluation" implied by paging and the hardware support for it.

3) It does not impinge upon the autonomy of other users: since data are moved to the application, if a significant amount of computation is to be performed on the data, it may be fairer to put the computational burden on the user of the data, not its owner.

On the other hand, if the criteria do not hold, then an IPC-based application is called for; SLS is useful because a large number of applications do have the simpler requirements that SLS can satisfy.

VIII. Some Performance Data

The section presents some performance data. In general, the results are not surprising and are quite similar to other reported results: that local networks can achieve high network file I/O throughput rates and low IPC costs, and that local network utilization is typically low. We provide the data mainly to provide another data point and for contrast with other systems. (See LOCUS [22] and the Distributed V Kernel [3] for comparison.)

A. Network Paging

Table I shows the costs of a page fault in three different situations. In all three cases, the program being measured used the SLS to sequentially "touch" (caused to be demand paged) each page of a 1 Mbyte file ten times. It was

Test name	Time (s)	ms/page	Data Mbits/s
L	99.0	9.7	0.85
RD	144.6	14.1	0.58
RM	73.6	7.2	1.14

arranged so that this caused 10 240 page faults; the cost of the page fault varied according to the amount of work needed to satisfy it in each case. Test L read a local file; it caused 10 240 disk read operations to a local 33 Mbyte Winchester disk. Test RD read a remote file; it caused 10 240 pages to be transferred through the network, as well as 10 240 disk reads on the remote node. Test RM also read a remote file; it too caused 10 240 pages to be transferred through the network, but it was arranged that all the pages of the file were resident in main memory of the remote machine, so that no disk I/O to the remote file was required. The average rotational latency of the disk is 8.3 ms; track-to-track seek time is 12 ms, and an average random seek takes 42 ms.

The results for test L show that a page fault on a local file costs 9.7 ms of elapsed time. The results for test RD show that a page fault on a remote file costs 14.1 ms of elapsed time, if disk I/O is required on the remote node. The results for test RM show that a page fault on a remote file costs 7.2 ms of elapsed time, if no disk I/O is required on the remote node.

From the above results, we can break down the cost into three components: disk I/O cost, network page-in request cost, and software page fault overhead cost. Since the only difference between the test RD and test RM was the need to actually read the disk, the difference in their costs must indicate the cost of doing disk I/O. That difference of 6.9 ms (14.1 − 7.2), indicates the average cost of disk I/O setup, disk transfer time, and disk latency for sequential reads.

The difference between the test L and test RD times is the cost of the network page-in request: the difference is 4.4 ms (14.1 − 9.7). (This includes 0.8 ms of network transfer delay for the request message and the reply data; thus, we can reconfirm our earlier observation that if the ring controller buffered message internally, it would cost 1.6 ms/page, about a 40 percent penalty.)

The difference between the test L times and the disk I/O cost calculated earlier is the software page fault overhead. That difference is 2.8 ms (9.7 − 6.9).

B. Socket IPC Performance

In this section we provide data on the performance of the socket IPC mechanism. The measurements were made by sending 2 byte messages from a user level process to an echo service.

The test was run twice: in the first case, no reply was returned; in the second case, the echo-service returned exactly the data sent. The times from the tests indicated a cost of 1.5 ms to send a packet with no reply; and 3.9 ms to send a packet and get a reply. Because the network transmission delay time itself is negligible for such a small packet and because the test program did not wait for a reply between transmissions, these times can all be attributed to software overhead.

C. Network Utilization

Figs. 5 and 6 show 6 min averages of network traffic and disk activity versus time of day on a typical work day; there were 124 nodes active on the day measured.

For each interval, the network paging curve shows the number of both page-in and page-out operations performed, the network I/O curve shows the total number of network messages transmitted, and the disk I/O curve shows the total number of disk read and write operations.

The data collected show fairly low network utilization. The peak network traffic was between 1 P.M. and 2 P.M. and climbed as high as 230 messages/s over a 6 min period. We do not know the packet size distribution, but a very conservative high bound for the average packet size is 550 bytes, which would correspond to all traffic being of the largest message type in use: paging requests and replies. Even with this estimate, less than 1/12 of the total available network bandwidth was used during the peak period. One other item to notice, from the network paging section, is that the paging traffic generated by the fastest test could still only consume 10 percent of the network bandwidth.

IX. CONCLUSIONS AND FUTURE DIRECTIONS

The current DOMAIN implementation fulfills the objectives of allowing sharing and cooperation, and providing network transparency while still keeping a substantial degree of autonomy. It is also an existence proof of the viability of the single level store concept for distributed systems. It remains to be seen how much further the SLS can be extended as we attempt to provide for higher levels of concurrency, atomic transactions, and replicated data, and gain further experience with distributed applications programs. Also, extending an "integrated distributed" system to one with long haul networks in an internet environment poses some problems to which we currently have no easy answers. However, we think that the current concepts

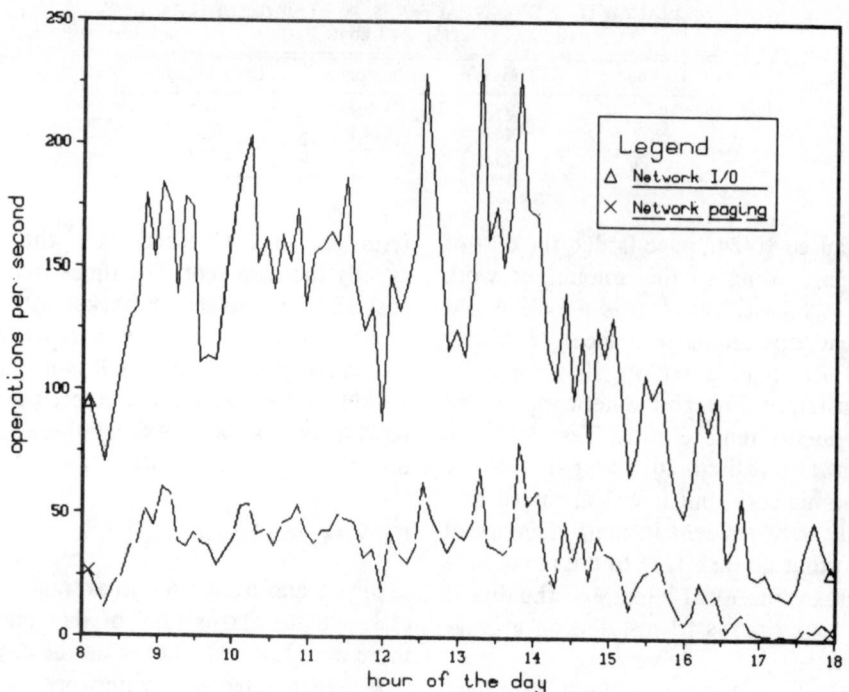

Fig. 5.   Network utilization (124 node network).

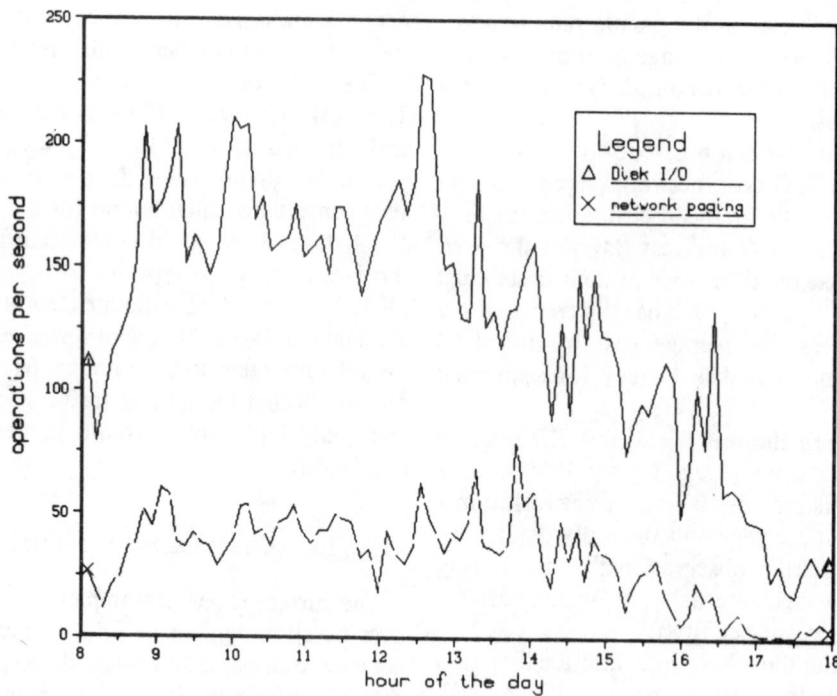

Fig. 6.   Network paging versus disk I/O (124 node network).

will most likely extend smoothly to a *local area internet* environment: local area networks connected by high speed gateways. We should have more definite conclusions on this in the near future.

We believe our implementation adds to the evidence of the desirability of problem-oriented protocols for high performance in a local area network operating system, of integrated distributed systems, and of network transparent file access. However, we do not argue for these to the exclusion of server model distributed computing; we support both models, and each has circumstances under which it is preferable.

ACKNOWLEDGMENT

The authors wish to thank D. E. Jabs and P. B. Madden

of the Apollo R&D group for many useful and insightful criticisms on the organization and content of this paper.

REFERENCES

[1] "Apollo DOMAIN architecture," Apollo Computer Inc., Chelmsford, MA, 1981.
[2] A. D. Birrel, R. Levin, R. M. Needham, and M. D. Schroeder, "Grapevine: An exercise in distributed computing," *Commun. Ass. Comput. Mach.*, vol. 25, pp. 260–274, Apr. 1982.
[3] D. R. Cheriton and W. Zwaenepoel, "The distributed V kernel and its performance for diskless workstations," presented at the 9th Symp. Oper. Syst. Principles, Oct. 1983.
[4] "The Ethernet—Version 1.0," Digital Equipment Corp., Intel Corp., and Xerox Corp., Sept. 1980.
[5] J. G. Fletcher and R. W. Watson, "Mechanisms for a reliable timer-based protocol," *Comput. Networks*, vol. 2, pp. 271–290, 1978.
[6] R. E. French, R. W. Collins, and L. W. Loen, "System/38 machine storage management," in *IBM System/38 Technical Developments*, IBM General Syst. Div., 1978, pp. 63–66.
[7] D. K. Gifford, "Weighted voting for replicated data," in *Proc. 7th Symp. Oper. Syst. Principles*, Dec. 1979, pp. 150–159.
[8] R. L. Gordon, W. Farr, and P. H. Levine, "Ringnet: A packet switched local network with decentralized control," *Comput. Networks*, vol. 3, pp. 373–379, 1980.
[9] C. A. R. Hoare, "Monitors: An operating system structuring concept," *Commun. Ass. Comput. Mach.*, vol. 17, pp. 549–557, Oct. 1974.
[10] M. E. Houdek and G. R. Mitchell, "Translating a large virtual address," in *IBM System/38 Technical Developments*, IBM General Syst. Div., 1978, pp. 22–24.
[11] W. H. Kohler, "A survey of techniques for synchronization and recovery in decentralized computer systems," *Comput. Surveys*, vol. 13, pp. 149–184, June 1981.
[12] B. W. Lampson and D. D. Redell, "Experience with processes and monitors in Mesa," *Commun. Ass. Comput. Mach.*, vol. 23, pp. 105–113, Feb. 1980.
[13] K. A. Lantz and R. F. Rashid, "Virtual terminal management in a multiple process environment," in *Proc. 7th Symp. Oper. Syst. Principles*, Dec. 1979, pp. 86–97.
[14] E. Lazowska, H. Levy, G. Almes, M. Fischer, R. Fowler, and S. Vestal, "The architecture of the Eden system," in *Proc. 8th Symp. Oper. Syst. Principles*, Dec. 1981, pp. 148–159.
[15] P. J. Leach, B. L. Stumpf, J. A. Hamilton, and P. H. Levine, "UID's as internal names in a distributed file system," in *Proc. 1st Symp. Principles Distrib. Comput.*, Ottawa, Ont., Canada, Aug. 1982.
[16] B. H. Liskov, "Primitives for distributed computing," in *Proc. 7th Symp. Oper./Syst. Principles*, Dec. 1979, pp. 33–42.
[17] R. M. Needham and M. D. Schroeder, "Using encryption for authentication in large networks of computers," *Commun. Ass. Comput. Mach.*, vol. 21, pp. 993–998, Dec. 1978.
[18] R. M. Needham, "Systems aspects of the Cambridge ring," in *Proc. 7th Symp. Oper. Syst. Principles*, Dec. 1979, pp. 82–85.
[19] D. L. Nelson, "Role of local network in the Apollo computer system," *Newslett. IEEE Tech. Comm. Distrib. Processing*, vol. 21, pp. 10–13, Dec. 1981.
[20] —, "Distributed processing in the Apollo DOMAIN," in *Proc. The CAD Revolution, 2nd Chautauqua on Productivity in Eng. and Design*, Kiawah Island, SC, Nov. 1983, pp. 45–51.
[21] E. I. Organick, *The Multics System: An Examination of Its Structure*. Cambridge, MA: M.I.T. Press, 1972.
[22] G. Popek, B. Walker, J. Chow, D. Edwards, C. Kline, G. Rudisin, and G. Thiel, "LOCUS: A network transparent, high reliability distributed system," in *Proc. 8th Symp. Oper. Syst. Principles*, Dec. 1981, pp. 169–177.
[23] D. D. Redell, Y. K. Dalal, T. R. Horsley, H. C. Lauer, W. C. Lynch, P. R. McJones, H. G. Murray, and S. C. Purcell, "Pilot: An operating system for a personal computer," *Commun. Ass. Comput. Mach.*, vol. 23, pp. 81–91, Feb. 1980.
[24] D. M. Ritchie and K. Thompson, "The UNIX time-sharing system," *Commun. Ass. Comput. Mach.*, vol. 17, pp. 365–375, July 1974.
[25] J. H. Saltzer and K. T. Pogran, "A star-shaped ring network with high maintainability," in *Proc. Local Area Commun. Network Symp.*, MITRE Corp., May 1979, pp. 179–190.
[26] J. H. Saltzer, D. P. Reed, and D. D. Clark, "End-to-end arguments in system design," in *Proc. 2nd Int. Conf. Distrib. Syst.*, Paris, France, Apr. 1981, IEEE Comput. Sci. Press, pp. 509–512.
[27] J. H. Saltzer, D. D. Clark, and K. T. Pogran, "Why a ring," in *Proc. 7th Data Commun. Symp.*, Oct. 27–29, 1981, pp. 211–217.
[28] A. Z. Spector, "Performing remote operations efficiently on a local network," *Commun. Ass. Comput. Mach.*, vol. 25, pp. 246–260, Apr. 1982.
[29] H. Sturgis, J. Mitchell, and J. Israel, "Issues in the design and use of a distributed file server," *Oper. Syst. Rev.*, vol. 14, pp. 55–69, July 1980.
[30] L. Svobodova, B. Liskov, and D. Clark, "Distributed computer systems: Structure and semantics," Lab. for Comput. Sci., M.I.T., Cambridge, MA, Tech. Rep. LCS/TR-215, Mar. 1979.
[31] D. Swinehart, G. McDaniel, and D. Boggs, "WFS: A simple shared file system for a distributed environment," in *Proc. 7th Symp. Oper. Syst. Principles*, Dec. 1979, pp. 9–17.
[32] K. Thompson, "UNIX implementation," *Bell Syst. Tech. J.*, vol. 57, pp. 1931–1946, July–Aug. 1978.
[33] M. V. Wilkes and D. J. Wheeler, "The Cambridge digital communication ring," in *Proc. Local Area Commun. Network Symp.*, May 1979, pp. 47–61.

Paul J. Leach (S'78–M'79) received the B.S. degree in electrical engineering and computer science from the Massachusetts Institute of Technology, Cambridge.

From 1977 to 1980 he was in the Research Department at Prime Computer, working on computer architecture and operating systems. From 1979 to 1980 he was also on the adjunct faculty of Boston University, Boston, MA. He joined Apollo Computer, Inc., Chelmsford, MA, in 1980 to do system architecture and operating system design for the DOMAIN system. His current interests are in distributed systems, programming methodology, and user interface design.

Paul H. Levine received the S.B. and S.M. degrees in electrical engineering and computer science from the Massachusetts Institute of Technology, Cambridge, in 1977.

From 1977 to 1980, he worked at Prime Computer, Inc., where he was involved with the development of Prime's networking products. He joined Apollo Computer, Inc., Chelmsford, MA, in June 1980 to do operating system and local area network software design.

Bryan P. Douros received the B.S. degree in electrical engineering and computer science from the Massachusetts Institute of Technology, Cambridge, in 1976.

He joined Lawrence Livermore Laboratory, Livermore, CA, in 1976, working for the weapons program on field diagnostics. In 1978 he joined Prime Computer, where he aided in the microcode development of the Prime 750 processor. He joined Apollo Computer, Inc., Chelmsford, MA, in 1980, where he designed Apollo's ring network and is currently working on future network and CPU architectures.

James A. Hamilton (S'80–M'82) received the B.S. degree in electrical engineering from the University of Colorado, Boulder, the S.M. degree in electrical engineering from the Massachusetts Institute of Technology, Cambridge, and the Ph.D. degree in computer and communications sciences from the University of Michigan, Ann Arbor.

Currently he is a Software Engineer for Apollo Computer, Inc., Chelmsford, MA. His research interests include operating systems architecture, object based systems, and user interfaces.

Dr. Hamilton is a member of the Association for Computing Machinery, and several of its special interest groups.

IN PRAISE OF RING ARCHITECTURE FOR LOCAL AREA NETWORKS

Incorporating the concept of wire centers and the wonders of fiber optics into a ring configured LAN eliminates the traditional bugaboos associated with circular network schemes.

by Howard C. Salwen

Ring networks boast several advantages over bus architectured networks. They are less complex and more flexible, and provide higher throughputs with guaranteed maximum access times.

It was once assumed that the carrier sense multiple access/collision detection (CSMA/CD) bus approach could provide higher reliability and would thus be adopted by the IEEE 802 committee. But the committee's initial ballots indicated that no single approach could be supported. The committee is now laboring to produce a standard document including separate sections for three techniques: token rings, token buses, and CSMA/CD buses. In the opinion of many designers, however, token rings are top achievers where reliability, maintainability, and availability are concerned.

Fig 1 illustrates three network topologies. Where many terminals desire access to a dominant central node, the star configuration (a) is applicable. A timesharing system is a good example of a star network. Obviously, such a system totally fails when the central

Howard C. Salwen is president and cofounder of Proteon Associates, Inc, 24 Crescent St, Waltham, MA 02154, where he is responsible for the design of communication and tracking systems. Mr Salwen is former chairman of the IEEE Communications Society, Boston Section, and holds BSEE and MSEE degrees from MIT.

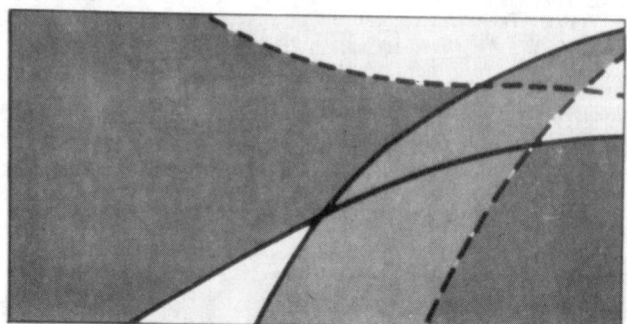

node fails. The ring (b) and bus (c) network configurations are examples of decentralized networks that avoid the hazards of central node failures. However, they require more complex control and access strategies.[1]

Trapping elusive reliability

For reliability's sake, each node in a ring network must be robust, since it must actively repeat each message. Bus topology does not require the message to be regenerated by each node. A node can fail without disrupting the bus if the failure presents high impedance to the bus. Of course, short circuits anywhere on the bus, or in the transceiver attached to the bus, cause the entire bus network to fail.

This reliability problem is often considered the major fault of ring topology. The argument against the basic ring design is that an open circuit anywhere in the ring, or failure of any repeater in the ring, disrupts service. While this is true of the basic ring design shown in Fig 1(b), most of the ring schemes in vogue are not basic

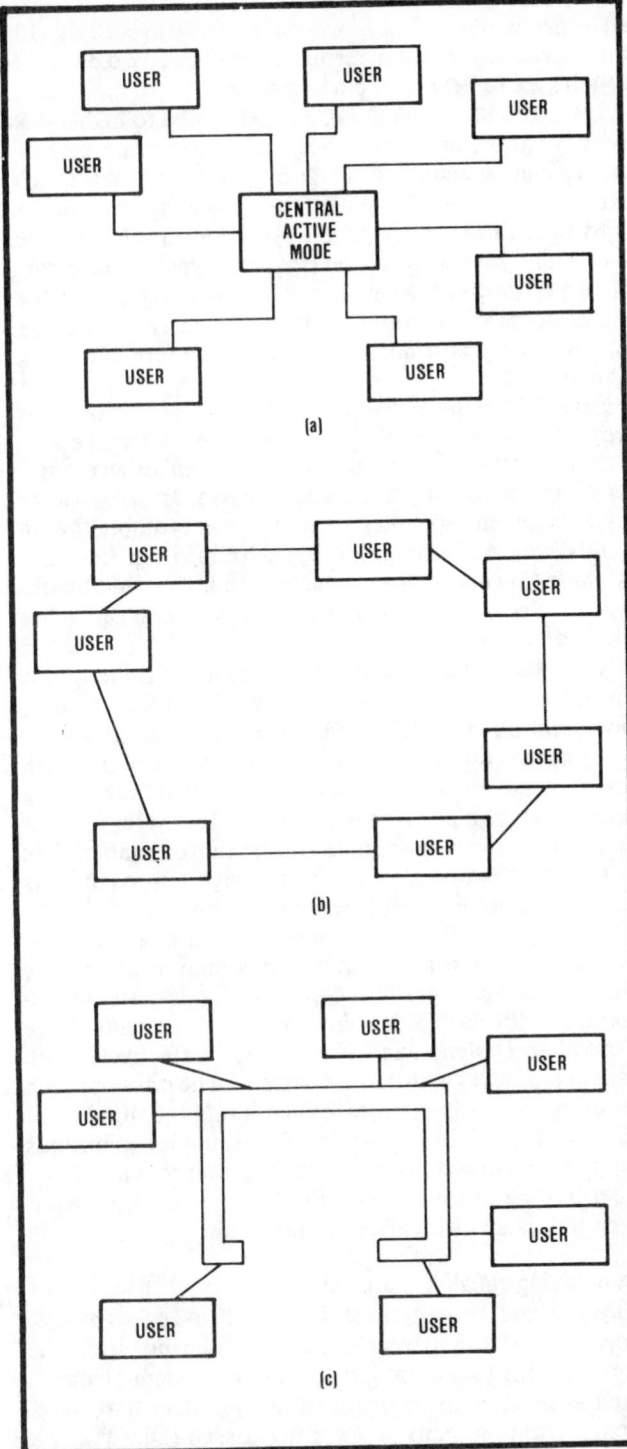

Fig 1 Three popular LAN configurations. Star scheme (a) is totally dependent upon the integrity of its central node. Ring (b) and bus (c) schemes do not suffer from this weakness in reliability.

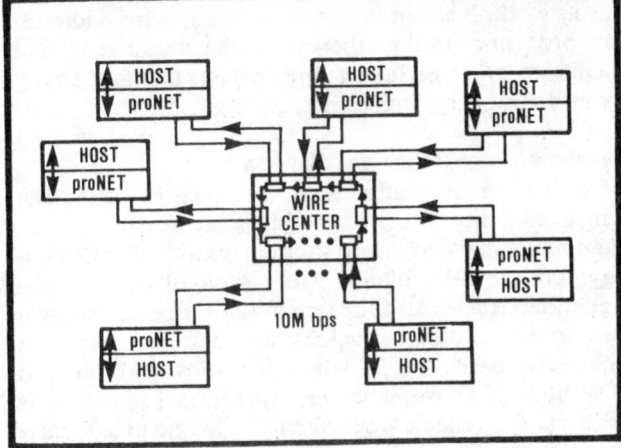

Fig 2 Star shaped ring LAN featuring a wire center. This configurations forgives failures in network nodes and it relay connections facilitate fault isolation. Many such rings can be connected by optical fiber data links.

ring is usually accomplished through a relay. Energization of the relay is accomplished by the user hardware through cable from the user to the wire center. The wire center itself does not have any intrinsic power requirement. When the user host is operating properly and desires to join the ring, it energizes its associated relay at the wire center. If the cable between the host and the wire center is broken, or if the host encounters software problems or power supply failure, the relay returns to its normal de-energized state, bypassing the user. In this way, most of the first-order failure mechanisms cause the automatic bypass of a misbehaving node.

Note that both baseband and broadband bus systems are vulnerable to a variety of single-point failures. For example, a short circuit anywhere in a bus system will disrupt the bus. Similarly, a transceiver that fails to stop transmitting jams the bus. Experience with both types of systems has shown that a duality exists between ring and bus systems. For instance, open circuits are detrimental to rings, while short circuits disrupt buses. Further, repeaters that fail to transmit disrupt rings, while transceivers that fail to stop transmitting disrupt buses.

The wire center concept applied to the ring topology results in a system with a graceful failure mode. That is, defective nodes are automatically bypassed without destroying the entire system. Current baseband and broadband bus topology systems are not designed with such devices. Consider, for example, the effect of a large mismatch (short or open circuit) on a bus system employing the CSMA/CD approach. In such systems, the user listens before transmitting. If the line is not busy, the user transmits a packet of data. The user continues to listen on the chance that someone else has started a transmission at the same time. Each of the users detects the collision of their packets in the ether and backs off for a short time.

Unfortunately, a user's signal that is reflected off mismatches can make the user think that a collision has occurred although it has not. The result is an aborted transmission. Digital Equipment Corp's Ethernet system includes the equivalent of a built-in time domain reflectometer at each node. This device facilitates the detection and location of short and open circuits on the

rings. Modern ring configurations use either redundant paths or fail-safe bypassing, thus avoiding first-level failure problems.

In a discussion of ring reliability, J. R. Pierce suggests that "simple circuits" can be used to bypass failed nodes.[2] The wire center approach is one such circuit.[3]

A basic star shaped ring shown in Fig 2 is actually implemented in a wire center at the hub of a star configured network. The wire center is passive and provides a way for users to break into the ring. Attachment to the bus network. None of the available bus systems addresses this problem. On the other hand, the star shaped ring facilitates graceful failure and built-in maintainability by means of very simple circuitry.

Synchronous operation and fiber optics

Effective communication is another measure of the system's reliability. Most of the bus systems discussed so far operate in the asynchronous burst mode. Ring topology, on the other hand, with its circulating control signal, lends itself to fully synchronous operation. Synchronous operation in the local network environment is not really necessary at data rates below 1M bps. At 10M bps and above, however, synchronous operation is required for reliable performance. This point is clearly made by the performance curves of Fig 3. These curves illustrate the effect of synchronization error on error performance probability in a Manchester encoded system. Manchester encoding uses 2 transmitted bits/data bit transmitted; ie, a mark could be represented by a mark-space pattern on the communication channel and a space could be represented by a space-mark pattern. Manchester encoding is used in many communication systems such as Ethernet and Proteon's proNET and in other applications such as disk recording systems where ac coupling is required.

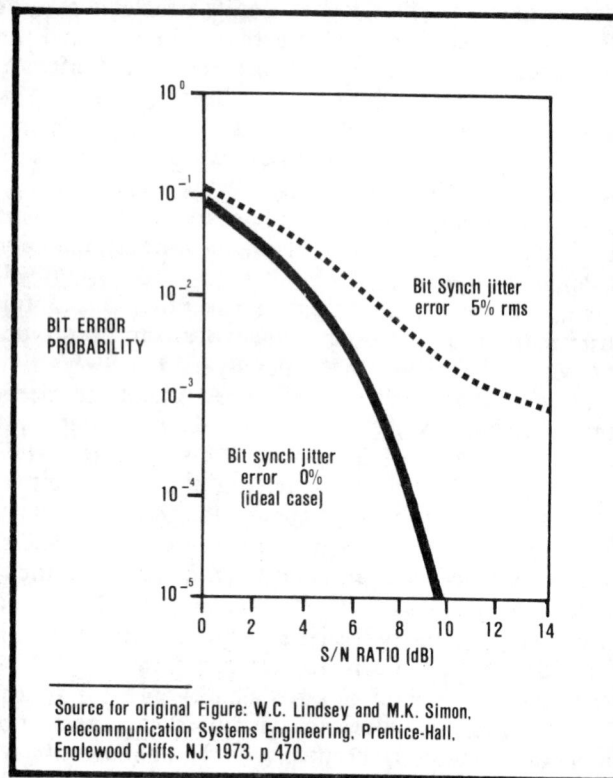

BIT ERROR PROBABILITY

Bit Synch jitter error 5% rms

Bit synch jitter error 0% (ideal case)

S/N RATIO (dB)

Source for original Figure: W.C. Lindsey and M.K. Simon. Telecommunication Systems Engineering. Prentice-Hall. Englewood Cliffs. NJ. 1973, p 470.

Fig 3   Effect of bit synchronization error on network performance. With jitter error of 5% (dashed line), unacceptable error rates are achieved even when S/N ratios are high.

In Fig 3, the probability of bit error as a function of signal to noise (S/N) ratio is plotted for two cases: the lower solid curve represents the ideal, and the upper dashed curve shows the effect of bit synchronization error. Note, for example, that a 5% root mean square (rms) bit synch jitter error (dashed curve) results in an

error probability of 10^{-3} when the S/N ratio is 12 dB. In the absence of such synchronization error, 12 dB would provide extremely high performance.

If the results shown in Fig 3 are extended to higher S/N density ratios, marginally acceptable error rate performance can be achieved at 5% bit jitter when S/N ratios exceed 50 or 60 dB. When the system is running at 10M bps, the estimate of bit synchronization must be less than 5 ns rms to achieve 5% bit synch jitter error. Such performance levels are difficult to achieve in the burst mode. Synchronous, phase locked systems easily achieve this performance level because more averaging time is used.

Severity of the phase jitter problem is not obvious from the Ethernet Phase I specification. DEC has a synchronization quality circuit built into their Ethernet system that automatically rejects messages when jitter levels threaten reliability. It is important to note that in a burst mode bus system, the synchronization error can be caused by noise, but it can also result from multipath-type reflections caused by impedance mismatches throughout the network.

Very soon, large local networks will probably use broadband techniques that employ fiber optic transmission technology. Current fiber optic technology allows the implementation of long transmission links with fewer repeaters when compared to similar links using coaxial very high frequency (vhf) technology. This means that fiber optic links will be more reliable. One important advantage of the ring design approach is its adaptability to existing fiber optic technology.

Specifically, all of the communication links in a ring network comprise a transmitter, a communication link, and a single receiver. This configuration is easily implemented with available fiber optic components. (See *Computer Design*, Jan 1983, p 75, "Effectively Link Microcomputers with Fiber Optics.") The bus approach requires an n-way coupler, which limits the number of users to around 10 per system if reasonable separations are to be achieved. The star shaped ring requires more fiber optic transmitter and receiver modules. But again, each link is an elementary simplex link.

Maintaining reliability a must

Any reliable system must be decentralized. That is, operation of the system should not depend upon the performance or availability of unique system elements such as master clocks or token management hardware. Token ring systems with fully decentralized clock distribution plus token management and error recovery can, and are, being designed. The techniques employed are substantially simpler than those required by a token bus system.

As mentioned, the wire center concept allows the system to fail gracefully. This ability reduces the maintenance burden, since not all failures require an immediate reaction. The wire center scheme discussed provides an even more useful function in this respect—it enables rapid fault isolation. The wire centers play the same role in the communication network as a circuit breaker panel plays in a power distribution network. If a defective node tries to attach itself to the ring, the wire center causes that node to be bypassed without disrupting the whole ring. Wire centers also provide

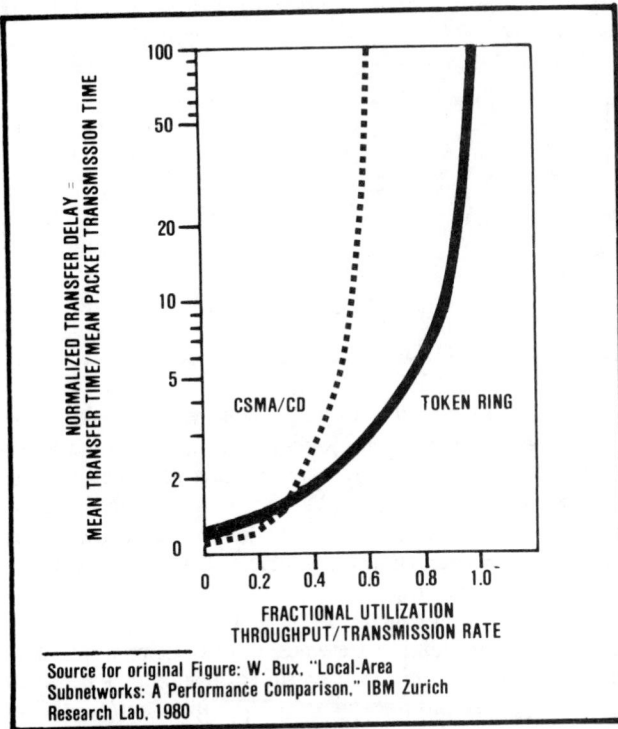

Fig 4 Performance comparison of CSMA/CD system versus token ring system. Given similar network parameters, token ring system offers higher performance and faster access.

system loading function for CSMA/CD systems versus token passing ring networks. The CSMA/CD system depicted is assumed to be 2 km in length; the token ring is assumed to be 2 km in circumference. Both systems have 50 active nodes and an assumed 1000-bit average message length. Under these conditions, the maximum achievable throughput on the CSMA/CD system is about 6M bps, achieved with infinite waiting times. Throughput on the token ring system asymptotically approaches a value just below 10M bps. Typical token ring protocols impose a maximum packet size. Given a 50-node network and a 1000-byte maximum packet size, the maximum time before access to the system is approximately 40 ms.

The proNET local area network (LAN) illustrates the various design concepts of ring network schemes. ProNET is a token arbitrated, ring local network operating at 10M bps. Up to 255 users can be supported by each ring. The proNET configuration in Fig 5 is an extension of the star shaped ring concept. In fact, it is a string of stars or a "constellation." Short runs from a wire center to various computers in a computer room can be interconnected with twisted pairs. Long runs from one wire center to another can be implemented with dual fiber optic links. Note that the wire center attachment point for fiber optic links includes a bypassing relay. If the fiber optic link connecting the two wire centers were to fail, the system would automatically partition itself into two star shaped rings. In this case, no interconnecting fiber optic link exists between them.

At each node or host there are two hardware modules: a control board (CTL) and a host specific interface board (HSB). The CTL hardware module performs bit-level network functions and signal modulation/demodulation required for data transmission through the transmission medium. The HSB module contains a full-duplex direct memory access (DMA) interface to the host. In addition, this board contains two separate

centralized locations where signals can be monitored, and a manual means for dropping or adding nodes to the ring. Thus, the wire centers substantially reduce the mean time to repair the network.

Rapid fault isolation and short mean time to repair improve the network's availability. The token approach further enhances availability by establishing a guaranteed maximum waiting time before access is granted. Fig 4 shows the normalized mean time to transmit as a

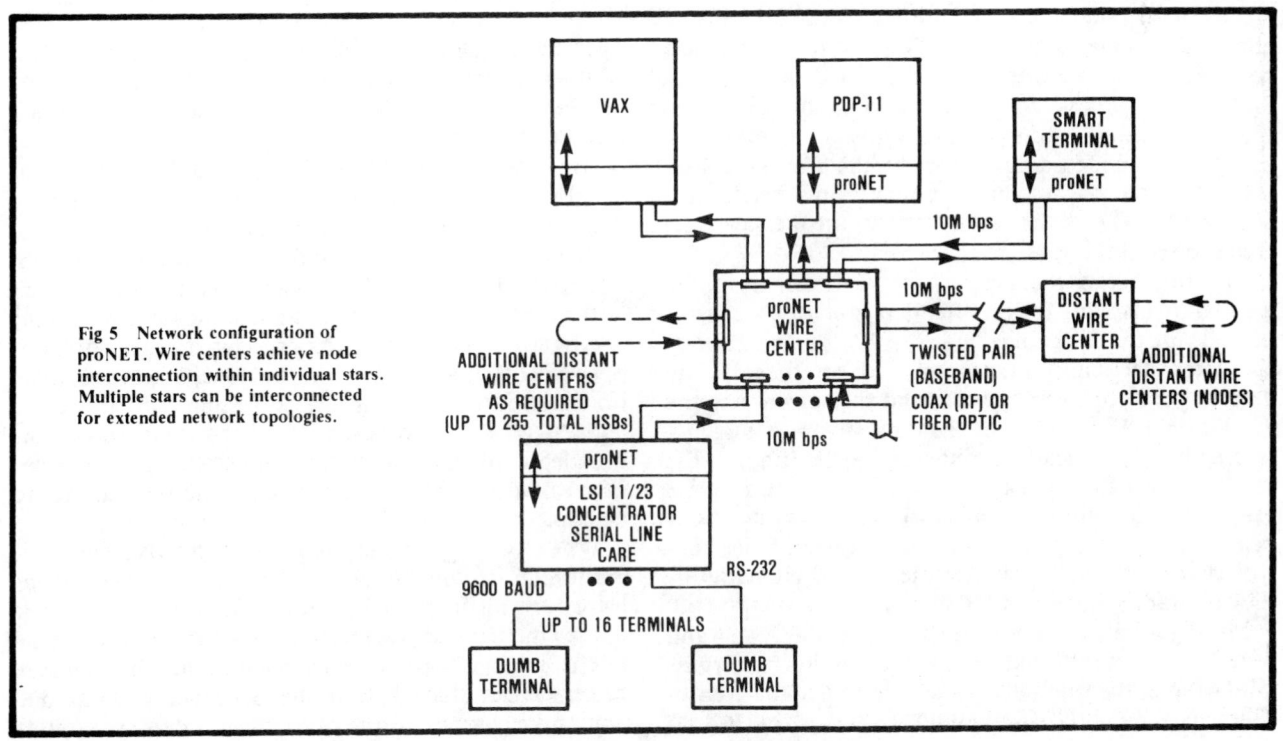

Fig 5 Network configuration of proNET. Wire centers achieve node interconnection within individual stars. Multiple stars can be interconnected for extended network topologies.

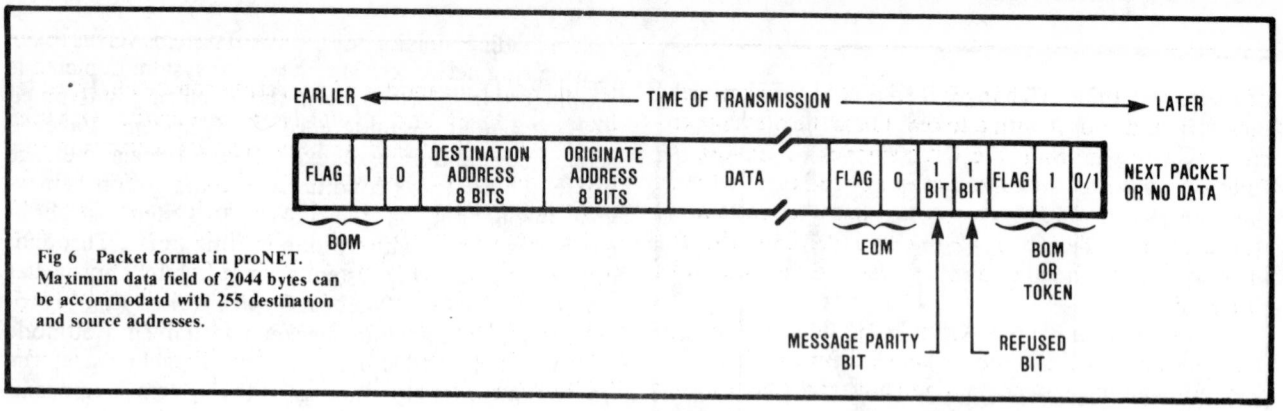

Fig 6 Packet format in proNET. Maximum data field of 2044 bytes can be accommodatd with 255 destination and source addresses.

2046-byte (1023-word) packet buffers, plus control and status registers. In short, all of the firmware needed for an automatic communications operation is supplied. This minimizes the host's software burden imposed by the communication network.

The wire centers shown in Fig 5 are passive. Control signals for the node relays are passed through the transmission medium to the wire center by each respective node. Maintenance switches included in each wire center override node relay control. This improves network fault isolation and reliability. Loopback testing is also implemented by the wire center. In this way, a host can check out the entire circuit right up to the attachment point before joining the ring.

Fig 6 illustrates the network's data link format and control characters. An important feature of the data encapsulation format is the absence of a word count field. Each packet can have a variable number of data bytes, since the end of message (EOM) control character serves as a data field boundary. Size of the packet buffer memory is the only restricting factor on the number of data bytes placed on the network. ProNET's HSB allows a maximum data field of 2044 8-bit bytes, plus 1 byte each of destination and source address data.

Every node within the ring network is identified by means of its node address. An 8-bit switch on the CTL allows 255-node address selection, with address 255 reserved as the network-wide broadcast address. An 8-bit source address follows the destination address in the data encapsulation format. The source address is equal to the node address as set by the 8-bit switch on the CTL card. Hardware automatically inserts this source address into the second byte of the message data received from the HSB.

Bit stuffing of the network data stream is implemented by inserting a 0 bit after detection of six consecutive 1s in the outgoing data. Destuffing and control character decoding is accomplished on the CTL by detecting a 0 followed by six 1s and then examining the 7th bit. A 0 here indicates the data stream contains a stuffed bit; a 1 indicates a control character (flag). If the sequence is a flag, the two bits following the flag are examined to determine whether the character is a beginning of message (BOM), EOM, or token. Since control characters consist of specific 8- or 9-bit patterns, they are rarely generated by accident.

Messages can be placed on the ring only if a valid token has been detected by the node wishing to transmit. At idle, the ring network circulates a token control character around the ring. If a node has a request to send

pending, the CTL will convert the next received token into a BOM character by changing its last bit, marking a BOM. Converting the token into a BOM ensures orderly queueing among nodes wishing to place messages on the ring. A token sent at the end of the message will allow nodes that are downstream of the originating node to place messages on the ring.

This data communication technique allows for simple 1-way communication between nodes. Low error rates are obtained on runs of several thousand feet between nodes at baseband parameters. The biphase modulation technique allows the nodes to be ac coupled. Frequency components below 1 MHz are rejected by filtering at each node so that the network is relatively immune to ambient noise. The communication medium for runs of under 300' (91 m) can be inexpensive twisted pair cable. Longer runs can be made with dual-axial cable. In addition, the network can be adapted to other transmission media, such as modulated radio frequency (rf) on coaxial cable or fiber optic links. In fact, 4-km links using fiber optics are available. Such links can be employed between wire centers so that networks many kilometers in length are feasible. In addition, token architecture does not limit maximum propagation delay across the network as CSMA/CD does.

Operational modes provide flexibility

In the network configuration described, four operating modes are available: repeat, copy, originate, and initialize. In addition, there are two possible test configurations: digital loopback and analog loopback. The CTL is usually found in the repeat mode, where the CTL repeats data on the ring. The data received from the adjacent node upstream are passed to the next node downstream.

The CTL automatically switches from the repeat mode to the copy mode if it determines that the message passing through it is intended for its associated host processor. Specifically, the message will be copied if the destination address in the message corresponds to the CTL's address. It will also be copied if the message has the broadcast address. Alternatively, the CTL can be strapped in the match-all configuration, allowing any message to be copied.

When copying or originating, the host's operations are similar in complexity to those required when writing to or reading from a disk. For example, when the host desires to transmit a message to another node, it carries out an originate operation. It begins when the packet to be sent is transferred from the host memory to an output packet buffer on the HSB. Then, upon recognition of the token, the CTL changes it to a BOM, transmits the message, and ends it with a token. Once the message circumnavigates the ring, the CTL removes it, leaving the following message or token intact. If the ring network does not have a valid token control character circulating it, the CTL module can create one by initializing the ring in response to an initialize request from the host processor.

The initialize mode is essentially the same as the originate mode, with one important exception: The CTL does not wait until an access control token passes into it before sending the message. In this way, the CTL module forces a message onto the ring. It removes the returning message, leaving only the valid token circulating on the ring.

Since every CTL module can initialize the ring in this fully decentralized network, it is important to avoid simultaneous attempts at initialization by two or more CTLs. Initialization of proNET is assumed to be random due to the random arrival of users. Typically, an originate request to the CTL is accompanied by an initialize request. However, if the CTL monitoring circuitry indicates that a valid token is circulating and flags are being seen at the required rate, the initialize request is blocked. If, at the instant of initialize request, the CTL indicates that the ring is not available, the origination is carried out immediately. Of course, it is still possible for two originators to arrive simultaneously at the network, causing each to think the ring is not available. As a result, each will attempt to initialize the ring, causing each CTL to drain the other's message. Each will then report a "message lost" to its associated host through the HSB, and the ring will remain without a token. The next originator who arrives at the ring will initialize it, while the first two are executing software-randomized timeouts.

In the normal mode of operation, the CTL receives data from its adjacent node upstream, and transmits data to the next node downstream. Two test configurations, digital and analog loopback, are also implemented under host control.

Digital loopback can be used to test all portions of the TL/HSB, except for the modem and cable intercon- nection. All four modes of operation can be analyzed in digital loopback and all hardware associated with the operation can be tested without actually disturbing the existing network. Analog loopback is a special operation implemented with a wire center. It allows the user to test all CTL circuitry and cables leading to a wire center, without disturbing the existing network.

Fully decentralized, token arbitrated ring networks provide superior reliability, maintainability, and communication availability. For these reasons, they are becoming widely accepted by network users.

References

1. D. D. Clark, K. T. Pogran, and D. T. Reed, "An Introduction to Local Area Networks," *Proceedings of IEEE 66*, vol 11, 1978, pp 1497-1517.
2. J. R. Pierce, "How Far Can Loops Go?" *IEEE Transaction on Communications,* vol COM-20, 1972, pp 527-530.
3. J. H. Saltzer and K. T. Pogran, "A Star-Shaped Ring Network with High Maintainability," *Proceedings of the Local Area Communications Network Symposium*, MITRE Corp, 1979.

Bibliography

P. Abramson and F. E. Noel, "Local Area Network Media Selection for Ring Topologies," IBM, July 27, 1982.

H. Meyr, H. Boutén, H. R. Muller, and U. Bapst, "Manchester Coding with Predistortion: An Efficient and Simple Transmission Technique in Local Digital Ring Networks," IBM research report RZ 1042, Nov 17, 1980.

P. V. Mockapetris, M. R. Lyle, and D. J. Farber, "On the Design of Local Network Interfaces," *Information Processing 77*, B. Gilchrist, ed, IPIF North-Holland Publishing Co, 1977.

J. F. Shoch and J. A. Hupp, "Performance of an Ethernet Local Network—A Preliminary Report," *Proceedings of the Local Area Communications Network Symposium,* MITRE Corp, 1979.

M. V. Wilkes and D. J. Wheeler, "The Cambridge Digital Communications Ring," *Proceedings of the Local Area Communications Network Symposium,* MITRE Corp, 1979.

Architecture and Design of a Reliable Token-Ring Network

WERNER BUX, MEMBER, IEEE, FELIX H. CLOSS, MEMBER, IEEE, KARL KUEMMERLE, MEMBER, IEEE, HEINZ J. KELLER, ASSOCIATE MEMBER, IEEE, AND HANS R. MUELLER

Abstract—Architecture, performance, transmission system, and wiring strategy of a token-ring local area network implemented at the IBM Zurich Research Laboratory are described. In the design of the system, particular emphasis was placed on high reliability, availability, and serviceability. To ensure robustness of the token-access protocol, we employ the concept of a monitor function which is responsible for fast recovery from access-related errors. Our protocol supports asynchronous transmission of data frames concurrently with full-duplex synchronous channels, e.g., for voice services or other applications requiring guaranteed delay. The delay-throughput performance of the token ring is shown to depend very little on data rate and distance. The transmission system of the ring is fully bit synchronous and allows insertion/removal of stations in/from the ring at any time. A mixed ring/star wiring strategy is used which provides the means for both fault detection and isolation, and system reconfiguration, and allows wiring of a building systematically.

I. INTRODUCTION

LOCAL communication systems for data employing various topologies have been used for a long time [1], [2]. The current activities in the field of local area communication networks can be viewed as an expansion to data networks to make high-speed packet-switching services available to the in-house domain. There are three driving forces. First, progress made in VLSI technology to implement low cost network adapters; second, the availability of

high-speed transmission media at reasonable cost; and third, the trend to distributed processing with intelligent workstations. The following objectives are to be achieved:

- To provide the basic communication functions for various types of devices, such as terminals, workstations, printers, communication controllers, host computers, etc.

- To solve the problem of crowded cable ducts, to allow easy system expansion, and to stop the proliferation of transmission systems for different sets of products.

- To allow manufacturers the design of compatible network components through standardizing media, transmission system, and access-control procedures.

This paper describes the major aspects pertaining to architecture, wiring, transmission, and performance of a local area ring system with token-passing access designed and implemented at the IBM Zurich Research Laboratory [3]–[10]. One of the first accounts of the basic token-access mechanism was presented by Farmer and Newhall [11], some other references are [12]–[15]. Our contributions focus on system reliability, availability, and serviceability. In particular, our investigations demonstrate that a local area network based on a token ring has the following attractive features:

1) robustness and efficiency of the access protocol, i.e., quick recovery from token errors and excellent delay-throughput characteristics compared to other access control schemes employed on bus and/or ring systems,

2) physical reliability and the potential for systematic

Manuscript received February 15, 1983; revised July 11, 1983. Parts of this paper were presented at the National Telecommunications Conference, New Orleans, LA, November 1981.

The authors are with the IBM Zurich Research Laboratory, 8803 Rüschlikon, Switzerland.

EHO228-7/85/0000/0166$01.00 © 1983 IEEE

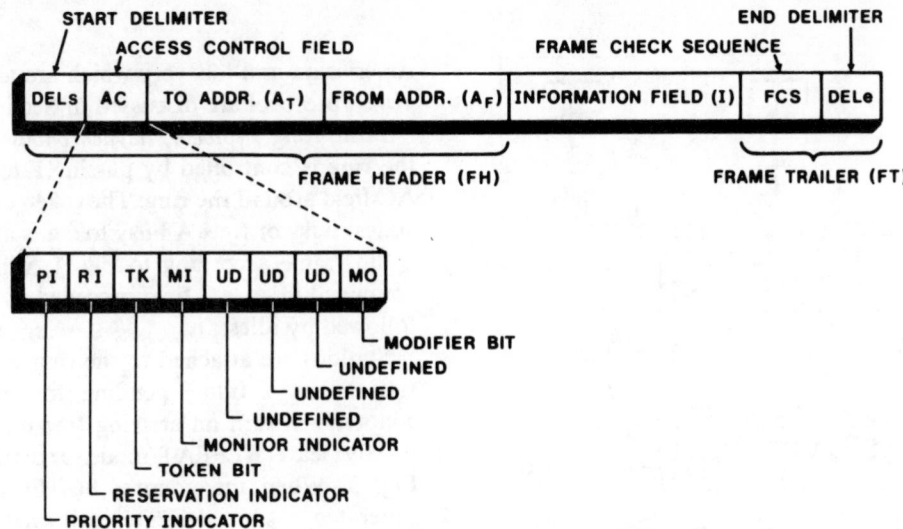

Fig. 1. Frame structure. After [5].

wiring through the concept of wiring concentrators to which stations are connected in a radial fashion and which are interconnected by the main ring cable,

3) electrical stability of a ring consisting of a chain of several hundred repeaters, and

4) the potential to provide synchronous channels in addition to the asynchronous (packet-oriented) data operation for applications requiring guaranteed delay or throughput. Examples are process control and real-time voice services.

In the next section, we describe the data format on the ring, the access method, and a monitor function through which we achieve a reliable ring operation. Section III discusses the wiring scheme, Section IV presents an outline of the ring transmission system, and, finally, we consider the delay-throughput behavior of the token ring in Section V.

II. TOKEN-ACCESS PROTOCOL

The design of the access method and the frame format was led by the consideration that the ring has to fit into the framework of a general network architecture, e.g., SNA [16], without requiring changes in higher level protocols. This has two basic consequences.

1) Protocols related to the ring access have to be confined to the bottom layers, physical and data link layers. In particular, the mechanisms for access-related error detection and recovery must also be embedded in these layers.

2) Access method and data link control functions should be clearly separated in order to be open-ended for the use of the most appropriate data link control procedures.

In addition to these architectural requirements, the desire to provide synchronous channels on the ring had a major impact on our ring architecture.

A. Frame Format

Transmission on the ring is in the form of variable-length frames, the structure of which is shown in Fig. 1. A frame is delimited by start- and end-delimiters (DELs, DELe) and consists of an access-control field (AC), TO- and FROM-link addresses (AT, AF), the information field (I), and the frame check sequence field (FCS). For ease of description, we subsequently refer to the combination of start delimiter, access-control field, and the two link addresses as "frame header" (FH) and to the combination of FCS field and end delimiter as "frame trailer" (FT). The meaning of the above frame elements is defined as follows.

Delimiters consist of four bit patterns representing violations of the differential (polarity-insensitive) Manchester code (see Section IV-A), followed by two unused bits and two "qualifier bits" which serve to distinguish between start and end delimiters.

Access-Control Field serves the following purposes: access control, multiplexing of asynchronous and synchronous traffic, ring supervision, and recovery. It consists of the following eight bits:

1) *Priority Indicator* (PI) which serves to distinguish between a frame carrying asynchronous traffic (PI = 0) and synchronous traffic (PI = 1).

2) *Reservation Indication* (RI) needed to guarantee timely access for stations with synchronous traffic.

3) *Token* (TK) which controls access to the ring and can be in either of two states: "free" (TK = 0) or "busy" (TK = 1).

4) *Monitor Indicator* (MI) is manipulated by the ring monitor for ring supervision/recovery purposes. For details, see Section II-C.

5) *Undefined Bits* (UD) of which the meaning is not defined.

6) *Modifier* (MO) allows the distinction between normal "user frames," i.e., the I field contains user data, and "access-control" frames, i.e., the I field contains well-defined control information related to the ring operation.

Link Addresses: The address space is based on the notion of a local network consisting of several interconnected subnetworks (rings). To simplify the routing function in the interconnecting units, we use structured TO- and FROM-addresses each four bytes long. The first two bytes of the link address denote the ring number (unique in the entire local network), the second two bytes are the station

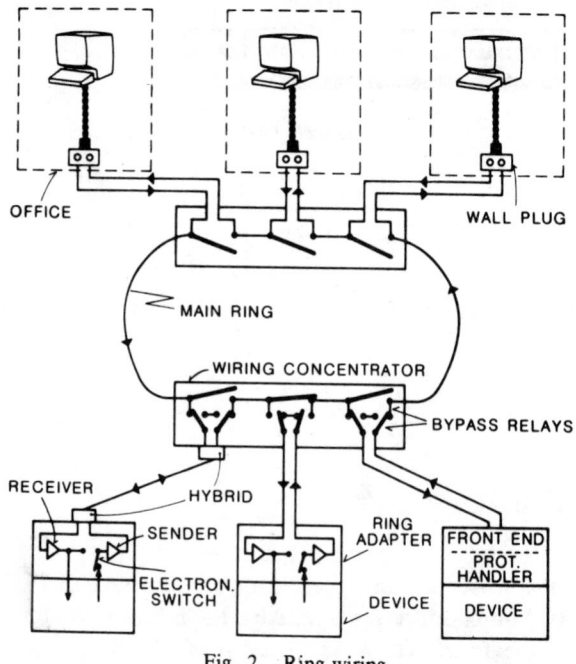

Fig. 2. Ring wiring.

number (unique at least on one ring, possibly within the entire network).

Information Field contains higher level data; it may contain any sequence of bits. The architecture does not impose any restrictions on the maximum frame size. It should be noted, however, that the setting of timers (see Section II-C) in an actual implementation does depend on the maximum frame length selected.

Frame Check Sequence Field is two bytes long and generated according to the standard HDLC/SDLC generator polynomial of degree 16. A two byte FCS was chosen because of readily available chips performing this function. The FCS protects the MO bit, the TO- and FROM-addresses, and the I field. Thus, the frame check sequence guarantees correctness of a frame received in a ring adapter, Fig. 2, and to be passed across the system interface into the station memory. Other errors, such as faulty transmission between ring adapter and station or lost frames, are detected by parity bits or by detection and recovery functions provided above ring access control, e.g., in the logical link control sublayer.

The frame structure shown in Fig. 1 is simpler than the one proposed in the draft standards of ECMA [17] and IEEE 802 [18]. This is due to various features which the standards groups added to the ring protocol, such as more priority levels, larger address space, four byte frame check sequence, and various indicators, e.g., the "address-recognized" and the "frame-copied" indicators. It should be noted that the key elements necessary for reliable token operation are basically the same in the draft standards and our architecture.

B. Access Control

In this section, we describe the basic ring-access protocol for both asynchronous and synchronous operation. Token supervision and recovery which are also part of the token-access protocol are discussed in Section C.

Basic Ring Protocol/Asynchronous Operation: Access to the ring is controlled by passing a token contained in the AC field around the ring. The token can be in either of two states: busy or free. A busy token is always associated with a full frame according to Fig. 1, whereas a free token is contained in an AC field preceded by a start delimiter and followed by idles.

Stations are attached to the ring via a ring adapter. If a station has a frame pending for transmission, then its adapter will turn an arriving free token to a busy one on the fly, leave REPEAT mode, and transmit its frame, see Fig. 3. When the adapter has finished transmission, it generates a start delimiter followed by an AC field in which all bits—including TK—are set to zero, provided that

1) the adapter has received back the entire FH including both addresses,

2) the received FROM-address equals the station's own address, and

3) the RI bit is still zero, i.e., the reservation indicator has not been changed (compare synchronous operation).

The reasons for imposing these conditions on the generation of a free token are as follows.

• Receipt of a FROM-address different from the station's address indicates that an error in the access protocol has occurred. Consequently, the transmitting adapter refrains from issuing a free token. (Recovery from this and other access-related errors is described in the next section.)

• As will be presented in detail later, the ring is switched into synchronous operation in regular time intervals. To guarantee timely start of the synchronous-access intervals, the synchronous bandwidth manager, explained below in the paragraph on synchronous operation, is allowed to set the RI bit in any AC field passing through with a busy token. This indicates to the transmitting adapter which receives back the header of its frame that it must not issue a free token.

Following transmission of the frame (and usually of a free token), the adapter keeps transmitting idles until it receives the next end delimiter which is the end of its own frame provided no access error has occurred. Upon detection of the end delimiter, the adapter enters REPEAT mode. In REPEAT mode, a ring adapter simply retransmits all data on the ring with a short latency, typically one bit time. It also monitors the TO-address fields of the frames passing through. When it detects its own address, it copies the frame, but does not modify the passing frame.

Rationale of Protocol Design: Two basic elements of a token-ring protocol have a major impact on its overall characteristics.

1) The repeater switching strategy, i.e., the rule according to which the adapter enters REPEAT mode following the transmission of a frame.

2) The token-generation strategy, i.e., the rule determining when and under which conditions the adapter issues a new free token. We subsequently give the motivation for

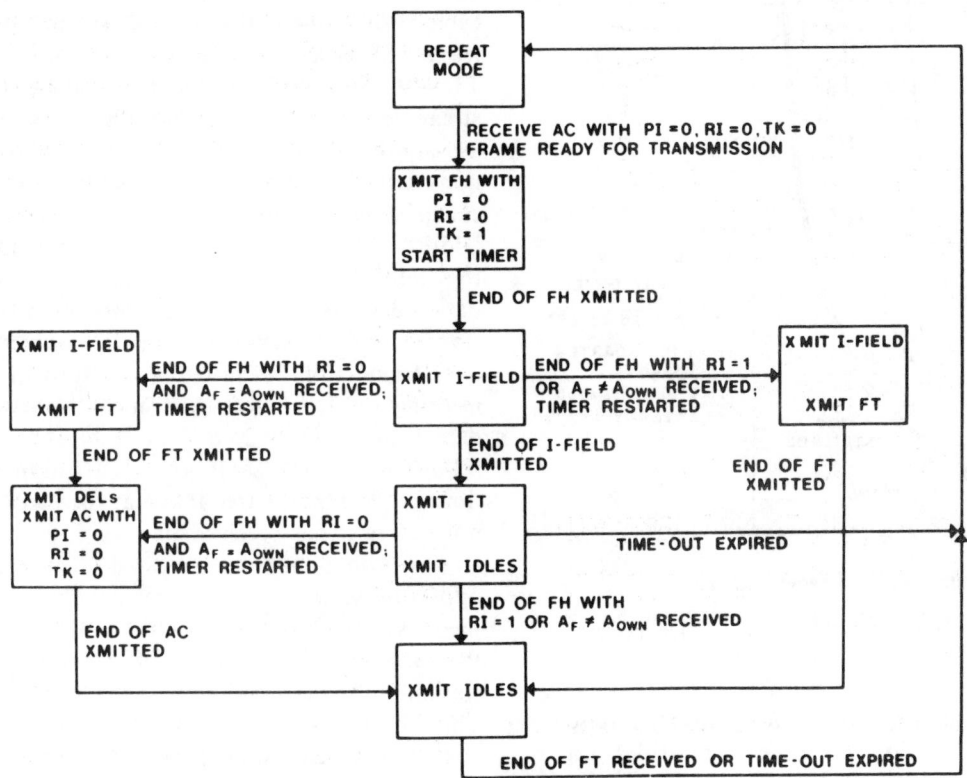

Fig. 3. Ring-access protocol. After [5].

choosing our particular solutions regarding these two issues.

Repeater Switching Strategy: There are two natural points in time when the adapter returns to REPEAT mode after transmission

1) immediately after the end delimiter of a frame has been transmitted, or

2) after the end delimiter has been received back.

Our major reason for preferring the second method is to guarantee that under error-free conditions, no garbage (i.e., fragments of previously transmitted frames) is left on the ring.

Token-Generation Strategies: Based on our repeater switching strategy, three approaches are conceivable regarding the point in time when an adapter generates a free token following the transmission of a frame.

1) "Single-frame operation" in which the sender of a frame issues the new token when it has completely received its entire frame and, hence, erased it from the ring.

2) "Single-token operation" in which the sender of a frame does not issue a new token before it has received back the header of its frame including the busy token. This rule becomes effective in cases where a frame is shorter than the ring latency.

3) "Multiple-token operation" in which a new free token is generated immediately after the end delimiter of a frame has been transmitted. This implies that depending on ring latency and frame transmission times, multiple tokens can exist on the ring; at most one of them, however, is in the free state.

Since the priority operation described below requires

that a free token is not issued before the frame header has returned to the sender, and since performance analysis shows nearly ideal delay-throughput characteristic for realistic speeds and distances [4], we decided in favor of the single-token operation. This decision is further backed up by the fact that token supervision and recovery will be greatly facilitated if the protocol ensures that only one token (free or busy) exists on the ring.

It has been mentioned above that the latency of a ring adapter in REPEAT mode is typically one bit time. Fig. 4 shows the sensitivity of the delay-throughput behavior of a token ring operating under the single-token rule at 4 Mbits/s with respect to adapter latency. The figure demonstrates that 1) there is a significant performance degradation when the latency is increased from one to eight bits, 2) this effect strongly depends on the number of active stations, and 3) the delay-throughput behavior is fairly insensitive to the number of stations, provided the latency is one bit. Therefore, our design decision was to select a latency of one bit per adapter (station).

Synchronous Operation: Our ring protocol offers two priority levels and thus allows provision of priority access for selected stations. Before we describe how these priorities can be used to concurrently provide asynchronous and synchronous operations, several general remarks should be made.

1) The priority mechanism based on the pair of reservation and priority indicators could be used to provide two asynchronous priority levels. In this case, the synchronous bandwidth manager described below is not necessary.

2) Currently undefined bits in the frame depicted in Fig.

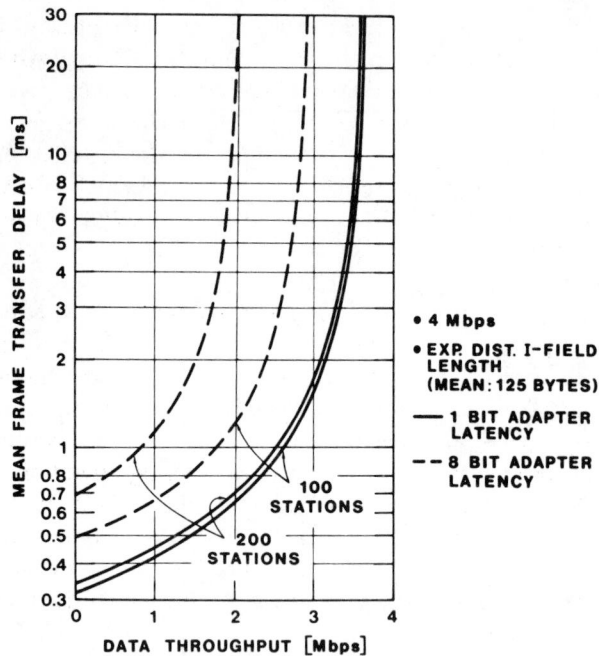

Fig. 4. Impact of adapter latency on delay-throughput characteristic. ©1983 World Telecommunication Union (I.T.U.).

1 could be used to obtain additional priority levels, thus providing the capability for several priorities for the asynchronous, and one priority level for the synchronous operation, respectively. (The token-ring draft standards [17], [18] provide eight priority levels through three bit priority and reservation indicators.) One important application of priority access is for synchronous operation requiring guaranteed bandwidth, e.g., 64 kbits/s in the case of PCM voice channels. Another application of the synchronous capability is to use it as a vehicle to attach data devices requiring guaranteed bandwidth and delay.

Stations desiring to establish a synchronous connection have to go through a call-setup procedure which involves a central control station, called the synchronous bandwidth manager (SBM). The SBM station will grant or reject a request for a synchronous connection, depending on the number of synchronous connections already established and on the bandwidth required for asynchronous data traffic. The assignment of bandwidth to the two traffic types is completely flexible, as will become clear from the subsequent description, which focuses on the mechanism of how synchronous full-duplex connections and asynchronous types of transmissions are concurrently provided on the same ring. It is assumed that the synchronous connections have already been established and all stations holding a synchronous connection are designated either as "calling" or as "called" stations. This property is defined during connection setup and is used to avoid ambiguities.

The SBM prepares switching of the ring into synchronous operation by making priority reservations at such points in time that it is possible to periodically issue priority tokens (PI = 1). To achieve this, the SBM uses the reservation indicator to interrupt the asynchronous operation. When the reservation indicator gets set (RI = 1) in a frame being currently transmitted, the transmitting station does not issue a free token but transmits idles until it

receives the end delimiter of its own frame (see Fig. 2). It also remembers that it was the last one in the asynchronous cycle. When the SBM detects the end delimiter of the frame, it releases a free priority token (PI = 1, RI = 0, TK = 0). Subsequently, the first calling station A downstream from the SBM changes the token to busy, appends TO-address B and FROM-address A, and puts its synchronous data into the information field. Station B —like every called station— monitors for its own address in the TO-address field. Upon detection of its own address, it copies the information field and puts its own synchronous data—destined to A—in the information field of the same frame. As in asynchronous mode, adapter A removes its own frame from the ring but instead of discarding the information field, A copies it since it contains synchronous data from its partner, B. Issuing of a new priority token follows exactly the same rules as for asynchronous operation, i.e., A sends a free token at the end of its frame but not before it has received its own FROM-address. When all synchronous stations have had exactly one transmission opportunity, the SBM will receive the free priority token. It then issues a start delimiter followed by an AC field with PI = 0, RI = 1, TK = 0, which cannot be used by any station but the last one in the previous asynchronous cycle. This station will flip the RI bit to zero, and thus issue the next free asynchronous token. It should be noted that this mechanism preserves the fairness of access among all stations operating in the asynchronous mode.

A performance analysis studying the tradeoff between number and bandwidth of synchronous channels, and the bandwidth left, or delay achievable for the asynchronous operation, is currently being pursued.

C. Token Supervision and Recovery

Our approach to achieve reliable operation is to have a monitor function responsible for supervising the proper token operation and performing fast recovery in case of errors. Implementation showed that both hardware and microcode necessary to provide the monitor function in addition to the token-access protocol only slightly increased the complexity of a ring adapter. Therefore, the monitor function is provided in each ring adapter, however, it is active in only one adapter at any one time.

Adapters in REPEAT mode play a passive role in token recovery. Transmitting adapters enter REPEAT mode upon detection of a protocol error and do not issue a free token. All active recovery measures are taken by the monitor itself.

Access to the ring is exclusively controlled by the token. Particular supervisory functions are therefore embedded in the protocol to invoke recovery actions when the token is mutilated. We classify the token-related error situations into three different types.

1) Lost-Token Situation when during a certain critical time interval, neither a free nor a busy token is transmitted over the ring. This can occur, for example, if a start delimiter is mutilated and also during ring initialization.

2) Circulating Busy-Token Situation when a start delimiter and an AC field with busy token continuously circulate around the ring. This may be caused by noise hitting the free-token bit.

3) Duplicate-Token Situation when two (or more) stations transmit simultaneously because both have received a free token. Such an error situation can occur, e.g., if a free token is generated by noise hitting a busy token.

How the ring recovers from these error situations is subsequently described.

Recovery from Lost-Token Error: One of the basic tasks of the monitor is to constantly check the data stream passing through for tokens. From the above description of the access protocol, it becomes clear that the time interval between subsequent observations of a free or busy token (or equivalently of a start delimiter) is upper bounded by the maximum frame transmission time plus the ring latency. Therefore, the monitor can detect a lost-token situation with the aid of an appropriately adjusted timeout $T1$ started whenever it observes a start delimiter. Upon expiration of the timeout, the monitor clears the ring from possible garbage by transmitting idles for a time interval longer than the ring latency, and eventually issues a new free token.

Recovery from Circulating Busy-Token Error: A permanently circulating busy token can be detected by the monitor with the aid of the monitor indicator bit (MI) in the AC field. Any adapter transmitting a frame sets MI to "zero." When the frame passes through the monitor, it changes MI to "one." In this way, the monitor is able to detect any AC field with a busy token circulating more than once around the ring by checking the MI bit. Recovery is again performed by the monitor through clearing the ring, and then transmitting a start delimiter followed by an AC field with a free token.

Recovery from Duplicate-Token Error: Duplication of a free token can lead to a situation where multiple stations are transmitting simultaneously. Two mechanisms in the access protocol are provided to recover from this error situation. The first mechanism is that a transmitting adapter checks the FROM-address field which it receives back. A second recovery mechanism is needed for those cases where a transmitting station does not receive back any intact FH at all. In such a case, the timeout $T1$ shown in Fig. 3 will expire. As shown in the state diagram of Fig. 3, the reaction of an adapter to either of these situations is to finish the transmission of the current frame and afterwards to enter REPEAT mode without generating a free token. Thus, the error is converted into a lost-token situation and recovered accordingly.

As described above, the ring is supervised by *one* adapter which, in addition to its normal access-control functions, acts as an active monitor. All adapters are identical, therefore, any adapter can assume the role of the active monitor. This allows automatic replacement of a failing active monitor, triggered by either of the following two events:

1) "watchdog" circuits sensing loss of synchronization of the bit stream, and

2) the absence of a free token for a period longer than the maximum free-token cycle time, detected by timeout. It should be noted that this situation is different from the lost-token condition described above.

The replacement process is split into two phases. In phase 1, all passive monitors continuously broadcast a "monitor-recovery" message. Upon receipt of such a message from another passive monitor which carries a FROM-address greater than its own address, a passive monitor terminates competition mode and enters REPEAT mode. Eventually, the monitor-recovery message which carries the largest FROM-address will succeed in traveling around the ring.

Phase 2 starts when a passive monitor has received its own monitor-recovery message. It first enters active-monitor mode and then informs all other adapters of this by broadcasting an "end of monitor replacement" message. Upon receipt of this message, the new active monitor generates a free token, thus restoring the ring operation.

The procedure described above is not only used for monitor recovery, but also to resolve contention when several adapters with monitor capability simultaneously connect to an inactive ring, i.e., to a ring which does not yet carry any signal.

There are, of course, alternative approaches to provide a reliable token operation. For example, it is possible to distribute the recovery functions among all active stations. This excludes use of the monitor indicator as described above, but requires recovery protocols entirely based on timeouts. Such an approach is viable but leads to significantly slower recovery. For this reason, the standards groups abandoned it in favor of a monitor-recovery solution very similar to ours [17], [18].

III. Ring Wiring

The installation of a local area network (LAN) in a building or on a campus requires a wiring strategy designed to offer sufficient flexibility for a wide variety of building structures. The LAN wiring plan must be open to reconfiguration and expansion. It must meet high standards of reliability, availability, and serviceability on a wide scale of environments ranging from office systems to more EMI-exposed plant control systems.

In our ring network, we use a two-level wiring hierarchy [7]. The main ring interconnects a set of wiring concentrators which can be placed at strategic and protected locations in a building, Fig. 2. Offices are wired to concentrators in a radial fashion. These lobes are terminated in the office by wall outlets. A station is connected to the ring by plugging it into any outlet. This hybrid ring/star wiring strategy allows wiring of a building in a systematic way without having to loop the main-ring cable through every office and to every outlet. Additional outlets can be installed according to evolving demand without having to restructure the ring.

Wiring concentrators are centralized points for maintenance and reconfiguration. In its simplest form, a concentrator contains bypass relays for each lobe, Fig. 2. It is a passive device in the sense that it does not amplify data signals. Lobe cables, wall outlets, and ring adapters can be isolated from the main ring. Relays are operated by the station for inserting/removing itself into/from the ring. Powering down a station leads to automatic disconnection of the station's lobe from the main ring. Breakage of a lobe has the same effect. All other parts of the ring network remain operational without the need for manual intervention.

The concept of passive wiring concentrators can be extended by introducing an active element such as a signal amplifier. It allows increasing of the maximum distance between concentrators. In our prototype, we developed an active concentrator with electrooptical transducers. With these devices, some sections of the main ring were implemented with optical fibers.

Fig. 2 shows additional relay contacts for configuring a "local-wrap" ring which consists of the lobe cable and the ring adapter. This configuration allows testing of ring-adapter hardware, the lobe cable, and significant parts of the ring-access protocol prior to inserting a station in the ring.

IV. THE TRANSMISSION SYSTEM

A ring adapter comprises two functional entities, the front end which implements the transmission system, and the protocol handler which executes the token protocol discussed in Section II, and supports the system's interface. Here, we first review the design decisions for the transmission system, and then address the key issues and findings of the ring synchronization method. For details, refer to the companion paper, [10].

A. Design Decisions

1) Clocking of the ring matches the principle employed with the monitor function. Each adapter contains a quartz oscillator; the actual ring clock, however, is provided by the adapter with the active-monitor function. The other adapters derive clocking information from the data stream with phase-locked loops (PLL). Switchover of the monitor function to another adapter, Section II-C, also causes a transfer of the ring clock. A comparison to other synchronization methods is made in the accompanying paper, [10]. From a transmission point of view, the ring consists of a chain of regenerative repeaters, subsequently for short repeaters, with the effects of timing jitter at each repeater and accumulated timing jitter at the end of the repeater chain. Jitter phenomena will determine the maximum number of stations which can be interconnected, and will be discussed in more detail below.

2) Stations are inserted in and removed from the ring randomly, i.e., these actions can be initiated at any time. Station insertion/removal leads to a momentary loss of synchronism, and requires a fast resynchronization method. It should be noted that this does not trigger monitor switchover.

3) We use differential Manchester code because it provides good clocking information, allows a simple and low cost implementation, is polarity insensitive, and allows transformer coupling. The frame delimiters can then be defined as violations of this code which represents a particularly simple and robust solution compared to other possibilities, e.g., zero-bit insertion.

B. Transmission Media

Transmission in a ring system is unidirectional and point-to-point. As a consequence, transmission media can be different in the various sections of the ring depending on requirements. In our ring prototype, we use the following media:

- shielded dual twisted-pair cables between wiring concentrator and stations,
- shielded twisted-pair cable for the main ring which interconnects wiring concentrators, and
- optical fibers between some wiring concentrators. In this case, the wiring concentrator needs a power supply for the optical drivers.

A fixed two-tap transversal equalizer is used in the transmitter to compensate for cable distortion [3]. The maximum distance between active stations can be about 1 km using twisted-pair media at a data rate of 4 Mbits/s. This distance includes the main-ring cable and twice the length of the cable between station and wiring concentrator. At this rate, transmission-error probability is $< 10^{-9}$ [10].

C. Ring Synchronization

The front end of each adapter derives clocking information from the received data stream. Clock recovery is impaired by signal distortion and noise. Zero crossings of the received signal and of the derived clock do not coincide precisely; they deviate in a random fashion called timing jitter. There are three sources of jitter: 1) intersymbol interference due to linear distortion of the cable, 2) imperfections of the clock recovery circuit, and 3) noise. A detailed analysis of jitter sources is presented in the companion paper, [10]. As each adapter uses the derived clock for receiving and transmitting data, timing jitter builds up along the chain of repeaters on the ring. Excessive jitter can eventually lead to intermittent synchronization failures, which will cause burst transmission errors.

Timing jitter limits the number of stations which can be placed on a single ring. The design of the synchronization scheme must, therefore, be guided by the objective to minimize jitter accumulation.

Phase-Locked Loop (PLL) Design: In each repeater, clocking information is derived from the received data signal by a phase-locked loop (PLL) [7]. Minimization of jitter build-up calls for narrow bandwidth PLL's. On the other hand, the need for fast resynchronization after station insertion or removal requires wide-band PLL's. These obviously conflicting requirements are resolved by the structure depicted in Fig. 5.

A phase detector is used for phase tracking during steady-state operation of the PLL. The loop filter F in Fig. 5 is designed to obtain a narrow-band PLL. An independent frequency detector can be switched into the PLL by means of the multiplexer replacing the phase detector. This frequency detector synchronizes the frequency of the voltage-controlled oscillator (VCO) of the PLL to the local crystal oscillator, and is used under the following conditions.

1) After a station has been powered up and before it is

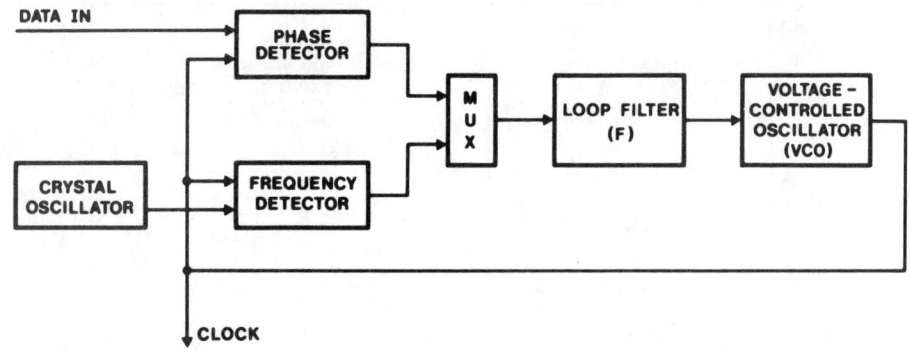

Fig. 5. Phase-locked loop with phase and frequency detectors.

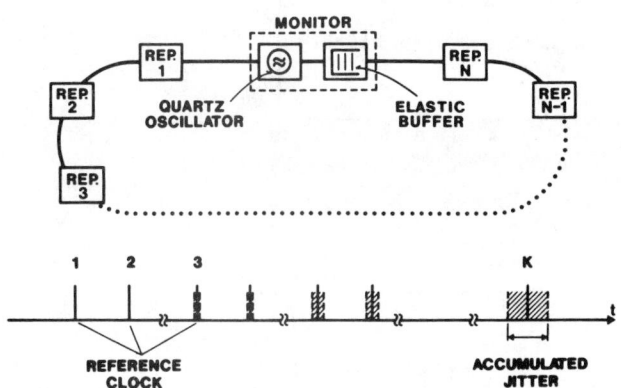

Fig. 6. Definition of accumulated jitter.

inserted into the ring. Therefore, the VCO frequency is already almost correct at insertion time, and only the phase remains to be locked to the incoming data signal.

2) If an adapter senses loss of energy, e.g., in case the adjacent adapter upstream is in the insertion process, then this adapter will send with the frequency of its local crystal oscillator.

3) During erroneous conditions, e.g., if a frequency offset larger than a predefined threshold occurs.

Timing Jitter Accumulation: The above design minimizes but does not eliminate jitter accumulation. Jitter can be defined in two different ways.

• Against the master clock in the active monitor as reference. This measure is called accumulated jitter. It increases along the chain of repeaters, Fig. 6.

• At the phase detector of a repeater using its voltage-controlled oscillator (VCO) as reference, Fig. 5. This jitter measure is called alignment or relative jitter.

1) Accumulated jitter. Each PLL acts as a low-pass filter for the jitter process. The transfer function of the PLL shows a small peak below the cutoff frequency. This peak becomes stronger, the more PLL's are chained. For a sufficiently large number of PLL's in cascade, accumulated jitter resembles a bandpass process whose variance increases with the number of repeaters in cascade.

The monitor derives its receive clock from data signals impaired by accumulated jitter (relative to its crystal-controlled transmit clock). A small elastic buffer is used in the monitor to compensate for accumulated jitter, Fig. 6. Data are written into the buffer with the receive clock, and read out with the crystal clock. It was shown analytically and by measurements [10] that 12 bits are sufficient to

compensate for timing jitter accumulated along a chain of more than 200 repeaters.

2) Alignment jitter is measured across the phase detector of a PLL. Large deviations between the zero crossings of the received and VCO signals may lead to cycle slips because the detector output may drive the voltage-controlled oscillator, Fig. 5, into the wrong direction. These cycle slips represent statistically occurring synchronization failures of short duration. Each slip introduces a burst of bit errors degrading transmission system performance. Analytic and measurement results [9], [10] have shown that more than 200 stations can be supported by a single ring without noticeable degradation due to cycle-slip phenomena.

D. Station Insertion and Removal / Detection of Signal Loss

Stations are inserted in and removed from the ring by relays in the wiring concentrators. Relay operation interrupts the data signal on the ring for about 1–2 ms. Special care was taken to prevent this error burst from propagating through the entire ring and, as a consequence, insertion/removal does not cause loss of synchronization in the whole ring. The PLL design described in Section IV-C allows resynchronization of the entire ring within 200 bit times after relay settling.

Each repeater is equipped with an energy detector to detect loss of the received signal. As above, the repeater prevents signal loss from propagating through the ring. Instead, it broadcasts a beacon message which allows identification of the location of the signal loss by analyzing the source address field of the beacon message.

V. PERFORMANCE CHARACTERISTICS

In a performance analysis [4], it was shown that the delay-throughput characteristic of a token ring compares very favorably to other access disciplines used on rings and media access-control procedures employed on bus systems. The most relevant performance features of a token ring, no speed and distance limitations over the range of parameters which is of practical interest, and fairness of access, will be explained below.

Fig. 7(a) and (b) shows the mean frame transfer time in ms versus the total data throughput in Mbits/s, i.e., throughput due to information carried in the *I* field. It should be noted, however, that the calculations were per-

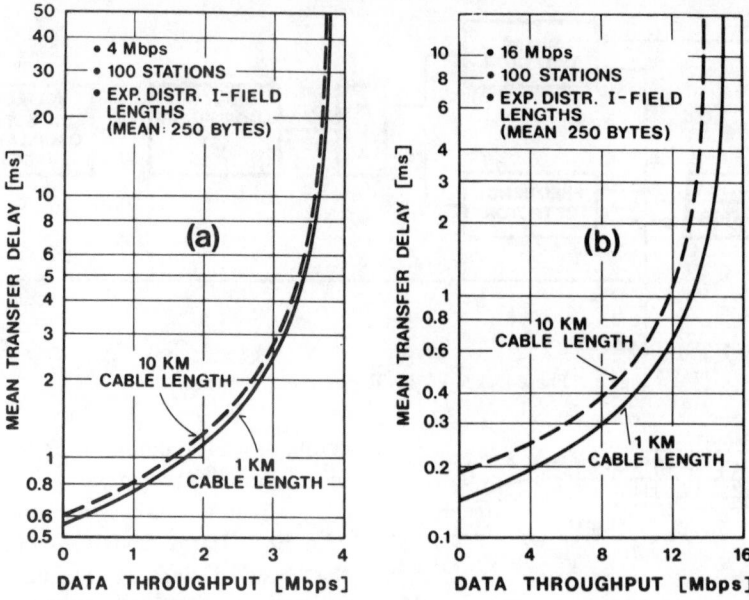

Fig. 7. (a) Delay-throughput characteristic for a 4 Mbit/s token ring. (b) Delay-throughput characteristic for a 16 Mbit/s token ring.

formed taking the frame overhead into consideration. The mean transfer time is defined as the time interval from the generation of a frame at the source station until its reception at the destination, and includes the queueing and access delay at the sender, the frame transmission time, and the propagation delay. In Fig. 7(a), the transmission rate is 4 Mbits/s, and the ring lengths are 1 and 10 km. The rings are assumed to operate according to the single-token rule. The curves clearly show that

1) the maximum achievable utilization is very high, and

2) the performance of the token protocol is practically insensitive to the length of the transmission medium.

Fig. 7(b) confirms this characteristic of the access protocol for a transmission rate of 16 Mbits/s, and also shows that maximum utilization will be only degraded insignificantly if we increase the transmission speed from 4 Mbits/s to 16 Mbits/s. We consider these performance characteristics as important advantages of a token-ring protocol compared to CSMA/CD on a bus (baseband or broadband), see [4].

Finally, Fig. 8 illustrates that the token protocol provides fair access in case of asymmetric traffic load. It is assumed that two of the 20 active stations, 1 and 8, each generate 40 percent of the total traffic, the other stations each contribute 1.1 percent. The results show that stations generating a small amount of traffic experience a much smaller transfer delay than heavy traffic stations, and do not get penalized by them. Furthermore, it can be seen that this property is preserved when the throughput approaches the saturation point. It should be noted that fair access in the above sense is only guaranteed when the transmission time per token is upper bounded for each station, e.g., to one frame, as assumed in Fig. 8.

VI. CONCLUSIONS

This paper has presented architecture, wiring, transmission, and performance of a token-ring local area network.

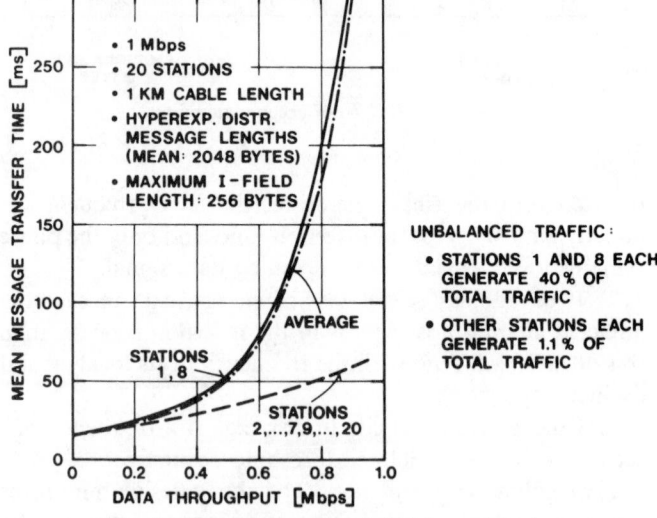

Fig. 8. Fair sharing of bandwidth in a token ring.

A 4 Mbit/s prototype has been implemented and is operational at the IBM Zurich Research Laboratory. The key features of our token-ring network are as follows.

1) Reliable token operation is achieved through a monitor function present in each ring adapter, but active in only one adapter to perform detection of and recovery from token-error situations.

2) Since the token-access scheme is a deterministic access protocol, it can, in addition to asynchronous data traffic, support applications requiring guaranteed delay or throughput.

3) The hybrid ring/star wiring scheme with wiring concentrators is the key to physical ring reliability, error isolation, system maintenance, and reconfiguration. It also allows prewiring of a building systematically.

4) The ring network allows the use of different media in different sections, and thus can be adapted to different environments, and is open to advances in transmission technology.

5) From a performance point of view, the token-access protocol compares very favorably to other major access-control schemes. Its key features are insensitivity with respect to speed and distance, and fair sharing of the bandwidth.

ACKNOWLEDGMENT

The authors express their gratitude to L. Recknor for implementing and testing of the ring adapter, to P. Zafiropulo for designing and debugging significant parts of the microcode implementing the ring protocol, and to P. Dill for supporting experimentation and replication of the adapter hardware.

REFERENCES

[1] K. Kümmerle and M. Reiser, "Local-area communication networks —An overview," *J. Telecommun. Networks*, vol. 1, pp. 349–370, 1982.
[2] R. J. Cypser, *Communication Architecture for Distributed Systems*. Reading, MA: Addison-Wesley, 1978.
[3] H. Meyr, H. R. Müller, U. Bapst, and H. Bouten, "Manchester coding with predistortion: An efficient and simple transmission technique in local digital ring networks," in *Proc. Nat. Telecommun. Conf.*, Houston, TX, 1980, pp. 65.4.1–65.4.7.
[4] W. Bux, "Local-area subnetworks: A performance comparison," *IEEE Trans. Commun.*, vol. COM-29, pp. 1465–1473, Oct. 1981.
[5] W. Bux, F. Closs, P. Janson, K. Kümmerle, and H. R. Müller, "A reliable token-ring system for local-area communication," in *Proc. Nat. Telecommun. Conf.*, New Orleans, LA, 1981, pp. A2.2.1–A2.2.6.
[6] W. Bux, F. Closs, P. Janson, K. Kümmerle, H. R. Müller, and E. H. Rothauser, "A local-area communication network based on a reliable token-ring system," in *Local Computer Networks*, P. C. Ravasio, G. Hopkins, and N. Naffah, Eds. Amsterdam, The Netherlands: North-Holland, 1982, pp. 69–82.
[7] H. R. Müller, H. Keller, and H. Meyr, "Transmission in a synchronous token ring," in *Local Computer Networks*, P. C. Ravasio, G. Hopkins, and N. Naffah, Eds. Amsterdam, The Netherlands: North-Holland, 1982, pp. 125–147.
[8] H. Rudin, "Validation of a token-ring protocol," in *Local Computer Networks*, P. C. Ravasio, G. Hopkins, and N. Naffah, Eds. Amsterdam, The Netherlands: North-Holland, 1982, pp. 373–387.
[9] H. Meyr, L. Popken, H. Keller, and H. R. Müller, "Synchronization failures in a chain of repeaters," in *Conf. Rec. GLOBECOM*, Miami, FL, vol. 2 of 3, pp. 859–869.
[10] H. Keller, H. Meyr, and H. R. Müller, "Transmission design criteria for a synchronous token ring," this issue, pp. 721–733.
[11] W. D. Farmer and E. E. Newhall, "An experimental distributed switching system to handle bursty computer traffic," in *Proc. ACM Symp. Problems Optimization Data Commun.*, Pine Mountain, GA, Oct. 1963, pp. 31–34.
[12] D. J. Farber, J. Feldman, F. R. Heinrich, M. D. Hopwood, D. C. Loomis, and A. Rowe, "The distributed computer system," *Proc. 7th IEEE Comput. Soc. Int. Conf.*, pp. 31–34, 1973.
[13] B. K. Penney and A. A. Baghdadi, "Survey of computer communications loop networks: Parts 1 and 2," *Comput. Commun.*, vol. 2, pp. 165–180, 224–241, 1979.
[14] D. D. Clark, K. T. Pogran, and D. P. Reed, "An introduction to local-area networks," *Proc. IEEE*, vol. 66, pp. 1497–1517, 1978.
[15] J. H. Saltzer and K. T. Pogran, "A star-shaped ring network with high maintainability," *Comput. Networks*, vol. 4, pp. 239–244, 1980.
[16] Systems Network Architecture. General Information, 1975, IBM Pub. GA 27-3102.
[17] ECMA Final Draft Standard, Local-Area Networks Token Ring, Mar. 1983.
[18] IEEE Project 802, Local-Area Network Standards, Draft IEEE Standard 802.5, Token-Ring Access Method and Physical-Layer Specifications, Working Draft, June 10, 1983.

Werner Bux (M'82) received the M.S. and Ph.D. degrees in electrical engineering from Stuttgart University, Stuttgart, West Germany, in 1974 and 1980, respectively.

From 1974 to 1979 he was with the Institute of Switching and Data Techniques, University of Stuttgart, where he worked primarily in the field of performance analysis of data communication networks and computer systems. He joined the IBM Zurich Research Laboratory, Rüschlikon, Switzerland, in 1979, where he is currently working on the architecture and performance evaluation of local networks. He has also been involved in local-network standardization through his work in TC 24 of the European Computer Manufacturers Association.

Felix H. Closs (M'72) received the M.S. and Ph.D. degrees in electrical engineering from the University of Stuttgart, Stuttgart, West Germany, in 1961 and 1969, respectively.

From 1961 to 1967 he was with the Institute for Theoretical Electrotechnology, University of Stuttgart, where he performed research work in the area of signal processing and speech encoding for pulse code modulation systems. In 1968 he joined the IBM Zurich Research Laboratory, Rüschlikon, Switzerland. After several years of research work in signal processing algorithms, he joined the IBM San Jose Research Laboratory, CA, where he became involved in the design of a computer network. After his return to Switzerland, he joined the Local-Area Networking Project. Presently, he is responsible for building a prototype for a token-passing local-area network.

Dr. Closs is a member of the Association for Computing Machinery.

Karl Kuemmerle (M'81), for a photograph and biography, see this issue, p. 701.

Heinz J. Keller (A'73), for a photograph and biography, see this issue p. 732.

Hans R. Mueller, for a photograph and biography, see this issue, p. 733.

The IBM Cabling System

The IBM Cabling System, which became available in the fall of 1984, permits traditional types of connections to be made between devices with a common cable consisting of twisted pairs of copper conductors. The cabling system connects wall outlets in offices to wiring closets. Called a star-wired system, the cable fans out from each closet to special outlets. The outlets are installed in the walls to connect to data devices and, optionally, telephones. Most currently available IBM products, including workstations and small and intermediate computers, can be plugged into the outlets.

Each office wall outlet is connected by standard cable to a distribution panel (see Figure) located in a wiring closet. A panel can accept up to 64 cables from different devices, and any two devices can easily be connected using patch cables at the closets where the cables converge. If an IBM 3270 Personal Computer, for example, is moved from one office to another, it is simply plugged into the wall outlet in the new office, and the patch cable in the wiring closet is reconnected. Wiring closets in the same building or different buildings on a campus can be connected with either twisted-pair or optical fiber cable.

Basic Elements of the IBM Cabling System

Transmission Cables:

- Type 1: For use between faceplates in work areas and wiring closets, or between two wiring closets in the same or different buildings; contains two balanced, twisted pairs for data transmission.

- Type 2: For use between faceplates in work areas and wiring closets in the same building; contains two twisted pairs for data transmission and four twisted pairs for voice transmission.

- Type 5: For use between wiring closets in the same or different buildings; contains two optical fibers for data transmission.

- Type 6: For use as patch cables in wiring closets; contains two twisted pairs for data transmission.

Faceplates and Connectors:

- Faceplates for mounting on electrical outlet boxes installed in work areas.

- Data Connector and telephone connector for installation in the faceplate; data connector allows termination of two data-grade twisted pairs. A telephone jack connector allows termination of three voice-grade twisted pairs.

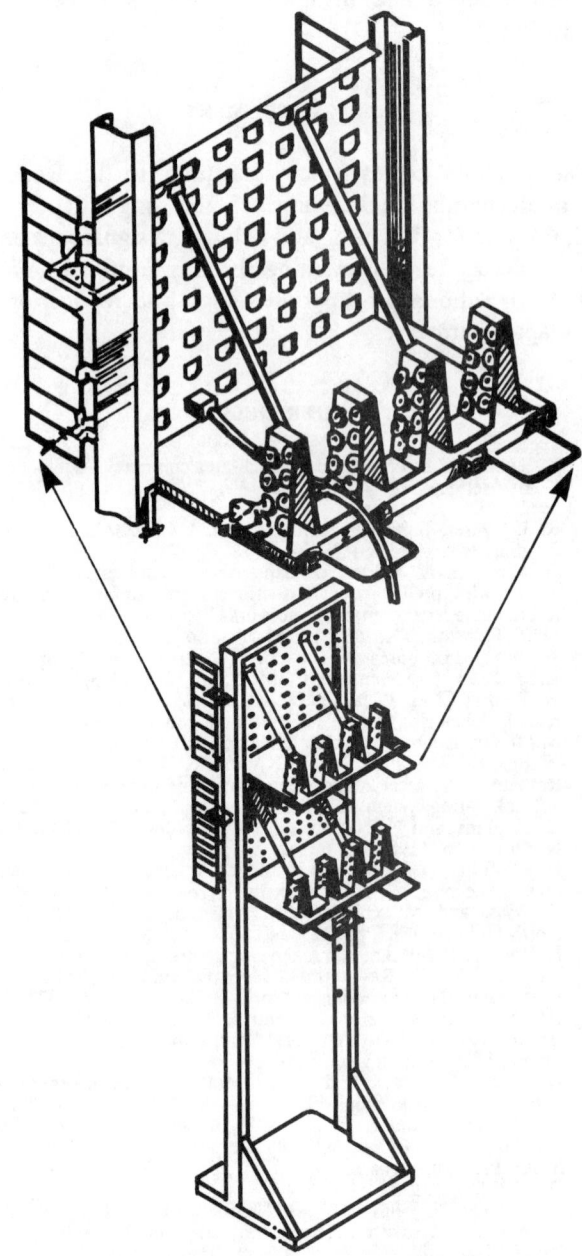

Figure: Distribution Panel For IBM Cabling System

Distribution Panel:

- Cable junction panel mounted on a rack in a wiring closet; each panel allows connection of up to 64 data cables.

- Patch cable for making panel cross connections.

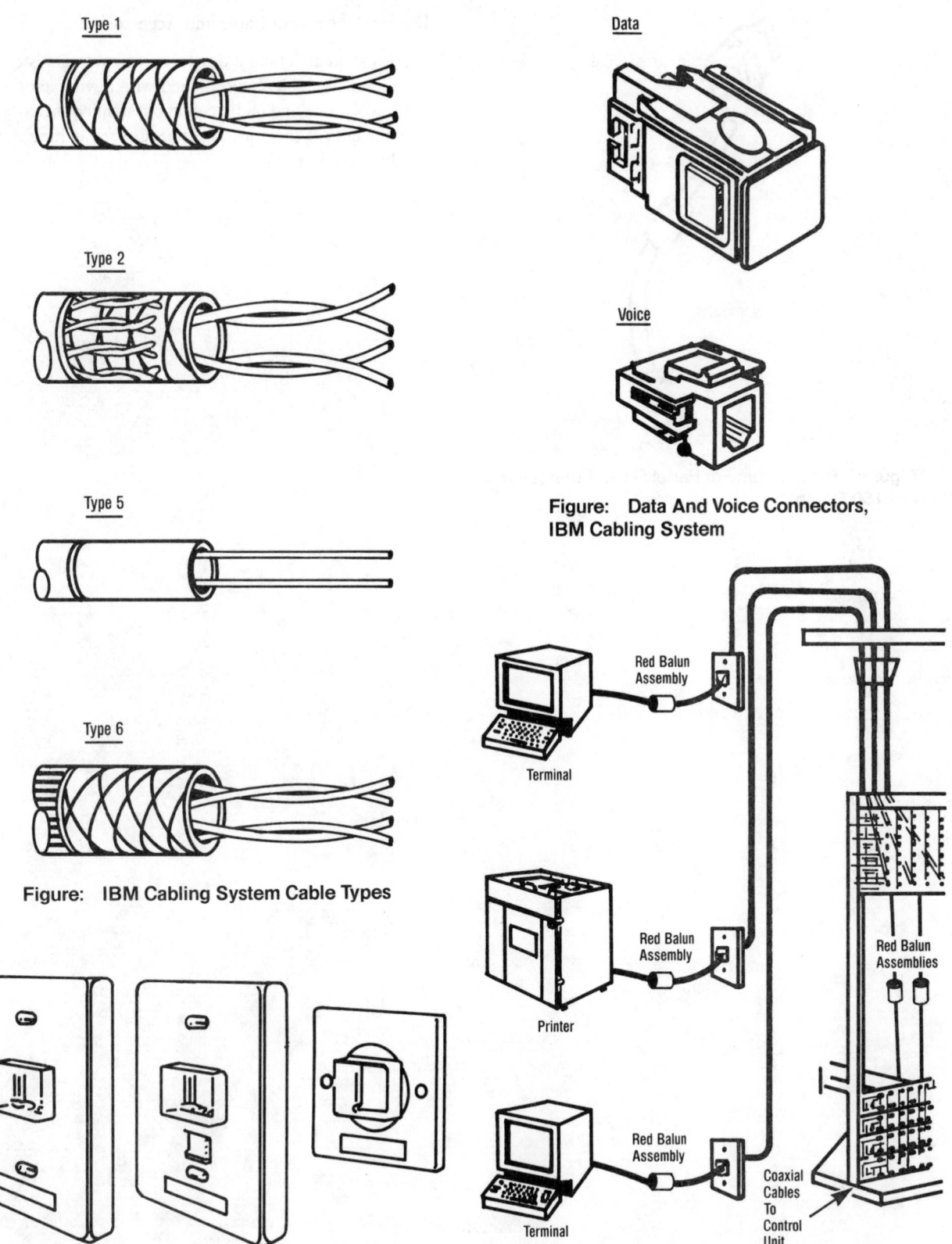

Type 1

Type 2

Type 5

Type 6

Figure: IBM Cabling System Cable Types

Data

Voice

Figure: Data And Voice Connectors, IBM Cabling System

Red Balun Assembly

Terminal

Red Balun Assembly

Printer

Red Balun Assembly

Terminal

Red Balun Assemblies

Coaxial Cables To Control Unit

Figure: Faceplates, IBM Cabling System

Figure: 3270 Attachment, Cable Junction Panel

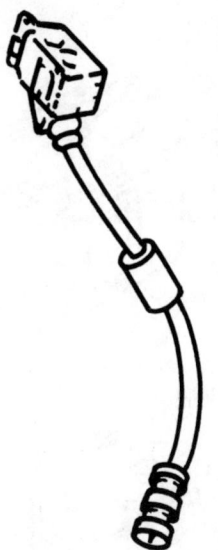

Device Attachment Cable and Accessories:

- For use in attaching a device to the cabling system; the attachment cable is terminated with a workstation connector at one end and a cabling system connector at the other end; it includes an impedance matching device, when required.

Figure: Patch Cable For Panel Cross-Connections (93:150 Balun)

ROLE OF OPTICAL FIBER LOOP IN C&C OPTONET

H. IKUTA, M. TADA, N. SHIMA and H. HATTA

Nippon Electric Company, Ltd. Tokyo, Japan

ABSTRACT

Integrating a variety of network technology, NEC has developed a universal local area network, named "C&C (Computer and Communication) OPTONET" which consists of three subnetworks, LOOP, BRANCH and STAR.

NEC LOOP6770, a member of the loop subnetwork, is a new optical fiber token loop designed primarily for high speed computer to computer communications at local area. It satisfies various requirements, such as geographical coverage, network expandability and maintenability as well as easy network modifications or reconfigurations, which are not fully solved by point to point connection networks. Transmission speed and reliability problems in conventional networks, such as pair-cable wiring star-shaped network, are also solved by this optical fiber loop network. It will play an important role in various computer distribution applications.

INTRODUCTION

Due to the technological progress, computer's cost/performance has been drastically improved. As a result, computer applications are rapidly expanding into new computer-aided office automation, laboratory automation, factory automation and so on. In the office, for example, because of a world wide economic slowdown and the stagnation of business, an increase in productivity has been expected through the higher investment in computers and office equipments.

The technological status and market situation as stated above have led companies, laboratories and government to purchase many automation equipments as well as large and small computers.

Eventually, the local networking of those equipments and computer systems is becoming important.

Each of various local area network technologies is a prime candidate for this need. It is, however, rather difficult to meet every application requirement with only one technology.

Integrating a variety of network technology, NEC has developed a universal (1),(2) local area network, named "C&C (Computer and Communication) OPTONET" which consists of three subnetworks, LOOP, BRANCH and STAR.

Each can be used as stand alone system or can be interconnected with any combination of the three through protocol conversion functions in order to satisfy various applicaion requirements.

A fiber loop subnetwork, named "LOOP6770", was developed to satisfy primarily high speed communications between computers in one customer's premises.

It is characterized with high reliability, high speed (32M/bits per second) with special consideration for bulk data transfer, peer to peer virtual circuit depending on token-passing discipline, and wide range of geograghcal coverage, with up to 126 nodes connectability.
Several LOOP6770 application systems are already installed in customer sites and are perfoming significant roles for the computer distribution applications.

C&C OPTONENT SYSTEM

The efficient and economical handling of coded data, image, voice and their mixture within the customer's premises has become quite desirable. The advent of the local area network having such total capability has been longed for.

User requirements to the local area network range quite widely. For example, let's imagine a 50-storied modern headquarter building wherein a total of 10,000 people work, each a member of one of 300 working sections. Various office automation machines are used by these workers. The activity in this building may produce a tremendous amount of various communication traffic.

Therefore, it is impossible, or at least economically infeasible, to satisfy every requirement with only one technology. For example, while PBX with pair cable wiring is still the best answer for handling ordinary telephone communication, optical fiber high speed and reliable computer-to-computer link is required as well in the same building.

This leads us to believe that the universal local area network cannot be realized without an adequate combination of such technology on hand as pair cable wiring, co-axial cable wiring, optical fiber cable wiring, wireless, star topology, loop topology, branch topology, baseband

Reprinted from *The Proceedings of COMPCON F'82*, 1982, pages 471-477.
Copyright © 1982 by The Institute of Elecltrical and Electronics Engineers, Inc.

transmission, broadband transmission, TDM, FDM, SDM, CSMA/CD, token passing, IPBX etc.

These technologies must be closely examined to determine their individual advantages and drawbacks and their mutual relationship must be clarified. Moreover, these technologies must be organized into the best combination and must be crystallized into products, which, while retaining all advantages, work independently and also are consistent when interconnected with each other.

NEC's C&C (Computer and Communication) OPTONET SYSTEM was developed in line with the above concept. The C&C OPTONET SYSTEM, abbreviated C&C-NET, consists of such three subnetworks as Star subnetwork, Loop subnetwork and Branch subnetwork (Fig. 1).

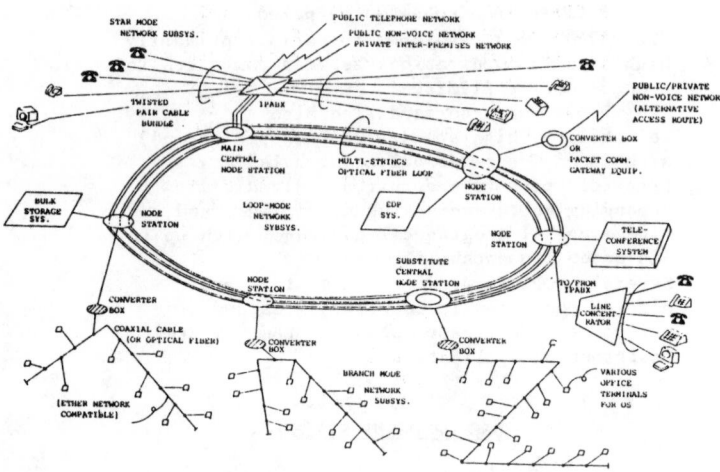

Fig.1. C&C OPTONET SYSTEM

Each subnetwork can work independently and they can also all be easily interconnected. Of course, in the latter case, all the computers or terminals attached to the network must follow the addressing scheme control system for the whole network, which is common to all subnetworks.

The Star subnetwork is a low speed IPBX and pair cable based communication system, which can easily be introduced even into an existing rather aged building already equipped with a bunch of pair cables. The Star subnetwork is a traditional and still most adequate answer to the customer's desires, when the major requirement is voice communication.

The Loop subnetwork is a high speed fiber optical communication loop (ring) which is most appreciated in computer-to-computer high-speed mass data transmission. The Loop subnetwork is also effective in the process control application since fiber optics technology is quite resistant to noise and corrosive gas.

The Branch subnetwork is a medium speed co-axial cable based communication system,

shaped as a branching tree. The Branch subnetwork can offer quite an ample communication facility to the terminal at a reasonable cost. Therefore, the Branch subnetwork will be the best vehicle for the terminal-to-terminal document communication.

Wireless communication technology is utilized in these three subnetworks. This means that cable communication, at least in some portion of these subnetworks, can be replaced with radio communication.

Interconnection of subnetworks can be made directly or through the gateway processor. In the latter case, local processings, such as higher level protocol conversion or address scheme conversion, can also be conducted in the same gateway processor.

The interconnection of the local area network to the global network is made through IPBX or the gateway processor. The interconnection can be made with the radio link as well as to the public network.

Thus, the C&C OPTONET can be the best answer to the headquarter building mentioned before and also to various other intra/inter premises communications needs (Fig. 2).

Many products are offered under the name of C&C OPTONENT SYSTEM. Most of all, LOOP6770 is a brand new optical fiber loop communication system catagorized as a member of the Loop subnetwork. LOOP6770 is a packet switching loop system based on the token passing technology.

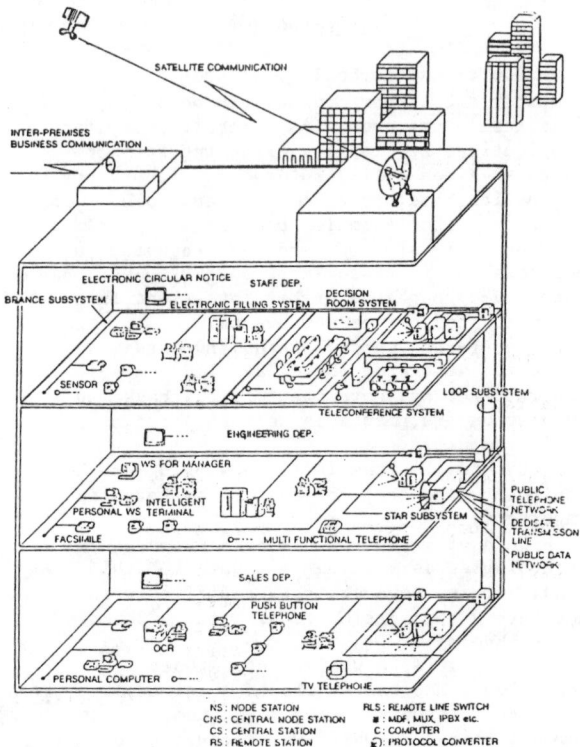

Fig.2. C&C OPTONET APPLICATION IN HEADQUARTER BUILING

C&C OPTONET LOOP6770 [3]

Characteristics

LOOP6770 consists of up to 126 nodes
(LIU: Loop Interface Unit), optical fiber
cables connecting LIUs in loop topology and a
network monitor. Figure 3 shows a system
configuration example, and Table 1 lists major
LOOP6770 performances.

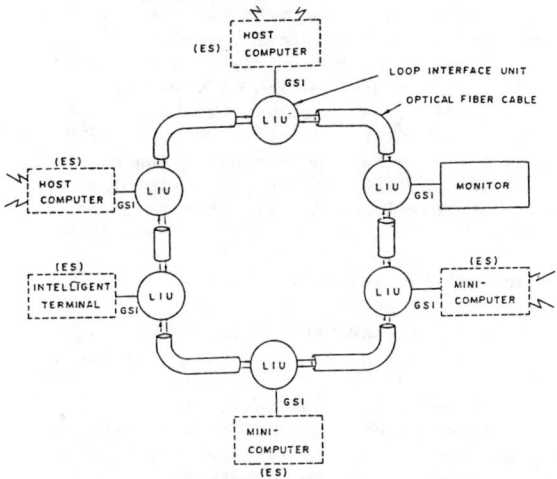

ES = External System
GSI = General purpose Serial Interface

Fig.3. System Configuration Example

Table 1. C&C - NET LOOP6770 major performance

Items	Specifications
Loop transmission rate	32.064 Mbits/s
Access control	Token passing
Interface	GSI (simplified HDLC) 6.312 Mbits/s 1.544 Mbits/s 0.772 Mbits/s
Number of LIUs	Max. 126
Cable	Optical fiber (graded index)
Cable span	Max. 2Km
Total loop length	Max. 100Km
RAS	Dual loop path Bypass Loopback Alternate path selection Periodic LIU health check Backup battery

Major LOOP6770 characteristics are as follow;
(1) Fiber optic communication
The LOOP6770 data transfer rate is as
fast as 32 megabits per second (Mbps).
Advanced fiber optic communication
technology made it possible to introduce
such fast communication speed to a local
area network. As fiber optic
communication is not affected by
electromagnetic disturbance and the
transmission loss is very low, LOOP6770
can configure a highly reliable and very
large local area network.

(2) Token loop
Topologically, LOOP6770 is a loop (ring)
network where communication is performed
between two nodes in burst mode. Message
transmission on the loop is controlled by
a "token", (which is a special electronic
signal frame) going around the loop
whenever no communiation is being handled
on the loop. When one of nodes attempts
to send a message to another node on the
loop, it waits for the "token". After
the sending node seizes the "token", the
node sends its message, followed by
"token", on to the loop. This mechanism
guarantees that only one node on the loop
is sending a message at a time, thus
avoiding signal collisions on the loop.
(Fig. 4)

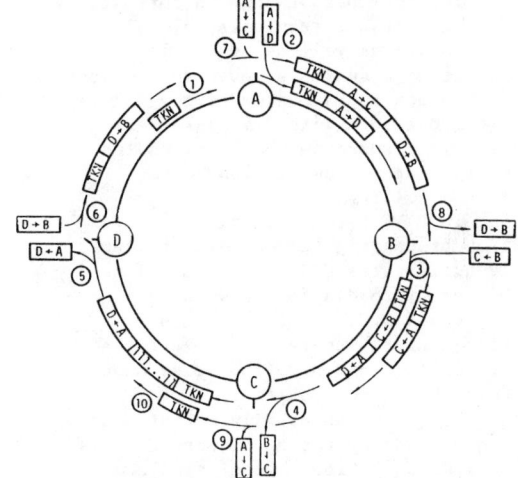

Fig.4. LOOP6770 Token Passing Mechanism

(4) Virtual circuit
Most conventional loop networks today,
provide permanent virtual circuits. LOOP
6770 offers virtual circuits with unified
GSI (general purpose serial interface),
so that a computer node can communicate
with any number of other nodes without
any additional hardware attachments, such
as communication line adaptors, and
without any centralized control station.

(5) Variable length packet communication
Message length on the loop is variable up
to 4K bytes. This message packet is sent
at 32 Mbps transfer rate, utilizing the
network capability at its maximum.

Therefore, a large volume of data can be sent in a very short time. Also, the network efficiency is very high.

(6) Overload characteristic
The LOOP6770 throughput capacity will not drop, even if the communication load exceeds the network capability, because no signal collision can occur on the loop through the use of "token" as a traffic warden.

(7) High reliability
The optical communication path is duplicated for both optical fiber and optical circuit modules. Furthermore, for higher network availability, LOOP 6770 offers such features as loop-back, battery-backup for optical modules and bypass.

LOOP6770 and Network Architecture

From the network architecture, such as ISO 7 layer model view point, LOOP6770 with GSI (General purpose Serial Interface) can be used as a data link server to computers. An alternate solution is to position the GSI at the network layer, since LOOP6770 has node to node routing capability. These approaches are selectable. If the communication is closed only within the loop net, the latter is preferable from the performance view point. However, from the view point of protocol conversion for internetworking and for already operating computers or terminals, global network protocols as well as higher level protocols are more suitable, even to the local network. The other discussion of the GSI is to make it compatible with X25 packet interface. This approach, however, causes the network component implementation to be difficult and costly.

Then, in DINA (NEC's Distributed Information processing Network Architecture),[4],[5] by merely putting the GSI at the data link level, higher protocols for network, transport, session, presentation, and application control layers can be kept the same as those for communication nodes under the global network environment.

Thus, LOOP6770 can easilly be introduced, even to an already operating network systems, replacing the conventional local area computer connection or adding a new computer to computer network at a local area with less modification in the rest of the network.

LOOP6770 APPLICATIONS

Three LOOP6770 applications presented here will verify that LOOP6770 can be a better tool to solve the following problems, compared with other networking facilities.[6]

(1) High speed channel and common interface
LOOP6770 offers computers a simplified HDLC-like common interface which can be easily mapped into the full HDLC service mechanism for communication control functions within computers. Under the limited transmission speed, STAR or BRANCH subnetworks can take the same role. High speed data transmission, on the other hand, is achieved with computer's I/O channels, where the interface is not always common to all computers.

(2) Number of I/O ports, channel length and speed
Since LOOP6770 supplies a high speed virtual circuit, a computer can communicate with any other computer through only one or a couple of (in case of redundant configuration) I/O ports. The communicating computers can be located far apart. Point to point channel wiring between computers can be an alternate solution, only in case of a few computers located very close to each other.

(3) Expandability, reliability and geographical coverage
In many cases, the network expandability, reliability and geographical coverage are key requirements for a local area computer network. Especially, the distributed processing environment for process control applications cannot condone any lack of those network functionalities.

1. Large Volume image data transfer system
Figure. 5 shows an example of a large volume data transmission network, which consists of a host computer and four distributed minicomputers. LOOP6770 satisfies the following communications requirements for this system:
. More than 3M bits per second data transfer rate between applications
. Processor distribution over several floors in one building

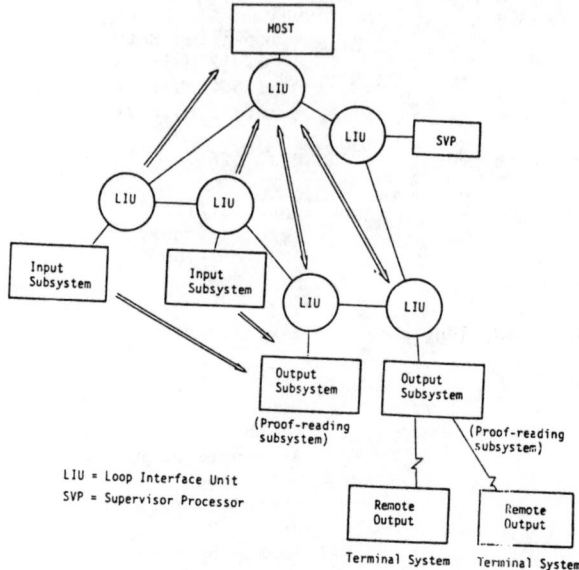

LIU = Loop Interface Unit
SVP = Supervisor Processor

Fig. 5 Image Transfer Network

(1) Network characteristics

The total system furnishes the following three major applications.
. Computer-aided proofreading of the daily newspaper
. Computer controlled press data transmission.
. Graphic data service.

Data carried through the network are mainly newspapers image data. One page of newspaper image consists of more than 15Mbytes.

Newspaper formats are created by the input subsystems. These formats are sent to the host computer and also to the output subsystems. The host computer fills the newspaper format frames with news and sends them to the output subsystems, where the proof-reading and test printing processes are performed. If test printing is successful, a ready-to-print exchange of protocols is carried out between the host and a terminal operator.

The final newspaper image, with news, pictures, advertisement etc., is output from the host to the output subsystems and also sent to the output stations located at various remote sites for printing.

(2) Multi-frame mechanism

A special bulk data transmission scheme, called "multi-frame mechanism" is applied to reduce the software-overhead for external systems.

Without the multi-frame mechanism, bulk data in the external system memory to be sent must be cut into less than 4K byte packets, since the LOOP6770 packet size is limited to up to 4K bytes.

The multi-frame flag within the data link control header is introduced to reduce interruptions to external system software, so that the software can send/receive bulk data with less overhead. The multi-frame mechanism is provided in the GSI channel controllers for external systems.

Using this mechanism, sender software first sends a bulk data request, to the receiver software. The acknowledgement signal is returned from the receiver software. Then, the sender software issues a "WRITE" signal to the GSI channel specifying a bulk data buffer. Similarly, the receiver software issues a "RECEIVE" signal to its GSI channel, specifying a bulk date buffer. The sender multi-frame mechanism creates packets and sends them one by one onto the network. The receiver receives these packets one by one from the network and stores them into the software buffer specified by the "RECEIVE" signal.

The bulk data transmission completion is notified to both sender and receiver software by an interruption from respective GSI channels.

Figure 6 shows the general data flow interchange.

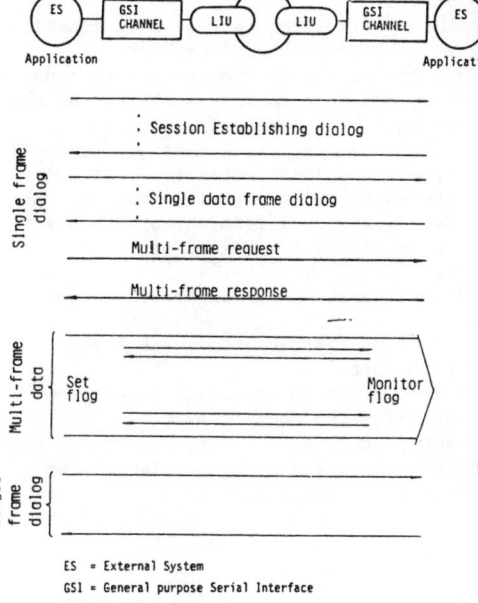

ES = External System
GSI = General purpose Serial Interface
LIU = Loop Interface Unit

Fig. 6 General Multi-frame Dialog Mechanism

2. Integrated Process Control System at Iron-Steel manufacturer

LOOP6770 utilization is very adequate in this network because:
. The working yard is spread over a few square miles.
. The network must be highly reliable with a guarantee of noise immunity and electrical safe guard.
. Transactions must be transmitted as quickly as possible.

(1) System configuration

A large host computer is attached through the network control stations (CS), which supervise the terminal nodes as well as passing information between terminals and the host computer. The network itself is monitored by the supervisor processor (SVP). More than 20 terminal control stations (TCS) are connected to the network. These terminal control stations work as gateway processors for protocol exchange with various input/output terminal devices and process control processors. (Fig.7)

(2) Network data flow

Result information, pertaining to an intermediate work process relating to a production flow, is reported to the host computer from terminals or process control processors. The host computer sends a succeeding work order or an invoice, for example, to the station located at the next work shop. It may broadcast an urgent message to all terminals. While the routine information is flowing, specific data or simulated data is transferred from the control station (CS) to terminals for a new application testing.

3. Distributed Processing network at a university

In the system shown in Figure 8, loosely coupled multi-hosts are used as high efficiency processing equipments for various applications and as data base servers. Remote users have their own terminals, such as KB/CRT, TTY, remote batch terminal or personal computers, which are connected to front end network processors through telecommunications lines. Two distributed terminal processors send and receive a large volume of remote-batch jobs and files.

LOOP6770 was chosen here, for the following reasons:

. Easy redundant configuration with less connection ports
. High speed communication channels between hosts and distributed processors.
. Distributed processors are to be located at different places from the computer center
. Future system expandability.

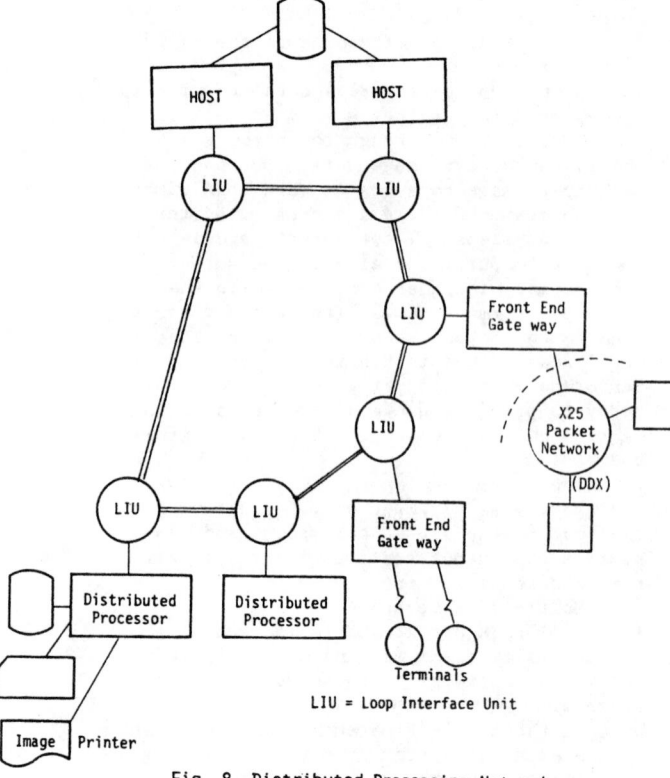

LIU = Loop Interface Unit

Fig. 8 Distributed Processing Network

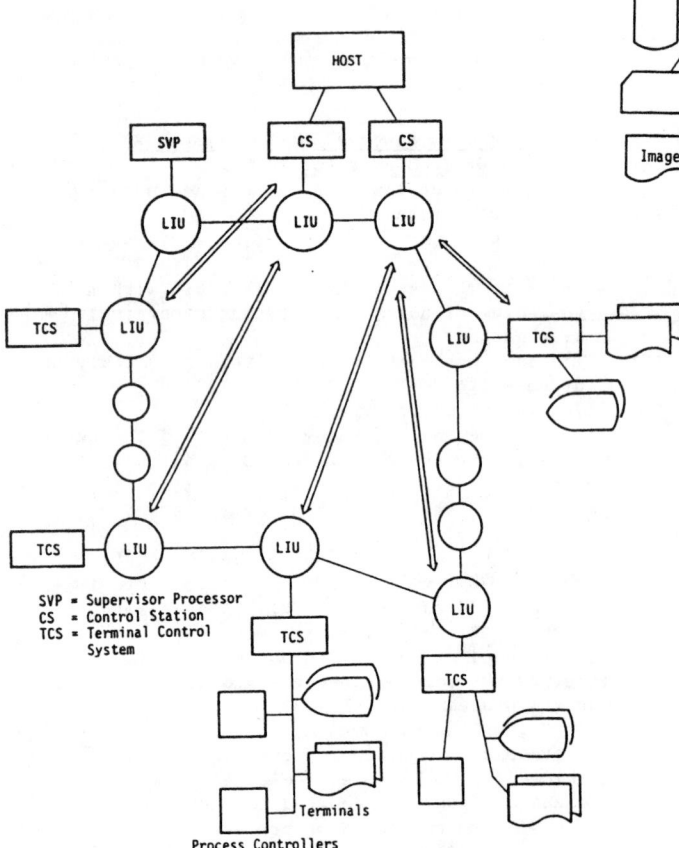

SVP = Supervisor Processor
CS = Control Station
TCS = Terminal Control System

Fig. 7 Process Control Network

PERFORMANCE EVALUATIONS

As a result of experience gained through several applications, the following performance results have been obtained. They are close to those expected.

(1) LOOP6770 path throughput can reach the almost maximum speed of 32M bits per second with the long packet (Fig. 9).

(2) GSI channel throughput is shown in Fig. 10. Where, in case 1, I/O instructin from the software to the GSI channel completes when the data link control response is returned from the network. In case 2, I/O completes without waiting for the acknowledgement from the network.

(3) Application throughput really depends on the computer nodes software overhead. One application, using the multiframe mechanism, attained over 250 Kbytes per second as point to point throughput.

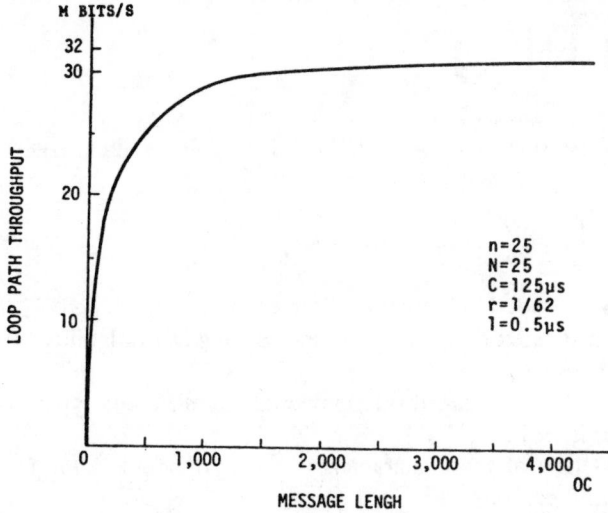

Fig.9. Loop Path Throughput

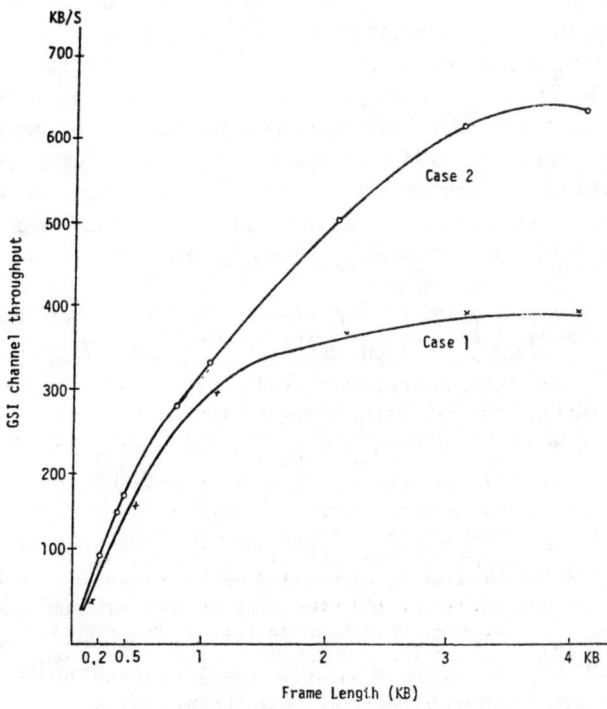

Fig.10. GSI Channel Throughput Examples

CONCLUSION

Based on the results from a number of application experiences using LOOP6770, it has been found that:

(1) The token passing is a good mechanism for use in a local area loop network, especially for computer communication.

(2) An optical loop network can take the place of the conventional point to point channel connection network or other low speed local area network. It provides better functionality, such as high speed, reliable communication, simple networking and expansion and wide geographical coverage.

(3) The optical loop network makes it easy to construct a distributed processing system. It is expected that LOOP6770 will open the door to various new applications for local area computer networks, such as laboratory automation, factory automation and office automation.

ACKNOWLEDGEMENT

The authors would like to thank Mr. T. Kitamura, Mr. E. Yoshikawa, Mr. O. Ohizumi and Mr. M. Kimura for their helpful discussion and suggestions.

REFERENCES

(1) H. Watanabe "Application of Computer and Communication Technology in Office Automation" OAC '82

(2) A. Koike et al., "Overview of NEC's Accomplishment on C&C related technology" NEC R&D No.56 Jan. '80

(3) M. Tada, et al, "N6770 DATALINK-A Homogeneous Optical Loop Network", ICC '82.

(4) S. Hamada, N. Shima and O. Ohizumi "A realization of C&C:DINA" Communicasia '81

(5) N. Shima "DINA, a realization of C&C" SUCESO '81

(6) K. Hwang, B. Wah and F.Briggs "ECN: A hardwired network of UNIX Computer Systems" NCC '81

SILK: An Implementation of a Buffer Insertion Ring

DANIEL E. HUBER, MEMBER, IEEE, WALTER STEINLIN, MEMBER, IEEE, AND PETER J. WILD, MEMBER, IEEE

Abstract — Ring topology local area networks (LAN's) using the "buffer insertion" access method have as yet received relatively little attention. In this paper we present details of a LAN of this type, called SILK—system for integrated local communication (in German, "Kommunikation").

Sections of the paper describe the synchronous transmission technique of the ring channel, the time-multiplexed access of eight ports at each node, the "braided" interconnection for bypassing defective nodes, and the role of interface transformation units and user interfaces, as well as some traffic characteristics and reliability aspects.

SILK's modularity and open system concept are demonstrated by the already implemented applications such as distributed text editing, local telephone or teletex exchange, and process control in a TV studio.

I. INTRODUCTION

WHEN surveys of LAN's [1] refer to the "buffer insertion" access method in ring topology networks, two early laboratory systems are sometimes mentioned. At the Research Laboratory of Hasler an experimental initial system using fixed length shift registers as insertion buffers was tested and the results were reported in 1974 [2]. At Ohio State University the "distributed loop computer network" DLCN was developed from 1975 onwards [3]. However, the subsequent development of SILK [11], "system for integrated local communication," reported at various conferences and in publications with limited distribution [4]–[10], with a considerably improved concept as compared to [2], is rarely referenced. We are aware of only one other product development belonging to the same class of buffer insertion ring networks [12]. As in most known LAN's with ring topology, SILK also employs synchronous unidirectional baseband transmission for the common ring channel. Compared with the early experimental system [2], the following improvements have been implemented in this product:

- single channel for synchronization, signaling, and data transmission [5]
- higher ring transmission rate of approximately 17 Mbits/s [5]
- variable packet length of up to 16 bytes [6]
- removal of packets by the receiving node [6]
- multiaccess nodes with a resident monitor and up to seven user ports per node [6]
- multipacket insertion, reception, and transmission buffers dimensioned according to simulation results [6], [9]

- "braided" interconnection of nodes combined with sophisticated system supervision for higher availability [4], [10], and
- interface transformation units for different types of user interfaces [7], [9].

Details of these characteristics are presented in the following sections.

II. ARCHITECTURE

Normally a SILK ring is divided into several segments which are interconnected by repeaters to form a single unidirectional digital ring channel. Users have access to this channel only at repeater locations, which are the nodes of this LAN. On the ring, information is transferred in small packets which are transmitted in time-division multiplex. Packet switching is done by each node and thus is distributed. The only functions performed at one specific location are master clock generation, overall system supervision, and means for removing packets which are not removed elsewhere. These functions can be taken over by suitable standby nodes as explained in the section on braided interconnection.

The system can be considered to be divided into three hierarchical subsystems, the so-called "planes" (Fig. 1).

The lowest plane, called the transport plane, performs transmission and distribution of information. It represents the nucleus of every system realized with SILK. It is connected to the next higher plane, the connection plane, through a number of identical interfaces.

The connection plane consists of all devices that accomplish transformation between the identical interfaces of the transport plane and the various application-oriented interfaces, including gateways to other networks. This concept allows the integration of user groups with considerably different characteristics on the same system.

The peripheral plane as the highest plane of this model consists of terminal equipment such as communication terminals, computers, and other networks attached to the connection plane.

III. TRANSPORT PLANE

Transmission

The nodes of the transport plane contain the circuitry for transmission and access to the ring (Fig. 2). The transmission sections between the nodes are of variable

Manuscript received February 24, 1983; revised June 28, 1983.

D. E. Huber and P. J. Wild are with Hasler Ltd., CH-3000 Berne 14, Switzerland.

W. Steinlin is with Department VL-26, Research and Development Division, GD PTT, CH-3000 Berne 29, Switzerland.

Reprinted from *IEEE Journal on Selected Areas in Communications*, November 1983, pages 766-774. Copyright © 1983 by The Institute of Electrical and Electronics Engineers, Inc.

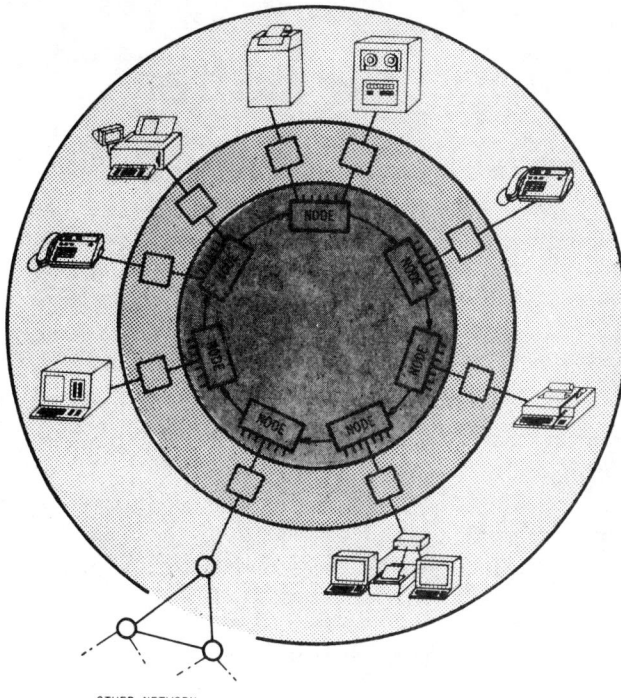

Fig. 1. Hierarchical architecture of SILK. Transport, connection, and peripheral planes.

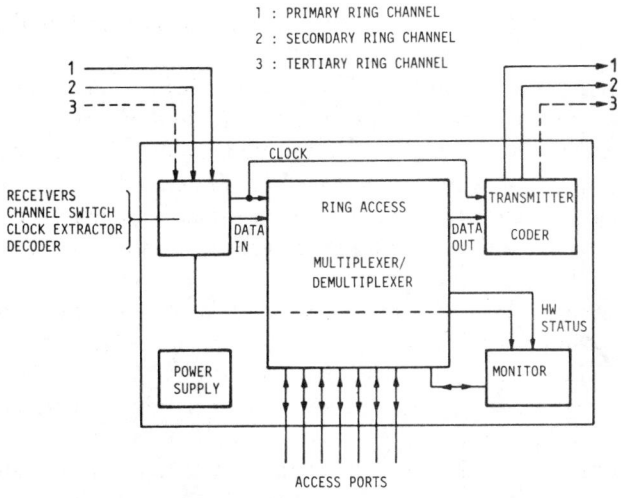

1 : PRIMARY RING CHANNEL
2 : SECONDARY RING CHANNEL
3 : TERTIARY RING CHANNEL

Fig. 2. Block diagram of a node with multiplexed access.

cable. To keep drivers and receivers simple, no equalizers are used. Transmission distance between the nodes is dispersion-limited with a cable parameter of $c = 0.5$ [5]. This corresponds to an attenuation of 15.4 dB at 17 MHz. With reasonable cable diameter a single section is therefore limited to approximately 500 m.

An add-on unit employing inexpensive optical modules (LED transmitter, p–i–n receiver) can extend section length to 2000 m. With graded-index fibers, sections are limited by attenuation only. Transmitters using laser diodes would allow even greater distances.

Transmission around the ring is synchronous. A quartz oscillator in a special node, the so-called master clock node, generates the master clock. PLL's in subsequent nodes extract timing information from the incoming Manchester-coded bit stream, thus forming a chain. Second-order PLL's with PI loop filters are used. With a narrow relative bandwidth of 10^{-3} the probability of timing errors due to electromagnetic interference is kept low.

In order to use inexpensive wide-tolerance voltage-controlled oscillators (VCO) in this narrow-band PLL, a frequency acquisition aid has been incorporated [16]. A simple phase and frequency detector is used (Fig. 4). If the loop is unlocked its output voltage $V_{PF}(t)$ has an appropriate bias $\overline{V_{PF}}$ to make the loop integrator slew the VCO frequency f_2 towards the data frequency f_1. After frequency acquisition the detector behaves much like a linear phase detector, without disabling the acquisition aid. For reasons of noise performance of the PLL in lock, the frequency slewing rate is deliberately kept small. A single PLL and also the entire ring lock within less than 410 ms. This is sufficiently short since the ring stays locked under normal operating conditions. PLL frequency drift without input signal has been made very small by freezing the loop integrator upon signal loss detection. In case of a ring interruption, sections following the defective location up to the master clock node stay locked for at least 2 s, which still allows the sending of diagnostic messages.

A special problem is jitter accumulation along the chain of PLL's as known for PCM repeaters [14] and other ring systems [15] but with the added difficulty of varying delay in the nodes due to the buffer insertion technique. Using narrow-band media such as coaxial cables, jitter is mainly due to intersymbol interference and is therefore systematic, i.e., the jitter sources are correlated [14]. The power spectrum of the jitter sources is application dependent and may even contain low frequency discrete lines. Relevant timing parameters are the accumulated jitter ϕ_k (phase variation of the output of the kth PLL relative to the master clock) and alignment jitter $\Delta\phi_k = \phi_k - \phi_{k-1}$.

The accumulated jitter, as well as the fraction of the ring delay which is not an integer multiple of a bit period, are compensated for in the master clock node. This compensation is not the limiting factor for system size.

Alignment jitter determines sampling at the receiver and the modulation of the phase detector of its PLL. Excessive jitter with $|\Delta\phi_k(t)| > \pi/2$ will first cause sampling errors and ultimately cycle slips. The variances of both the accumulated and the alignment jitter of the PLL's increase along a chain of repeaters [14]. Delay due to the insertion

length with data regeneration and retiming in the nodes (Fig. 3). A serial bit stream is transmitted at a bit rate of 16.896 Mbits/s, which is an integer multiple of the commonly used data rates and a European PCM multiplex standard.

The design target of less than 10^{-9} bit error rate for each ring transmission section has been reached. The main sources of errors are impulsive noise and timing jitter in large systems. Signal levels will normally be far above any continuous noise levels.

Manchester coding is used for transmission [5]. Neither system architecture nor access strategy impose any restraint on the choice of a transmission medium and its propagation delay. In contrast to LAN's with CSMA/CD techniques, network size depends on attenuation and dispersion considerations only. The presently used nodes contain circuitry for baseband transmission with 75 Ω coaxial

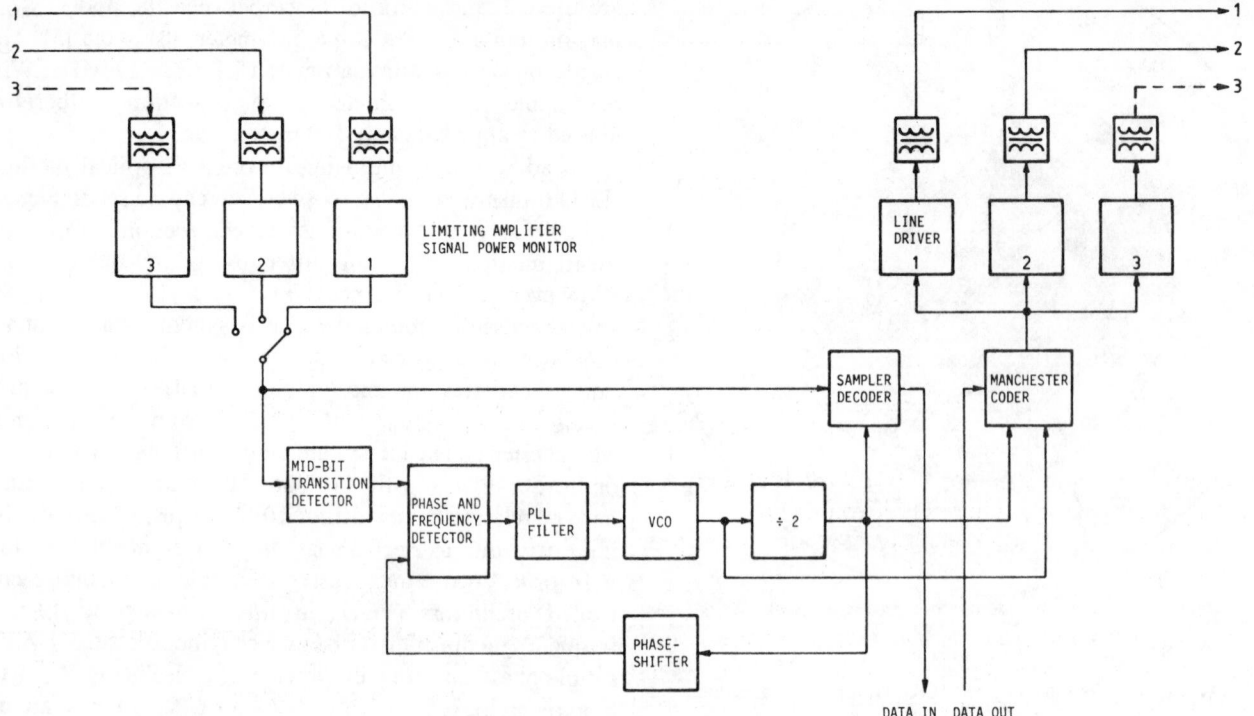

Fig. 3.   Repeater part of a node.

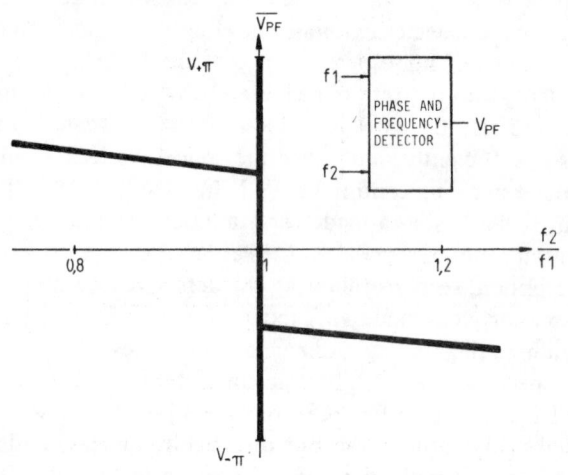

Fig. 4.   Frequency characteristic of the phase and frequency detector. $V_{\pm \pi}$: V_{PF} for $f_1 = f_2$ and a phase difference of $\pm \pi$ between the inputs.

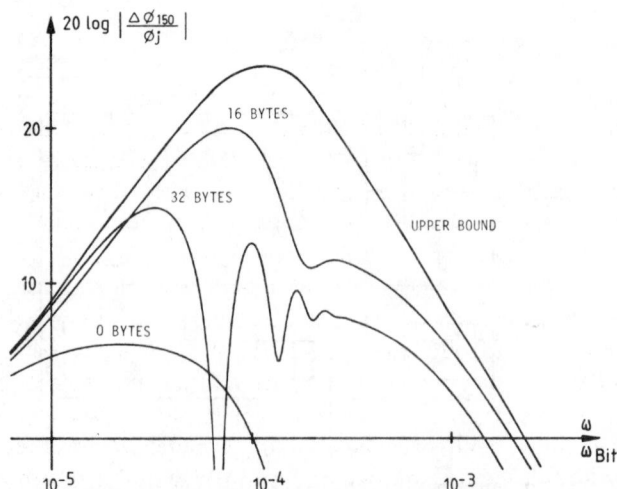

Fig. 5.   Alignment jitter transfer functions computed for the case of 150 nodes. Simplified model with identical jitter excitation and insertion buffer filling for all sections. The upper bound assumes worst-case buffer filling for each node. ϕ_j: amplitude of jitter excitation of one section. $\Delta\phi_{150}$: amplitude of alignment jitter of the 150th node. Parameter: insertion buffer filling.

buffers may cause considerable additional amplification of certain jitter frequencies. Fig. 5 depicts this effect.

A comprehensive analysis of the system limits due to timing errors has to consider the variable delay in the nodes as well as different data patterns and lengths of the individual ring sections. The simplified and pessimistic upper bound of Fig. 5, assuming $c = 0.3$, would limit the system to 150 sections for worst-case periodic data ($\sigma_{\phi j} = 5.2°$). For practical purposes a few hundred sections are reasonable.

The above considerations determined the PLL design: a high damping factor of 7 and a relatively small bandwidth tolerance of ± 6 percent reduce peaking of the alignment jitter transfer function, while the narrow relative band-width confines the possible spectrum of amplified jitter.

Data Structure

Data are processed in the nodes byte by byte. Each node periodically transmits a pair of synchronization bytes to which the next node synchronizes. Synchronization is performed independently on each ring section, which prevents propagation of byte-synchronization errors.

Four types of bytes exist in the transport plane:

● the already mentioned synchronization bytes, characterized by a unique bit sequence,

● header bytes containing packet format and control information,

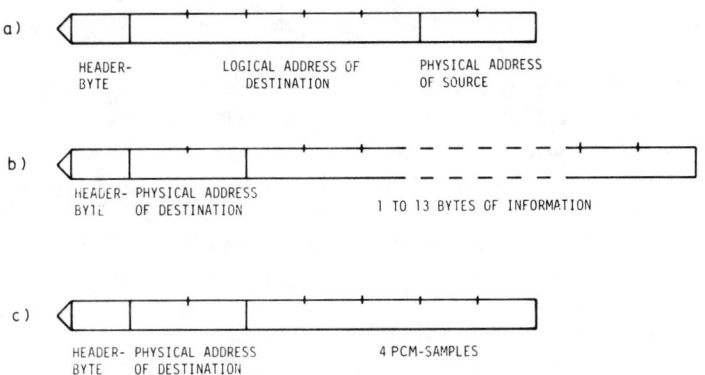

Fig. 6. Examples of packet formats. (a) Broadcast packet for establishing a virtual circuit. (b) Addressed data packet. (c) Addressed voice packet.

● empty bytes containing no information but a special bit pattern that causes a minimum of jitter, and

● information bytes, whereof 7 bits contain addresses or user information.

Packets on the ring consist of one header byte and information bytes and are of variable length so that transmission capacity is used optimally. Packet length is restricted to 16 bytes in order to allow real-time applications requiring short transmission delays. For telephone communication, packets of 8 bytes containing four PCM samples are used [Fig. 6(c)].

Packets are either broadcast to all users or sent to a particular physical address. The system strictly distinguishes the logical from the physical address so that users can be reached anywhere on the system as follows. Setting up a virtual circuit requires the exchange of the physical addresses of the participating users. Therefore, a caller sends a broadcast packet [Fig. 6(a)] containing the logical address of the called user (5 bytes) and his own physical return address (2 bytes for node and access port). Upon recognition of his logical address, the called user sends back an addressed packet (total of 10 bytes) to the caller containing his physical return address, thus establishing a virtual circuit between two particular access ports. The subsequent packets contain 3 bytes of overhead (header + physical address) and up to 13 bytes of information [Fig. 6(b)].

Access Scheme and Its Implementation

In addition to its repeater function, each node allows access of up to seven local users to the ring. As an eighth participant each node has its own monitor. Buffer insertion is used as the access strategy [2], [3]. In contrast to an earlier laboratory implementation using a shift register of fixed length [2], a FIFO buffer temporarily stores the incoming ring traffic in order to allow a local user to transmit a packet onto the ring. This strategy normally gives local users priority over ring traffic. In practice the insertion buffer is of limited capacity. To prevent packet loss on the ring, ring traffic is given priority as soon as the insertion buffer fills up. The filling of the insertion buffer can be reduced when empty or synchronization bytes between packets arrive on the ring channel or when packets

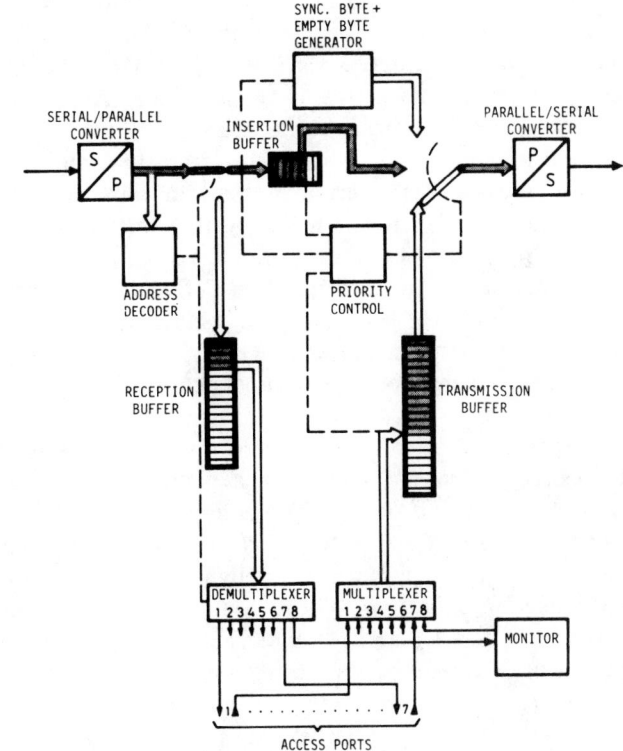

Fig. 7. Access part of a node. Buffer insertion with priority switching.

are removed from the ring because they are addressed to this node.

Access to the ring involves three buffers (Fig. 7). As the node has to perform speed conversion as well as multiplexing and demultiplexing of user traffic, buffer memory is necessary in both the transmitting and receiving data paths.

An analytical model based on Markov chains [6] has shown that mean packet delay and packet loss probability in the transport plane depend on the sum of insertion and transmission buffer capacity only (in this context, packet loss probability means the probability that a packet from a local user finds the transmission buffer already filled up). These results have been verified by computer simulations.

To keep the delay of ring traffic at a minimum in nodes with heavy traffic from the connection plane, the minimal capacity of the insertion buffer is chosen. It has to be able to store two full-sized packets of 16 bytes each. This FIFO buffer of 32 bytes capacity can dynamically handle individual bytes.

Transmission and reception buffers are shared by all eight ports of a node. In contrast to the insertion buffer, they consist of blocks of 16 bytes each, which are dynamically assigned to users on request. The size of the transmission buffer has been chosen according to simulation results to be 32 blocks, an average of four blocks for each port. The size of the reception buffer is 16 blocks, which represents the minimal size.

The following behavior is observed. If there is no traffic from the connection plane to be sent onto the ring, the insertion buffer is empty. An average time interval of $1\frac{1}{2}$ bytes is needed for serial/parallel and parallel/serial conversion as well as byte synchronization. The time used for header or address decoding and temporary buffering of the incoming data is 2 bytes, which is necessary for the deletion of truncated packets as explained below. As a consequence, a minimal mean traffic delay of $3\frac{1}{2}$ bytes/node, i.e., 1.6 μs is required. When traffic from the connection plane increases, the insertion buffer can cause an additional packet delay to the incoming ring traffic. A maximum is reached when priority should be switched to ring traffic due to a half-filled insertion buffer, but the transmission buffer has just started transmitting a full-sized packet. The insertion buffer can be filled with up to 32 bytes, which determines the maximal delay of 35.5 bytes or 16.8 μs/node.

However, it has to be considered that the transmission time of a full-sized packet from a node to an interface transformation unit or vice versa is approximately 500 μs. The transmission between the interface transformation unit and the terminal equipment normally is even slower. For a virtual circuit under normal load conditions, this transmission time of more than 2×500 μs is much longer than the packet delay caused by the ring channel.

The header byte, possibly in conjunction with an address, defines whether a packet has to be removed from the ring channel at a specific node.

A particular bit of the header byte serves as a label which indicates whether a packet has passed the master clock node. If this label is true, the master clock node deletes the packet. Broadcast packets are only transferred to the access ports after this label has been set, i.e., after the first pass through the master clock node. They are removed at the second pass. This procedure ensures that broadcast packets reach each access port only once.

Another bit of the header byte indicates whether a packet contains a physical address. In this case the first two bytes after the header are interpreted as node and access port address. Addressed packets are removed from the ring channel at their destination. Up to the third byte it is unknown if an addressed packet has to be sent to a local port or forwarded on the ring. Therefore, it is possible that truncated packets are sent to the next node when transmission and insertion buffers are empty and the packet is addressed to a local port. These packet fragments are

deleted at the following nodes without causing delay of any other packet.

The discussed procedures for removing regular packets are also effective in deleting packets that are corrupted by transient failures. Header bytes that are no longer recognizable as headers or headers with an erroneously reset label are taken care of in such a manner that no packet circulates more than twice.

In contrast to some other implementations of ring topology LAN's, there is no need for central regeneration of a control entity.

In case of node overload, the insertion buffer fills up first. Then ring traffic gets priority and the transmission buffer begins to fill up. Therefore, a node becomes overloaded if its transmission buffer overflows. As a consequence, overload occurs at individual nodes only. If a particular node is overloaded, the rest of the system still works as usual. In particular it is not possible that a single user can overload and paralyze the whole system by defective transmission of random data. Packet loss might occur, but only to users connected to the overloaded node.

To avoid packet loss due to overload, the node generates a busy signal when it can receive just one more packet from each local port. This busy signal is transmitted to all local users allowing packet flow control.

A hardware status word is generated in each node. It can be polled by a central supervisory terminal. Error events between polls are recorded by the monitor in the node.

Braided Interconnection

Common to most systems with ring or loop topology is their problematic reliability due to chaining of active repeaters. Several countermeasures have been proposed in the literature [1], e.g., bypassing of repeaters by relays [17], doubling of the ring channel [1], [18], or skipping of repeaters and ring sections by means of bypass transmission sections [4], [9], [10].

The braided structure of Fig. 8 has been chosen. A primary channel connects all nodes to form a ring. Each node is bypassed by a so-called secondary section. The secondary section that bypasses the master clock node contains a standby master clock node. Tertiary sections may be used as an option to protect the system against failures affecting groups of subsequent nodes such as power supply interruption in parts of a building.

Braid switching is under distributed control. All ring transmission sections originating at a given node carry the same signal. The monitor of the master clock node sends unaddressed test packets to all monitors, which therefore are able to measure the bit error rate of this test traffic. Depending on the results, switching to another transmission section is initiated. A special protocol prevents unintentional switching of subsequent nodes downstream. Switching causes an alarm which is indicated on a central alarm unit.

Another alarm is indicated if the bit error rate is higher

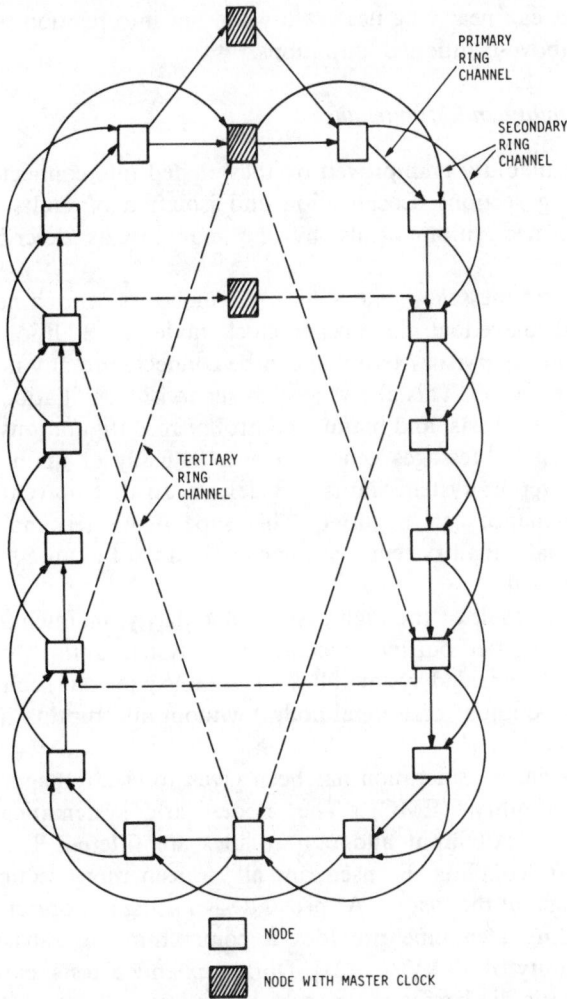

Fig. 8. Braided interconnection of nodes to enhance ring channel availability.

Fig. 9. Actual implementation of a SILK node. Board with hybrid thick-film technology.

than a preset level (typically 3×10^{-6}). There is even a scheme to supervise proper operation of the node monitors. Total traffic load on the ring generated by these monitoring functions is about 20 kbits/s, a small fraction of 17 Mbits/s.

Hardware of the Nodes

Each node is contained in a unit that fits into a 19 in rack. The housing measures $178 \times 482 \times 230$ mm (Fig. 9). No forced-air cooling is required due to a sophisticated thermal concept based on thermal conduction. Extensive use is made of thick-film hybrid technology employing 4×4 in substrates and automatic laser trimming. Different IC families are used depending on subsystem requirements. The high-speed bit stream is processed by ECL logic. To reduce chip count, LSI semicustom circuits are used.

IV. CONNECTION PLANE

The connection plane includes all equipment that translates the SILK-specific interface of the transport plane to the interfaces used in applications. Only a subset of the various characteristics of the transport plane interface is used for a given application. Therefore, the overall system characteristics are application-dependent and can be chosen accordingly. That is why different user requirements for file transfer, process control, or voice communication can be met on the same system.

At the interface to the transport plane, traffic is handled at a maximal data rate of 256 kbits/s with packets of variable length.

It is possible to supply power for connection plane devices from the node (e.g., for telephone handsets). However, they are normally ac-coupled to prevent ground loops.

The interface transformation units contain microprocessors. As the hardware between transport plane interface and microprocessor bus is always identical, semicustom IC's are used.

An interface transformation unit always has a logical address assigned to it which remains unchanged when the unit is moved to another access port.

It is an important design goal to provide internationally standardized interfaces. The CCITT interface X.21 [19] has been implemented for synchronous duplex traffic of up to 48 kbits/s or half-duplex operation up to 96 kbits/s. As many as 220 duplex links with 48 kbit/s data rate can be handled concurrently by the system.

Datagram traffic based on HDLC frames is possible at the same data rates. An X.25 interface [19] using this datagram concept is presently under development.

Physical integration of an interface transformation unit and the associated terminal equipment is possible as well. For a prototype system, a digital telephone handset has been developed which connects directly to the transport plane interface of a node [13]. Assuming no concurrent data traffic, 120 simultaneous telephone calls are possible on a single ring so that systems of more than a thousand subscribers (at 0.1 Erlang) are technically feasible. If a

PCM sample does not arrive in time (i.e., within the 125 μs sampling interval) the previous value is kept unchanged. With this method the loss of up to four samples is not audible. Due to the high ring bit rate and the short packet length used for voice communication, no priority scheme was necessary.

V. SYSTEM ASPECTS

Traffic Characteristics

Traffic characteristics of SILK are mainly influenced by variable filling and byte-wise organization of the insertion buffer. In particular, gaps between packets of the incoming data stream can be either closed or extended to insert packets from local users in order to efficiently use the common ring channel farther downstream.

Compared with other ring access schemes that remove packets at the transmitting node, average throughput is improved by a factor of two as addressed packets are already removed by the receiving node. This has been taken into account for a full duplex voice communication traffic analysis [6] assuming a packet pair occupying the whole ring during one packet transmission interval. A more recent paper [20] pointed out the potential disadvantage of the buffer insertion scheme for highly asymmetrical load. However, these results hardly apply to SILK because the offered load of any user does not exceed 256 kbits/s, which is a small fraction of the total ring channel capacity. In practice, SILK user data rates so far have been below 96 kbits/s.

Another favorable characteristic of SILK is its flexible adaptation to varying traffic loads. Under low-load traffic conditions, overall packet delay is on the order of 1 ms, determined mainly by the transmission times on the 256 kbit/s interfaces between the transport and connection plane. Even under high-load conditions near the limit of system capacity, the user priority scheme allows fast access to the ring channel which behaves like a delay line with a delay that is artificially increased by the insertion buffers. As a consequence, a variable number of packets can be accommodated on the ring. Even close to the limit for continuous traffic, additional short-term load can be handled. This is in contrast to "slotted" rings, where the number of simultaneously circulating packets is mainly determined by cable propagation and, therefore, is constant.

Analysis and simulation results of the performance of the SILK transport plane are given in [6].

Major throughput limitations of implemented SILK systems are imposed by microprocessors and their software in sophisticated interface transformation units and in gateways to other networks. For the applications served by SILK so far, the performance of these units together with the characteristics of user terminals are the decisive factors of system throughput. Delay caused by buffers in the nodes can nearly be neglected when put into relation with the above-mentioned limitations.

Reliability and Maintenance

Availability is improved by the braided interconnection of ring sections. Localization and isolation of faults are performed automatically by the monitors as described above.

Alarm messages generated in the monitors of each node are displayed at the master clock node. In addition, a special supervisory terminal can be connected to any node of the system. This allows system supervision, initiation of additional tests, and manual control of reconfigurations of the braid. Messages generated automatically or upon request report system status and defects, so that preventive maintenance can be done. This supervisory terminal is optional. Small systems with few nodes do not require such a terminal.

As a result of the high system modularity, maintenance can be carried out by replacing faulty system units. Moreover, the braided system allows system expansion (such as introduction of additional nodes) without interrupting ring traffic.

Special consideration has been given to electromagnetic compatibility (EMC). The nodes are systematically shielded. All input and output lines are filtered. Transformer coupling is used in all transmission sections throughout the system. A special design using a proprietary shielding technique provides a common-mode transient immunity of 40 kV/μs [21]. During extended tests, external static discharges of up to 16 kV had no influence. Due to ac-coupling the system is insensitive to low-frequency potential differences. SILK has been tested for compliance with VDE 875 and VDE 871 standards and has been approved by the German "Bundespost" [22].

To reduce maintenance to a minimum, no moving parts were used throughout the whole system. No forced-air cooling is required up to ambient temperatures of 50°C. To prevent damage, the internal temperature of the nodes is supervised and the nodes are switched off in case of overtemperature. Short power supply interruptions of approximately 100 ms duration do not affect operation.

Modularity

SILK was designed to accommodate a range of applications and system sizes. The smallest configuration consists of one master clock node with its ring output connected to the ring input. Up to seven users can be connected to a single node. The transport plane interface allows a distance of up to 300 m between a node and its remote interface transformation unit, depending on the cable used. A single node with its attached peripheral devices is a cluster configuration with star topology. Since there is no need for a supervisory terminal or any other type of additional network administrator, such a minimal configuration can be an interesting LAN solution by itself.

A network can grow by adding nodes with seven external access ports each. No modifications of the already installed equipment are required. In small systems with a few nodes only, it might not be necessary to have a braided ring interconnection.

Using the same system units, very large networks with over a thousand access ports in one ring can also be realized. Identical interfaces to all access ports are another reason for the high flexibility that allows easy reconfiguration of such systems.

Due to the distributed monitoring and automatic braid reconfiguration technique with central indication and message recording for maintenance personnel, such large systems remain manageable.

VI. APPLICATIONS

Distributed Text Editing

A system with 33 nodes has been installed at a German broadcasting station [7]–[9]. It spans a distance of nearly 3 km and carries out transfers of text files between text editing work stations, data banks, and special communication processors that are linked to press agencies. External information exchange of the system is about three million characters per day. Internal traffic is much higher. In-house communications are carried out over synchronous 96 kbit/s half-duplex channels. They have circuit-switching characteristics. Interfaces conform to CCITT standard X.21. The SILK part of the system was installed in late 1981. Operated on its own with simulated data traffic, an inspection after 7 months showed that not a single bit error occurred in the monitor test traffic of approximately 20 kbits/s which was continuously controlled. Subsequent debugging of the whole system, including application software, did not reveal any problem in the transport plane.

Process Control

A process control system has been installed in a new studio of an important German television network [9]. It includes 67 nodes and allows, among other tasks, remote computer control of complex technical studio equipment such as video tape recorders and film scanners. A reaction time of less than 20 ms (i.e., one video half-frame) is required in order to synchronize different video sources for "live" transmission of a television program. Communications are based on HDLC frames that are transmitted at a rate of 48 kbits/s across X.21 duplex interfaces. As every HDLC frame carries its destination address, it represents a datagram. This means that the terminal equipment has a multiplex connection to the SILK system. Such a requirement exists because some of the processors have to control

more than one video source at the same time. Furthermore, a message containing the current time of day has to be distributed on the entire system every 40 ms. This problem has been solved with a broadcast type of packet. Besides excellent real-time performance, reliability, and availability are of major importance since television broadcasting quality depends heavily on the proper operation of the system. The SILK part of this system was installed in 1982 and tests were successful.

Local Teletex Exchange

In another type of application SILK is used as a private automatic branch exchange for teletex, a new CCITT-defined public service. Message transfer is memory-to-memory at 2400 bits/s. The first implementation of such a teletex exchange with SILK is intended for countries which use a circuit-switched public data network and X.21 interfaces. An X.21 gateway is used to connect to the public network. Gateways can be operated in parallel to enhance throughput. Software facilities already developed for voice communications such as "group call," or "transfer on busy" have been adapted for this purpose. In order to allow local communications between teletex terminals, addressing with an alphanumeric prefix is necessary to differentiate internal and external calls. Prefixes for addresses are also used for calls to other SILK rings that are connected via internet gateways.

VII. CONCLUSION

It has been shown that ring topology LAN's characterized by a buffer insertion access technique have found practical application in various systems with demanding requirements. Very short delays in the active repeater and access nodes are not decisive for real-time performance, as shown by the process control tasks solved with SILK.

Braided interconnection with automatic bypassing of faulty ring transmission sections is a useful concept for maintaining high availability of the system.

The capability of using fiber-optic links between nodes, where required, is shared with other ring systems.

ACKNOWLEDGMENT

The authors wish to thank the many co-workers who contributed to this project. In particular we acknowledge valuable comments by Dr. F. Braun (especially for contributing the results of Fig. 5), J. Clavadetscher, and H. Ryser.

REFERENCES

[1] B. K. Penney and A. A. Baghdadi, "Survey of computer communications loop networks," *Comput. Commun.*, vol. 2, pp. 165–180, Aug. 1979, and pp. 224–241, Oct. 1979.
[2] E. R. Hafner, Z. Nenadal, and M. Tschanz, "A digital loop communication system," *IEEE Trans. Commun.*, vol. COM-22, pp. 877–881, June 1974.

[3] M. T. Liu, *Distributed Loop Computer Network* (Advances in Computing, vol. 17). New York: Academic, 1978.

[4] E. R. Hafner and Z. Nenadal, "Enhancing the availability of a loop system by meshing," in *Proc. Int. Zurich Sem. Digital Commun.*, Zurich, Switzerland, 1976, pp. D 4.1–D 4.5.

[5] F. G. Braun, W. Steinlin, and H. Ryser, "Transmission in local digital loop communication," in *Proc. Int. Zurich Sem. Digital Commun.*, Zurich, Switzerland, 1978, pp. C 2.1–C 2.6.

[6] F. G. Braun, E. R. Hafner, and E. Schultze, "System and traffic aspects in SILK: System for integrated local communications," in *Nat. Telecommun. Conf. Rec.*, 1980, vol. 3, pp. 65.1.1–65.1.6.

[7] I. Reibert, "IDA: A local digital information system for communication and data exchange in a German broadcasting station," in *Nat. Telecommun. Conf. Rec.*, 1980, vol. 3, pp. 65.2.1–65.2.5.

[8] W. Hack, W. Schott, and H. Schneeberger, "Software aspects of IDA: Principles and implementation," in *Conf. Rec., Nat. Telecommun.*, 1980, vol. 3, pp. 65.3.1–65.3.5.

[9] Special Issue on SILK, *Hasler Rev.*, vol. 14, no. 1, pp. 1–40, 1981.

[10] F. G. Braun, "Zuverlässigkeit von lokalen Kommunikationsnetzen," presented at Telecom 82 Deutschland, Köln, Germany, Oct. 27–29, 1982, Kongressdokumentation Bd 2, Workshopreihe D2, Seite 52–60.

[11] SILK is a registered trademark of Hasler Ltd. in various countries.

[12] IBM Series/1, "Local communications controller."

[13] H. J. Matt and K. Fussgänger, "Integrated broad-band communication using optical networks—Results of an experimental study," *IEEE Trans. Commun.*, vol. COM-29, pp. 868–886, June 1981.

[14] T. Shimamura and I. Eguchi, "An analysis of jitter accumulation in a chain of PLL timing recovery circuits," *IEEE Trans. Commun.*, vol. COM-25, pp. 1027–1032, Sept. 1977.

[15] H. R. Müller, H. Keller, and H. Meyr, "Transmission in a synchronous token ring," in *Proc. IFIP TC 6 Int. In-Depth Symp. Local Comput. Networks*, Florence, Italy, April 19–21, 1982, pp. 125–147.

[16] W. Steinlin, Int. Patent Appl. PCT WO 82/01289.

[17] W. Bux, F. Closs, P. A. Janson, K. Kümmerle, H. R. Müller, and E. H. Rothauser, "A local-area communication network based on a reliable token-ring system," in *Proc. IFIP TC 6 Int. In-Depth Symp. Local Comput. Networks*, Florence, Italy, Apr. 19–21, 1982, pp. 69–82.

[18] G. David and B. Pando, "An on-board digital transmission system," *Philips Telecommun. Rev.*, vol. 37, Aug. 1979.

[19] Recommendations X.1–X.29, *CCITT Yellow Book*, vol. VIII, Fascicle VIII.2, Geneva, Switzerland, 1980.

[20] W. Bux and M. Schlatter, "An approximate method for the performance analysis of buffer insertion rings," *IEEE Trans. Commun.*, vol. COM-31, pp. 50–55, Jan. 1983.

[21] H. Ryser, U.S. Patent 4342976, Aug. 1982.

[22] "Zentralamt für Zulassungen im Fernmeldewesen," Deutsche Bundespost, FTZ-Serienummer C-145/82.

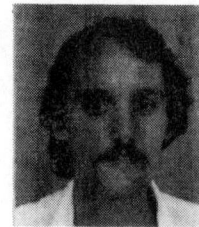

Daniel E. Huber (S'79–M'80) received the Dipl. Ing. degree from the Swiss Federal Institute of Technology (ETH), Zurich, Switzerland, in 1978.

From 1979 to 1981 he worked at the Hasler Research Laboratory, Berne, Switzerland, on the development of a local area network. In 1982 he joined the Engineering Department for Local Area Networks at Hasler, where he is working as a System Engineer.

Walter Steinlin (M'80) received the Dipl. Ing. degree from the Swiss Federal Institute of Technology (ETH), Zurich, Switzerland, in 1977.

From 1977 to 1983 he worked at the Hasler Research Laboratory, Berne, Switzerland, on the development of a local area network and on fiber optic transmission. He is now with the Research and Development Division of the Swiss PTT, Berne.

Peter J. Wild (M'64) received the Dipl. Ing. degree from the Swiss Federal Institute of Technology (ETH), Zurich, Switzerland, in 1963, and the M.S. degree from the University of California at Berkeley in 1968.

From 1964 to 1968 he worked as an Electronics Engineer in Swiss and U.S. companies. From 1969 to 1980 he held positions as Senior Member of Technical Staff at the Corporate Research Center and Development Manager for Display Devices at the Electronics Division of Brown Boveri Company, Baden, Switzerland. In 1980 he joined Hasler Ltd., Berne, Switzerland, where he is now Engineering Manager for local area networks and communication terminals.

Mr. Wild is a member of Eta Kappa Nu and the Society for Information Displays.

Design and Use of an Integrated Cambridge Ring

ANDREW HOPPER AND ROBIN C. WILLIAMSON

Abstract —The Cambridge ring is a local area network used both in universities and industry. It is based on the empty slot principle and data are transmitted using minipackets containing two bytes of data. This paper describes the design process, decisions, and tradeoffs in implementing an integrated system which incorporates both analog and digital components. The technology chosen is a bipolar gate array. A number of options are provided for the implementor who can optimize network parameters such as minipacket size and transmission speed to his needs. He can also choose the style of interface between the communicating device and the network.

An important option provided by the integrated Cambridge ring is the ability to simultaneously transmit short control minipackets and long data packets. A system exploiting this feature has been built and is described. Its proposed uses are to interconnect telephones and other real-time systems as well as computers where the partitioning of bandwidth and precise performance specification are important.

I. INTRODUCTION

THIS paper describes the design and use of an integrated version of the Cambridge ring and outlines some of the local area network structures that can be implemented with it. The initial impetus for an integrated ring was to reduce system cost, to increase the ease of constructing ring networks, and to gain experience of integrated circuit design techniques.

One of the most important parameters in any network design is the cost of connection. This can be divided into several levels. The first level is the cost of connection to the transmission medium which may involve looking at the costs of using a wide range of transmission media. Above this comes the cost of implementing the network architecture in either hardware or software. Most networks have a number of similar features which only vary in detail. These are framing, addressing, error checking, and maintenance. In general, these features are implemented in hardware for reasons of speed. Occasionally, to reduce cost, they may be performed in software, but such systems tend to be rather simple, and shifting problems to software does not always mean a lower total cost. Once a system for delivering data between nodes has been devised, the cost of interfacing machines can be considered. Here the problem is more general, as we may require both very simple and also sophisticated devices to be connected easily. For a simple device, it may be sufficient to ensure the network buffers at

least the smallest unit the hardware delivers at full speed. For more sophisticated devices, appropriate interrupt or direct memory access (DMA) handling techniques are important.

II. THE CAMBRIDGE RING

The Cambridge ring (CR) [1]–[3] is a baseband mode local area network based on the empty slot principle. A CR consists of a set of *repeaters* connected by a communications medium, such as twisted pair or optical fiber cables, and a *monitor station* which has the responsibility for synchronizing and maintaining the network. Each repeater is connected to a ring *station* which controls the transmission and reception of data via the ring. The interface between the repeater and station is serial and consists of "data in," "data out," "clock out," and "gate new data" signals. The interface between the station and the user is parallel with 49 active signals. The station is connected to the target device through an *access box*. This is the logic required to interface the bus which is provided by the station with the host machine. The structure of the CR is shown in Fig. 1.

A CR repeater has a delay of 3 bits and a typical ring configuration with about 30 nodes and 1 km of wire operating at 10 Mbits/s has about 150 bits of delay. This delay is used to accommodate a whole number of 38 bit slots which are divided up into fields for source and destination addresses, two bytes of data, and control information. Use of two bytes of data as the lowest level hardware transmission unit is the principal difference between a CR and most other local area networks. Each slot has a start of slot bit (always one) and a bit to indicate whether it is currently in use. When several slots exist on the ring at one time, they form a head-to-tail train. The delay remaining after the maximum number of slots has been inserted is called the gap, which always consists of zeros and is used for synchronization. The slot structure is set up initially by the monitor station. For transmissions to proceed correctly, stations have to be synchronized to the slot train. This is done by each station having two modes, in-slot and in-gap. When in-gap, a station waits for the next one, assumes this is the start of slot, and counts 38 bits before repeating the algorithm. Because during synchronization slots leaving the monitor station are full and zero elsewhere, the first station downstream will synchro-

Manuscript received March 4, 1983; revised June 24, 1983.

The authors are with the Computer Laboratory, University of Cambridge, Cambridge CB2 3QG, England.

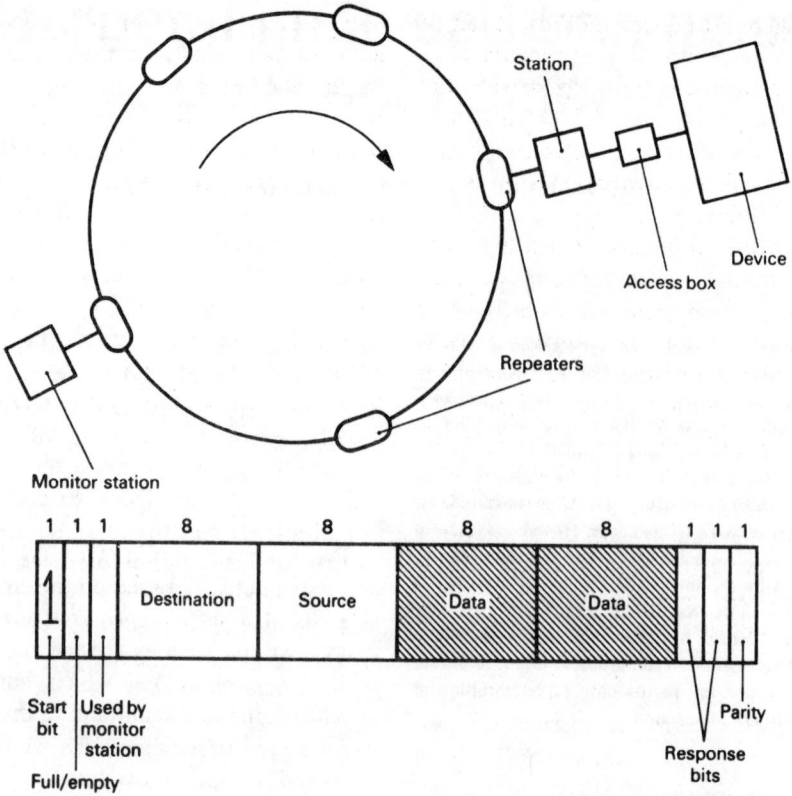

Fig. 1. Cambridge ring structure and minipacket format.

nize, leaving an uninterrupted slot structure for the second station and so on.

To transmit, a station must wait until an empty slot arrives, then, having filled it with a *minipacket*, it waits until the slot returns and always marks it empty. When the slot has returned, two response bits, which are located after the data bytes, are inspected to see whether the minipacket was accepted, rejected, or marked busy by the destination station. Each station is provided with a unique address as well as information about the number of slots in the system so that it can mark empty slots it has used without increasing repeater delay.

For reception, each station looks at the destination addresses of all full minipackets circulating the ring and recognizes its own ring address. When this match takes place and the station is able to receive data, the source address and data fields are copied. Having recognized the destination address, the response bits of the minipacket are set according to whether it was accepted or not.

In order to diagnose breaks and parity faults on the ring, a self-maintenance system is provided [4]. The parity bit is inserted correctly for each slot leaving a repeater and is checked as it enters the next repeater. Thus, if a parity fault occurs, it is localized to a link which causes a special minipacket to be transmitted to destination zero (the error logger). A ring break generates a continuous train of minipackets to destination zero.

From the user's point of view, the CR provides a frequent opportunity to transmit a small amount of data. This can be used directly in simple systems, but often these minipackets are formed into longer variable length *packets*, similar to those in other networks [5]. However, in many other systems only one station can transmit at a time, while several transmissions can take place at once in the CR.

III. WHAT CAN BE INTEGRATED?

When considering an LSI chip design, it is important to integrate as much of the system as possible so that the complexities of the design are hidden from the user, who has a simple and well-specified interface. We shall consider each layer of the architecture in turn.

The most common transmission medium is twisted pair wire. It is thus important to consider the design of line drivers and receivers for this medium. On the driving side, we must make sure that sufficient signal is injected into the wire to ensure that at the receiving end the data are decoded correctly with minimum distortion. With baseband signals and twisted pair wire, we would like to be able to transmit down several hundred meters of wire at up to 10 MHz and in some systems also decode the clock. Normally, a 100 mV signal at the receiving end is sufficient to decode transitions correctly. With typical line impedances of around 100 Ω, a 20 mA TTL totem-pole output will give a satisfactory signal at the end of several hundred meters of wire. At the receiving end, an amplifier can be used to receive the signals and this may incorporate some hysteresis so that noise or a broken cable does not introduce erroneous data.

An important feature to be considered is the amount of

jitter the transmission system introduces and how it can be minimized. Jitter can be made up of components from logic, drivers, the line, or receivers. Both the drivers and receivers may have different propagation delays for a positive edge and for a negative edge. The line itself may also introduce this effect, as well as attenuating signals for changing bit patterns in different ways.

In addition to the line driver and receiver, a chip design should also consider the clocking system. In some schemes, the clock is passed round on separate wires and can be regenerated easily. However, if the clock and data paths are shared, some form of clock extraction mechanism is required. If jitter has been introduced, some averaging may have to be performed. This can be done either digitally using a high-speed counter or gate delay chain, or in a more conventional way using analog phase-locked loop techniques [6], [7]. In summary, it is important that any chip design consider the line driving, receiving, and clocking systems, as often these are the most difficult or sensitive parts of the system and are typical of the kind of complexity that should be hidden from the user.

At the network design level, it is desirable that the chip perform the basic network functions of address recognition, framing, error checking, and maintenance. Such functions normally have to be done within one bit or minipacket time and are thus implemented in hard logic.

Once minipackets are addressed correctly, we can consider the buffers which store data to be transmitted or received. Such buffers can hold just one minipacket or they can be large enough to hold one or more packets. In some systems, the buffer is smaller than the smallest unit that can be transmitted, but this normally poses severe timing constraints on the user. If a simple 8 bit interface is permissible, then an integrated buffer is only constrained by chip space. However, in many applications, a wider bus is required and we are faced with pin-out problems.

DMA is a feature that is used on high-speed interfaces, and if provided in LSI may be used more widely. The requirement is usually for several DMA channels, some for transmit, some for receive, and some for control. It should be possible to perform scattered read and write operations with minimum delay when manipulating the DMA registers. Because of pin count constraints, these registers would normally only be available through shared pins and the resulting indirection may make rapid changes in DMA routes expensive.

On the CR, no error checking facilities are provided for the user who normally implements an external sumcheck over a packet. This error check could be implemented in hardware within the network chip. However, because the error rate is low (1 bit in 10^{11}), performing the error check close to the network may be unsatisfactory since there will be an unchecked path between the hardware error checker and the memory of the device, which may be as error prone as the ring itself. This poses a difficulty in that it may be impossible to perform the error check in hardware unless it is done in the memory itself.

At the next level, the interface has to be specified to the user in a way that is both convenient and allows high-speed data transfer. However, there is an overall constraint that the number of pins is minimized. An interface which is both easy to use and allows high-speed access logics to be built is one in which there is a general purpose data bus, and separate control signals for commands to the station logic. The CR interface is designed in this way. Access to the data and address buffers is through duplex 16 bit buses which can be folded to give 16 and 8 bit duplex or half-duplex systems and all of the control signals can be used independently. A reduction in the number of wires needed for control signals can be achieved using indirection and control registers. This means the control signals are allocated positions in registers, and since the registers are typically 8 bits wide, the number of pins is divided by eight. When a user wishes to perform some control function, he must identify which register he is using before writing into the appropriate position to specify the action to be performed. This can be duplex, but if further interface simplification is required, half-duplex operation permits a single 8 bit data bus to be used. By carefully arranging the position of bits within registers or only assigning one function per register, it is possible to ensure that the delay in manipulating registers is minimized.

Once the user interface is specified, it is possible to consider how much of the access logic can be placed in LSI. For the register-oriented interface, it is sufficient to add a chip enable signal and the network looks similar to any other peripheral chip. Once in LSI, this is probably the simplest way of interfacing a network.

A sophisticated access logic may require a microprocessor for control together with its own memory and buffer space. This is normally used to implement a stream protocol. Such protocols for local networks could be implemented in a modestly sized controller. Thus, it seems feasible that a stream protocol can be implemented in hardware.

IV. Design of the Integrated Cambridge Ring

A. Technology Choice and Partitioning

The design constraints for the integrated Cambridge ring (ICR) were to encapsulate as much of the design as possible in a chip, while enabling the implementor to have many options. It was not an original design goal to make the ICR system directly compatible with the TTL based system at the wire level, although it was thought this would be desirable at the access box level.

The choice of technology was constrained by a number of factors. It was thought that the package size should not exceed 40 pins since larger sizes become prohibitively expensive. The target design speed of the system was 10 MHz, which suggested a typical gate delay of under 10 ns. At the time, easily available CMOS technology was not capable of providing this performance, particularly with 5 V power rails, which suggested a bipolar process. The technology would also have to provide facilities for analog circuits to enable the line drivers and receivers to be integrated. An estimate of the gate count indicated that the whole system would be integrated on several thousand gates and that a system with external minipacket buffers would require under 1000 gates. It was also a requirement that the design be completed rapidly, perhaps at the expense of silicon area. For these reasons, the technology chosen was the Ferranti gate array current mode logic [8]. These arrays are uncommitted at the transistor level and thus can be used to construct analog structures as well as gates. Various sizes were available at the time; the largest provided about 500 gates for the designer.

On examining the original system, it was clear that some partitioning would have to take place to minimize the pin count. As access to the shift registers used for storing minipackets was through two 16 bit buses, a large reduction in pins could be achieved by retaining these shift registers in TTL. In addition, because silicon area was limited, it was inappropriate to use it for such regular structures. It was thus decided to implement the shift registers externally. A design based on this structure was made, but the number of pins was still large and the gate count was too high for a single gate array. The logic was therefore partitioned into two sections: the repeater, which would perform the transmit and receive functions; and a station for decoding minipacket frames and transmitting and receiving user data. Because the gate utilization on the two chips was still uneven, some of the station logic was implemented on the repeater chip. This partitioning required duplication of logic and dedication of a number of pins for communication between the two chips. With this partitioning, most criteria of pin count, gate count, and cost were met.

B. Analog Design

For transmission media such as twisted-pair wires, it is desirable to provide differential line drivers of sufficient power to cope with typical line impedances of 100 Ω. Attenuation is not a problem because of the short line lengths normally involved in local networks. With a typical twisted-pair, it is sufficient to source and sink about 10–20 mA to provide satisfactory voltage swings at lengths up to several hundred meters. Also, if a modulation system with a restricted set of pulse widths is used, the differential attenuation with frequency is small at frequencies up to 10 MHz. On the repeater gate array, a single-sided drive has been provided to help maintain the pin count at 40. On short links, this can be used directly, but on long links it is preferable to use a transformer or similar means to convert to differential drive.

Line receivers must be optimized in terms of three parameters. These are gain, hysteresis, and the difference in propagation delay for positive and negative edges. The gain should be enough to reliably detect a signal down to several tens of mV. Hysteresis is used to prevent a partially or completely broken cable from apparently receiving spurious bit patterns. Such patterns may be interpreted as bits, which may upset maintenance transmissions. With no hysteresis, this happens because the inputs to the line receivers at the end of a broken link are likely to float to the most sensitive region. With a partially broken cable, some changes on the wire will be detected, but providing the other side is steady, this will be read as a string of zeros and the maintenance mechanism will operate properly. With this implementation, up to 300 m of standard twisted-pair wire can be driven and decoded correctly at speeds up to 10 MHz.

The design of a phase-locked loop consists of three components. These are the voltage-controlled oscillator, the filter, and the phase comparator. The voltage-controlled oscillator should be implemented in such a way that noise in the chip does not cause arbitrary phase changes in the oscillation. In some oscillator designs, there may be a sensitive region in the cycle and noise at this time may make phase-locking difficult. With the ICR implementation, the oscillator has its own 5 V and GND supplies. The chip and oscillator GND supplies are internally connected although the extra pin improves decoupling. The phase comparator chosen is a sawtooth one based on EXCLUSIVE-OR gates. The delays through the various paths are matched to minimize jitter on the control waveform and the filtering and integration of the comparison signal is done by an external *RC* network.

C. User Options

A number of user options have been introduced during the design of the ICR. These may be used to implement a variety of systems and are described in the following.

1) The number of data bytes per minipacket now lies in the range from 1 to 8. The system designer defines this length by setting three static pins of the repeater chip. The performance changes with minipacket size in two ways. As the number of data bytes increases, the ring becomes more efficient in use of data and the effective system bandwidth improves. Increasing the number of data bytes also means that a single user can transmit more data each time he acquires a slot. However, as the slot size increases, the number of slots for any ring size will decrease, and thus the degree of sharing of bandwidth will tend to decrease. This means sharing will be at a coarser level and the upper bound on service time will increase. Another effect of changing the number of data bytes is on the design of the interface. However, as the shift registers for holding minipackets are external, the bus structure can be very wide because there is no direct limitation on the pin count. The ICR minipacket format is shown in Fig. 2.

2) The addition of two user control bits to the minipacket format is the main change which makes the ICR incompatible with the CR. The two extra control bits are available to the user who can load them and read them as required. The hardware treats these bits as an extension of the data field and does not change them in any way. Their primary use is to mark minipackets as belonging to some category, by higher level protocols, for instance. Another way of using the control bits is to allow hardware to interpret them in a specific way. For example, one could

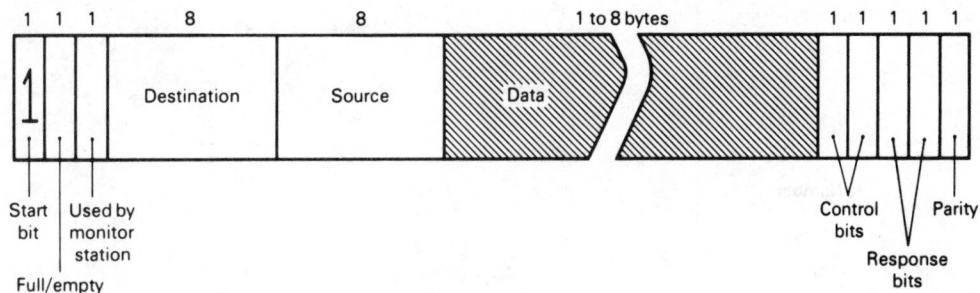

Fig. 2. Integrated Cambridge ring minipacket format.

envisage a system where voice minipackets are marked as a special pattern of control bits.

Because the control bits are just an extension of the data field, it does not matter where they are in the minipacket structure. For compatibility reasons, however, they are normally implemented so that they precede the response bits.

3) A broadcast address has been implemented to permit a single minipacket to be recognized by every destination. It is characteristic of a ring that all minipackets pass all destinations. Thus, it is easy to reserve one address (255) which is detected by each station. Minipackets are then received in the normal way. There is a problem with responses, as it is difficult to inform the source what the response was at each station. To make this option more useful, the responses have been changed so that for broadcast minipackets only one bit is used. It is set by any station which accepts the minipacket. Thus, the response information available at the source indicates whether at least one station has received the minipacket.

4) One of the most important limitations of the transmission speed on the CR is that the transmit command cannot be issued until the previous minipacket has returned. Since this command is asynchronous to the network clock, by the time it has settled, the next full/empty bit has passed. To improve this, a transmit-on-accepted mode has been introduced in which two extra signals are provided. These are the transmit-on-accepted command and the buffer empty response. The transmit-on-accepted command is a conditional command and can only be issued while a previous minipacket is making its way round the ring. Its effect is to launch the next minipacket if the previous one was accepted. Because the transmit-on-accepted command can be early, synchronization can also take place early. The buffer empty response indicates when a minipacket has been shifted out and a new one can be loaded.

5) Another mode of operation has been provided in the ICR for use where either very high bandwidths are required or where the service times of the ring must have a very precise specification. This is called channel mode and allows a station to replenish data in a slot. Thus, once a station has acquired a slot, there is no compulsion for this slot to be released. The service time is deterministic and part of the ring bandwidth has been allocated to that station. To use this mode, the interface initially has to issue a normal transmit command which will use the next availa-

ble slot. When the buffer empty response indicates that the minipacket has been moved out of the transmit shift register, a new minipacket is loaded and the channel-transmit command issued. The returning slot is not marked empty, the new data are inserted, and the next transmit command can be issued.

In channel mode there is a difficulty in handling responses. Because new data are inserted into a slot before the responses are read, there is a possibility that minipackets are sent out of order. This happens whenever a minipacket is not accepted at a destination. Thus, in this mode it is important that either the destination can receive from the ring at full speed or that a protocol which deals with minipackets being received out of sequence is used.

D. LAN Implementations

Various board implementations of the ICR are possible. We shall discuss a number of these in the following.

Because of the extra control bits, it is impossible to design a ring node completely compatible with the TTL system. However, the control bits can be made transparent to the user and thus the access box interface can be made the same as the CR design. For this, the transmit and receive shift registers and a number of other components are required to implement echo signals, line buffers, etc. Like the TTL version, the integrated system can be based on a 16 bit transmit data bus and a 16 bit receive data bus. The access box interface has two extra lines which are used for access to the control bits. With the integrated system, the total chip count for a ring node can be reduced from the 80 used in the TTL implementation to 12.

The design is easily altered to increase the number of data bytes in a minipacket. This requires the appropriate buffering and the pins indicating minipacket length to be set correctly. The bus architecture can be arranged as required; in particular, a very wide structure can be used. This is attractive when an interface for a 32 or 64 bit machine is being constructed or when very high throughputs are required.

V. A HYBRID RING

A. Traffic Considerations

A recent survey [9] of the distribution of the size of packets transmitted on the CR suggests that while 79

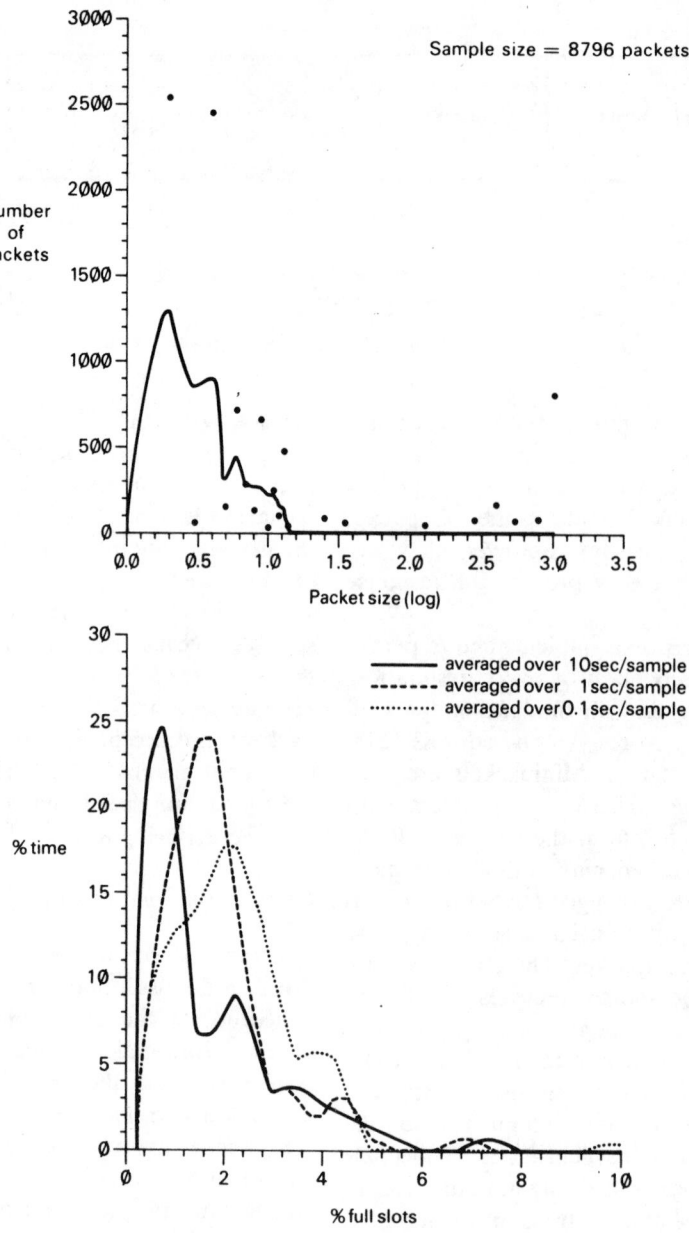

Fig. 3.   Packet length and ring utilization distributions.

percent of the packets contain less than 28 bytes of data, 96 percent of the total data are sent in the remaining 21 percent packets. The large packets mainly consist of data transfers to and from the file storage devices on the ring and a high proportion of these are the maximum length, 2048 bytes. The short packets are used to transmit mainly protocol control information. Fig. 3 shows distributions of packet length and ring utilization measured under average traffic conditions on a 50 node ring.

As the slot utilization of the CR is relatively low, approximately 20 percent at peak times, these figures suggest that the delay in transmitting a large packet would be considerably reduced if the number of data bytes per minipacket was increased. Although the ring would then accommodate fewer slots, the additional delay in transmitting a minipacket is likely to be small because the number of devices using the ring at any one time is low. A further upgrade in the packet transmission time can be achieved

by using the ICR channel mode. If the length of the ring was limited to one slot having an 8 byte data field, then the point-to-point bandwidth available to a user could be as high as 70 percent of the system bandwidth. Unfortunately, with ring traffic consisting predominantly of very short packets, the overall performance of the network would be severely degraded as the number of stations wanting to transmit increased. A solution to this problem would be to support a second type of slot for which retention was not allowed. If the length of this slot was short compared to the length of the channel mode slot, then the bandwidth available to channel users would still be high while access to the short slot would be rapid. A partitioning of the system bandwidth to various types of traffic in this way is possible with the integrated ring. This is achieved by changing the pins on the repeater chip which define the slot length at the appropriate time.

A system has been designed and built which incorporates these features using short minipackets holding one data byte and long minipackets with eight bytes of data. The number of each type of slot is specified before synchronization of the ring is performed. The structure of the ring is similar to that of the CR, a cyclic network consisting of a number of repeaters. Attached to each repeater chip is a station chip and some extra logic, the combination of which is refered to as a ring *tap*. A host device may then be connected to the ring via an interface. One tap on the ring performs certain executive functions, which include synchronization, maintenance of the slot structure, and servicing errors. This special tap is called the *monitor station/logger* (MSL).

In a CR, a user can transmit once every $Q+2$ slots where Q is the number of slots in the system. Thus, a typical CR with three slots, each of two data bytes, and a gap of 8 bits can support up to five users each transmitting 800 kbits/s. When slots can be replenished, this improves to once every Q slots for such channel mode transmissions. So, for a hybrid ring with one long slot, one short slot, and a gap of four bits operating at 10 Mbits/s, the point-to-point bandwidth for a station transmitting a large packet is 5.2 Mbits/s. The maximum bandwidth available to stations using the short slot is 325 kbits/s. Thus, for low traffic loads, there is a considerable reduction in the transmission delay of large packets, while the time to transmit a minipacket for other users will change little. It could be suggested that this type of network is similar to a token ring. Whereas this is true in that a long slot operates in the same way as a token, i.e., a user must wait until the empty slot arrives at the repeater and can then reserve it, when a channel mode slot is in use, it does not preclude all other traffic from the ring. Indeed, several channel mode slots and short slots can coexist with little interference. In allowing both short and long minipacket transmissions to be made simultaneously, the hybrid ring appears more flexible than the token ring. One particular area in which this facility would be most advantageous is in protocol control.

B. The Ring Tap

The ring tap is similar to the ICR node described above. As well as the repeater and station chips, there are minipacket buffers, in which minipackets are assembled and deassembled, bus buffers, and the analog components necessary to phase-lock and drive the ring. At each tap there is also the logic associated with detecting the slot structure (framing logic). This includes two 4 bit counters, one for each slot size, the values of which are used to switch the repeater chip control lines that define minipacket size. The contents of the counters may also be gated onto the data bus for inspection by the host. A diagram illustrating the structure of a ring tap is given in Fig. 4.

Since in channel mode the data transfer rate is potentially high, the shift registers of the conventional CR have been replaced by two sets of 16×16 FIFO registers, one each on the receive and transmit sides. The use of FIFO's on the transmit side enables data to be queued by a high-speed interface before the transmit command is given.

The interface can then enter a wait state until an empty channel slot is received, possibly releasing a DMA hold over the host device. Once the transmission is underway and the first data have been unloaded from the FIFO's, a line of the control bus will indicate that the FIFO is no longer full and the interface can resume transfering data from the host to the tap. The rate at which the rest of the data are transfered is then governed by the same FIFO-full control signal. On the receive side of the control bus, a similar signal (receive-FIFO-ready) indicates whether any data are waiting in the FIFO's and controls the rate at which the interface reads it. The receive and transmit buffers can easily be extended by connecting additional FIFO's in series with the existing buffers. If enough local storage is provided, entire packets could be assembled prior to transmission or reception, leaving the host free during the transfer of the packet.

C. The Monitor Station/Logger

The monitor station/logger is the central control node of the hybrid ring. Its main role as seen by the other taps is to set up and maintain the slot structure of the ring. The MSL can be functionally divided into two sections: a repeater with the external logic associated with setting up the slot structure and a ring tap similar to the other taps connected to the network which is used for error logging.

Overall control of the MSL is performed by a Z80-type microprocessor with which a network supervisor can communicate through a console. The control software continuously monitors the state of the ring and under some error conditions will attempt synchronization. The errors that can be detected by the MSL hardware are

1) lost start of minipacket bit,
2) incorrect parity bit in minipacket,
3) minipacket has already passed MSL, and
4) minipacket marked empty that should be full.

The network supervisor can, through a console, interrogate the MSL on the state of the ring. The information available describes the current number of each size of slot, the size of the gap, the number of each type of error detected, and the number of times that the ring has been resynchronized due to an error condition. The number of each size of slot and the gap length can also be updated at the console. The maximum number of slots that can be implemented on the ring is 16; this is dictated by the ICR specification, although the proportion of each size of slot is arbitrary. The MSL incorporates a long shift register so that if an addition is necessary to accommodate a particular slot train (because of insufficient total delay through repeaters and wire) a variable length extension can be provided. In the case where the supervisor does not know the physical length of the ring and therefore cannot calculate the length of shift register required for a minimum sized gap, the value is computed automatically.

A further facility contributing to the constant surveillance of the ring allows the insertion of random bit patterns into empty slots that are passing the MSL. Such slots are not marked full and can thus be used, but the mainte-

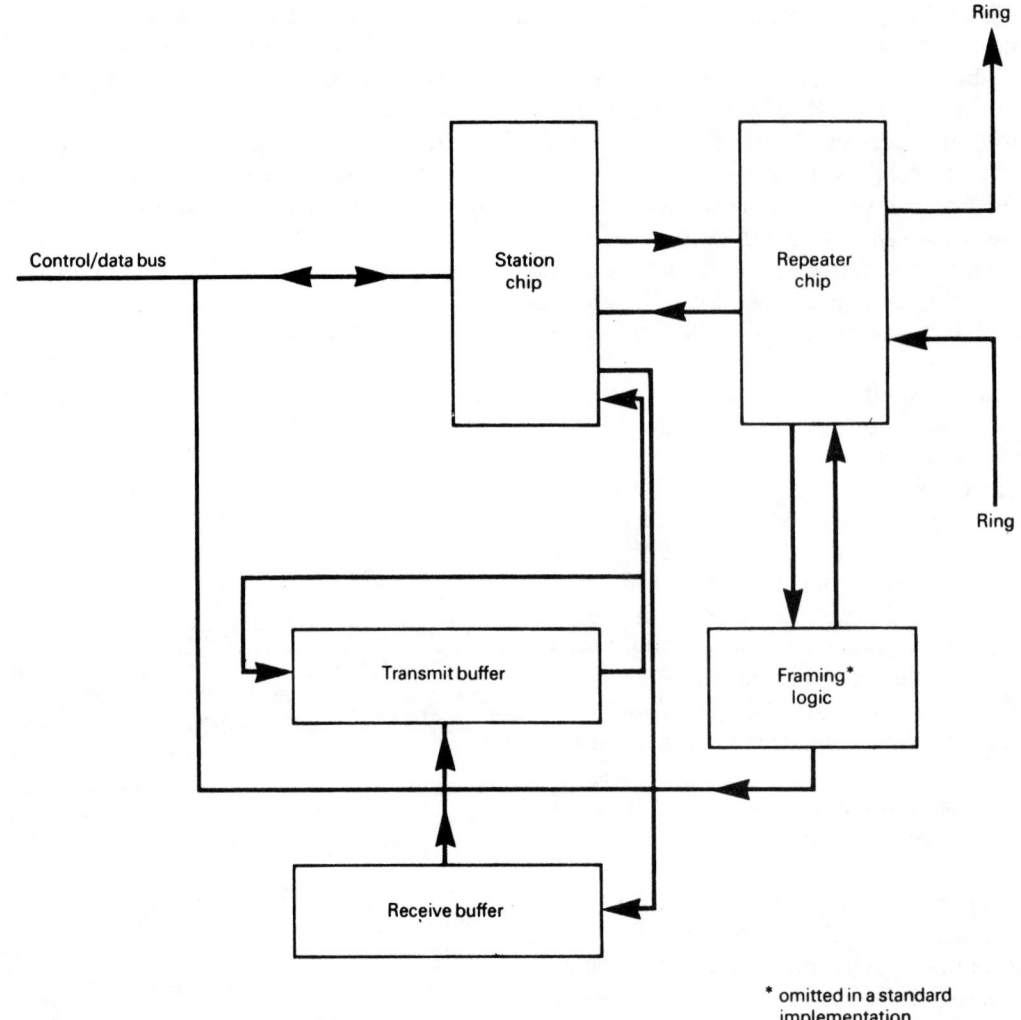

Fig. 4. The structure of a hybrid ring tap.

nance mechanism is exercised with changing patterns. The error logging function is supported by the ring tap part of the MSL. The repeater in the tap is allocated ring address zero and so all maintenance minipackets generated by taps around the ring will be received by it. The source address of these packets can then be used to pinpoint the location of the error condition indicated by the data field so the MSL can take appropriate action.

On start-up or after errors which affect the frame structure the ring will be synchronized. Synchronization is the process by which all taps on the ring achieve a common view of the frame structure. For a ring with homogeneous slots, the number of slots is the only parameter required. However, for a ring with multiple slot sizes the position and number of each size must be determined. If the relative position of each group of similarly sized slots is kept constant, as in the hybrid ring, then this task is reduced to establishing the number of each size. As the format of a minipacket does not include a field indicating to which category it belongs, this information can be temporarily inserted during synchronization and each tap must retain a copy of the frame structure once synchronization is complete.

In a hybrid ring tap, the number of each size of slot is stored in a lockable counter which is unlocked at the beginning of synchronization by the MSL transmitting a train of zeros which is longer than the maximum permissible gap. The tap then enters a learning state in which it can interpret a stream of minipackets containing length markers which are issued by the MSL. It can be shown that the ring will be synchronized to the MSL after one complete frame structure has been transmitted and that the tap framing logic will take at most two complete frames to deduce the number of each of the sizes of slot. One gap later, the slot counters are locked. During the synchronization process, the taps will have their repeaters disabled so that no spurious transmissions can take place and so reduce the amount of garbage data on the ring. Once the slot counters are loaded and locked, transmissions are reenabled.

Resynchronization is only performed when certain errors occur, such as lost start of minipacket bit or when high numbers (a few hundred) of the other error types are detected. Fluctuations in the length of the gap, which probably mean that a tap has lost synchronization, can be detected by the MSL. If any change is noticed, reframing will be initiated.

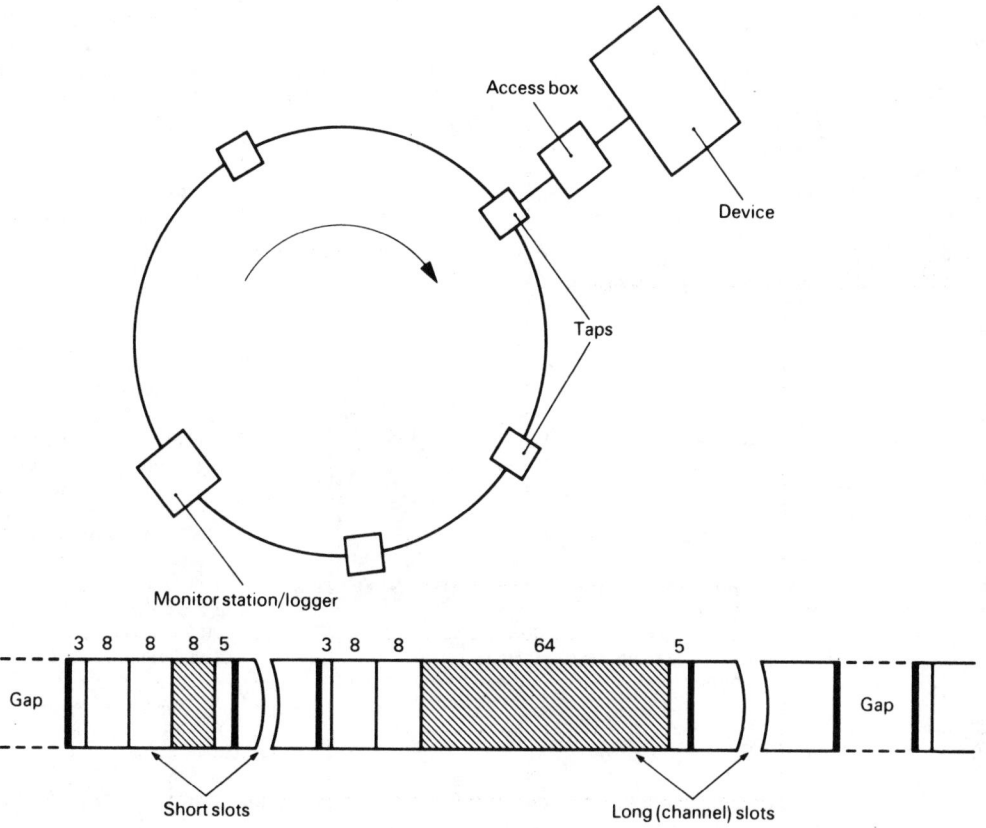

Fig. 5. Hybrid ring structure and slot train format.

The complete structure of the hybrid ring is shown in Fig. 5. At present, power is distributed on separate wires, although distribution through the transmission wires is possible as used in the original CR design. The ring is started by powering-on and booting the MSL program from an external source. It is planned that the MSL will also become a station in the ordinary way so that the control program can communicate with other nodes on the ring to collect and distribute traffic and error information.

VI. Conclusion

This paper has shown the development process used to implement an integrated version of the Cambridge ring. The chips have been used to construct ring systems by a number of universities and commercial organizations. The design of a new type of local area network using many of the new features of the ICR was discussed. A hybrid ring partitions the system bandwidth by supporting two types of slot: long slots, which hold eight bytes of data and which can be used in channel mode; and short slots with one byte data fields, which must be released after use. Different types of traffic such as voice, facsimile, and data can be allocated bandwidth in accordance with their traffic patterns. In advanced systems, the configuration of slots can be changed dynamically with needs. The traffic partitioning made possible by the hybrid ring makes the implementation of an integrated services local network attractive.

Whereas the facilities of the hybrid ring were superim-posed onto the ULA implementation of the more simple CR, the next step in the process of development would be to integrate the whole system. Recent advances in gate array technology suggest that a complete local area network chip could be produced incorporating the repeater/station functions, a ring monitor station, and internetwork bridges. With the availability of high-quality fiber optic transmission cables, the new ring could operate at very high data rates, for example, above 50 Mbits/s. The system bandwidth could then be partitioned to provide slots which would support traffic ranging from interprocessor communication, high-quality video, and fast file transfer to protocol control information and voice traffic.

Acknowledgment

M. V. Wilkes, D. J. Wheeler, and R. M. Needham are responsible for numerous suggestions, ideas, and support related to the design. The idea of changing minipacket size on-the-fly is due to S. G. Zaky.

References

[1] M. V. Wilkes and D. J. Wheeler, "The Cambridge digital communi-cation ring," presented at Local Area Commun. Network Symp., Boston, MA, May 1979, sponsored by the National Bureau of Standards.
[2] A. Hopper, "Local area computer communication networks," Ph.D. dissertation, Cambridge Univ., Cambridge, England, Apr. 1978.
[3] Cambridge Ring 82, Interface Specifications, Science and Engineer-ing Research Council, Sept. 1982.
[4] A. Hopper and D. J. Wheeler, "Maintenance of ring communication

systems," *IEEE Trans. Commun.*, vol. COM-27, pp. 760–761, Apr. 1979.

[5] R. M. Needham, "System aspects of the Cambridge ring," in *Proc. 7th Symp. Opt. Syst. Princ.*, Pacific Grove, CA, Dec. 1979.

[6] I. M. Leslie, "Frequency stability in a unidirectional ring of phase locked loops," unpublished project note, Comput. Lab., Univ. Cambridge, Cambridge, England.

[7] ——, "A master clock repeater for the Cambridge digital communication ring," unpublished project note, Comput. Lab., Univ. Cambridge, Cambridge, England.

[8] *ULA Design Manual*, Ferranti Semiconductors Ltd., Ref. A/FØØ'2.

[9] N. J. Ody, "Monitoring ring traffic using a promiscuous station," unpublished project note, Comput. Lab., Univ. Cambridge, Cambridge, England, June 9, 1981.

Andrew Hopper received the B.Sc. degree in computer technology from the University of Wales, University College of Swansea, Swansea, Wales, in 1974 and the Ph.D. degree from the University of Cambridge, Cambridge, England, in 1978.

From 1977 to 1979 he worked at the University of Cambridge as a Research Assistant, from 1979 to 1983 as an Assistant Lecturer, and from 1983 a Lecturer. He is one of the directors of Acorn Computers Ltd., a company specializing in the design of personal computer systems. His research interests include local area networks, VLSI design, computer architecture, and microprocessor systems.

In 1981, Dr. Hopper was elected a Fellow of Corpus Christi College and a member of the Institution of Electrical Engineers.

Robin C. Williamson received the B.Sc. degree in computing and electronics from Hatfield College, University of Durham, Durham, England, and is presently studying for the Ph.D. degree at the University of Cambridge, Cambridge, England.

In 1983 he worked as a summer student at IBM's Zurich Research Laboratory. His research interests include local area networks, distributed computer systems, microprocessor systems, and LSI design techniques.

Mr. Williamson is a student member of the British Computer Society.

Section 4: Broadband Networks

A relatively recent development in local area networks has been the introduction of intelligent broadband networks. In broadband technology, frequency division multiplexing (FDM) techniques are used on the single transmission cable to handle concurrent video and data communications. The field has grown very rapidly because most of the needed technology had already been developed by the cable TV industry, and broadband manufacturers simply had to adapt this technology to meet local area network requirements. There are, at the time of this writing, only 17 identified producers of broadband networks and nine of those are presented here.

The reprinted article by Biba discusses Sytek's Localnet System 20 and System 40. Although the System 20 is a well established network with more than 630 installations, the System 40 was never released. The technology for the System 40, however, was used by Sytek to develop the broadband network for IBM PCs that is now known as the IBM PC Network and which is described in a subsequent article.

The Localnet System 20 is intended for low duty, low cost terminal-to-host communications. It uses CATV coaxial cable as its transmission medium and has a single rooted-tree topology. The cable bandwidth is separated into multiple communication channels using FDM, and a portion of these channels are reserved for digital communication. User equipment interfaces to the cable through microcomputer-based Packet Communication Units (PCU) with tunable RF modems and communicate using a CSMA/CD protocol. Each PCU can find and directly communicate with any other PCU on the same or on a different channel, or even on a different cable.

In the following article, a network control center for broadband networks is described. The development of these control centers is thought to be one of the essential features of any future network. This article explains some of the issues involved in deciding what functions a network control center should provide, and it offers a description of Sytek's own network control center.

The third article describes the IBM PC Network developed by Sytek and sold by IBM. Although limited in extent (less than 1000 feet), number of nodes (72), channels (1), and speed (2 Mbps), because it is sold by IBM, it will have a major impact on the market. This network is being sold through IBM's retail distribution system and allows a low cost network for IBM PCs to be purchased and easily installed. One should keep in mind, however, that IBM's stated corporate philosophy is toward the token ring de-scribed in the previous section and not this type of broadband network.

In the next article, a variation on CSMA intended for use particularly in broadband networks is discussed. This access scheme, known as CSMA/CA, allows failed receipt of a data packet to be correctly diagnosed as due to system failures and not due to simultaneous contention. Computer Automation uses this access protocol in their broadband network SyFanet. The network has a bus topology and operates with a data rate of 3-Mbps.

Yet another access scheme is employed in the next network. Interactive Systems/3M has applied Datapoint technology to their broadband network Videodata LAN/1. The network interface units (NIU) are microprocessor-based units which handle all message processing and formatting tasks, traffic acknowledgment, and automatic port contention. The network also has an optional network monitor which aids in system-maintenance tasks. IS/3M recently applied this technology and developed its LAN/PC broadband network to compete with IBM's PC Network. In fact, with the ability to work on multiple channels and to operate in conjunction with the LAN/1, the LAN/PC is a more powerful and useful broadband network for PCs.

Concord Data Systems Token/Net also uses a token-passing access scheme. It is, in addition, the first network to be fully compatible with the IEEE 802.4 Standard. Token/Net was designed for high capacity use on broadband cable systems, and it provides users with reliable errorand flow-controlled data transport services. It supports all serial asynchronous and synchronous DTE equipment and specific parallel interface data peripherals.

Wang's broadband local computer network, Wangnet, uses a dual-cable, branching tree topology and operates with a CSMA/CD access protocol. Currently, there is an overall bandwidth of 390 MHz available. The bandwidth is divided up into "bands" which are reserved for the application of special services. Also, a good deal of the frequency spectrum is reserved for future services.

Another broadband local network, TRW's Concept 2000 was developed out of TRW's long experience in developing networks for United States federal government and defense-related industries. It operates in either a dual- or single-cable mode. A feature that TRW will have with this network is the capability to implement an Ethernet network on a portion of the broadband cable. TRW will be able to support as many as three 33 MHz bands in the 300 to 400 MHz range to carry the necessary Ethernet data and collision information.

EHO228-7/85/0000/0205$01.00 © 1985 IEEE

KEENET, produced by KEE, Inc., is a network that is offered in both dualcable and mid-split single-cable configurations. It conforms to the first three layers of the ISO reference model and uses the CSMA/CD access scheme. Many types of computer peripheral equipment can interface to the network bus through the KEENET BIU. The BIU is responsible for assembling/disassembling packets to/from data devices using the HDLC frame format.

UniLAN by Applitek, as described in the last article, is a network that uses a unique access method which gives token passing and CSMA/CD-like performance concurrently. UniLAN's RF broadband modem operates at 10-Mbps and can transmit and receive in sub-split, mid-split, or super-split mode, or on dual-cable.

LocalNet™: a digital communications network for broadband coaxial cable

K. J. Biba

Sytek, Incorporated   Sunnyvale, California

ABSTRACT

LocalNet™ is a low cost, high performance data communications network. Based on a synergistic combination of broadband analog, digital and packet switching communications technologies, LocalNet offers substantial functional, performance and operational advantages over conventional local networks. Utilizing industry standard cable TV (CATV) data distribution facilities, LocalNet builds a transparent, high performance, communications system incorporating distributed network intelligence. This approach provides for the interconnection of a wide range of user equipments, end-to-end data security, configuration flexibility, and ease of installation.

1. INTRODUCTION

LocalNet is an integrated, local data communications system that services not only the future intelligent workstation, but also the rather substantial installed base of "dumb" terminals, timeshared computer systems, and minicomputers comprising today's data networks. Integrating component technologies of wideband broadcast local networks, packet switching, and broadband CATV, LocalNet provides services inexpensively enough for today's needs but with the flexibility required for future applications. The generality of the LocalNet system enables it to effectively service a wide range of user applications: timesharing networks, management information systems, and integrated office communications systems. The particular advantages of the broadband communications system further extends its usage to industrial control and monitoring systems and inter-campus and intra-city data distribution systems. Broadband CATV is unique in its capacity to integrate a wide variety of data communications applications on a single medium [1].

The paper provides an overview of the LocalNet system:

o requirements motivating LocalNet's design,

o architecture of LocalNet's fundamental local data communications services, and

---

* LocalNet, Tbox, Tmux, Tbridge, Tgate and Tverter are Trademarks of Sytek, Incorporated.

o advanced services built atop this basic communications architecture.

2. REQUIREMENTS

The anticipated local network role as an integrated data communications backbone for all local communications lays some rather unique requirements on the network implementation. Local networks must support a rather wide range of applications, including but not limited to: terminal/host communications, computer/computer, office automation, process control, and others. The local network should provide a common data communications system serving all user applications, establishing a ubiquitous interconnect system substantially lowering lifecycle communications costs.

In providing this integrated data communications system, local networks can address three ranges of geographic coverage: a single room (e.g. a shared logic word processor), a complete high-rise building (e.g. integrated office communications) or a rather large multi-building area (e.g. a corporate campus or small city). We expect the most installations to be the first of these, however more nodes will be served by the latter two.

The network should provide a wide range of performance, customized to the needs of each application. Wideband, low delay applications should coexist with narrowband, delay tolerant applications without requiring the latter to pay the cost of the former. Low-cost, low performance devices, such as interactive terminals, require a quite modest attachment cost while for high performance computer-to-computer applications, the cost can be greater.

Contemporary data communications includes a variety of applications, not all of which can be simply solved by packet-switching techniques. A flexible network should accomodate not only the packet-switched services but also special services including point-to-point dedicated circuits, security and educational television, PABX trunks and other services.

As more data traffic, users and applications are migrated to an integrated data communications network, an increasing number of them will require privacy and security features to safeguard their

Reprinted from *The Proceedings of COMPCON S'81,* 1981, pages 59-63.
Copyright © 1981 by The Institute of Electrical and Electronics Engineers, Inc.

data from other users. These features should be modularly included so that users not requiring these services do not pay for them and further, that the full interconnectivity of the network is not compromised. That is, a secure user should be able to optionally invoke the security and privacy services of the network.

An integrated network must provide for reliability both of individual components and of the network as a whole. The failure of one user attachment must effect neither overall network integrity nor the integrity of other nodes.

3. LOCALNET ARCHITECTURE

In its simplest form a LocalNet consists of broadband coaxial cable system, network nodes called Packet Communication Units (PCUs), and protocol software. It may also include one or more bridges, gateways and specialized server nodes.

3.1 A LocalNet Cable System

LocalNet utilizes broadband coaxial cable as its physical communications medium. In wide use in many commercial CATV applications, this medium provides the high bandwidth (300 to 400 MHz), proven reliability and multidrop capability required for growing data communications requirements. Broadband cable provides high noise immunity, and each user branch is electrically isolated from the main signal, reducing the possibility of total system failure from accidental or malicious causes. Analog video or voice applications can share the same cable using dedicated channels.

Broadband CATV is a directional broadcast transmission system based on single rooted tree physical topology. Each user device can broadcast his transmission in one direction, up the tree towards the CATV head-end. The head-end contains an analog translation device that, similarly to a satellite transponder, rebroadcasts the transmission from the root of the tree, downstream to all attached user devices.

LocalNet exploits the directional aspect of the CATV transmission system to achieve full connectivity. LocalNet transmissions are contained in two frequency bands: an upstream (low frequency) and a downstream band (high frequency).

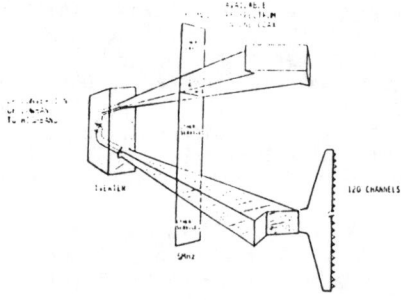

Figure 1. Channel Organization

The band from 40 to 106 MHz is used to transmit data from a user device to the broadband translator (LocalNet Tverter). The Tverter converts the entire 66 MHz lowband to a highband occupying 196 to 262 MHz for retransmission along the cable for reception by each attached user device. This technique is totally compatible with mid-split and dual CATV cable installations. A modified version can be used with subsplit CATV cable systems.

LocalNet divides the 300 MHz cable bandwidth into multiple logical channels through Frequency Division Multiplexing (FDM). Standard phase and frequency modulation methods can be used to create data channels at a wide variety of data rates, with each channel accessed by multiple devices spread over a geographic radius of up to 50 kilometers. Devices requiring low data rates can thus share the cable with high-performance devices, and channels can be logically connected if desired to provide a single network servicing thousands of users.

LocalNet currently supports two classes of such channels. LocalNet System 20 is based upon over one hundred 128Kb/s channels and provides packet-switched data communications service to many (tens of thousands of active users) low-duty cycle users (e.g. terminals) over a wide geographic area (a 20 Km. radius) on a single broadband CATV cable. LocalNet System 40 is based upon five 2.5Mb/s channels and provides similar services to high duty cycle (1Mb/s throughput) users over a smaller geographic area on the same broadband cable as System 20. LocalNet also provides for the interconnection of System 20 and System 40 to provide a single, integrated communications network.

A simple coax outlet (F Fitting) in each area to be served provides access to underlying analog broadband network and hence to any LocalNet service, specifically System 20 and System 40 channels. The independence of the transmission system from the services offered allows LocalNet to meet today's data communications needs, and provides the capacity for tommorrow's new and growing requirements. The user may easily connect or disconnect his unit, moving if necessary from room to room with no wiring changes. Functional upgrades or the addition of new services, such as voice and video teleconferencing, may be made without addition or change to the analog CATV transmission system.

3.2 Packet Communication Units

LocalNet provides communications intelligence at each user interface point implementing protocol interpreters for required protocols from the LocalNet protocol architecture. Services typically provided include: packet assembly, disassembly, buffering, virtual circuit management, error and flow control, protocol and code conversion, speed matching, data security and others.

LocalNet currently provides two implementations of packet communications units: System 20 - oriented towards low duty cycle, low-cost users, and System 40 - oriented towards high duty cycle, high throughput users. Each system has full connectivity to other systems and to common LocalNet services.

3.2.1 System 20 System 20 is designed to provide low-cost communications to low throughput users (< 20Kb/s). It is comprised of two packet communications units: the Tbox and the Tmux. The Tbox is the basis of LocalNet System 20. This unit provides all the necessary media access, network intelligence, and user interface functions to service a variety of user devices: asynchronous terminals, synchronous terminals, host ports, printers and other shared resources.

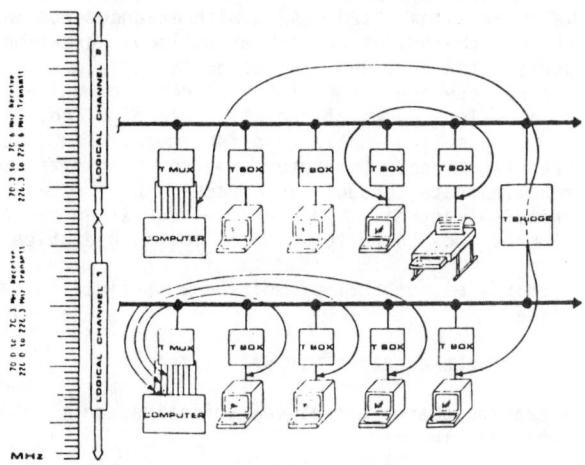

Figure 2. LocalNet Architecture

Tbox is designed to perform the following functions:

o selects, under network management control, one System 20 128Kb/s LocalNet logical channel on which it will operate

o establish, maintain, and disconnect virtual circuits between LocalNet packet communications units and the user devices they interface

  o format and address packets for their destination, using the internal LocalNet data communications protocol suite

  o control the allocation of channel bandwidth using CSMA/CD mechanisms

  o control the flow of data over the channel and supported virtual circuits to prevent congestion and data loss, both local (at the terminal or host-port) and global (aggregate traffic on the backbone channel)

  o detect errors through the use of Cyclic Redundancy Checks (CRC) and correct errors through retransmission of lost or damaged packets

o support optional value-added services including protocol and code conversion, directory services and end-to-end encryption

o export these functions to the user equipment utilizing access protocols appropriate to the attached user device.

Tbox can support one or two user ports. Where several terminal or computer ports are in close physical proximity, a multiplexer, Tmux, is available. System 20 packet communications units are implemented with 8-bit microprocessors and associated LSI components to minimize cost of user device attachment yet provide appropriate performance.

3.2.2 System 40 System 40 packet communications units are designed primarily for high duty cycle, high throughput connection to host computers. They provide the same functions as the System 20 units, with the following differences:

o select a LocalNet System 40 channel (2.5Mb/s) on which to operate;

o provide a host specific hardware and software attachment and access protocol; and

o System 40 packet communications units are implemented with a multiple 16-bit microprocessor architecture with 16-bit data paths to provide the performance necessary for this class of user device.

System 40 units are designed to provide a high performance local network front-end for host computer systems. Such an architecture offloads time consuming communications processing from the host and provides a single standard implementation of the data communications protocols among heterogeneous computers and operating systems. System 40 units can provide host throughput, including protocol processing overhead, of up to 1Mb/s with minimal support from the host computer and its operating system.

System 20 and System 40 packet communications units each implement the same elements of the LocalNet protocol architecture, permitting these units to intercommunicate through the use of interchannel gateways.

3.3 LocalNet Protocols

LocalNet implements a common packet-switched protocol architecture throughout its component elements. The protocol architecture is based on the ISO Open Systems Interconnection Reference Model [3] with modifications and extensions for the local network environment. Seven protocol layers are supported:

Access	modular interfaces to various user device types, exporting internal LocalNet services to user devices
Presentation	virtual terminal, format translation, end-to-end encryption services
Session	name to address mapping, network monitor and control services

Transport	flow and error controlled virtual circuit and transaction services
Network	end-to-end addressing, routing and datagram services
Link	per channel addressing, datagram services, error detection, transmission control (CSMA/CD)
Physical	multipoint, half-duplex communications with distributed access control.

The protocol suite is designed to be extensible; offering new

o internal services

o transmission media and

o user device access methods

with only localized changes to the LocalNet architecture and implementation.

Channel transmission is allocated in a distributed manner using CSMA/CD [2], "listen-while-talk" distributed access technique. This technique permits each packet communications unit to independently contend for transmission access on one of LocalNet's high-speed channels. The minimization of centralized network control provides for high system reliability, low transmission delay and channel utilization in excess of 95%. Each LocalNet channel is independent from all other channels with respect to transmission access thus supporting simultaneous transmissions on each configured channel.

3.4 Bridges

LocalNet provides three methods by which packet communications units (and their associated user devices) can communicate. First, for users connected to the same LocalNet logical channel, the basic link broadcast protocol provides complete one-hop connectivity. Second, for users attached to different channels on the same same cable, an internal store and forward packet gateway is provided to route packets between LocalNet channels. This internal gateway is termed a bridge and services both System 20 and System 40 channels. Third, for users attached to different cable systems each supporting LocalNet, a variant of the bridge provides for interconnection of these distinct LocalNet systems into one common LocalNet through use of one or more transit networks: AT&T DDS, a public packet-switched VAN, or other data communications system.

4. THE USER INTERFACE

LocalNet is designed to service a variety of user devices in a manner imposing the least change and overhead to the user device. The mechanisms by which user devices access LocalNet services are termed access protocols. Three classes of access

protocol can be distinguished: asynchronous, synchronous and wideband DMA.

4.1 Asynchronous Access Protocols

This class of access protocol provides a user-friendly interface to internal LocalNet services. The connection to the standard LocalNet packet communications unit is either a bit serial asynchronous interface at rates to 19.2 KBaud or a byte serial interface using a LocalNet byte stream interface protocol. The serial interface provides standard transmit data, receive data, carrier detect, request to send, clear to send, and x-on/x-off flow control functions.

A user command language based upon CCITT Recommendation X.28 [4], with enhancements that exploit the unique properties of local area networks, is provided to allow the user device to control the operation of the packet communication unit. Two modes of operation are provided: command mode and data transfer mode. In data transfer mode, the user device transmits and receives data through its packet communications unit. At any time the user may request entry into command mode to perform the following operations:

o initiate a virtual circuit to a destination device

o terminate a extant virtual circuit

o examine/change packet communications unit internal parameters

o exit to data transfer mode.

The packet communications unit parameters supported are a superset of those defined by CCITT Recommendation X.3 [5].

4.2 Synchronous Access Protocols

The generalized access protocol interface of LocalNet permits the usage of synchronous terminals as well as asynchronous. One of the synchronous of protocols of particular interest is X.25.

4.3 Wideband Host DMA Access Protocols

Host computer systems require one of two attachment strategies: emulation of an existing telecommunications interface, or a custom interface designed for high performance and minimal host overhead. The LocalNet System 40 interface for Unibus* based hosts is example of the latter. The System 40 packet communication unit is closely coupled to its host, having complete access to host memory and relieving its host of the vast majority of time-consuming interrupt-based protocol processing.

---

* Unibus is a Trademark of Digital Equipment Corporation.

5. ENHANCEMENTS

The distributed intelligence within LocalNet's implementation provides the capacity for significant enhancements to the basic services outlined above. The incorporation of these services through specialized server nodes permits the network user to configure only those services required for his application.

5.1 Network Interconnection: Gateways

LocalNet products (Tgate) provide gateways between not only multiple LocalNet installations, but also to external networks including X.25 packet networks. These gateway products both extend the size and geographical coverage of LocalNets as well as supporting their interconnection with other types of networks.

5.2 Symbolic Resource Naming and Access Control

The standard LocalNet packet communication unit uses uses numeric addresses, similarly to most long-haul networks, to identify network nodes. A compatible LocalNet upgrade provides a distributed symbolic name to numeric address conversion system permitting users to be unaware of the location and address of services requested of the network. This service is provided by a server LocalNet node, the Directory, that may be shared among several cable systems within a Local-Net. It provides the protocols and storage for the maintenance of the LocalNet Directory data base. For LocalNets not requiring these features, the Directory node is not required.

5.3 Network Security and Privacy

A compatible upgrade provides substantial security features through incorporation of end-to-end encryption for those user terminals requiring such protection. This capability requires no change to existing terminals and further, secure terminals and non-secure terminals may compatibly and securely coexist on the same network. User devices requiring data security are attached to LocalNet via a secure packet communications unit incorporating the necessary protocols and hardware to perform authentication, key management and encryption. A server LocalNet node (the Key Distribution Center) provides for key distribution and network access control. For LocalNets not requiring these measures, the KDC is not required.

5.4 Network Monitoring and Control

LocalNet provides the tools for network managers to easily diagnose and solve network problems through the provision of network traffic monitoring, node status and performance, as well as full range of tools for monitoring cable connectivity and signal quality. A server node (the Network Control Center) for each LocalNet, which could comprise multiple cable systems in several installations, provides the user interface and data base for the storage and processing of this information. For LocalNets not requiring this monitor and control capability, particularly small networks, the NCC is not required for LocalNet operation.

5.5 Special Purpose Networks

Many applications require special data transmission services that cannot always be optimally provided by the general purpose LocalNet system. For these users, LocalNet's use of broadband provides the quite reasonable solution of dedicated (possibly multipoint) FDM channels on the common LocalNet broadband cable system. One such channel, for example, could utilize a reservation TDM system (rather than LocalNet's standard CSMA/CD) to provide guaranteed bandwidth and delay to process control nodes of the integrated LocalNet. Other such channels could provide for 3270 terminal access through the common cable system.

5.6 Advanced Services

Other special services can be supported by either such special FDM channels or through use of the shared CSMA/CD network. Services of particular interest include: packetized voice, digital imagery, teleconferencing, robot control and others.

6. SUMMARY

LocalNet offers an integrated local data communications system based on the special properties of broadband CATV cable. It provides not only a sophisticated packet-switched network for current communications needs, but also the flexibility required to meet future data communications growth and needs.

7. REFERENCES

[1] M. Dineson and J. Picazo, "Broadband Technology Magnifies Local Networking Capability", Data Communications, February 1980.

[2] R. Metcalfe and D. Boggs, "Ethernet: Distributed Packet Switching for Local Computer Networks", Comm. ACM, 19, 7 (July 1976), 395-404.

[3] Reference Model of Open Systems Interconnection, ISO ISO/TC97/SC16 No. 309, August 1979.

[4] CCITT Provisional Recommendation X.28 (Geneva, 1977), "DTE/DCE Interface for a Start-Stop Mode Data Terminal Equipment Accessing the Packet Assembly/Disassembly Facility (PAD) in a Public Data Network Situated in the Same Country", Data Communications Standards, McGraw-Hill, New York, 1978, 286-309.

[5] CCITT Provisional Recommendation X.3 (Geneva 1977), "Packet Assembly/Disassembly Facility (PAD) in a Public Data Network", Ibid, 190-195.

A NETWORK CONTROL CENTER FOR BROADBAND LOCAL AREA NETWORKS

Mary Bernstein
Carl Sunshine
David Kaufman
Sytek Inc
USA

A Network Control Center for broadband local area networks should provide a wide range of functions including configuration control, security and access control, administrative recording, and performance monitoring. Furthermore, the NCC should be designed for easy expansion as both the number and types of devices attached to the network increase. The Sytek LocalNet (tm) NCC is described as an example that meets many of these goals.

Mary Bernstein has been with the Los Angeles Operations office of Sytek since 1982. Her position as Network Control Center Project Leader includes responsibility for definition, design, and implementation plus coordination of testing, manufacturing, and technical support of the 50/100 Network Control Center product line. From 1979 through 1982 she was at System Development Corporation where she participated in network protocols standardization and secure networking projects. She received her B.S. in Information and Computer Science from UC Irvine.

Carl Sunshine has been Principal Engineer with Sytek since 1982 where he is engaged in design and implementation of local area computer networks for commercial, residential, and military environments. His research interests include network control centers, access control, network interconnection, protocols, and network front ends. Prior to joining Sytek, Dr. Sunshine was with USC Information Sciences Institute working primarily on the DARPA Internet project. His professional activities include scientific, standards, and journal activities, and he has lectured and published widely.

David Kaufman has been Manager of Los Angeles Operations for Sytek since 1981. He heads development of local area network communication products and network control and monitoring components, and investigation of network architectures and military applications. Prior to joining Sytek, Mr. Kaufman was program manager at the System Development Corp. for several DoD, NBS, and internal projects involving protocols, network front ends, cryptography, security, and electronic funds transfer.

1. INTRODUCTION

A broadband local area network (LAN) can support thousands of different user devices over an area of up to 50 kilometers. A Network Control Center (NCC) for such a network must provide a network manager with a number of tools to monitor, control, and tailor the network to local requirements, and must provide users with assistance in utilizing the services available on the network.

The main network control functions needed fall into the categories of configuration control, performance monitoring, and security and access control. This paper discusses each of these functions in turn, using the NCC provided in Sytek's LocalNet (tm) system as an illustration. Hence we first provide some background on the LocalNet system and its NCC.

Unlike wide area networks where the major network management function is monitoring switching nodes and the lines that interconnect them [1], LANs typically employ a simpler communications medium with primary intelligence at each user node rather than within the network itself. Hence the focus of network management also shifts from internal network activity to user interface points.

2. SYTEK LOCALNET SYSTEM

Sytek's LocalNet(tm) system [2,3] uses low cost, easy to install, CATV coaxial cable as its communication medium. A small portion of the total cable bandwidth is typically allocated to digital communication and separated into multiple communication channels through Frequency Division Multiplexing, with each channel shared among hundreds of user devices via the CSMA/CD technique. A microcomputer based packet communications unit (PCU) with a tunable RF modem interfaces user equipment to the cable to provide a completely distributed communications architecture. In the basic system, each PCU is capable of finding and forming sessions directly with any other PCU on the same channel, different channels, or different cables [4].

Beyond this capability for fully distributed operation, an NCC can provide several useful additional services. Each PCU is a highly configurable device, supporting many options for data presentation, user device interface, and inter-PCU communication characteristics. The NCC can ensure the setting of these parameters in each PCU to achieve optimal network performance. The NCC can also provide performance monitoring, access control and security, and call establishment support as discussed below.

3. LOCALNET NCC

To accomplish these functions, a NCC needs a variety of software and hardware tools. At the heart of the NCC is a database containing information on PCU characteristics, network users, destinations, access groups, etc. There must also be a variety of programs which access this database to perform the various NCC functions. These programs are invoked by several tasks running concurrently in the NCC. Since LANs typically expand and evolve, it should be possible to add both new units of existing types and also to add new types of units or features to the NCC.

These NCC design goals may be summarized as follows:

o Moderate database (1-10 Mbyte)
o Many programs
o Concurrent tasks, some real-time
o Flexible interface for net manager
o Simple interface to help users making calls
o Expandability to add more user nodes
o Upgradability to add new types of nodes and features
o Reliability and security of operation
o Good cost/performance for wide range of net sizes

These design goals suggest that a microprocessor class computer with small fixed disk, good file system, and support for multitasking is the minimal system requirement for LANs with up to 5000 nodes. For the LocalNet NCC, we chose a M68000 based processor with 10 or 20 Mbyte fixed disk capacity and streaming tape for backup. The system can be configured with 8 or 16 serial I/O ports to provide LocalNet system access through ordinary LocalNet PCUs.

The software runs under the UNIX(tm) operating system which provides a multi-tasking environment and structured file system maintenance. Due to its central importance, the database was carefully designed to be self-defining and extensible. Thus, the format and content of the database files are not rigidly imposed by software structures in the programs which use the database, but instead are flexibly defined by data dictionaries. These data dictionaries incorporate information such as field name, field size, field structure, legal values, display format, and intra-record and interfile relationships. Thus, changes made to existing LocalNet devices and the introduction of new devices are reflected in changes to the data dictionaries, not to each and every software program.

4. CONFIGURATION CONTROL

Each PCU must be configured to best support the nature of the attached
user device. Terminals, printers, modems, and computers obviously
differ in their interface requirements; different brands and applications of these devices require a further level of individualized configuration. In addition, some flexibility for user preference must be
supported. Thus, the task of establishing and maintaining LAN configuration is a complex and time-consuming one.

In the design of the configuration control tool, Sytek identified the
following design goals:

transparent	- no disruption of active sessions
flexible	- several modes of operation
fast	- configure a large net overnight
robust	- operate in spite of busy net conditions or unexpected PCU responses

The LocalNet NCC provides a configuration tool, called CONFIG, to aid a
network manager in performing this task. CONFIG, as are all NCC
software tools, is driven by the NCC database. Each PCU is represented
by a record in the PCU file of the database. Within this record each
aspect of configuration (e.g., baud rate, flow control, command escape
code, commands allowed) is recorded as well as administrative information such as serial number. To save space, commonly used groups of
settings are defined once in separate attribute files and merely referenced by each PCU record.

Within the PCU's configuration records, the network manager defines the
required value for a particular parameter. In addition, he can specify
whether a parameter is to be unconditionally set to the database definition or whether it may vary. This "care/don't care" feature allows a
network manager to leave certain parameters for the user to tailor to
his preference. For example, baud rate can be changed by the user
depending on application: e.g., 1200 baud to access a dial-out modem,
or 9600 baud to access a host terminal port.

CONFIG is invoked by the network manager with a list of one or more PCU
identifiers to be configured. CONFIG creates a LocalNet session to
each PCU and remotely issues commands to collect status data and to set
individual parameters. To protect against inadvertent or malicious
damage, a PCU's configuration can only be remotely set from a unit
operating in a special privileged mode. This capability is normally
reserved for the NCC.

The CONFIG program can be invoked in several modes of operation. The
"init" mode is used to initialize a PCU upon installation to the LAN.
Each and every configurable parameter is absolutely set according to

215

the database record definition. The "update" mode is used for day-to-day maintenance of PCU configuration. In this mode, CONFIG first queries for the current parameter settings, then resets only those which are marked as "care" and differ from the database definition. With the "poll" mode, CONFIG operates as in "update" mode, but merely records discrepancies for the network manager's reference.

5. PERFORMANCE MONITORING

A LAN cable layout can span an area with a diameter of up to 50 kilometers. In a practical sense, this may cover a multi-story high rise, an entire college campus, or several city blocks. When effectively integrated into an institution's communications system, the LAN may carry the majority of a site's digital traffic including data processing, word processing, MIS data, and so on. As such a pervasive communication tool, LAN failure or poor performance affects the entire institution's effectiveness and productivity.

In the development of performance monitoring tools, Sytek identified the following design goals:

transparent	- no disruption of network traffic
fast	- operation at real data transfer rates
expandable	- easy incorporation of additional channels
flexible	- capability to monitor over a range of periods

The LocalNet NCC supports a Digital Monitoring Package which includes software programs that interact with monitoring devices on the LocalNet system to record, collect, interpret and display status. One portion of the Digital Monitoring Package is the statistical monitor program, called SM. It uses the 50/120 statistical monitor device to determine performance characteristics of a single LocalNet channel. The 50/120 is an eavesdropping device that peruses channel traffic to record periodic, peak, and cumulative information regarding data transmission quality, data packet size and type, number of data characters, and number of active sessions. The 50/120 can be configured to report at periods ranging from one minute to one hour.

Each channel and 50/120 device is represented by a record in the NCC database. The channel record defines alarm thresholds for channel traffic characteristics including percent utilization, number of sessions, and number of bad packets. The 50/120 record defines the the operating parameters and location of the 50/120 device.

When invoked by the network manager, SM sequentially forms a LocalNet session to each 50/120, initializes the operating parameters according to the database definition, and starts the recording cycle. At the end of the every recording cycle SM polls each 50/120, collects the sta-

tistical data, and records it in the NCC report files. At the same
time, if the collected data exceeds alarm thresholds, an alarm report
is generated.

A summary of the data recorded and alarms reported by SM is continually
maintained by CONTIN, the continuous display tool. This summary can
incorporate data from up to five channels and can be displayed once a
minute. The display includes percent utilization, packets per minute,
percent good packets, and number of open sessions, and a summary of
other NCC activities in progress. With this display the network
manager can determine at a glance the "health" of major LAN channels.

6. SECURITY AND ACCESS CONTROL

A LAN can support a wide variety of devices and resources. Some or all
of these resources may offer services or house information of a sensitive nature. This capability imposes three requirements on network
use: first, access to the LAN itself must be controlled; second, access
to sensitive resources must be controlled; and third, data exchanged
between a user and a sensitive resource must be protected from inadvertent or malicious perusal, modification, or interception. The LocalNet
NCC can support these three requirements for a network manager within
certain logical configurations.

Controlling general access to a LocalNet system is difficult. By
design, new taps can be added to a cable in just a few moments. With a
LocalNet PCU and such a tap, an intruder has potential access to every
other unit on the network. A combination of the solutions for the
second and third requirements, discussed below, solve this problem.

The second requirement, access control to LAN resources, is supported
by the LocalNet NCC's User Interface program, UI. This program uses
three parts of the NCC database: the PCU file, the destination file,
and the user file. As noted in previous sections, each PCU is
represented by a record in the database. Within this record is a
definition of the access groups to which the PCU belongs. Each destination, a mnemonic identification of a host or other resource on the
LocalNet system, is also represented by a record. A destination record
defines a destination with a set of LocalNet addresses and membership
in a set of access groups. A network manager can also optionally
assign each LocalNet user a record, allowing each user to belong to
access groups independently of the PCU he happens to be using at the
moment.

To effectively enforce access control, the network manager must disable
the ability of a PCU to call other PCUs directly. Instead, all PCU
calls must be made via the NCC through UI. This approach makes use of
the permanent call feature of the PCU which automatically calls a given

LocalNet address (in this case the NCC's) upon terminal power-up or user command.

With this configuration, a call scenario works as follows: the user initiates a call to the NCC. The UI service, constantly scanning for incoming calls, verifies the PCU's validity for LocalNet system use by finding a corresponding PCU record. If the PCU is not valid, UI immediately terminates the session, thereby denying LocalNet system use. If the PCU record is valid, UI responds with a short "message of the day" and a query for desired destination.

The caller then supplies the desired destination name. UI compares the access group membership of the calling PCU and the destination, and if common group membership is determined, causes a session to be formed between the caller and the destination. If that comparison fails, UI will query for the caller's name and password. If the caller's user record indicates common access group membership with the destination, the session is also formed. Thus, with a centralized name serving and access control service, a network manager can enforce access control by limiting individual PCU operation.

The third requirement, protection of session data, is provided by the Key Distribution Center Package (KDC) which is used together with Secure PCUs to provide encrypted data sessions. Each Secure PCU is equipped with a DES encryption chip and enhanced communication protocols.

The KDC and Secure PCU scenario [5] can be summarized as follows: a calling secure PCU initiates a secure session to a destination secure PCU. That PCU requests a session key from a KDC server on the NCC. The KDC server software validates both the calling PCU and the destination PCU with information in the database. After validation, the KDC server issues a session key to be used only for the duration of the session to both secure PCUs. Thus, a secure session can only be established if both secure PCUs are registered and valid to the KDC.

Two additional features of the secure PCU further strengthen network security. Secure PCUs support a feature called "secure privilege" so that a Secure PCU's configuration parameters can only be changed by another Secure PCU that has formed a session to it with secure privilege authority. Secure privilege is granted by a KDC server during secure session establishment. Thus, secure PCUs cannot be reconfigured inadvertently or maliciously even by a PCU with standard privilege. A second feature, called "secure listen," forces a Secure PCU to accept only secure sessions. Thus, the calling PCU must be valid to the KDC which prevents bootleg PCUs from accessing correctly configured Secure PCUs.

Access control and secure sessions can be used together to provide a strong protection mechanism that supports all three access control and security requirements. Only authorized users with registered PCUs have access to LocalNet resources and all inter-PCU communication is protected with per-session unique encryption.

7. ADDITIONAL SERVICES

The following paragraphs discuss additional services that are valuable to a network manager and that are under evaluation as future enhancements to LocalNet's NCC.

7.1 Fault Isolation

In addition to monitoring LAN traffic behavior, a network manager needs tools to monitor physical properties of the LAN. These properties include signal level, cable connectivity, and LAN device malfunction.

Monitoring analog properties of a LocalNet system can be performed through the use of an analog monitoring device with a digital command interface. This device could be located anywhere on the LocalNet cable, and by way of a PCU, be controlled from the NCC. Cable connectivity can be determined through a simple polling of PCUs located on the endpoints of the LocalNet cable branches.

Detecting the malfunction of an individual PCU can currently be performed only to a limited degree because of PCU restrictions. If a session can be formed to a PCU, and it responds appropriately, it is assumed to be fully functional. While not supported by the current PCU design, the NCC should ideally be able to form a session to the PCU, initiate self-tests, and issue data loopback commands.

7.2 Accounting and Global Configuration Management

As with any computing resource, network management needs LAN activity information for the purpose of billing network users for LAN use and for the purpose of determining usage patterns for long-term planning.

Since LANs are normally administered and used by a single organization, usage-based billing is somewhat less important than with public networks, and is often omitted. Current PCUs do not collect accounting data. However, a centralized server could perform this function to collect on a per session basis a summary of session endpoints, number of packets transmitted and received, number of data bytes transmitted and received, and session duration. This information could then be forwarded to the NCC for recording and interpretation.

Summary data on peak call loads to particular servers can also be used to determine when more network interface ports are needed, or whether available ports should be shifted from one channel to another. On-channel vs. off-channel usage statistics and source/destination traffic patterns can also be used to determine how to redistribute the channel utilization of the system to improve performance.

7.3 Queuing

A queuing service provides fairness in allocation of high demand network resources. That is, when a destination is busy a user may add his session request to a list so that when the destination becomes available he is connected in order of request. Without a queuing service, a user must periodically recall a busy destination and rely on the fairness of the system for eventual success.

To be effective in the LocalNet's fully distributed system, the queuing service must be performed at a central processor. Each session request must be routed through the queuer which either immediately connects the user, or adds him to the queue until the destination is available. The queuer would then periodically call a busy destination until successful, passing off the connection to the first user on the queue.

7.4 Downline Loading

There are definite advantages of easy modifiability in having the software for PCUs and other specialized network components loaded into them over the network each time they power up. If this is done on an individual demand basis, performance after global problems (e.g., power outage) can be unacceptable.

With the multiple channels available in broadband systems, it becomes attractive to use one channel for broadcasting node software images. All nodes use one of a small number of software packages, so this is very efficient and fast since as many nodes as necessary can capture the software as it is transmitted once. The NCC could itself transmit the boot images, or could control their dissemination to and transmission by a simple dedicated booter.

8. CONCLUSIONS

A Network Control Center for broadband LANs should provide a wide range of functions including configuration control, security and access control, administrative recording, and performance monitoring. Sytek's LocalNet NCC is one example that meets many of these goals. Furthermore, the LocalNet NCC is designed for easy expansion as the overall LocalNet system family of devices grows and expands in capability.

REFERENCES

[1] S. Bernstein and J. Herman, "NU, a network monitoring, control, and management system," Proc. Int. Communications Conf., June 1983.

[2] K. Biba, "LocalNet, a digital communications network for broadband coaxial cable," Proc. COMPCON 81 Spring, IEEE.

[3] G. Ennis, P. Filice, "Overview of a broadband local area network protocol architecture," IEEE Journal on Selected Areas in Communication, November 1983.

[4] C. Sunshine, D. Kaufman, G. Ennis, and K. Biba, "Interconnection of broadband local area networks," Proc. 8th Data Communications Symp., October 1983, ACM/IEEE.

[5] T. Berson and R. Bauer, "Local network cryptosystem architecture," Proc. COMPCON 82 Spring, IEEE.

IBM PC Network

The IBM PC Network, introduced in August, 1984 is based on technology developed by Sytek, Inc. The PC Network is designed for the IBM PC, PC XT, Portable PC, and the new Personal Computer AT. IBM does not intend to support the PCjr; however, possible networking of the 3270 PC has not been precluded.

As a major PC network supplier to IBM, Sytek supplies the PC network adapter card and the network translator unit, or headend, to IBM. The network translator comes with a connector assembly for attaching as many as 8 PCs within a radius of 200 feet. A network base expander and various cable kits are used to increase the number of networked PCs from 8 to 72, as well as to increase the distance to a 1,000 foot radius. In addition, IBM is an OEM of Sytek for LocalNet/PC protocols—modified Sytek LocalNet/20 protocols that are used in the adapter card for higher-level protocol implementation.

The IBM PC Network operates at 2 Mbps on one channel of a mid-split broadband system for distances up to 1,000 feet. With the components available from IBM, the maximum number of PCs will be 72. These limitations appear to be due to IBM's decision to make this broadband network as "easy" as possible to install by end-users, thus eliminating the special "tuning" and "sweeping" and careful cable layout details associated with larger broadband local networks.

For larger installations, IBM recommends consulting with a "third-party" company—namely, Sytek: Sytek is prepared to design and implement these networks for large installations where up to 1,000 PCs can be connected on one channel using the adapter card and network translator unit and Sytek's protocols. Basically, the only items needed to extend the distance are amplifiers, to ensure a relatively constant signal strength throughout the network. However, the maximum distance possible is 5 Km (3.1 miles), a limitation of the Ethernet CSMA/CD data link protocol running at 2-Mbps.

Hardware

In addition to the on-board RF modem, the adapter card contains an abundance of processing power with four processors: an Intel 80188 processor, an Intel 82586 datalink controller, a Sytek Serial Interface controller (SIC), and an Intel/IBM Host Interface Controller (HIC).

The 80188 controls the overall operation of the adapter and also implements layers 4 (transport) and 5 (session) of the ISO reference model. It has its own 32-Kbyte firmware in ROM and 16-Kbyte RAM used for packet buffering and tables.

The 82586 is Intel's high-performance VLSI Ethernet datalink controller that is also used by other vendors such as Ungermann-Bass and Interlan. It implements layer 2 (datalink) of the ISO reference model with functions such as data encapsulation, preamble and address generation, checksum calculation, etc.

The Sytek Serial Interface Controller interfaces to the RF modem and, together, they implement layer 2 (physical) of the ISO model. The SIC receives its data from the 82586.

The host interface controller, in conjunction with several TTL circuits, provides the "glue" between the adapter board and a PC expansion slot. It allows the adapter to appear as an array of I/O address spaces in the PC. The HIC and TTL circuits also contain registers to allow commands and data to be passed back and forth. Interrupts and DMA may be used for high performance.

The Figure below is a block diagram of the adapter board.

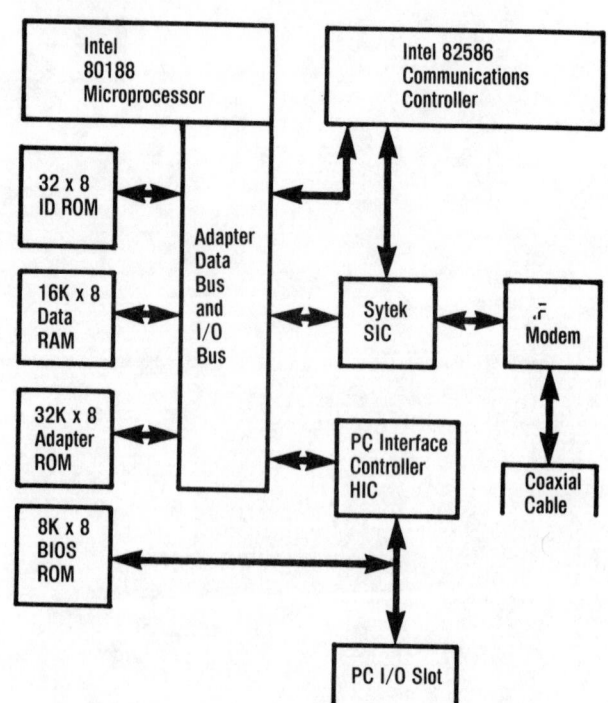

Figure: Adaptor Board, Block Diagram

Cable Kits

Several cable kits are available that allow the network to reach up to a 1,000-foot radius from the translator unit. The short-distance kit attaches directly to the base expander;

cable can be added from the expander to a PC up to 200 feet away. The medium-distance kit attaches to the base expander through 400 feet of cable; another 200 feet can be added for a total distance of 600 feet. The long-distance kit attaches to the base expander through 800 feet of cable; as with the other kits, up to 200 feet can be added, for a total distance of 1,000 feet between the PC and the translator unit. An example layout is illustrated in the Figure. A subtle detail is that one cannot deviate from the cable length offered by the various kits. To do so would upset the cable plant design, possibly causing the network to fail. IBM has carefully chosen this limited distance configuration with special detail paid to cable length, splitters, taps, attenuators, etc., so that special expertise is not required to install this system.

Translator Unit

The translator unit or headend, uses a 6-MHz channel with a offset of 168.25 MHz on an input frequency of 50.75 MHz (T14) to yield an output frequency of 219 MHz (Channel J). Most broadband networks, including Sytek's Local-Net/20, use 156.25 as the offset, while the IEEE 802.4 token bus specification calls for an offset of 192.25 MHz. One must be very careful in allocating bands to have this PC network work on top of an existing broadband network. What is even more interesting is that by reading the fine print in IBM's technical reference material for the PC network, one discovers that other data channels, voice, or video cannot be added to the network using the standard translation unit; again, one must resort to an "outside" vendor for such a design.

Software

In addition to DOS 3.1, the IBM PC Network Program will be available for sharing data, messages, printers, and other devices on the network. Publications provided with the program contain information needed to develop application programs for the network.

The IBM PC Network Program is a set of software that supports the operation of the IBM PC, the IBM PC XT, the IBM Portable PC, and the IBM PC AT on the IBM PC network. The services provided by the network program are used for sharing data and devices among applications in network machines and for the transmission of user messages among the network machines.

The IBM PC Network Program defines four machine configurations in an IBM PC network. Any machine can be on the network as any one of the four configurations (if the minimum hardware for the configuration is available) and can change to another configuration if desired. All of the configurations permit access to and use of network disks, network directories (data file access), and network printers.

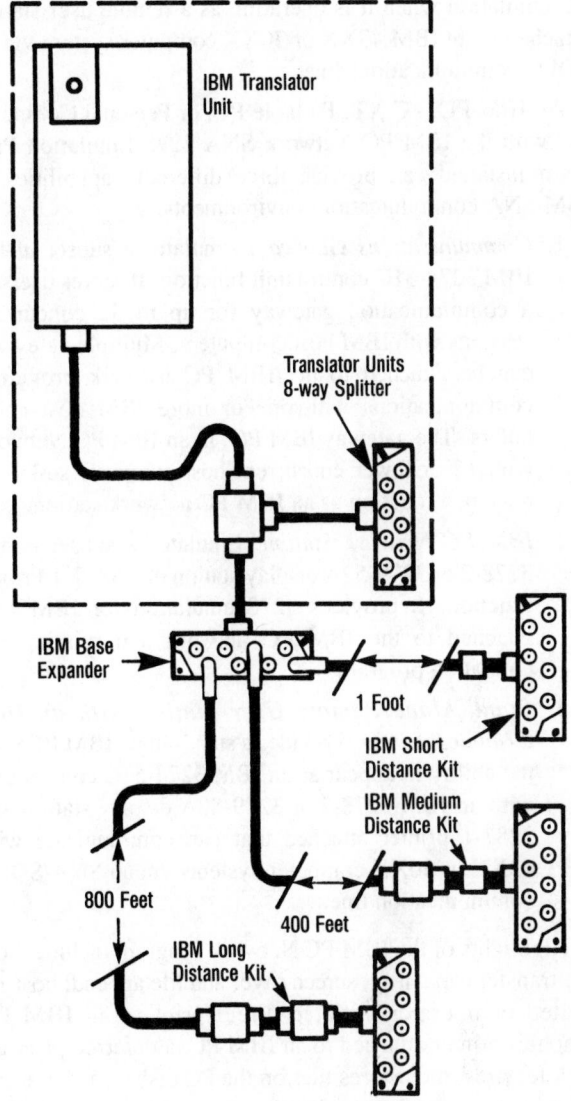

Figure: Cable Kit, Example Layout

The operation of the network programs can be concurrent with many applications.

IBM also announced the IBM PC Network SNA 3270 Emulation Program, which can be installed on PCs in the network to give them communications access to a large IBM host computer system via the company's Systems Network Architecture communications protocol.

When installed on an IBM Personal Computer in the IBM PC Network, the IBM PC Network SNA 3270 Emulation Program provides the user with a subset of full 3270 functions to share SDLC communications facilities to IBM 43XX and 30XX computer systems with other users on the same IBM PC Network. It also provides a stand-alone IBM

PC emulation when it is operating as a remote user station attached to an IBM 43XX or 30XX computer system via an SDLC communications line.

An IBM PC, PC XT, Portable PC, or Personal Computer AT with the IBM PC Network SNA 3270 Emulation Program installed can provide three different capabilities in IBM SNA communications environments:

1. *Communications Gateway*: Emulates a subset of the IBM 3274-51C control unit function. It serves users as a communication gateway for up to 32 concurrent sessions with IBM host computers. Multiple gateways can be attached to the IBM PC network providing communications with one or more IBM host computers. The gateway IBM PC, in an IBM PC Network with 12 or fewer concurrent host computer sessions, may also function as an IBM PC network station.

2. *IBM PC Network Station*: Emulates a subset of the 3278-2 or 3279-52A display station or a 3887-1 Printer function. It provides 3270 emulation for IBM PCs attached to the IBM PC network and running the emulation program.

3. *Stand-Alone Remote User Station with an IBM Graphics Printer*: Provides a stand-alone IBM PC with the ability to appear as an IBM 3274-51C control unit with an IBM 3278-2 or 3279-S2A display station and 3287-1 printer attached that can communicate with 43XX or 30XX computer systems via an SNA/SDLC communication line.

Highlights of the IBM PC Network Program include: host file transfer capability, screen save, and file append; host-initiated or operator-initiated direct print to an IBM PC graphics printer attached to an IBM PC; a deferred print-to-disk feature which stores files on the PC disk or diskette and permits the appending of files to existing files on the disk or diskette; a keyboard mapping capability which permits the user to redefine most of the keys on the PC keyboard; and the capability, with the suspend and resume feature of the program, to switch back and forth from a PC-DOS application to 3270 emulation without interrupting the 3270 session. The PC stores the cursor location on the screen and returns the cursor to the same point when switching between DOS and 3270 applications. While performing a PC-DOS application, the 3270 emulation is suspended, and vice versa.

An IBM PC running the IBM PC Network SNA 3270 Emulation Program cannot be used simultaneously with the IBM PC network programs that provide print server or file server function.

Protocols

The following discussion details the functions provided by the various layers of protocol mentioned in the adapter hardware description.

- *Link Layer—Link Access Protocol (LAP)*: Provides basic CSMA/CD, packet framing, addressing, and error detection services. LAP is responsible for the exchange of data frames between two nodes. LAP is used to provide service for the Packet Transfer Protocol (PTP).

- *Network Layer—Packet Transfer Protocol (PTP)*: Provides routing, address discovery, and unacknowledged packet transfer services. PTP is used by the Reliable Stream Protocol (RSP) and Datagram Transport Protocol (DTP).

- *Transport Layer--Reliable Stream Protocol (RSP)*: Provides error-free virtual connection services to other users through end-to-end acknowledgments and retransmissions. RSP provides transport layer services to the Session Management Protocol (SMP).

- *Datagram Transport Protocol (DTP)*: Provides unacknowledged datagram services between session layer entities, including the User Datagram Protocol (UDP) and the Diagnostic and Monitoring Protocol (DMP).

- *Session Layer—Session Management Protocol (SMP)*: Provides support for user sessions between nodes. SMP allows users to establish connection to a named process (names) and is responsible for interacting with the Name Management Protocol (NMP) within the local node to determine the address of the named process. Once the destination node address is determined, the initiating SMP can communicate with the SMP within the destination node to provide session level services to both users.

- *User Datagram Protocol (UDP)*: Provides support for user datagrams between nodes. UDP allows users to send datagrams to a named process (alias) and is responsible for interacting with the NMP within the local node to determine the address of the named process. Once the destination node address is determined, the initiating UDP can exchange datagrams with the UDP within the destination code.

- *Name Management Protocol (NMP)*: Provides the binding of alias names and network addresses within the entire local network. NMP provides all name management services, including the translation of remote names to network addresses, to both SMP and UDP.

- *Diagnostic and Monitoring Protocol (DMP)*: Provides protocol mechanisms that allow the collection of diagnostic and status information, and provides support for other network management functions.

SMP, UDP, NMP, and DMP services are accessible to the Host Interface Process. The relationship between the various protocol services is shown in the Figure.

Up to 16 names, or aliases, can be assigned to each adapter (station). One can have up to 32 sessions at one time. The session layer also supports reliable data transmission between sessions, and up to 64 Kbytes of data can be sent at one time. Datagram service is also available (broadcasting for example, is supported using datagrams).

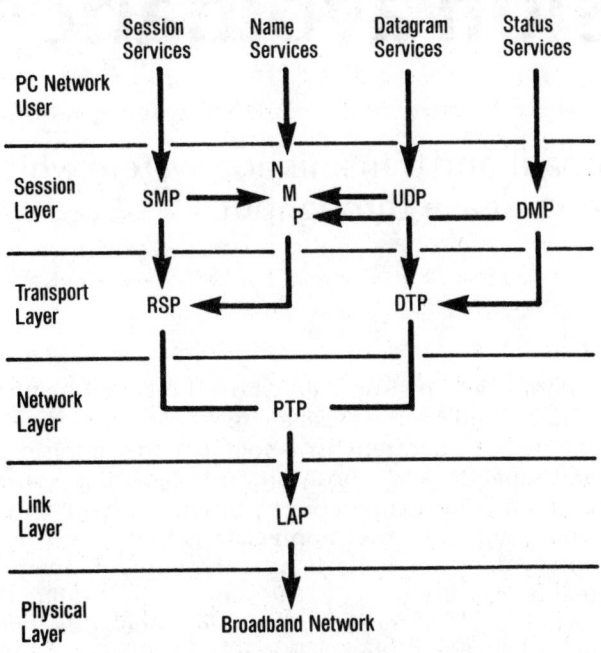

Figure: Relationship Between Various Protocol Services

Diagnostics and Statistics

Diagnostics are performed at power-up time, concurrently with the PC's own power-on diagnostics. The following tests are performed: 80188 self-test, ROM checksum, unit ID PROM test, RAM test, HIC tests (registers, GO interrupt, data transfer interrupt, data transfer DMA, and host interface control), + 12 and -12 presence check, and digital serial loopback (82586 to SIC and back). An optional test allows testing of the cable to the translator and back: A failure of any test will interrupt the PC and send a numeric code to screen, much like the existing power-on test for the PC itself.

Several traffic and error statistics can be maintained. These include: number of CRC errors, packet alignment errors, number of collisions detected, number of aborted transmissions, number of successfully transmitted and successfully received packets, number of retransmissions, and number of times the receiver has "exhausted its resources" (counters exceed 64K).

Conclusion

The PC Network adapter board is a very powerful networking product with its on-board processors and extensive diagnostics. It is also interesting to note that, for the first time in IBM's family of PC products, it is using proprietary devices (the HIC and SIC); this will certainly hamper third-party hardware development, at least from a cost standpoint. However, IBM has openly published the interface specifications at all levels, which leaves the door wide open for third-party software development.

IBM has demonstrated that it will be capable of making first deliveries on time (first quarter 1985)—a final beta-test PC Network consisting of three PC ATs running DOS 3.1; and the PC Network Program was demonstrated at the 1984 PC World Exposition in Dallas. By using DOS 3.1, IBM has "endorsed" Microsoft's MS-NET, an OEM local network operating system that is being considered by a number of competing PC local network vendors as a de facto standard for PC networking in general. By providing a common local network operating system similar to Novell's NetWare/OS, one can port applications across several vendors' networks.

One drawback to the whole system may be the illusion of "low-cost." The installation of the cable may cost more than all of the adapter boards of the PCs, and when users discover that they want more than 1,000 feet, multiple data channels, video, voice, etc., costs will escalate substantially. However, with IBM aiming at retail markets, it may establish PC Network as a de facto standard for broadband networks for the IBM personal computer.

CSMA with collision avoidance

Alan Colvin describes the operation of a broadband transmission system which uses collision avoidance to increase throughput

Advances in local area networking have allowed users to run many different applications on one system. Users are now asking for greater access, more functions, more power and greater reliability. This requires that the system tasks should be distributed, and means that the interconnection system used should be highly reliable; 'passive', so that no failed component can bring the entire system down; support high throughput; and operate on low-cost cable. This paper describes a broadband transmission system based on a single, passive coaxial cable which detects possible collisions before the data is sent. Examples of two remote stations and two adjacent stations competing for transmission are given, along with performance comparisons of CSMA/CD and CSMA/CA.

Keywords: data communications, local area networks, CSMA/CD, CSMA/CA

Before descending into the intricacies of LAN design, it is sensible first to view the whole (the computing system); it then becomes easier to appreciate the rationale behind the design of one of the fundamental parts (the LAN), viewed in the proper context.

The customer, whose interests the system supplier should keep paramount, is often needlessly burdened with the problems of selecting and integrating the ever-increasing number of new technologies. As a businessman, the customer views his information database as one of his most vital assets. His need is, quite simply, to create, access and interrogate this information as simply, quickly and informatively as possible. He does not need computers *per se*, but views them rather as a convenient and efficient means of accessing his vital information.

The supplier's role therefore, must be to offer complete business solutions to the business user. In the

author's view, the suppliers who will succeed are those who best utilize the available technologies to provide simple, yet comprehensive solutions to the businessman's needs, and whose products least impede the user's freedom of operating his business. The vital issue which suppliers must appreciate is that a new technology does not, in itself, offer the end user anything that he can use directly. The supplier must refine the technology and encapsulate it in value-added products which provide the user with the benefits which accrue from the technology, but which effectively mask its complexity.

Figure 1 shows a typical multifunction, multitasking, multiuser business computing system, based on a single minicomputer. The SyFA system shown enables up to 32 users to share the common system resources, and each user may be developing application programs or executing application programs or system utilities concurrently with all other users. The system is designed to extract the highest possible performance from relatively modestly powered low-cost hardware, and its wide range of communications emulators enable the system to be used in its prime role as a node in a corporate communications network, using asynchronous, bisynchronous (2780, 3780, HASP 360/20), SNA/SDLC and X.25 protocols.

As the raw cost of computing hardware continues to fall, users at last feel able to afford to extend the use of their computing systems to an ever-widening base of internal staff; ultimately to any employee who routinely needs to handle information. Potentially, almost every member of the 'office' staff is a candidate for his own terminal, on which he can perform all his normal day-to-day office functions, including both internal and external correspondence. Thus, users wish to increase (dramatically) the number of terminals from which their information system may be accessed.

Providing increased access is, however, only part of the user's aspiration; he is most unwilling to proliferate a number of incompatible 'specialist' systems, one for

Computer Automation Ltd, Hertford House, Denham Way, Maple Cross, Rickmansworth, Herts WD3 2XB, UK

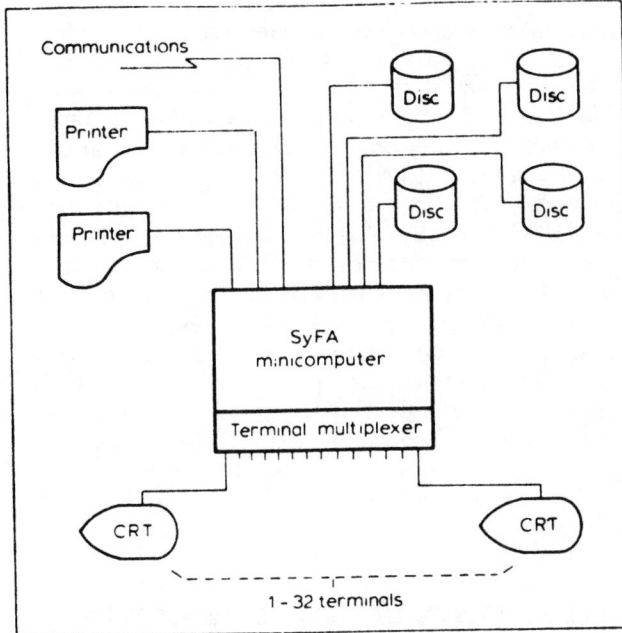

Figure 1. SyFA minicomputer sytem

data processing, another for word processing, another for shop-floor data collection etc. The inconveniences and costs associated with dealing with several different suppliers and their unique products are self evident. Increasingly therefore, users are looking to suppliers to integrate most, if not all, of their business computing functions into a single system.

One final introductory thought: users have learned from earlier experience with smaller scale computing systems. Before committing so many of their business eggs to one computing system basket, they are going to take a long, cool look at the design of the basket. The system will be required to have very high availability, which in turn dictates both high intrinsic reliability and resilience to failures. Most attention will focus on the possible causes of a complete system failure, which (at worst) could bring the entire business to a stop. Hence, although the design of each terminal and computing node will receive careful scrutiny, the design of the interconnecting system (which may well be linking several hundred users together) will be subjected to the most minute and cautious analysis.

THE PROBLEM

It is almost immediately apparent that the single-CPU architecture shown in Figure 1 is a less than ideal match for the set of requirements described. No matter how well 'tuned' the operating system, how well the hardware is designed or how well thought out the users' application programs, no single CPU system could cope with the simultaneous heavy demands of:

● more access — extending the number of users from 32 to several hundred,

● more function — integrating data processing, communications, office systems, data collection etc.
● more power — improving the system response times,
● reliability — ensuring high availability.

Clearly, the system must be partitioned, and the system tasks distributed and allocated to dedicated processing elements, each of which is purpose designed for its specialized role.

In so doing, it is essential that total compatibility be maintained with existing systems, so that the customers who have placed considerable investment in the current product (partly in the initial cost of acquisition but much more so in their application design, programming and implementation) can obtain the benefits of the new system at minimal cost and inconvenience.

APPROACH TO A SOLUTION

The fundamental components of the computing system were easily identified and isolated, and formed two discrete entities:

● the management of the system's resources, which necessarily have to be shared by all users; these include the disc storage system, the printers and the communications links to the other mini and mainframe network nodes,
● the execution of the applications programs for each user (or task) on the system.

These two entities exhibit markedly differing characteristics.

The shared system resources will, in practical systems, be concentrated in one or a few discrete locations. The resource processing system requires hardware which will efficiently perform

● multitasking
● input/output in high volume and at high speed
● memory management
● peripherals management
● communications

A modern minicomputer provides a cost-effective match for this set of requirements.

Program execution, however, is best removed from the mini. It is a CPU-intensive task which demands an inordinate share of the available power. Worse, as additional tasks (e.g. more users) are loaded onto the mini, the existing users receive a progressively smaller share of the available 'horsepower' until, inevitably and eventually, they become disenchanted with the system.

Application program execution is far better suited to the characteristics of a microcomputer. Microcomputers combine the ability to execute single-threaded (i.e. single-task) code at high speed with rapid updating of a screen image. These two attributes, coupled with the inherent low-cost of microcomputers, made them an obvious choice on a one-micro-per-terminal basis.

Figure 2 shows the approach adopted. Called SyFAnet, the system employs a minicomputer for each resource processor (RP) and a microcomputer for each task processor (TP). The principle of operation is simple; after the system has been powered up, any TP may request an application program from an RP. The program, in its entirety, is then passed from the disc system, via the interconnection path, to the requesting TP, in whose local storage the program now resides. From this point on, the program executes in the TP, using the network only when it needs to obtain or deposit data, to print or to communicate externally.

Each TP incorporates a dedicated microprocessor, and since there is one TP for each executing task, the TP carries no operating system overhead. The application program executes rapidly, at the speed of the 16 bit CPU chip, and predictably, since the CPU is not shared by other tasks. Each additional user brings an additional TP to the system, thereby providing the computing power to discharge the incremental task without draining CPU power from the existing users.

The RP is implemented by removing hardware and operating system modules from the system shown in Figure 1, and the TP by designing a single-board microcomputer around a powerful 16 bit industry-standard chip, with high-volume, on-board memory, a network-access 'datalink controller' and an interface to local mass-storage devices. The design of both of these elements is such that compatibility with the existing product is assured at both the application program (high-level, business-oriented language) level and at the hardware level (the RP is a reconfigured version of the current SyFA system).

The designers found it no insuperable technical challenge to provide a cost-effective implementation for the TP and the RP. The design of the interconnecting system, however, proved to be a severe technical challenge: it was deemed essential that the interconnecting system should be intrinsically and absolutely reliable, and that this objective was to be achieved without compromising any of the other present or future cost and performance goals. Examination of the complete set of requirements reveals the nature of this challenge.

REQUIREMENTS OF INTERCONNECTION SYSTEM

Figure 2 shows that the interconnection system (the serial backplane) is the key element in the entire system. Put very simply, if the interconnection system

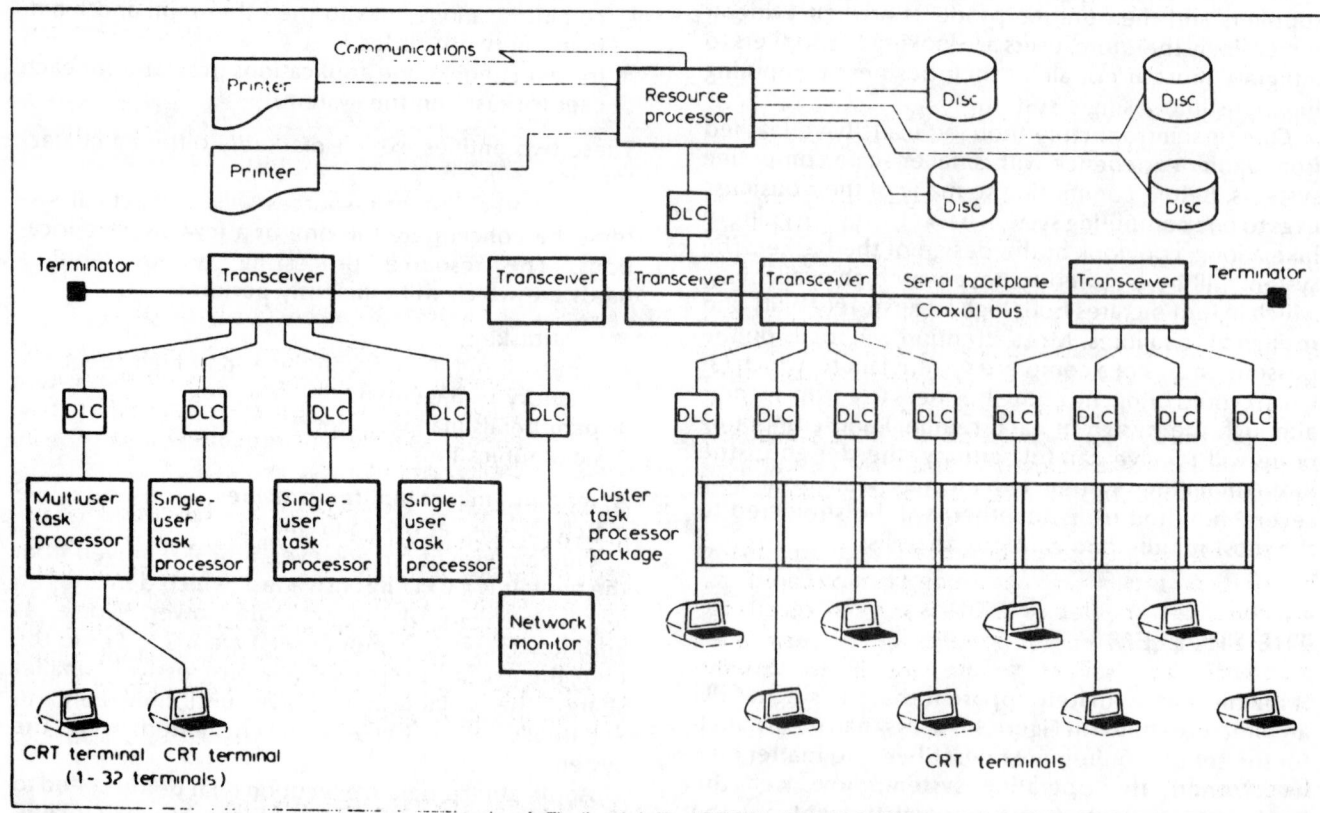

Figure 2. SyFAnet distributed multicomputer system, based on coaxial-cable-based LAN and broadband transmission technique. Transceivers interface net to datalink controllers, which in turn connect to single-user task processors, multiuser task processors, groups of task processors housed in a single cabinet, resource processors and a network monitor

fails, then the system is useless. The failure of an individual task processor may prove to be a temporary inconvenience to its user, and the failure of a resource processor can be accommodated, if the user so desires, by designing two or more RPs into his system and distributing and/or replicating his databases and programs accordingly.

In the designers' view, the essential requirements, *all* of which the interconnection design must fulfil, include the following.

- It must allow all system components to be loosely coupled. In other words, there must be no 'master' unit which could fail and prevent the entire system from operating.
- It must not contain any active components; an active component could fail and render all or part of the system inoperative.
- It must support high datarates, guarantee data integrity and ensure high data throughput, even during traffic peaks.
- It must operate on low-cost cable, with freely-positioned, low-cost taps for the access points. The cable must be easy to install, sufficiently rugged for business and industrial environments, immune to external electrical noise and free of self-radiated electrical noise.
- It must be capable of supporting very considerable growth in traffic of all types (data, facsimile, voice, video etc.). Future growth must be achievable without loading additional costs onto the initial implementation.

The implementation options available were to select either ring or bus topology, and either baseband or broadband transmission.

A ring topology solution was discarded early in the project, not because ring systems were intrinsically deficient, but because their characteristics were adjudged to be unsuitable for the specific requirements of SyFAnet. In particular, ring systems do not enable nodes to be added or removed from the network without powering the system down, they invariably require a 'master' control module (e.g. to generate empty data packets) on which the availability of the system totally depends, and they are normally constrained to modest datarates and relatively few nodes.

The relative merits of baseband and broadband transmission techniques have long been debated and will continue to be debated. This is scarcely surprising, since each system has its benefits and its associated problems. The salient points are listed, briefly, below.

Baseband

Method The digital signals are placed directly on the cable, using simple, low-cost transmitter and receiver circuits.

For A single transmission cable is used; installation is relatively simple and inexpensive.

The CSMA/CD access method enables a reliable, efficient contention system to be supported on a single cable, without the need for active components.

Against The cable specification usually results in a high cable cost.

The signalling method generates standing waves, which restrict the positioning of the access taps to points at fixed intervals along the cable.

The signalling method precludes any further traffic expansion, irrespective of the available bandwidth of the cable itself.

Broadband

Method The digital signals are used to modulate a radio-frequency carrier signal. The RF signal is placed on the cable. RF modems are used to modulate the signals on transmission and demodulate the RF signals on reception.

For The full cable bandwidth is available for transmission, such that, even with one fast channel initially installed, considerable expansion is available to accommodate traffic growth.

Any mix of any type of traffic can be carried, by selecting modems with appropriate modulation systems, centre frequencies and bandwidth.

Access taps may be freely positioned anywhere along the cable.

Against RF modems are relatively expensive.

CSMA/CD is difficult to implement, and can normally be supported only with the use of active components (head-end amplifiers, frequency changers or repeaters) and/or twin cable systems.

Within Computer Automation, the baseband versus broadband debate raged as strongly as elsewhere until, early in the development of SyFAnet, a conscious decision was made to divert the energy being expended in the continuing debate to more productive use, by attempting to design a transmission system which incorporated the best of both systems without incurring the pitfalls of either.

SOLUTION TO THE PROBLEM — CSMA/CA

The target was to design a broadband transmission sys-

tem based on a single, *passive* coaxial cable (i.e. free from any 'master' or active components such as amplifiers, frequency changers or repeaters) using the proven low-cost baseband access method CSMA/CD.

If this could be achieved, the advantages would be significant.

- A passive system would provide an intrinsically reliable interconnection system; if there were no amplifiers, repeaters etc. in the system, the reliability of the system would be beyond doubt. Furthermore, if these active components could be 'designed out', then the user would not have to pay for them.
- Broadband transmission would enable the use of very low-cost television cable and connection components, and would provide a high cable bandwidth for immense traffic expansion in the future. Cable television cable is rugged and shielded, making installation simple and relatively inexpensive.

Carrier sense, multiple access with collision detection is a system which is highly effective and well proven (Ethernet being an obviously successful example). CSMA/CD is relatively easy to implement on baseband systems but, until recently, very difficult to implement economically on broadband systems, and impossible to implement on broadband systems without the use of active components.

To understand how CSMA/CD works, and to appreciate the excellence of its simple, passive mode of operation, consider the following analogy.

Imagine a business meeting at which all the participants have a lot to say, and for which it has been decided that there shall be no chairman. This is an excellent recipe for chaos! For the meeting to be successful, i.e. for all participants to succeed in having their say, being clearly heard and understood, all present would have to agree to conduct themselves according to a simple set of rules (the human equivalent of CSMA/CD), as follows.

- Anyone wishing to speak must first listen (carrier sense) and ensure that no-one else is speaking. When this condition is satisfied, he may then start speaking.
- All present have an equal right to speak: no-one has preferential priority (multiple access). It follows that several participants may be simultaneously listening for silence and wishing to speak.

Occasionally, therefore, and particularly when passions are running high, two or more participants will start speaking at once. Should this occur, each will hear the other talking (collision detection) and, to restore order and effective communication:

- all those who have started to speak now stop talking, pause for a (random) brief period of time, and then listen for silence before speaking again.

It is also desirable, to avoid the meeting being 'hogged'

by the verbose, that all participants subdivide their speeches into brief sentences (packets of data rather than entire messages). This analogy precisely parallels the operation of CSMA/CD.

While CSMA/CD is quite workable, as network traffic becomes heavier the chance of a collision increases and, in peak traffic, throughput degrades as the collision-detection mechanism (and consequent retries) comes into frequent operation.

More significant, however, is the effect of signal attenuation. In baseband systems, using relatively low-speed digital signalling, attenuation is rarely a problem. For collision detection to function, the 'colliding' signals must each disturb (corrupt) the other sufficiently for the collision to be detected. In a high-frequency broadband system, the signal attenuation may be quite severe, such that for widely separated stations the collision-detection system could not be relied upon.

The fundamental and crucial difference in transmission characteristics between baseband and broadband systems is best explained by returning to the analogy of the business meeting.

In the earlier 'baseband' example, it was taken for granted that all participants could clearly hear each other. Thus, if two or more began to talk at the same time, each would hear the other and would then stop talking. Imagine now that the same meeting is transferred to another, quite unsuitable, room. The participants find, to their discomfort, that the new room is only six feet wide, and is several hundred feet long, with a long, thin table running the length of the room. Again, no chairman is present and the meeting restarts under the previous 'CSMA/CD' rules.

It will not be long before two participants, several hundred feet apart from each other, having listened for silence, begin to speak at the same time. It is now quite likely, due to their separation, that each may not hear the other speaking, the distant speaker's speech having lost so much amplitude in travelling the length of the room that the local speaker's voice completely swamps it. Collision detection is no longer dependable.

Faced with this problem, the meeting organizer could exercise his ingenuity in a variety of ways (e.g. amplifier/loudspeaker system, individual headphones linked to a multimicrophone sound system etc.) to restore effective communications.

Similarly, in broadband transmission systems, many different solutions to this problem have emerged in LAN-based products, including the use of 'head-end' amplifiers, frequency changers and amplifier/repeaters. All of these approaches regrettably introduce an active element into the transmission system; most of them use twin coaxial cables, thereby doubling the cable cost. None of them satisfies the set of requirements earlier described.

CSMA/CA is a variant of the CSMA/CD technique. It utilizes all of the benefits of CSMA/CD, but resolves contention *before* any data is transmitted (rather than by detecting colliding data packets), thus improving the efficiency of the system, especially at the most critical time, i.e. when the network traffic is heaviest. This it achieves by a combination of three additional and innovative elements, for which patent applications have been lodged.

The problem posed by the attenuation of the signals over distance is resolved by a timing technique; each node listens (carrier senses) *twice* before transmitting a packet. As will become apparent, this enables CSMA/CA to operate on a single, long, passive broadband cable system.

The second addition is a technique to detect potential collisions during the initial 'carrier burst' (instead of during the ensuing data transmission). This is achieved by generating a specially modulated carrier burst, such that the merging initial carrier bursts from two locally contending stations generate a 'beat' signal, with a high-frequency component which is readily detectable by both stations during their brief initial carrier bursts. By this means, minimal bus time is 'wasted', and maximum bus time is left available for productive data transmission.

The third addition is a reserved 'time slot' appended to each information packet sent, during which the receiving station, having checked the incoming packet for integrity of content, returns an acknowledgement (or, if necessary a negative acknowledgement) to the transmitting station. This, of course, requires that the receiving station should be equipped with the intelligence to compute the data-integrity checking algorithms and build the appropriate response frame 'on the fly'. The result is attractive, in that every packet sent across the network is confirmed as correctly received by the correct recipient, virtually instantaneously and without the receiving station having to reacquire the LAN bus.

The effect on system performance, and the removal of the traditional 'end to end' acknowledgement delays, is considerable.

CSMA/CA OPERATION

In this section, the detailed operation of the collision avoidance system is described. The mechanism is best understood by illustrating its operation in the two bounding cases of:

● two contending stations immediately adjacent to each other on the cable,
● two contending stations at the maximum permitted cable distance from each other.

Each processor's datalink controller accesses the coaxial cable via a port on a shared broadband transceiver (modem). The datalink controller and the higher level layers of the system architecture prepare correctly formatted packets of information and submit these to the transceivers for access to the bus. The transceivers have the sole responsibility for implementing the CSMA/CA system.

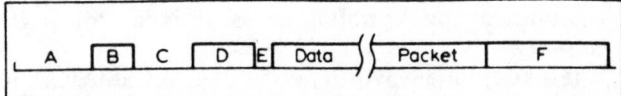

Figure 3.   Information packet — format and timing

Figure 3 shows the composition and timing of all information packets.

● At time *A*, the transceiver listens before attempting to transmit.
● At time *B*, the transceiver, having found the cable free, sends its initial carrier burst.
● At time, *C*, the transceiver again listens to the cable.
● At time *D*, if the cable is still free, the transceiver transmits a second carrier burst, during which the receiving transceivers adjust their automatic gain control circuits to the strength of the received signal, retaining this setting for the duration of the current packet.
● Time *E* is used by datalink controllers to detect and respond to their unique addresses,
● The data packet then follows.
● Time *F*, is reserved for a response frame; the receiving station computes an 'on the fly' cyclic redundancy check on the incoming packet, and appends an appropriate response for the immediate benefit of the originating station.

Two adjacent stations

Figure 4 shows CSMA/CA operation for two adjacent stations, where both stations simultaneously attempt to transmit a packet.

It would normally be the case that, for two adjacent stations simultaneously commencing to transmit, their respective signals would be in-phase, of equal amplitude and at the same frequency, i.e. indistinguishable. This makes detection of an impending collision an intriguing challenge. Normally, in CSMA/CD, the collision is detected much later, when the two (nonidentical) data packets are both present on the network. Valuable bus time is wasted transmitting data which will have to be aborted and retransmit-

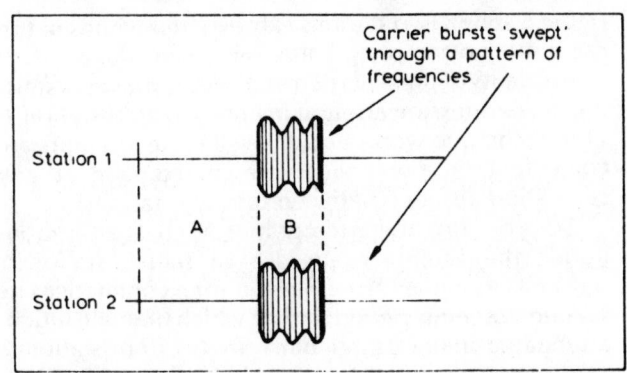

Figure 4.   Two adjacent stations start transmitting simultaneously

ted later. In normal light-traffic conditions this is irritating; at peak traffic times it is a downright nuisance.

It is additionally worth noting that, in CSMA/CD, to ensure that a data collision will be detected, it is mandatory that all packets transmitted should be above a defined minimum length (this being twice the maximum end-to-end propagation delay of the cable). This is a severe restriction for control (as opposed to data) packets, which could otherwise be much shorter, with consequential throughput benefits.

Clearly, the requirement is for the two adjacent stations to detect each other's transmission *during the initial carrier burst*, rather than to sort out the wreckage after an ensuing data collision. CSMA/CA achieves this with the following technique.

As previously noted, both carrier frequencies are nominally identical. In practice the two frequencies will differ fractionally, owing to component tolerances. If one were to wait long enough, the difference frequency could be detected as the two carriers 'beat' against each other. The detection time would, however, be ridiculously long.

The solution is simple; the 'beat frequency' principle is merely enhanced, as follows.

At time *B*, both stations transmit their initial carrier burst. The carriers are not transmitted with a fixed frequency; each carrier burst is swept through a proprietary 'pattern' of frequencies. The result is a beat pattern with a high-frequency component which is readily and rapidly detected by both transmitting transceivers; they both immediately abort the attempt to transmit. As with CSMA/CD, both stations then wait a pseudorandom time before reattempting the transmission. Note that no data has been sent; a potential collision has been avoided with minimal bus occupancy.

Note further that, because detection of data collisions is no longer required, there is no necessity for packets to be of a minimum length. Very short packets can be (and are) a normal feature of the CSMA/CA system, contributing to a high throughput of data.

Two remote stations

Figure 5 shows two stations at the extreme ends of the cable, both attempting a transmission.

For clarity of presentation, station 2 is shown as starting its transmission attempt fractionally after station 1. (The technique works equally well if the attempts are coincident or more widely separated, and at any separation distance between the two stations).

Consider first the attempt by station 1: after monitoring the cable for absence of traffic, station 1 transmits its initial carrier burst. It then commences its second 'listening' period, during which time the much-attenuated initial carrier burst arrives from station 2 at station 1, delayed by the cable propagation time. Because the station 1 transceiver is now listening,

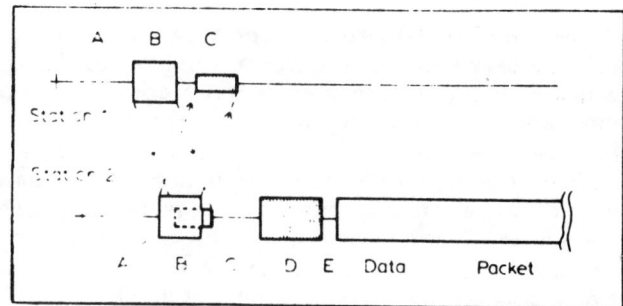

Figure 5.   Two remote stations — station 1 starts first

it *can* detect the attenuated carrier signal from station 2. Thus, recognizing that a collision would occur were it to proceed, the station 1 transceiver *avoids* this by abandoning its attempt to transmit.

Meanwhile, during station 2's initial carrier burst, the much-attenuated initial carrier burst (delayed by the cable propagation time) arrives from station 1. Let us assume that station 2's signal completely swamps the weak signal received from station 1, such that no beat frequency is generated and the first element of the collision avoidance technique is thus ineffective. (This, of course, is the very same problem with which CSMA/CD cannot cope.)

Station 2 therefore proceeds; its transceiver listens for the second time, sees nothing from station 1 (which has by now aborted its attempt), and continues with its transmission until the entire packet has been sent.

Note once again that a potential data collision is avoided *before* the data is sent, and that once transmission of data has started, it continues free of any risk of collisions until the packet has been sent in its entirety.

This, then, is the prime difference between CSMA/CA and the more traditional CSMA/CD. No data is transmitted until it has been unambiguously determined that the transmitter has exclusive use of the cable. The initial listening period is exactly the same as that for CSMA/CD (and determined by the round-trip propagation delay time of the cable). Nothing comes entirely free, however, and CSMA/CA requires a second, albeit brief, listening period prior to each data packet. This small extra overhead is compensated by the increased throughput inherent in the technique.

SYSTEM CONSIDERATIONS

The network topology is a branching, nonrooted tree. The original design decision to reject any amplifiers, repeaters or other active components in the cable imposed a finite limit on the cable length. The upper limit selected is 1 km, along which up to 254 addressable processor nodes may be freely configured.

Typical datarates of up to 10 Mbit/s are achieved through simple serial interfaces to all processors in the SyFAnet. Planned enhancements will enable individual SyFAnets to be locally interconnected via 'bridge' processors, and connected to remote SyFAnets, other *de facto* standard nets and public data networks via a family of 'gateway' processors.

SyFAnet's proprietary radio-frequency broadband transceivers employ a carrier centre-frequency of 48 MHz, the choice of frequency being determined by the availability of a plethora of low-cost 'building brick' components from the television industry (48 MHz is one of the standard internal frequencies used in US television equipment). This contributes to the low-cost design of the transceiver. A secondary, but welcome, benefit is derived from the use of standard television circuits within the transceivers. The TV circuits provide such a high bandwidth that each transceiver (with the incorporation of minimal multiplexing logic) can support the data bandwidth requirements of four attached processors. The transceivers are therefore designed to be shared by up to four node processors; the cost-per-connected-user is therefore lower than that to be expected from more conventional broadband systems.

The higher layers (both hardware and software) in the system architecture are modelled on the ISO reference model for open systems interconnection. The combination of the CSMA/CA technique (which eliminates the need for any 'master' network controller) and the layered, peer-protocol software architecture results in an intrinsically reliable, and therefore high-availability system.

PERFORMANCE BENEFITS

It cannot be too highly stressed that the SyFAnet local area network was designed from the outset as an integral part of a total multicomputer distributed computing system. In particular, the design goals for the LAN included a requirement for high traffic throughput, coupled with lowest possible latency. The designers were free to disregard any need to incorporate features and functions to provide for generality of traffic and terminals, and hence were able to implement a finely-tuned LAN which did not have to bear the burden of the overheads associated with such generality, unlike almost all proprietary 'open' networks. It was decided that the gateway processor was the correct point at which to accommodate the less efficient (lower data/control bit ratio) characteristics of other *de facto* network standards.

These decisions were amply justified by the resulting performance of the networked product when compared with the existing single CPU system, itself no sluggard.

The comparison is best shown by a 'real life' example. Laboratory benchmarking of the two systems had already proved thoroughly satisfactory, but offering the new system for existing customers to evaluate confirmed beyond further doubt that all of the original design aims had been met or exceeded.

A good illustration of this is provided by a customer

with some 90 installed systems, all running an identical application suite (insurance broking). The kernel of this application is a single program of around 60 kbyte of code. This is a large CPU-intensive program, typical of many commercial applications. As more terminals are brought into use, each executing the same application, the terminal response degrades due to heavy CPU loading caused both by executing the application program code and by the paging of the program from disc.

In the multicomputer networked system (shown in Figure 2), each terminal first loads the *entire* program code into its dedicated task processor. Execution of the program, for each active terminal, now takes place entirely within the task processor's local memory, and at the speed of the task processor's internal 16 bit microprocessor. Note that the program is no longer paged from disc, and that each user has his own 'personal' application computer. The LAN is used only to fetch or deposit data from the disc system, and is normally so lightly loaded that each task processor is, for the most part, totally unaffected by its neighbours.

Figure 6 shows the comparative performance of the two systems, running the identical program. The performance characteristics of the two architectures is strikingly apparent. In the single CPU case, the time for all terminals to complete the benchmark becomes almost a linear function of the number of active terminals. In the multicomputer, LAN-connected system, the response time is flat, and almost independent of the number of active terminals. Better still, the performance with only one terminal is better than that of the single CPU system.

In the general case, as the number of terminals increases, the factor which most often limits perfor-

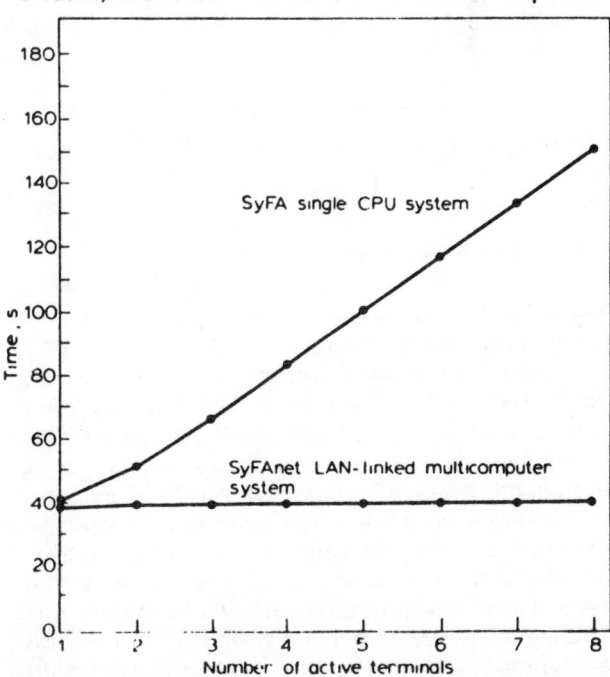

Figure 6. Performance comparison — single CPU and multicomputer system

mance is the input/output traffic to and from the disc system. This limit is reached well before the LAN loading becomes a significant consideration. For systems with large numbers of connected task processors, where disc contention becomes problematic, SyFAnet offers an advanced resource processor, incorporating a large bank of fast RAM memory which is used to 'cache' data from the disc system.

The disc caching algorithm retains disc data in memory on a 'most frequently used' basis. When a resource processor receives a request for disc data from a task processor, it scans its internal tables to determine if the data is already in the disc cache memory. If it is, the data is available at the 'microseconds' access time of the memory system rather than at the 'milliseconds' electromechanical access time of the disc system.

Moreover, the caching algorithm automatically 'locks' index files into the disc cache memory, so that multilevel indexed access to data (characteristic of commercial applications) will usually take place in memory at high speed, instead of via several physical disc reads, each taking an average of some 50 ms.

Lastly, since the resource processor CPU is often 'idle' and awaiting a task processor request, the idle time is put to profitable use by scanning the historical pattern of data requests from the task processors, and anticipating the ensuing data requests. The predicted data is thus fetched from disc and placed in the disc cache memory. The prediction will often be incorrect, but this is inconsequential, since all this activity takes place in idle time. There is always a net gain in performance.

CONCLUSIONS

CSMA/CD is a well-proven and effective network access technique, but it suffers from inherent deficiencies which limit its effectiveness as traffic densities approach the limit of the transmission capacity, and which make it difficult to implement at low-cost in reliable, high-capacity broadband systems.

CSMA/CA resolves these deficiencies and, in the implementation described, enables a versatile, intrinsically reliable high-capacity broadband transmission system to be implemented on a single, passive cable at a cost comparable with baseband systems.

This alone, however, does not constitute a useable product; the local area network is merely the 'plumbing', albeit excellent plumbing, linking the modules within the confines of a high-performance business computing system. This is as it should be. The user need not, indeed should not, have to pay any undue regard to the intricacies lurking within his system; merely to enjoy the resulting benefits.

RECENT DEVELOPMENTS
WITH THE VIDEODATA
BROADBAND NETWORK

B K Hackett
Laboratory Manager
Interactive Systems/3M
USA

Reprinted with permission from *The Proceedings of Localnet*, 1983, pages 261-271. Copyright © 1983 by On-Line Publications.

Recent developments in LSI technology have permitted powerful new local area networks to be developed. The present state of 3M's Videodata system with emphasis on LAN/1 local area network is presented.

Brian Hackett is Manager of the IS/3M Development Laboratory. His responsibilities include Business Development manager for LAN/1 and Director of Technical Operations at IS/3M. From 76-79 he was manager of the RF development group and in 1980 he became Product Development manager of all Broadband Products.

Preface

With the advent of LSI network controllers, the cost of high
performance local area networks is diminishing rapidly. As the
technology of high speed and low cost RF modems advances, the
advantages of broadband communications for local area networks is
more marked. This paper discusses recent enhancements of the
Videodata network with primary focus on LAN/1 broadband local area
network.

The 3M Videodata network is comprised of many services that can
coexist on the same physical media. The 440Mhz bandwidth available
to users is ample room for services such as local area networks,
video conferencing, surveillance, energy management, factory
automation, etc. Through the late seventies and early eighties, the
Videodata network supplied users with point to point FDM channels in
the data rate ranges of 10Kb and 100Kb and TDM channels used mainly
for data transmission from many remote sites to one centralized
controller. These two methods of data transmission methods still
have a place today on broadband cable systems.

Local area networks arose from the need for high speed data traffic
that can reach anyone connected to the network. During the early
eighties it became very clear that baseband and broadband networks
would have to offer full connectivity, network data rates beyond 1Mb
and port connection costs of under $500.00. The achievement of
those results could only come from use of LSI devices in network
interface units (NIU).

LAN/1 NETWORK OVERVIEW

LAN/1 is a fully distributed token passing broadband local area
network. This high speed, packet-switching network provides a
versatile, reliable, and cost-effective method for transporting
digital data. Each LAN/1 network channel occupies one 6MHz transmit
/ 6MHz receive channel pair on a broadband cable system. Multiple
LAN/1 network channels can coexist on the same broadband cable, and
each channel supports up to 254 NIU's. Each NIU can have up to 8
logical addresses; thus each channel pair can support over 2000
users.

The broadband cable system is used as a bus with all network
interface units receiving what they send. Frequency translation is
provided by a channel converter located at the headend of the cable
system. A single channel converter unit (CCU) can be used if one
local network is desired or a five band converter can be utilized to
allow expandability without any hardware modification. Full
redundancy of the converter is provided at the headend by installing
a redundant switchover unit (RSU).

All upstream traffic (towards the CCU) is frequency translated by
the CCU and rebroadcast downstream (towards the NIU's). In order that
LAN/1 coexist on a broadband system, RF channels were allocated as
indicated in the following frequency plan:

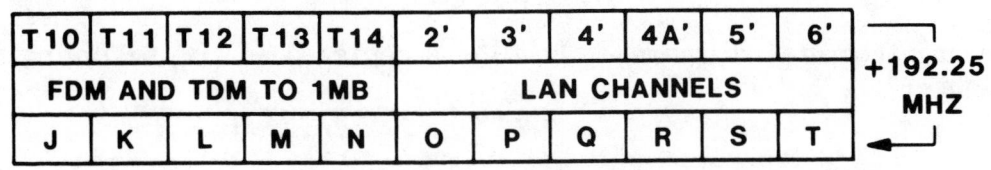

T10	T11	T12	T13	T14	2'	3'	4'	4A'	5'	6'	
FDM AND TDM TO 1MB					LAN CHANNELS						+192.25 MHZ
J	K	L	M	N	O	P	Q	R	S	T	

216 222 228 234 240 246 252 258 264 270 276 282

The indicated channels have a 192.25 MHz offset which is consistent
with the recommendation of the IEEE802 committee on broadband
standards. All services that were available previously on Videodata
can maintain their required channel separation from the local area
networks.

The physical broadband coaxial cable can be laid out in a "branching
tree" type of structure. Thus, the cable can be easily routed to
cover plant or office floor area, or three-dimensionally routed
through high rise office buildings and other multi-floor structure.
NIU's can be located anywhere on the cable system within a 7 mile
radius of the CCU.

The system architecture is depicted as follows:

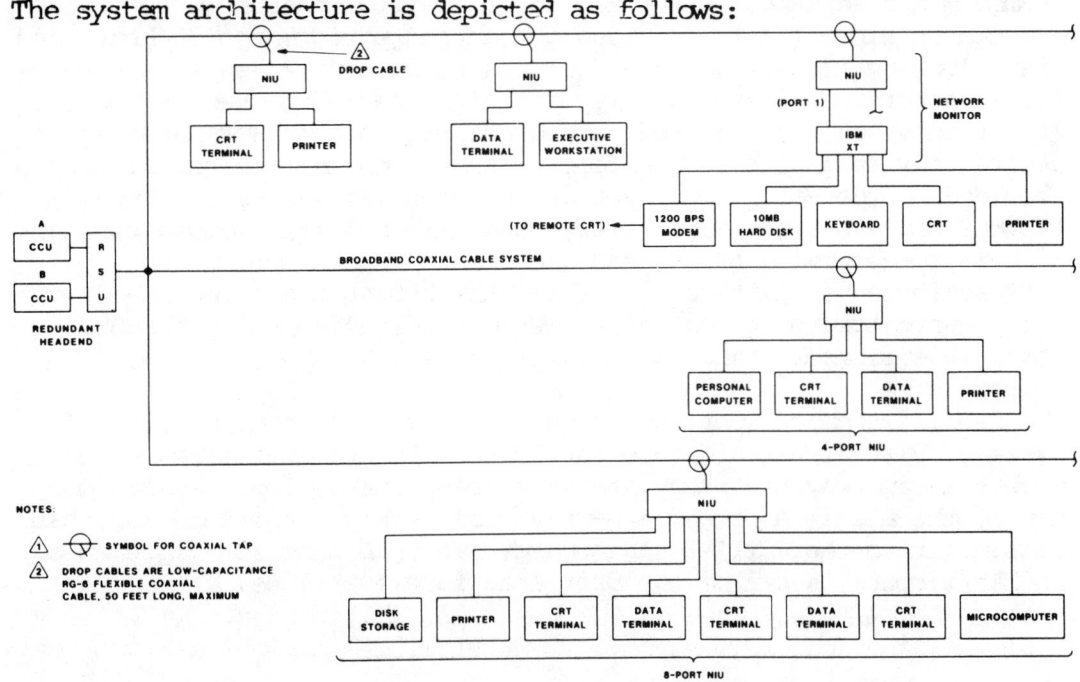

Each user device is attached to the network through an NIU.
Currently, NIU's support asynchronous serial communications
connections. NIU's are available in 2, 4, or 8 port versions.
Support of synchronous serial and byte parallel devices is a matter
of swapping the NIU's interface card. Each NIU contains an RF
modem, and a network controller card.

An architectural diagram of the NIU is depicted in the following
figure:

	PAD (SIMILAR TO X.3)	
DATA LINK LAYER	IEEE 802 LLC	CONFIGURATION PARAMETERS (SIMILAR TO X.28 & X.29)
	RIM TOKEN CONTROLLER	
PHYSICAL LAYER	2.5MB FSK MODEM	RS232

The physical layer is provided by a unique combination of a 3Mb FSK
RF modem and an ARCNET RIM token controller. The ARCNET protocol
was chosen since (1) it provided guaranteed performance at heavy and
light loading (2) it had been well tested in over 7 years of service
(3) it interfaced inexpensively with high speed broadband RF modems
(4) it provided the required throughput on a bus network and (5) it
was readily available in LSI form. Connection oriented services are
provided by the data link layer above the physical layer. The
IEEE802 LLC was chosen for a few reasons - (1) it provided virtual
circuit connectivity (2) it had excellent error recovery and
retransmission facilities (3) having the LLC in place would aid
future work towards a gateway between LAN/1 and a fully IEEE802
compatible system.

The LAN/1 system as mentioned previously is a connection oriented
system. Virtual circuits are easily established and disconnected in
much the same way that they are in a telephone system. Layered on
top of the LLC is a packet assembly/disassembly (PAD) function that
is similar to the CCITT X.3 standard. The PAD function implemented
in LAN/1 contains all of the user interface functions.

Packets sizes can be from 1 to 253 information bytes varying
dynamically with network loading. When the network is lightly
loaded packet sizes are very small - < 5 bytes. As the network
traffic increases the packet size increases to the maximum of 253
bytes. The relatively small packet size is an aid in rapid response
and fairness in the system. The most demanding interactive process,
a screen oriented editor or word processor, is easily accommodated.

Many features similar to CCITT X.28 were implemented to be an aid in
configuring the NIU for individual needs. Special capabilities such
as echo filtering, autobaud, auto drop of DTR on disconnect,
automatic port selection and contention chaining were added to
enhance the NIU's utility. Either in-band (XON/XOFF) or out-of-
band (RTS/CTS) flow control can be used to supply speed matching
through the network. Slow 300 baud devices can have logical
attachments to user devices running at 19.2Kb since LAN/1 provides
the necessary buffering and flow control. Also, remote configuration
of PAD parameters as outlined in CCITT X.29 are supplied. Any NIU
on the network can, with the proper password, configure any other
NIU on the network.

To aid in system maintenance, a network monitor (NMU) was developed.
The NMU is an optional device and is not required for the network to
function. The primary objective of the NMU is gathering statistics
from each NIU and reporting this information to the system manager.
An IBM XT computer is used for the monitor because of its low cost
and suitable computing power. Many displays such as number of
network reconfigurations, virtual circuit connections, number of
packets sent and received, and token wait times are available to
the operator. A powerful database management package is also
integrated into the monitor so that the user can define specific
displays and reports from the collected data.

Another relted service that is available in the NMU is cable system
monitoring of the whole Videodata network. A key ingredient in
network performance is up-time of the whole cable network whether it
be used for local area networks or any other services. The cable
monitoring system consists of transponders that are located at the
far ends of active branches of the cable system. These transponders
are interrogated by the network monitor through a separate 10Kb data
channel that is allocated specifically for that purpose. Each
remote transponding unit (RTU) is interrogated and its response is
noted. Then the NMU inserts a specified amount of attenuation and
again interrogates the RTU. If the transponder responds, the cable
branch from the NMU to RTU is displayed as active and has ample
signal margin for proper operation. RTU's not responding or failing
the attenuation test are prime suspects for cable system
malfunction.

NIU TOKEN CONTROLLER OPERATION

All network functions such as token passing, packet transmission and reception, and network reconfiguration are handled entirely by the RIM. When the network is in its stable state with all token linkages established each node has saved a value NID, which is the address of the next (numerically ascending) node present on the network, and is the node to which it will pass the token. When a node receives the token, it will check to see if any data is queued for transmission. If no data is ready to be sent, the node will pass the token to NID. If when a node receives the token, it has data queued, it will first send a "Free Buffer Enquiry" to the destination node. The receiving node will have free buffer space if no packets have been received since its microprocessor (uP) last wrote a packet to the receive buffer. If the destination has free buffer space, it will respond with an ACK (acknowledge), and if no space is available it will send a NAK (negative ack). If the transmitting node receives the NAK, it will simply pass the token. If the ACK is returned, the node will transmit the packet and append a 16 bit CRC. The receiving node will verify the length of the message and check the CRC, and if both are correct will send an ACK to the source node. If either length or CRC fail the node will return NO message, and the transmitting node will time out. If when the transmitting node sends a free buffer enquiry and no response is heard, this is equivalent to a NAK.

Reconfiguration of the network must occur when any node enters or leaves the logical ring of token circulation. For the case of a node leaving the network, when its predecessor attempts to pass the token to this now nonexistent node, it will listen for network activity for a period of time, T_resp. If no activity is detected within this period, the node will increment its NID value and attempt to pass the token to this address. The node will repeat this process until it detects activity, and will now have the address of its successor in its NID register. For the case of a node entering the network, the process is somewhat different. When a node is powered up or has not received the token for a period of time T_token, it will send a reconfiguration burst consisting of a data pattern of eight marks and one space repeated 765 times. This transmission is longer than any other possible on the network, and is designed to collide with and destroy the token, thereby rendering the system "tokenless". Now no node has control of the network. When the nodes hear no activity on the network for a period of time T_recon, each node will set its NID to its own ID and begin an internal countdown equal to a time of T_delay multiplied by 255-ID. This timeout will expire only in the node with the highest address on the network, which will then attempt to pass the token to the node with its ID = NID.

This will fail in the first attempt due to the fact that the node previously set NID = ID. The node will then wait for T resp, and if no response is heard it will increment NID and try again. This will continue until it finds its successor, and the process will continue until all nodes have once again found their successors, and normal network operation will resume.

NIU DATA LINK OPERATION

The logical link control (LLC) layer provides the connection oriented service in each NIU. The LLC provides communication services for the packet assembler / disassembler (PAD) above it, and interfaces to the RIM controller below it. The RIM controls the main channel token protocol and provides basic physical packet addressing, transfer, and primary error detection (CRC). The LLC provides additional addressing for routing data to user ports within an NIU, provides virtual circuit setup and disconnect, and provides control procedures to ensure that data packets are transferred error free and in their correct sequence.

The IEEE802.2 LLC is comparable to standard protocols such as HDLC (X.25). It operates in a "balanced" mode which means that either end can issue CALL, DISCONNECT, and other supervisory commands.

The IEEE802 specifications define the LLC protocol data unit (PDU) formats. This LLC packet is embedded in the data area of a RIM physical layer packet. Each LLC packet is structured as follows:

- 1 byte of DSAP (Destination Service Access Point).
  This address byte normally identifies a user port within an NIU. Note that the NIU address is contained in the RIM packet header.

- 1 byte of SSAP (Source Service Access Point).
  This identifies the sender (along with the SID byte in the RIM packet).

- 1 byte of Control field
  This identifies the PDU type, and may also contain control and status bits.

- N bytes of information

There are three primary types of LLC packets: Information, Supervisory, and Unnumbered. Bits in the control field identify precisely what type the packet is.

All "user" data is carried in information (I) type packets. The control field of each I packet contains a 3 bit sequence number. This number is incremented by 1 (modulo 8) for each new I packet sent. This is used to guarantee that packets are delivered in the correct order. A different 3 bit receive number field in the control bytes of information and supervisory packets is used to acknowledge the correct receipt of information packets.

There are 3 types of supervisory packets: RR, RNR, and REJ. The RR (receive ready) type is used to indicate that I packets may be received. The RNR (receive not ready) is used to indicate that no more packets may be received. Flow control is implemented by using a combination of RR and RNR packets. The REJ (reject) type is used to request the re-sending of one or more information packets.

The unnumbered (U) type packet provides basic link control and responses. An SABM packet is used to request or make a virtual circuit, and a DISC packet is used to disconnect a circuit. The UA type packet provides a positive response to these and other types of operations. The FRMR type is used to reject frames that have correct CRC at the physical level, but are incorrectly formatted.

Unformatted information (UI) type packets are used for special functions not necessarily associated with the virtual circuit. For example, the LAN/1 network monitor uses UI type packets to poll and receive statistics from remote NIU's

Most packets also have an attribute bit which indicates that the packet is being sent as a "command" or as a "response". For example, an I packet may be sent either as a command or as a response. In general, when a packet is sent as a command, a timer is also started. If a packet with a "response" bit set is not received before the timer times out, appropriate recovery action can be taken (re-transmit, abort, etc.)

NIU PAD SERVICES

The prime user interface is the PAD. The following are representative examples of some of the PAD characteristics. The PAD is responsible for all local and remote port configurations, establishing and breaking virtual circuits and viewing port statistics. Procedures similar to X.28 and X.29 were used where possible with additional parameters added to further enhance the NIU's utility. One added parameter was an echo filter that allows a user to set the NIU to local character echo and filter out any returned characters that are normally echoed from the remote end.

If the network is heavily loaded or if the remote end of the circuit is electrically seconds away such as a satellite, the user views the echoed characters immediately. For hosts that can not accept a constant throughput that equals the line data rate, a configurable intercharacter time can be programmed that effectively slows the character rate.

The NIU resides in the console mode (phone on-hook) when there is not virtual circuit or in the data mode when a virtual circuit has been established. The user can easily switch back and forth between these modes with the NIU responding with appropriate messages. The console messages can also be disabled if the NIU is connected to a host that can not process them properly. If console messages are disabled, the NIU will always remain in the data transparent mode.

"Drop DTR on disconnect" was added to the NIU to allow a complete disconnection of all devices attached to the virtual circuit. If a virtual circuit consists of the local NIU connected to a remote NIU that is then connected through long haul modems to another service, a virtual circuit disconnect initiated at the local NIU end will propagate through the entire network and result in the disconnection of both local area network and long haul link. Also, carrier detect can be programmed to be affected in the same manner.

Automatic port selection (port contention) can be programmed. A user wishing to connect to a central resource such as a mainframe database should be able to dial one port on the mainframe and if busy the NIU should automatically search for an inactive port and make the connection. Each port on an NIU can be programmed to enable port contention. Also, in some instances, port selection over more than eight ports is desired. The NIU can be programmed with a chaining address that provides this utility. Therefore, any number of ports can be selected by calling one global number or name. Port identifications follow a simple numeric format such as 45,2 (NIU node address 45, port 2) or can be named by using the name table facility. The name table consists of 20 locations that can be used to equate NIU numbers to logical names. The names are local to the NIU; thus users can assign unique names to network facilities or other user nodes. Thus instead of calling 45,2 the user calls "Bill".

All port configuration parameters are stored in battery backed up ram. With the exception of call, hang-up, data mode, and help, all parameters are password protected. Master and local passwords are maintained as an aid in system maintenance. The network monitor can enable a special password in each NIU to allow repairmen to access the local NIU port configuration information or "help the user remember his local password".

NETWORK MONITOR

Many local area networks today offer good performance in sending packets from node to node but lack reasonable means for displaying the health of the system. Network management personnel are demanding automated systems of performance measurement that are very user friendly and require little operator training. The network monitor should be able to isolate existing system problems, but it also should play a key role in preventative maintenance. The LAN/1 network monitor, although not required for system operation, is a key element of a well managed local area network.

Two major pieces of hardware are required for the NMU (1) a two port NIU and (2) an IBM XT computer. The NIU used for the monitor is identical to any other NIU in the network except it is addressed as node 1. Connection is made to the XT over an RS232 cable connected to port 1 of the NIU. Over this cable flows broadcast packets from the NMU to all remote NIU's. Also sequenced packets from each remote NIU are received and stored in memory. These returned packets represent current status of a number of parameters stored in each NIU. Status packets received from remote NIU's contain information such as:

- Destination node and port number of active virtual circuit
- Number of reconfigurations
- Number of buffer overflows
- Token wait time
- Max token wait time
- Number of ports in NIU
- Number of packets sent/received
- Number of information packets sent/received
- Number of transmit retries
- Address of responding NIU

A number of the above statistics is kept individually per port. The collected information is then written to a data file from which the user can specify a number of viewing options.

The IBM XT computer was fitted with a multitasking operating system - Concurrent CPM-86. Four virtual consoles are available to allow for multiple display viewing. The prime data collection task (DCT) operates independently from display tasks. Console 0 is used primarily for initializing, stopping and starting the DCT and configuring data logging parameters. Optionally, with the DCT halted, (1)individual NIU's can be disabled or enabled (2)scan cycle times can be changed (3) selective NIU's can be interrogated for parameters such as port configuration tables or (4) the XT can be made to function as a dumb terminal.

Collected data is then displayed using virtual console 1 that allows viewing of (1) reconfiguration table (2) virtual circuits (3) token wait times and (4) individual NIU statistics. The data display task (DDT) formats the data and displays the information in graphical form. The reconfiguration table indicates all active NIU's in the system plus the number of reconfigurations each NIU has noted. With the virtual circuit display, the network manager can view connection activity including destination address, number of packets(info or token) sent or received. As an aid in monitoring system delays, token wait times are viewed either numerically or graphically. If network management personnel are interested in the health of an individual node, a display is provided that gives him all the information viewed in the other displays.

Preventative maintenance on a network can be very difficult if statistical information is not accumulated and reviewed periodically. A data logging task (DLT) and a powerful database management package was added to the NMU in console 3 for this purpose. Each scan of the DCT places all NIU packets on the XT's hard disk with a date and time stamp. The database management (DBM) package can then access these records and perform a variety of functions. The DBM can sort, select, merge, concatenate and report any data contained in the NMU's database. Also, a menu generator is included that allows individualized reports of such things as network usage, packet latency, department billing, MTTR, trend analysis, etc.

Remote operation of the NMU is allowed through the use of a second serial port on the XT. When connected to a Bell type 1200 baud modem, the information contained in the NMU is available to any remote location. If the line is connected to port 2 of the attached NIU, anyone on the network (through a password structure) can also have access. The distributed monitoring function that this provides it very useful for maintenance personnel that are very seldom in one place permanently.

Concord Data Systems Token/Net

Introduction

Concord Data Systems, Inc. was founded in 1981 to design, manufacture, and market high technology data communications equipment—specifically a new local area network (LAN) system, Token/Net, which is based on the IEEE 802.4 token-passing access method and implemented on broadband CATV cable. Because of the time and cost of taking a concept of this sophistication from the drawing board to the marketplace, Concord Data first developed a "bread and butter" product line to sustain the company. Thus, Concord Data built a strong financial base through the development and sale of modem products. The revenue generated while developing the LAN product ensured the company was on a sound financial footing to introduce Token/Net.

Token/Net was formally introduced at the March 1983 Interface show. It is the first system in the industry to fully comply with the IEEE (The Institute of Electrical and Electronics Engineers, Inc.) Committee's 802.4 Standard for token passing on broadband cable. Token/Net is designed to provide high-speed, real-time, simultaneous, collision-free communications between computers and other digital devices in large management information/data processing, office automation, engineering, and factory applications.

Token/Net provides users with highly reliable, flow-controlled data transportation services, coupled with sophisticated switching and connection services, implemented in a fully modular distributed fashion. While the Token/Net System could operate on either baseband or CATV-compatible broadband cable systems, it is oriented toward CATV sytems in order to achieve the extended distances and bandwidth required for larger facilities.

One of the benefits of the token passing access method is the ability to prioritize user data awaiting access to the medium. Four levels of priority are available to be assigned to each data port. The highest priority frames are transmitted whenever a node holding them gets the token. Other classes have individual performance target times which allow those frames to be sent based upon a measurement of network congestion. This means of load-controlled shedding is an important benefit in many time-critical applications.

Token/Net operates at a data rate of 5 Mbps over cable distances of up to 20 miles. It is designed to work in a mid-split CATV single cable system, where the two-way directionality of the cable system is achieved with a headend remodulator.

Its major differences compared to other local area network offerings are full IEEE 802 and ECMA compatibility, token-passing access methods, and operations on CATV broadband cable.

Hardware

The basic hardware in the Token/Net system is the Token/Net Interface Module (TIM). The TIM connects to the broadband cable which serves as the broadcast media to all other TIMs on the network. Each TIM contains all the necessary hardware and software to allow network managers to implement a variety of flexible, controllable, and easily understood network functions according to user need and sophistication.

Within each TIM is a high-speed radio frequency (RF) modem, a TIM access controller board, a TIM control unit, and a power supply assembly as shown in the Figure. These elements provide network access, control, management, and diagnostic functions, as well as a wide variety of network enhancement functions. These include mnemonics known as "name services" which allow users to call various network addresses in a more user-friendly fashion than numerical addresses, queuing, and restricted services.

Each Token/Net TIM supports both synchronous and asynchronous RS-232C/V.24 serial interfaces at speeds from 75 to 19,200 bps. It also supports RS-449, 422 at speeds up to 230.4 Kbps. There are a variety of connection options, including permanent or switched, point-to-point, multipoint, or broadcast (multicast), to connect data terminal equipment (DTE) ports. Current TIM models include the TIM 200 a 3-slot, non-expandable, 4-port unit, and the TIM 220, a 5-slot, field-expandable, from 2-to-10-port unit. Both support RS-232 and RS-449 at the above speeds. Future TIM models are expected to include additional port interfaces.

RF Modem: The TIM RF modem is designed to the specifications of the IEEE 802 duo-binary AM-PSK modulations standard. It is frequency agile over six IEEE 802 recommended 6 MHz CATV channels, and operates at 5 Mbps. Specifically, the modem can operate over any of the following channels pairs:

Transmit		Receive	
Name	**Freq (MHz)**	**Name**	**Freq (MHz)**
3'	59.75 - 65.75	P	252 - 258
4'	65.75 - 71.75	Q	258 - 264
4a'	71.73 - 77.75	R	264 - 270
5'	77.75 - 83.75	S	270 - 276
6'	83.75 - 89.75	T	276 - 282
FM1	89.75 - 95.75	U	282 - 288

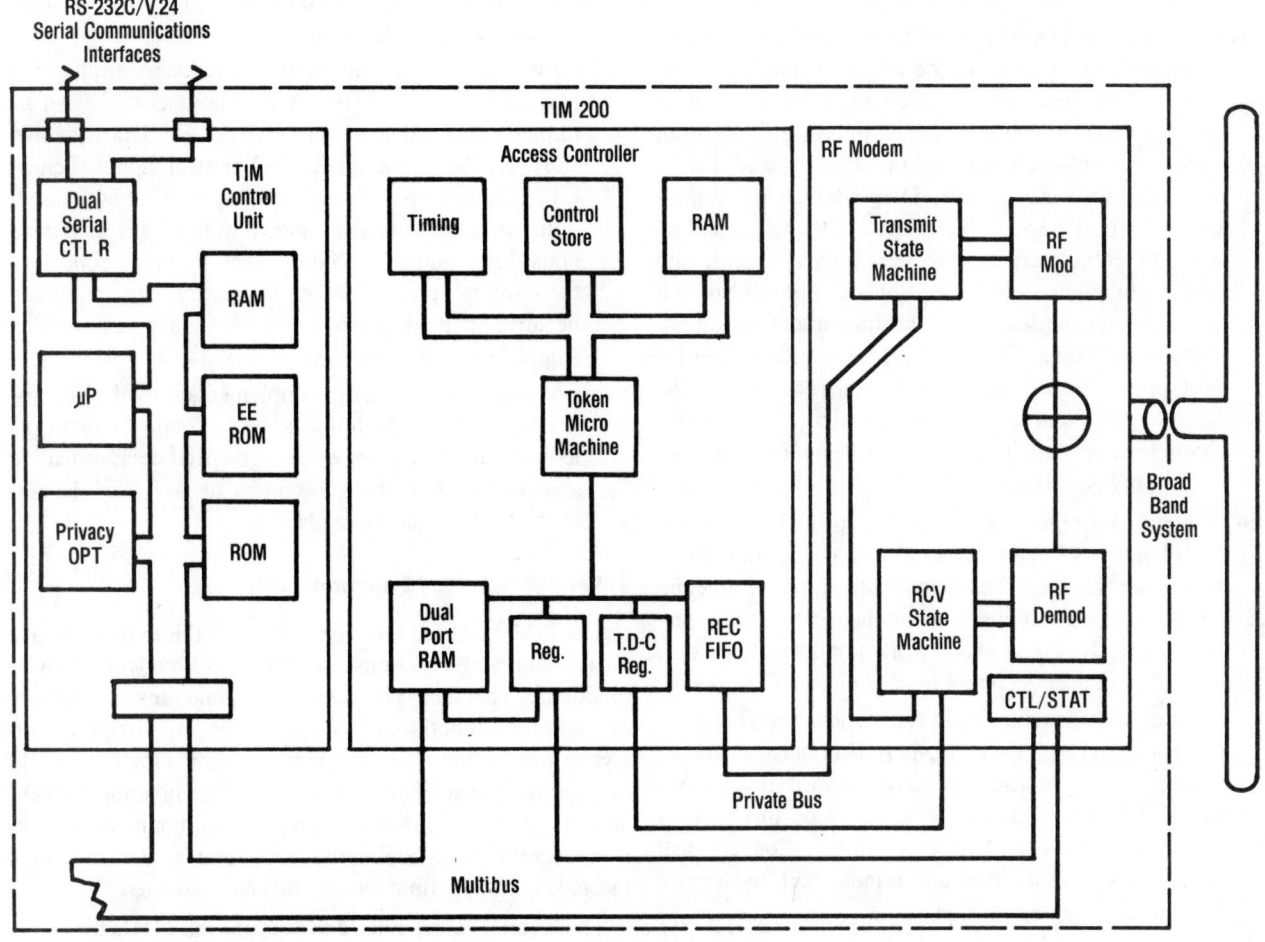

Figure: TIM Block Diagram

Out-of-band transmissions are strictly controlled so that adjacent channel operation is possible. Since the token-passing access method, under normal conditions, does not cause signal "collisions" (as in CSMA/CD systems), intermodulation products which may affect the quality of other CATV services on the cable are eliminated.

The modem transmitter is designed to operate in a switched carrier mode, where the transmitter is under control of the access unit. In essence, the modem transmitter is only enabled when the TIM has received the token.

The modem receiver can operate in two modes: a constant carrier mode with a remodulator headend, or a switched carrier mode with a frequency translator headend. The Concord Data RF modem provides several powerful functions that ensure maximum system reliability. A sophisticated modem self-check, controllable via software, for example, provides a loopback at the RF connector that verifies virtually every active component in the modem. Anti-jabber circuitry forces the modem transmitter off if any transmission exceeds a specified time value.

- *Access Controller*: The TIM's access controller board implements the IEEE 802 specified Token Passing Access control method, which provides high throughput and stable operation under all network loads. The access unit constantly monitors receive signals from the modem. It watches the media for proper token operation and listens for data packets addressed to itself as well as for broadcast addresses it has been configured to receive. It checks to determine that all receive messages pass a 32-bit frame check sequence, and it passes good frames to the control unit via shared memory queues. When the access controller receives the token, it automatically forms transmit packets from the appropriate priority transmit queues. If no data is ready for transmission, it immediately passes the token to the next TIM on the network. Each access controller uses a distributed algorithm to detect and resolve network faults, ensuring that there is no central point of failure on the network. Diagnostics include start-up tests, firmware checks, and the ability to loop test packets through a modem check loopback.

- *Control Unit*: The control unit provides TIM management functions as well as the first user interface ports (the first of these ports can alternatively serve as a console port). It also provides an interface to the front panel, non-volatile configuration memory, and a wide variety of software services. On power-up, the control unit tests the TIM and solicits entry to the token polling list. The entire start-up process is fully automatic and takes only a few seconds to complete. The control unit also provides the session establishment and packet addressing functions for its own serial interfaces and for port option boards within the same base unit. The console port process provides local control of configuration memory and local diagnostic testing. It can connect to any ASCII terminal.

- *Network Management*: Token/Net provides sophisticated network maintenance functions. Among these functions are local and remote diagnostics, integral signal level measurement, name management utilities, network statistic utilities, network monitoring facilities, and network access control management.

  Integral software diagnostic tools allow test frames to be sent from one TIM to another. This function can be invoked remotely from a properly authorized user. Accurate delivery statistics are gathered on this process and can detect even periodic failures. Conventional diagnostics such as local and remote port and device loopbacks are also available.

  Real time performance statistics of the system are available from each TIM. Network attributes, such as current token rotation rate and stations in the ring, can give an accurate sense of network loading and the number of TIMs participating in the system.

  Higher level performance measurements are also available. These include counts of transmitted packets per port, received packets per port, re-transmission rates, and queue overflows and underruns.

- *Options*: Additional optional port boards include a quad serial port (which can interface with up to four data terminals, in either synchronous or asynchronous modes) and a high speed serial port (with a RS-449, 422 high speed serial interface).

  When configured for ASCII asynchronous operation, the user has the capability to alter his/her port's configuration parameters via an X.28 like command structure. These parameters control various port functions such as echo on/off, line feed-carriage return padding, procedures on break, etc. In addition, session set-up and addressing information can be entered directly from the terminal's keyboard. This allows the user to, in es-

sence, dial the desired connection via direct network address, a name, or a rotary.

Flow control is a configurable parameter on all serial ports. Flow control for asynchronous devices can be implemented either via an XON/XOFF data signaling (for ASCII), or via an RS-232 control signal such as CTS. If configured, flow control operates in both directions, in other words, to and from the DTE. Synchronous flow control is accomplished by clock control to the terminal devices. When so configured, timing can be advanced or retarded as necessary, as well as stopped entirely if congestion persists.

Concord Data System's implementation of synchronous flow control techniques, when coupled with priority mechanisms, allow even high-speed delay-sensitive synchronous devices to communicate with minimal network delay on the Token/Net.

Token/Net Layered Functions

The TIM's layered functions are divided into two primary areas: data port functions and local area network (LAN) functions. The data port and LAN functions are further divided into functional "layers." This organization into layers allows one to implement complex functions while keeping them conceptually separable. The functional layers define logical, and in some cases physical, boundaries. Data flows across these boundaries according to defined interfaces, keeping the functions in the layers isolated.

The layering concept used to describe the TIM's functions is similar to the International Standards Organization Open Systems Interconnection Reference Model (ISO OSI-RM), and is compatible with the General Motors Manufacturing Automation Protocol (MAP). Equivalent layers are given the same names. The Figure details the layers in a TIM. OSI-RM layers, which are omitted from the Figure, are null layers in the TIM implementation.

- *Port Interface Layer*: The port layers implement the interface between the user's equipment and the TIM. Since the layer decomposition of all types of ports are not the same, the layering structures are described in the individual port functional specifications. Generally, the ISO layering, or some subset thereof, is used.

- *Port Application Layer*: The port application layer serves to interface the user port to the network. It provides the port with both data and control interfaces to the LAN layers, and provides some necessary port-related support services to the LAN as a whole.

  The port application layer provides any port specific command functions. For example, a port configuration and session control command language is specified for

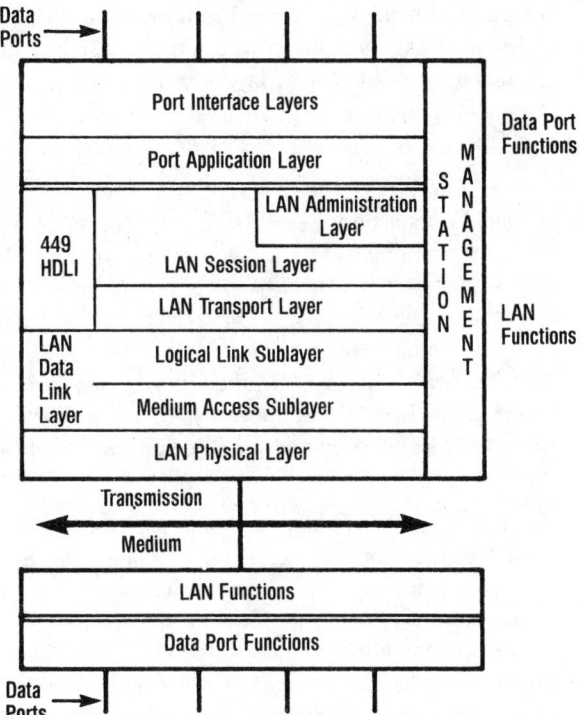

Figure: TIM Logical Block Diagram

ASCII serial ports. The application layer transforms ASCII serial commands to control information to be passed to the LAN session layer. The application layer also implements any necessary interfaces to TIM administrative processes.

A high-speed serial or other type port, on the other hand, implements a different command language or none at all. The command language is oriented toward a tightly coupled machine interface. The port application layer masks differences between ports from the LAN layers.

Data flow is controlled by the application layer. Buffers are allocated and passed between the application layer and the LAN session layer. Data blocks from the port interface layers are formatted as necessary for this interface.

The HDLI function, as shown in the Figure, is a special purpose, high-performance interface into the LLC layer. It is optionally provided for applications where external computer equipment already implements some of the higher layer network functions. This arrangement allows the TIM to become, in essence, a local area network communications "frontend" to the attached processor.

- *LAN Administrative Layer*: The LAN administrative layer is the collection of TIM and network administra-

tive functions. It is not concerned with passing data, but rather with control of the TIM hardware and software. Its functions include the following:

1. *TIM Administrative Control*: Initialization and startup of hardware and software.

2. *Station control and management functions*: These include the ability to access and reset system counters, control paths, and other mechanisms for station service and diagnostics.

3. *Statistics Collection*: Maintain event counters, handle counter read requests, and perform error logging operations.

4. *Network Configuration*: Implement a slave configuration process to service configuration information requests.

5. *TIM Configuration and Maintenance*: Implement maintenance console primitives and provide both local and remote console interfaces.

- *LAN Session Layer*: The LAN session layer is concerned primarily with the establishment and termination of data flow paths between higher level entities using the local area network. Within a TIM, each such data flow path is represented by an addressable service access point of the session layer.

To establish a session, all of the end-points of the session have to be identified, and suitable state information must be created at each end-point such that data presented by other TIM functional layers to that end-point can be sent across the LAN and delivered to the other end-point(s) of the session.

Different types of TIM-to-TIM communication service are available for Token/Net sessions, and for some of them, negotiation of the service attributes occurs during session establishment. Once a session has been established, each end-point may send data to the other end-point(s) by presenting that data to the LAN session layer, which, in turn, passes it on to the LAN transport layer.

The session layer also provides accounting and statistical information to special processes in the TIM. These processes are generally linked to a central process in the Network Management Processor for centralized accumulation and reporting of such data.

- *LAN Transport Layer*: In establishing a session, the transport layer sets up any necessary local state and, in certain cases, establishes a transport connection with the other end-point of the session.

Once the session is established, the port application layer passes data through the LAN session layer to the LAN transport layer; this takes the form of messages to be sent via a specific network address specified by the local LAN session layer. The source and destination transport layers then cooperate to convey the information across the LAN or interconnected set of LANs by using the lower-layer data link services. The receiving transport layer passes the messages through its local session layer to the higher-level entity connected to the particular Address.

The transport layer uses the buffering allocated by the application layer for messages to be sent and received on the LAN by the data link layer. The transport layer offers two types of data transfer service: virtual circuit and datagram. Token/Net's transport layer is compatible with the ISO and ECMA transport specifications.

- *LAN Data Link Layer*: The LAN data link is divided, according to IEEE 802 recommendations, into two sublayers. The higher sublayer is the logical link control sublayer which is common to all IEEE 802 specified access techniques. The lower sublayer is the media access sublayer which performs, in the case of Token/Net, the token-passing access control.

- *Logical Link Control Sublayer*: The logical link control sublayer takes messages from the transport layer, adds a standard LLC prefix, and queues the messages for the medium access sublayer. The logical link sublayer provides only datagram transmission service. On message reception, it takes properly error-checked frames from the media access sublayer and routes them to the appropriate higher-layer transport, HDLI, or station management entity. It also provides a software broadcast message filtering facility. The LLC sublayer provides loopback and other diagnostic services as well.

- *LAN Media Access Layer*: The media access sublayer controls the TIM's receiver and transmitter. Media access monitors the medium (channels on the cable) for messages addressed to the TIM. If a data message is heard addressed to the TIM, the check sequence is tested; if correct, the message is passed to the LAN logical link Level. (For messages addressed to the TIM which the TIM originated, this action occurs only in a logical sense).

Media Access controls the TIM's transmitter. The media access layers of all TIMs in the network cooperate so only one TIM is transmitting at a time. The right to transmit is passed from one TIM to another by sending special non-data messages (tokens) on the network. These messages are sent and processed totally within this sublayer.

- *LAN Physical Layer*: The LAN physical layer is concerned with the data transmission rate, modulation method, transmission and reception frequencies, and other physical signaling considerations. As such, it is mainly a hardware-related layer.

System Operation

- *Connection Services*: The TIM offers the network user a variety of connection services, i.e., the mechanisms to set up communication paths to another location. The types of connections may be either permanent circuits, switched virtual circuits, or multi-cast circuits. Permanent and multi-cast circuits are typically static, and usually pre-configured by the system manager. No overt action needs to be taken by the network user to initiate this kind of service. The connection is always available.

Switched virtual circuits allow the user the ability to switch connections on a session-by-session basis. Since the remote devices in different sessions are sometimes of different types, capabilities, or characteristics, the network user additionally needs the ability to adjust the session parameters based upon whatever the new session requires. An example of a session specific characteristic is flow control. Some network connections may provide their own flow control, while other devices must rely on the Token/Net for proper flow control. The network user is provided with a very simple command interface to allow easy setting of specific session parameters. Among these characteristics are: flow control, line feed padding, echo, and sequence on break.

- *Name Services*: Switched virtual circuits provide a capability to address the remote resource by either physical network address or via a name. Name services are used to assign a particular resource a widely known and easily remembered mnemonic. Names can also be assigned to a pool of resources, such as computers or computer ports. Names are only restricted to 12 ASCII characters in length, where the first character must be a non-numeric value.

Token/Net uses a sophisticated session arbitration routine which allows different types of ports to be assigned to the same name. Calling ports are assigned, according to their characteristics, to the closest available port in the name group. This process occurs on every switched virtual circuit session establishment.

Conclusions

Token/Net is the first system in the industry to fully comply with the IEEE 802.4 Standard for token passing on broadband cable. Other distinguishing characteristics include a 230.4 Kbps interface, pseudo-multi-point service, transparent synchronous, and the ability to handle any synchronous RS-232/RS-449 interface. Token/Net is designed to provide high-speed, real-time, simultaneous, collision-free communications between computers and other digital devices in large management information/data processing, office automation, engineering, and factory applications.

Inside Wang's local net architecture

Mark Stahlman, Wang Laboratories Inc., Lowell, Mass.

Wangnet uses a broadband technique based on a dual-cable, branching-tree topology to provide multiple services.

Local-networking concepts and technologies are not new. What is new is putting these technologies to work in addressing the overall needs in today's office environment. In taking this step, local networking takes on a product life of its own, independent of the specific applications or devices that use the network. From Wang's point of view this meant going back to the drawing board and examining the requirements for information interchange in the office.

As a result of this basic re-examination, Wangnet has been designed to meet two principle objectives: it must be able to handle the diverse forms of information in the office environment and it must handle these forms simultaneously. Broadband was chosen as the technology that satisfies these objectives.

There are a number of reasons for that choice. First, data in the office is by necessity highly diverse in form. This diversity is typically indicated listing key office automation technologies—word processing, data processing, audio processing, and image processing. People communicate through words, numbers, speech, and visual images. In the design review that preceded the decisions to build Wangnet, the expressed needs of a wide cross section of office automation users were weighted. This survey emphasized the present and future requirements for video and related image technologies, including graphics. A broadband design uniquely permits this wide variety of information forms.

Another dimension of this diversity is reflected by the proliferation of devices and their associated communications protocols in today's office. This protocol diversity is based not only in history but in utility. As any communications design engineer will say, there are significant performance and cost tradeoffs in matching protocols to their applications, and small details can make a large difference. For any office-automation user who wishes to install functionally integrated networks and true multifunction workstations, the market today offers powerful solutions. But any network that only supports one vendors' equipment is by its nature limited. The choice is not limited to functional integration or transmission integration because broadband designs allow for both.

Second, the flow of information in its many forms is simultaneous. Consider that protocols refer to the time domain; or, in other words, a specific protocol will typically employ a time-division multiplexing scheme to permit many devices to share a communications channel. The simultaneous character of information flow in the office cannot be practically solved by an extremely fast, very sophisticated time-division scheme. The traditional solution to this problem could be called the space-division multiplexing approach—a separate wire for each device or channel. Broadband solves this problem by replacing this jungle of cables and wires with a single medium. Unlike baseband networks, which are inherently limited to a single channel and therefore a single protocol, broadband employs one of the oldest communications techniques, frequency-division multiplexing (FDM).

Examples of frequency-division multiplexing to achieve multiple channels are very common, and it is

1. Standard. *Wangnet is designed around industry-standard protocol specifications using a packet format. The company plans to follow the Open Systems Interconnection model as the basis for its future software releases in the communications arena. Fully configured Wangnets are currently installed in a number of beta test sites.*

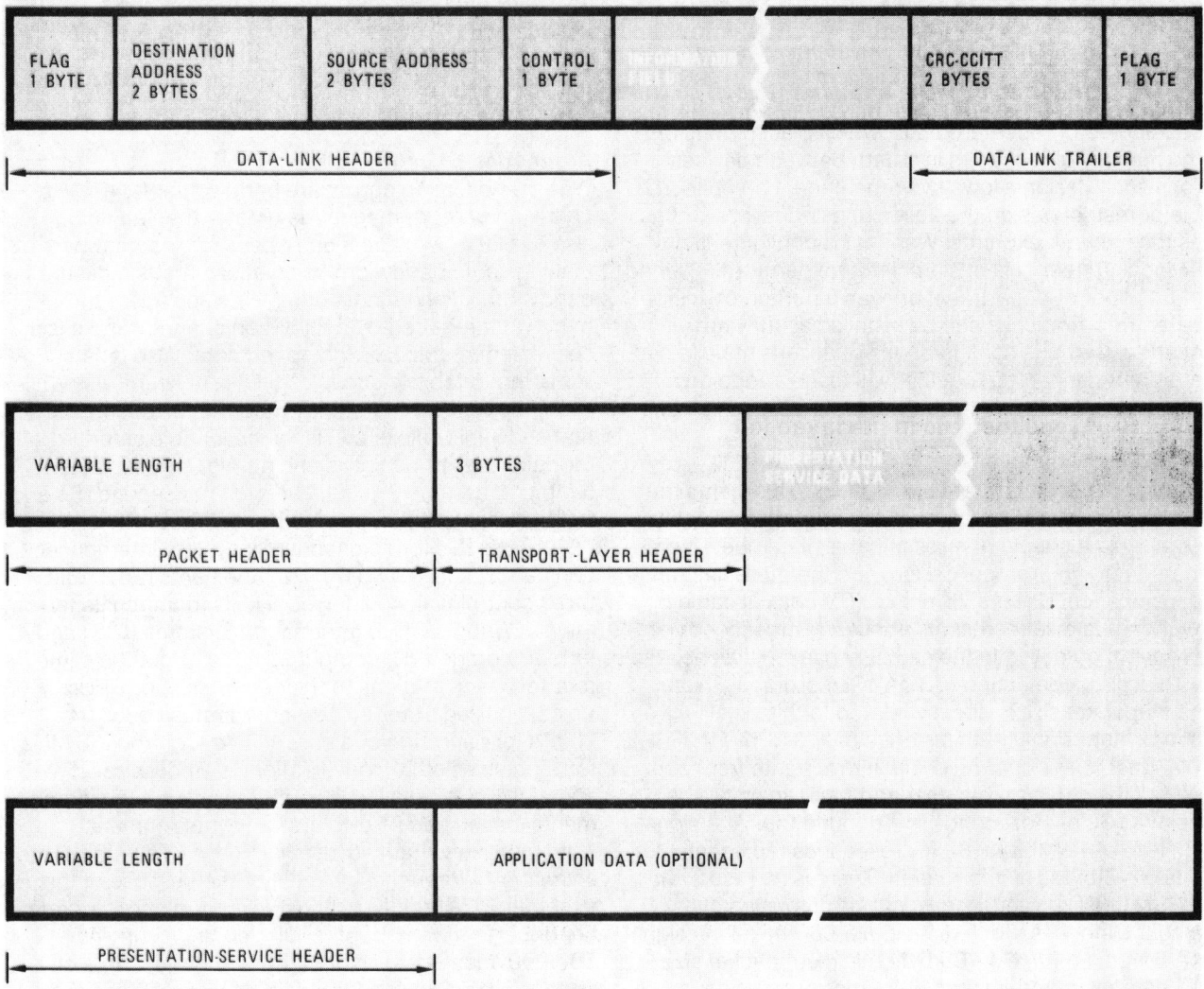

the development of frequency-division equipment on a large scale by the cable-TV industry that makes broadband particularly attractive. With more than 20 percent of United States households wired for cable today, significant economies of scale have been realized by cable and component manufacturers. Semiconductor makers have made a contribution to reducing parts' cost for radio frequency (RF) devices. Integrated circuits—many designed for television or radio—are being used extensively in modern RF modems. These modems are an important factor in the price per network connection for broadband networks. Contrary to the claim that broadband is more expensive on this account, at a price of $250 to $600 per user, the price per connection for broadband is currently below that for baseband networks.

When compared with the normally expected reliability of computer equipment, the use of CATV technology also brings with it higher reliability. Mean-time-between-failure figures in excess of 20 years are common

for active components, and these typically refer to an outside plant installation considerably more hostile than the average office. The single most commonly cited cause of CATV failures is lightning strikes.

Outlet cost

Another advantage afforded by the use of CATV technology is the cost effectiveness of the true network outlet. It is attractive for information users to consider cabling an entire office complex with such outlets. The ongoing need to move equipment, as well as people, when added to the continuing introduction of new equipment can produce significant rewiring costs and intolerable delays. In order for this widely popularized network outlet notion to become a reality a few simple requirements must be met. The network outlet must have an installed cost that is about equal to the cost of wiring a facility for electrical power. Also, the outlet has to be there when and where its needed, without any need to get a building crew to rewire an office.

Finally, a network outlet has to be inexpensive enough to be left on the wall, unused, without worrying about underutilized capital.

Distance and topological restrictions often play havoc with plans to introduce local networks into offices. It is generally considered that bus topologies are superior to star or ring (often folded into a star-like pattern) arrangements. But all buses are not created equal. A segmented or repeatered bus, which places limits on the number of repeaters in a path between devices (one such design allows two repeaters), can put some major restrictions on the ability to grow new branches as the network expands. Wangnet is configured as a branching tree. This bus architecture permits the wiring of one floor or department or even a portion of a floor. Later, new branches can be installed as they are needed. Campus configurations of dozens of buildings are often connected together with such a topology. It is certainly cost effective, however, to begin small and expand as needed.

Inasmuch as Wangnet is a local network, it like any such network has distance limitations. This stems from two root causes. One cause is the propagation delay. Over even a couple of miles of cable, it can be a significant factor in protocol design, and therefore network performance. Using a 75-ohm CATV coaxial cable in Wangnet, a mile represents about 8 microseconds of propagation delay. In the carrier sense multiple access with collision detection (CSMA/CD) protocol, the minimum packet size is directly related to this delay. Given a maximum signal path distance of two miles for Wangnet, any signal which must propagate from one end of the cable to the other and back again will be delayed 32 microseconds in the round trip. At a signaling rate of 12 Mbit/s, 32 microseconds represents 384 bits or 48 bytes of information. There is no reason why a CSMA/CD protocol could not be employed over longer distances. For example, a 2,000-mile-long signal path would require a 48-kbyte minimum packet size. To demonstrate this more dramatically, consider a satellite in orbit 22,300 miles above the equator. For a round trip propagation delay of 540 milliseconds, CSMA/CD would require an 810-kbyte minimum packet size at a signaling rate of 12 Mbit/s.

The other source for distance limitations on local networks could generally be called signal quality. Broadband networks use amplifiers and baseband systems use repeaters, but the purpose of both is to extend the distance that a signal can be transmitted. It is a fact of transmission engineering that cables attenuate and distort signals. Moreover, these effects are not the same at all frequencies. In addition, noise from a variety of sources is also a constant concern. As a point of comparison, the probability of a bit being received in error is 1 out of every 1,000 for a dial-up telephone line, and 1 out of 100,000 for a conditioned leased line. Local-area networks are typically designed for errors rates in the range from 1 out of 100 million to 1 billion. Some interesting results emerge as signal quality declines. In general, video signals will visibly suffer first, with audio signals worsening next, and data signals being seriously affected only under considerably poorer conditions. The most sensitive of these, video, is routinely transmitted over tens of miles of metropolitan CATV networks.

The structure of the branching-tree topology is actually a Siamese twin of two parallel cables. Each is amplified in one direction only, so that one becomes the transmit and one becomes the receive cable. The cables are joined in a simple loop at the base of the tree.

A question of bandwidth

Wangnet offers an aggregate bandwidth of 340 MHz. This is an order of magnitude greater than anything else available. Why so much? Let's answer that by making some bandwidth calculations. Let's measure bandwidth in increments of 6 MHz since this is the bandwidth required by a television channel, and it is a convenient metric for high-speed data. Also let's assume that 5 Mbit/s occupies 6 MHz of spectrum. While all RF modems don't employ modulation techniques that show this efficiency, it is a reasonable standard for data rates at 5 Mbit/s and above. At rates below 5 Mbit/s, assume 2 Hz for every bit per second. So a 9.6-kbit/s modem might use about 20 kHz.

A 10- to 12-Mbit/s channel for system interconnection needs at least two 6-MHz increments. Each IBM 3270 control unit would need 6 MHz to attach its terminals. Wang's Office Information Systems (OIS) and Virtual Storage (VS) computers need about the same to attach workstations to their controllers or CPUs. Voice digitized at today's standard rates needs 64 kbit/s for each side of a conversation, or about 6 MHz for both sides of 24 conversations. A thousand slow-speed full-duplex devices might take six 6-MHz increments if each had its own frequency assignment.

It's not likely that two installations will have the same inventory of frequency needs. For the purpose of this example, let's take a perhaps not so typical corporate headquarters with about 3,500 people occupying 500,000 square feet of office space. Projecting a bit into the future we can foresee a density of office automation equipment that averages one device per 200 square feet, or approximately 2,500 devices. Let's assume that 1,000 of these are slow speed synchronous or asynchronous terminals (printers, etc). The other 1,500 of them are intelligent Wang workstations, IBM 3270s, or similiar equipment connected over the network to approximately 75 controllers. These in turn are connected to each other over a local channel. We need six television channels for video conferencing and other applications, and a distributed PBX uses sixteen TI-speed (1.544-Mbit/s) carrier links over the network. This adds up to approximately 97 pieces of 6-MHz bandwidth or more than even a full Wangnet could handle.

At this time it is appropriate to introduce a notion that addresses the problem posed by the numbers game above: hierarchical spectrum allocation. Just as any corporation is organized into smaller units—be they divisions, departments, and the like—a local-area networks can be divided into public and private frequency spectrums. In the example above, 75 of the 6-MHz increments were used for connecting worksta-

2. Wang Band. *Intended for connecting Wang products, Wang Band can facilitate Wang's Mailway service—an electronic-message distribution system for VS, OIS, and Wang 2200 systems. Other Wang Band applications include remote data processing for the VS systems, document editing on the OIS offering, and file transfers.*

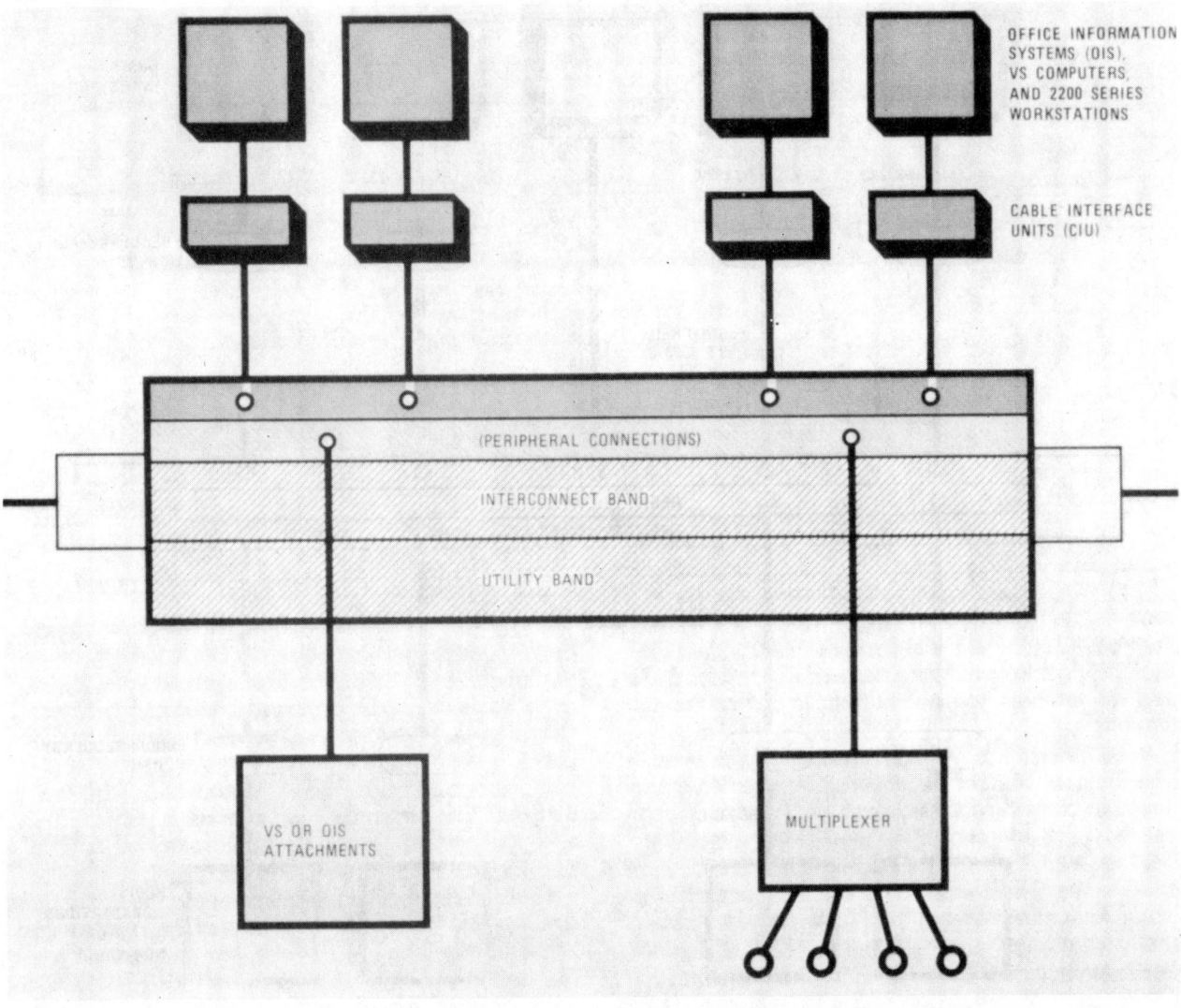

tions to their controllers or CPUs. In general, these controllers will be distributed at the departmental or divisional level and there is no reason to use a corporatewide public spectrum for what is clearly a private data requirement of a particular part of the organization. On the other hand, interconnection of these systems' controllers or CPUs, video conferencing, PBX functions, and mainframe-based terminal attachment will likely need to exist in the public-frequency spectrum because their use crosses departmental boundaries.

Since there is one public and many private spectrums, the total network capacity can be expanded almost indefinitely. Medium- to large-scale Wangnets will support 300 to 400 increments of 6 MHz when they are fully grown.

Service approach
Wangnet, as a broadband local network, consists of not one but a number of communications services.

These services are grouped into the Wang Band, the Interconnect Band, the Utility Band, and the Peripheral Attachment service. A good deal of the available frequency spectrum has been reserved for the future introduction of additional services.

The Wang Band—a 12-Mbit/s channel for the interconnection of systems—employs a CSMA/CD protocol to control contention and uses a variable length HDLC-derived packet format (see Fig. 1). Up to 16,384 devices can be attached to the Wang Band. A Cable Interface Unit (CIU) connects systems to the communications channel, as shown in Figure 2. The CIU is a generalized network processor built around the ISO's Open Systems Interconnection Reference Model concept. Wang's implementation of the lower five layers execute in the CIU. This allows the CIU to be used without change with each of the three otherwise quite distinct Wang systems, the OIS, the VS, and the 2200 product lines. The CIU also assumes the responsibility for extensive network diagnostic and network admin-

3. Interconnect Band. *The Peripheral Service is not in itself a band, but rather a means of hooking peripherals to larger systems on the network. The Interconnect Band is for Wang as well as non-Wang devices and dedicated and switched channels. Any protocol common to both sending and receiving units is allowed.*

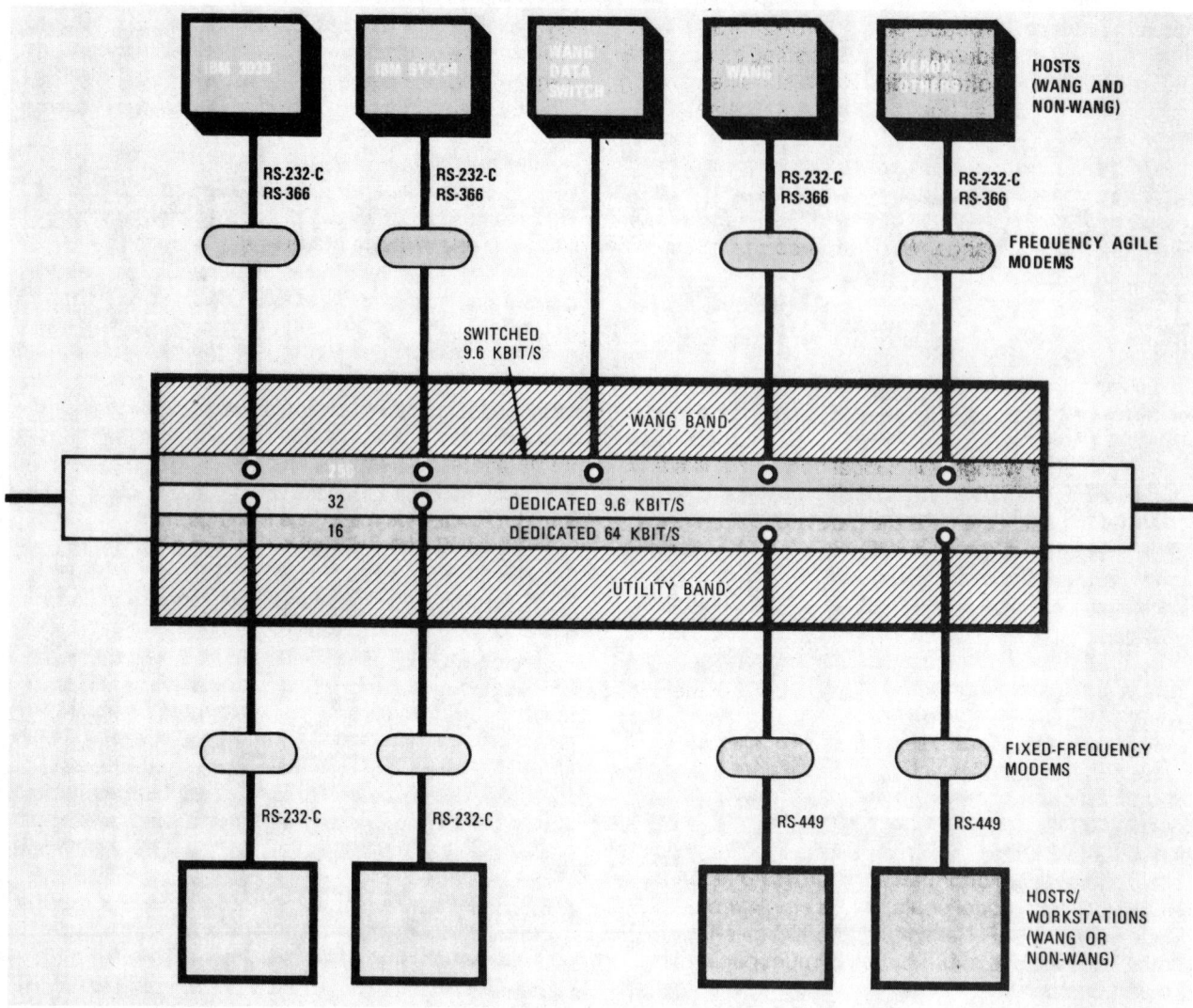

istrative functions.

The advantages of interconnecting between and among these systems families are considerable. While all of these product lines have already integrated word and data processing, they each have specific strengths and weaknesses. Particular applications, databases, interfaces, and peripherals can now be accessed from terminals attached to any of the systems. A multifunction workstation can now edit or even typeset documents at an OIS, run Cobol programs at a VS, or log-on through 3270 emulation to an IBM mainframe—all from the same workstation.

The CIU sells for $3,800. Since this is a system-level network interface, its cost is shared by all workstations attached to that system. Average configurations of VS or OIS systems might have 10 terminals, making the cost approximately $400 per user for each CIU network interface.

The Interconnect Band is divided into three separate services which are comparable to leased-line, wide-

band, and a special sort of circuit-switched channel. Each of these services are protocol independent, and therefore support equipment from virtually any manufacturer. As shown in Figure 3 the first service is made up of 32 dedicated full-duplex channels for handling data at speeds up to 9.6 kbit/s, sync or async, and point-to-point or multipoint. In the second, there are 16 channels with the same attributes but with maximum signaling rate of 64 kbit/s. The equipment to interface to these two sets of channels are known as fixed frequency modems (FFM). The 9.6 kbit/s FFM sells for $850, and the price of the 64 kbit/s FFM is $1,200.

In the third interconnect service, there are 256 switched channels operating at speeds up to 9.6 kbit/s, sync or async. The data stations for this portion of the Interconnect Band are known as frequency agile modems (FAM). The full FAM consists of a small enclosure and a desktop control unit. The enclosure has five data interfaces—two for the network (transmit and

4. Utility Band. *Each Utility Band channel is capable of handling one composite video-and-audio signal. The band has seven channels. Any approved cable-television head-end equipment is permitted. Interconnection is accomplished with the use of type F 75-ohm dual-captive manually terminated plug.*

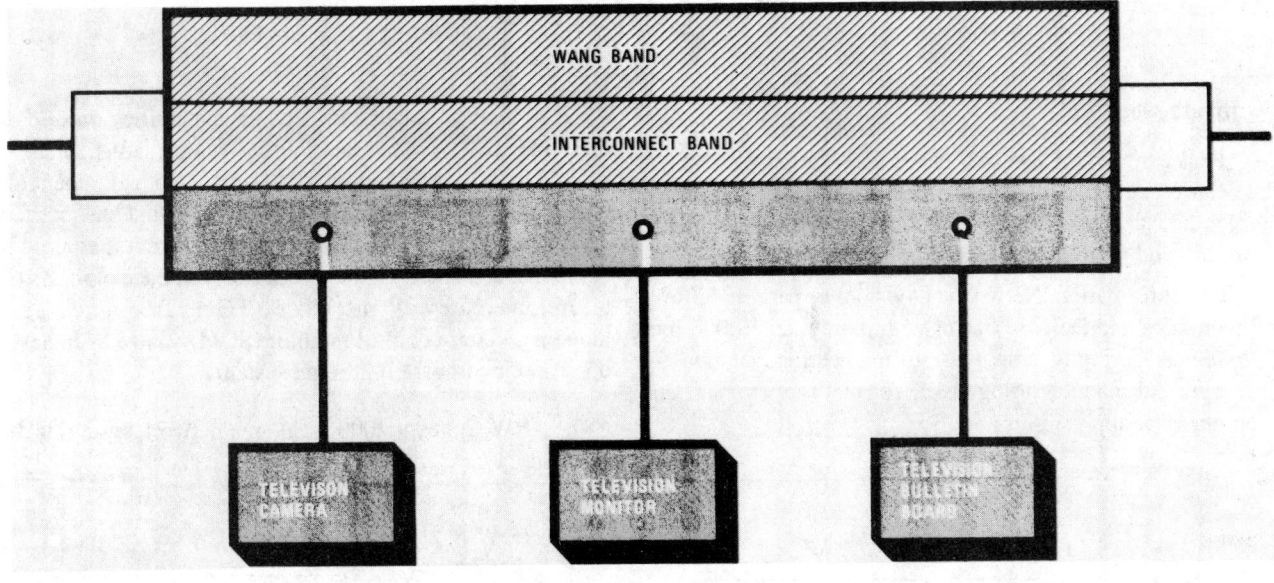

receive), an RS-232-C connector (DCE), an RS-366 connector (automatic dial), and an analog/data interface. The control unit has a numeric keypad for dialing and various indicators and buttons to control the data station.

In addition to the FAMs, a Dataswitch is required. This master controller continually polls the FAMs and keeps track of the status of each FAM and each channel. A typical operating cycle would look something like this: a FAM signals the Dataswitch over a control channel that it wishes to be connected across the network. After handshaking, the FAM tells the Dataswitch that it wants a connection to another FAM at number 2487, for instance. The FAM sends this data after either an operator has manually keyed it at the control unit or an attached DTE signals at the RS-366 interface. If this number is free or the start number of a hunt sequence, the Dataswitch will assign an unoccupied frequency to both FAMs and step out of the connection. At this time, data and control leads are connected between the two FAMs and the circuit looks like a long RS-232-C cable. Polling continues and the reverse process is invoked to disconnect a circuit. The FAM sells for $1,250, and the Dataswitch price is $12,000.

These Interconnect Band services can be used for Wang and non-Wang products alike. For instance, Wang 2200 terminals can attach to their CPUs over the Interconnect Band since they are interfaced using RS-232-C. A typical Interconnect Band configuration might have IBM remote 3270 control units multi-dropped using 9.6-kbit/s FFMs, two 3705 or similar units tied together at 56 kbit/s with the 64-kbit/s FFMs, and a hundred or more asynchronous terminals attached to a variety of minicomputers using the FAMs and a Dataswitch.

The Peripheral Attachment service is used to attach Wang OIS and VS workstations, printers, and other peripherals to their controllers or CPUs directly over Wangnet. Series 5300 and 5700 workstations for OIS or VS systems can be optioned to individually attach to Wangnet. Additionally, a four-port network multiplexer is available to attach printers and other workstations or peripherals. The workstation options sell for $600. The network multiplexer has a price of $1,050, which can give a cost of approximately $250 per workstation if all four ports are used.

Finally, Wangnet has a service called the Utility Band (see Fig. 4). This is a 42-MHz slice of the spectrum set aside for non-Wang RF devices. The frequencies correspond to VHF television channels 7 through 13. Video signals will often be carried by this band, but other RF devices that meet CATV power levels and frequency specifications can be used as well. While teleconferencing and video conferencing are best used across distances far beyond the reach of a local-area network, local distribution of video signals for this and other educational, security, or experimental purposes is growing in demand.

Office-automation vendors have long depended on local networking. Proprietary networks linking word processors and other intelligent devices are widespread in today's office. Over 20,000 such networks have been installed as the basis of Wang's OIS and VS products alone.

Wangnet is part of a new generation in local networks. Such networks are open to many vendors and multiple purposes. It is now practical to install network outlets to handle a range of information needs. Whether they are supporting an office complex or a handful of systems, such networks are the cornerstone of the future in office automation. ∎

TRW Concept 2000

Introduction

TRW, Inc. is a Cleveland-based corporation with annual sales exceeding $5 billion in electronics, defense, automative, industry, and energy. It has total assets of more than $3 billion, and more than 90,000 employees.

The Information Networks Division is part of TRW's Electronics and Defense Sector with more than 10,000 professionals currently employed in engineering, design, research, and manufacturing tasks, for both government and commercial applications.

TRW's initial local area network technology was developed in 1973-1974 for the Shuttle Avionics Bus. In 1978, using TRW research funds, TRW initiated development of a broadband local area network system. The first bus interface unit (BIU) was built in 1978. Since then, other product components—such as the processor interface unit (PIU), telephone gateway interface (TGI), frequency-agile modems, system control/monitor (SCM)—have been developed and incorporated into the system.

The TRW Concept 2000 local area network system is the

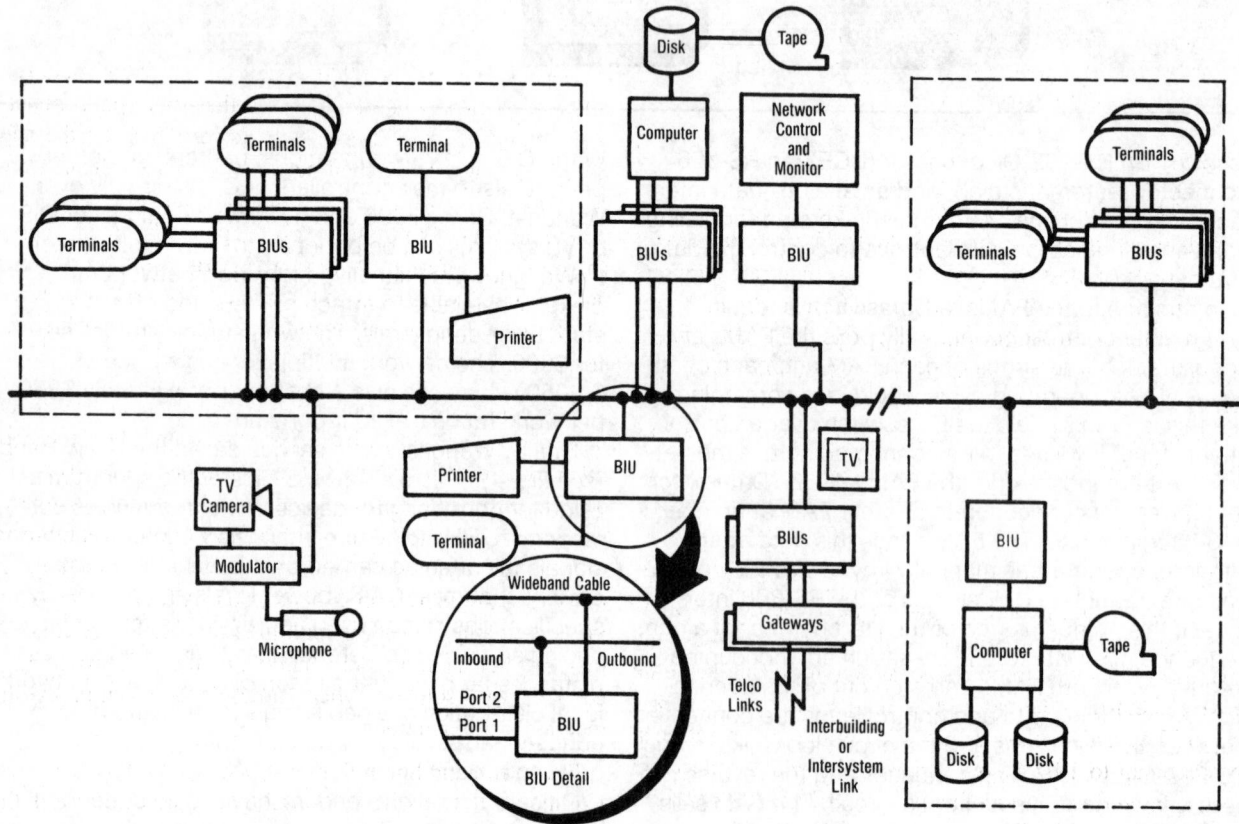

Figure: Typical TRW Dual Cable Concept 2000

commercial entry to the market via the newly formed information networks division. Several thousand BIUs have been installed at commercial sites such as the Cleveland Clinic Medical Foundation in Cleveland, Alcoa Technical Center in Pennsylvania, and Eaton Corporate Headquarters in Cleveland, as well as in government agencies.

System Overview

The TRW Concept 2000 is a family of local area network products that support high capacity information carrying intrafacilities communication system. The TRW Concept 2000 is comprised of three types of products:

- A cable plant, consisting of single or dual coaxial cable, and fiber optic cable.

- Interface units that connect user devices, such as terminals, computers, word processors, video equipment, voice devices, and other networks, at various levels of user protocol, to the cable plant.

- Network support and management tools such as the network status monitoring and control capabilities, network accounting and resource servers.

Cable Plant

The TRW Concept 2000 local area network can be installed either in non-translated dual cable configuration where greater bandwidth applications are required, supporting up to 40 independent 6-MHz channels, or the mid-split single-cable configuration supporting up to 20 independent channels. In either case, each channel can support up to 500 user devices with data rates of up to 20 Mbps for any video and voice traffic. Fiber optic is used to interconnect networks on a point-to-point basis.

Interface Units

The basic interface unit is the bus interface unit (BIU) which houses the internal RF modem, and the device interface. Using optional frequency-agile modem modules, the BIU allows a device to be connected on up to four separate 6-MHz channels. The basic serial device interface supports two to 32 devices with simultaneous full-duplex operation at speeds of up to 19.2 Kbps, and with the widest selectable electrical interface options including RS-232, RS-422/423, MIL-STD-188/114, and Burrough's Poll Select TDI.

Access to the cable plant is via the highly reliable carrier sense multiple access with collision avoidance (CSMA/CA) techniques. A variation of the HDLC protocol is used for this access method. For specific applications token-passing access method can be made available to access the cable plant configured either in a logical ring or a bus topology.

TRW Concept 2000 also includes a variety of data, video, and voice interface units. To interface with other computing services either the RS-232 interface or a direct high data rate interface can be used. At present the processor interface unit (PIU) allows direct interface of DEC unibus systems to the broadband LAN. It supports up to 255 virtual circuits.

The video interface unit (VIU) is one of the building blocks of TRW Concept 2000 for a video distribution system. The VIU consists of the basic BIU, a control interface, a 40-channel translator, a modulator, and a demodulator. The VIU command line interpreter (CLI) provides the command set necessary to establish a link between two VIUs or the broadband LAN. There are three ways to control a VIU: 1) through CLI input from an asynchronous terminal attached to the VIU; 2) through remote control from a local terminal and, 3) through the network system control monitor (SCM). With these products, TRW Concept 2000 is able to provide a general video distribution system, video teleconferencing, security monitoring, and other video applications.

The TRW Concept 2000 Gateways products include a telephone gateway interface (TGI), that enhances connectivity by providing additional network resources via the telephone company's switched network. It is user friendly and performs symbolic address translation and dialing of the phone numbers. It provides two telephone line connections to the switched network offering 300/1200 baud asynchronous support in Bell 103/Bell 212 format or Racal Vadic 3400 format, as well as 1200 baud synchronous service.

Another gateway product is the Ethernet on broadband modem interface unit, which allows existing Ethernet equipment to be directly connected to broadband LAN. This is a direct "plug-in" replacement for the usual baseband modems. This gateway product allows Ethernet equipment to gain the increased capability, bandwidth, and flexible topology offered by a broadband LAN. A four-port configuration is available to allow multiple Ethernetcontrolled cards to share the same modem hardware, thereby providing a cost-effective solution where multiple connection in one location is a requirement.

The command line interpreter (CLI) provides basic control for the BIU. Three operation modes are available in the BIU. The command modem (default mode) allows communication between the user and the BIU. No information is transmitted onto the network. The call modem provides communication between a BIU and a computer on the network. Information can be exchanged with another user on the network using the talk mode. The CLI provides more than 200 command combinations to be executed on the BIU, that operates either in local or remote mode providing user functions such as resource and data rate bit selection, control functions such as password and command set privilege selection, and diagnostic functions such as self test and test data loopbacks.

Network Management Tools

TRW Concept 2000 provides different levels of network management tools. The network status monitor (NSM) provides network status management functions by surveying each BIU on the network providing failure- and performance-related information.

For larger networks the system control monitor (SCM) provides advanced network management functions such as dynamic network configurations and reconfigurations, security access control and password assignment, network re-source allocations, and network accounting features.

TRW Concept 2000 management tools are written in high-level language and run under UNIX.

Conclusion

TRW is positioning itself to capitalize on its R&D capabilities, system experience, and field maintenance coverage to enter the commercial broadband local area market.

TRW is selling its TRW Concept 2000 product line through three distribution channels: a direct sales force covering major cities, a network of value added reseller in the communication markets, and OEM accounts.

The products are competitively priced. Also, TRW has the resources and experience to provide the necessary support for a complete turnkey system.

KEE KEENET

Introduction

KEE Incorporated, owned by IDEAS, Inc. for more than four years, and previously operated independently for nine years, is engaged in the general area of high technology office automation products. The company has two major product lines: a keyboard training system and a local area network system. The company currently has fifty employees, the majority of whom are engineers and technicians. All of the personnel previously involved in IDEAS' local area network activities are now employed by KEE.

The KEE LAN system is a reliable, multi-purpose communication system that allows for various types of computers, terminals, and peripherals to communicate in a very efficient and cost-effective manner. The system uses broadband coaxial cable as the transmission medium, providing communication for data, video, and many other sources of information. KEE manufactures a variety of network products that allow for equipment to communicate via the LAN. The basic bus interface units (BIUs) provide from 1 to 32 serial communication ports to the LAN. The KEE products support a variety of protocols, ranging from simple asynchronous to sophisticated binary-synchronous and bit-oriented protocols.

The three most important features of the KEE LAN systems approach are:

- *No Central Controller*: The intelligence of the network devices is totally distributed. Thus, no central controller is necessary, and therefore, there is no single point of failure. The KEE network monitor product is a valuable tool for rapid fault isolation, troubleshooting, and configuration control of the network. However, each of the devices on the network has enough "intelligence" to function without the use of a controller or network monitor.

- *Modular Design*: The KEE network products have a very modular design to allow for easy expansion and special interfacing. All products in a given LAN system have the same CATV modem.

- *Easily Configurable*: The operating characteristics of each port on the LAN devices are easily configurable on site. The characteristics may be down-line loaded (from the network monitor) or changed from a terminal device by use of a special password technique. The operating parameters are retained in the device when AC power is removed.

Product Overview

KEE supplies four basic local network products: terminal bus interface units, computer bus interface units, gateway bus interface units, and high-speed, point-to-point CATV modems. Each of these products—with the exception of the modems—is discussed below. A typical configuration employing these devices is illustrated in the Figure.

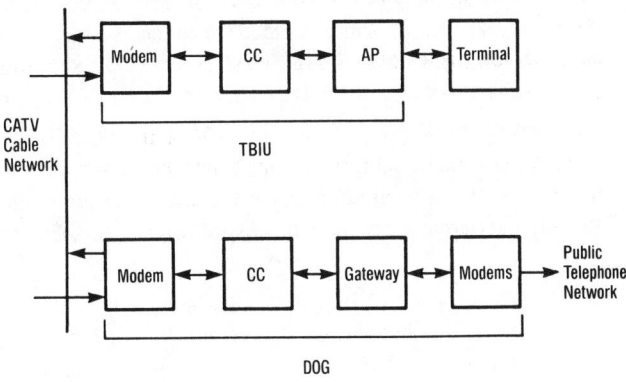

Figure: Typical KEENET Configuration

Terminal Bus Interface Units

KEE is offering a series of local network products based upon its fundamental terminal interface unit (BIU). This desktop device performs the CCITT X.3 packet assembler/dissassembler (PAD) function for a cable-based local network. The device is based on the original MitreNet dual-Z80 architecture. A single Z80-based board implements the carrier sense multiple access (CSMA) cable protocol. The second Z80 board implements the terminal and/or computer interface protocol. Custom software and hardware permit a great diversity in protocol support. The two boards "talk" over a high-speed parallel link. The bus interface is self-contained and includes hardware that is capable of interfacing up to level 3 of the ISO model.

A CATV modem implements level 1 (the physical interconnection). The modem uses a frequency shift keying (FSK) modulation technique to operate at speeds up to 1.544 Mbps. It occupies 6 MHz of bandwidth just below the commercial television band (50 MHz, channel T14). This dual-cable version can also be tuned to operate on a lower frequency channel, such as T13 (44 MHz).

A plug-compatible mid-split modem is currently in prototype development. It will support both the *de facto* 156 MHz split and the proposed EIA standard of 192.25 MHz split.

The second component of the BIU is the communications controller, or CC card. It operates in HDLC format, using an unslotted, non-persistent type of CSMA/CD. Acknowledgement is on a per-frame basis. The capability exists to download network software to the CC card.

The third component, the user interface board, is also Z80-based, with up to four serial ports supported. These serial ports are capable of operating at up to 19.2 Kbps each, simultaneously; in fact, the individual ports may operate at higher speed, i.e., 56 Kbps synchronous, but the aggregate throughput of the BIU is limited to 80 Kbps.

The board implements flow control with either XON/XOFF or RTS/CTS. Various electrical interfaces are available, including RS232, RS422/3 and MIL-STD 188. It has the capability of handling HDLC, SDLC, BISYNC, and X.25 line protocols.

The board is straightforward in design. The software and hardware are easily modified to meet custom requirements. In a typical application, the BIU cost is targeted for $500 per port.

In February 1984, KEE, Inc. announced a new product option that will extend its local network market range. The KEENET mid-split modem will enable KEE to interface its LANs with single-cable CATV systems.

The mid-split modem is essentially an enhancement to the bus interface unit (BIU). The BIU is the key to the operation of the firm's KEENET LAN. The device allows communication between dissimilar terminals, computers, and other equipment. The integral transmitter and receiver module designs of the BIU were used in development of the new modem. While the new modem supports the T8/I channel, it allows the user to access many other channels.

Computer Bus Interface Unit

The computer bus interface unit, which is multi-bus-based, allows for the connection of up to 16 serial lines to a communications front-end at a host processor. At the cable end of the device, the interface is identical to the BIU.

Gateway Bus Interface Unit

The gateway bus interface unit (GBIU) provides access to the public telephone network for a LAN-connected device. It centralizes the modem function and eliminates the necessity of providing a telephone modem to each user. The unit establishes, maintains, and disconnects seven simultaneous virtual circuits over the broadband cable network.

For the gateway, KEE has replaced the single-user interface of the terminal bus interface unit board with six boards to implement the gateway function.

The gateway hardware consists of three 19-inch rack chassis containing the modems, a microprocessor, and disk drives. The modem chassis contains seven Vadic modems and a dialer. The modems are compatible with Bell 103 for 300 baud service and Bell 212 or Vadic for 1200 baud service. The microcomputer chassis contains eight plug-in PC boards. The computer is an S-100 bus-based system running a CP/M disk operating system. The third chassis contains two eight-inch floppy disk drives.

Two of the gateway Boards are slightly modified copies of the communications card and a modem card. The other six boards are commercial boards which make up the AP portion of the gateway. The CPU board contains a Z-80 microprocessor and an eight-level vectored interrupt controller. The RAM board contains 64 Kb of memory. The floppy disk controller board contains a double density floppy disk controller and the operating system boot. The system support board contains timers for real-time interrupts and a time-of-day clock. The serial input/output boards each contain six RS 232 serial channels and two eight-level vectored interrupt controllers.

Because of the flexibility of the KEE product, the communications card software is virtually unchanged from the original terminal bus interface unit code. The only modification is an allowance for up to seven virtual circuits to be established through the communications card.

The major portion of the work involved implementing the gateway software. The software controls the transfer of data between the communications card and the phone lines. The software functions are discussed below.

- The software must establish, maintain, and clear simultaneous virtual circuits for up to seven users. This includes call-establishment with the network user and dial-out handling for the phone line circuits.

- As the interface between the communications card and the phone line, the auxiliary processor must be the data demultiplexer between the communications card and the phone lines for outbound data, and the data multiplexer between the phone lines and the communications card for inbound data.

- The software must provide flow control for data movement between the auxiliary processor and the network terminal bus interface unit.

- The software must transfer data between the auxiliary processor and communications card, and between the auxiliary processor and phone lines on a byte-by-byte basis under interrupt control.

The Auxiliary Processor software is divided into two major sections, the routines driven by the real-time interrupt and the background tasks. The interrupt-driven routines are:

- Send and receive packets to/from the communications card.

- Send and receive characters to/from the phone lines.

- Maintain the system real-time clock.

The background tasks are:

- Process inbound packets.
- Manage data buffers.
- Manage phone lines.
- Assemble outbound packets.

A real-time monitor acts as the interface between the various software modules or tasks that make up the auxiliary processor software. The real-time monitor provides a clean, well-defined interface for intra-task communications and provides a structure that allows additional tasks to be easily added to the gateway software.

Dial-In/Dial-Out Gateway

The dial-in/dial-out gateway allows communication between the broadband network and the public telephone network. Remote users can now access LAN resources by "dialing in" to the gateway and establishing a virtual circuit with any device on the network. LAN users can access remote resources by "dialing out" via the gateway.

Interface between the gateway and broadband network is accomplished via a CATV modem and a Z80-based communications controller (CC). The CC transmits and receives frames of data in HDLC format. This interface is identical to the cable interface used by other LAN devices. The gateway features a floppy disk interface, eight serial I/O lines (accommodates seven modems and a dialer), and a second Z80 processor. The gateway uses an S100 bus structure.

The floppy disk drives can be used for program loading, software development, or statistical accumulation of network functions. The second Z80 performs functions such as packet assembly/disassembly, call requesting, call accepting, and call clearing for up to seven simultaneous virtual circuits.

The electrical interface to the public telephone network consists of seven Vadac modems and a dialer; the modems can transfer data at 300 or 1200 bps, and they feature Bell compatibility.

Conclusion

KEE has delivered a significant system to the United States House of Representatives. The House of Representatives Local Area Network (LAN) is a Mitre-type LAN using a dual-cable CATV system supporting both video and digital devices. The current configuration of the network consists of approximately 50 terminal bus interface units, a network monitor, two computer bus interface units, and a dial-out gateway. The system is expected to expand to more than 2,000 terminal bus interface units, several gateways, and an X.25 interface to replace the computer bus interface units.

An Integrated Data/Voice Local Area Network

Reprinted with permission from *Telecommunications*, May 1984, pages 50-56. Copyright © 1984 by Horizon House--Microwave, Inc.

ASHRAF M. DAHOD
Applitek Corporation
Wakefield, Massachusetts

Local area networks developed in the 1970's are no longer adequate to meet the increasing demands of both voice and data communications. Applitek Corporation has developed a new universal local area network, called UniLAN™, which can handle data and voice integration efficiently on one network.

EMERGING INTEGRATION OF DATA AND VOICE

Two major trends are leading the way to all-digital networks. The first trend is the increasing use of data and digitized voice for wide-area networking. The other is the expanding use of personal computers and workstations. These trends substantially add to the amount of data that travels within and outside any organization.

To date, private branch exchanges (PBX's) and data switches, illustrated in **Figure 1**, have supported data and voice communication adequately. However, the growing need for data communications will inflate the cost of using PBX's and data switches due to the rising need for centralized switching and the subsequent cost of wiring.

The telephone network is evolving. Major forces are the digitization of voice and the expanding need for data communication. Increasing use of T1 digital lines will extend the integration of data and voice on a single line. Distributed processing and the greater processing power available at user stations will magnify the need for data communica-

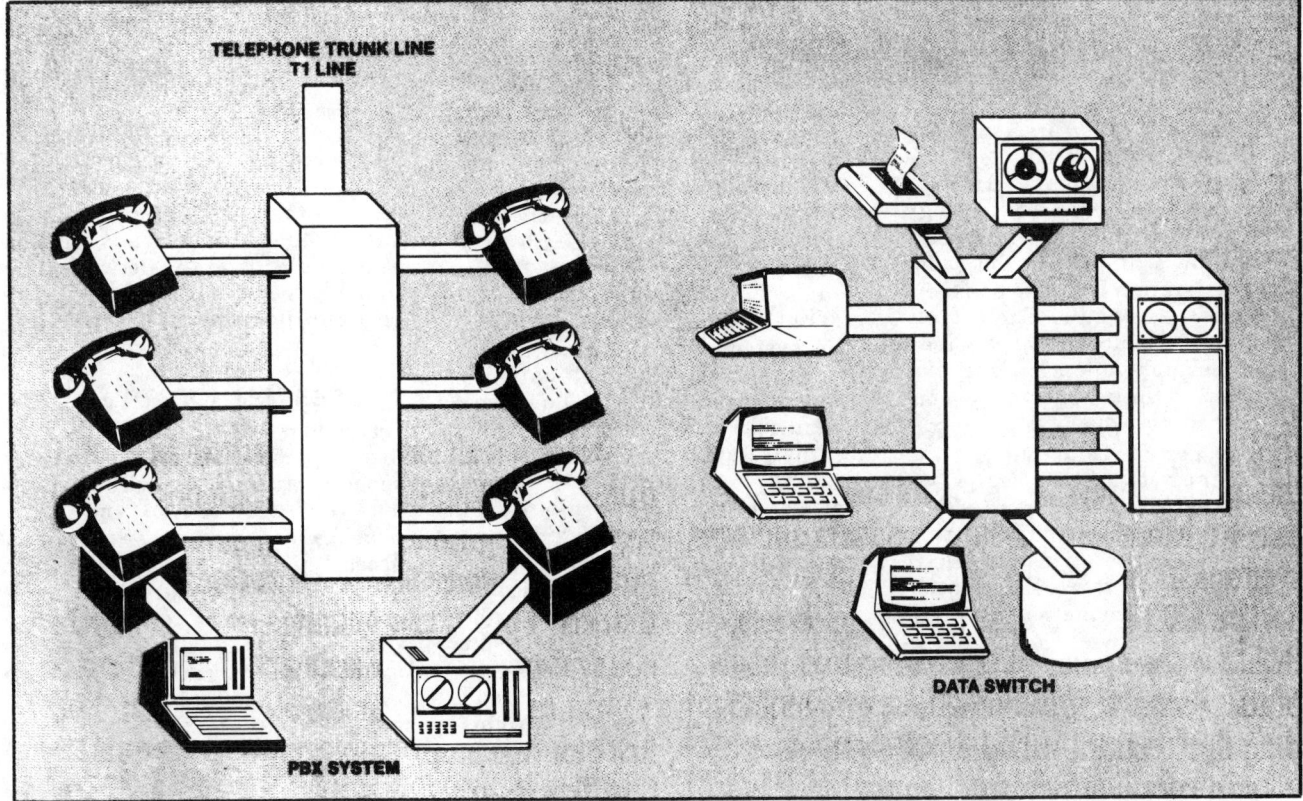

Fig. 1 A PBX and a data switch

tions on wide-area networks. This, in turn, will drive the industry toward digitized communication on wide-area networks. Although one T1 line may cost more than 24 voice lines, its cost is much less than 24 high-speed data lines. This trend in wide-area networks will permit digital lines to come into any one facility at very high speeds.

Digital interfaces, combined with growth of data communications within a facility, also will push the development of all-digital intrafacility networks. Personal computers, workstations, and integrated data/voice stations have heightened the need for data communications within the workplace. Greater use of intelligent stations has led to a greater need to transfer large files of data and to the sharing of expensive resources like printers, storage devices, and communication facilities.

These developments, coupled with the need to communicate with host systems having common, large data files and application programs that users may want to access, will result in a dramatic increase in intrafacility communication.

Any company looking to install a communications system must view a time-use horizon of 10 years, not just the next two or three. If an appropriate time-use horizon is not considered, any communications system installed today will be overwhelmed in a few years by the volumes of data that these systems will be required to support.

For the next few years, incremental changes in PBX technology will be more than adequate. However, their point-to-point star topology and the need for high-volume, centralized switching will soon cause third-generation PBX's to be expensive and inadequate. These problems will be hastened by the spread of simple applications like graphics — requiring the transfer of files containing bit-map displays.

Many people realize that, in the future, the network will be the system. Supporting the network will be its communications system, controlling network operation and allowing access to the network. No matter how sophisticated the network highway is, its economic payoff — performance — will be limited if access and control are not efficient.

AN INTRAFACILITY COMMUNICATION HIGHWAY

Local area networks which can support digitized voice, data, and video using a common cable promise systems which not only provide interconnectivity but also link communication points within a facility.

Local area networks hold the promise of being a communication highway within a facility; a few local area network cables have sufficient capacity to replace thousands of small twisted-pair cables within a facility. Local area networks allow the connection of different types of devices, using one common interconnecting medium, within a limited geographical area. The usual interconnecting medium is some form of coaxial or optical-fiber cable. The limited geographical area could include a campus encompassing a few miles. By this definition, a PBX or a data switch is not considered to be a local area network.

Local area networks not only offer a solution to integrated data/voice/video communication systems; they also greatly reduce wiring requirements and give substantial interconnectivity and reconfiguration benefits. Further, the distributed switching feature of a local area network reduces the need for large centralized switching power to support increasing traffic needs.

SELECTING A LOCAL AREA NETWORK

Before choosing the appropriate local area network for a facility, one should study the types of traffic such a communication highway will have to support. The nature of communication to be supported could include not only digitized voice and data, but also video or energy management systems. The network could cover distances of 5 to 7 miles and may be required to support thousands of devices.

Other requirements could be that the system must be reconfigured easily, and that the installation of the cable plant must follow some standard procedures.

Analyzing these needs, the two leading contenders for the transmission medium of a local area network are broadband coaxial cable and optical fiber. Optical fiber promises substantially greater total bandwidth than broadband coaxial cable in the future but, for the next few years, tapping the optical-fiber cable will be too complex. Thus, broadband coaxial cable is most promising. Installation procedures for broadband coaxial cable are standard and thousands of miles of broadband coaxial cable exist in the country. Broadband coaxial cable also allows tree topology and will simplify video communication and installation of energy management systems.

Baseband coaxial cable, twisted pair, and optical fiber still may be used within subnets coming off the broadband coaxial cable highway. Traffic on a broadband network will include not only digitized voice but also block transfer of data for graphics applications or file transfers, and bursts of traffic from terminal or terminal-like devices.

The ability of a network to handle terminal-like traffic is important for two reasons. First, there is an extensive installed base of terminals (about 7 million devices). Second, there is a need for these terminal devices to be used for data entry into host systems where personal computers or workstations might be far too expensive.

Figure 2 shows how different types of devices produce different types of traffic on a network. Data-entry terminals generally send short packets infrequently on the network. This is illustrated in **Figure 2a**, where the time between packets sent by one terminal may vary between 100 and 400 ms. When a computer responds to a data-entry terminal (**Figure 2b**), it sends long packets, also very infrequently.

When a file transfer is in progress, however, long packets are sent out regularly until the file has been transferred completely, as shown in **Figure 2c.** Separate file transfers on a network could occur often or infrequently. Digitized voice traffic requires that, while a connection exists, medium-sized packets must be sent regularly on the network. The time between the packets should be between 10 and 20 ms (**Figure 2d**).

ACCESS METHOD

Local area networks available today use two access methods, carrier sense multiple access with collision detection (CSMA/CD) and token passing. An analysis of these two access methods shows that bursty terminal traffic is serviced best by contention access techniques like CSMA/CD, while digitized voice is supported best by access techniques like token passing that have deterministic delays on the network.

An analysis of such traffic as file or block transfers shows that, during the transfer, network efficiency could be increased if the determinis-

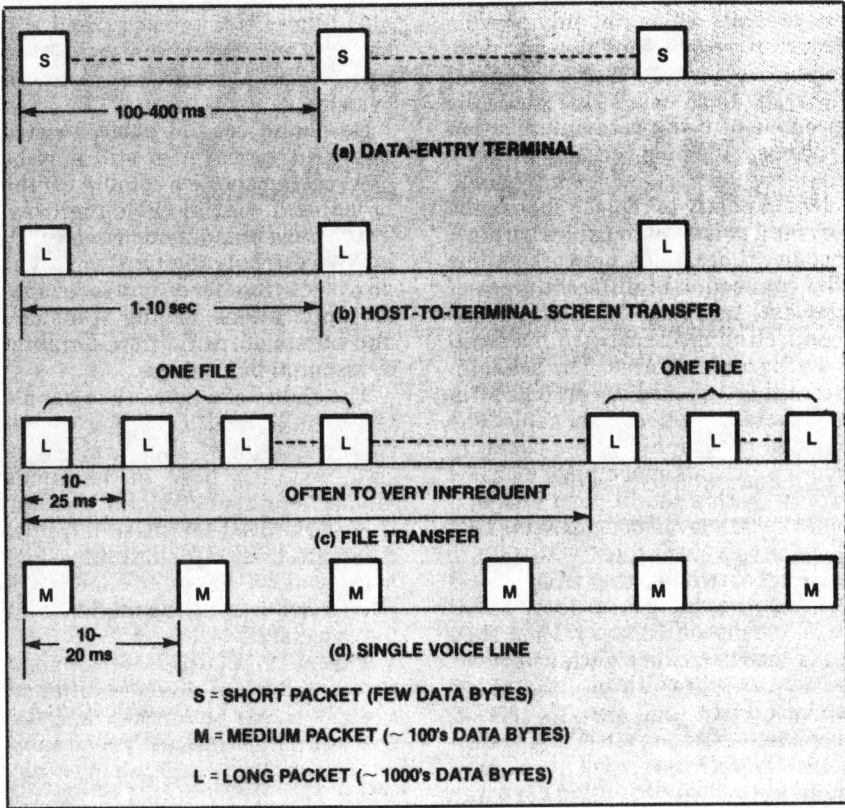

S = SHORT PACKET (FEW DATA BYTES)

M = MEDIUM PACKET (~ 100's DATA BYTES)

L = LONG PACKET (~ 1000's DATA BYTES)

Fig. 2 Different types of network traffic.

tic access of token passing could be provided, but not at all times, especially when no transfer is occurring and devices are idle. To do this on a token bus would result in devices entering the logical ring far more frequently than a token bus protocol can allow sensibly. A technique is required which could adapt not only to the type of active devices but to the type of traffic generated by these devices at any point in time.

One such technique is Adaptable Message Division Multiple Access (UniLINK™). UniLINK is a distributed local area network access method which provides the benefits of both CSMA/CD and token passing on one network concurrently. UniLINK can be implemented on baseband or broadband coaxial cable or optical-fiber cable.

The UniLINK method uses two rules to access the network. The first rule requires that time on the network be broken into messages, with the implicitly numbered messages grouped into message blocks. Message division is illustrated in **Figure 3**. A message is defined as the period of time during which a data packet of variable length may be transmitted. Messages are numbered consecutively within a message block. Message numbers are known by each network interface unit at all times, using a distributed process called *pacing*. Pacing is performed by all network interface units to track message numbers on the network correctly.

The second rule requires that an interface unit transmit a packet only during the time of the message number assigned to it. Message numbers are assigned to network interface units for use on a dedicated or contention basis. A message has a dedicated assignment if only one interface unit can use that message number to send information through the network. If a message number is assigned to more than one interface unit, then any one of the units to which it is assigned can transmit during the time of that message number. This is known as a *contention assignment*.

During a contention message number interval, the interface units trying to transmit can detect multiple transmissions. If they detect multiple transmissions, they cease transmitting and wait a random amount of time, based on a random back-off algorithm, before trying to send again in contention assignment. However, if a dedicated message number belonging to an interface unit comes up before that unit's wait period is over, the unit transmits in the time of the dedicated message number.

Automatic Message Number Allocation

Dedicated messages can be assigned to interface units on the basis of need. For example, an interface unit supporting devices generating regular traffic requiring known transmission delay (e.g., synchronous equipment, factory control equipment, or real-time voice) needs dedicated assignments and can send a request for them onto the network. Similarly, an interface unit supporting devices with bursty traffic (asynchronous terminals) that normally can use contention assignments but that have a backlog of packets created by network collisions also can send a request for a dedicated assignment on the network. The network responds to such requests on a first-come, first-served basis and assigns to the requesting interface units the required dedica-

| 0 | 1 | 2 | 3 | - - - - - - - | 65535 | 0 | 1 | - - - | 65535 | 0 | ·· |

| HEADER | DATA UP TO 32K BITS | CRC |

Fig. 3 UniLINK's message division.

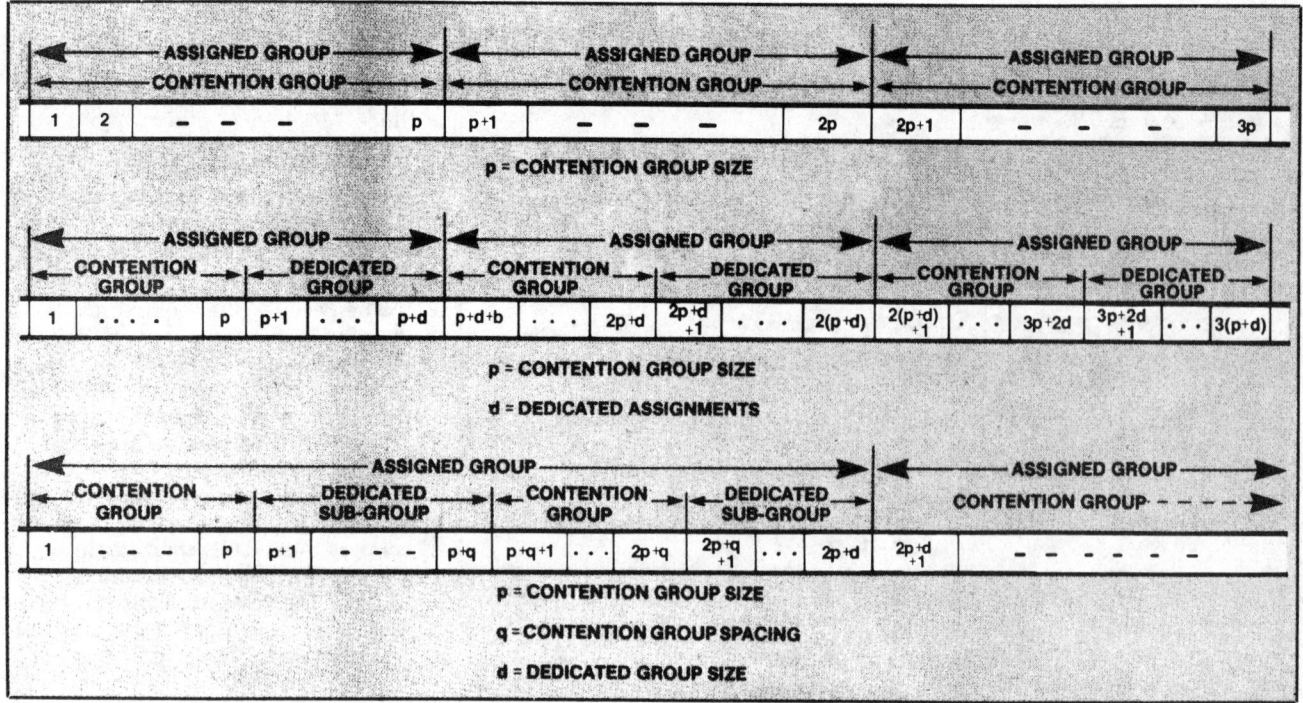

Fig. 4a Message group sizing and spacing.

ted message numbers.

If a network is operating with no dedicated assignments, then all message numbers are assigned as contention message numbers. These contention message numbers are divided into a repeating set of equal-sized groups. The size of each group is a programmable parameter, called the *contention group size*. Dedicated message numbers are assigned, when requested, after the first contention group. Assignments in this dedicated subgroup continue until the group size equals contention group spacing. Spacing is also a programmable parameter.

Once this limit is reached, additional dedicated assignments are made after repeating a contention group. The set of nonrepeating, dedicated message numbers between contention groups forms a continuous, sequential set of dedicated message numbers. The complete set of assigned message numbers — from the first contention to the last dedicated message number — recurs on the network. **Figure 4a** illustrates message groups, their sizing and spacing.

The automatic message allocation scheme used by UniLINK ensures dedicated assignments are obtained and relinquished automatically. Interface units are aware when they under-utilize their assigned message number bandwidth and automatically relinquish some

or all of this bandwidth.

If a unit wishes to keep a dedicated message number, it must transmit a packet — either normal or null (no useful information) — in that message number interval. However, if it wants to give up a particular assignment, it ceases to transmit anything in that assignment. The other interface units sense this period of no activity and readjust themselves. This effectively "fills up" holes created by unused dedicated message numbers. This scheme also works in situations where power to devices with dedicated message number assignments is turned off. **Figure 4b** shows how the network readjusts itself when dedicated assignments are reliquished.

Part of an Integrated System

UniLAN can be used to support the three types of traffic — digitized voice, file transfers, and terminal-like transmissions — that any communication highway will encounter. Digitized voice-type traffic is supported by assigning dedicated message numbers to network interface units supporting voice communication while the voice circuit is in session. When voice communication is terminated, the message number used by this session is relinquished and becomes available to a new voice connection.

For file transfers, the first few packets generated by the file transfer device might go off on a contention message number basis. As soon as

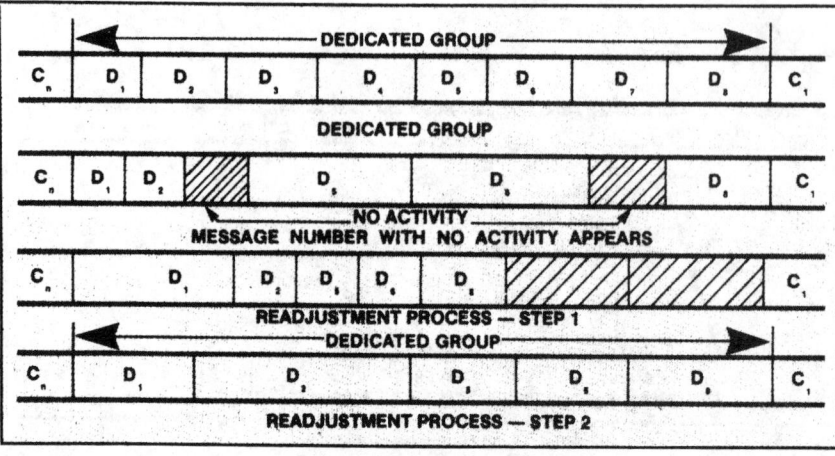

Fig. 4b Deleting dedicated assignments.

the nature of traffic becomes apparent to the interface unit supporting the file transfer, it gets a dedicated message number to allow the file transfer to continue on a noncontention basis. As soon as the file transfer is complete, the dedicated message number is relinquished.

Bursty, terminal-like traffic is supported by having the interface units share a common set of messages. If a device is performing like a terminal emulator, its supporting interface unit operates on contention message numbers. If at any time a series of packets are generated by the device to transfer some files or transfer blocks of data, the interface unit supporting that personal computer or workstation gets a dedicated message number during that file transfer.

Using UniLINK, devices can get contention or dedicated assignments. The type of assignment depends not only on the inherent nature of the traffic presented by a device, but also on traffic patterns at any point in time. If a device needs dedicated assignments, these dedicated assignments (equivalent to additions and deletions from a logical token bus) can be done quite easily to adapt the network state, depending upon the demands placed on the network. **Table 1** illustrates the performance implications of UniLINK.

Such an adaptable access method can support thousands of different types of devices. As the natures of devices change, or the speeds at

TABLE 1
PERFORMANCE IMPLICATIONS OF UniLINK

Message Length	Message Number Allocation		Performance Similar to	Applications
	Dedicated	Contention		
Variable	•	•	Token passing & CSMA/CD	Mixed Environments
	•		Priority Token Passing	Synchronous Devices, Real Time Voice, Factory Control
		•	Priority CSMA CD	Asynchronous Bursty Devices
Fixed	•	•	Dual Mode STDMA*	Highly Synchronous
	•		Reservation STDMA	Applications or
		•	Contention STDMA	Long Networks

*STDMA: Slotted Time Division Multiple Access.

which devices communicate change, the UniLINK access method will adapt automatically and, therefore, will help protect the investment in the communication highway.

The UniLAN local area network will be able to support simultaneous transmission on the communication highway of up to 4500 sessions at 64 kbps using a mid-split broadband cable. Using UniLINK, a UniLAN network can configure its dedicated message number assignments to optimize network utilization. Each device is allowed to obtain dedicated message numbers to assure guaranteed access or contention message numbers for infrequent packets.

CONCLUSION

Explosive growth in intrafacility data communications, due to the increased use of personal computers, workstations, and distributed data processing, sparked the initial interest in local area networks. Integration of data and voice in digital form has emphasized the need for communication systems, both local and wide-area, that can handle a growing volume of digital traffic. Local area networks like UniLAN, which can handle heavy digital traffic effectively and efficiently, may be the choice for a communication highway within a facility. □

Section 5: PBX-Based Networks

The Private Branch Exchange (PBX) has been in place in major office buildings for years. However, only recently have people noticed that telephones are the natural companions of computer terminals on the modern office desk. In addition, these in-place PBX systems already supply most of the needed wiring for new integrated voice/data PBX systems. In this section, we examine some of the products available in this area. The field of PBXs is very competitive, especially since the AT&T divestiture. Currently there are at least 13 manufacturers of these PBX systems, though in the last year alone, Rockwell International, Plessey/Stromberg-Carlson, and Datapoint have backed out of the market, discontinuing their PBX products.

Although the PBX environment has been around since the 1920s, people generally do not know much about how it actually works. Therefore, a brief basic introduction to the operation of a PBX is presented here.

An analog signal must be continually amplified without any allowance for noise on the line. If noise is present it also is amplified. A digital signal is regenerated only after it is determined if the pulse of a constant width and amplitude is on or off.

A digital signal—which also lends itself to incorporating control signals via time division multiplexing, resulting in a logical separate control channel without dedicating a separate physical channel—is easily multiplexed. This multiplexing of control information allows insertion and deletion of a digital message stream independent of transmission media, thus permitting independent design of signaling equipment. Control information is inherently digital since it is inherently binary (on hook/off hook) and digital (station address).

Since the telephone has consistently been a window to the world, interfaces to public digital services are inherent to a digital PBX design. The standard PCM system rate of 64 Kbps that most PBX manufacturers have adopted, readily interfaces to network services. Some PBXs already can accommodate direct digital trunk interfaces at 1.544 or 2.048 Mbps for future requirements.

The technology of digital signal processing assists in tone generation/detection, echo control, amplification/attenuation, equalization, filtering, companding, and digital voice encoding format conversion.

The technique used for switching digitized voice may be space-division switching, time-division switching, or a combination of the two.

Space-division switching involves setting up a single path through one or more sets of crosspoint switches between the line and the trunk. The path, a physical connection, is used by the caller for the duration of the call. This path is released for use by other callers after the call is terminated. Because it is a circuit switch which could remain analog throughout, this connection need not be digital. The disadvantages of single-stage switching are: 1) the number of crosspoints, ($n(n$-1)/2 for a triangular array and $n(n$-1) for a square array where n is the number of inputs and outputs), required in a large system becomes prohibitive because only one connection may be made per crosspoint; 2) the large number of inlets and outlets create a capacity load on the message path; 3) one specific crosspoint is required for a particular connection which cannot be made if there is a failure in that crosspoint; and 4) crosspoints are inefficiently used, since only one crosspoint in each row or column is in use when all lines are active.

A non-blocking switch incorporates space-division switching in the form of a multiple-stage switch. Non-blocking is achieved, for example, in a three-stage switch in which the central stage contains 2i-1 arrays. The advantages of a multiple-stage switch over a single-stage switch are fewer crosspoints are needed, and those that are necessary are used more efficiently. Crosspoints are shared so that more than one path is available for any potential connection, and alternate paths reduce blocking and provide protection against failures.

Time-division switching is done by sampling the signal over time. For continuity of the signal, synchronous time-division multiplexing (TDM) is usually incorporated in voice transmission although asynchronous data transmissions, or voice store-and-forward may be intermixed. In time-division multiplexing, a framing scheme must be accepted whether it be synchronous (fixed frame), or asynchronous (variable frame length), in which the data may be encapsulated; the frame is the smallest unit in which each station is serviced at least once. Each time slot within the frame is uniquely assigned to each data source, and a timing procedure is developed to sample each data source at the appropriate time interval. Control bits for framing and synchronization are inserted in the frame to enable the receiver to recognize the beginning of the frame, each slot within the frame, and each bit within the slot. Also, to reduce errors, provisions for handling small variations in the incoming bit rates to the multiplexor should be made.

The bit rates of the transmitting devices are much lower than those of the line. A typical frame for a synchronous system, for example, contains 10 bits of information in each data slot and 10 bits in the control bits at the beginning and end of the frame. With the data sources transmitting at 4800 and 9600 bps as indicated, the line data rate is 24 Kbps.

EHO228-7/85/0000/0271$01.00 © 1985 IEEE

One way in which PBXs increase their switching capacity is by time-slot interchanging to accomplish time muliplexing. The methods of doing such an interchange vary widely and in some cases, such as Northern Telecom, the type of interchange may induce blocking.

In AT&T Information Systems' System 85, the CSM contains the time slot interchange unit (TSIU), which performs intramodule switching by placing the voice and data samples for each active port on a time slot in a time-multiplexed channel. The TSIU establishes connections between ports by rearranging the order of the time slots in the channel.

In Northern Telecom's SL-1, the type of time slot interchange introduces blocking. Blocking occurs because each two-party call requires two time slots. One time slot is required from each network, and these time slots must form a matching pair such as (2,3), (3,2), (5,4), (4,5). . .(30,31), (31,30). Time slots 0 and 1 are reserved; thus, only 30 slots are available for voice connections. If a matching pair is not available, then the call is blocked.

Two major classes of multiplexing are evident in long-haul communications, those that travel over voice-grade lines and those that travel at much higher data rates for data transmission service. The voice-grade channels are those lines designed to carry the range of frequencies that accommodate the human voice (up to 3.3 KHz) that may be dial-up or leased, regular or conditioned. The higher data rates are the type that evolve from the digital hierarchies created by AT&T for North America and Japan and by the CCITT for Europe.

Space- and time-division switching may be incorporated in two ways: the singleor multiple-stage space division switch crosspoint outputs are multiplexed on the same line, or a multiplexed line is switched through space division switching. Either type of hybrid switching is necessary in larger digital switches.

As was mentioned before, non-blocking is achieved in a multiple-stage switch in which each input may connect to an output. A blocking switch has more inputs and outputs than the number of simultaneous connections, which is actually a function of the type of call and its transmission rate. At first glance, it appears that a non-blocking switch would be more desirable, but a non-blocking switch may not always allow a connection. A non-blocking switch will block a connection when all trunks are busy, a DTMF receiver is not available, or the processor (not the switch) is overloaded. In these cases a blocking switch would be just as effective (and sometimes more so due to queuing algorithms) as a non-blocking switch.

Queuing of calls is provided in a blocking system when trunking facilities are busy, so that users are not required to redial for facilities. InteCom's IBX offers two queuing options, on-line priority and call-back priority. On-line queuing offers queuing while keeping callers on hold, possibly with a recording or music or both; this method is used in quantities by both the phone company and airline reservation desks. Call-back priority queuing is effected by the switch monitoring the trunk or other requested facility and ringing the caller back (usually an internal party) when the facility is available. If multiple facilities are requested, for instance, a trunk and a modem, the switch would not call back until both were available.

In the first article in this section, Intecom s PBX is described. Intecom's integrated business exchange (IBX) was the first large-scale, non-blocking switching system to fully integrate voice/data communications. The basic hardware interface to the IBX is a family of terminals which support simultaneous voice/data communication. The IBX, which is especially attractive for large sites, provides total office automation and InteMail Voice Messaging. Intecom has recently improved the IBX, and it now has IBM 3270 and Ethernet connections and emulations.

While Intecom is geared mainly for large-scale applications, Northern Telecom has developed a family of PBXs to serve an entire spectrum of users. The SL family combines PBX, key telephone, Centrex, and custom-calling services. The SL-1 is a modular system which can handle from 100 up to 5000 lines. The SL-100 was developed for large users. It was designed to easily connect multiple SL-100s together, with a single system supporting up to 30,000 integrated voice/data stations. Both the SL-1 and SL-100 are non-blocking systems, perform 3270 protocol conversion, and offer a variety of interface devices for data communications.

The Saturn III, developed by Siemens Communication Systems, was designed to meet the current requirements of business office data switching. The network uses twisted-pair wiring to transmit unmodified and modem-treated digital data and analog signals. The software package provides the integrated voice and data communications ability and offers data traffic measurements, data-message digital recording, and other programmable features.

In the next summary, AT&T's System 85 is briefly described. AT&T has incorporated both advanced digital switching technology and stored program control in the System 85. It allows simultaneous voice and data communications with a distributed control architecture that makes extensive use of microprocessors to offload the simple and repetitive tasks from the main processor. The system architecture provides for flexiblity and modular growth.

Ericsson's MD110 is an integrated voice/data PBX which has a distributed architecture that allows the system to be modularly expandable up to 10,000 lines, in increments of

200 lines. The system supports both standard analog and proprietary digital phones which allow simultaneous voice and data communication over a single pair of wires. Modemless switching, modem pooling, and autodialing enables the user to use existing data terminals and CPUs for different applications.

The SX-2000 by Mitel is designed to be dependable and flexible, as well as providing PBX requirements over the range from 150 to 10,000 lines. Augmenting the SX-2000 are special proprietary communication sets that require no more than two pairs of standard office wiring for connection to the system interface card. Other features include electronic mail, low power and heat, extensive maintenance and diagnostic aids, and the capability of having fully duplicated hardware down to the interface card level. IBM originally counted on Mitel's SX-2000 to be its PBX offering. However, development problems and missed schedules forced IBM to abandon Mitel and sign with and finally purchase ROLM.

ROLM introduced one of the oldest PBXs, the computerized branch exchange (CBX), in 1975, and it quickly gained popularity, with over 16,000 systems installed to date. Recently, however, ROLM designed a new architecture and made many improvements to the old CBX. The result is the CBX II which is completely compatible with the CBX but has modular expandability to support from 16 to more than 10,000 users. The details of the new CBX II are described in the article.

Taking a step forward, Ztel's PNX was the first of the 4th generation (i.e., distributed integrated voice/data switches) PBXs to appear on the market. The PNX design unifies the voice capabilities of a PBX with the baseband token-ring architecture of the IEEE 802.5 (and IBM) Standard. Some of the resulting abilities of the PNX include the automatic selection of the most cost-effective route for each communication, redistribution of traffic loads for better performance, and making dissimilar devices appear to be compatible. The PNX uses multiple rings of packet and circuit-type formats, operating at 10 and 9.2 Mbps per ring.

The second of the 4th generation PBXs to be produced is CXC's Rose. The transmission medium is a broadband cable ring which operates at 50 Mbps and can be configured to conform to the IEEE 802.5 Standard. The heart of the system is a per-line switch which, in effect, is a PBX per line. The chip used in CXC's node and proprietary personal teleterminals provides the system with programmable bandwidths to each station.

InteCom IBX

Introduction

InteCom has taken its place in the large circuit switch local network market with its IBX (integrated business exchange), which is designed to provide each port with both voice and data port functionality.

More than 50 IBX systems have been installed, the first (summer 1981), at CIT Financial in New York. One of the larger systems (approximately 8000 lines) is installed at the University of Chicago.

System Concept

The integrated business exchange (IBX) is the first large-scale switching system to fully integrate voice and data communications. Designed around a totally non-blocking digital architecture, the IBX supports simultaneous user speech and data, up to 57.6 Kbps. With LANmark, the local area networking capability, receiving data speeds of up to 10 Mbps are possible.

The IBX provides inherent ability to accommodate data in a circuit-switched mode. Through packet switching techniques, the IBX is able to perform both format conversion and protocol translation.

By providing the capability for intrafacility and interfacility voice and high-speed data communication in one integrated system, the IBX represents an advanced generation of switching equipment. Without the necessity for a modem at their stations, users can initiate or receive an asynchronous or synchronous data call on a per-station basis at selectable speeds ranging from 50 bps to 57.6 Kbps and simultaneously initiate or receive a voice call. This is accomplished using one two-pair telephone wire structure instead of present multiple wiring structures. LANmark receiving speeds of up to 10 Mbps are provided via the same universal cable plant.

The IBX, through T1 compatibility, provides interfacility data and voice communications via interfaces to commercially available network offerings (X.25).

The IBX S/40 architecture features a non-blocking switching matrix and redundant Perkin-Elmer Corporation 32-bit supermini processors, with a capacity of four megabytes of directly addressable memory and up to 67 megabytes of disk-resident memory, which provide coordinating functions for as many as 16 distributed interface multiplexers. Each interface multiplexer is equipped with Zilog Z-80 microprocessors and provides 256 wideband (128 Kbps) interface ports for a system-wide total of 4096 ports. The IBX S/80 provides up to 8192 ports using 32 Interface Multiplexers.

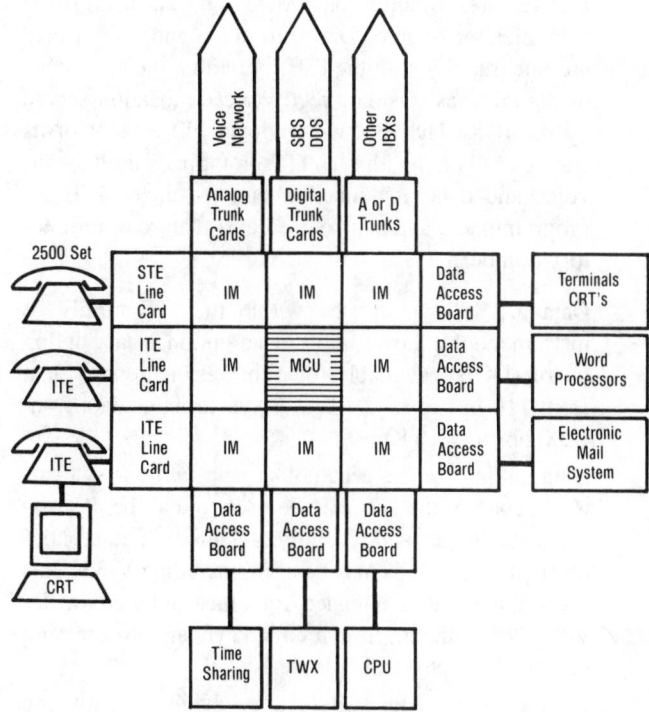

Figure: IBX Series 40

In the IBX, voice is digitally encoded at a user's station by electronic instruments termed ITE (integrated terminal equipment). The ITEs can provide RS-232-C or RS-449 or V.35 interfaces and multiplex up to 57.6 Kbps of user data with digitized voice, over universal two-pair telephone wire, from the ITEs to the interface multiplexers. The interface multiplexers can be interconnected over distances up to 2,500 feet, via laser-driven fiber optic cable.

In the fall of 1983, InteCom announced plans to market a new digital PBX called the IBX S/10. This switch is a small version of its IBX digital PBX and is aimed at users having as few as 250 lines or as many as 1000 lines.

The IBX S/10 incorporates all the features of the IBX S/80 (a larger version of the S/40 capable of handling 8192 ports with up to 32 interface multiplexers), including its LANmark (local networking package which supports the Ethernet protocol, 3270, and InteMail voice store-and-forward system OEM'ed by VMX, Inc. InteCom's LANmark (LAN) software is available with the switch.

Features

Numerous features and specific equipment distinguish the IBX concept.

- *Integrated Terminal Equipment (ITE)*: The integrated terminal equipment (ITE) family of electronic instruments is supported by the IBX switching system. The ITE features simultaneous voice and data using two-pair telephone cable. Digitized voice and digital data are integrated within the ITE, providing the advantage of digital transmission directly to each location served by the IBX. The IBX will support 100 percent of its stations as ITEs, with each ITE providing simultaneous voice and data. All function buttons on the ITE are programmable and can be used as a feature or a directory number.

  Data are fully integrated within the ITE family of instruments by the addition of an optional data option board (DOB), available for either asynchronous data from 110 bps to 19.2 Kbps or synchronous data from 1200 bps to 57.6 Kbps.

  Data calling can be accomplished in two ways. First, the keypad of the ITE may be used to dial the destination data device; and secondly, a number of automatic-origination methods may be used, including V.35. This second method is intended for office automation devices or for dialing from a CRT keyboard. Addressing can be either physical or logical.

  Data calls use standard features available with any ITE-equipped IBX. Features such as queuing, busy recall and call detail recording are available.

  An ITE can be located up to 27,000 feet from the IBX using a combination of standard telephone wire and fiber optic cable.

- *Uniform Alternate Routing and Queuing*: The IBX switching system is capable of routing calls via predefined trunking facilities in predefined priorities based upon the user dialing a single digit access code. The uniform alternate routing (UAR) feature of the IBX is table driven and selects a transmission path based on a least-cost routing scheme built into user-programmable routing tables. Queuing of calls is provided when trunking facilities are busy, so that users are not required to redial for facilities. Several queuing options are available, such as "On-Line Priority" and "Call Back Priority."

- *Automatic Call Distributor (ACD)*: The automatic call distributor feature is an IBX system group option requiring an ACD configuration in the data base. Although ACD is available on both the Standard Telephone Equipment (STE) and ITE sets, most of the special ACD features, which are designed for productivity enhancement, require the ITE feature button functions.

An ACD group is defined as a number of stations (telephone sets) designated as agent or supervisor positions sharing a common directory (pilot) number. Any call to the pilot number is automatically routed to agents via an equalized workload distribution scheme, assuring that calls are processed through the receiving station and connected to their destination numbers with a minimum of expended time and effort. One of the many ACD features is a group/agent performance statistics report for use in the evaluation/management of an agent force.

- *Call Detail Recording and Accounting*: IBX supports a comprehensive call detail recording (CDR) and administrative and accounting package (AAP). CDR collects details regarding system calls. This information is available for use on an off-line system or as input for AAP. AAP processes the CDR data and outputs administrative reports.

  With the selection of AAP, the following reports are available: individual reports, account reports, cost center reports, and exception reports.

- *Man/Machine Package (MMP)*: The man/machine package (MMP) is the human/computer interface to the IBX system. MMP is a data base management system using an English language dialogue. Special programming languages are not required. Commands in the MMP are selected by the data base administrator for managing and update IBX features and functions. A "menu selection" of commands can be quickly displayed for viewing, thus aiding the administrator in selecting the proper command for data base manipulation. Each command in the MMP data base pertains to a feature or function of the IBX and determines what features or functions a user is allowed or denied.

- *Directory Lookup System (DLS)*: The directory lookup system (DLS) provides a quick method of operator assistance. The information available for display to the DLS operator is programmable and can be restricted to those items necessary to extend calls efficiently. The DLS operator can search for information by entering a number of information items such as name, directory number, department, or location. The entered item does not have to be complete; for example, when entering a name, only as much of the name as can be spelled needs to be entered. A search begins with the entered portion, and a list of names that start with the entered letters will be displayed. The DLS operator can then sequence forward or backward until the desired listing is displayed.

Other DLS features consist of support programs such as wiring and spares. The wiring program is an inventory of the IBX building-wide wiring plan, providing an electronic roadmap of the entire IBX installation. The spare inventory feature provides a displayed status list of all "spare" items associated with the IBX installation; items such as available "spares" quantity and type, their physical location and state of repair.

- *Multi-Functional Data Transmission*: The IBX provides a communications structure for a variety of resources, using the two-pair telephone cable already in place for building-wide voice communications.

A user's CRT may be directly plugged into the IBX via a DIU or DAB or into an InteCom-provided electronic station instrument, called integrated terminal equipment (ITE). On a port-contention basis, this CRT terminal may be connected by user-command to any other data resource on the IBX.

If a destination port supports a dissimilar format or protocol the IBX can be equipped with a variety of InteNettm Packet Controllers (IPCs) that provide communications between the natively incompatible devices (see below).

If the destination requires the use of an analog facility, the routing parameters are defined to insert a modem of the proper speed and type. The IBX automatically allocates and connects both the analog and digital sides of a selected modem in a mode that is transparent to the user.

By entering the proper commands from the IBX man/machine control terminal, data circuit automatic dialed services can be implemented on the IBX.

Since the IBX is a completely non-blocking system, a permanent data connection feature can be implemented without any fear of degrading performance. A permanent connection is data base-defined at system generation time and is useful for application connections such as a remote printer or a remote job entry (RJE) station.

Whether data connections are permanent (automatically dialed) or dialed manually by the station user, the IBX records complete information about each data call. Stored information contains the identity of the originator, destination, and duration of the call.

- *3270 InteNet Packet Controller*: The 3270 IPC communicates with the customer's host processor at speeds of up to 9.6 Kbps in bisynchronous format and appears to the host as an IBM 3271 Model 2 Control Unit, without requiring host software changes in the basic configuration.

Since IPCs are shared resources for multiple station users of the IBX, 3270 IPCs may be connected to different 3270 compatible host processors. Thus, governed by a class of service designation, all CRT terminals connected to one IBX can become multi-functional and may switch, on a dial-up basis, to any number of customer host processors.

A 3270 IPC is capable of supporting 8 to 12 user CRTs or printers on a dial-up basis, depending on the specific applications and desired response times. Traffic-engineerable quantities of 3270 IPCs are installed in standard card slots of the 256-port interface multiplexer data auxiliary cabinet (IM) portion of the IBX. Tandem grouping capabilities allow a selectable grade of service to be engineered for all terminals using the 3270 emulation capability. For example, an IBX system may have 200 user CRT terminals contending for 48 emulation ports. Four 3270 IPCs, each supporting 12 ports, provide these 48 emulation ports. The user can enter an automatic queue to be called back when a 3270 IPC emulation port is available. This feature eliminates user aggravation and maximizes port usage during peak periods.

All common features (such as formatted screens, protected fields and program function keys) of the IBM 3270 Information Display System are supported by the InteNet 3270 IPC.

- *X.25 InteNet Packet Controller (IPC)*: The X.25 IPC provides "terminal interface" capability for asynchronous devices attached to the IBX that is interfacing to packet data networks (PDNs). The number of X.25 IPC assemblies required depends upon the grade of service desired. The user can minimize the number of X.25 ports required by using the port-contention and queuing techniques of the IBX.

The X.25 IPC provides the packet assembly/disassembly (PAD) function to access PDNs. Each X.25 IPC assembly has up to 16 ports for terminals or printers and, since the PAD function is provided via the X.25 IPC assembly, all ports of an X.25 IPC assembly use a single PDN access channel. This minimizes the number of PDN access lines required. The companion recommendations X.3, X.28, and X.29 are also supported.

Asynchronous devices connected to ports of the IBX can access a remote host or terminal. First the IBX interconnects an asynchronous device to the X.25 IPC, and then the X.25 IPC, performing the PAD function, interfaces to the PDN networks in compliance with X.25 standard specifications. The PDN then carries the assembled packets to the host computer or terminal for processing and response. Packets coming back from the host computer via the PDN are received and disassembled by the X.25 IPC for delivery to the proper asynchronous device.

Device operation via the X.25 IPC complies with X.3 parameter recommendations, and transmission speed up to 9600 bps is supported. Also, the X.25 IPC uses a combination of hardware and software to support a synchronous link to the host computer via the PDN at speeds of up to 46 Kbps. The physical, functional, and electrical interface is EIA RS-232-C.

The Word Processor Conversion InteNet Packet Controller (WPC IPC) provides users with the capability to convert files from one word processing format to another as the information passes through the IBX. The conversion of data is transparent to the operator and allows inter-system communication capability.

Protocol translation for Wang, and IBM families of WPCs is provided. The WPC IPC provides the communication path between the dissimilar systems. Many features of electronic mail and message distribution terminals may exist on current word processing equipment. The WPC IPC provides the format conversion and communication capabilities necessary to allow universal communication between these systems.

- *LANmark Package*: The LANmark feature of the IBX enables the PBX to emulate Ethernet with burst speeds up to 10 Mbps. With this feature, the IBX can connect to or become an Ethernet network.

InteMail

InteCom, Inc., will market VMX, Inc.'s voice store-and-forward system as an integrated system on its IBX digital PBX. It will be offered to new and existing customers under the name InteMail, and will be developed jointly by personnel from InteCom and VMX.

InteMail features will include automatic call answering, a voice messaging center (to which unanswered, incoming calls are routed), a waiting-message indicator, and a Name-Scan feature whereby users can learn the identities of people who have left messages before playing them back.

Conclusion

A highly advanced voice/data system, the IBX is a significant entry into the rapidly developing area of PBX technology. The system 3270 and X.25 data connection capabilities give it a clear advantage in a market in which such capabilities are critical to success. In addition, LANmark provides the system with true local area networking capabilities.

The IBX system used for initial entry into the PBX market, targeted the large-user environment. Subsequent expansion of the IBX product line permits InteCom to serve small-, medium-, and large-user markets.

Northern Telecom SL-1 and SL-100

Introduction

Northern Telecom (NT), after performing for a number of years in the voice and data communication fields, is now integrating the two in an effort to meet the low- and medium-speed communication requirements of the automated office. NT's most successful products are the SL-1 and the SL-100, which may act as stand-alone PBXs, as nodes on the Electronic Switched Network (ESN), or both. The SL-1 and SL-100 were designed for expandability, with special attention given to the ability to upgrade previous models.

dressing capabilities, increased the number of lines, developed interfaces to public and private networks and to various types of computers and terminals, and enhanced and expanded software packages.

The SL-1 operates by digitizing the voice and multiplexing its control signals with the data transmission. Since two pairs of wire run to an integrated telephone set, one is used solely for voice conversations and the other for data with information about the voice call. The two separate channels allow a station to receive voice calls while transmitting data

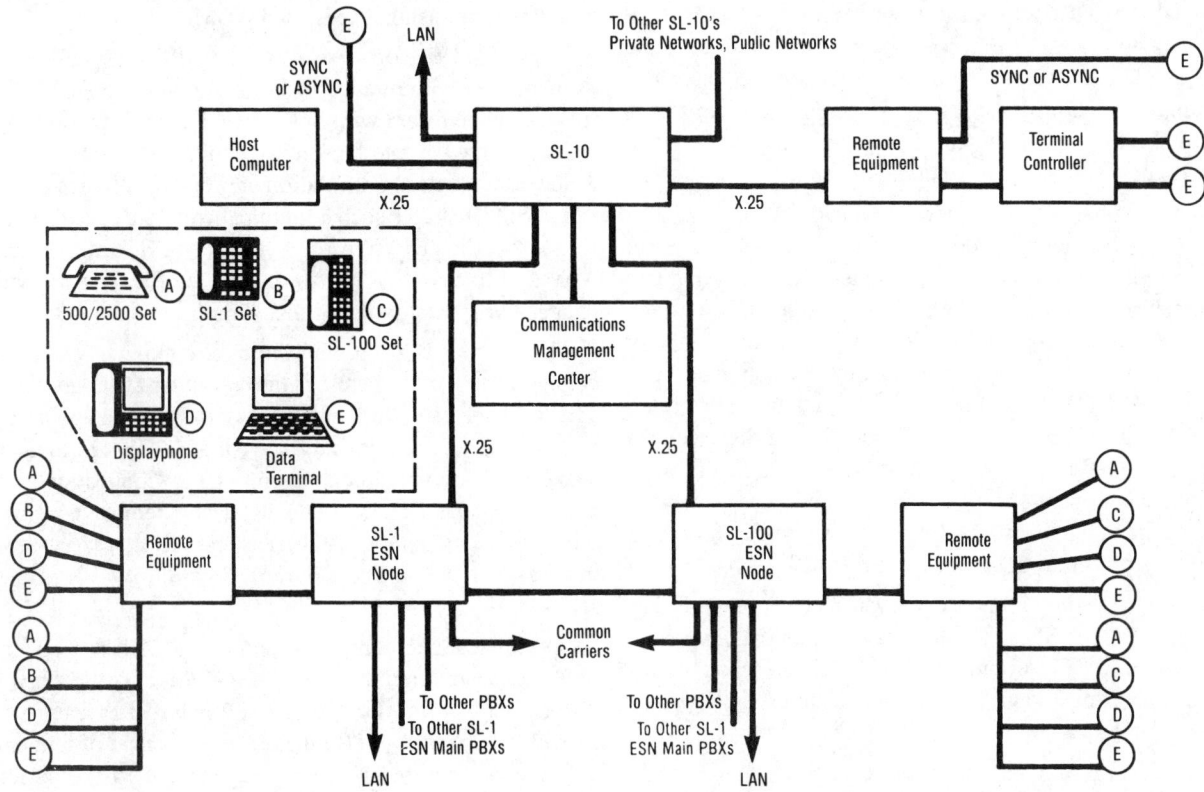

Figure: SL Family

SL-1

The SL-1 is a digital, computerized business communications system that uses a flexible system architecture, which can be configured to meet required traffic levels.

The SL-1 was originally a voice-only PBX, but was designed from the start to be capable of handling integrated voice and data applications. It has evolved into a significant telecommunications product. NT has increased memory increments from 4K cards to 192K cards, enhanced the processing capabilities, resulting in increased speed and ad-

or to receive data while engaged in voice transmission.

Voice is digitized in accordance with the North American Standard for 64 Kbps, 8 bit code Pulse Code Modulation (PCM) using mu-law compression. This forms the basis for the T1 carrier compatibility used by the SL-1 in its distributed network Remote Peripheral Equipment (RPE) feature, which allows the PBX to be extended up to 80 miles.

To allow for expansion, redundant common equipment, a segmented bus structure and a Distributed Switching Network (DSN) were implemented. Each network multiplex loop with 32 time division multiplexing (TDM) slots handling 2.048 Mbps transmission rate can support up to 160 station instruments, 80 trunks, or a mixture of station instruments and trunks. The modular card slot concept of the peripheral equipment shelf permits any combination of line, data, and trunk cards up to the shelf capacity of ten cards. Sixteen network loops form a network group and the SL-1 can support up to 5 network groups. The SL-1 can physically interface up to 19,200 terminations and can handle up to 1500 simultaneous conversations.

To incorporate data into the original voice-only PBX, the SL-1 telephone set and standard two-pair wiring are used, and two system components are installed: a data line card (DLC) at the switch and a terminal interface device at the terminal. The DLC supports two voice and two data ports or four data ports. The DLC microprocessor presents voice and data as two individual information streams to the SL-1 system; the type of transmission, voice or data, is transparent to the system. This technique eliminates the need to develop new software for data transmission.

One terminal interface device, called the add-on data module (ADM) attaches directly to the SL-1 telephone set and provides the interface to the data terminal (or equivalent equipment), as well as to the SL-1 set and the transmission line. The ADM is compatible with most terminals, computer systems, or other communication devices equipped with RS232 interfaces. This microprocessor-controlled unit replaces modems, acoustic couplers, and limited distance data sets. The ADM, which has an assigned data directory number, may operate in a stand-alone mode, as in answer-only applications. The ADM can operate synchronously at up to 56 Kbps or asynchronously at up to 19.2 Kbps.

A new version of the ADM was recently announced. Designated the V.35 ADM, the data communications device provides CCITT's Standard V.35 interface capabilities while supporting all synchronous data features and capabilities of the SL-1 ADM.

The CCITT V.35 interface protocol is designed to enhance data communications capabilities for devices that communicate at rates exceeding 20 Kbps. It is the most commonly used interface for these speeds. The V.35 ADM incorporates new circuitry and cabling to match the V.35 interface requirements, permitting synchronous data transmission at rates up to 56 Kbps.

The V.35 ADM can be used with any synchronous protocol, including Bisync, SDLC, HDLC, and DDCMP. It provides such features as dedicated modem access, inbound and outbound modem pooling, and a hotline with automatic connection for users who regularly communicate only with a single point.

For data transmission in areas where an electronic telephone is not required, an asynchronous interface module (AIM) can perform many of the functions of the ADM, operating independently of a telephone set. The AIM can handle data at speeds up to 110 to 19,200 bps and permits keyboard dialing from the terminal. A 500 or 2500 standard telephone set may be plugged into the AIM to allow voice and digital data communications using three-pair wiring. Terminals connect through an RS-232 interface. An asynchronous interface line card can support four AIM units.

For high-density applications, the multi-channel data system (MCDS), which uses only two power supplies, allows 64 asynchronous devices, such as printers, to be connected to the SL-1. Answer-only applications thus can be maintained without using a dedicated ADM.

Previously, local access for PCs required an asynchronous communications adapter and a modem, or an integral modem card with low-speed data transmission capability. A new PC interface card permits faster data transfer, at speeds up to the PC limitation of 9,600 bps. It also permits use of SL-1 features such as automatic dialing speed call and ring again directly from the computer keyboard. The card works with any SL-1 system and requires no software changes or special tools for installation.

The PC interface card plugs into the computer, and a wire connected to the device plugs into a standard telephone jack. The interface card works with standard IBM data communications software to transmit data using the RS-422 industry-standard data communications interface. Connection to the SL-1 gives the PC access to local and remote terminals, other PCs, computers, databases, and via shared modems, databases such as The Source, CompuServe, and Dow Jones.

Specialized components support digital 128 Kbps full duplex transmission between the ADM and the DLC at distances of up to 4000 feet. Use of the RPE feature can extend the distance to 80 miles. The full range of transmission characteristics, which are transparent to the system, include 5-8 bit character codes, 1, 1.5, 2 stop bits, 50-19200 bps asynchronous data rate and 56 Kbps synchronous data rate, Echoplex/no Echoplex, odd, even, no parity, auto answer, complete path testing diagnostics, strappable RS232 signals, etc. The originating ADM downloads these characteristics to the module on the receiving end, which adjusts accordingly. Control settings are located under a lift-up panel on the ADM.

The SL-1 also features inbound and outbound modem pooling. Inbound pooling allows a user to call into a modem pool and be connected to a computer port by a dedicated terminal; therefore, dedicated lines to each unit are not necessary. In outbound modem pooling, the data user acquires a modem from the modem pool, dials the external telephone number, and establishes communications from the terminal. The integrated voice and data system supports asynchronous data communications over analog lines (WATS, FX, TIE, etc.) at speeds up to 1,200 bps.

The SL-1 does not support computer-to-computer communication, because Northern Telecom feels that this is a high speed application for which other technologies are better suited.

An integrated messaging system permits two-way communications between the SL-1 PBX and an attached information processor through an RS-232C interface. The SL-1 PBX converts coded data from phone sets into messages for the attached processor, and transmits data from the indicators on the appropriate phone sets. A single-station system can handle messages for up to 200 people.

SL-1 reliability requirements are met by means of a fully redundant memory/CPU (in SL-1N and SL-1XN) and an optional battery back-up power supply, which can be configured to meet the individual requirements of the customer. In the case of power failure, the system is immediately converted to back-up power and no service is interrupted, even that which was active at the time of power failure. A software package of remote fault diagnostics is able to pinpoint 90-95 percent of the problems according to claims.

SL-1 Enhancements

In 1983 there was a change to the SL-1 family. Three switches were available in the first quarter of 1984: The SL-1M doubled the number of simultaneous data connections over the current SL-1M version. A new CPU, 60 percent faster than the current one, is used. This particular model serves the 40- to 300-line switch market.

The SL-1N is non-blocking to 840 lines or ports; the SL-1XN is non-blocking to 3000 lines. These two switches essentially replace the SL-1LE and SL-1VLE models. Again, performance improvement of 60 percent is claimed over the switches replaced.

The second new product was 3270 emulation on the SL-1. Through a converter manufactured by southern California-based PCI, up to seven 3270-type devices can be connected.

Another new product was a box to allow 3270s to be switched through the SL-1 PBX. Coaxial cable is used to connect the 3270 device to the converter box, which then reduces the speed to 56 Kbps to transmit over twisted pair to the SL-1. The SL-1, in turn, sends information at 56 Kbps to another box, which converts back to 3270 speeds for transmission over 93 ohm coax to an IBM mainframe.

The ASIM announced in September 1984 permits asynchronous and synchronous terminals such as the IBM Personal Computer, IBM Display Writer, and Xerox 560 to communicate quickly, easily, and economically with various databases through the SL-1. ASIM was designed for SL-1 customers who want to alternately operate their data terminals in the synchronous mode and in the asynchronous mode.

A stand-alone module, the ASIM provides a single RS-232 interface for synchronous and asynchronous terminal. By supporting both data communication protocols, the ASIM eliminates the need for different interfaces to support synchronous and asynchronous terminals: this can eliminate the need for modems in local data networks, thereby lowering the cost to the user of an integrated system.

SL-1 Gateways

The SL-1 System 36 gateway permits integration of personal computers, printers, and other ASCII terminals with IBM System 34, 36, and 38 host computers. The gateway enables the SL-1 to transmit and switch data from these ASCII terminals to the IBM host computers at speeds up to 9,600 bps. With the SL-1 System 36 gateway connected to a variety of computers over standard twisted-pair telephone wiring, users can access local databases or databases in other buildings, cities, or countries.

The SL-1/X.25 gateway offers asynchronous ASCII terminals direct, digital format access to packet-switched networks through the SL-1. Access to the SL-1 is accomplished via a packet assembler/disassembler which assembles data in blocks or packets. The SL-1 then routes the data to a public or private packet-switched network. With the network connection established, the terminals can communicate with workstations and host computers over a wide geographic area. The X.25 gateway deliveries are scheduled in the first quarter of 1985.

SL-100

The SL-100 system uses a time-division multiplex (TDM) switching matrix which switches pulse code modulation (PCM) traffic and directly interfaces with T1 lines or the equivalent. The SL-100 switching network derives its efficiency from several key features. Its solid-state technology provides highly reliable circuits and crosspoints. Since it requires less than 10 percent of the space that a crossbar-switching equivalent would require, major space savings are achieved. The network is inherently four-wire. The regeneration of the digital signal through the system permits close control of cross-talk, distortion, and attenuation. Its flexible, modular design permits it to grow from a very small to a very large system incrementally by adding network modules. The switching network is duplicated to increase reliability.

A characteristic of the SL-100 is the use of stored program control and software modularity to enable the system to accommodate a wide variety of new services and advancements, allowing the system to evolve without major redesign.

The SL-100 system consists of a stored-program-controlled central control complex (CCC); a duplicated, four-stage, folded, solid-state, inherently four-wire, digital time-division switching network; a peripheral module (PM) consisting of trunk modules (TM), digital trunk controller (DTC), line concentrating modules (LCMs), line group controllers (LGC), and remote modules; input/output controllers (IOCs); and a modular system comprised of operating system, call processing, maintenance, and administration software programs.

The central control complex (CCC) consists of a group of four units which act together to formulate the proper response and issue instructions to subsidiary units. Each member of the synchronized pair of central processing units (CPUs) has a solid-state dedicated memory where stored programs and network data are located. The program store memory module is associated with a CPU and is a repository for the program instructions required by the CPU for call processing, maintenance, and administrative tasks. The data store memory module, also associated with a CPU, contains transient information on a per-call basis, as well as customer data and office parameters. Additional memory modules can be added to accommodate growth.

The CPUs have been designed to execute a high-level language called PROTEL. Interfacing with the peripheral units is achieved via duplicated central message controllers (CMCs). The CMC controls the flow and priority of messages between the other units of the CCC and the network message controller (NMC) in the various network modules (NM).

The peripheral modules (PMs) provide the interface between the switching network and subscriber lines, analog trunks and service circuits, and digital carrier facilities. These include a digital trunk controller (DTC), a trunk module (TM), a line concentrating module (LCM), a line group controller (LGC), and a remote line module (RLM). The message system provides the control interface between the peripheral modules and the rest of the system. The PMs are microprocessor-controlled and are responsible for scanning the lines in the modules for changes of circuit state, performing timing functions for call processing, collecting and storing digits, generating digital tones, sending/receiving signaling and control information to/from the CCC, and providing integrity checking of the network.

The digital trunk controller (DTC) provides a direct interface between the SL-100 digital switching network and digital carrier signals referred to as DS-1 or T-1. It also provides the following features:

- Ability to software-assign, by means of data modification order (DMO), any two DS-1 systems in the switching system as primary and secondary timing links for interoffice synchronization.
- Ability to use any channel within a DS-1 system as any existing type of inter-office trunk or special service facility.
- Ability to mix any of the trunk types listed above within a DS-1 system and within a DTC.
- Correction of existing defects such as provision of high tone and elimination of MF echo during outpulsing.
- Transmission levels maintained as per DCM, i.e., no loss or gain in the DTC.

The trunk module (TM) encodes and multiplexes incoming speech from a maximum of 30 analog trunks into 8-bit PCM. It combines them with internal control signals and the trunk supervisory and control signals for transmission at 2.56 Mbps to the network. In the other direction, the 30 digital speech signals and the two control channel signals received from the network are demultiplexed and decoded by the TM into 30 individual channels. It also accommodates service circuits such as MF receivers, announcement trunks, and test circuits, either on dedicated TM or with analog trunks.

The line control module (LCM) provides the line interface to SL-100 subscribers. Each LCM shelf is equipped with a controller which provides line-related control functions such as scanning, ringing control, and channel assignment. The controller is also responsible for messaging to and from the Line Group Controller. The LCM operates in dual-shelf mode, with control duplication through load sharing.

The line group controller (LGC) is used in the SL-100 office as the peripheral processor module for all subscriber lines, including remotes, and as direct digital interfaces to other digital subscriber carrier systems. In addition, it supports services such as electronic set and data lines.

The remote modules home onto an SL-100 host switch. The design of the RM is based on that of the LCM. RMs provide the same grade of service as the LCM subscribers.

The switching network employs four stages of time switching in providing the 4-wire voice paths between the originating PM and the terminating PM, under control of the central processing unit (CPU). The network also distributes the control messages to and from the PM. The network is fully duplicated from the originating PM to the terminating PM in order to achieve the necessary reliability.

Each of the planes forms an identical and independent half

of the network. Each plane is a set of network modules (NMs) which are the major building block of the plane and consist of an incoming and outgoing side. The provision of separate paths for each direction of transmission gives the network its inherent 4-wire characteristic. Each side of an NM provides two stages of time switching by using 16 time switches, arranged as 8 in x 8 out, per stage. Thus, the NM provides full availability from 64 digital network ports to 64 junctions. Each network port operates at 2.56 Mbps and carries 30 voice channels plus two signaling and control channels.

Each NM provides 1,920 voice channels in each direction (64 ports x 30 channels). Growth of the network is accomplished by the addition of NM in each plane and arrangements of connections between planes. The full network consists of 32 NM in each plane providing 61,440 voice channels in each direction in each plane.

The LCM and TM convert the incoming voice frequency signals and supervisory signals to 8-bit PCM signals and combine them with internal control signals. These digital signals are multiplexed into a high-speed digital bit-stream which is transmitted to an input port of the network, where they are demultiplexed and converted into individual channels of combined speech and signaling. Each LCM equipment frame has a capacity of 1280 subscriber lines, and each shelf TM has a capacity of 30 analog trunks. The DTC provides an interface for signaling and alignment between digital carrier lines and the network highways. Each DTC has a capacity of 20 digital T1 carrier lines.

Data cards fit into the system in exactly the same manner as the voice cards, which gives rise to a trade-off factor. The only limitation in size is the real-time limitation to the switching element. Up to 240 calls may be initiated in one second, which does not include those already in operation; more than that loads down the system. Terminals are connected through the system using an RS-232-C connection, and they may transmit up to 56 Kbps synchronous and 19.2 Kbps asynchronous.

Using a standard twisted pair, the station set may be placed at a distance of 2.5 miles from the switch, which is very attractive in a campus environment. For the geographically separated sites, the system presently supports a T1 interface and operates on CCITT X.25 internally. Future plans include development of an X.25 gateway and an interface to Northern Telecom's smaller SL-1 system. Alternate media which are currently being used with SL-100 systems are radio and infrared.

The system also supports uniform dialing, incorporating seven-digit numbers on the network and 10-digit numbers off the network. This uniform dialing requirement limits the system to 640 locations, with 40,000 connections at each location, which translates to 26 million stations.

The operation of this system is similar to the operation of other PBX systems. The system supports special station sets and common rotary and touch-tone phones, compromising only the ease of using the features that are available on each. If a standard telephone is used, it is necessary to use the flash hook and two-digit authorization code. However, if an electronic proprietary phone set is used, programmed buttons determine the functions. LCD lamps also indicate which features are invoked at any particular time.

SL-100 Software

The SL-100 software is made up of many individual processes which perform the various functions necessary for operation. These processes communicate with each other, or with similar processes in peripheral devices, via a message-passing facility, and they compete for machine resources such as storage registers, common control equipment, and real-time.

As a call progresses from its set-up to take-down, processes involved with the call move from state to state. State transition occurs when a process receives a message from another process, indicating the occurrence of an event. The control of processes and allocation of machine resources falls to an overall controlling mechanism, the operating system.

Each of the programs within each major functional area (call processing, maintenance, etc.) varies in size, depending on the complexity of the function. All programs are on-line; however, the flexibility exists for the future use of off-line programs if the need arises (e.g., extended maintenance capabilities or extended administration capabilities).

The software is modular and located within several different modules in the SL-100 system. A typical software module consists of a procedural interface and a number of implementation sections. The implementation sections contain data declarations, code for procedures declared in the interface, and additional procedures. Interface procedures are available outside the module, but data and code declared in the implementation sections are private to the module and are not accessible from outside.

If the selection algorithm or data structures are ever modified, the effects of such a change are strictly contained within the module, and the only requirement is to implement the functions as specified by the interface procedures. Each module can be compiled separately and can be incorporated in the operating system through a binding (linking) procedure. Therefore, changes of software modules or implementation of new modules do not require the complete software system to be recompiled and reloaded.

SL-100 Communication Protocols And Gateways

NT now has an SL-100 feature that will permit switched access to IBM 3274 and 3276 controllers from IBM 3270 terminals over twisted-pair telephone wiring. This feature eliminates the need for more costly coaxial cable and makes terminal moves less expensive; it also allows the terminals to access multiple host computers and data bases because data can be routed by the SL-100 in the same way as any other voice or data call. Deliveries are scheduled for the third quarter of 1985.

An IBM 3270 protocol conversion feature for the SL-100 will permit most ASCII asynchronous terminals to operate as IBM 3178or 3278-type on-line terminals. A single protocol conversion unit connected to the SL-100 PBX permits as many as seven asynchronous terminals to be connected to various host computers. The conversion unit transfers the terminals' data into the standard format of data from an IBM 3178- or 3278-type terminal. Several conversion units can be connected to a single SL-100. Deliveries are scheduled for the third quarter of 1985.

Another protocol converter, the SL-100 System 36 gateway, will allow these same ASCII asynchronous terminals, personal computers, and printers to function as IBM System 34-, 36-, or 38-compatible products. They will communicate through the SL-100 system network with standard SNA/SDLC protocol capabilities. Deliveries are scheduled for the third quarter of 1985.

Another device allows the IBM PC or IBM PC XT to connect to and communicate in digital format with the SL-100 PBX via twisted-pair telephone wiring. The device, the SL-100 PC interface card, plugs into the computer, and a wire connected to the device plugs into a standard telephone jack, which is connected to the SL-100. The PC then has access to local and remote terminals, other PCs, computers, and data bases such as The Source, Dow Jones, and Compu-Server. Deliveries are scheduled for the third quarter of 1985.

A new asynchronous interface line card (AILC) allows low-cost connection of the IBM PC interface card and other asynchronous RS-422 compatible devices to the SL-100 PBX system. RS-422 is an industry-standard data communications interface using four wires in its connections. The AILC allows users of connected terminals to dial through the terminal keyboards and guides users in establishing connections through simple instructions. Deliveries are scheduled for the third quarter of 1985.

A new X.25 gateway unit connects to the SL-100, enabling ASCII asynchronous terminals to communicate through the SL-100, in digital format, with public or private packet data networks. Users can benefit from a more cost-effective, efficient, and reliable form of data communications through connection to twisted-pair telephone wiring. Deliveries are scheduled for the third quarter of 1985.

The computer-to-PBX interface (CPI) is a feature that can be incorporated into the SL-100 system to permit economical data communications from computer terminals through the SL-100 to a compatible computer. The CPI communicates the data over telephone wiring or other transmission media, using the industry T-carrier standard. T-carrier is the digital transmission rate adopted for the North American public telecommunications networks, based on a 1.544-Mbps channel that can be subdivided into smaller units. Deliveries are scheduled for the second quarter of 1985.

Conclusion

To improve the SL-1 and SL-100, Northern Telecom plans to incorporate selected local network interfaces and expand protocols under its OPEN World strategy. By developing asynchronous data interfaces and enhancing voice communication terminals, NT hopes to make greater use of its integrated voice/data Displayphone.

An office communications system for the '80s

Office communications needs during the 1980s
will be more diverse and more sophisticated.
To meet those needs, new systems must provide
an integrated office communications solution

Reprinted from *Telephony*, June 7, 1982. Copyright © 1982 by Telephony Publishing Corporation, 55 East Jackson Boulevard, Chicago, IL 60604.

MICHAEL P. LUDLOW

PROMPT, ACCURATE, efficient and economical communication is essential to sustaining a viable and competitive business. These factors are even more important when office worker productivity levels are stagnant, labor costs are increasing, and the shift to a white-collar worker, service-based economy continues.

To increase productivity levels, many businesses are making a substantial investment in new forms of office equipment such as word processors, electronic mail systems, distributed data processing equipment and multifunction workstations. The affordability of these devices was made possible mainly because of technology advances during the '70s in

---

MICHAEL P. LUDLOW is Director of Planning and Research, Telephone Div., Marketing, in Boca Raton, Fla., for Siemens Corp., Iselin, N.J.

the areas of microprocessors, memory systems (high-density random access memory and read only memory, and low-cost bulk memory), and software engineering techniques. These same technology advances today are being harnessed and effectively utilized to economically provide an integrated office communications solution with the potential to enable flow of information among the new types of office equipment, as well as handling voice communications—the integrated voice and data private branch exchange (IVD-PBX).

At the International Communications Assn. (ICA) show held May 2-7 in New Orleans, (see p. 78), Siemens Corp., Iselin, N.J., introduced its version of the IVD-PBX—Saturn III. It has been designed for the North American market with the full range of office communication needs of the '80s in mind—today's needs and those which will evolve during the decade. A key criteria in the system

design has been to ensure economical voice switching. Studies have shown that voice communications will continue to be the primary form of electronic transmission of information in the business and office environment.

Because of the present high priority for voice communications, a digital PBX must be cost-justifiable and competitively priced if configured as a voice-only system. However, the capability of transmitting and switching high speed data is intrinsic to the digital architecture. This has been achieved by providing high-speed transmission of voice and data information, in a digital format, via standard telephone wiring to optional digital telephones. Data switching can be configured and enabled through the addition of optional peripheral modules and an enhanced software load. Evolution of this system from a voice-only business switching system to a fully configured integrated office communications system

FIG. 1 *Saturn III hardware configuration.*

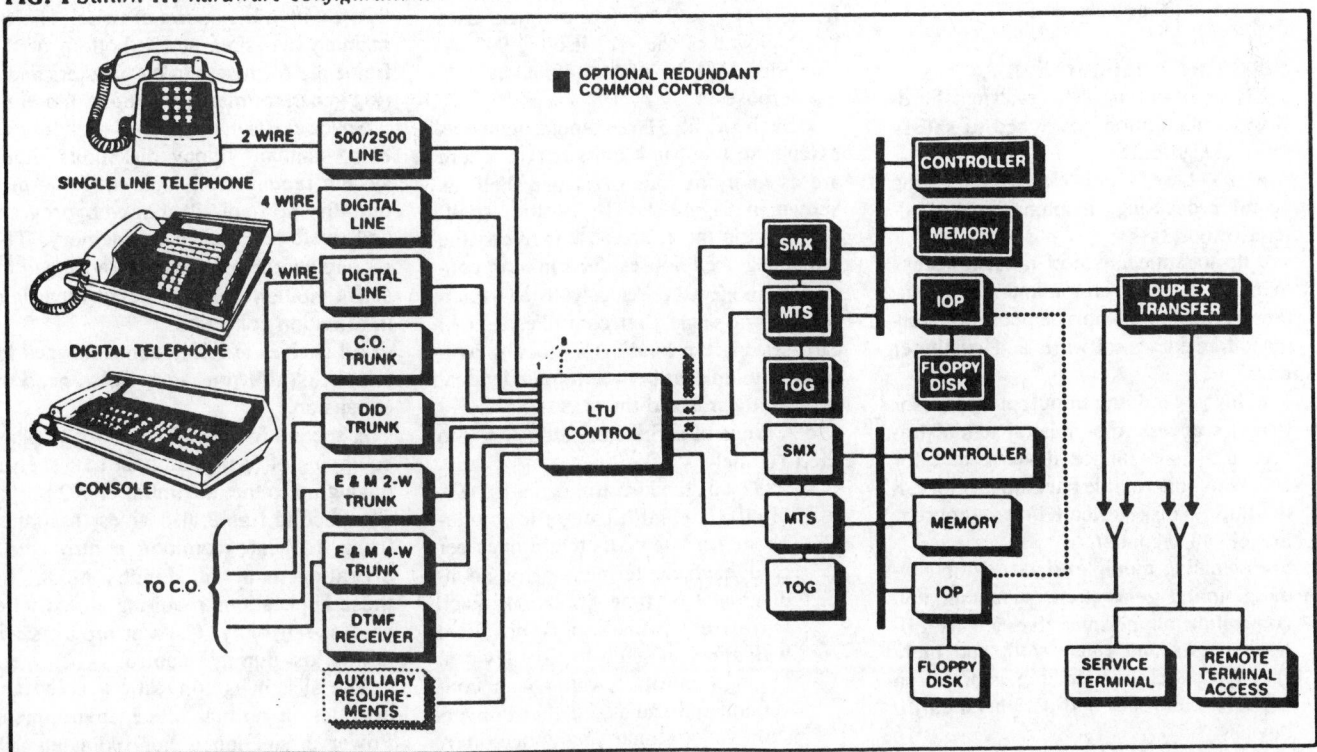

can therefore be achieved in low-cost, small incremental steps matching the growth in needs of the end user. The requirement to invest a large quantity of funds in a separate data-only switching system with its associated wiring and cabling costs, perhaps serving only a limited population of data users initially, therefore can be avoided.

This article will review briefly the architecture, key features, maintenance and administration, and general system capabilities of Saturn.

Design criteria

The key design criteria resulting from the evolving market environment outlined earlier, were as follows:

• capable of economical basic and full-featured voice operation;

• fully modular—hardware, software, and applications—to meet expansion/growth requirements;

• capable of operation in a modern office environment;

• high reliability;

• easy installation, maintenance, and administration;

• design capable of taking advantage of future technology evolutions;

• compatibility with existing and future data equipment interfaces, networks, and operating methods;

• human engineered for easy user training and acceptance; and

• digital technology to provide extensive voice and data integration potential —optimized for the data call environment (similar to the voice call environment in terms of holding times, bit rate limitations, casual access from office desk, use of shared resources and optimum connection/route selection).

Hardware configuration

Figure 1 outlines the system's hardware configuration developed to satisfy these design criteria:

• 8086-based controller for executing all call processing, maintenance, and administration tasks;

• up to 1 megabyte of random access memory (RAM), with minimum of 3 minutes power-fail memory support, for storing all resident software and customer data.

• high-speed imput/output processor (IOP) for access to peripheral administration and maintenance devices, and for access to non-volatile back-up memory, 8 in. floppy disk (reload time — approximately 40 seconds).

• signaling multiplexer (SMX) for handling timing generation, scanning, and controlling all peripherals such as off-hook, digits and ring on/off, and high-speed transfer of signaling information between controller and peripheral cards/devices.

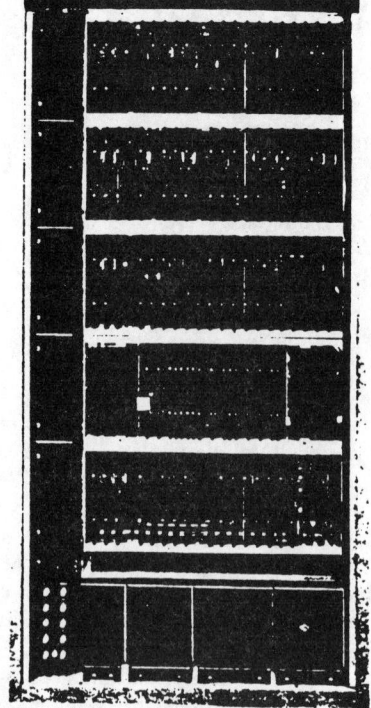

FIG. 2 *Saturn equipment frame.*

• memory time switch (MTS) made up of 32 highways each operating at 2.048 megabits per second (Mbps), 32 time-slots per highway, 64 kilobits per second (kbps) per time-slot—giving a total of 1024 ports. It is a totally non-blocking network capable of 512 simultaneous two-way (four-wire) connections (64 kbps each way). The potential exists for all ports to be in use at the same time. The MTS also provides digital level control for adjusting insertion loss and conferencing functions.

• Tone generator (TOG), with potential for as many as 32 different tones, uses one highway of the MTS leaving 992 usable ports for telephony and data switching purposes.

• Each of the 31 remaining highways extends to line trunk units (LTU). There are as many as four LTUs per shelf, as shown in Figure 2. The bottom shelf, plus the top three, are LTU shelves—the remaining shelf houses the common control components previously listed. Each shelf has a single LTU controller (LTUC) card serving the four LTUs—acting as a simple multiplexer between the individual peripheral cards and the MTS/SMX.

• A range of peripheral cards plug into the LTU shelves:

1. 500/2500 standard rotary and DTMF (dual tone multifrequency) telephone set line cards (eight lines per card, each line terminating on an individual LTU time-slot port). Each two-wire termination is provided with appropriate protection devices, ringing control, 2 watt/4 watt conversion, plus analog/digital conversion via a single-line codec/filter.

This operates at a standard 8 kHz (kilohertz) sampling, 8 bit companded μ Law, 255 segment, 64 kbps PCM (pulse code modulation) rate.

2. Digital telephone line cards (two lines per card). Each line terminates a four-wire connection supporting 192 kbps full duplex digital transmission to either a digital telephone, attendant console or busy lamp field. The 192 kbps consists of three 64 kbps time slots, one for voice, one for voice or data, and one for synchronization and control signaling. The voice and voice-or-data time slots each terminate on separate LTU time-slot ports, permitting separate but simultaneous switching of voice and data calls from the same telephone termination. The third time slot (control signaling) provides a medium speed communications control channel between the controller and the various peripheral apparatus, via the SMX.

3. Various standard trunk cards are provided, four trunks per card, using single line codec/filters for analog/digital conversion.

4. DTMF receivers, four per card, also plug into the LTU and are provisioned on a traffic-engineering basis.

Referring again to Figure 2, a single frame version of the system provides up to 480 usable ports, and can be equipped with a variety of peripheral cards. Power supplies are provisioned on a per-shelf basis. The bottom of the frame contains miscellaneous control and power units. The -48V (volt) supply is modular, and can be equipped on a traffic engineering basis, with a maximum of three. The remaining two slots at the bottom of the frame are for fuses/circuit breakers and a ring generator/memory support module.

Space exists in the control shelf for two 8 in. standard floppy disk units. Each system requires a minimum of one disk unit for non-volatile back-up program and customer data base memory. The second can be optionally provisioned for SMDR (station message detail recording) information collection.

All shelves are fully connectorized for easy installation and field growth/expansion.

A second frame can be added to allow equipping of four additional LTU shelves (giving up to the maximum of 992 ports). The second frame also gives the option for a duplicate common control shelf, operating in a hot standby mode, for those applications requiring an extra degree of reliability. Calls in progress will not be lost during a control switchover.

The system is convection-cooled and operates in normal office environment. Power dissipation is approximately 800 watts per frame. This, together with the small frame size—36 in. × 27 in. × 72 in.—is the highest density equipment packaging of any equivalent convection-cooled PBX system. Power source can be 110 VAC (volts, alternating current) 60 HZ (57-63 HZ, 96-127 VAC) or 220 VAC, 60 HZ (57-63 HZ, 196-254 VAC). A 50 HZ and a DC (direct current) power option also are available.

Software configuration

As with any PBX required to offer an extensive set of business features and interface with a wide variety of peripheral devices and networks, software engineering is a key technology.

Software is highly structured and self-documenting for easy maintenance and feature upgrade. The system uses state-event, device-oriented decision tables with a single clock interrupt, event and command queues, and multiple processing levels. A clock interrupt occurs every few milliseconds. This activates the pre-processor software level which processes changes in state detected in peripheral cards and queues them for action at the next level (base), subject to priority and function. For example, an off-hook state is detected by the pre-processor, and is sorted, prioritized, and queued for base level action. When the action request is removed from the queue, the base level checks that the line appearance and class of service are valid and then determines from the state-event table the appropriate action required—in this case, to return dial tone to the off-hook line appearance. Base level then sends appropriate messages to form a network connection between the line appearance port and the dial tone TOG port.

A third level of processing occurs during idle time, when free processing time is used for low priority maintenance, administrative and other background testing activities.

The system has a wide range of features for single-line telephones (500/2500), a proprietary key telephone, an attendant console, maintenance integrity and administration. Only a few of these features are described here to illustrate the system's capabilities.

Features are provided which allow single-line sets to emulate most of the capabilities of key systems. Features such as distinctive ring, distinctive camp-on/call back, call hold, call forwarding, message waiting, speed calling, pickup, do not disturb and hunting are accessed through one or two digit codes.

A three-model family of digital telephones are available for more sophisticated features. Each set is microprocessor controlled and contains its own codec/filter for voice analog/digital conversion. Some key points include:

• system powered via four-wire connection up to 2000 ft. (local power up to 4000 ft.);

• uniform station system wiring;

• couples to digital data interface for transmission of data over same four-wire connection;

• digital station pushbutton dialing;

• available with LCD (liquid crystal display) alphanumeric display (16-character);

• 10, 18, or 26 programable feature buttons with LED (light emitting diode) indicators, flexibly assignable as either feature or line pickup buttons; and

• programable features include: transfer, call forwarding, hold and park, last number redial, save number redial, system speed call, station speed call, hands free, message waiting, time of day, DSS (trunk, speed call, station, UCD [uniform call distribution] group), and voice calling.

The digital telephone also may access other features via one- or two-digit access codes.

If equipped with a display, each digit dialed or the identity of an incoming caller is displayed. The display also is used for indicating call forwarding number and many other call states encountered during the processing of telephone calls. If there are messages waiting for the digital telephone user, the message waiting key LED is illuminated. By repeatedly pressing this key, the numbers of the parties leaving the messages can be scrolled through on the LCD display. Pressing the message call-back key will automatically place a call to the party leaving the message.

Data calls are made possible through an optional digital data interface (DDI) module which simply plugs into the digital telephone. It has the following features: simultaneous voice/data transmission; asynchronous transmission (up to 9.6 kbps currently); automatic data call answer; bit transparency; data call origination—station; signal for incoming data call; half/full duplex operation; data resource pooling; and RS232C compatible.

A data call is initiated by pressing the DDI data call key and then, using the digital telephone keypad, dialing the telephone number of the required data re-

source. DDI LEDs provide continuous indication of the status of the data call. Simultaneous voice calls to the same or different destinations can be set up.

The system can be equipped with as many as eight consoles. Each console has a 40-character alphanumeric display used for continuous updates of lengths of call queues (incoming, recall, local). It also is used for identifying incoming call trunk group and other call status information.

Alarm indicators are included on the console, and the attendant has the ability to request display of a failure history buffer to allow reporting of any faults to maintenance personnel.

All 34 keys are fully assignable, although a preset arrangement of the important operational keys is recommended for ease and efficiency of use.

Consoles are microprocessor controlled and contain a codec/filter for voice analog/digital conversion. They are connected to the PBX via standard four-wire connections and are system-powered up to 2000 ft. Local power extends the range up to 4000 ft. The connection to the PBX is through the same digital line card as the digital telephone.

A full set of maintenance features are provided, which cover: automatic fault analysis; system alarms and reporting; failure history buffer; automatic background routine exercise of equipment; sanity checks; manual initiation of testing; local or remote maintenance access; optional redundant control (automatic switchover); and non-volatile memory back-up (floppy disk).

Comprehensive system management and control features simplify administration and ensure optimum performance. The features include: customer memory updating (local and remote); plain English format man-machine interface; on-line traffic metering; SMDR (output via RS232C interface or optionally to second floppy disk for off-line processing); feature usage measurement; least cost routing (LCR); and special night answer position.

The unit is a PBX designed for the diverse office communication needs which will emerge during the '80s. The importance of voice communications has not been forgotten—a highly modular digital switching architecture permits provision of economical voice operation while retaining the ability to grow in small incremental steps in directions matching the evolving communication needs of business organizations. □

TELEPHONY

Issued by Telephone Division
1001 Broken Sound Parkway N.W., Boca Raton, FL 33431 (305) 994-8100

Siemens Corporation

CC/4000-024-121
ESP 10M 7/82 Printed in U.S.A

AT&T Information Systems System 85

Introduction

With the divestiture of AT&T, American Bell Incorporated (ABI) was formed on January 1, 1983. At that time, ABI introduced its first new product, the Dimension System 85. (In August 1983, ABI became AT&T Information Systems.) This system is meant to enhance current dimension systems and may directly upgrade a dimension system with Feature Package 8, Issue 3, by replacing only the switch (from analog to digital).

System Concept

The System 85 is a communications and information management system incorporating digital switching technology and stored program control. It integrates simultaneous voice and data communications and offers functions designed to meet current and future needs.

The System 85 design is based on a distributed control architecture that uses microprocessors to offload tasks from the main processor. The system architecture provides for flexibility and modular growth.

Large-scale integration technology is evident in a new family of digital voice and integrated voice/data terminals. A standard communications protocol has been developed to complement this use of LSI technology. The Digital Communications Protocol (DCP) allows a multiplexed stream of digitized voice and high-speed data to be transmitted over normal telephone wiring to the digital switch. The combination of the DCP and the microprocessor-controlled digital terminals supports an integrated workstation concept. Simultaneous voice and data communications are possible through a single terminal, via a common wire into a single port on the communications processor. The architecture also allows rearrangement of both voice and data terminals with a common wall plug.

System Components

Control Complex contains a group of components that control, supervise, and coordinate system operations. Those components are the system processor, the system memory, the tape system, the data communications interface unit, and the input/output data channels.

- *The System Processor*: The System Processor is the 501CC which is a Bell System designed processor using bit slice technology. The 501CC provides a high capacity call processing system, boosting the System 85's Busy Hour Capacity (BHC) to 20,000 calls. The processor is a 16 bit processor utilizing 24 bit address words. The 501CC heads System 85's hierarchical control structure of microprocessors, performing the highest level of call processing, administrative, and maintenance functions. It acts as the master controller for the distributed microprocessors that control specific functions within the switching module.

- *The System Memory*: The memory array provides a capacity of 2 million words of random access memory. This memory stores the system programs, parameters, translations, and operating status. The memory consists of dynamic circuits requiring periodic refreshing. Protection is provided by nominal power hold over or optional long term power supply. Back up is provided by the Control Complex Tape system.

  High-speed cache memory may be provided to further decrease the time required to access program instructions and data. The cache duplicates 16K words of the main memory, maintaining "copies" of frequently-accessed storage elements. Therefore, when a storage element is repeatedly requested, the cache can quickly return its copy of that element, replacing the slower main-memory access. Because programs contain loops, storage elements that have been recently referenced will likely soon be required again.

  Cache memory will usually not be needed when the System 85 is configured with nine or fewer modules. With ten or more modules, cache may be included depending on call volume requirements.

- *The Tape System*: The Tape System includes a tape cartridge, a High Capacity Mini Recorder (HCMR) and a tape interface circuit pack. The major function of the tape system is to reload memory whenever power to the system is interrupted or whenever memory is lost for any reason.

- *The Data Communications Interface Unit (DCIU)*: The DCIU is a processor with its own memory and I/O circuits. It provides advanced packet switched links between the 501CC and the Applications Processors. In addition, Release 2 provides Distributed Communications System (DCS) capabilities, utilizing the DCIU to provide the data link to other DCS nodes. The R2 DCIU provides up to eight ports. This capacity allows the connection of up to seven APs and up to eight DCS links in any combination as long as the total does not exceed eight.

- *The Input/Output Channels*: The I/O Channels are the interface circuits connecting peripherals to the system processor. These peripherals can include Attendant

Consoles, Station Message Detail Recording (SMDR) output and the System Management Terminal (SMT). Ports for the Maintenance and Administration Panel (MAAP) and Remote Maintenance, Administration, and Traffic System II (RMATS-II) are also provided by these channels.

- *Time Multiplexed Switch*: The new component introduced to the system architecture is the Time Multiplexed Switch (TMS). TMS provides the link between the Control Complex and the Communications Switching Modules in a multi-module configuration. R2 can be configured as a single or a multi-module system.

The TMS is a time multiplexed space division switch that interconnects modules. It is the space element of the time-space-time digital switch architecture, providing connections between ports on different modules.

Fiber optic data links are used for the time slot information transfer. The fiber optic links provide extremely fast data transfer (32 Mbps) and almost no susceptibility to electromagnetic interference.

The System 85 architecture provides multi-module capability utilizing a single fiber optic link between the TMS and each module. This structure provides a system that is easily expanded to meet your customers' requirements.

- *Communications Switching Module (CSM)*: Two components are added to the CSM when a multi module configuration is required. These additions are the inter-module data store and the light guide interface which are added to the module to provide the interface to other modules.

- *Reserve Power*: The System 85 operation depends on the continual supply of commercial power. To protect the system and the customer's communications in the event of commercial power failures, two degrees of protection are available to your customer. The first, Nominal Holdover, protects against brief power outages. The second, Extended Power Reserve, is designed to provide for continued System 85 operation during a longer power outage.

  a) *Nominal Holdover*: This capability is designed to maintain power should a short-term loss of power occur. The holdover power sustains operation of the main system cabinets for 3 to 5 minutes.

  b) *Extended Power Reserve*: The Extended Power Reserve capability maintains power for the System 85 during a long-term loss of commercial power. In the event of an interruption of power, the extended reserve will sustain operation of System 85 up to eight hours. Extended Power Reserve is provided by

a battery plant designed individually to meet the needs of your customer. The size of the battery plant is based upon the size of the System 85 it supports and the length of time for which your customer requires protection.

The System Protocol, Digital Communications Protocol (DCP), integrates intra-premises voice and data communications by providing workstations with digital transmission over unconditioned telephone wiring. The DCP format will interface with emerging international standards.

DCP can be provided to any workstation along with voice via a universal walljack and standard building telephone wiring. The DCP allows data communications at speeds up to 19.2 Kbps asynchronous or 64 Kbps synchronous.

The APs and the DCIU use a modified CCITT X.25 layered protocol for data transfers. As the standard synchronous communications interface protocol for host-to-host and host-to-data switching network data transfers, this protocol uses a packet-switching structure to provide a virtual circuit with several logical channels. By packetizing data, multiplexing independent data streams, and performing error control, it allows high-speed transfer of data between APs or between an AP and Net/1000.

The Applications Processor handles the advanced capabilities of the system. These functions can be implemented in a single processor or with multiple APs, depending on the user requirements. These can be tightly coupled to the 501CC processor via a connection to the DCIU to provide integrated voice/data services. The AP initially supports software for nine applications:

- The message center
- Call detail recording and reporting
- Terminal change management
- Facilities management
- An electronic directory
- The electronic document communications feature
- Terminal emulation
- Building management
- Automatic transmission measurement system (ATMS) (the first four applications require connection to the DCIU; the latter five do not.)

The interconnection of the APs with the other elements of the system is illustrated in the Figure. All services except building management can be offered on a single AP if the capacity of multiple processors is not required.

The AP is controlled by a proprietary 16-bit main processor using a version of the UNIX operating system. The main processor communicates with internal and external equipment through 8-bit microprocessor-based systems. For mass storage the processor contains a 40 or 160 Mbyte hard disk and a high capacity mini-recorder or 9-track tape deck. The mini-recorder contains 26 Mbytes of memory for disk backup. Peripheral controllers, which are built around a common design using an 8-bit microprocessor, perform all device-dependent functions.

Besides disk and tape controllers, there are line and terminal controllers. Line controllers provide communication channels for synchronous and asynchronous modes at speeds up to 19.2 Kbps. A line controller controls two line ports which interface to the DCIU, a customer host, data modules, or modems. Besides DCP, the line controller can also operate with a multipoint private line emulating the binary synchronous (3270) and 2780/3780 protocol locally or over a synchronous private data facility.

Data modules enable data terminal equipment to be connected to the DCP link. They convert the terminal data into the DCP format via an RS-232 interface and permit it to be transmitted through the digital switch matrix to another data endpoint. The data modules support full- and half-duplex operations at standard asynchronous and synchronous rates up to 19.2 Kbps. The data modules are designed using a microprocessor with memory on the same chip. The software that controls the functions of the data module is loaded during manufacture. The three types of data modules available with the System 85 are the Digital Terminal Data Module (DTDM), the Processor Data Module (PDM), and the Trunk Data Module (TDM).

The DTDM is attached to a digital voice terminal. It has a Data Communications Equipment (DCE) interface and provides for data call origination from any asynchronous ASCII terminal keyboard or tel set dial. With this module, the

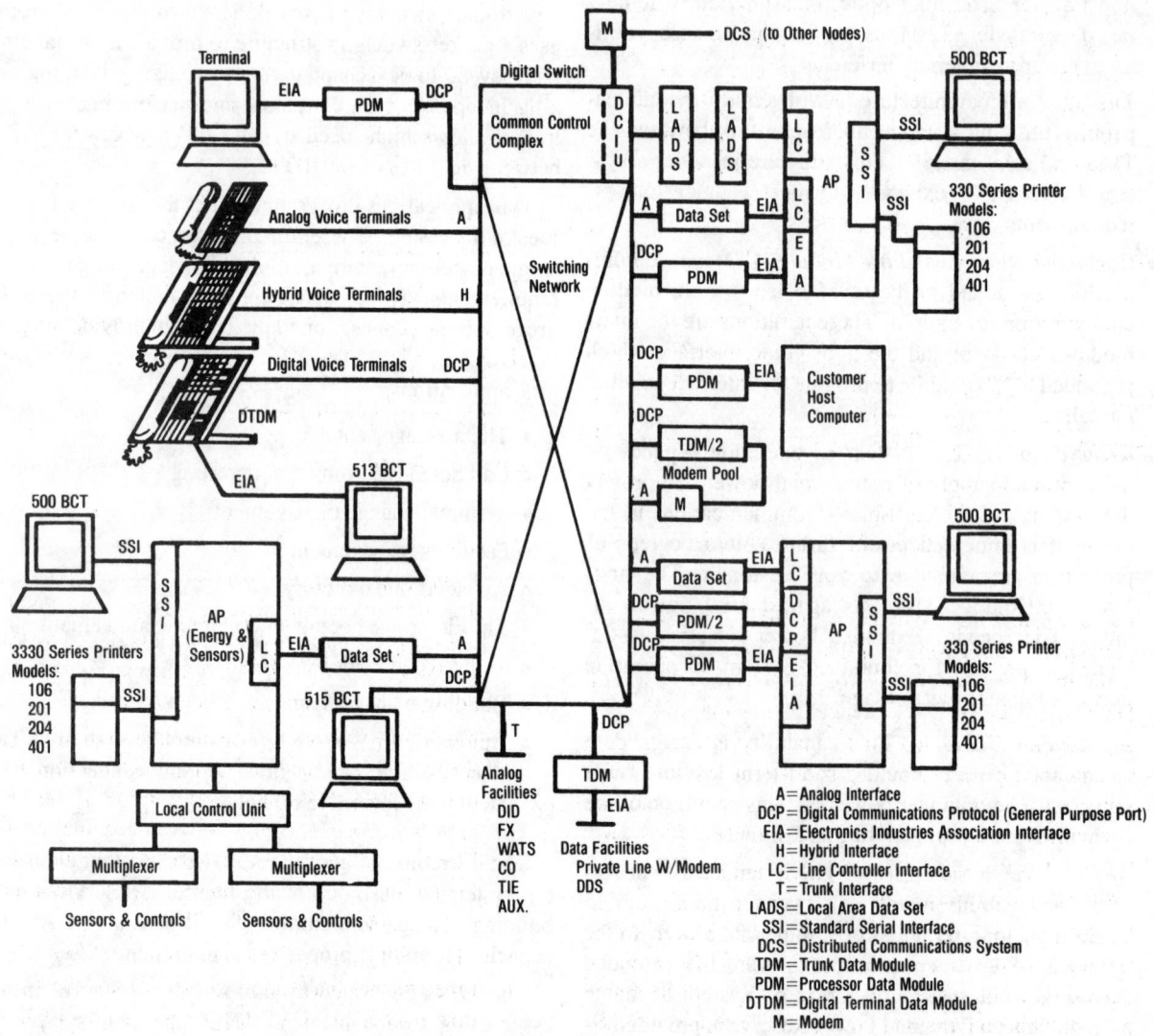

Figure: System 85 Communications System Release 2

290

associated voice terminal may be used while a data call is in progress.

The PDM has a DCE interface and is used to connect terminals, APs, or user host computers to the digital switch. It connects directly to the DCP link without an associated telephone. The PDM provides the optional call origination capabilities using asynchronous ASCII dialing. APs can initiate intra-premise calls in this manner or associated tel set dial.

- *DS-1 Interface*: The DS-1 Interface was announced in June 1983. Available on Dimension System 85 Release 2, DS-1 provides the interface from a 1.544 Mbps DS-1 type facility into System 85. An integral part of System 85, the DS-1 Interface offers an economical alternative to businesses needing dedicated voice and data circuit connections in a point-to-point configuration.

The System 85 DS-1 Interface provides tie trunk type appearances to connect either two System 85s or a System 85 and a Dimension PBX. Between two System 85s (see Figure), the DS-1 Interface can use the "common channel" signaling technique to provide 23 fully digitized channels at 64 Kbps, without using modems. Either "clear channel" data less than or equal to 64 Kbps or digitized voice can be sent through this configuration. In this type service, the channel is referred to as an alternate voice/data (AVD) channel.

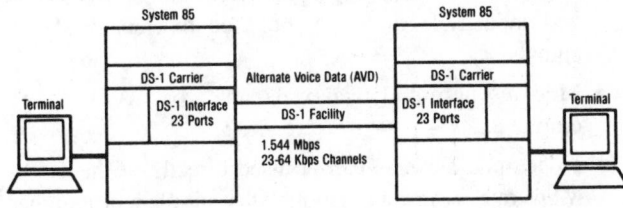

Figure: System 85 AVD Example

For a System 85 to Dimension PBX connection, a compatible D4 Channel Bank provides an interface from the DS-1 facility to the Dimension PBX. The DS-1 Interface to D4 Channel Bank connection only supports the use of the bit robbed (in-baud) signaling technique. This provides 24 channels of up to 56 Kbps voice and voiceband data traffic on circuit switched connections. Serving as a direct replacement for analog type tie trunks, this type of channel is referred to as a "voice grade" channel.

Digital data calls set up over a voice grade DS-1 facility linking a System 85 and Dimension PBX must be converted to voiceband data before they can be transmitted. This conversion is required due to the possibility of the bit robbed signaling technique distorting any

information present in a pure digital data stream. To accomplish this conversion, modem pooling is required at both the System 85 and Dimension PBX.

a) *Physical Description*: A special carrier and circuit pack arrangement is used to provide for the DS-1 Interface with System 85. A DS-1 Interface circuit pack terminating in a DS-1 carrier logically appears to the System 85 scanner software as six SN233 tie trunk circuit packs, each having four trunk terminations. This means the only access to a DS-1 facility through the System 85 is circuit switched access.

A System 85 can accommodate up to 255 DS-1 Interface circuit packs. A DS-1 carrier can hold up to 2 DS-1 circuit packs. The Figure below illustrates a DS-1 configuration within System 85.

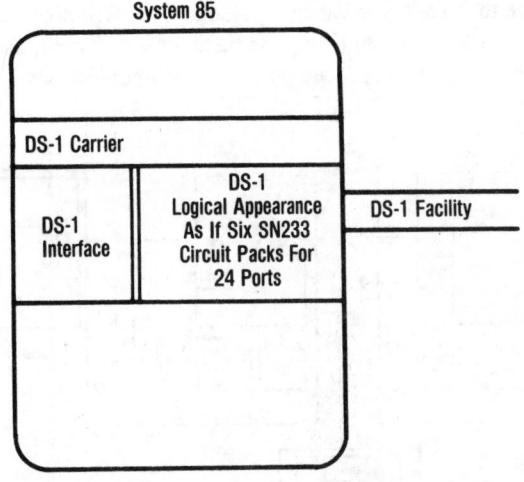

Figure: System 85 DS-1 Configuration Example

b) *Typical Installations*: The DS-1 Interface is integrated into System 85s architecture. The DS-1 Interface is used to provide circuit-switched access to a 1.544 Mbps DS-1 type facility and can support both voice grade and AVD signal formats.

The Figure shows a typical configuration linking two System 85s and using AVD type service. A connection is established via software in the System 85 to provide for a connection between terminal devices. The System 85 system manager can control access to the DS-1 channels through using trunk group codes and restrictions.

The DS-1 Interface is also compatible with a D4 type channel bank and can provide for the connection over a DS-1 facility of an analog PBX to a System 85.

c) *Considerations*: 1) Voice grade and AVD signaling cannot be mixed on an individual interface. 2) Calls cannot overflow from voice grade trunk group to AVD type trunk groups due to far end modem requirements. 3) Modem pooling is required for data calls on voice grade service. 4) The DS-1 Interface is integrated into System 85s architecture, providing circuit switched access to a DS-1 channel. The DS-1 Interface does not support direct dedicated data connections.

- Digital Network Interface: Digital Multiplexed Interface (DMI) provides high speed digital communications between a host computer and a System 75. System 85 also supports DMI.

The DMI specification was developed in collaboration with host computer vendors to establish an open and efficient interface to AT&T's advanced systems. DMI will provide a vital link for interconnecting workstations and computers which will result in reduced costs for communications networks.

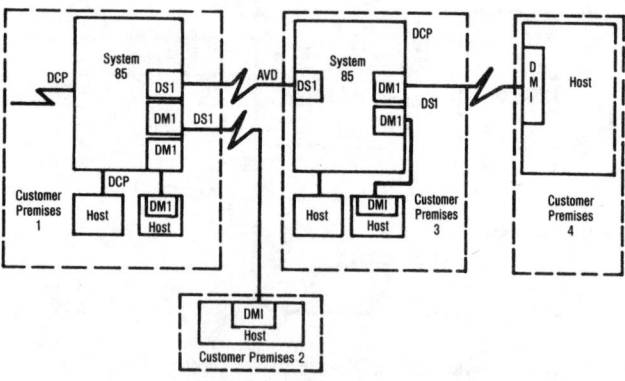

Figure: Dimension System 85 Digital Multiplexed Interface

DMI provides twenty-three 64-kilobit-per-second data channels and one 64-kilobit-per-second common signalling channel. It is based on the use of standard digital carrier systems, such as T1 1.544 Mbps systems, as a transport medium using standard channel and frame structures.

DMI utilizes three data formats to convey user data. They are: Mode 0: provides clear 64 Kbps full-duplex, synchronous transmission; Mode 1: provides 56 Kbps full-duplex, synchronous transmission and is compatible with 56 Kbps DATAPHONE Digital Service (DDS); Mode 2: provides general data transmission at rates up to 19.2 Kbps. It supports asynchronous or synchronous data, full- or half-duplex operation, and existing data terminal interfaces.

The DMI greatly reduces the cost of interfacing a System

75 to a host computer when compared to today's channel techniques. It replaces space consuming hardware and reduces interconnecting wiring. DMI is designed to meet international (ISDN) standards being defined by the CCITT. It allows economical high speed access to hosts from terminals distributed across a System 75.

In telephone technology, the DS-1 facility is called a T1 facility. T1 is the standard method of interconnecting digital communications systems within the telephone industry of North America. The line or facility operates at a rate of 1.54 Mbps which allows twenty-four 64-kilobit-per-second channels to be multiplexed on a single line. The 64-kilobit-per-second rate is compatible with generating toll quality voice signals.

In the telephone industry, DS-1 signals are usually transmitted over a twisted pair of wires. One pair is required for each direction (transmit and receive). Inexpensive repeaters are used, permitting the signals to be sent over hundreds of cable miles. System 75, System 85, and Dimension 2000 with Feature Package 8, Issue 3 may be connected to a variety of DS-1 channels.

- Terrestrial and satellite 1.544 Mbps service may be leased from common carriers.
- 18 GHz and 23 GHz microwave radios provide low cost local distribution.
- Digital radios operating in both common carrier bands and industrial bands can be used to transmit DS-1 signals.
- Modems permit the coaxial cable for CATV to be employed.
- Fiber optic systems can be used directly at the 1.544 Mbps rate, or in conjunction with multiplexers at higher rates.

DS-1 type compatibility provides a number of different alternatives to linking client premises locations.

The two methods of DS-1 signaling are in-band signaling ("bit robbed") or common channel. The DS-1 facility chosen does not determine the signaling format used. Rather, the interface devices located at each end of the facility determines this. For example, a D4 Channel Bank only employs "bit robbed" signaling while a System 85 DS-1 interface can employ either "bit robbed" or "common channel" signaling.

Digital transmission facilities are widely available with the introduction of the AT&T Terrestrial Digital Service (TDS) tariff. This tariff, as well as facilities provided by telephone companies, other common carriers and privately owned transmission systems, offers 1.544 Mbps digital private lines between two locations. These private lines can be used to transport voice, data, or video signals.

A significant client benefit of DS-1 permits sharing voice and data transmission on a single digital facility. The cost(s) of separate voice and data facilities are significantly more expensive versus a single shared DS-1 channel.

The Uniform Wiring Plan for the System 85 revolves around a uniform walljack to simplify terminal changes or moves and to encourage user participation in rearrangements and changes. This walljack is able to connect data terminals, voice sets, or an integrated terminal to the main system.

AT&T has brought the software supporting the System 85, single- and multi-module configurations, up to speed with that previously available for Dimension Feature Package 8, Issue 3. The switch capacity was increased to 7,000 lines from 900. Three configuration modes are now offered: blocking, essentially non-blocking, and non-blocking. The blocking configuration is claimed to be adequate for typical applications requiring 10 percent or less data communication. The essentially non-blocking is offered for those installations needing heavier data performance and offers a "one-in-a-million" chance of blockage. For critical installations that require a totally non-blocking switch, it is now provided with a 10 percent premium on the price tag. The 301CC processor was replaced with the 501CC processor which uses bit-slice technology and cache memory and is able to address up to two million words of memory as opposed to one million addressable by the 301CC; the 501CC also increased the Busy Hour Call capacity to 20,000. The number of AP ports supported by the DCIU was increased from four to eight. Modem pooling is now offered for System 85 as well as AT&T provided Extended Reserve Power that was previously provided by the user. The memory capacity of the APs was increased from 40 Mbytes to 160 Mbytes; this memory upgrade is also available for Release 1 and Feature Package 8, Issue 3.

Three major network enhancements introduced in Release 2 that were previously available on Feature Package 8, Issue 3 but not on Release 1 include: Distributed Communication Service (DCS) capability, a T1 interface, and ETN enhancements. Release 2 supports DCS configurations with up to 12 nodes and 25,000 lines or more. System 85 and the Dimension can both be nodes in tha same configuration. DCS can now be extended beyond a campus or large industrial environment within a metropolitan area to reach across the continental United States. The T1 interface—Digital Service (DS-1)—provides a format for multiplexing twenty-four 64-Kbps digital channels onto a 1.544 MHz T1 carrier. The ETN enhancements include expanding the number of trunks to 255, expanding ARS Deluxe number of 6-digit tables to 64, conversion of 10-digit ARS Deluxe to 7-digit AAR, and introducing 5-digit dialing.

Expanded System 85

AT&T Information Systems announced in November 1984 an enlarged System 85 that offers as much as four times the line capacity of the largest previous version, along with enhanced features for communications networks and system administration.

The expanded version of System 85 can be configured to accommodate as many as 32,000 lines in a single system. System 85 can provide up to 100,000 lines of service through distributed communications systems.

AT&T's customers can easily upgrade to the newer versions of System 85 via added system memory and a new software tape. The expanded system also offers increased busy hour capacity, more sophisticated automatic call routing to reduce long distance costs, and a centralized management function that gives users greater control over the system. In addition, the new Remote Group feature permits small clusters of voice/data terminals to be located up to 100 miles from the central switch with total feature transparency.

The new version of System 85 can handle up to 45,000 calls per hour. It offers 640 patterns for sending long distance calls over the most economical route through its Automatic Route Selection and Automatic Alternate Routing functions. Automatic Call Distribution, with management information functions, is available to handle and track heavy incoming call flows.

The new version of System 85 is compatible with AT&T's System 75, enhanced Dimension PBX, and 5 ESS processors in a network configuration. It also offers high-speed data communications and a built-in DS-1 interface for direct connection to digital transmission services. System 85 can act as a control point or remote site in a distributed communications environment, where several processors in different locations act as a single unified communications system.

Conclusion

The System 85 is the first glimpse of the much-talked-about, before divestiture, AT&T Antelope project. However, this is not the entire development. AT&T intends to continually upgrade the system, gradually easing the user into office automation. AT&T views its system as analogous to crystallization with all systems—voice management, data management, office management, building management, and network management—fitting together in a systematic and uniform fashion.

Ericsson MD110

Introduction

Ericsson (changed from Anaconda-Ericsson in late 1983), formed in 1980, is a joint-venture company of Atlantic Richfield Company and LM Ericsson. In 1982, the company released an integrated voice/data PBX, the MD110. The MD110 has been in service in Europe for several years and was enhanced for applications in the more complex American market.

System Concept

The MD110 is controlled by distributed, stored-program microprocessors with modularly expandable to 10,000 lines in increments of 200. The MD110 employs time division multiplexing in pulse code modulation format based on the CCITT European Standard of a 2 Mbps internal transmission rate.

The MD110's design uses fully distributed processing to enhance reliability and cost effectiveness, and its modular hardware and software are intended to accommodate expansion without disturbance to the existing configuration. It also features a processor provided on each device board for improved reliability and ease of maintenance; voice and data transmission over a single pair of wires; easy access to custom calling features via standard instruments; a family of digital instruments available for special features and applications; and pulse code modulation (PCM) with u-law encoding to simplify compatibility with T1 carrier, microwave equipment, and fiber-optic transmission systems.

In addition to basic functions of the PBX, the MD110 will support a variety of applications. These include voice and data networking among remote locations, transit/tandem switching, main/satellite operation, and integrated office with text communication.

System Components—Hardware

Based on two building blocks, the Line Interface Module (LIM) and the Group Switch (GS), the system is fully distributed with no centralized common control at any level. Each LIM is self-contained and supports 150-200 extensions as a stand-alone, non-blocking PBX. When LIMs are joined with other LIMs, a network of up to 10,000 lines is formed. When more than two LIMs are required, a GS is added as an interface between LIMs.

The LIM is a microprocessor-controlled unit that can be equipped with any combination of line circuits, trunk circuits, and other telephony devices. The LIM possesses an internal digital switch and can function as an autonomous

PBX or as an integrated part of a larger system. The capacity of the LIM, in normal traffic conditions, is 200 extensions. Larger systems are achieved by interconnecting LIMs via 32-channel PCM links for traffic and control purposes. Two LIMs can be interconnected directly, whereas larger systems need to employ a group switch.

Since the LIM can operate autonomously, it contains all the necessary call processing hardware subsystems. These include the Line Signaling Subsystem (LSS), the Switching Subsystem (SWS), the Processor Subsystem (PRS), the Input/Output Subsystem (IOS), and the Service/Maintenance Subsystem (SMS).

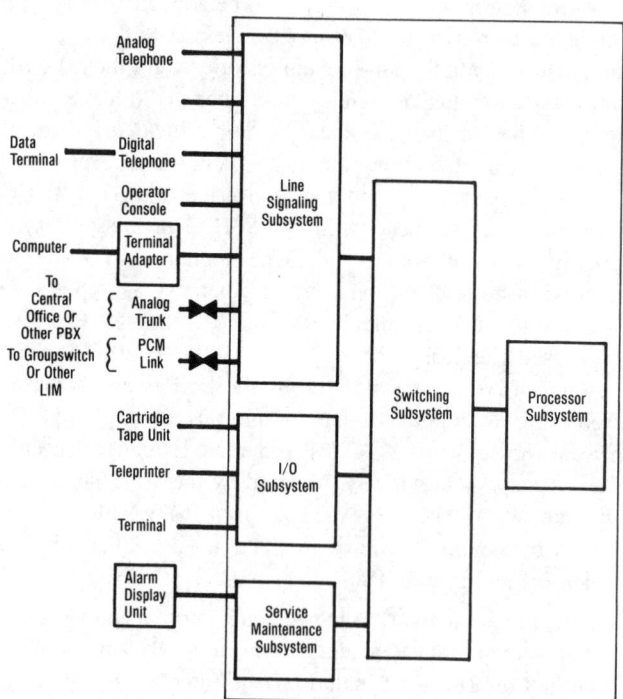

Figure: Line Interface Module (LIM) Block Diagram.

The LSS consists of a number of circuits of various types. These circuits fall into two general categories: those that interface the LIM with external communication devices, such as telephones and operator consoles, and those that provide important call processing functions, such as tones and ringing.

The interface circuits on the LSS include analog and digital line circuits, trunk circuits, and group junctor circuits. The analog line circuit and the trunk circuits used with the MD110 function primarily to convert the calling party's voice into PCM-encoded form so that it can be handled by the SWS. In addition, these circuits perform signaling functions, informing the LIM control of any changes of state on the associated line or trunk.

The digital telephone (DTU) and the operator console (OPI) used with the MD110 each contain analog-to-digital conversion circuits within their internal circuitry. The digital line circuit, which is used to interface these devices in the SWS, functions primarily to handle the digitally-encoded information transmitted between the devices and the SWS. As these devices transmit and receive over a single pair of wires, the digital line circuit functions to separate the two directions of transmission, in time, by a technique called burst signaling. Burst signaling allows PCM-encoded data to be sent alternately from DPU/OPI to digital line circuit and from line circuit to DTU/OPI in high-speed bursts.

The Group Junctor Circuit (GJU) is a unit designed to interface PCM links with a LIM. It does this by multiplexing speech samples from up to 30 lines and/or trunks onto the associated PCM link, together with signaling and synchronization data.

The LSS also includes service circuits that provide important call processing functions. These are tone receivers to receive DTMF signals, tone senders to generate dial tones and busy signals, conference circuits to allow up to eight parties to converse simultaneously, and ringing equipment control circuits to generate and control the application of ringing voltage.

Tone senders and tone receivers are devices for digital generation and reception, respectively, of tones (dial tone, busy tone, etc.) and, also, dual tones for DTMF signaling. A tone sender unit, TSU, consists of one board and supplies one LIM with all tones. A tone receiver unit, TRU, consists of two boards and contains eight DTMF receivers and four receivers for dial tone. One TRU is normally adequate for one LIM.

A multi-party conference unit, MPU, occupies one board and is used, by digital methods, to achieve a flexible number of conferences with three-to-eight participants. One MPU is normally included in each LIM.

The SWS, or time switch, is non-blocking and has 512 time slots (multiple positions) capable of supporting 64 Kbps. The SWS consists of one basic board, the Basic Switch Unit (BSU), and two supplementary boards, Supplementary Switch Units (SSU). The BSU contains the voice and control memories for the time switch, as well as a microprocessor that controls the internal functions of the switch and has contact with the signal processor. The SSU boards each serve 256 time slots and undertake serial/parallel conversion of the PCM signals to and from the device boards. In combination, the SSUs and the BSU cause the PCM samples from one device—arriving on a particular bus during a given timeslot—to be switched to the bus and timeslot assigned to another device. This, in effect, creates a speech path between the first and second devices over which information can be transmitted. Two such paths permit the two-way transmission required for conversation between devices.

The PRS directs all the functions of the LIM processor. It does this according to programs stored in its memory, and in response to changes of state detected by the device circuits. The PRS consists of two functional areas, the LIM Processor Unit (LPU) and the Memory Unit (MEU). The LPU contains a processor system built around two commercial 8-bit microprocessors. One processor functions as the LIM's main processor, and the other works as a signal processor whose task is to handle the direct communication with the control circuits of the switch and the telephony devices. The memory boards in whose circuits the LIM programs and data are stored contain RAM-type storage components. Each board contains 512 Kbytes of RAM.

The IOS provides the necessary man-machine interface to permit external administration of the system. This interface is used for loading the system software into the PRS's memory and also for the entry of commands to initiate functions such as diagnostic programs and database alterations. The IOS includes the Input/Output Interface Unit (IOU) and the I/O devices themselves, which include the Cartridge Tape Unit (CTU) and external CRT terminals and/or teleprinters. It also includes a Serial Interface Unit (SIU) and Magnetic Tape Unit (MTU).

An I/O terminal interface unit (IOU) consists of one board. It facilitates connection of cartridge tape units for backing up programs and data, CRT terminals or teleprinters for making keystroke entries into the system, the SIU for an RS-232-C output port for connection of processing equipment, and the MTU for Station Message Detail Recording. One or several IOUs is/are included in one MD110.

The SMS continually monitors system hardware and software, detects faults, generates alarms, and aids in fault clearing. In addition, the SMS acts to limit the effect of faults by restarting individual devices, programs, LIMs, or the entire system, and by removing faulty hardware from service.

The Group Switch (GS) connects PCM voice, data, and control signals between the LIMs via a 32-channel, four-wire PCM link. For LIMs located within 1300 feet (400 m) of the GS, the PCM links can be coaxial cable. For remote LIMs up to 1.56 miles (2.5 km) away, twisted-pair cable can be used with a line terminal amplifier at each end. By adding repeaters every 1.24 to 1.56 miles (2-2.5 km), it is possible to use twisted-pair cable on spans up to 12.4 miles (20 km), with the repeaters powered from the ends of the cable.

Optical fiber can also be used for PCM links up to 4.38 miles (7 km) without repeaters. Alternately, the PCM links can be adapted to T1 span lines or microwave equipment. The time slots T1-T15 and T17-T31 are used for speech and data, while T16 is used for control signals and T0 for synchronization signals.

The GS contains from one to eight Group Switch Modules (GSMs). The basic GSM consists of one to eight Time Switch Units (TSU) and up to 31 Group Junctor Units (GJUs), one for each PCM link the TSU serves. Each GJU interfaces its associated PCM link with the TSU, converting the incoming 32-channel serial data to parallel form for switching by the TSU, and reconverting the switched data from the TSU to serial format for transmission over the receiving PCM link.

The GS is a non-blocking switch consisting of one or a number of time-switch units each with 1,024 ports. The units are arranged in a matrix. The PCM links from LIMs are connected via terminal boards, GJUs. One Group Switch module has capacity for 31 PCM links, two modules with two time switches each having capacity for 62 PCM links, and so on. The GS can be expanded to a maximum of eight modules which can then manage 248 PCM links, each with a transmission speed of 2.048 Mbps.

The GS contains from one to eight Group Switch Modules (GSMs). The basic GSM consists of one Time Switch Unit (TSU) and up to 31 Group Junctor Units (GJUs), one for each PCM link the TSU serves. Each GJU interfaces its associated PCM link with the TSU, converting the incoming 32-channel serial data to parallel form for switching by the TSU, and reconverting the switched data from the TSU to serial format for transmission over the receiving PCM link.

The TSU is a time division switching matrix capable of serving 1,024 time slots (31 PCM links). The time-division switching that takes place in the TSU is similar, in concept, to that of the switching subsystem in the LIM. As the system grows and more PCM links are added, the number of TSUs is increased.

The GS itself possesses no control equipment; it is controlled fully by the LIMs. However, the GJU contains a microprocessor that manages the communications with the processor of the connected LIM via time slot T16. The processors on the GJU boards extend control information internally within the group switch.

One GS cabinet can house the eight time switch modules that form a row in the switch matrix, and the corresponding 31 GJU boards. A fully-built GS comprises eight cabinets.

The establishment of a connection between two LIMs commences with the LIM processors informing one another about which time slots have been selected on the relevant PCM link. The GJU processors are then ordered to establish the connections via the involved time-switch modules. A connection through GS is, by its nature, one-way, and it is consequently necessary to establish two paths through the switch in order to obtain a two-way connection.

At the station level, the MD110 is equipped with either analog or digital station line circuit cards. The analog line circuit cards are used for regular phone sets, both rotary and DTMF. The digital line circuit card serves the MD110 Proprietary Station Instrument (PSI), which is able to send and/or receive simultaneous voice and data transmission. This PSI also features visual displays and a variety of operation keys for simpler operation.

The system supports simultaneous voice and data on one-pair wiring at a rate of 9.6 Kbps. With an additional pair, transmission speeds up to 56 Kbps are possible. Because of engineering restrictions, the maximum distance between the stations and the switch is 3,500 feet.

System Components—Software

The software for the MD110 is written in high-level assembly language and PLEX (Programming Language for Exchanges). PLEX was developed for the LM Ericsson AXE-10 Digital Central Office.

The software is divided into central and regional portions. Regional software is resident in each LIM and controls functions internal to that LIM; central software consists of programs related to inter-LIM calls and is stored in two or more LIMs, for reliability.

All program units that make up the MD110 sortware fall into one of two main functional categories: the Audio Communication System (ACS) and the Service System (SES). The ACS software controls all functions related to the establishment of connections between stations, trunks, and other terminal equipment that is connected to the system. The SES software is composed of the operating system, the I/O programs, the maintenance and administration routines, and the switch control.

The ACS contains the Line Signaling Subsystem (LSS), the Traffic Control System (TCS), and the ACS Handling System (AHS). The LSS software controls the signaling functions of the LSS hardware, such as the application of tones and ringing. The TCS software sends program signals to the SWS to control the set-up, monitoring, and release of connections in the switching matrix, as demanded by the LSS hardware. The AHS software identifies such basic data as directory numbers and classes of service and allows this data to be changed on command.

The SES software consists of the Switching Subsystem (SWS), the Processor Subsystem (PRS), the Service/Maintenance Subsystem (SMS), and the Input/Output Subsystem (IOS). The SWS software controls the operation of the switching matrix hardware in response to program signals from the TCS software. The PRS software consists primarily of the Executive Program (EXS), which directs the overall operation of the LIM processor, scheduling the running of the various subsystem programs and performing certain timing functions. The SMS software includes programs that continuously monitor system operation, detect any faults that may occur, and cause alarms to be generated as necessary. The IOS software serves primarily to direct the loading and dumping of software and to provide access to the stored data that requires periodic changes and additions.

System Management

System management of the MD110 includes both manually-initiated operations—such as moves and changes—and automatic functions (e.g., power failure recovery). All human-machine communication is undertaken from interactive I/O devices.

Authorization classes are incorporated to prevent unauthorized access to the system. A user is assigned to one of eight authorization classes, with each class being assigned a password of up to sixteen characters which must be entered before the system will acknowledge the entry of the commands in that class.

A common use for commands is the effecting of moves and changes, changes which are frequently necessary when the system is growing rapidly or the application/configuration is changing often. Changing telephone numbers, initiating new service, adding trunks, and establishing classes of service are examples of often-used commands dealing with moves and changes.

Commands are available in the MD110 to initiate collection and print-out of traffic measurement data. This traffic measurement data provides a measure of the traffic load being carried by various elements of the system. It is a useful management tool that aids in planning for future growth and in determining the relative efficiency of the current equipment configuration. The user can set the start and stop time of the measurement, the periodicity of the recording, selection of the equipment to be measured, and the method of output of the data.

With system expansion, commands are available to install and place into service new equipment which can range from an individual circuit board to a complete LIM. When adding a complete LIM, it is necessary to load its PRS memory with the regional software necessary for its call-processing functions.

When the MD110 is placed into service, the programs and data stored on the cartridge tape are loaded into the memories in the LIMs. This loading is initiated by a bootstrap program stored in a nonvolatile PROM in that I/O LIM. Programs and data are first read from the cartridge tape into the LIM's I/O memory; they are then transmitted over PCM lines to the other LIMs. Reloading can be initiated by a command entry from a terminal to restart all or a portion of the system's call processing resources. Commands are available to reload the entire system, a single LIM, a program unit, or a portion of a program unit.

Conclusion

The major advantage of the MD110 is its distributed control, which eliminates the single point of failure. Its ability to swap analog and digital line cards allows the user to use previously acquired phone sets now, upgrading to digital in the future. Future enhancements include store-and-forward switching and packet switching.

TOMORROW'S PABX/DATA SWITCH

J Mackie
Vice-President

Reprinted with permission from *Local Networks and Distributed Office Systems*, Volume 2, 1982, pages 137-145. Copyright © 1982 by On-Line Publications.

Mitel
Canada

Describes the MITEL digital PBX, its existing role in the office and as the integrating factor in an automated office in which the PBX handles a mixture of rotary dial and more specialised sets. Future developments to the SX-2000 system are discussed with particular reference to its role in local networks.

I should like to start by reviewing the history of the private branch exchange. A private branch exchange is private because the subscriber owns it and it is a branch of another exchange, the telephone company's public exchange. Connected to that exchange are normally trunks, except in the case of a residence telephone, in which case it is a private subscriber line. The distinction between trunks and subscriber lines concerns who is likely to be found on that telephone. In the case of a residence the subscriber loop is dedicated but in the case of trunk lines it could be any person in that specific building because that trunk line is a shared resource. The PBX is the focal point of the shared resource: it is a star operation.

This PBX exercises a control function in switching calls to the outside world normally by using a console as part of the switching procedure. Even today cord boards are still commonly found in which the human operator performs the switching by plugging and unplugging cords. When mechanical PBXs appeared, steppers automatically performed the intermediate switching stages. We got into the jargon game a few years ago when such devices were named private automatic branch exchanges. Then that was not good enough and they were called electronic private branch exchanges but some other people thought it might be nice if they were called computerized branch exchanges. I say let us be done with all that; they are just private branch exchanges.

Most of the traditional suppliers of branch exchanges are big names: $2 - $16 billion companies. We think they are slow moving, conditioned to passively taking orders rather than actively seeking customers and they are not suited to swiftly harnessing high technology as are many of their smaller competitors. At the moment, these companies are sustained by the momentum of the huge world telephone and data network: 400 million telephones and 4 million data terminals with an annual growth rate of 5 - 20%. At the moment this market is sufficiently large to keep us all happy but let me focus your attention on some very important facets of this market.

There is an old saying "love is blind". Whether this refers to perceptions of our spouses, lovers, parents or children, it is true that affection filters out the less admirable traits of our loved ones. I assume that the reader has some degree of affection for technology. Such a condition tends to blur our ability to see what is the real situation.

If you objectively examine the potential PBX market you will find, for example, that in the USA:

- 55% of all companies have 1 - 4 employees
- 20% have 5 - 9 employees
- 12% have 10 - 19 employees
- 8% have 20 - 49 employees
- all other companies employing 50 and more employees account for only 5% of the total business establishement.

The kind of group we are talking about today, with our distributed networks and our large PBXs, is a tiny piece of that 5%. One of the reasons why Mitel has been involved in small PBX equipment until now is that their view of the world is based on market realities.

The digital PBX area has been one of furious activity. The Mitel SX-2000 has been launched in 1982, Datapoint and Intecom in 1981, and Rolm in 1975. All these companies share a vision of the PBX as the hub, or integrating factor, of the automated office.

People question the value of integration; the concept of integration is best summed up as a concept of control. Ultimately humans drive the office not computers. The important conversations occur between you and me rather than between computers and I would humbly suggest that these conversations start with the simple black rotary telephone. If you examine how you spend your working day, chances are that you will discover that you spend most of your day in the communications mode, either directly with other people in the office, or phoning people. Unfortuantely many people are attempting to make office communications work with very primitive PBX equipment. Our position is to start with a good PBX.

Mitel designs and manufactures integrated circuits as well as PBXs. To make this particular voice and data PBX possible we employ extremely dense and sophisticated microelectronic technology.

- The MT8980 digital crosspoint chip is the building block of the SX-2000. It contains the equivalent of 65,500 crosspoints and can handle 32 channels of PCM input on a 1/4 inch square piece of silicon. It is used in many configurations within the PBX to provide a variety of functions including simple switching matrices, non-blocking matrices and concentrators.

- The MT8960 Codec Filter chip combines both the filtering and digital/analog conversion functions on one chip and adds a significant number of control functions as a bonus. This chip is available in either A Law or MU Law companding codes because we design for the international market from the start.

- The MH88500 Hybrid Subscriber Line Interface circuit is a 20 pin package that combines with the DX and Filter/Codec chips to provide interface for a 2.048 MHz serial PCM Link; it is uniquely compact and effective.

- The Digital Line Interface Circuit (DLIC) provides for 256 Kb/s transmission on a standard four wire interface to accommodate the Supersets which are an extension of the SX-2000 switching system technology.

- The Digital Trunk Interface (DSI) permits the switch to handle the Europen 2.048 Mb, 32 channel signalling standard or the North American T1 standard of 1.544 Mb, 24 channels with equal facility.

- The bus monitor incorporates a large chunk of logic analyzer circuitry on a chip; this was done to achieve the desired architecture in the PBX and to serve as a maintenance aid during operation. There will be further applications of this resource in the areas of data encryption, system logic analysis, and illegal access detection.

All the proprietary circuitry is fabricated in ISO-CMOS so it is rugged and consumes little power in addition to being compact.

The result of all this semiconductor technology and system architecture is an initial PBX cabinet which contains all the system controls plus a possible 768 ports which is nominally 600 subscriber lines. Additional cabinets enlarge the system by a maximum 1200 lines per cabinet and are driven by the two control shelves in the initial cabinet. The original control shelves can handle up to 5,376 ports and have an optional redundancy feature that reduplicates the control system right down to the line cards which provide the external interfaces. At the line card level we are pioneering disposeable circuit modules for fast and easy maintenance. The telephony standard of reliability is demonstrated by the fact that we assume the telephone will work when the power goes off in our homes but the phone only works because the industry provides extensive backup. The PBX manufacturers strive to give that level of relability even as the equipment becomes more complex and the loads become both heavier and more diverse.

The cabinet is 69 inches high and approximately 30 inches square on the bottom. There are thermostatically controlled fans to maintain the optimum temperature to give the longest life to the equipment. While the equipment consumes little power, each telephone that goes off hook dissipates 5 watts and when a lot of telephones go of hook a lot of heat is generated. Incidentally that is why our power specification shows different requirements for standby and operating power; systems based on non C-MOS technology consume a fairly high amount of power at all times.

Let us now look at some of the interfaces to the outside world. This system starts with POTS (plain old telephone service) epitomized by the black rotary dial telephone costing $40 (the world's simplest and cheapest terminal) hooked up through the PBX. Our PBX handles mixes of DTMF (touchtone) and rotary dial telephones. We offer message registration, and can use voice synthesis to provide some primitive messaging with POTS. As far as office automation is concerned, the prime instrument is still the telephone augmented by a functionally contributing PBX and the PBX is the hub on which all else effectively turns.

Each of the modules on the subscriber line interface card is a thick-film hybrid module and there are 16 of them on this card. Simple mathematics demonstates that 16 modules transmitting at 64Kb/s TDM which is one half the available capacity of the 32 channel 2.048 Mb/s serial stream. The capacity which is excess to telephony requirements eventually becomes the data transmission function which provides 128 Kb/s to each subscriber line on 2 wires. By putting a codec on this same 128 Kb/s two-wire line we can service a feature phone, we allocate the necesary 64 Kb/s to voice and have abundant bandwidth for both control and data transmission on the same subscriber line. This is not an especially radical solution but it does demonstrate that we have invoked a wide range of solutions and that, within the SX-2000 as a large network system, we also have a massive number of mini networks.

Our strategy is to encourage the PBX user to migrate upwards from the rotary dial telephone to special sets which offer easy access to specific features. The Superset 4 has some dedicated buttons but it also has a liquid crystal display which indicates the current function of the soft keys, such keys change their function at various times. The liquid crystal display offers prompts to steer the subscriber through the choice of features at his disposal and in another mode offers primitive messaging capability in the form of a serial string - like the early word processors. All of this depends on the line card previously described.

The four-wire system is more sophisticated as evidenced by our Superset 7 professional workstation which has a CRT and a 256 Kb/s data capability. Within that workstation is a 68000 microprocessor with 128 K bytes of RAM and we can load that whole memory from the main CPU in four seconds. This sophisticated workstation is supported by those familiar beasts of burden: the codec, the digital line interface card and the digital line card. The later card serves eight of these 4 wire sets at a tranmission rate of 256 Kb/s or double that of the two wire sets.

Once the user has migrated to any set beyond the rotary dial telephone he then gains data access through an RS232 connector on the back of the special set. In this case we treat the set as a little modem which brings the protocol conversion capability of the SX-2000 to bear on foreign equipment in the building. For instance, if you have a word processor which you wish to link to a teletype terminal housed in a different office in the same building with a common SX-2000, it is feasible that by pushing one button on your set you can connect the two through the RS232 connections and the PBX. At the moment we have not constructed the protocol conversions because of the pressure of other tasks but a number of manufacturers are lined up at the door willing to co-operate on this. We hope to begin within the next three months on some of the interfaces but we do not want to interface with a manufacturer who will not co-operate because interfacing is some of the thorniest prblems in the whole data processing industry. With co-operation both the word processor manufacturers and the general data-using population will benefit from an integrative hub like the SX-2000.

Another facet of our program is that the same set is used for an attendant console, a maintenance console, an administative console or a general office workstation. Many people are bewildered by the concept of there being no TTO, no zero based reference for the terminal. Rather than a dedicated console in a specific place, the console can be located anywhere and used for any number of applications by an operator possessing the required passwords. A four wire interface card supports this console.

The SX-2000 has aroused much curiousity by offering 1 Mbyte of memory in RAM or, optionally, in non-volatile bubble memory. We have chosen bubble memory to address another real problem in our industry: the need for increased environmental tolerance by telecommunications equipment. We use bubble for bulk data storage, voice messaging, and for billing and accounting systems: that is, for data you can't afford to lose. Bubble memory is very rugged and compact; it is particularly popular with the military and the industrial control people. In addition to bubble memory and ISO-CMOS technologies, Mitel makes thick film hybrid circuits by silk screening the conductive parts of a circuit on a ceramic substrate then adding miniature discrete parts to form thin but durable minicircuits. Most PBXs have to be installed in the same room that some electromechanical antique switch has been torn out of. Mitel and Northern Telecom are the only PBX manufacturers currently designing for that 'broom closet' environment, the rest insist on a computer room environment which simply translates manufacturer's design savings into hidden costs to the customer.

The focal point of all the office automation discussion is to find an effective means of increasing productivity in the office. Everyone seems to be aware that capital investment in the worker in other parts of our economy has brought about gratifying increases in productivity. Investment per farm worker of about $35,000 brought a productivity increase of about 185% in agriculture and much the same results were obtained by capital investment in the factory. In the office there has been an investment of about $2000 per worker for a 4% productivity increase largely resulting from word processing. People are contemplating an investment of $10,000 per worker in the near future but no one knows exactly what is the most profitable kind of investment to make, or what percentage of productivity increase to expect.

We believe in starting with simple things done well. The first is plain old telephone service - POTS. Then personal aids are added. Now everyone's PBX has lots of features but we have transferred the features from the SUPERSWITCHES (TM) which preceded the SX-2000, the features that made them favourites in the marketplace, and are building upon that established base of features with human factors in mind. Instead of hearing funny beeps, the user will be given prompts by voice or text to guide him/her in the use of the system: errors will be discernable and correct operation will be made obvious. Having an automated office in mind, the first release of software will contain a 'dial by name' feature whereby the operator can optionally dial the name or the telephone number of the intended party and the switch will recognize both if the party is in its directory.

Our professional workstation in conjunction with the first release software unearths latent capabilities of the SX-2000 and puts them at the operator's fingertips. Timed reminders, text messaging and voice messaging have incredible potential to overcome personal time constraints, international time zones and linguistic barriers respectively, in addition to other obvious applications. Primitive protocol conversions will allow us access into commercial data bases and electronic mail services operated by outside suppliers.

The initial offering is a pledge on the complete office automation package we will provide in the future, and for us the future is little more than a year away. Then we expect to offer more extensive networking, multi-grouping, packet switching, and satellite operation for significant system upgrading. Centralized attendant service, travelling class marks that offer entry to appropriate telephone services for detached workers, remote grouping, and local area networks will all be brought to the task of increasing productivity.

To return to the theme of doing simple things well: small size, light weight, low power consumption and environmental tolerance, make SX-2000 installation and maintenance both simple and economical. A default database brings the system into basic business operation immediately upon power-up; additional data can be entered at a high level through PASCAL which is our programming language. Basic PROM can be stored in bubble but we have a Winchester disc capability for database storage, if desired, but the disc storage does not have the same enviornmental tolerance as the rest of the system.

I am personally convinced that our system must inform your communications manager what the system is doing well and what the system is not doing. Station message detail recording, station message detail accounting, toll restriction, and automatic route selection are now becoming essential to the proper supervision and control of a modern business telephone system.

There are some administrative features common to PBXs such as the ability to remotely poll the system, find out how healthy it is and how well it is doing. The telephone companies like to be able to phone the PBX and to change its program without the expense of sending someone out.

In our system we have carried that a step further in that each card has a self-identifying PROM on it. We can interrogate any SX-2000 remotely and instruct it to map out its card complement as a check against an assembly error or, alternatively, if we have the number of a card of which we are unsure we can locate that card anywhere in the world by having the switches read out their card numbers over the telephone. There is a wide range of diagnostics so that impending circuit malfunctions can be detected long before degradation of service is noticeable, and the malfunction will be located by cabinet, shelf, card and circuit.

The title 'office automation' has a romantic ring and the theories that buttress the loop, ring, and star proposals are downright seductive; but PBX people have solid credentials for performance and useful innovation. Less theory and more practice is the characteristic of the PBX industry.

The multiprocessing architecture existing in the SX-2000 is feasible up to 32,000 lines with PBX central office compatibility. The remarkable circuity that I have described above has a great potential for expansion of service by software enhancement.

Conclusion

My recommendation for networks in the office is to start simple, to buy a system that lets you grow. Office automation is for everybody and, invariably, most people's telephone system needs upgrading. If they have a Mitel system we have probably devised a new software package by which they can benefit. The PBX always leaves room for improvement either reducing floor space and power consumption, or by opening the gate for migration to working more productively with special sets.

The PBX industry is going to make increased use of powerful microprocessors distributed through every product area. This will give more features and extensive protocol conversion within the PBX and, ultimately, as much as 10 Mhz bandwidths for voice and data transmission through peripheral shelf expansion.

Networking is the logical extension of office automation. We are developing a comprehensive networking system. Our Satellite or Skyswitch division is building an earth station model that is specifically dedicated to telecommunications. In addition to linking up large digital switches like the SX-2000, it will resolve the economics of using small PBXs like the SX-20 which will be a tremendous break-through for third world countries.

The PBX inherently has the potential to use networking in a way that optimizes all telecommunications media. Our software people are currently exploring concepts for making the SX-2000 a network manager. In particular, we are looking at Ethernet as a networking protocol. Already we use Ethernet as our local area broadband network and intend to market this Ethernet port by the spring of 1983. Whether Ethernet or Cambridge Ring or whatever, the broadband loop will be the future source of office automation linkages but I expect the telephone to be the liaison instrument. The initial link will be established by you telephoning me; the PBX will check the class of service, establish the protocol conversions, identify your terminal and verify that the correct passwords are in its database, then make the connection with astonishing speed and ease.

We will support any market that is there, but primarily we would like to be the host, secondarily the switcher and finally the voice carrier within that market. We cannot handle all those things but the market, reckoned at billions of dollars, is big enough for us all.

Howard W. Johnson, Rolm Corp.

AN INSIDE LOOK AT THE NEW ROLM CBX II ARCHITECTURE

In 1975 ROLM Introduced its digital PBX, the Computerized Branch Exchange (CBX). At that time, customers were seeking replacements for their electromechanical PBXs and their old-fashioned cord boards that required an operator to connect calls by hand.

From its inception, designers recognized that a digital PBX could play a key role in transferring and transmitting data as well as voice communications. With the proliferation of word processors, personal computers, terminals and other digital devices in the early 1980s, digital PBXs began to serve as the voice and data communications hub of the office. To a large extent then, the long awaited "office of the future" is here now. Today, about 10 percent of all office workers have data devices on their desks.

The key requirements for business communications systems in the second half of this decade and on into the 1990s are exactly those two required in the past: the ability to act as the communications controller for the office and to easily incorporate new technical advances. The volume of data communications between devices in the office and between devices in the office and external sources will increase exponentially. PBXs must be equipped to handle not only voice communications at every desk but data communications as well. Unlike telephones, which are used sporadically, terminnals or personal computers are oftentimes used throughout the day. Thus, the PBX must possess sufficient data communications capability to permit all data devices to be simultaneously active. In addition, the transmission speed for such devices will surely exceed the 9,600 bits per second which is, for practical purposes, today's upper limit. Although some suppliers believe that a PBX that can handle 64,000 bps will be adequate for future desktop devices, Rolm believes that to achieve the kind of performance needed in the second half of this decade and in the 1990s, it will be necessary to support data rates of at least hundreds of thousands of bits per second from the PBX to many desktop devices.

Another key trend in the marketplace is the need for the communications controller to deal with a much wider universe of communications needs. Within the office this means that a PBX must be capable of providing communication between all devices in the customer's establishment, regardless of vendor. Thus, a PBX must be able to accommodate standards such as asynchronous, synchronous, X.25, and T1/D3 that are now evolving. The ability to connect to the IBM world, using existing protocols, such as 3270 and SNA, and allowing compatibility with future ones, such as IBM's proposed token ring, will be crucial here.

In addition, an organization with more than one building should still be able to use a PBX as its communications controller. Whether for a university or large corporation, one PBX system, with distributed processing, should be able to control the communications of many sites separated by thousands of feet.

If we are to live in a "global village," the PBX must be able to connect to a global business communications network as well. Coaxial cable, microwave, satellite, and fiber optic links to other systems and private and public data bases and networks will become increasingly important. Brokerage houses, banks, major industrial corporations, and other Fortune 500 companies will want access to these data bases and networks from any site in the world.

A business communications system, then, must follow flexible growth, provide easy-to-use devices, integrate voice, data text and even video applications, and permit access to the outside world through networks.

Rolm Corporation recently announced a new product called CBX II™ to meet these needs. Major engineering advancements on four separate fronts have been incorporated into a new business communications architecture that will provide total switching capability at high bandwidths and line sizes. This architecture is the basis of CBX II, the successor to the Rolm CBX telephone and data switching product line. CBX II is typified not only for the large increases in system capacity that it affords, but for the modular, extensible nature of its architecture, and the important fact that the new capabilities can be retrofitted into any existing Rolm CBX. Customers no longer need to worry that they might "run out" of vital communications systems bandwidth (communication capacity) or that they might not have sufficient growth capacity in their CBX system.

CBX II Physical Structure

The CBX II, which provides both voice and data switching capacity for a variety of applications, accepts data, asynchronous or synchronous, at speeds up to 64,000 bits per second (bps). Voice connections may be either analog or digital. All voice and data connections are brought to the CBX II system over single twisted-pair wiring and terminated on replaceable electronic circuit cards, called line cards. The line cards are arranged in racks, called interface shelves, of up to thirty-two cards each. Six shelves make up a cabinet, and three side-by-side cabinets make up a CBX II switching node. Every CBX II node contains a master processor, which can be either the Rolm 8000 (16-bit) or 9000 (32-bit) processor. Each interface shelf has its own backplane capable of switching 74 Mbps. A special circuit card, or expander, on each shelf passes information from the shelf backplane to a system backplane, called the ROLMbus™, which is used for exchanges of information between shelves. There are two choices of system backplanes: ROLMbus 74 and ROLMbus 295. ROLMbus 295 provides four times the connection capacity of ROLMbus 74, and is an option for high-performance applications.

Large systems are built by joining up to fifteen nodes in a distributed processing network. Between nodes, there are several possibilities for voice/data communication. For small systems the Digital Intertie, which multiplexes several calls onto one digital T1 link is used. For larger systems, CBX II uses a fiber-optic inter-node link (INL) that can carry up to 295 Mbps between nodes. For installations of more than 4,000 lines there is an inter-node network (INN), which can service more than 10,000 users providing non-blocking voice and 64 Kbps data to every desk.

CBX Philosophy

The CBX II project started with six primary objectives, two which were design guidelines, and four which were functional objectives. The design guidelines were to build a modular product, and to maintain full compatibility with previous products. The four functional objectives were to: (1) increase the bandwidth of each node; (2) develop extremely high bandwidth connections between nodes; (3) retain and enhance distributed

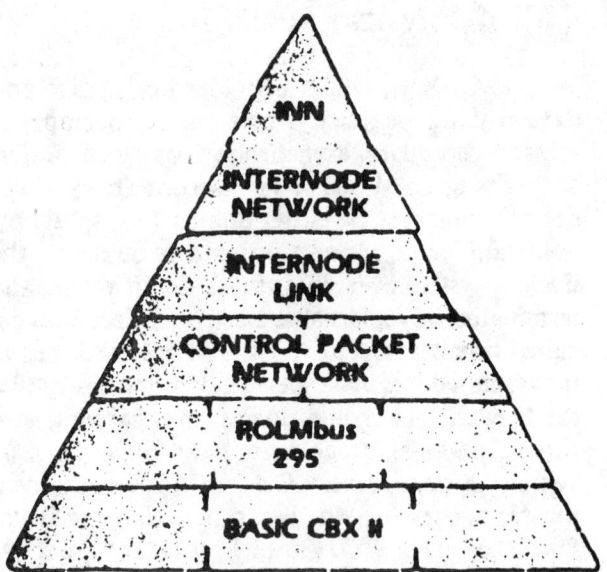

Figure 1. The hierarchical structure of the CBX II architecture.

control of the system by multiple processors communicating over a packet network; and (4) design in new modes of data handling to accommodate future functional enhancements.

Modularity

Large PBX systems that are modular and expandable benefit customers in many ways. From an engineering standpoint, a modular design ensures fault isolation, self-testing and reliability. A more direct benefit is that it is not necessary to configure a system with all the layers of the hierarchy.

If a customer's switching needs can be filled by some subset of the hierarchy, then the upper layers do not need to be installed or can be installed later as the need arises. In some systems, ultimate control over the entire system is vested in the top layer, so that even for modest applications the entire package must be purchased.

The ROLMbus 295, INL and INN modules are examples of hierarchical layers in CBX II that are not necessary for small systems (see Figure 1).

Compatibility

Since it is directly compatible with previous CBX systems, CBX II retains the powerful software feature set and innovative distributed control functionality common to the Rolm CBX family. CBX II also uses telephony and data in-

terface circuit cards common to the entire Rolm CBX family, so no installed system has been obsoleted. Even line cards in the new architecture are the same as those in older systems.

Bandwidth

Bandwidth, the fundamental communication capacity inside any PBX switching node, is the logical means by which information (data, telephone conversations, FAX, video) is moved from place to place. Units for measuring information transfer capability, or bandwidth, in a digital system are bits per second. When fully configured, CBX II has a total capacity exceeding 4.4 billion bits per second. That's enough bandwidth to switch 3,000 high-quality video channels, or 23,000 data channels of 192,000 bps each — more bandwidth than any other system today.

Inter-Node Connections

The switching bandwidth of ROLMbus 295 would be wasted if there were no means of carrying it to another node. The CBX II uses an internode link (INL), which comes in basic modules of 73.728 Mbps (plus parity and framing). Four INL Modules between a pair of nodes extend the full node bandwidth of 295 Mbps to each. The link can use either coaxial cable for short distances or fiber optics for distances up to 20,000 feet. Up to twelve links can be placed on every CBX II node. INL hardware, available in a redundant configuration, can be used for voice, data, or any combination.

For very large systems, the inter-node network (INN) expands the connection possibilities of each node.

Control Flexibility

It is sometimes difficult to balance the two naturally opposing system requirements of centralized control and modularity. While it is advantageous to have one extremely fast, centralized processor to handle the entire system, it is also beneficial to have each section of the system control itself. The CBX II system uses distributed processors connected via a packed switched network to achieve both goals. Each node retains the intelligence it needs for local call processing, while the network of controllers can share common processing tasks and centralize some duties (such as call detail recording). This control flexibility will be the key in providing new and innovative software features and functions. The distributed packet network will allow Rolm CBX II processors to link up with specialized external processors to configure cost-effective integrated communications solutions.

CBX II Architecture

There are ten major parts to the CBX II architecture. They are ROLMlink™, the Interface Shelf, Expanders, ROLMbus, Turnaround, Time Division Multiplexing (TDM) Controller, Control Processing Unit (CPU), Inter-Node Link, Inter-Node Network and the Control Packet Network. These are listed roughly in terms of their status on the hierarchical tree.

ROLMlink

ROLMlink is not specific to any one product, but is a pervasive new way of connecting most types of terminal devices to the CBX. ROLMlink provides a basic communications channel of 256 Kbps bidirectionally from the CBX to the terminal equipment. The digital communications channel back to the switch is carried on ordinary voice-grade twisted pairs of wire at distances up to 3,000 feet. The link protocol is synchronous, with the line interface card in the CBX acting as master for 16 ROLMlink channels. The data transmission is divided into distinct frames, with each frame containing a fixed amount of bandwidth for voice, data, and control. The link adds its own

parity check to each stream independently. The link operates over a single twisted pair in a bidirectional mode. Both sides transmit simultaneously, and the signals are separated by specialized data hybrids at each end of the line. Voice-grade twisted pair was chosen because of its low cost, ease of installation and servicing, and the fact that many buildings are already wired with it. No special shielding is required for a ROLMlink since the link meets all applicable FCC standards regarding emitted radiation. ROLMlink can be bundled into twenty-five and one-hundred pair cables with no loss in performance.

The ROLMphone family of digital desktop devices (ROLMphone® 120, 240 or 400) shown in Figure 2 uses ROLMlink and is compatible with both the previous CBX and the new CBX II architecture.

The ROLMphones use an integrated codec chip to both sample and digitize the analog speech wave forms from the handset. The same chip is used to drive the handset ear piece. By itself, digitized voice may be transmitted long distances without distortion or noise effects. Not only does the ROLMphone communicate voice, but any ROLMphone can be configured to accept and transmit data at speeds up to 64 Kbps *simultaneously* with voice conversations. For data connections, the user's data equipment plugs into a telephone socket which accepts data according to the appropriate physical standards. From there, the data can be switched through the ROLM integrated voice/data network to any

Figure 2. The ROLMphone 120, 400 and 240, from left to right.

properly configured data port, be it another ROLMphone, a desktop data terminal interface (DTI), or a Cypress™ Personal Communication Terminal.

The digitized voice signals and the user's data stream, along with control information vital to the operation of the phone, are all multiplexed together into the common ROLMlink digital data channel. The ROLMphone 400, for instance has a 60-character display and forty soft-function keys, in addition to the dialing pad. Key stroke capture, off-hook sensing, and display handling are performed by an on-board microprocessor, which communicates with its counterpart inside the CBX through the ROLMlink control channel. This pre-processing greatly reduces the real-time operating burden on the CBX II main processor, allowing it to devote more time to high-level routing and management decisions. The processors at both ends of the ROLMlink are continually checking each other to maintain dependable service and participate in fault isolation and determination, to reduce service time. Transient errors are likely to be caught by the parity checking hardware integral to the link, and immediate retransmissions will prevent any service interruption to the user. This feature is built into every ROLMlink and does not require additional user support.

Intershelf/Expander

A main function of the switch is to collect the data from all cabinet shelves and send it back to the appropriate places. The Expander Card in a CBX II (see Figure 3) acts as a bus master for the shelf bus, and is the only device capable of driving the shelf address and enable lines. The Expander exchanges data and control information with other shelves via the ROLMbus.

ROLMbus 74

The bandwidth (74 Mbps) and clock speed (4.608 Mhz) of ROLMbus 74 are identical to an interface shelf. The TDM Controller (Time Division Multiplexing Controller) for ROLMbus 74 contains a complete connection table for all system events and continuously supplies the Expanders with addressing information, which is forwarded by the Expanders to the shelves. This addressing information specifies which devices are to communicate in what time slots. The Expanders are relatively simple circuits that can buffer data

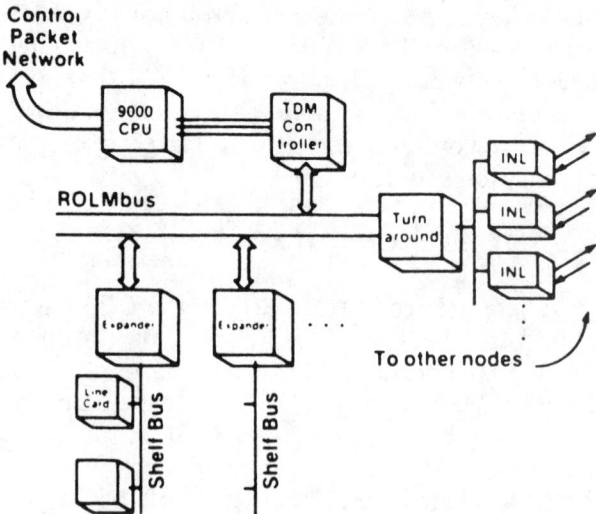

Figure 3. The Expanders act as the interface between the individual shelf busses and the ROLMbus.

bidirectionally from the shelf to the ROLMbus, and drive the shelf address and card select lines based on information from the TDM Controller.

ROLMbus 295

ROLMbus 295 has a bandwidth of 295 Mbps, four times that of the ROLMbus 74, and can be installed as original equipment in new systems, or retrofitted in any previous CBX or CBX II. ROLMbus 295 provides substantially greater service in those applications where it is needed. To install ROLMbus 295 in CBX II, the Expanders and TDM controller are changed, and a new circuit card called the turnaround is plugged in. ROLMbus 295 uses the same flat ribbon cable harness used by ROLMbus 74. ROLMbus 295 is classified as a *undirectional* bus. It is also a *traveling wave* bus. Because the total bus length is longer than the wave length of one clock period, several successive signals can actually be present on the bus at one time. The signal pulses are pipelined through the bus in such a way that they do not interfere with each other.

CPU

The CPU, TDM Controller, ROLMbus, and one Expander for each shelf all go together to form the control subsystem. The ROLMbus can be either a type 74 or 295 and the CPU can be either the 8000 (16-bit) or 9000 (32-bit) processor. This entire control subsystem is completely and independently mirrored by a redundant system.

Each shelf has two Expanders. Only one of the control subsystems is active at a time, the other is a "hot standby," ready to take over at any instant, and constantly running diagnostics and self tests. The active CPU also constantly runs self tests and diagnostics on all the components of the system.

In a CBX II 9000 processor environment with several nodes, each CPU has a packet network interface called the Control Packet Network for communicating with its peer processors in other nodes, and also for talking to specialized applications processors. The Control Packet Network is an ideal place to connect external processing power such as mainframe resources, or remote diagnostic computers for off-site servicing. Once a sound network has been established the growth potential for the system becomes practically unlimited.

The Control Packet Network is carried by the INL between remote nodes, capitalizing on the fiber optic technology and high bandwidth available over those connections. This is an excellent example of synergistic relationship that exists between the Rolm CBX II and the LAN world.

The Control Packet Network is used for node-to-node system traffic, and not for user device communications or voice traffic.

Inter-Node Link (INL)

The INL hardware must interface through a turnaround, and is available only on systems equipped with ROLMbus 295. The INL is designed to permit extremely high bandwidth connections between nodes. It is most often used to perform a data swapping operation, and is, therefore, able to effectively double the ROLMbus bandwidth. Data going out from the ROLMbus can be buffered in the INL subsystem, passed through a time slot interchange, and sent across a 73.5 Mbps serial (coax or fiber optic) link to the destination node. Data coming back from other nodes through the INL may be subjected to another time slot interchange before being placed on the local ROLMbus.

INL links may be installed in a redundant mirrored fashion. There is a turnaround for each half of the mirrored ROLMbus 295, and each turnaround interfaces to both of the redundant INL networks. The INL equipment can be used in a local sharing arrangement. Up to 12 fully redundant INL links can be installed on any CBX II node. A fiber optic INL using all glass 100 uM cable can be run as far as 20,000 feet.

Inter-Node Network (INN)

What if 12 redundant INL links aren't enough? What if the user wants fifteen nodes, all fully inter-connected with 294 Mbps of non-blocking service between each pair? Research indicates that such requirements may exist in the forseeable future. To meet this requirement, Rolm has developed an inter-node network (INN) that can absorb and switch the full 294 Mbps from each of 15 CBX II nodes. The INN is a slave type device, and responds to requests from the community of CBX II nodes which arrive over the Control Packet Network. The INN is connected to each CBX II node with a full complement of four INL links.

CBX II Growth Plan

A user might start with a single cabinet version of a CBX II using the ROLMbus 74 and 8000 processor and expand it to include more shelves and up to three cabinets. As the total traffic or feature load grows, the ROLMbus 295 can be installed, followed by the 9000 processor. The next step is to add the Control Packet Network, a second node, and the INL connecting them together. More INLs and nodes will suffice until the requirement grows beyond a few thousand users. For very large systems, the INN becomes appropriate, and the user can expand to 15 nodes.

CBX II Meets Needs of Today and Tomorrow

The distributed architecture and flexible hierarchical structure give the customer a system tailored exactly to individual needs, not tailored for some hypothetical "average" customer. The CBX II architecture can grow consistently from 16 lines to more than 10,000 users by adding successive layers of the hierarchy — up to 4.4 billion bits per second of non-stop performance, connecting users eight miles apart (or further with T1 links and microwave equipment). Distributed processing and fully redundant switching capability keep problems local, eliminating shutdowns.

More Than You Probably Want to Know About the CBX II

The Rolm CBX II is both a product and an architecture; the latter being the basic capabilities which are implemented by the specific product. The key architectural element is a high-speed, parallel, time-division-multiplexed bus, called the ROLMbus™.

Voice and data devices and resources are connected, typically by twisted-pair telephone wiring, to appropriate interface cards, all connected to the ROLMbus. A central processor runs the software that defines the intelligence of CBX II, and it allocates via commands to the time division controller, the bandwidth of he ROLMbus, providing appropriate connections between the various interfaces.

There are two types of ROLMbus available, ROLMbus 74, which provides 74 Mbps of capacity, is the standard configuration and provides the information capacity and capability required for today's voice and data devices.

Because the ROLMbus 74 is used in a bidirectional manner, it is not possible to increase the system clock speed without distorting the signal pulses. If the signals could be made to travel along the cable in only one direction, they could be pipelined through at a much higher rate without distorting. That is the basic idea for ROLMbus 295. With a bandwidth of 295 Mbps, ROLMbus 295 has the designed-in flexibility to handle demanding future communication requirements.

At first glance into a digital PBX, one will see the interface shelf. The shelf supplies a basic interface to the CBX II switching capabilities. The shelf definition includes card dimensions, connector types, power, grounding, shielding and other mechanical specifications designed to make the interface circuit cards reliable and easy to service.

In the Rolm system, each interface card has two connectors. One is the actual line interface connector and goes off to various types of telephone and data service equipment. The second connector goes to the "shelf bus," which is a motherboard used to bring voice samples, data and control information to and from the card. The total bandwidth potential of this connector is 74 Mbps, although no one card would be expected to make sense of such an enormous flow of information.

Any bus cycle can be used either to transmit voice, data or control information at any time. The "Expander" is hardware that is contained on each shelf, serving as the bus master, which sequences the flow of the bus cycle so that each voice or data connection is sampled at an even rate. The flexibility of using any bus cycle for any type of operation means that CBX II can be adapted to many different uses.

The motherboard format includes a 16-bit bidirectional data bus, a 10-bit address bus, and a special "enable" line to each card. The enable line serves three basic purposes: (1) cards do not have to be configured with a special physical address when they are plugged in, as the enable line performs that function for them; (2) the reliability of the system has been enhanced relative to letting each card do its own address decoding, because the enable line interface is simpler on the card; and (3) because the card select decoding is done on the Expander (the bus master) instead of on each interface card, the enable line is actually replacing five coded card select lines, which saves connector pins on each interface card.

The bus cycle rate is 4.608 Mhz. Addresses (and enables) appear on the bus synchronously with data, but one cycle earlier. By convention, 832 of the possible 1024 address patterns are used in conjunction with the enable lines. This is a subtle, but important point, as it is the key to the new CBX II broadcast and shared-access modes of operation. The remaining 192 patterns are called non-enabled commands and can be used for broadcast and multi-access. The 832 commands are more than enough to program intelligent interface cards, such as the ROLMphone interface group.

For a typical data transfer, the Expander first outputs a card enable and 10-bit address indicating which word it wants. In the next shelf, the enabled card places its data on the shelf bus. From there the Expander transfers the data out to the ROLMbus. At the destination shelf, the corresponding Expander captures the data word off of the ROLMbus and places it on the destination shelf from which it may be read by the intended interface card.

The Expander is the first point on the hierarchical ladder at which redundant (i.e., duplicated) hardware can be supplied. The entire common control structure of a node can be supplied with mirrored redundancy including the CPU, ROLMbus and Expanders. Two Expanders sit on each shelf, one for each side of the common control system. Only one common control side is active at a time; the other side spends its day checking for errors.

The Expanders form what is called a fully connected redundant interface between the non-

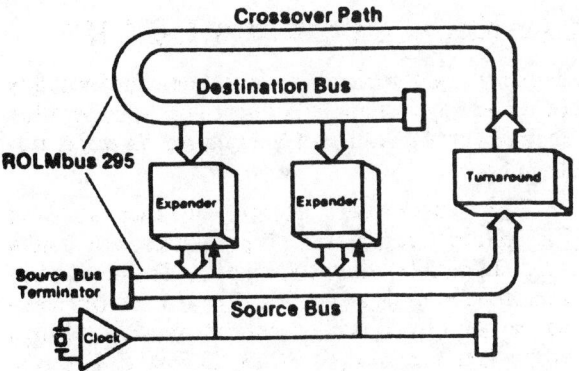

Figure A. The two halves of the ROLMbus.

redundant shelf bus and the redundant ROLMbus system. The two Expanders are completely independent and may be replaced without a service interruption.

Figure A illustrates the connection of Expanders onto the bus, which is split into two halves: a source half and a destination half. The turnaround card is used in conjunction with the Inter-Node Link (INL) equipment, but from the perspective of the ROLMbus 295, it is just a repeater. Clock signals are generated by the turnaround and propagate from left to right along the bus. Each expander uses the ROLMbus 295 clock for all timing, so that while the Expanders are all "out of phase" with each other, they maintain the correct phase relationship with the data, which travels along the ROLMbus 295 in the same direction as the clock.

Up to 17 devices can be connected directly to the ROLMbus 295. A data word traveling on the ROLMbus 295 would be split out by the source shelf Expander onto the source half of the ROLMbus 295 and progress to the right until it is absorbed by the turnaround. The turnaround then repeats the word back onto the destination bus from which it may be captured by the destination shelf Expander.

Because ROLMbus 295 goes four times faster than the interface shelves, it has time to service four shelves during each shelf cycle. This means that four shelf transfers can take place simultaneously, multiplying the CBX II internal bandwidth by a factor of four.

Inside the ROLMbus 295 Expanders, a complete connection table for all regular voice and data connections affecting the shelf is stored (see Figure B). The Expander uses the information in its connection table to generate addresses for the shelf. This means that address information is not required to flow on a regular basis between the controlling CPU and the Expander. That saves a great deal of bandwidth on the ROLMbus because the addressing information for a one word data transfer is much longer than the data itself.

The ROLMbus taps are not unidirectional, so some waves actually do propagate to the left along the source bus. These reverse waves are harmlessly absorbed at the source bus terminator at the left end of the ROLMbus. The Expander transmitters are linear current sources so that they can transmit correctly even when other reverse waves are passing by. There can be as many as three sets of forward and reverse waves traveling on the bus at any one time. The turnaround repeats all the signals only to the destination bus and they propagate on the crossover link back to the left end of the ROLMbus and then back from left to right. This is necessary to preserve the correct phase relationship between clock and data at every Expander. Only the turnaround is allowed to transmit on the destination bus, and since the turnaround is located at the end of that bus, waves can propagate only in one direction on the destination bus.

All interfaces to the ROLMbus have been designed to sustain local power outages, failed components and other local disasters without affecting the operation of other devices on the ROLMbus. The ROLMbus 295 always uses parity.

The turnaround is needed only on systems equipped with the high performance ROLMbus 295. The turnaround has the duty of absorbing information from the source bus and putting it back onto the destination bus. But nothing in the architecture requires the turnaround to put back the same information it pulled off. The capacity of the switch effectively can be doubled by doing just that!

Suppose a call is in progress between a local node with phone "X" and a remote node with phone "Y." When "X" transmits a voice sample it flows out to the local source bus and down to the turnaround. If the turnaround could capture that sample and send it directly to the remote node, then

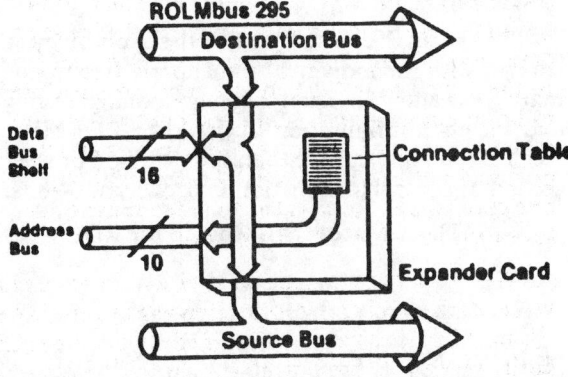

Figure B. The connection table inside the Expander.

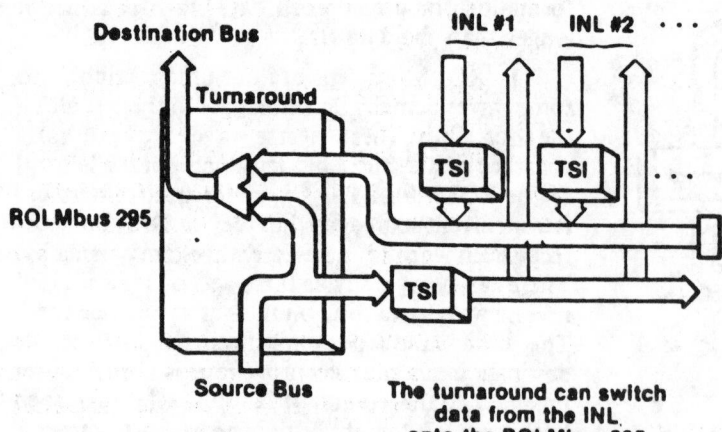

Figure C.   Signal flow paths inside the turnaround.

the local destination bus could lie idle for the remainder of the cycle (because the sample certainly isn't needed anywhere else in the local node).

The empty destinations bus cycle could be filled in with a sample from "Y," if the turnaround had such a sample. This is a way to do a full conversation using only a single timeslot, but it only works if the turnaround knows exactly what to do.

Figure C shows the signal flow paths inside the turnaround that allow it to communicate with the INL Hardware. The INL exchanges information with other nodes and is capable of supplying data for the turnaround to perform this efficient swapping operation. The net result is that a two-way conversation takes up only one timeslot if the call is being placed to another node, instead of two timeslots like an ordinary intra-node call. In multi-node systems, many of the calls are between nodes, and the efficiency of the turnaround/INL combination is almost twice as high as tie lines or digital interties.

The ROLMbus 74 TDM Controller (TC) contains the full system connection table and acts as bus master for the entire ROLMbus 74, generating and driving all the address and select lines systemwide.

ROLMbus 295 vests more of the cycle by cycle control with the individual Expanders, freeing the main CPU and TC to perform more polling, testing and system configuration duties. The ROLMbus 295 TC can handle more than three million bits per second of control information in packets of 64 bits.

The TDM Controller attaches to the ROLMbus

295 exactly like an Expander. Control commands from the TC propagate through the ROLMbus 295 system just like regular data. The TC is responsible for three activities: loading the connection tables on every Expander, configuring the turnaround and INL hardware, and communicating with all the various line card groups. The TC does not contain its own connection table, and does not participate in the normal connection oriented data flow.

The TC uses the ROLMbus 295 special control field line (CFL) to signal its activities. When the TC has a message to send it raises the CFL line and broadcasts a packet of 64 bits of control information. The CFL is wired as a seventeenth data bit that only the TC is allowed to use. The packet contains addressing control and data information to do operations like loading the Expander connection table, or reading the status of a line card. The TC is careful to never set up regular connections in the timeslots that it uses for control packages. In most respects the TC behaves very much like an Expander.

There are two important points about the control packet strategy: First, any number of timeslots can be used for control. The control bandwidth could be expanded to a full 295 Mbps if necessary. The current TC version is configured in hardware to use a maximum bandwidth of slightly more than three bits per second, about one percent of the total system capacity. Second, there can be multiple TCs inside one node (as long as they use non-overlapping timeslots). This provides yet another important direction of expansion possibilities for the CBX II architecture.

Further software developments eventually will open up even more configuration possibilities. For instance, the INL could support a chain of CBX IIs with INL connections between adjacent pairs

stretching out for tens of miles. Combining two INN subsystems might pave the way for configuring systems of twenty or thirty nodes, even though such huge installations are difficult to imagine today.

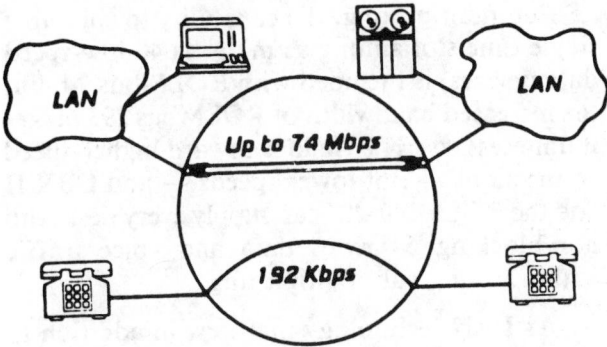

Figure 4. Supermultiplexing capability.

External computing facilities could be interfaced with the Control Packet Network; such arrangements are already under study. That could provide for more comprehensive on-site billing and recordkeeping. Automatic call distribution systems could be integrated with the terminal handling equipment for airline reservations and other applications. Text processing applications may be integrated with voice systems, enhancing the value of both. A telephone could be used to access computer files (using voice responses from the computer and the DTMF pad on the telephone). A computer terminal could be used to screen calls, or to help file and retrieve voice recordings.

New Data Communications Capabilities

Many people believe that a PBX can only be used to set up low-speed point-to-point data connections. While that may be true of some systems, the CBX II architecture will allow it to expand and grow as office automation matures.

Super-multiplexing is one of three new switching modes included in the CBX II ROLMbus 295 for future expansion. Blocks of bandwidth can be allocated to provide high-speed switching services. Bidirectional high speed data streams of up to 37 Mbps can be configured (see Figure 4). Super-multiplexing works well for providing bridge and gateway functions between local area networks (LAN), such as Ethernet or the IBM token ring network. For multiple LANs spread out over a large geographical area, the CBX II and its INL hardware can act as a high-speed backbone network for the LANs. Suppose a site had several LANs located three miles apart. The CBX II, with INL links, could be used to provide a basic high-speed data connection from place-to-place with each LAN having a bridge interface to the CBX.

Video transmission is possible with super-multiplexing. Out of 295 Mbps per node, a mere 1.5 Mbps for high quality video could hardly be missed. In addition, enormous amounts of burst traffic between computers, like magnetic tape transfers, could be easily handled with super-multiplexing.

The broadcast mode allows one device to transmit to a number of listeners simultaneously as shown in Figure 5. This mode uses non-enabled card commands to instruct a number of cards to read data from a single source simultaneously. If an Expander has a non-enabled command programmed into its connection table, all the cards on that shelf sensitive to the command will respond. The broadcast mode may prove to be extremely effective for solving automatic program load problems. Many intelligent workstations could use the broadcast feature for obtaining system update information. Another use for this mode is to synchronize events in different parts of the system by sending out global timing information. Mail distribution and document circulation are other potential applications.

Broadcast groups can be configured at any speed up to the full interface shelf bandwidth of 74 Mbps.

Shared-Access mode also uses the non-enabled commands. This mode provides common broadcast bandwidth to a number of cards and allows the cards to arbitrate among themselves for access. The only difference between shared-access and plain broadcast is that in broadcast an enable command is typically sent to the source device,

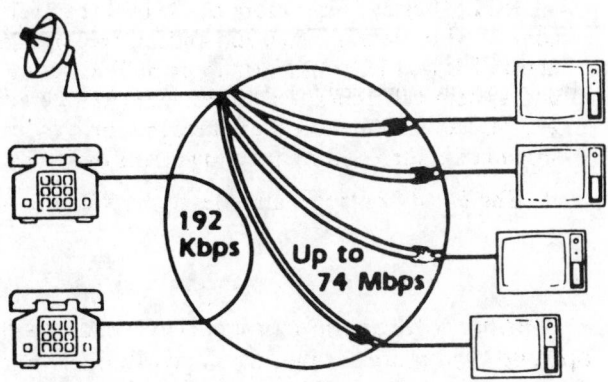

Figure 5. Shared access capability.

315

while in the shared-access mode it is not. In shared-access mode, the non-enable command is broadcast to the whole group. From the CBX II perspective, any device in the group can transmit when it wants. By combining super-multiplexing with shared-access, a number of one megabit shared communication channels can be configured. CBX II can partition the ROLMbus 295 bandwidth into many non-interacting segments of super-multiplexed shared-access groups — broadcast groups, bidirectional super-multiplexed channels and ordinary data or voice connections. This capability is called "dynamically allocatable bandwidth."

The shared-access mode can be used to implement a packet switching service directly embedded in CBX II. As long as the devices doing the transmitting have an agreement not to transmit simultaneously, every station can hear every other station. The access control could be via token passing between the sharing devices or access control could be statistical, as in Carrier Sense Multiple Access methods. Or a new TC type card could be plugged in to the ROLMbus 295 and programmed to poll devices and grant transmit requests, providing centralized arbitration.

Sub-multiplexing, the capability to split up a single time slot among as many as 40 low-speed data devices, is included with ROLMbus 74, but the increased bandwidth of ROLMbus 295 makes it unnecessary. The trend is toward higher-speed connections — not lower speeds — and CBX II and the ROLMbus 295 can supply every desk with non-blocking 64 Kbps data and voice traffic without using sub-multiplexing.

As LAN technology matures, in addition to providing backbone and gateway functions, the CBX can act as a center for administration and maintenance of the various LAN networks that will coexist with the CBX at the customer site. It can function to configure, allocate, and monitor vital LAN resources such as satellite links, printers, diagnostic equipment, and other network servers. The need for these services is virtually independent of the type of LAN, and is fundamentally the same for CSMA broadcast bus networks, token passing ring networks, and even cellular mobile radio installations. The CBX will continue to be a point of departure for external communications, such as X.25 networks, just as it is today.

DR. HOWARD W. JOHNSON is a senior member of the Rolm Corporation Technology and Advanced Development Group. He earned his BSEE, MEE and Ph.D degrees from Rice University. He joined Rolm in 1979 and completed his graduate studies under a Rolm fellowship. Dr. Johnson is a member of Tau Beta Pi, Sigma Xi, IEEE ASSP Society and a winner of the ACM computer art contest.

Reprinted with permission from *Business Communications Review* 950 York Road, Hinsdale, IL 60521, Tel: (312) 986-1432

A NEW DISTRIBUTED PBX FOR VOICE/DATA INTEGRATION

Philip M Kay
Manager
Third Party Marketing
Ztel Inc
USA

Integration of voice and data communications is a logical estension of the trends of the 1970s. Ztel's Private Network Exchange (PNX) is designed specifically to accomplish this task by combining the voice features of a sophisticated private branch exchange (PBX) with an industry-standard local area network (LAN). Its token-ring or LAN architecture is based on IEEE-802.5 standards. Ztel-designed station equipment compliments the PNX.

Philip M. Kay is Third Party Product Marketing Manager for Ztel, Inc. His responsibilities include the marketing of Ztel's PNX to Bell Operating Companies, independent telephone companies, mainframe computer manufacturers, and telecommunications interconnect companies. Mr. Kay was previously product manager for Voice Communications Systems development at Wang Laboratories, where he was responsible for the development of stand-alone and integrated voice products. Prior to joining Wang, Kay was a member of the professional staff of Arthur D. Little's Telecommunications Sciences section. At ADL his consultation included the technical and economic evaluation of both AT&T and Interconnect telephone systems. He is the author of the 1980 ADL publication "The Outlook for the U.S. Telephone Interconnect Equipment Industry." While at International Business Telephone Co. (now Rolm New England), he was vice president of marketing. Kay was also territory sales manager for Burroughs Corp. Kay received a bachelor of arts degree from Colby College and and MBA from Boston University.

Although the necessity of integrating voice and data communications has been recognized for the past ten years, it is only now becoming a reality.

Several factors have mitigated against this integration. One impediment was the lack of coordination between the data processing and telecommunications departments of user organizations. Ten years ago these were completely separate functions, with separate managers. Each manager was concerned with meeting his unique communications needs and typically was not familiar with the functions of -- and the technology used by -- the other department.

This reflected a division between suppliers. On the one hand there were computer companies, and on the other telecommunications companies. PBXs handled data in a manner totally inadequate for true office automation, and local area networks did nothing about the communication of voice in the business communications department.

However, in the 1970s a new function, the management information system department, developed in user organizations as a result of the merger of technologies between data processing and telecommunications. Since then, a host of new applications have arisen -- word processing, message generation, and graphics, to name only a few. And the trend has been to integrate these functions, rather than have them all run on separate systems.

A logical extension of this trend into the 1980s is the integration of communications into one system. For true office automation to occur, there must be total integration of voice and data. To users, such an integrated system will be transparent; they will not be aware of how data is moving or whether it moves over telephone or data lines.

It has not been easy for industry to integrate with existing technologies. A number of computer vendors have signed agreements with telecommunications vendors, and are attempting to cobble two existing systems into one. And telecommunications vendors have attempted to adapt the traditional PBX star architecture to handle data communications as well as voice. In most cases these attempts have not been particularly successful.

VOICE/DATA INTEGRATION IN PNX

Ztel, however, has designed its Private Network Exchange, or PNX, from the ground up as an integrated voice/data network. We have not started with one system and then attempted to graft another onto it. We believe we have developed the first system to fully integrate into a single, unified system the voice features of a computerized private branch exchange and an industry-standard local area network for communicating high-speed data. Building the PNX required the coordination of extremely diverse talents because of the technologies involved. Our personnel are approximately equally divided between the voice and the data processing industries.

There are a number of advantages in combining the two technologies. PBX wiring is already in place in most businesses, and the PBX voice functionality will always be required. The LAN technology facilitates the linking of devices such as facsimile and personal computers which require high speeds.

By combining the PBX and LAN, the PNX will lower the cost of both voice and data communications, be more compact, offer more features, and have far better reliability and serviceability. These improvements are accomplished through the use of custom large scale integrated circuits, software implementation techniques, and new types of fault-tolerant, distributed system architecture.

Because the PNX system software strictly follows the International Standards Organization's Open System Interconnection model and is implemented in the high-level C language, OEMs can easily add industry-specific customizations to the PNX. No other PBX allows this level of accessibility.

THE CHANGING PBX ENVIRONMENT

In the typical PBX star architecture, telephones and terminals connect to a central processor. The information flows through some common carrier to its destination, where it is then distributed to the proper recipient.

But this typical PBX environment is changing very rapidly. The PBX function will always be needed for voice communications. Users must interface to telephone companies and common carrier type of networks. But there is now a major, rapidly growing trend to add productivity aids such as electronic mail and calendaring to the PBX.

Another trend is to use the PBX as a gateway to other types of networks. Sooner or later voice and data information has to exit a facility, so a gateway will always be needed. A third major trend is a marketplace that will require significantly more information. Right now there is probably one data device for every 10 to 15 office workers. Within a few years there will be one device for five workers or even fewer.

With this explosion in devices it becomes very costly to implement separate solutions to business communications needs. Thus, a revolution in the marketplace is now occuring. The voice PBX has had many data PBX features grafted onto it, and now the local area network is being integrated. This step is inevitable, due to the need for very high speed data communications to handle the new types of office products on the horizon.

But there is another evolution in the marketplace, one that few have recognized. Very soon applications will be the primary means of differentiating PBX-type products, making them unique to an industry or a business. The user can translate the applications, such as protocol conversion and on-line directory, very easily and quickly into profit or added productivity. Applications in business communications will require new types of hardware and software capabilities that do not exist in today's traditional PBX or LAN.

AN INTEGRATED SOLUTION

The evolution outlined above leads directly to integrated solutions for the decision making process, from lower management levels right up to the CEO. If a system cannot support the decision making process, it will be of little value to the user.

The only solution that supports this process within a corporation is total network communication that starts within a building, extends to a campus of buildings, goes out nationally, and then internationally. Without a totally integrated network, it will be more difficult to achieve the information flow and transfer required to support decision making.

The design of Ztel's PNX is based on this forecast of an evolution to integrated and instantaneous transmission of business information over vast distances, or between departments in one building. And we made several determinations about the requirements such a network should meet.

First, it must have voice communications equal or superior to that of a traditional PBX, or it will not be accepted.

Second, it must be extremely reliable because all of a company's communications requirements -- voice, data, image, video -- will be moving through one system.

Third, it must have local area networking.

Fourth, the LAN must be as compatible as is realistic. Adopting the IEEE-802.5 standard is a major step in this direction. Additionally, IBM has focused on networking as a prime ingredient for success in in the communications market. Because of its size, IBM will tend to dominate the networking market with the standard it chooses. Therefore, compatibility with IBM at the connection level will be mandatory.

Before describing how these requirements have been met in the PNX, it may be useful to look at current PBX architectures. Bar none, they consist of a central processing resource to which are attached I/O boards. These boards may be resident in the central site or be remotely connected to the central site via a T-1 channel. In either case, this is the star architecture used by the telephone industry for 100 years and by the data processing industry since the early 1960s.

Star architecture has several problems, including performance, cost, and capacity. Because the central resource is finite, performance is finite, making it difficult to add new applications such as electronic mail. Because the architecture is not modular, the user must pay for the entire central resource even before the first line is put on the system. Capacity is limited to the number of lines the central resource can handle; to go above that number is difficult. Capacity and capability bought today are what the user will have tomorrow, even though new applications and additional lines may be needed.

TOKEN RING LAN ARCHITECTURE

In its search for a solution that would solve these problems, Ztel decided to base the internal system structure of the PNX on a local area networking technique.

The technology used is the baseband token ring LAN architecture as defined by the IEEE-802.5 standards committee. This was selected after evaluating both CSMA/CD (Ethernet) and token bus standards and rejecting both because of performance inadaquacies and reliability problems. Each ring in the network operates at the IEEE-802.5 standard rate of 10 megabits per second, the minimum rate for transmitting voice. Anything less does not make sense.

In a token ring network the transmission medium forms a circle through each connected device. Information is communicated in sequential order around the ring. Devices transmit and receive information by appending or extracting messages from the medium as tokens circulate through the network.

Data and analog information are digitized upon entering the network. Data is also packetized, and these packets are intermixed with packets from other transmissions and routed through the network, allowing efficient use of available bandwidth.

NETWORK CONTROL

To implement a LAN based on a token-passing protocol of a ring structure, we had to add devices to our system processing units that provide the functionality of a data switch. Each system processing unit
can perform three types of processing. Switch processing which performs the actual handling and connection of voice and data calls.
Applications processing which performs tasks such as least cost routing, directory look-up or other value added applications. And data
conversion processing which packetizes/depacketizes information and
provides protocol conversion between differing types of equipment.

The PNX has a distributed architecture, typically utilizing multiple
system processing units or SPUs. These can be added or taken away to
make a system larger or smaller. Because no one SPU controls the
system, the failure of any one processor will not shut down the system.
If one processor fails, its workload can be distributed among other
processors.

Devices such as phones and terminals can be interfaced to the system
processing unit via standard quad telephone line up to 5,000 feet
long which carries two channels of information. The Ztel channel
structure includes one digitized voice channel, one data channel,
and two control channels of the correct size to guarantee correct
data operations at 56 kilobits simultaneous with voice.

Non-Ztel user device such as a workstation or a computer that meets
protocol requirements can be attached directly to the token ring.
Simple wall connectors, defined by the 802 standard, are used. Any
device with that physical interface can be attached to the PNX system
and take advantage of it as a high-speed transport mechanism to access
system information at megabit speeds. And if it is appropriately
programmed, any device can communicate with applications we provide
on our applications processor.

There are six main features to this architecture.

First, it provides fully integrated voice and data.

Second, it strictly follows two standards. One is the IEEE-802.5 LAN,
and the second is the expected IBM LAN, with which we are committed
to being compatible. I'll talk more about this later.

Third, the PNX features multiprocessing, so it has virtually unlimited
expansion capabilities.

Fourth, features can be added in a modular fashion as requirements
increase.

Fifth, the PNX offers very high throughput. Token ring LANs are the only determinstic LAN, which means you can forecast the worst case performance of the network independent of its load. This is a very valuable characteristic in both telephone and data communications. Thus, a deterministic network can achieve transmission rates high enough for transmission of video, graphics, and file services without fear of deteriorating performance.

The last main feature is the extreme reliability of the PNX. Token ring networks have proven to be one of the most reliable techniques available in local networking standards.

MULTIPLE RINGS

Ztel achieves its tremendously high throughput by using multiple rings, which may be installed according to the required level of service. Our initial release will allow up to 40 rings to operate in one PNX system, each ring operating at 10 megabits per second, for a total throughput of 400 megabits per second. Thus the PNX has the throughput potential to handle the extremely high data rates that will be required in the near future by automated equipment. Plus it has the high level of system reliability that only a multiple ring network can provide. Even if one ring fails, backup mechanisms will redistribute that ring's traffic over other active rings.

The other aspect of using multiple 10 megabit rings is low cost; the user only need implement the number of rings needed to achieve the desired throughput and functionality. Also, a multiple ring network is easy to expand. As more bandwidth is required, more rings are added incrementally and at low cost. And the limit of 40 rings is artificially imposed by packaging. The architecture allows hundreds of rings, and as time goes on the artificial packaging barrier will be removed.

RING TYPES

Rings can be implemented in two media, coaxial cable and fiber optics. Coax can be used in rings up to about one mile long. For longer distances or in severe environments, or indeed any time a ring goes outside of a building, we recommend fiber.

There are two types of rings, packet and circuit. The totally transparent circuit rings handled digitized voice -- one 10 megabit circuit can handle 113 simultaneous conversations, each in a 64K bps slot. Any data call can also be put on the ring, but it is wasteful to transmit a 4800 bps data transaction over a 64K bps slot. The circuit ring is also used to transmit video.

The packet ring is where LAN compatible devices are connected. It transfers packetized data from source to destination. The PNX itself determines whether the circuit or packet ring will be used, and packetizes the information. Depending on the characteristics of the network, there may be any number of circuit and packet rings.

PNX IMPLEMENTATION

The PNX can adapt to the exact geographical structure of the site where it is installed. For example, rings can be lobed out from a system processing unit at a central site to a SPU at a remote site. And from this remote site rings can be lobed out to a site even further away. All elements of the system are connected -- totally transparently -- to one another.

If a user prefers, all of the PNXs System Processing Units can be collapsed into central equipment cabinets typically found in a telecommunications room. The wiring from the central cabinets to the stations is the typical quad telephone wire that is currently installed. The LAN resides inside the cabinets, interconnecting all of the chassis. Whenever the need arises, cabling can simply be extended out to the areas where true LAN operations are required.

The PNX can also network all corporate facilities to the outside world. It accommodates T-1 channels, packet-switched networks, satellite and microwave communications. High-speed data capability can be brought directly to a company, avoiding the high cost of that last mile of satellite transmissions.

STATION EQUIPMENT

Ztel has also designed station equipment, the primary devices users see when they interface with the system, to complement the PNX. Three telephone sets have been developed to correspond with the three organization levels that require different functions in their station equipment. All sets are easy to learn and easy to use; any operation can be implemented using only one button.

The top-of-the-line telephone set has 28 feature keys. There are no prompts, no multi-step operations, and no confusing sequences. The user simply pushes a button to implement a feature. Among the innovations in this telephone set is level I electronic mail. Keys represent requests such as "call me back," "please see me," and "returned your call". Users can also construct their own messages.

If a line is busy or there is no answer, the user simply pushes one of these keys. A message light on the recipient's station turns on. At his convenience the recipient presses the message key and a LED display gives the name, number, date, time, and message. In addition, messages can be sent to this telephone set via a standard CRT.

Other unique PNX functions include a complete on-line directory, a message center, and full electronic key set emulation. Menu-driven screens step the user through the entire administrative aspect of the system. The attendant console, which includes a CRT screen, lets the operator know what is happening with all of the calls the system is handling.

Release 1 of the PNX has two categories of data features. The first category provides cost savings and convenience and includes X.25, ISO level 1 protocol conversion, automatic route selection, and external access.

The second category includes call convenience features such as speed dial, hold, and queuing. The equivalent of these voice call features is available for data handling operations. There are almost 100 voice operations on the telephone sets, and nearly 40 of these can be used for data operations. The PNX also allows the user to place a call from the telephone set or from the keyboard of a terminal.

The PNX also provides several different methods for attaching data devices. Terminals and workstations that operate at up to 56K bps can plug into the back of a telephone set. Where there is no telephone, a workstation or terminal can plug into a full feature data attachment without a keypad and can be used with a dedicated terminal.

To sum up, any type of data or voice device can be connected to the PNX using a variety of means. Because the PNX has a multi-ring, multi-processor architecture, users can be assured that their communications will be reliable. And for the first time, users have one system for voice and data communications.

CXC Rose

Introduction

CXC Corporation, Irvine, California, was founded in June 1981 to develop, manufacture, and market a business communications and information processing system that combines communications and computer technologies. The result of the company's efforts to date was the formal introduction in May 1984 of its "Rose" product line and the preparation for production shipments that began in mid-1984.

System Concept

The Rose's fourth-generation architecture integrates a local area network (LAN) and distributed processing with multi-function workstations; voice processing (PBX); voice and data switching and networking; dynamic allocation of bandwidth; an integrated packet channel to each terminal; voice and text store-and-forward mail; and programmable processors for value-added applications. It also provides access to external networks like Telex, Telenet, and local area networks like Ethernet and IBM's contemplated token ring.

The Rose's user-interface equipment was designed to be easy to use, requiring but minimal training. System prompting, integrated HELP programs, and software-driven keys aid in voice and data call processing. Among the system's advanced architectural features are a proprietary local area network integrating a 33 Mbps circuit-switched ring and a 16 Mbps token ring over a 50 Mbps broadband cable, VLSI custom circuitry for integrated voice and data switching with dynamically allocatable bandwidth; an integrated messaging system with a personal teleterminal (a digital display phone), and an integrated packet channel to each personal teleterminal.

System applications range from a full complement of traditional PBX voice functions and communications cost management packages of full-featured voice and text messaging and mail. Both circuit and packet switching support a communications network that is capable of integrating word processing, graphics, personal computer applications, and, in future releases, video teleconferencing systems.

Architecture

A CXC Distributed Communications Processing Node supports the Rose family of digital voice and message stations, personal teleterminals, digital telephones, and analog telephones. As illustrated in the Figure, the CXC Processing Node may be connected with other CXC nodes to form a distributed integrated voice and data system. These nodes are interconnected via CXC's proprietary local area network which combines both baseband and broadband technologies to support up to 64 nodes in a single network ring (see Figure). The broadband ring operates at 50 Mbps and supports circuit-switched internodal communication of voice and data at a combined throughput of 33 Mbps using a CXC proprietary RF modem and standard CATV technology. The additional capacity of more than 16 Mbps is reserved for future token ring implementation (e.g., it can be configured as four 4 Mbps token ring bands, each consistent with IEEE 802.5).

The 10 Mbps, CSMA/CD Ethernet baseband LAN is used on an interim basis for control interfaces between nodes and for packet-switched data. Provision of both baseband and broadband local area networks allows the architecture to apply the benefits of each approach cost effectively. In a future release, compatible IBM and/or IEEE 802.5 token-passing rings will be integrated into a CXC broadband channel to provide a single coaxial broadband transmission system for voice, data, and packet data. The Ethernet interface then will become an optional gateway.

The distributed per-line-switch architecture provides the ability to define a TDM slot as 8 Kbps and combine these slots in multiples of 1-, 2-, 4-, or 8-bits, and then 1-, 2-, 4-, or 8-bytes. This yields switchable pathways of 8 Kbps to 512 Kbps to CXC teleterminals or data ports. This addressing switching architecture permits, for example, the CXC Rose processing node to dynamically configure multi-drop and loop data communications network topologies, in addition to traditional point-to-point connections.

Bridges connect network rings into one integrated system by attaching to the broadband circuit-switched highway and signaling channel and exchanging data and voice messages and, in future releases, video between the rings. Individual nodes within rings can be configured as gateways to interface to other networks, including standard analog telephone connections, X.25 packet networks, digital communications links, and Telex/TWX facilities. The capabilities within a node can be shared by all the other facilities within the network.

- *Switching*: Voice is digitized in the personal teleterminal, and all forms of information are handled in a digital mode. Two-pair wire connects a personal teleterminal or digital telephone to the Station Interface Module (SIM) (See Figure). Information is transmitted between the teleterminal and node at 192 Kbps full duplex. Each frame of information contains a 32-Kbps packet channel (up to 9.6 Kbps are initially available for direct user access), a 32-Kbps channel for

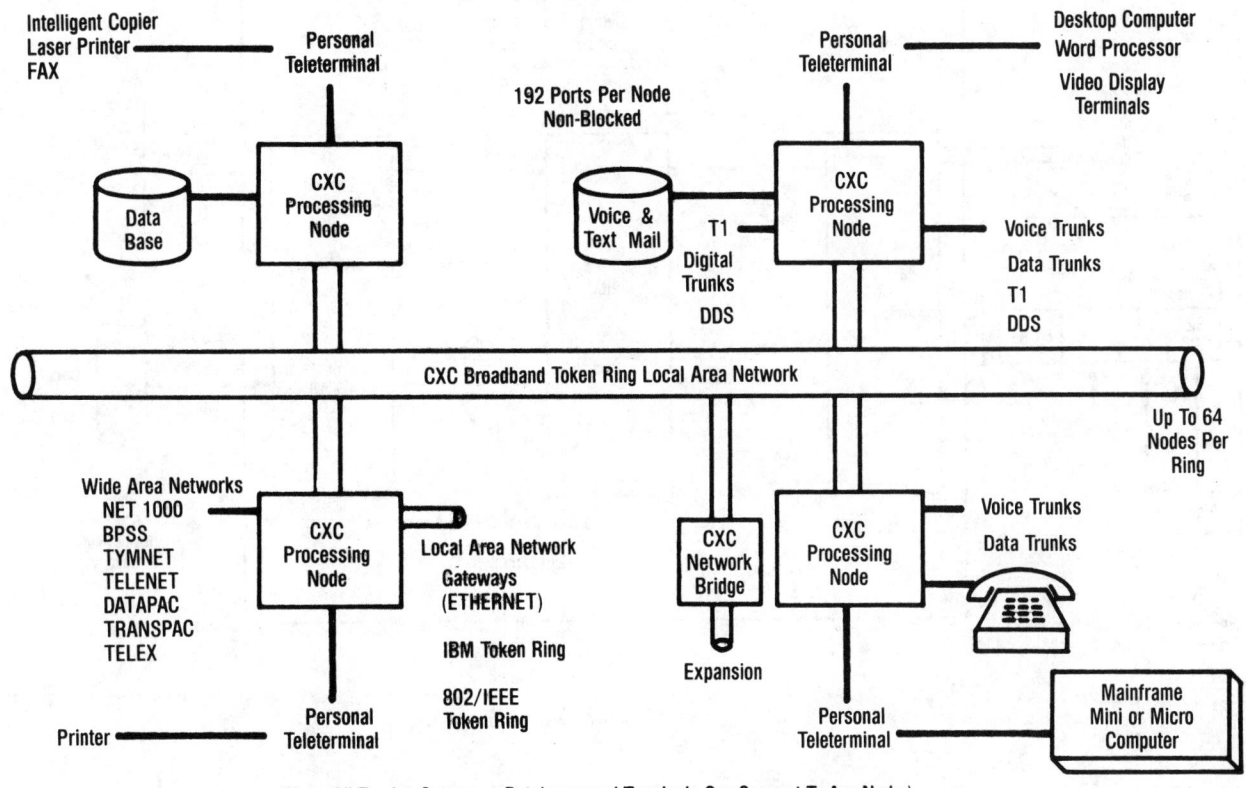

Figure: CXC's View Of Office Communications

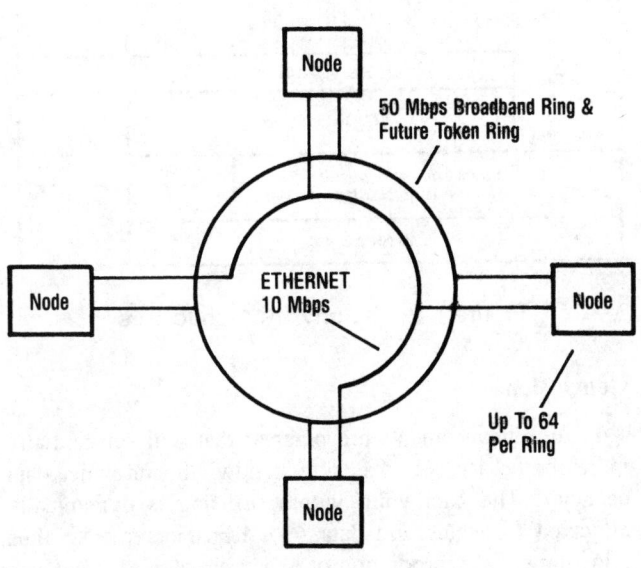

Figure: Initial Rose System Ring

synchronization and packet link control, a 64-Kbps channel for voice or data, and a 64-Kbps channel for data. Alternatively, the two 64-Kbps channels can be configured under software control into one 128-Kbps channel. Each personal teleterminal or digital telephone is controlled by a per-line-switch (PLS). There are four PLSs per custom VLSI circuit, called the QPLS, and there are four QPLSs for each microprocessor-controlled SIM. A QPLS can be configured under software control to support 320 Kbps or 576 Kbps circuit switched over standard two-pair wiring.

The Network Interface Module (NIM) is also microprocessor controlled and provides interfaces from the TDM highways and CPU memory to the clear channel circuit-switched broadband cable and CSMA/CD baseband cable. The bandwidth from the NIM to the broadband circuit switched system is dynamically allocatable in 8-Kbps increments. This provides the ability to vary the ratio of intranode and internode simultaneous voice conversations and data sessions. Each node treats the entire 33 Mbps ring as a pool of traffic capacity which it draws from on an "as needed" basis.

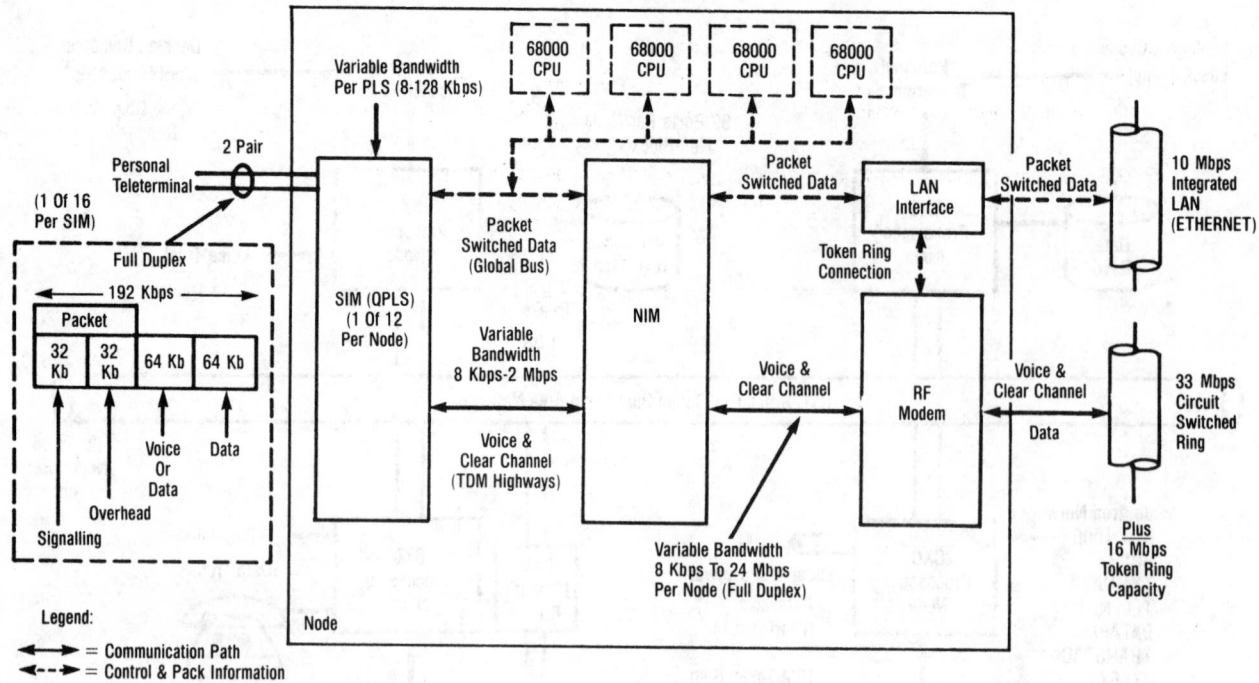

Figure: Rose System Block Diagram

- *Software and Applications*: The network and applications software provided by CXC are shown in the Figure. The layering of the software is mapped to a hardware layering to provide a modular system structure that will interface with multiple protocols and networks with minimal impact on the product base. Further, the layered structure allows for the distribution of functions across nodes with no requirements for symmetrical configuration. Multiple nodes can be interconnected by sharing a wide variety of storage, terminals, personal teleterminals, Rose digital Telephones, applications software, and network interfaces, all of which are based on a common operating system, system level functions, call processing database, and call processing applications software.

The Rose system provides the capabilities to support value-added applications programs. Integral M68000 microprocessor-based application processors in one or more nodes can be shared throughout the network (this processor will be supported in a subsequent release). Also, external application processors, such as personal computers or multi-terminal computer systems, can be connected to the Rose system via a personal teleterminal or a data communications adapter. Either way, the application processors will be able to exchange information with the call processing software in the Rose system and with personal teleterminals, terminals, computers, and other connected networks.

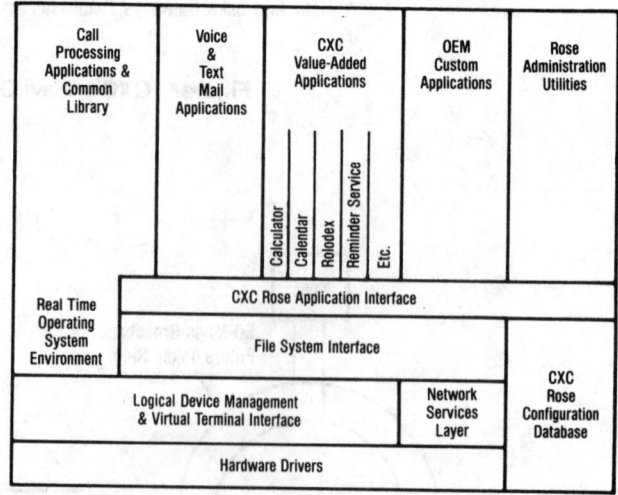

Figure: Rose Software Architecture

Conclusion

Future enhancements are planned that will substantially increase the Rose's total ring bandwidth and voice/data capacity. The bandwidth within the ring is dynamically allocated for voice and data in 8 Kbps increments, thus allowing easy incorporation of new technologies, such as a 32 Kbps adaptive PCM voice code or fiber optics, and substantially increasing system capacity. In addition, future releases will allow up to eight network rings to be interconnected by bridges that will allow an integrated voice/data system capacity of more than 25,000 ports. Protocol converting gateways will also be supported to connect CXC's local area network with wide-area networks such as Telenet.

The CXC Rose is running neck-and-neck with Ztel's PNX to be the first of the fourth-generation integrated voice and data switches to be widely accepted. Its initial integration of Ethernet technology allows it to be used with the thousands of Ethernet-type systems already installed. Its future token ring implementation then will allow entry into the IBM environments when IBM's local network becomes available in two or three years.

Section 6: Available Chips

For the first few years following their introduction, the entrance of personal computers into the local networking field has been hindered either by the large power consumptions of MSI level boards or by the cost of interface units which had nearly the same price tag as the personal computer itself. The development of VLSI technology and the introduction of VLSI-based network controller chips have cleared the way for personal computers networks, making it the most dynamic area in the field of local area networks. This section gives a sampling of a few of the controller chips available today for use either in personal and mini computer network connections.

One of the first chips to come out, the MB61301 developed jointly by Fujitsu and Ungermann-Bass is a link controller chip that implements the data link layer of ISO's reference model. Its companion chip, the MB502, implements the physical layer, and together they make a two-chip set for Ethernet networks. Since the chips were quickly developed to get them onto the market, they are less flexible than the next two chips described and they do need some additional circuitry to make a complete Ethernet interface board.

The second chip, made by Intel, one of the companies which formulated the Ethernet Specification, is a more versatile chip, capable of implementing not only Ethernet, but almost any CSMA/CD access scheme. The chip is optimized for operation as a Ethernet controller and offers some extra features, such as priority mechanisms, link management mechanisms, and others that make Intel's 82586 VLSI chip attractive for developers of network interface boards.

Another intelligent Ethernet chip, Mostek's Local Area Network Controller for Ethernet (LANCE) chip works in conjunction with a 16-bit microprocessor to form Ethernet interfaces in a wide variety configurations. Using the LANCE chip, it is possible to implement the first four layers of the ISO reference model on a single board, though the particular way in which these layers are implemented is left to the board designer.

Western Digital's LSI controller chip was designed for use in token-passing networks. This chip also works with a microprocessor in a cooperative manner to form the interface. The chip, known as the WD2840, is very versatile, supporting features such as dual DMA/highly efficient memory, diagnostic support, prioritization, and global addressing. Western Digital has recently introduced their own local area network which uses this chip.

EHO228-7/85/0000/0331$01.00 © 1985 IEEE

Link-controller IC combines versatility and flexibility

by Allen B. Goodrich
Ungermann-Bass Inc., Santa Clara, Calif.

Recognizing that different Ethernet implementations can meet the standard's specifications yet vary greatly in other important aspects, Ungermann-Bass in cooperation with Fujitsu Ltd. has developed a versatile two-chip set that meets the standard's specs while offering the designer maximum flexibility in realizing the other facilities. The two integrated circuits, the MB61301 data-link controller (DLC) and the MB502 encoder-decoder (Fig. 1), will suit a broad spectrum of applications.

For example, an Ethernet interface node for a terminal or a personal computer requires drastically different design tradeoffs than for a mainframe controller handling computer-to-computer traffic or large numbers of multiplexed circuits. Thus the two ICs integrate only the strictly specified parts of the Ethernet approach, leaving open the detailed interface with the node's processor. As different interfaces become standardized and as higher-level protocols are agreed upon by major vendor communities, they, too, can be committed to silicon.

In particular, system design using the 61301 and 502 gains flexibility in buffer management and interface control, as these are highly dependent on the particular application and environment. Except for providing signals to indicate retransmission after collision and to discard packets after erroneous reception, packet-buffer management is left to the system designer as required by the application.

A second architectural decision was to provide the 61301 DLC with the capability of transmitting and

1. Manchester formatting. Developed by Ungermann-Bass and built by Fujitsu, the MB502 encoder-decoder chip converts non-return-to-zero code to Manchester code and vice versa. It performs Ethernet's layer 1 protocols with bipolar technology.

receiving packets at the same time. This allows important features such as efficient communication between devices at the same node (especially broadcast or multicast communications) because special filtering code in the transmission software is not needed for delivery to the receiving software.

In addition, a simultaneous transmission and reception capability permits more thorough diagnostic functions, such as loopback tests. Also, because the transmit and receive byte streams are distinct, systems needing extensive buffering can treat each byte stream as an independent event.

Another basic architectural decision was to keep the data paths separate from the control paths. The 10-megabit-per-second data rate specified for Ethernet is high relative to most microcomputer systems. Thus it requires some special handling of the byte streams to accommodate the required 1.25-megabyte bandwidth or the possibility of a 2.50-megabyte bandwidth in the case of a node's transmission to itself during self-testing, broadcast, or communication between devices on the same node. So separating the special requirements of data handling from the usually simple system timing requirements reduces the complexity of all interfacing.

The final architectural decision was to defer as many design decisions as possible to the system designer. For example, all three buses—transmit data, receive data, and control—may be tied together by three-state enable signals. Each bus has the signals required to implement a complete extension of the Ethernet timing requirements to a buffer-management chip. Alternatively, a controlling processor manages the buffer by using internal status indicators instead of the actual signals of the byte-stream interfaces.

The controller's design

Implementing layer 2 of the International Standards Organization's open-system network interconnection reference model, the DLC design is based on an existing Ethernet controller implemented in medium-scale integration that has been in volume production since July 1981. As mentioned, the algorithms and state diagrams exist in the Ethernet specifications for the signals on the coaxial cable, but no such simple definition of specs exist for the node interface. The 61301 design uses the MSI implementation's proven interface because silicon could be produced quickly with no interface problems. For example, provisions for packet-flow control and testing are already specified and proven in the existing design.

For this chip, complementary-MOS technology was chosen for its low power consumption. The architecture is based on a gate array for several reasons. For one, logic conversion is simplified because designing with a gate array is similar to MSI design. In particular, the fact that gate arrays may be easily configured to perform macroinstructions makes conversion simple.

Another reason for the use of gate arrays is that complete simulation before fabrication may be achieved by the design team. The geometry of a gate array is

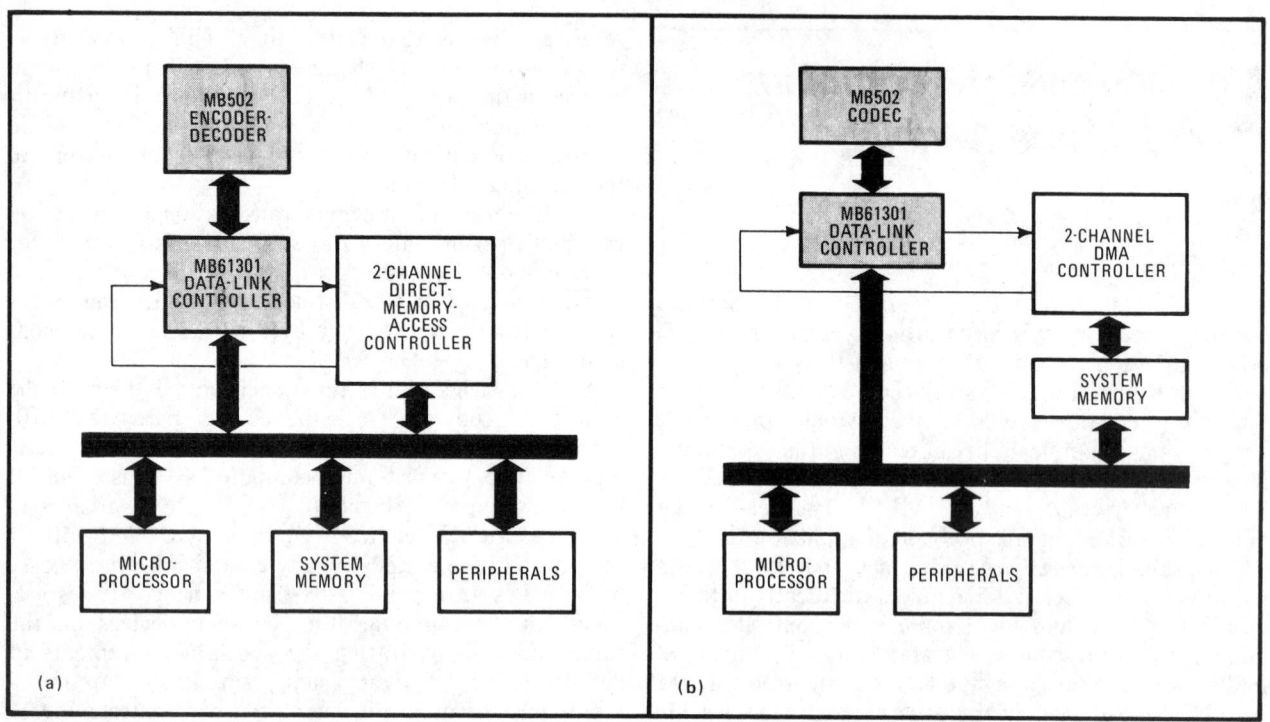

2. Low end . . . A simple Ethernet work station has a single memory for program access and real-time data handling. For many data rates, a single-port memory is adequate (a), but for higher rates a two-port memory may be needed (b).

fixed; as such, extremely reliable simulations are possible during design.

Also, gate arrays have a short fabrication cycle. The process time is less than that needed for fully custom designs, and the data base of the associated computer-aided design system makes changes easy.

Finally, the gate-array approach minimizes the penalty paid for adaptations. For example, any changes in the data-link level required in order to conform to the local network standards being drafted may be quickly accommodated in the Ungermann-Bass approach.

The C-MOS IC is configured as two principal sections — a transmitter and a receiver. Each section provides asynchronous buffering, provisions for byte-parity preamble generation or stripping, cyclic redundancy generation or checking, and conversion between serial and parallel data or vice versa. In addition, the transmitter provides contention resolution by means of the Ethernet-specified binary exponential backoff algorithm. For its part, the receiver provides various modes of address filtering.

The DLC chip has its architecture set up to optimize hardware and software interfacing in the Ethernet link. For example, the length of the receive first-in, first-out buffer (6 bytes) allows the reception of 10-byte packets (6 data and 4 CRC) for diagnostic purposes. The CRC is always tested and stripped from incoming packets. Also, for diagnostic purposes, a test bit inhibits the CRC accumulation in the receiver so that new packet data will be used as the test data.

There are other DLC features that make life easier for the network designer. A set of pins, controlled by the node's processor, gates the receive and transmit status bits in order to generate interrupt signals from such important events as packet transmission and reception and errors of various types. What's more, a time-domain reflectometry function in the transmitter measures the distance to a fault on the Ethernet coaxial cable.

Also, a status bit is cleared at the start of each transmission and set at the end if the receiver successfully receives a frame. This feature reduces software overhead since the receiver can still perform address decoding. Because the DLC is full-duplex, the receiver is active during transmission and will have the correct status for the packet being transmitted. Therefore, the software can be told after transmission that a copy of the transmit buffer should be made available to the receive function before release of the buffer.

Make the connection

The DLC chip has five groups of pins: power, control, receive, transmit, and transceiver. Its package is a 64-pin grid array, chosen to allow for the separate data paths for the control, transmit, and receive groups. The four power pins are broken down into two each for power and ground — a standard arrangement.

More novel is the design of the control group. Nineteen of these pins provide a byte-wide microcomputer interface port, including eight for data and four for register. To gate these, there are seven pins, a number that minimizes the number of external gates required for decoding and control.

There are also five special-function control pins, including a reset input for refresh, a receive interrupt output, and a transmit interrupt output. The others are

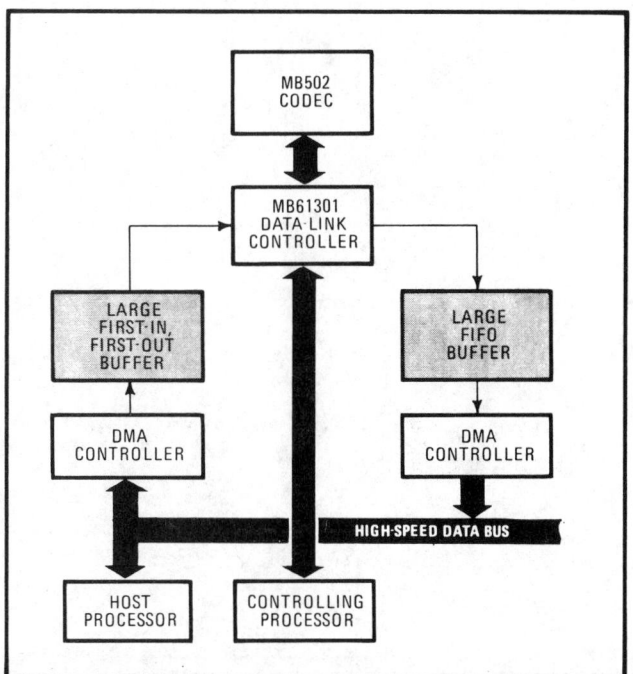

3. . . . and high. For a high-data-rate computer hooked up to an Ethernet, large first-in, first-out buffers may be needed to provide the mode with adequate bandwidth to do its tasks.

an output intended to control power to the transceiver by external switching and an output resulting from reception of a frame of a particular Ethernet type. The latter pin is intended for use as a remote reset function.

The transmit pins handle 8 data bits, a parity bit, and a last-byte flag, plus two byte-control signals that are the interface to a 2-byte asynchronous FIFO buffer. In addition, two packet-control signals are available for use in buffer-management tasks.

Incoming signals

The receive group of pins also includes the 8 data bits, a parity bit and a last-byte flag, plus three byte-control signals, which include a three-state output enable. Only one signal, discard, is required in the packet controls, because the last-byte flag indicates successful packet reception.

The transceiver pin signals are shared between the DLC and encoder-decoder IC. The transmit data is non-return-to-zero form and carries an enable signal with it. It receives its clock from the encoder chip. The receive data is accompanied by an enable (carrier detect) and a clock. A collision signal is received from the encoder-decoder chip.

The 502 encoder-decoder chip implementing the ISO layer 1 is a reversal of the DLC in that its external interface is specified without the algorithm being described. As in designing the 61301, an existing MSI design, in this case 10K emitter-coupled logic, was the best starting point for producing the decoder. However, a gate array is not feasible because of the Ethernet coaxial cable's voltage requirements, the multiple volt-

age levels required, and the internal speed requirements. As a result, a full custom design was appropriate, and a direct design translation was done from MSI to LSI in order to minimize the risk and decrease the design time.

The basic function of the 502 is to convert between Manchester and NRZ data. Beyond this function, there are two others: to serve as the interface with the baseband transceiver and to handle the signal distortion found in long cables with many taps.

Serving as interface

For transceiver interfacing, the encoder-decoder IC can send and receive for either dc- or ac-coupled amplifiers. To do this, the receiver adjusts the voltage threshold between the idle and active states while the transmitter maintains a 0-volt differential in the idle state.

To handle distortion, the 502 has a dual-bandwidth phase-locked loop, which can acquire phase in eight bit times or less. It can handle up ±15% waveform distortion during the preamble of the Ethernet packet and ±20% thereafter.

The encoder-decoder has a signal pin to put it in a loopback mode, in which it ignores inputs from the cable and tests the complete encode-decode path. It has five groups of signals: power, data-link, oscillator, cable, and controls in a 24-pin standard dual in-line package.

Most of the pin functions are straightforward. Thus, single power and ground pins are all that are required; and, in the oscillator group, three pins are used for direct connection of a crystal and a resonant circuit. The eight data-link group signals between the two chips were described earlier. There are also six pins in the cable group, and these interface directly to the three signal pairs of the transceiver cable.

In the control group of pins, two provide for a timing capacitor used to control the transmit pair to allow for ac-coupled transceivers. The last three pins are used for testing. Two of them also have other defined uses. For example, reset may be tied high, and dc link tied low to inhibit all ac-coupling provisions on input and output. The third pin is left open and used only for testing.

System interfaces

A typical low-end Ethernet interface has a single memory used both for program access and data buffering (Fig. 2a). A standard one- or two-channel direct-memory-access controller can support network access and be intelligent enough to supervise retransmission of discarded frames. Because the data rate of the network may be excessive for the bus protocols of some microcomputers, dual-port memory (Fig. 2b) may be a better design option.

Figure 3 shows a typical high-end use as would be found on network controllers for high-performance computer systems. The supervising processor may be the host processor or an intermediate processor resident on the controller board, as used here. In this design, the FIFO buffers provide network bandwidth and the elastic frame buffering to absorb peak traffic. □

A HIGH FUNCTIONALITY VLSI LAN CONTROLLER FOR CSMA/CD NETWORK

M. Stark, A, Kornhauser, and D. Van-Mierop

Intel Israel LTD.

Abstract

A revolutionary VLSI device for the emerging
LAN field is described. The 82586 performs autonomously, communication tasks in Ethernet and
other CSMA/CD networks. The innovation lies in the
integration of on-chip buffer management, network
management, diagnostic support, architecture and
debug-oriented features.

I. Introduction

Local Area Networking is an emerging technology that provides a communication facility of
relatively high speed data exchange, among host
computers and other digital devices located within a moderate distance. It has spawned much
interest because of its applicability in many areas
like distributed processing, office automation,
factory automation, inter-processor communications, etc.

The Local Area Network (LAN) is composed of
a physical transmission medium (the link) and a
set of LAN stations. Each station includes the
user hardware/software and a LAN controller.
The controller serves as the interface between the
user and the medium. It is designed to relieve
the user from tasks like resolving contention
on the link, encapsulation, data addressing, error
detection, network management and detailed timing
of the interface signals. Designing a limited
performance LAN controller, using standard MSI/SSI
technology, takes at least two PC boards, a substantial amount of software and a substantial
amount of development time.

There is a variety of proposed methods for
designing LANs: contention, token passing, loops,
etc.. By far the simplest and most mature technology is CSMA/CD (Carrier Sense, Multiple
Access with Collision Detect), which is based on
distributed resolution of contention on a single
cable link. The more than five years experience
of XEROX with this method, combined with Intel's
VLSI expertise and DEC's system know-how, has
yielded the first LAN standard: Ethernet[TM].
Ethernet is the specification of a CSMA/CD LAN
that transports frames of 64 to 1518 bytes, between hosts of up to 2.5Km apart, at a bit rate
of 10Mb/s, with minimum Interframe Spacing of 9.6
microseconds.

Intel's 82586 VLSI chip (see microphotograph in Figure 1) is an intelligent, high
performance CSMA/CD LAN controller. It is optimized for Ethernet. This component implements all
of the network related controller functions as
well as a user interface, whose friendliness and
autonomy is unprecedented in the semiconductor
industry. Figure 2 shows a general structure of
the complete solution for an Ethernet station
(see the box for the detailed structure). The
82586 interfaces to the link via a 20 pin Ethernet
Serial Interface chip (82501) and an Ethernet
transceiver. It interfaces to the CPU and the
memory via an 8 or 16 bit system bus.

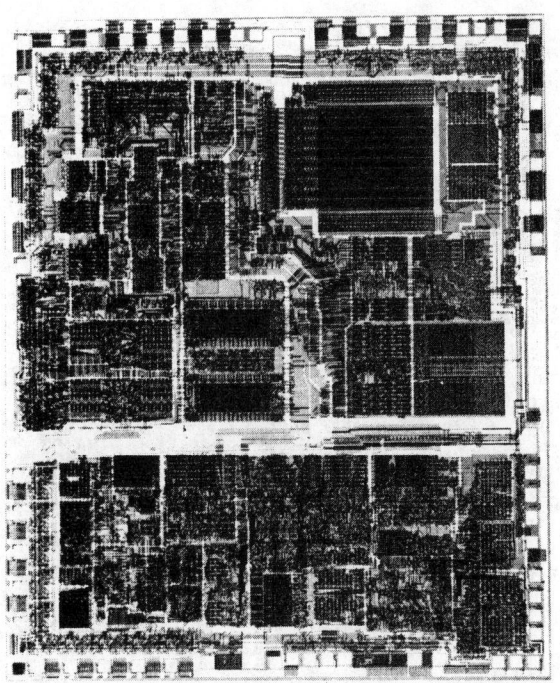

Figure 1: 82586 Microphotograph

Reprinted from *The Proceedings of COMPCON S'83*, 1983, pages 510-517.
Copyright © 1983 by The Institute of Electrical and Electronics Engineers,
Inc.

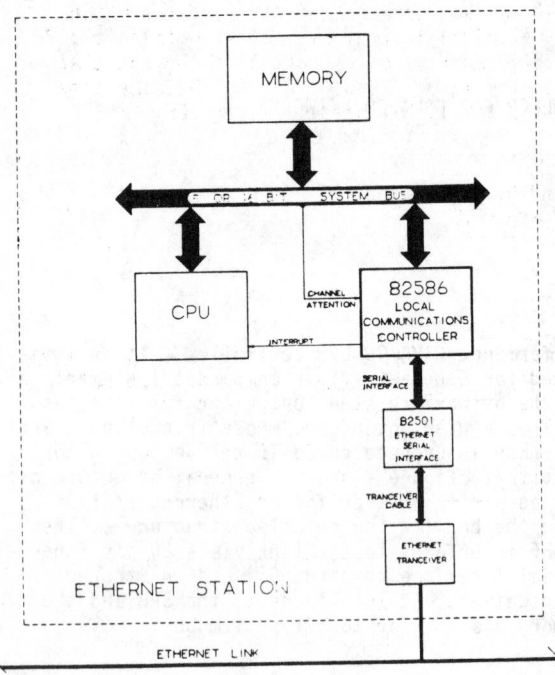

Figure 2: 82586 Based Ethernet Station
Block Diagram

The 82586 offers tremendous advantages over any other implementation of a LAN controller. It saves the cost of developing a LAN controller (which is a pretty complex system). It guarantees compatibility with the Ethernet standard. The 82586 reduces the hardware cost significantly by replacing two dense PC boards with a single chip. It reduces software cost and CPU execution overhead by providing an intelligent and friendly user interface. It provides performance (bit rate and interframe spacing) that is not achievable with standard components. The chip enhances reliability of network operation by providing diagnostics and management functions. It enhances system reliability by providing self test, register dump and loopback. For users who have special requirements, the 82586 is configurable to support CSMA/CD LANs at various speeds, topologies, traffic patterns and frame formats.

The 82586 is composed of two major parts: the Ethernet Interface and the User Interface. This paper presents the major features of each part, in addition to the functions that enhance performance, reliability and flexibility.

II. Ethernet Interface

The Ethernet specification defines two layers of the network architectures: Data Link and Physical Channel. The Data Link layer specifies the data encapsulation format and the link management protocol. The Physical Channel layer specifies the data encoding and the channel access. The 82586 provides all of the Data Link functions and some of the Physical Channel functions. A companion 20 pin chip (the Intel 82501) provides the balance of the Physical Channel functions. Using these two chips saves the user from spending the time and money for designing an Ethernet interface out of MSI logic and relieves him from any worry concerning compatability with the Ethernet standard. Intel has solved these problems for him.

In order to perform transmission of a frame, all that the Ethernet interface needs from the user is the destination address, type field and information field. The 82586 performs the framing, channel allocation and contention resolution. After the transmission, the chip returns status. Even when it has nothing to transmit, the 82586 monitors the link. Whenever the link is busy the chip defers to passing traffic by delaying any pending transmission. After the last Ethernet interface generates a 62 bit alternating ones and zeros preamble, followed by the flag of 2 ones. It inserts its individual address as the source address (between the destination address and type field). It calculates the 32 bit CRC frame check sequence during the transmission of the addresses, type field and information field, and inserts the CRC after the information.

If the transmission is completed successfully, then an OK status is passed to the user. If a collision occurs, then the 82586 performs the jamming, calculates the exponential backoff using an on-chip random number generator, and performs the retransmission according to the requirements of the standard. If the number of retries exceeds the maximum, then the chip gives up and notifies the user. It also reports an abortion of transmission due to DMA underrun, dropping of Clear To Send or dropping of Carrier Sense.

The Ethernet interface performs the reception of a frame completely on its own, and passes to the user the destination and source addresses, the type field, and the information field. It performs frame decapsulation, address 'filtering' and error detection. After the reception, the chip provides status. The 82586 strips the preamble, detects the opening flag, discards the CRC and discards any dribble bits. The 82586 checks the address of all the frames that go by on the link, and passes to the user only the frames that pass the address match. All the other frames are ignored. A match occurs in either of three cases: first, if the incoming address is an all ones broadcast address. Second, if the incoming address is equal to the controllers individual address. Third, if the incoming address is a multicast address and passes the multicast filtering mechanism.

The multicast filtering mechanism is based on hashing the 48 bit address into a 6 bit value. The hashing is required because it is not possible to store all the desired multicast addresses on chip.

This multicast filtering mechanism may accept frames that were not intended to be recognized, but it guarantees the acceptance of all the required frames. If the multicast addresses are judiciously selected, then the probability of accepting unwanted frames, can be reduced to zero. In any case, this mechanism relieves the user from having to check all the multicast frames that appear on the link.

The 82586 checks the incoming frames for various error conditions and notifies the user about these errors: First, it checks the frame check sequence of the frame, and reports the existence of a CRC error. Second, if the length of the frame is not a multiple of 8 bits and the CRC is incorrect, it reports an ALIGNMENT error. Third, it checks the length of the frame and reports an error if it is shorter than 64 bytes (presuming it is a collision fragment). Fourth, if any data is lost due to congestion on the system bus, an OVERRUN error is reported.

The whole Ethernet interface must sustain incoming data at 10Mb/s, therefore, the only alternative to the 82586 is a big set of MSI chips. This alternative is very expensive and may turn out not to be compatible with the standard.

III. User Interface

A significant part of the chip is devoted to an intelligent user interface. This interface reduces required CPU overhead, saves memory space, assures high performance and makes the chip easy to use.

The chip is viewed logically as two separate units: the COMMAND UNIT (CU) and the RECEIVE UNIT (RU). The user interface may be engaged in two activities simultaneously: the CU may be fetching and executing commands out of memory, and the RU may be storing received frames in memory. User intervention is only required after the CU executes a sequence of commands or the RU stores a sequence of frames. This means a big relief for the CPU compared to current LSI data comm controllers. They require user intervention every byte. Even with the use of DMA controller, current data comm controllers require the user to take care of buffer switching, initiation of transmissions of each frame, and cleaning up after every transmitted or received frame. The 82586 does all this on its own.

The communication of the host CPU with the 82586 is done via shared memory. The common memory structure is composed of three parts: The System Control Block (SCB), the list of commands for the CU, and the received frames area used by the RU (see Figure 3). The only hardware signals that connect the CPU and the 82586, are the INTERRUPT and CHANNEL ATTENTION (see Figure 2). The former is used by the 82586 to draw the CPU's attention, to a change in the SCB. The latter is used by the CPU to draw the 82586's attention. The SCB serves as a bi-direct-

ional mailbox between the user and the 82586. During initialization, the 82586 obtains the 24 bit base address of the 64K byte segment that holds the memory structure. At the same time it obtains the 16 bit offset of the SCB.

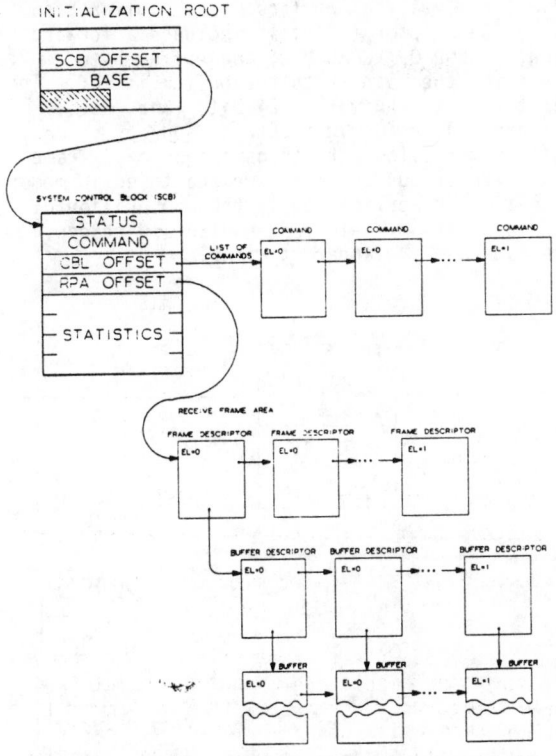

Figure 3: 82586 Controlled Memory Structure

The SCB is composed of two parts. First, instructions from the CPU to the 82586. These include: control of the CU and RU (START, ABORT, SUSPEND, RESUME) a pointer to the list of commands for the CU, a pointer to the received frames area, and a set of interrupt acknowledge bit. Second, information from the 82586 to the CPU, that includes: state of the CU and RU (e.g., IDLE, ACTIVE, READY, SUSPENDED, NO RECEIVE RESOURCES), interrupt bits (command completed, frame received, CU gone not ready, RU gone not ready), and accumulative tallies.

The list of commands serves as a 'program' for the 82586. It is prepared by the user and executed by the CU. The commands are linked together starting with the COMMAND LIST POINTER in the SCB and ending with an END OF LIST bit. It is possible to form a circular linked list that is used for repeated execution of the construction of a queue of commands. All the commands have the same basic structure called a Command Block (see for example Figure 4): the command code; instructions for command completion (QUIT, SUSPEND, GENERATE INTERRUPT); the forward link; and the state of execution (NOT STARTED, BUSY or COMPLETED). In addition, most Command Blocks include command specific parameters and command specific statuses.

The Transmit command triggers the transmission

of a frame by the 82586, as described in the previous section. The representation of the frame in memory is very flexible (see Figure 4). The destination address and type field reside in the Transmit Command Block. The Information resides in a linked list of buffers. Each buffer has Buffer Descriptor (BD) that includes a forward link, an END OF FRAME bit, the buffer byte count and the pointer to the buffer itself. The pointer in the buffer is 24 bits long, i.e., buffers can reside in a 16Mbyte address space. This format allows the transmission of a frame from several buffers that are scattered in memory. A particular application is the composition of the information field from a standard header, the data and a standard trailer.

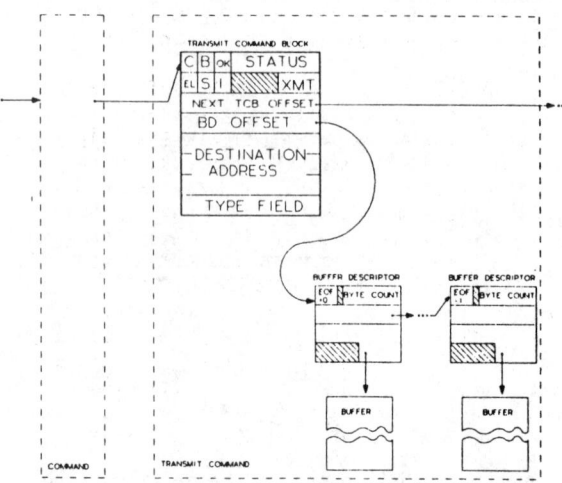

Figure 4: The Transmit Command Structure

The Receive memory structure is organized so that all that the user has to do is prepare the receive frame area. The 82586 fills the buffers upon reception of frames and reformats the free buffer list into received frame structures. The user must prepare two linked lists (see Figure 3): a list of Frame Descriptors and a list of Buffers with their descriptors. Each frame descriptor has a forward pointer. The first frame descriptor is referenced by the SCB, and the last one is marked with an END OF FRAME bit. The Buffer Descriptors are almost identical to the ones in the Transmit Command. They include an extra field that specifies the size of the empty buffer and an END OF LIST bit.

When the 82586 is ready for reception, it must have a pointer to the first free Frame Descriptor, which includes a pointer to the first free Buffer Descriptor. When the data starts arriving from the link, the 82586 performs the following: It strips the preamble, checks the destination address, stores the destination address, source address and type field in the Frame Descriptor, stores the information into as many free buffers that are needed, checks the Frame Check Sequence, updates the status bits in the Frame descriptor, and links the next Frame Descriptor to the next Buffer Descriptor.

Receive buffer chaining (i.e., storing an incoming frame in a linked list of buffers) improves memory utilization significantly. Without buffer chaining, the user must allocate for each frame size (1514 bytes in Ethernet). This is significant because a typical frame size may be about 100 bytes and the controller may have to be ready to receive a burst of several frames. The 82586 allows buffers to be even shorter than the minimum frame length (64 bytes), and uses only as many of them as necessary for the actual received frame. The drawback of the buffer chaining is usually its processing overhead and the problem of the time involved in the buffer switching (especially at 10Mb/s). The 82586 overcomes this drawback by performing the buffer switching on its own (completely transparent to the user).

In order to prevent overruns during switching of the buffers, the 82586 prefetches the reference to each buffer in parallel to filling the previous buffer. The actual switching is extremely fast because of the tight coupling of the Receive Unit and the memory access unit (see 82586 Internal Architecture).

IV. Performance

An important measure of performance of a data communication system, is the throughput. Throughput at the data link level depends on two factors: first, the serial bit rate, which is the rate at which data is actually transferred on the link. Second, the Interframe Spacing, which is the period of time required by controllers to recover from a transmission or reception of a frame, before it is ready for a new transmission or reception. Ethernet is aimed at a pretty high throughput: bit rate of 10Mb/s and Interframe spacing of 9.6 microseconds. The 82586 operates at a bit rate of up to 10Mb/s which is about an order of magnitude higher than is provided by any MSI/LSI data communication controller currently available. Any alternative implementation to the 82586 will require a lot of chips in order to meet this bit rate.

The 9.6 microsecond Interframe Spacing poses even a greater challenge to the implementor of the controller. This time is very 'short', enough to execute only a couple of instructions in any currently available microprocessor. This means that all the Interframe activities (e.g., updating frame status, updating statistics, deciding whether to continue or suspend reception, switching the pointers to the next frame, etc.) must be done in the controller itself. Most board level implementation of Ethernet controllers had to compromise: either not meet the required Interframe Spacing or, at best, only allow bursts of two frames (after which a long recovery time is required).

The 82586 is able to receive infinitely long bursts of frames whose interframe spacing is 9.6 microseconds. This is due to the four on chip DMA channels that are tightly controlled by the user interface. Moreover, the pipelining of the operation of the Ethernet interface and the User Interface, as well as the concurrent processing units, contribute to the performance too. See details in the box.

The 82586 can operate with high performance system buses on the one hand, and is very tolerant to limitations of system buses on the other. The absolute minimum required data transfer rates (in order to sustain a serial bit rate of 10Mb/s) is 1.25MByte/sec. The 82586 is optimized for an '8MHz bus', whose transfer rate is 4MByte/sec. This leaves much bandwidth for overhead and CPU processing.

The 82586 shares the bus with the CPU, and possibly other peripheral devices. The bus arbitration is done with the HOLD/HLDA mechanism. In order to increase the burstiness of the access to the bus, the 82586 utilizes two on chip 16-byte FIFOs.

The trigger mechanism associated with the FIFOs, determines when the chip requests the bus and when it relinquishes it. There is a certain latency between the bus request and the grant. The trigger mechanism assures that there will be no bus overruns or underruns if the latency is below a particular value. This mechanism also ensures a minimum time that the 82586 will not request the bus between bursts. This also minimizes the overhead due to bus switching.

Although the 82586 performs command chaining, frame chaining, and buffer chaining on the fly, it can operate with buses that transfer data as low as 2MByte/sec.

V. Reliability, Testability & Diagnostic Support

Data communication networks are typically very complex due to their distributed and asynchronous nature. It is particularly hard to pin-point a failure if it occurs. The 82586 was designed in anticipation of these problems and includes a set of features for improving reliability and testability. All these functions are performed under software control. They do not require any diagnostic hardware or any modifications. The chip offers the following services: (See Figure 5) First, monitoring the transmission and reception of frames. Second, support for statistics gathering and diagnostics of the whole network. Third, diagnostic support for the particular station on the network. Fourth, means to test the proper operation of the chip itself.

The 82586 presents the user with status after the completion of transmission or reception of every frame. The details of the status bit were given in a previous section on the Ethernet section. For the received frames, the chip also accumulates a set of tallies that indicate the number of frames lost due to CRC errors, alignment errors, DMA overrun, or no receive resources.

The 82586 has mechanisms to collect statistics about the behavior of the whole networks as well as a means to locate problems in the network. The status of every transmitted frame provides the following network activity indicators: whether the transmission was deferred because the channel was busy, the number of collisions experienced before the frame was transmitted and, whether the transmission was not performed because this frame experienced too many collisions. The 82586 can be configured to 'promiscuous mode', i.e., to capture all the frames that are transmitted on the network. This is useful to implement a monitoring station. Each 82586 is capable of determining whether there is a short or open circuit anywhere in the network, using the Time Domain Reflectometer (TDR) command. In case there is a problem the chip can determine the distance of the problem from the controller.

To support testing of both the software and hardware of the station itself, the 82586 provides the following features: first, the chip can be configured to internal loopback, where it is disconnected from the link and any frame transmitted is immediately received by the same controller. This can be used in conjunction with the possibility to inhibit the source address insertion and/or CRC insertion by the chip. Second, the chip can be configured to external loopback. This mechanism provides the capability to test all the external logic between the 82586 and the link itself. The chip also checks the correct operation of the Carrier Sense and Collision Detect signals from the transceiver for every frame that is transmitted.

The 82586 provides several features for users who desire checking the chip itself (either during acceptance or during an attempt to debug the system). First, the Dump command causes the chip to write almost all its internal registers to memory. This is a very powerful capability that could serve as the basis for a comprehensive diagnostic package. There are parts of the chip, in particular the logic that depends on the random number generator, that cannot be checked from the outside. The Diagnose command triggers a self test procedure that exercises a whole set of unaccessable counters. Finally, the internal loopback is also a very good mechanism to verify the correct operation of the chip.

VI. Flexibility

Although the 82586 is optimized for Ethernet, its design took into account the possibility that the user may want to apply it to different environments. The chip can be used as a 'non-Ethernet' CSMA/CD controller by using the flexible configuration parameters of the Configure command.

An alternative frame format can be configured, using the following parameters: the preamble length (including the opening flag) can be set to either 2,4,8 or 16 bytes; the address length can be set to any length between 0 and 6 bytes; the

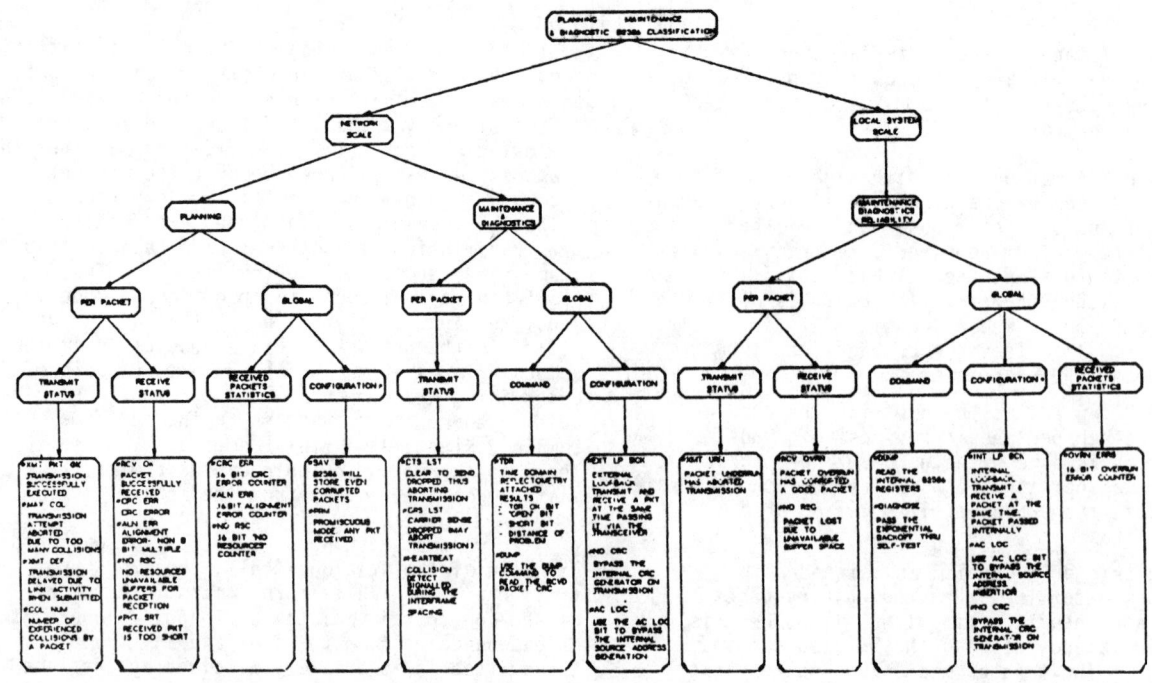

Figure 5: 82586 Planning, Maintenance & Diagnostic Features Classification

CRC can be set to either 16 bit CCITT or 32 bit Ethernet (adopted from Autodin II); the minimum frame length can be set to any length up to 255 bytes. The frame encapsulation method can be set to either Ethernet method of the HDLC flag and bitstuffing method. In the latter case, the chip can (optionally) perform an automatic padding with flags, thus relieving the user from assuring enough information to fill a minimum size frame.

The link management mechanism is programmable to different topologies and traffic patterns: the interframe spacing can be set up to 255 clock units. For Ethernet, one clock unit is 0.1 microseconds. The Slot Time can be set to any time in the range of 1 to 2048 clock units. The Slot Time and the bit rate determine the maximum diameter of the network. For impatient users, the maximum number of retires can be set to be smaller than 15. For users with urgent frames: the 82586 provides a linear priority mechanism.

The user has all the flexibility regarding the bit rate of the chip. Any rate, from DC to 10Mb/s can be used.

VII. Internal Architecture

The 82586 performs transmission and reception at 10Mb/s. Unlike the conventional communication chips, where the serial processing rate is significantly lower than the system processing rate (by one or two orders of magnitude), the serial and system processing rates are comparable. Potential transmission underruns, reception overruns, long Interframe Spacing, high system-bus consumption and significant processing overhead

problems were resolved by the 82586 innovative architecture.

The 82586 copes with the problems by this highly integrated multiprocessor/pipelined architecture (see Figure 6). Thus, several units are working concurrently on the same task or on two tasks (transmission and reception).

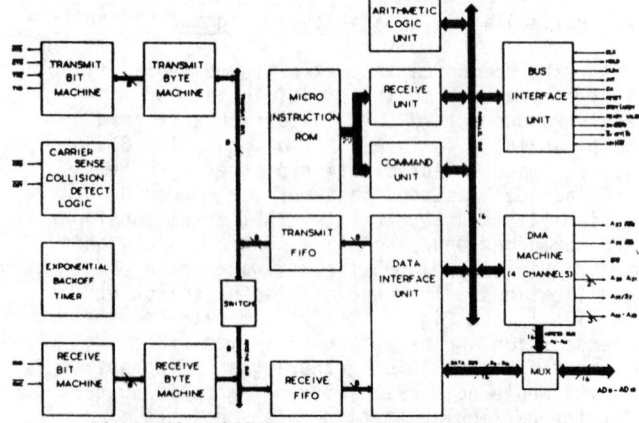

Figure 6: 82586 Internal Architecture

The chip consists of two major blocks: The PARALLEL PROCESSOR, which is the system interface and the SERIAL CHANNEL which is the serial interface. Both parts communicate via TRANSMIT and RECEIVE FIFOs.

The following operations are performed by the various blocks.

The BUS INTERFACE UNIT generates bus control signals based on received statuses. It also generates internal control signals and statuses for the internal logic.

The DATA INTERFACE UNIT is a switch which routes the data from the system bus to Transmit FIFO to internal Parallel Bus (PBUS) or routes the data from the Receive FIFO to the system bus or to PBUS.

The DMA machine is an address generator that performs DMA transfer to/from the 82586 from/to the memory. There are four (4) DMA channels available.

The COMMAND UNIT fetches commands from the memory, and writes status to the memory. It also has full control over the DMA machine, loads the starting pointers and byte counts, and triggers the DMA start. It also analyses the command status (which has been executed by the Transmit Byte Machine) and calculates address pointers using the ARITHMETIC/LOGIC UNIT services. It sends execution commands via the TRANSMIT FIFO to the TRANSMIT BYTE MACHINE.

The RECEIVE UNIT performs similar tasks for the Receive memory structure, the COMMAND UNIT performs for the Command Block. Both machines fetch microinstructions from a shared MICRO INSTRUCTION ROM.

The TRANSMIT FIFO regulates the traffic which flows from the PARALLEL PROCESSOR (via DIU) to the TRANSMIT BYTE MACHINE.

The TRANSMIT BYTE MACHINE interprets the execution commands which are coming via the TRANSMIT FIFO, executes the commands and sends the status back via the SWITCH and the RECEIVE FIFO. For transmission, the TRANSMIT BYTE MACHINE is responsible for frame assembly including preamble starting flag and Source Address insertion. It also commands the TRANSMIT BIT MACHINE to shift out the Frame Check Sequence.

It may stop transmission or other command executions based on status received from the serial port or via the TRANSMIT FIFO from the COMMAND UNIT.

The TRANSMIT BIT MACHINE serializes and encodes data, performs Zero Bit Insertion (in Bitstuffing mode), generates the Frame Check Sequence and transmits the data. It also controls the Request To Send, Clear To Send modem like handshake, and generates the internal Transmit Clock phases.

The TRANSMIT BYTE MACHINE timeliness is based on signals received from the CARRIER SENSE and COLLISION DETECT LOGIC and the EXPONENTIAL BACK OFF TIMER.

The CARRIER SENSE and COLLISION DETECT logic performs CDT and CRS filtering, Interframe Spacing Timeout generation and internal Carrier Sense and Collision Detect generation.

The EXPONENTIAL BACKOFF TIMER is responsible for backoff and priority timeout.

The RECEIVE BIT MACHINE is responsible for Preamble and Flag congesture, received Frame Delineation, decoding Zero Bit Deletion (in bitstuffing mode) and Frame Check Sequence testing. The RECEIVE BIT MACHINE deserializes the information and delivers it in bytes to the RECEIVE BYTE MACHINE.

The RECEIVE BYTE MACHINE compares the Destination Address with the various possible address types and if the address matches, it transfers the received data to RECEIVE FIFO. At the end of frame reception the Frame Check Sequence testing is summed up and Receive Status is delivered via the RECEIVE FIFO to the RECEIVE UNIT.

The RECEIVE UNIT decisions are based on the Receive Status and on the operational mode, what to do when the packet is received.

The whole 82586 machine operation is highly concurrent. For example at the same time:

* TRANSMIT BIT MACHINE transmits bits.
* TRANSMIT BYTE MACHINE assembles a frame.
* TRANSMIT FIFO regulates the data flow from the outside world.
* DMA MACHINE performs DMA transfers from the memory to the TRANSMIT FIFO via DIU.
* COMMAND UNIT is looking at the data that is transferred to the TRANSMIT FIFO, fetches pointers to the next Buffer Descriptor and loads another DMA channel.
* RECEIVE UNIT writes the Receive Status (optional, receive dependent) to the memory or fetches the next Receive Packet Descriptor and the next Receive Buffer.

The opposite situation can also be handled, where on the Receive background the next command is prepared for execution.

In Internal or External Loopback mode transmission and reception will be performed concurrently all the way.

VIII. An Ethernet System Node Example

A powerful Ethernet system node can be built on the basis of Intel's highly integrated microprocessor, the iAPX 186 and the 82586 (see Figure 7).

Since the 82586 and the iAPX 186 timings and controls are the same, both chips may share the same address latches, data latches and bus controller. Optionally, a bus arbiter may enable multisystem node. The 82586 system clock is driven by iAPX 186 internally generated system clock output.

Also all the necessary handshake and control signals match in timing and behavior, thus avoiding any hardware between the two.

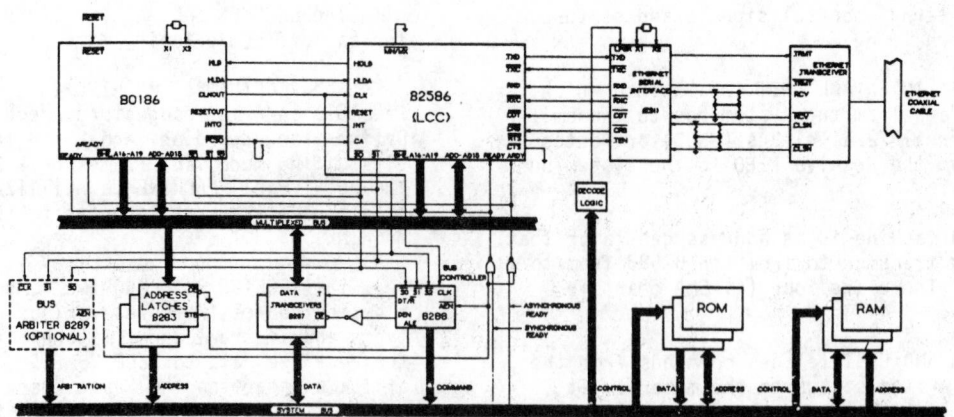

Figure 7: iAPX 186/82586 Based Ethernet System Node

On the Serial Interface side, the 82501 Ethernet Serial Interface (ESI) chip, performs the electrical interfacing to the transceiver cable. This chip also generates the Transmit Clock and performs Receive Clock recovery from data for the 82586 using on chip Phase Locked Loop circuit. It also generates the Carrier Sense and collision Detect Signal for the Local communication Controller. The Serial Interface Pins of 82586 and the 82501 match, thus allowing easy board layout.

IX. Conclusions

A powerful system implemented with VLSI technology has been presented. This device not only reduces Ethernet node implementation costs but also provides flexibility and services beyond and above Ethernet. High VLSI technology and innovative architecture were used to meet the high performance goals.

X. Acknowledgement

The authors would like to thank all the Intel Israel 82586 design team members, who made this device a reality, by their beyond-limits dedication, teamwork and creativity.

XI. References

1. DIGITAL/INTEL/XEROX: The Ethernet, A Local Area Network Data Link Layer and Physical Layer Specifications, Version 1.0, September 30, 1980.

CONTROLLER AND MICRO TEAM UP FOR SMART ETHERNET NODE

The LANCE chip adapts 16-bit power of micro to form a true Ethernet connection.

by James A. Fontaine

A common problem associated with high speed data transfers in Ethernet-like local area networks is receiver-end data congestion, caused by a system's failure to process messages and reallocate receiver-buffer space at an adequate rate. This is due to either insufficient processing capability or inadequate computer system bus bandwidth. An intelligent VLSI processor with dedicated memory can alleviate data congestion, thereby allowing efficient attachment of intelligent node devices. A number of local area network control chips are available to perform this kind of operation (see Panel, "Ethernet controller chip comparison"). One possible configuration utilizes the Local Area Network Controller for Ethernet (LANCE) MK68590 chip in conjunction with a single-chip, 16-bit microcomputer like the MK68200.

Ethernet's performance level often depends directly on the throughput of a host computer. In addition, transmitted messages can only be generated by the host during the time it controls the system bus. However, if each message consists of large amounts of data, the amount of bus bandwidth available for host computer processing may become the factor limiting throughput.

An effective method to reduce bus congestion is the use of a 16-bit microcomputer, such as the

James A. Fontaine is senior architectural engineer at Mostek Corp, a subsidiary of United Technologies Corp, 1215 W Crosby Rd, Carrollton, TX 75006. He holds a BS in electrical engineering from Marquette University.

68200, for an Ethernet node's local processor. The chip's architecture provides for onchip ROM and RAM, as well as an onchip baud rate generator and timers that produce the interrupt time-outs necessary for implementing upper levels of the Ethernet protocol. The 68200 can handle message acknowledgment, buffer manipulation, frame-related errors, and software implementation of upper level protocols. This frees the main CPU to handle only the core of the messages.

Utilizing the leadless chip carrier (LCC) version of the 68200, both the private bus and the system bus can access an external memory-mapped I/O (see Panel, "A closer look at LANCE and the micro"). Up to 111 Kbytes of memory can be addressed with two independent bus structures, enabling concurrent host and node processor activity. Thus, the 68200 does not have to stop processing when the host or LANCE requires control of the system bus to load or unload messages. The 68200 has its own private bus and program space from which it can continue to execute. This architecture makes the 68200 an ideal processor in situations where concurrent activity from both a local processor and a host processor is required.

Two types of configurations can be supported with the 68200-68590 interface. One configuration is the standalone mode, used when interfacing a terminal or number of terminals via an Ethernet link to a main processor located up to 2.8 km away. In this configuration, the 68200 handles local processing of both transmitted and received messages, achieving economic interfacing of many terminals to the main processor. The second configuration uses the interface as a peripheral or a frontend processor to the host.

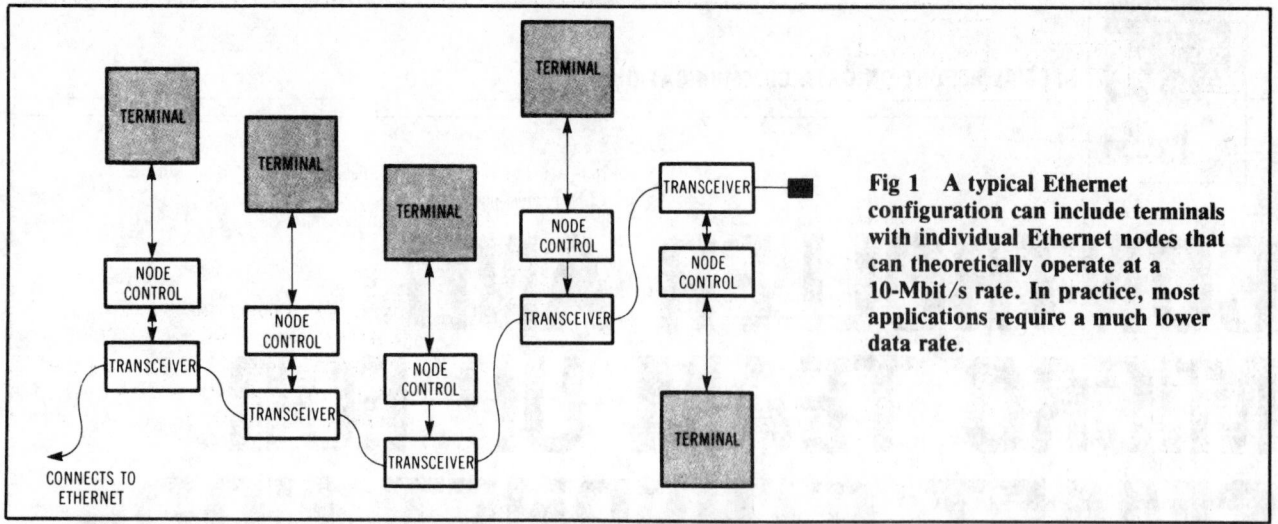

Fig 1   A typical Ethernet configuration can include terminals with individual Ethernet nodes that can theoretically operate at a 10-Mbit/s rate. In practice, most applications require a much lower data rate.

In some applications, it may be desirable to interface one or more user terminals to an Ethernet link, each with an individual interface (Fig 1). The 68200's onchip serial port and baud rate generator make this configuration simple to implement. The chip's serial channel provides for a double buffered receive and transmit interface with data rates up to 1.5 kbits/s if the clock is asynchronous, and up to 1.5 Mbits/s with a synchronous clock. It also provides for internal or external baud rate generation.

For user terminal and similar interfaces, the 10-Mbit/s message rate that Ethernet offers is not typically required. Therefore, a cost-effective configuration may be implemented in which a local node services many terminals (Fig 2). A series of universal synchronous/asynchronous receiver/transmitters (USARTs) can be placed on the private bus to accommodate more than one terminal. Also, a modem interface can be provided to link the Ethernet to other local area networks (LANs) via telephone lines. This provides a link to additional LANs at a reasonable cost, but at data rates

much lower than those that can be attained by a direct Ethernet link.

Such a standalone configuration can also be used in other applications to reduce Ethernet's cost. For example, designers can configure a printing station composed of a letter-quality printer, a fast line printer, and a plotter. Although the need to use all three simultaneously may not arise very often, each device can be accessed at any time.

System peripheral configuration

The second configuration, where the 68200-68590 interface acts as a peripheral or frontend processor to the host, greatly unburdens the host CPU as well as the system bus. The host can gain access to the local bus and transfer messages and commands to the 68200 by dumping them into memory space and then notifying the 68200 that a transfer has occurred. This is done by either interrupting the 68200 or setting a bit in a shared status block (Fig 3). The 68200 would have control of the node's local bus, which may be accessed by both the LANCE and the

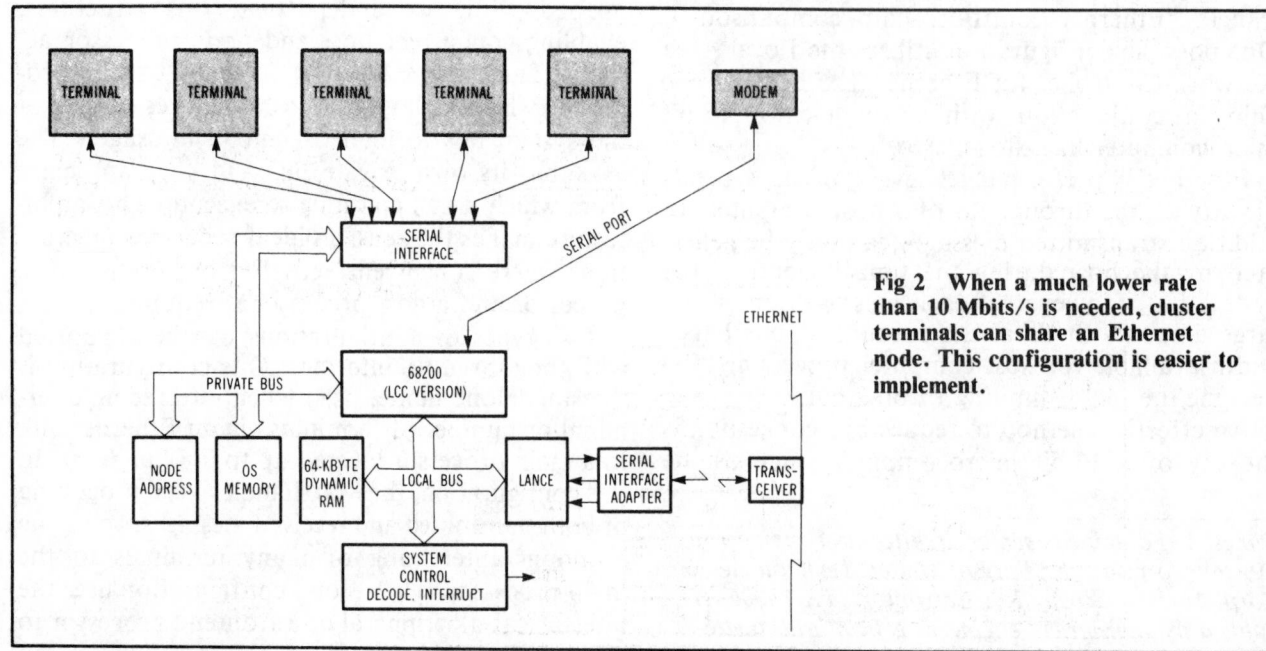

Fig 2   When a much lower rate than 10 Mbits/s is needed, cluster terminals can share an Ethernet node. This configuration is easier to implement.

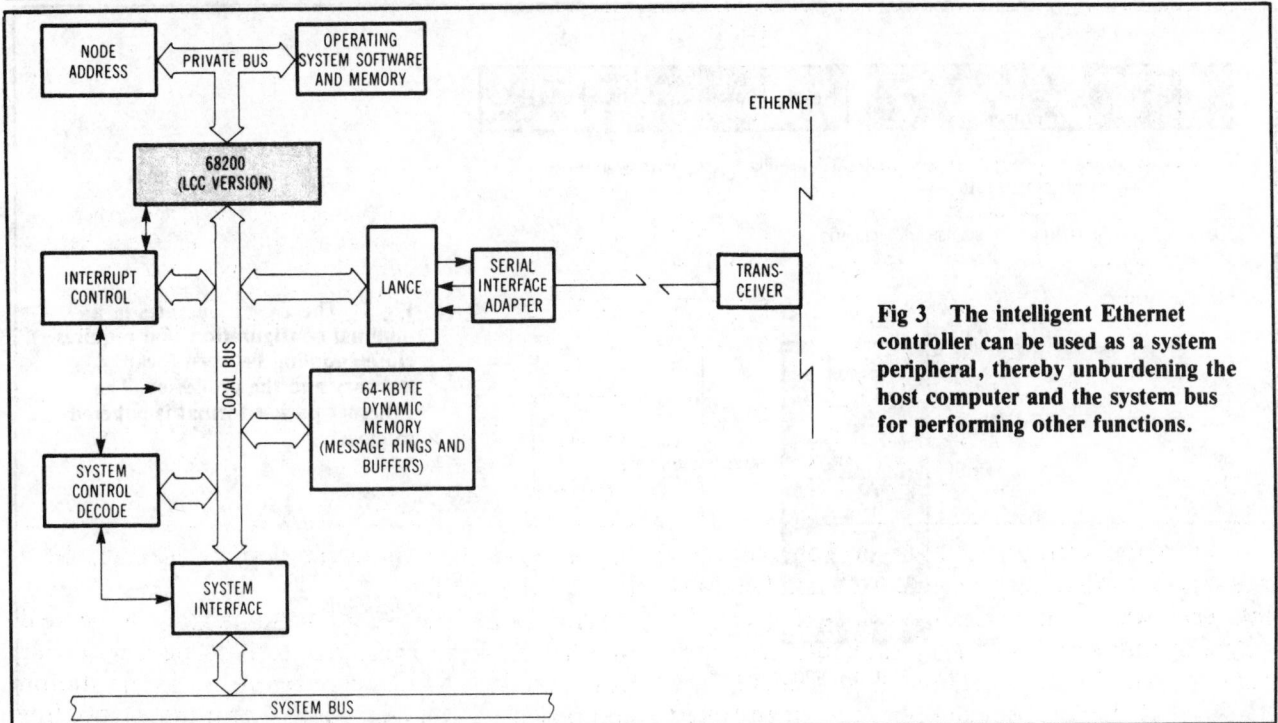

Fig 3   The intelligent Ethernet controller can be used as a system peripheral, thereby unburdening the host computer and the system bus for performing other functions.

host CPU. Using this configuration, the 68200 does not access the system bus; thus, the host must use its DMA function to pass messages and commands in and out via a two-ported memory.

While the 68200 can access both the local node bus and its own private bus, it has sole control of its private bus. The private memory will contain the node's operating system software required to implement the bottom three layers of the Ethernet specification (Fig 4).

Interface and control logic must be incorporated to perform local bus accessing as well as all of the memory access decoding that is required for the host, the 68200, and the LANCE to access memory.

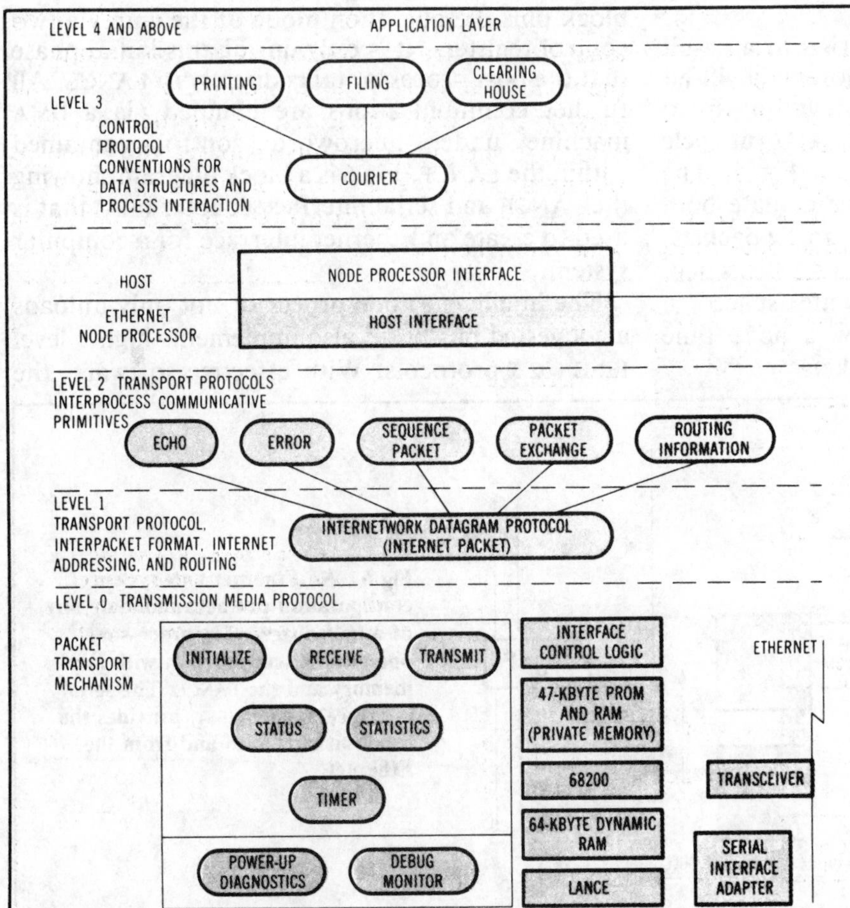

Fig 4   The Ethernet node processor can implement the first four levels of the ISO protocol model. Depicted here are the software functions that are needed to implement the Ethernet specification.

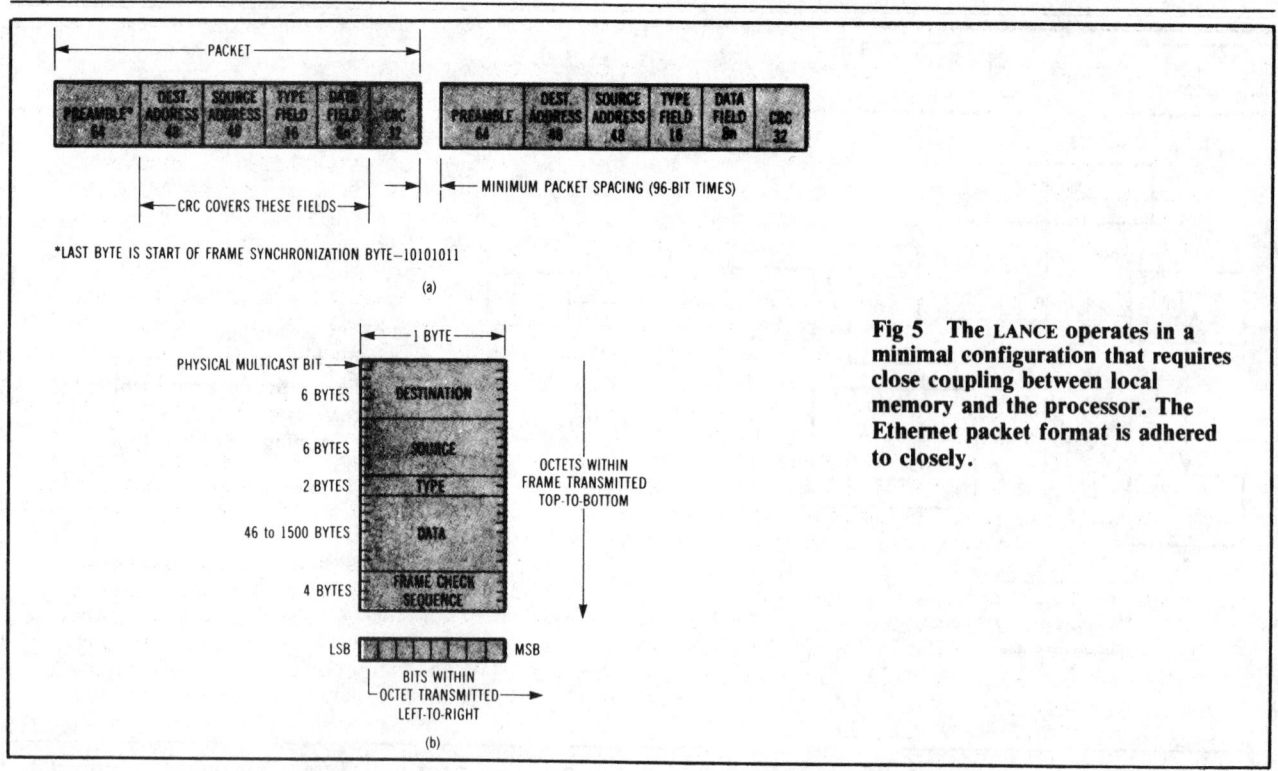

*LAST BYTE IS START OF FRAME SYNCHRONIZATION BYTE—10101011

(a)

Fig 5 The LANCE operates in a minimal configuration that requires close coupling between local memory and the processor. The Ethernet packet format is adhered to closely.

(b)

If one were to implement the node processor scheme using true dual-ported memory (memory that can be simultaneously accessed from two sources without ill effect), the host would not have to gain access of the local bus. It could instead simply read and write to memory via one access port while the 68200 reads and writes to the memory via the second access port.

The Ethernet packet format consists of a 64-bit preamble, a 48-bit destination address, a 48-bit source address, a 16-bit type field, and a 46- to 1500-byte data field terminated with a 32-bit cycle redundancy code (CRC) as shown in Fig 5. The variable widths of the packets accommodate both short status, command and terminal traffic packets, and long data packets to printers and disks (eg, 1024-byte disk sectors). Packets are spaced a minimum of 9.6 μs apart to allow a node time enough to receive back-to-back packets.

The LANCE is intended to operate in a minimal configuration that requires close coupling between local memory and a processor. The local memory provides packet buffering for the chip and serves as a communication link between chip and processor. During initialization, the control processor loads into LANCE the starting address of the initialization block plus the operation mode of the chip via two control registers. It is only during this initial phase that the host processor talks directly to LANCE. All further communications are handled via a DMA machine under microword control contained within the LANCE. Fig 6 is a block diagram showing the LANCE and serial interface adapter (SIA) that is used to create an Ethernet interface for a computer system.

The intelligent node processor not only unloads a congested bus but it also implements higher level IEEE 802.3 protocols. With effective software, the

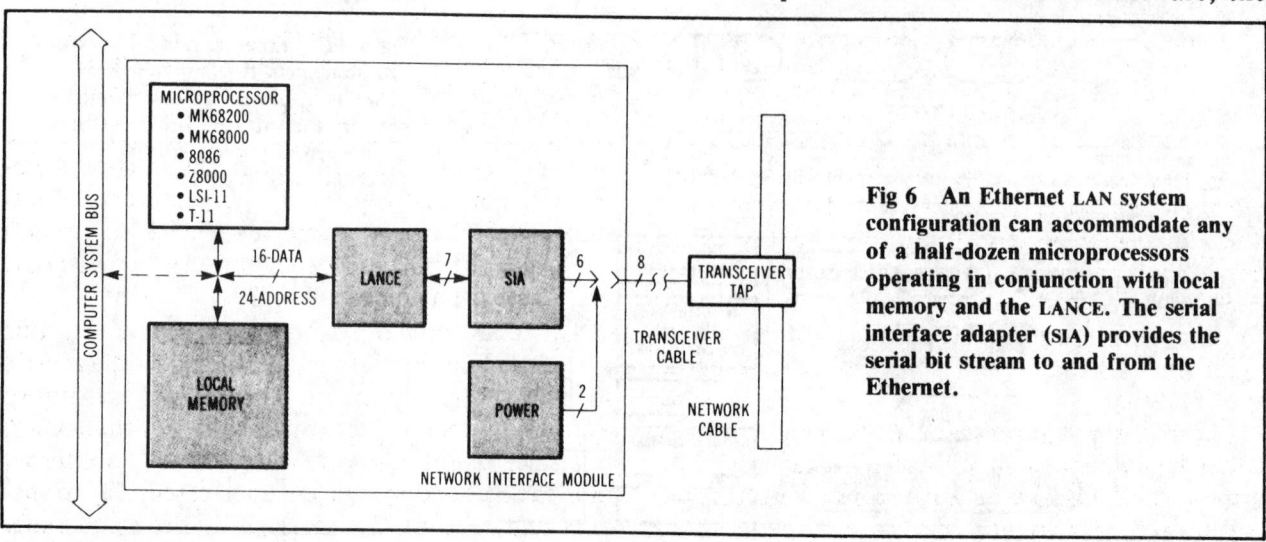

Fig 6 An Ethernet LAN system configuration can accommodate any of a half-dozen microprocessors operating in conjunction with local memory and the LANCE. The serial interface adapter (SIA) provides the serial bit stream to and from the Ethernet.

Ethernet controller chip comparison

The designer has a variety of VLSI Ethernet controller chips from which to choose. There are presently five Ethernet controller chips available: MK68590 (LANCE) from United Technologies/Mostek, i82586 (LAN) from Intel, the R68802 (LNET) from Rockwell International, the 8001 (EDLC) from Seeq Technology, and the MB61301 (DLC) from Ungermann-Bass/Fujitsu. These devices can generally be grouped according to performance by comparing the performance specifications of their respective data sheets. The LANCE and i82586 can manage multiple simultaneous transmit and receive buffers while the EDLC, LNET, and DLC can manage only one transmit or receive buffer at any one time. The Rockwell, Seeq, and Ungermann-Bass/Fujitsu devices meet the IEEE 802.3 specification, and although they support the implementation of ISO layers 1 and 2, they leave implementation of multiple buffer management to the designer. The LANCE and i82586 also provide all of the layer functions mentioned above, but do so with a sophisticated buffer management technique along with the physical Ethernet protocol functions.

Both the LANCE and i82586 access the transmit and receive buffers by first accessing the descriptor rings to determine the starting address of the message buffer. This method provides multiple buffers for both transmit and receive, and does not require the host to provide a buffer address for each message. The Rockwell, Seeq, and Ungermann-Bass/Fujitsu devices support only one memory address at a time for transmit and one for receive. Thus, the host must supply this address each time a buffer is allocated for either receive or transmit.

The Seeq, Rockwell, and Ungermann-Bass/Fujitsu controller chips require external hardware to implement DMA capabilities, while both the Mostek and Intel parts have controlling microcode to perform onchip DMA operations on both sequential receive buffers and sequential transmit buffers. The LANCE has a contiguous ring arrangement allowing up to 128 transmit and receive buffers. The i82586 uses a linked list arrangement that allows software control of the unlimited number of buffers for each side. Both devices provide for multiple buffers within a single transmit or receive frame.

Both the Intel and Mostek devices provide flexible memory arrangement, allowing the designer to interface them to operating systems with little software effort. Meanwhile, the Seeq, Ungermann-Bass/Fujitsu, and Rockwell devices require the hardware designer to plan a memory access arrangement that accommodates the local software environment, all at the expense of added board real estate. The LANCE requires contiguous, 8-byte-aligned, buffer descriptor rings that localize all the buffer descriptors at any properly aligned location within a 16-Mbyte address space, and also requires three word memory accesses to acquire the next buffer address. The i82586 device allows the buffer descriptors to be placed anywhere within a 64-Kbyte address range, with a linked list arrangement. It requires at least four word memory accesses to obtain the next buffer address. This is one more than the LANCE requires; the number of memory accesses is critical in sequential message handling.

Both the Intel and Mostek controllers have complete station, broadcast, and multicast address recognition capabilities. The Seeq chip requires external multicast address recognition. In contrast, Rockwell's chip supports only the single node and indiscriminate address recognition modes. LANCE, i82586, and the R68802 perform the binary exponential backoff algorithm, while the Seeq device performs only part of it. The Seeq device notifies the CPU of collisions and waits for CPU completion of the computed backoff interval.

Mostek's LANCE and Intel's i82586 must be regarded as superior devices to other available controllers. The LANCE and i82586 are equal in performance, with the exception of LANCE's greater allowable bus latency, which directly reduces the possibility of first in, first out (FIFO) overrun. According to Dale Taylor, Dave Oster, and Larry Green in their article, "VLSI Node Processor Architecture for Ethernet" (IEEE *Journal on Selected Areas in Communications*, Nov 1983, p 733), "The FIFO buffer in an Ethernet controller provides two valuable functions: more efficient bus/memory usage through multiple transfers for each bus acquisition (bursts) and more tolerance to long bus latencies. The deeper the FIFO is, the larger a burst transfer may be and the longer peak latency will be." Intel's FIFO is 8 words deep, while Mostek's FIFO is 24 words deep. It can be shown that the average allowable latency that LANCE offers is almost equal to twice that of the i82586, while the allowable peak latency is greater than three times that of the i82586. They continue, "the larger the allowable peak latency of an Ethernet controller is, the less likely it will suffer a FIFO overrun/underrun in a system with a heavily utilized bus."

node processor can implement International Standards Organization (ISO) layers 1 to 4—the physical, data link, network, and transport layers. These correspond to layers 0 through 2 in the Ethernet specification. As shown in Fig 4, there are software routines that must be executed in order to implement the bottom three layers of the Ethernet specification.

Layer 0, the transmission media protocol level, could be implemented by executing a basic software kernel. This kernel provides an interface between user software and hardware elements of the node processor. The kernel performs all nonsystem-bus I/O port addresses and interrupt vector locations. Basic hardware elements needed for level 0 are the 68200, LANCE, SIA, transceiver, memory, and interface and control logic.

To verify proper operation of the node, this kernel should contain basic power-up diagnostic software. The routine should include a memory test, an I/O register test, timer test, and the LANCE test. The LANCE test would implement an internal loopback checking routine that essentially transmits and receives the message at the same time.

A closer look at LANCE and the micro

The MK68590 LANCE is a 48-pin VLSI device designed to greatly simplify the interfacing of a microcomputer (such as the 68200) or minicomputer to an Ethernet LAN. This chip is intended to operate in a local environment that includes a closely coupled memory and microprocessor. The LANCE uses scaled NMOS technology and is compatible with several popular microprocessors.

The LANCE interfaces to a microprocessor bus characterized by time multiplexed address and data lines. Typically, data transfers are 16 bits wide, but byte transfers occur if the buffer memory address boundaries are odd. An added advantage is that the address bus is 24 bits wide.

One of the key features in LANCE is its onboard DMA channel and the flexibility and speed that it gives in communicating with the host, or the dedicated microprocessor, through common memory locations. The basic organization of the buffer management is a circular queue of tasks in memory called descriptor rings (Fig A). There are separate descriptor rings to describe transmit and receive operations. Up to 128 tasks may be queued up on a descriptor ring awaiting execution by the LANCE. Each entry in a descriptor ring holds a pointer to a data memory buffer and an entry for the length of the data buffer. Data buffers can be chained or cascaded in order to handle a long packet in multiple data buffer areas. The LANCE searches the descriptor rings in a "lookahead manner" to determine the next empty buffer in order to chain buffers together or to handle back-to-back packets. As each buffer is filled, an "own" bit is reset, signaling the host processor to empty this buffer.

The 68200 is a recent addition to the 68000 family line (see "Microcontroller Addresses Control and Instrumentation" by Don Folkes and John Bates, *Computer Design*, Oct 1983, p 229). The chip is a

Fig A   The LANCE memory management feature allows flexible communication between the host and common memory.

This would verify proper controller chip operation. The kernel should also contain some basic debugging software.

Software must also execute the basic operating routines of the transmission level. These include the initialization module, which initializes the LANCE to a particular mode of operation; the transmit and receive modules, which handle all buffer management of the descriptor rings; the network statistics module, which keeps track of collisions and other errors occurring on the net; the status module which keeps track of the node's activity; and the timer module, which generates timer interrupts needed for execution of upper level protocols.

Layers 1 and 2, the internet and transport layers, are implemented by the Ethernet node's user software. The function of layer 1's internet datagram protocol is to address, route, and deliver standard internet packets. Each of these packets is treated as an independent entity with no relation to other internet packets traveling throughout the system. The protocol must determine if the node has been addressed by either the broadcast or multicast method through the use of a software filter.

Implementing layer 2

In order to implement layer 2, primitives must be generated and contained in the Ethernet node's firmware to execute the following procedures: routing information, error, echo, sequenced packet, and packet-exchange protocols. The routing information protocol provides a means by which the data base is maintained in a dynamic manner and therefore the way routers direct

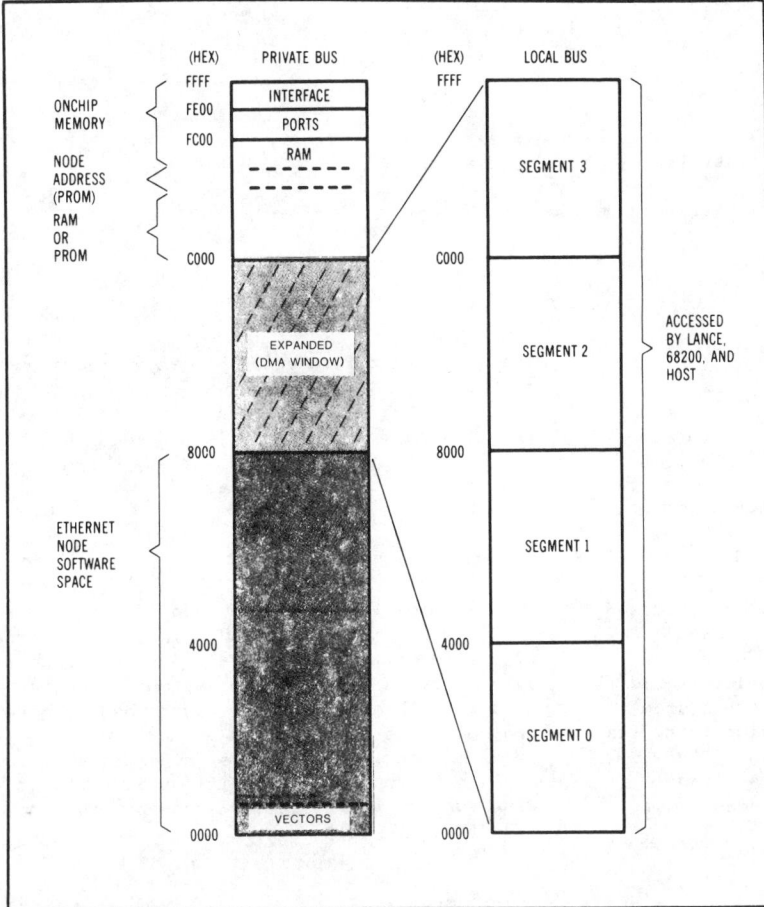

(HEX) PRIVATE BUS
FFFF
FE00 INTERFACE
FC00 PORTS
RAM

ONCHIP MEMORY

NODE ADDRESS (PROM)

RAM OR PROM

C000

(HEX) LOCAL BUS
FFFF

SEGMENT 3

C000

EXPANDED (DMA WINDOW)

ACCESSED BY LANCE, 68200, AND HOST

SEGMENT 2

8000

8000

ETHERNET NODE SOFTWARE SPACE

SEGMENT 1

4000

4000

SEGMENT 0

0000

VECTORS
0000

Fig B   On the memory map of the 68200 and the GP-LCC configuration, DMA window expansion allows access of up to 111 Kbytes of memory.

16-bit microcomputer chip with onchip CPU, ROM, RAM, and I/O that provide parallel expanded bus modes operating with a full complement of multiprocessing features. The user can select I/O architecture allowing the device to operate both as a high performance single-chip microcomputer with a fully expandable CPU that can address external memory and I/O, and as a dedicated I/O controller that can share a 16-bit system bus with a 68000 or other types of 16-bit microprocessors. This architecture makes it an apt choice as a node processor for standalone or peripheral configurations. In addition, the 68200 provides an onchip serial I/O port that significantly reduces the amount of interfacing hardware needed to connect the Ethernet node to a serial device such as a terminal.

Forty of the 48 available pins on the device can be used for I/O, and their functions are programmable. I/O capabilities include parallel I/O, three timers, a serial channel, and an interrupt controller. In the single-chip configuration, all 16 bits of Port 0, and 9 bits of Port 1, are used for general purpose I/O. Up to three of the pins on Port 1 can be programmed as external interrupt sources, and up to four pins can be programmed as I/Os for the onchip serial channel. All 8 bits in Port 4 can be used as simple inputs or outputs or can serve as timers. For example, TAI can be used as an input for timer A, an interrupt source, or a general purpose input pin. If it is used as an interrupt source, it can be selected simultaneously with either of the other two functions. With the LCC 68200 version in the bus grant mode, the processor can access up to 64 Kbytes using the system bus and up to 47 Kbytes using the private bus and onboard RAM (Fig B). Thus, the 68200 can access up to 111 Kbytes of memory. The LCC allows the 68200 to grant system bus use to a host or peripheral, and private bus use for concurrent operations.

packets to other routers on their way to the final destination. The error protocol provides a means for error reporting when a packet has been discarded. It is intended as a diagnostic tool for analyzing network performance. The echo protocol is used simply to echo, or return each received packet to its source in order to verify proper operation. The sequenced packet protocol provides transmission of successive internet packets by the use of sequence numbers.

Using these numbers ensures proper rearrangement of a packet once it reaches its destination. The final software required for the intelligent node processor's operation is the interface software. This is necessary to ensure proper communication and message transfer between the host and the node processor.

The chip count for implementing intelligent nodes is low enough so that the entire intelligent Ethernet controller can be placed on a single standard PC board such as VME, Versabus, or Multibus. This facilitates an easy system integration of Ethernet throughout the entire product line, regardless of the particular application. Standard software may be written for the Ethernet frontend processor, and unique software may be written to enable the host to implement particular applications.

An LSI Token Controller

Mark Stieglitz
Western Digital Corporation
2445 McCabe Way
Irvine, California 92714

ABSTRACT

A token based access protocol for bus (shared
media) based local networks is described. A past
stumbling block for acceptance of token protocols
has been their complexity when consideration is
given to exception conditions. These complexities
are examined and solutions are offered.

These complexities, as well as the other necessary
functions of data buffering via DMA, packet
filtering, etc., are performed by a device
referred to as a Token Access Controller (TAC).
The TAC is a highly microprogrammed sub-system
incorporating internal diagnostics along with its
network support and control functions. The TAC
is implemented in a single LSI device using
conventional commercial processing techniques.

INTRODUCTION

To be widely used, a local network access protocol
must be easy to use. This ease of use may be
derived from an LSI implementation which can be
made cost effective only when sufficient volume
exists for its manufacture. Sufficient volume may
be acheived only by the creation of a device with
multiple diverse applications--a device that may
be user customized and optimized by the user for
his unique application. This network "parameter-
ization" requires a sufficiently complex protocol
for implementation. Thus a carefully designed
protocol, with an implementation in LSI, is needed
to get local networks off-the-ground, and with
its ease of use, to create new applications for
network technology.

The easiest method of interconnecting multiple
stations on the local network is via a broadcast
medium [1]. A broadcast medium is one where all
stations hear all transmissions virtually
simultanously (e.g., not store and forward).
While the sorting of information on the network
as to its destination is easily accomplished with
addressing information included in each frame,
some coordination, refered to as an access method,
is required to keep multiple devices from
transmitting at the same time.

The access method meeting the above requirements
is based on the use of tokens. A token is the
explicit right of a station to initiate a
transmission. This right is passed amoung all
stations on the network but at any given time,
one and only one station has it.

TOKEN ACCESS

Tokens allow a very simple, and therefore reliable, access method. This reliability is acheived
by its deterministic nature and by ensuring a high
visability on any error conditions which may
occour. (These are usually evidenced by garbled
transmissions--collisions, or the lack of
transmissions.) Since error conditions are clearly
separable from normal conditions (a fact not true
with some competing access schemes), they may be
expeditiously delt with.

Normal Operation

A local network is usually in a "normal operational mode". This means that tokens and data
frames are being exchanged and no stations are
instantanously being added to or removed from the
system. Since this "normal" condition occurs most
always, it is fortunate that it is the simplest
and most efficient mode.

Normal operation may be described with the aid of
Figure 1. We assume in this figure that the
network has already been initialized (meaning that
the linkages in the access ring have already been
established) and the token is held at this instant
by station 4 (SN=Station Number).

When station 4 has finished sending its data
messages (if any) it is ready to pass its access
right on. Station 4 sends a message to the
station number given in its internal "next
address" register (NEXT), in this case 11.
The message, and thus the token, is received by
station 11 who can now transmit his message(s).
When station 11 is ready to pass the token, he
sends a message to station 19, as directed by his
internal register NEXT. The cycle continues, in a
circular fashion, from station 4 to 11 to 19 to 54
to 4. In this way, the token is passed from one
station to the next in a logical ring.

Reprinted from The Proceedings of COMPCON S'82, 1982, pages 115-120.
Copyright © 1982 by The Institute of Electrical and Electronics Engineers,
Inc.

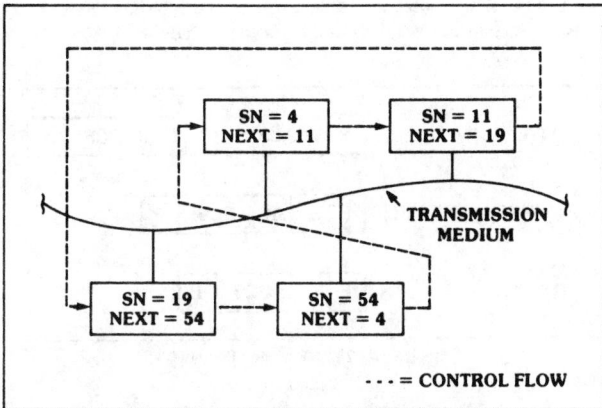

Figure 1. Access Control Flow

Notice that the station numbers need not be contiguous. The relatively arbitrary station numbering (in the example) poses no inefficiency to the access method. The value of this is the ability to add and remove stations (re-configure) to/from the network without re-arranging the remaining nodes' addresses.

One may ask "If tokens are so simple to use, why are they not more popular?"

The answer is in the complex algorithms required to set up the station linkages initially and to recover from network exception conditions. Since an LSI device has not been previously available to address these challenges, the entire token based access protocol has been usually cast aside in favor of something simpler. Let's see what these challenges are and how they are handled by the TAC.

Challenges for a Token system

There are three primary network exception conditions that the TAC must handle: network initialization, the addition of new stations into the access ring while the network is in use, and the ability to recover from failed stations.

The occurance of a failed station is detected by the token passing TAC when it attempts to pass the token to that (failed) station. The sending TAC times out the acknowledgement of the token and automatically searches the network address space for a station that does respond. When found, the sending TAC updates his NEXT register, patching over the failed station(s).

If the station that fails happens to be holding the token at the time, the token is considered lost which results in a silent network. This condition is recovered with the aid of another timer which commands a properly enabled TAC to "assume" the token. Several (or all) stations may be set up to assume the token if too much silence is detected as long as each waits a different interval before attempting recovery. (An easy way to ensure this is to set the timer value in each TAC to a multiple of its address.)

Initialization is handled in the same method as recovery from much silence. One TAC will assume the token as described above and search the network for someone to pass it to. This recipient will receive the token, use it (if he has anything to say), and will also search for someone to pass it to. This procedure continues until the token returns to the origional initiator which indicates all linkages have been set up.

The adding of stations to an already initialized and operating network is accomplished with assistance from the host. The simplest scheme requires a host to periodically poll all the possible stations in the address space. When a new station is found who desires to be added to the access ring, the host sends a message to the appropriate host to update his NEXT register (internal to the TAC) to the address of the new station. There are several other methods of implementing the add station function involving varrying degrees of host effort and network impact which are summarized in [3].

The above challenges are addressed and handled by the TAC, freeing the user from concern. Thus, the primary obstacle to token protocol usage is removed.

DATA TRANSMISSION

Data is transmitted between controllers within special messages called information frames. The TAC supports two primary classes of service in transporting this data.

The first is the simple datagram. When this method is selected, the sending TAC completes its responsibility for the message as soon as it completes the transmission of it. The receiving station easily validates the message (by checking the CRC) but has no way of informing the sender of an error. This method enjoys current popularity since many users perform high level message sequencing as a matter of course. Also, some applications do not demand that absolutely every frame sent be correctly received. Examples of this include digital voice (some loss can be tolorated; further, a late speech segment has little value) and repetitive update of control points (where the message will shortly be re-sent anyway).

The TAC does provide an acknowledge option on each frame transmitted which is handled in real time by the receiving device. This second class of service is often refered to as an "acknowledged datagram." Each frame so optioned is acknowledged before another is sent removing the need for sequence numbers (a non-acknowledged frame may be immediatly re-tried). This scheme is efficient since local network applications do not encounter the extreemly long transmission delays (such as satellite links) as in conventional data networks (such as X.25).

A third class of service can be implemented with some help from the destination's host. A source may pass the token to a station who expects it and is set up to immediatly pass it back. The message passing the token back to the origional source may contain data, making this procedure a simple type of data polling. It is useful in many repetitous applications, such as process monitoring, where one cannot afford to or does not need to have all the on-line stations in the access ring.

Priority

The token access protocol described prevents self-induced transmission collisions and ensures fair and guaranteed distribution of transmission time amongst all attached controllers. Many applications, however, require that some stations have "premium" status; that some stations are more important than others for whatever reason. To support this requirement, the TAC allows adjustment of several access parameters on a per-station basis. Two examples of "fairness" parameters are:

o Maximum Frame Transmission Limit. This value indicates the maximum number of queued frames that may be sent per access interval. This is often refered to as exhaustive (send all frames queued) or non-exhaustive transmission.

o Access Hold-off. This allows some stations to defer transmission a multiple of the token cycle interval.

Stations set to always send all their data or who are allowed to send messages everytime they receive the token, will use more of the transmission bandwidth than those who send only a little at a time. The sending of only a limited amount of data may cause a backup of frames (a large transmission queue) within that station requiring action by the host (but not clogging the network). This backup is proportional to the network activity (since access intervals, or token circulation, depend on the current network utilization). Therefore, the host in a "less important" station may defer, or cause the TAC to defer, message transmission until the network is less busy.

Frame Types

All messages are transmitted over the network in organized groups of bytes called frames. The frame format used is similar to the industry standard HDLC; a 16 bit CRC is implemented and flag patterns with standard zero insertion are used for framing.

For maximum efficiency, three unique frame types are implemented (Figure 2). The frames differ both by their length and by the definitions of the header bytes in each. This byte saving in messages saves valuable transmission bandwidth, especially at lower transmission rates.

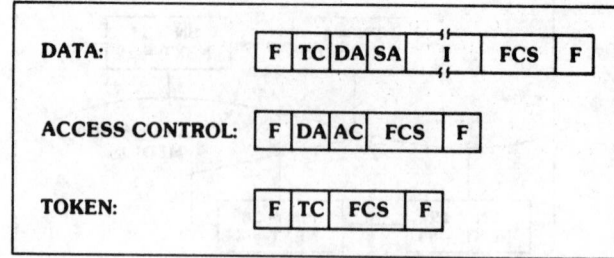

Figure 2. Frame Formats

Field Descriptions and Encoding

    F   = Flag, binary pattern 01111110
    TC = Token Control (8 bit)
    AC = Access Control (8 bit)
    DA = Destination Address (8 bit)
    SA = Source Address (8 bit)
    I   = Information Field
    FCS = Frame Check Sequence (16 bit)

The Access Control (AC) field is used to send ACK/NAK and control information to or from the TAC. Examples of NAK's are "out of receive buffers" and "receiver not enabled." An example of a status indication is "I desire to be admitted into the access ring" on response to a poll.

The Token Control (TC) field contains either the address of the station to whom the token is currently being passed (if any) or a flag indicating a response is requested from the message's destination station (e.g. ACK/NAK). (Note that there is no interaction between the between the TC field and the DA or SA fields. Thus the token may be transfered to one station and data sent to the same or a different station in a single frame.)

The Information field (I) is variable in length and is passed to the host, undisturbed, by the TAC. The user may build a structure into this field as required by his application. Examples of user defined structure would be link level control fields and/or protocol multiplexing at the host level if needed. The use of this field may be as elaborate or as simple as the user desires.

Higher levels

Due to limitations of the specific hardware implementation, a complete link level could not be included in the same LSI device as the token controller. It is likely in fact that this logical partitioning will be an asset in the long range applications of the device since specific higher level protocol functions greatly influence a communication systems overall efficiency. The requirements and allowable expenses for these functions are today very application dependent.

This lack of an integrated high level protocol (usually refered to as a "link level") is not deemed a problem since classical connection oriented applications can tolorate some delay between information receipt and transmission of an acknowledgement (e.g., transmission windows). Therefore, these additional functions can be implemented in the host if needed without sacrifice from those stations, even on the same network, who do not need the link level function.

IMPLEMENTATION

The Token Access Controller is a single chip NMOS LSI sub-system intended to be used with other intelligent devices (e.g., microprocessors) in a cooperative mannor. This assumption allows the networking tasks to be effectively partitioned between the TAC and its supporting processor (refered to as the host).

Usually, in partitioning a job between multiple processors, some inefficiencies are created. These have been minimized or avoided compltetely by attention to the following points:

1. The network must not wait for a given host to respond to an action request. (The host may at any given time be busy with unrelated tasks that cause his response time to be variable.) Therefore, the TAC must perform all real-time functions on its own. Examples are token passing and error recovery, generating ACK/NAK responses, performing packet filtering (address matching), and handling any DMA buffer chaining overhead.

2. The host is an asynchronous device; it may read and/or modify memory locations without notice of the TAC. Control blocks are therefore designed to prevent "deadlock" conditions by using separate locations for each processor's use.

3. The more processing that is done in the TAC, the longer its response times (and it turns out, the higher its cost). The host usually has some spare processing power available (with the restrictions noted in point one) so everything that is not time dependent is deferred to it. Examples of this are link level functions and the addition of new stations into the network.

Operational Modes

To preserve the implementation simplicity of a half duplex system and maintain low network latency while at the same time providing comprehensive LSI diagnostics (some of which require full duplex operation), the algorithms are divided into three independent modes, or states (see Figure 3).

At power up, the isolated state is entered. Here, the TAC is essentially idle allowing external memory tables as well as internal parameter and pointer registers to be initialized. This state is a mintained until a specific command is received from the host requesting a transition into the diagnostic or network states.

The diagnostic mode allows the selective execution of routines by the TAC intended to validate the functionality of itself and of the host system it is a part of. The tests are all local in that they do not depend on the presence of a second station on the network (nor will they interfere with any active stations on the network).

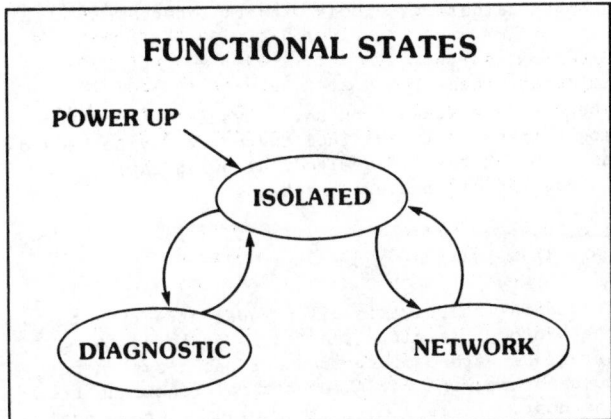

Figure 3. Operational Modes

Network mode is where the TAC monitors the incoming serial stream for data and tokens addressed to it. Correctly addressed frames are processsed resulting in DMA buffers being filled or transmissions initiated, as appropriate. Some network diagnostics are activated in this state such as duplicate station detection and various network time-outs.

Users Interface

The use of the TAC allows a clear seperation of engineering diciplines while realizing the local network interface (See Figure 4).

One side of the controller interfaces to a conventional microprocessor bus with the usual data and address lines, control lines such as chip select for I/O, DMA grant, etc. These are quite common and comfortable for computer systems engineers to work with. The host software interface is also very familiar to systems software people.

The other side of the controller also looks familiar to hardware engineers. For many applications, the modem consists of simple RS-449 drivers/receivers and a manchester clock encoding circuit.

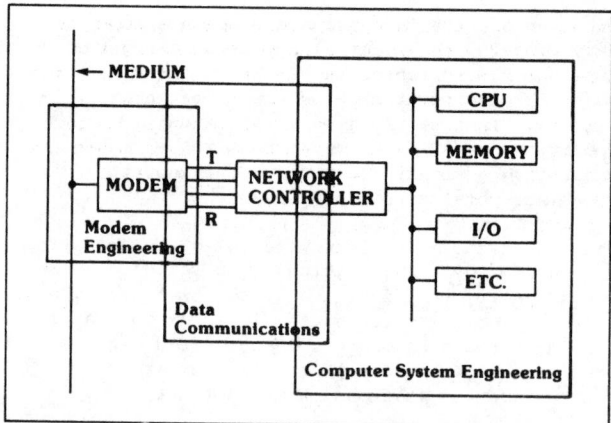

Figure 4. Local Network Interface

There are two primary interfaces to the TAC--
programmed I/O control/status register operations,
and a chained buffer DMA (Direct Memory Access)
structure. The control/status registers are used
to set modes (such as network or diagnostic), to
set "long term" network options (such as frame
transmission limits), and device addresses. With
few exceptions, these are set before the device is
placed into network mode.

The DMA interface performs all data fetch/store
functions. The DMA system also reads individule
control bytes from each frame buffer which allows
some options to be adjusted on a per-frame basis.
An example of this is the acknowledge request.

To optimize memory buffer usage, multiple buffers
may be linked teogether to form a frame. This is
useful where most frame are short when compared
with the largest posible frame allowed on the
network. The TAC will transend buffer boundaries, both on receive and transmit, until a
frame end signal is detected.

The operation of these chains may be better described by example with reference to Figure 5.

The complete token processing system (the protocol
logic internal to the TAC) therefore may be viewed
as a "black box" if desired, allowing rapid
integration into users' systems.

Host Interface

The users interface is given equal attention to
the protocol itself. The TAC is designed to
interface with a microprocessor based system but
does not require any time critical functions from
the host. In many cases this means that a local
network may be easily added to existing systems
without upgrading the existing processor.

When appropriatly addressed frames are received,
the TAC DMA's the data bytes into the memory
buffer pointed to by internal register "NEXT
RECEIVE." Buffering continues until the frame
ends. When the frame does end, the TAC marks the
Frame Status Byte (FSB) as complete and updates
its internal register NEXT RECEIVE to the value in
the LINK field of the buffer At this point, the
TAC is ready to receive another frame.

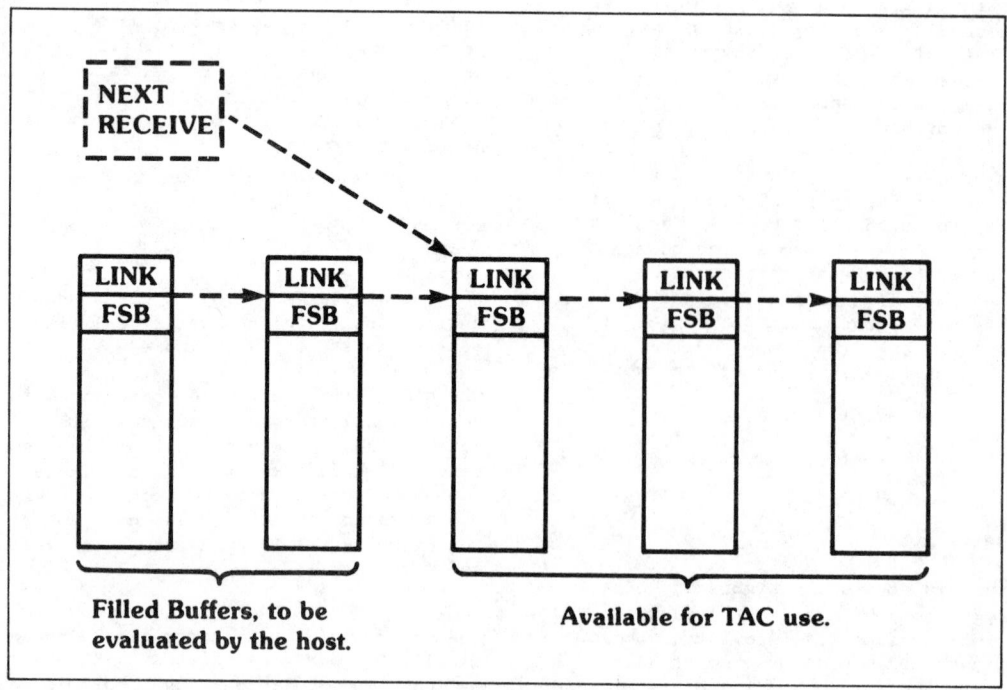

Figure 5. Receive Buffer Chain

The host evaluates and processes received buffers by following the receive chain via the LINK's, consuming the buffers as long as each FSB indicates it has been filled. The host recycles these buffers (or creates new ones) by attaching initialized ones to the head of the chain. The length of the chain can be arbitrarily long giving the user latitude in trading off host response requirements, queue length, and network traffic patterns.

Modem Interface

The modem interface is the conventional NRZ type with seperate clock and data. An added input is used in the receive subsection as a "signal quality" indicator from the modem. This allows easily detectable low level errors (such as exceeding a low carrier level limit or the absence of a clock transition in a manchester decoder) to be conveyed to the TAC, strengthing its frame integrity beyond the CRC.

SUMMARY

A token access and data transfer protocol that is implementable today in LSI has been described. Several trade-offs were made and limitation were imposed on the applications scope to insuer a useful mix of features can be had for a reasonable cost.

The usefulness of the Token Access Controller is the direct result of an intentional division of design efforts between the protocol functions, and the user's system interface simplicty. All real-time requirements of the protocol as well as the complex recovery and initialization algorithms are shielded from the user. This allows ease of integrating the controller, and hence local network functions, into a users system.

REFRENCES

[1] "Tradeoffs in local network access methods," Mark Stieglitz, Computer Design, October 1981.

[2] "WD2840 Token Access Controller, Functional Specification," Western Digital Corporation, 1981.

[3] "Token Challenges," Mark Stieglitz, December 1981, Available from the author.

[4] "OSI Reference Model--The ISO Model of Architecture for Open Systems Interconnection," Hubert Zimmerman, IEEE Transactions on Communications, April 1980, pp 425-432.

Appendix: Local Network Manufacturers Listing

3COM
    1365 Shorebird Way, Box 1390, Mountain View, CA 94039
    Ethernet Controllers, EtherSeries Ethernet for IBM PC

A.B. Dick
    5700 West Touhy Ave., Chicago, IL 60648
    Knowledge Worker (Convergent N-GEN)

Acorn Computers
    Fulbourn Rd., Cherry Hinton, Cambridge, CB1 4JN U.K.
    Econet and the Cambridge Ring

ACT Computers (North America)
    3375 Scott Blvd., Santa Clara, CA 95051
    Apricot Point 32 (Omninet-based)

Advanced Computer Communications
    720 Santa Barbara St., Santa Barbara, CA 93101
    Ethernet products

Aetna Telecommunications Labs
    131 Flanders Rd., P.O. Box 723, Westborough, MA 01581
    Fiber Optics Couplers for Local Networks

Alspa Computer, Inc.
    477 Division St., Campbell, CA 95008
    Alspa Computer w/OMNINET or Zero-Net interface; Add-Net

Altos Computer Systems
    2360 Bering Dr., San Jose, CA 95131
    Altos-Net, Ethernet

AMD
    901 Thompson Pl., Sunnyvale, CA 94086
    Ethernet components: Am7990 LANCE, Am7991 SIA

American Photonics, Inc.
    Milltown Office Park, Route 22, Brewster, NY 10509
    64Net (fiber optics for Commodore 64)

Ampheonol
    33 East Franklin St., Danbury, CT 06810
    Ethernet cable components

Amtel Systems Corp.
    1293 Anvilwook Ave., Sunnyvale, CA 94086
    Messenger II Private Network Electronic Mail System (through A.C.)

Anderson Jacobson, Inc.
    521 Charcot Ave., San Jose, CA 95131
    IOX voice/data PBX;

Anixter Brothers, Inc.
    4711 Golf Rd., Skokie, IL 60076
    LAN Cable Plant

Apollo Computer, Inc.
    15 Elizabeth Dr., Chelmsford, MA 01824
    DOMAIN

Apple Computer, Inc.
    20525 Mariani Ave., Cupertino, CA 95014
    AppleTalk

Applied Intelligence, Inc.
    1043 Stierlin Rd., Mountain View, CA 94043
    PC/NOS Network Operating Systems for PCs

Applitek Corp.
    107 Audubon Rd., Wakefield, MA 01880
    UniLAN

Armor Systems, Inc.
    324 North Orlando Blvd., Maitland, FL 32751
    Excalibur Plus accounting software for PC LANs

AST Research
    2121 Alton Ave., Irvine, CA 92714
    PCnet-II

AT&T Information Systems
    100 Southgate Pky. Rm 2D07, Morristown, NJ 07960
    Dimension System 85; integrated voice/data PBX

Augat, Inc.
    901 South Ave., Horseheads, NY 14845
    Broadband passive components

Auragen Systems Corp.
    Two Executive Dr., Fort Lee, NJ 07024
    System 4000 with cluster bus and optional Ethernet

Auscom, Inc.
    2007 Kramer La., Austin, TX 78758
    8911A Ethernet to IBM Channel Interface

Autocontrol, Inc.
    11400 Dorsett Rd., St. Louis, MO 63043
    Autolan

B-Komp, Inc.
    5949 Sherry La., Suite 1535, Dallas, TX 75225
    Net-Worker

Banyan Systems, Inc.
    135 Flanders Rd., Westboro, MA 01581
    Banyan Virtual Networking System

BBN Communications Corp.
    70 Fawcett St., Cambridge, MA 02238
    Pluribus IMP, C/30 Packet Switch Processor

Bedford Computer Corp.
    Tirrell Hill Rd., Bedford, NH 03102
    the Meteor Graphics workstation for Ethernet

Belden Corp.
P.O. Box 1980, Richmond, IN 47374
Ethernet Cables and Assemblies

Braegen Corp.
525 Los Coches St., Milpitas, CA 95035
ELAN System (8500 series of 3270-compatible controllers and LANs)

Bridge Communications, Inc.
1345 Shorebird Way, Mountain View, CA 94043
Ethernet System Product Line (ESPL)

Broadband Engineering, Inc.
P.O. Box 1247, Jupiter, FL 33458
Broadband components and amplifiers

Burroughs
1 Burroughs Pl., Detroit, MI 48202
Inter-System Control (ISC)

Cableshare Ltd.
P.O. Box 5880 20 Enterprise Dr., London, Ontario N6A 4LC, Canada
Local Area Network

Cadlinc Inc.
1872 Brummel, Elk Grove Village, IL 60007
Ethernet Graphic Computer

Cadmus Computer Systems
600 Suffolk St., Lowell, MA 01852
Cadmus 9790 CAD w/Ethernet or fiber-optic net

California Microwave
990 Almanor Ave., Sunnyvale, CA 94086
CD5800 Digital Encryption System (NBS DES)

California Network Systems
372 Turquoise St., Milpitas, CA 95035
OEM/SNA Gateway for PC LANs

Callan
2645 Townsgate Rd., Westlake, CA 91361
UNISTAR 200 Multiuser System w/Ethernet Option

Cambridge Electronic Design
Science Park, Milton Rd., Cambridge CB4 4BM U.K.
Worknet

Canadian Micro Distributors
500 Steeles Ave., Milton, Ontario L9T 3P7, Canada
MUPET

Canoga Data Systems
21218 Vanowen St., Canoga Park, CA 91303
Fiber optics systems

Canstar Communications
1240 Ellesmere Rd., Scarborough, Ontario M1P 2X4, Canada
Hubnet

CASE
Woodcock Hill Est, Harefield Rd., Rickmansworth, Herts WD3 1L U.K.
Casenet

C-COR Electronics, Inc.
8285 SW Nimbus Ave., Suite 131, Beaverton, OR 97005
C-LAN

Centram Systems West, Inc.
2372 Ellsworth Ave., Berkeley, CA 94704
Transcendental Network (multi-PC, multi-OS)

ChipCom
19 Brook Rd., Needham, MA 02194
Communication components including broadband RF modems

Codenoll Technology
1086 N. Broadway, Yonkers, NY 10701
Codenet

Codex
20 Cabot Blvd., Mansfield, MA 02048
Codex LAN

Commercial Dynamics, Inc.
168 Bowen St, Providence, RI 02906
TurboNET (S-100)

Commtex, Inc.
2411 Crofton La., Crofton, MD 21114
Cx-80 Data Exchange (clustering device with ARCNET interconnect)

Communication Machinery Corp.
1421 State St., Santa Barbara, CA 93101
Ethernet Node Processor, XNS, TCP

Companion Computer Co.
192 Deerfield Rd., Apex, NC 27502
A.NET

Complexx Systems, Inc.
4930 Research Dr., Huntsville, AL 35805
StationMate (XLAN)

Compucorp
2211 Michigan Ave., Santa Monica, CA 90404
OmegaNet

Computer Automation
1800 Jay Ell Dr., Richardson, TX 75081
SyFAnet

Computer Communications, Inc.
2610 Columbia St., Torrance, CA 90503
CC-8 Enhanced Emulation Processor

Computer Network Technology
6440 Flying Cloud Dr., Minneapolis, MN 55344
CNT LAN System

Computrol
15 Ethan Allen Highway, Ridgefield, CT 06877
Megalink, RF Modems, 'Computrol System'

Concord Data Systems, Inc.
303 Bear Hill Rd., Waltham, MA 02154
Token/Net

Contel Information Systems
130 Steamboat Rd., Great Neck, NY 11024
ContelNet

Control Data Corp.
P.O. Box 0, Minneapolis, MN 55440
Loosely Coupled Network

Convergent Technologies
3055 Patrick Henry Dr., Santa Clara, CA 95050
MiniFrame with Ethernet option

Corvus Systems, Inc.
2100 Corvus Dr., San Jose, CA 95124
Omninet

CPT Corp.
8100 Mitchell Rd., Eden Prairie, MN 55344
Office Dialog Link

CPU Computer Corp.
420-438 Rutherford Ave., Charlestown, MA 02129
CPUnet (OMNINET)

Cromemco, Inc.
280 Bernardo Ave., Mountain View, CA 94043
C-Net

Crowntek Networks, Inc.
650 McNicoll Ave., Willowdale, Ontario M2H 2E1, Canada
Prod/Net

CSEE
17 Place Pernet, 75015 Paris, France
Coralis coaxial interface

CXC Corp.
2852 Alton Ave., Irvine, CA 92714
Rose integrated voice/data PBX

CYB Systems, Inc.
6448 Highway 290E, D-106, Austin, TX 78723-9990
Unite 16i

Cybernetic Micro Systems
P.O. Box 3000, San Gregorio, CA 94074
CY232 Network Controller

Daisy Systems Corp.
139 Kifer Ct., Sunnyvale, CA 94086
CAE Workstations w/Ethernet

Data Access Corp.
8225 SW 129th Terr., Miami, FL 33156
DataFlex multiuser DB for PC LANs

Data General
440 Computer Dr., Westboro, MA 01580
Multiprocessor Communications Adapter

Data Transfer Corp.
180 Bent St., Cambridge, MA 02141
LINC (Local Integrated Network Communication)

Data-Control Systems
P.O. Box 860, Danbury, CT 06810
RAM 11/22 wireless AC multidrop modem

Datamac Computer Systems
680 Almanor Ave., Sunnyvale, CA 94086
Datamac 1200 series

Datapoint
9725 Datapoint Dr., San Antonio, TX 78284
ARCNET

Datastream Communications Inc.
1115 Space Park Dr., Santa Clara, CA 95050
Network access systems (T7 IBM Gateway)

Davong Systems, Inc.
217 Humboldt Ct., Sunnyvale, CA 94086
Multilink

Davox Communications Corp.
6 Continental Blvd., Box 328, Merrimack, NH 03054
DavoxNet (twisted pair voice over data)

DEC
1205 Andover St., Tewksbury, MA 01876
Plug Compat. Ethernet (PCE) transceivers and boards, DECnet

DEC MS Two/B12
1925 Andover St., Tewksbury, MA 01876
DEC DataWay

Destek
830 C E. Evelyn Ave., Sunnyvale, CA 94086
DESNET

Develcon Electronics
Swamp Rd., Rt. 313, Doylestown, PA 18901
Dataswitch

Digilog Business Systems
P.O. Box 355, Montgomeryville, PA 18936
System 1800 LAN

Digital Communications Assoc.
303 Research Dr., Suite 225, Norcross, GA 30092
Network processors (multi-drop masters)

Digital Microsystems, Inc.
1755 Embarcadero, Oakland, CA 94606
HiNet

Digital Products, Inc.
600 Pleasant St., Watertown, MA 02172
Netcommander (terminal cluster device with LAN capabilities)

Digital Research, Inc.
160 Central Ave., Box 579, Pacific Grove, CA 93950
CP/NET, Soft/Net

Digital Sound Corp.
2030 Alameda Padre Sierra, Santa Barbara, CA 93103
DSC-2000 VoiceServer for SL-1

DY-4 Systems, Inc.
888 Lady Ellen Pl., Ottawa, Ontario K1Z 5M1, Canada
Dynasty

Eagle Computer
983 University Ave., Bldg C, Los Gatos, CA 95030
EagleNet I

Electrosound Systems, Inc.
4030 North 27th Ave., Suite E, Phoenix, AZ 85017
Data Loop Exchange (DLX) 320 local network

Elicon
4800 S. Lapeer Rd., Pontiac, MI 48057
Ethernet cable assemblies (coax and transceiver)

En-Link, Inc.
4706 Bond, Shawnee, KS 66203
Apple II Ethernet Interface

Energy Methods, Inc.
177 Main St., West Orange, NJ 07052
Two-way power line carrier equipment (AC)

Equinox Computers
16 Anning St., London EC2A 3HB, U.K.
Equinet

E-Systems, Melpar Division
7700 Arlington Blvd., Falls Church, VA 22046
E-BUS

Excelan, Inc.
2180 Fortune Dr., San Jose, CA 95131
Ethernet Products

Executone, Inc.
Two Jericho Plaza, Jericho, NY 11753
Eclipse (Siemens) PBX; Enterprise EPABX

Exxon Office Systems
777 Long Ridge Rd., Stamford, CT 06902
Summit

Fairchild Test Systems
299 Old Niskayuna Rd., Lantham, NY 12110
FastNet (In-circuit testers linked via Ethernet)

Fedder Group, Inc.
6707 White Stone Rd., Baltimore, MD 21207
Ultra-net

Ferranti
Bridge Ho Pk. Rd., Gatley Cheable, Cheshire SK8 4HZ, U.K.
Interface chips (for ring based system)

Four-Phase Systems
10700 North DeAnza Blvd., Cupertino, CA 95014
Net IV

Fox Research
7005 Corporate Way, Dayton, OH 45459
10-NET, 10-BASE

Fujitsu America, Inc.
2075 Oakmead Village Dr., Santa Clara, CA 95051
Optical Data Highway

Fujitsu Microelectronics
3320 Scott Blvd., Santa Clara, CA 95051
Ethernet VLSI

Future Computers Ltd.
14 Imperial Way, Croydon Airport, Ind. Estate, Croydon, Surrey, U.K.
Token Ring or Ethernet for Future Computer

Gandalf Data, Inc.
1019 S. Noel Ave., Wheeling, IL 60090
PACX IV, 3200 Coaxial Mux, PACXNET

Gateway Communications, Inc.
16782 Red Hill Ave., Irvine, CA 92714
G/NET (IBM PC)

GE
1225 Service Ave., Warwick, RI 02886
Energy Management Local Network

General Automation
1045 South East St., Box 4883, Anaheim, CA 92803
ARCNET for Zebra Computers

General Dynamics Corp.
12101 Woodcrest Exec. Dr., St. Louis, MO 63141
Focus, Infotron PBXs

General Instrument TACO Div.
1 Taco St., Sherburne, NY 13460
Broadband equipment

Gifford Computer Systems
1922 Republic Ave., San Leandro, CA 94577
Net 8-16

GN Netcom AS
Solvang 4-61, DK-3450 Allerod
X-Net

Gould Programmable Control Div
P.O. Box 3083, Andover, MA 01810
MODWAY

Gould, Design & Test Sys. Div.
4600 Old Ironsides Dr., Santa Clara, CA 95050-1279
9540 Engineering Workstation w/Ethernet (TeamNet)

Grass Valley Group, Inc.
P.O. Box 1114, Grass Valley, CA 95945
Wavelink broadband fiber optic communications system

GTE
8229 Boone Blvd., Vienna, VA 22180
Telenet TP4000; GTD family of integrated voice/data PBX products

GTE Communications Systems
12502 Sunrise Valley Dr., Reston, VA 22096
GTD-4600 PBX, XT300 ActionStation

Harris Corp. Info. Sys. Group
    1025 W. Nasa Blvd., Melbourne, FL 32919
    Harris 9070 baseband/broadband

Harris Corp., WP Division
    505 John Rhodes Blvd., Box 2400, Melbourne, FL 32901
    9000 Series Office Systems w/LAN

Hasler A.G., Ltd.
    Commerce Way, Croyton, Surrey, U.K.
    SILK (System for Integrated Level Communication)

Hawker Siddeley Engineering
    HSDE House, Bridge Rd. East, Welwyn, Garden City, Herts, U.K.
    Multilink

Hewlett-Packard
    19447 Pruneridge Ave., Cupertino, CA 95014
    DS/1000-IV, Ethernet

Hewlett-Packard, Colorado Networks Operation
    3404 E. Harmony Rd., Fort Collins, CO 80525
    LAN 9000, 3Com for HP 150

Hewlett-Packard, PC Group
    11000 Wolfe Rd., Cupertino, CA 95014
    EtherSeries/150 for HP 150

Hitachi America, Ltd.
    2696 Peachtree Sq., Doraville, GA 30360
    Digital Communications Controller; features similar to a PBX

Honeywell, Action Comm Systems
    4401 Beltwood Pky. South, Dallas, TX 75234
    Roadrunner; tandem switching system

Honeywell, Inc.
    P.O. Box 8000/A-79, Phoenix, AZ 85066
    Enterprise System (PBX and LAN integration, initially with Ethernet

Hughes Aircraft Co.
    2601 Campus Dr., Irvine, CA 92715
    Facility Management System

IBM Data Products Division
    1113 Westchester Ave., White Plains, NY 10604
    8100 SDLC Loop; Series 1 Ring

IBM Entry Systems Division
    P.O. Box 2989, Delray Beach, FL 33444
    PC Network; Cluster Control Program (PC)

ICS Electronics Corp.
    1620 Zanker Rd., San Jose, CA 95112
    IEEE 488 Bus Extender (Model 4887)

ILC Data Device Corp.
    105 Wilbur Pl., Bohemia, NY 11716
    1553 VLSI Controller

Incommnet, Inc.
    2772 Johnson Dr., Ventura, CA 93003
    Lotus System for mixed vendors

Inconix Corp.
    10 Tech Cir., Natick, MA 01760
    CINCHNET

Inforex
    186 Middlesex Tpk., Burlington, MA 01803
    Ultranet

InfoSoft Systems, Inc.
    P.O. Box 640, S. Norwalk, CT 06856
    Multi/NET

Infotron Systems
    Cherry Hill Industrial Center, Cherry Hill, NJ 08003
    TL 460 Intelligent Data PBX, Infotron LAN

InteCom Inc.
    601 Intecom Dr., Allen, TX 75002
    IBX (Integrated Business Exchange)

Intel
    3065 Bowers Ave., Santa Clara, CA 95051
    BITBUS

Intel Corp.
    3066 Bowers Ave., Santa Clara, CA 95051
    Ethernet: Development systems, boards, VLSI (82586 controller, 82501 SIA)

Interactive Systems/3M
    225-4S-06 3M Center, St. Paul, MN 55144
    Viedeodata LAN/I, LAN/PC

Intercontinental Micro Systems
    4015 Leaverton Ct., Anaheim, CA 92807
    MicroNet (S-100 and IBM PC)

Interlan, Inc.
    15 Swanson Rd., Boxborough, MA 01719
    LCN controller boards and software

International Computers Inc.
    415 E. Airport Fwy., Irving TX 75062
    ECMA Ethernet support within product line

International Computers Ltd.
    Computer House, 322 Euston Rd., London, NW1 3BD, U.K.
    DRS20—Distributed Resource Systems

International Electronics
    1518 E. Broadway, Tucson, AZ 85719
    M-Net (GPIB)

International Micro Systems
    Anaheim, CA
    MicroNet (ARCNET datalink) for IBM PC, S-100

International Software Ent.
    350 West Sagamore Pky., West Lafayette, IN 47906
    DBnet (DBMS for Net/One)

Interphase Corp.
    13667 Floyd Cir., Dallas, TX 75243
    LNC 5180

Intertec Data Systems
   2300 Broadriver Rd., Columbia, SC 29210
   Compustar

ITT
   7635 Plantation Rd., Roanoke, VA 24019
   Optic Fiber Digital Modules

ITT Electro-Optical Division
   7635 Plantation Rd., Roanoke, VA 24019
   Broadband fiber optics bus

ITT Telecom Products
   3100 Highwoods Blvd., Raleigh, NC 27604
   Multitenent PBX

JC Systems
   469 Valley Way, Milpitas, CA 95035
   JCS A-10 Broadband

Kantek
   1370 NE 20th, Suite J, Bellevue, WA 98005
   Kannet

Kaypro Corp.
   533 Stevens Ave., Solana Beach, CA 92075
   The Web

KEE, Inc.
   10739 Tucker St., Beltsville, MD 20705
   KEENET

Keybrook Business Systems
   2035 National Ave., Hayward, CA 94545
   Keybrook FileServer

Kurzweil Computer Products
   185 Albany St., Cambridge, MA 02139
   Scanning and Processing System with Ethernet

Lancore Technologies, Inc.
   31324 Via Colinas, Westlake Village, CA 91362
   PC Core Mass storage products for PC LANs

Lanier Business Products, Inc.
   1700 Chantily Dr., N.E., Atlanta, GA 30324
   Lanier Business System 5000 token passing LAN

Lee Data
   10206 Crosstown Cir., Eden Prairie, MN 55344
   COAX ELIMINATOR (for 3270 based products)

Litton Amecon
   5155 Calvert Rd., College Park, MD 20740
   UBITS (Universal Bus Information Transfer System)

Logic Replacement Technology
   9 Arkwright Rd., Reading Berks RG20EA U.K.
   Filtabyte Ethernet controllers

Logica VTS Ltd.
   86 Newman St., W1A 4SE, London U.K.
   Logica VTS Polynet (10 Mpbs)

Logical Business Machines
   1294 Hammerwood Ave., Sunnyvale, CA 94086
   L-NET

M/A-Com DCC
   11717 Exploration Ln., Germantown, MD 20767
   Cable Access Packet Communications system (CAPAC),
      INFOBUS

M/A-Com Linkabit Corp.
   10453 Roselle St., San Diego, CA 92121
   IDX-3000

Malco, A Microdot Co.
   306 Pasadena Ave., So. Pasadena, CA 91030
   Ethernet coax and transceiver cable supplier to Xerox

Martec International
   20 William St., Wellesley, MA 02181
   iBEX 7500 (multiprocessor network architecture)

MASSTOR Systems, Corp.
   5200 Great American Pky., Santa Clara, CA 95050
   MASSNET

Master Systems Ltd.
   100 Park St, Camberley, Surrey, U.K.
   Xibus

Maxicom
   17060 Dallas Pky., Suite 111, Dallas, TX 75248
   System/48

MDBS/Consumer Products
   Box 248, Lafayette, IN 47902
   LAN version of Knowledgeman and MDBS III

Metapath
   737 Lincoln Centre Dr., Foster City, CA 94004
   Robin Network

Metaphor Computer Systems
   2500 Garcia Ave., Mountain View, CA 94043
   Integrated Professional Information System w/Ethernet

Micom Systems, Inc.
   4100 Los Angeles Ave., Box 8100, Simi Valley, CA
      93062-8100
   Data PABX, voice/data multiplexing, multi-drop con-
      trollers

Micro/Sys
   1101 Grand Central Ave., Glendale, CA 91201-3010
   STD Bus Multidrop Coaxial Modem

Microcom, Inc.
   1400A Providence Hwy., Norwood, MA 02062
   Microcom Networking Protocol (MNP)

MicroRIM, Inc.
   1750 112th Ave. N.E., Bellevue, WA 98004
   MicroRIM Multi-user DB for PLAN 4000

Microserve, Inc.
   276 Fifth Ave., Suite 1005, New York, NY 10001
   Sysnet 2000

Microsystems, Inc.
175 Columbia St. W., Waterloo, Ontario N21 3B6 Canada
Waterloo Port OS/Development System with multiuser LAN capability

Millidyne Services, Inc.
9855 Carroll Canyon Rd., San Diego, CA 92131
LADD (Local Area Data Distribution)

Mitel
5400 Broken Sound Blvd. N.W., Boca Raton, FL 33065
SX 2000 (digital PBX), Superswitch

Modular Computer Systems, Inc.
1650 W. McNab Rd., Ft. Lauderdale, FL 33310
MAX NET

Molecular Computer
251 River Oaks Pkwy., San Jose, CA 95134
Infonet I, Infonet II

Mollard Systems Design
1210 South Bascom, San Jose, CA 95128
Power Line Network (PLN) for RS-232

Morrow
600 McCormick St., San Leandro, CA 94577
Morrow Network (PC-Bus and PC/NOS)

Mostek
1215 W. Crosby Rd., Carrollton, TX 75006
MK 68590 LANCE (Local Area Controller for Ethernet)

Motorola Semicond. Products
Box 20912, Phoenix, AZ 85032
VME Ethernet Controller Board

Multicomputer Ltd.
24 Windmil Rd., Brentford, Middlesex TW8 0QA U.K.
M200

MuSYS
1752 B. Langley, Irvine, CA 92714
NET/81, NET/82, S-100 Ethernet

National Semiconductor
675 Almanor Ave., M/S 15-236, Sunnyvale, CA 94086
LC-8545 Intelligent Communications Controller Board

National Semiconductor
2900 Semiconductor Dr., Santa Clara, CA 95051
Ethernet VLSI

NBI
P.O. Box 9001, Boulder, CO 80301
NBI NET

NCR
1700 South Patterson Blvd., Dayton, OH 45479
Personal Computer Network

NEC
5 Militia Dr., Lexington, MA 02173
N6770

NEC
8 Old Sod Farm Rd., Melville, NY 11747
NEAX 2400 IMS voice/data PBX

NEC Information Systems
5 Militia Dr., Lexington, MA 02173
Astra

Nestar Systems, Inc.
2585 Bayshore Rd., Palo Alto, CA 94303
PLAN Series

Network Development Corp.
Box 1785, West Chester, PA 19380
DNA (IBM PC and compatibles)

Network Research Corp.
1101 Colorado Ave., Santa Monica, CA 90401
Fusion (Ethernet and Unix)

Network Systems Corp.
7600 Boone Ave. No., Brooklyn Park, MN 55428
HYPERbus, HYPERchannel

Network Technology Ltd.
Unit 8 Suttone Park Ave., Reading Berkshire RG6 1AZ, U.K.
Automated telex system (ABCS)

Nixdorf Computer Corp.
169 Middlesex Tpk., Burlington, MA 01803
Ethernet support

Noakes Data Communications
3330 Stovall, Irving, TX 75067-4093
Envax 500—Intelligent box to interface a LCN to Telex/TWX/others

North Star Computers, Inc.
14440 Catalina St., San Leandro, CA 94577
NorthNet

Northern Telecom, Inc.
1001 E. Arapaho Rd., Richardson, TX 75081
SL-1 (integrated data/voice system); SL-100

Novell, Inc.
1170 N. Industrial Park Dr., Orem, UT 84057
NetWare

ONYX Systems, Inc.
73 East Trimble Rd., San Jose, CA 95131
C8002 local network, OMNINET

Open Systems
430 Oak Grove, Minneapolis, MN 55403
Software Fitness Program (accounting software) for 3Com, PCnet,

Orange Compuco, Inc.
1135 Deana Ct., Morgan Hill, CA 95035
ULCnet

Orbis Computers Ltd.
Fulbourn Rd., Cherry Hinton, Cambridge, U.K.
Orbis Cambridge Ring

Orchid Technology, Inc.
    487 Sinclair Frontage Rd., Milpitas, CA 95035
    PCnet

OSM Computer Corp.
    665 Clyde Ave., Mountain View, CA 94043
    PC-Link for OSM-PC

Paradyne Corp.
    8550 Ulmerton Rd., Largo, FL 33541
    PIXNET Communications System

PEP Elektronik Systeme GmbH
    Am Klosterwald 4, 8950 Kaufbeuren, West Germany
    PVDNET (network board for Eurobus systems)

Perex Inc.
    1798 Technology Dr., San Jose, CA 95110
    S2 S100 Ethernet Controller (Perinet)

Perkin-Elmer
    2 Crescent Pl., Ocean Port, NJ 07757
    Ethernet support

Perq Systems
    2600 Liberty Ave., Pittsburgh, PA 15230
    PERQ LINQ with Ethernet

Personal Micro Computers, Inc.
    475 Ellis, Mountain View, CA 94043
    the Downloader (TRS-80 compatible)

Philips Information Systems
    4040 McEwen, Dallas, TX 75234
    Philips Local Area Network

Phoenix Digital Corp.
    2315 N. 35th Ave., Phoenix, AZ 85009
    OPTONET

Phoenix Software Assoc. Ltd.
    P.O. Box 207, North Easton, MA 02356
    PAXNET networking software for 8086-based micros

Plexus Computers, Inc.
    2230 Martin Ave., Santa Clara, CA 95050
    UNIX file server for Ethernet

Power Line Communications, Inc.
    123 Industrial Ave., Williston, VT 05495
    Building energy automation

PRAGMATRONICS, Inc.
    2015 10th St., Boulder, CO 80302
    TIENET

Prime Computer, Inc.
    Prime Park, Natick, MA 01760
    PRIMENET, Ringnet

Prolink Corp.
    5757 Central Ave., Boulder, CO 80301
    Prolink system (on Proloop)

Proteon
    4 Tech Cir., Natick, MA 01760
    proNET (ring-based)

Quadram Corp.
    4355 Intl. Blvd., Norcross, GA 30093
    Quadnet I (300 Kbps), Quadnet IV (2 Mbps), Quadnet IX
    (10 Mbps proNET)

Quanta Microtique
    3332 Prospect St. NW #1, Washington, DC 20007
    QM10 Advanced Communications Controller (TCP/IP)

Quic-n-easi Products, Inc.
    136 Granite Hill Ct., Langhorne, PA 19047
    Q-PRO 4 (database for PC LANs)

Quorom Computers
    Polygon House, Commercial Rd., Southhampton, S01
    OGG U.K.
    Q-LAN (CP/M-based)

Racal Data Comms Group
    Richmond Ct., 309 Fleet Rd., Fleet, Hants, U.K.
    Cambridge Ring

Racal-Milgo
    8600 N.W. 41st St., Miami, FL 33166
    PLANET

Radionics
    1800 Abbott St., Salinas, CA 93901
    Cable modem series

Raycom Systems
    6395 Gunpark Dr., Boulder, CO 80301
    ARCNET active hub with fiber optics

Raytheon Data Systems Co.
    2540 Mission College Blvd. #101, Santa Clara, CA
    95050
    RAYNET

Real Time Developments Ltd.
    Lynchford Hse, Lynchford Ln., Farnborough, Hants
    GU14 6JA U.K.
    Clearway (RS-232 ring box), Clearway Gateway

Ridge Computers
    2451 Mission College Blvd., Santa Clara, CA 95054
    Ridge 32 with Ethernet

ROLM
    4900 Old Ironsides Dr., Santa Clara, CA 95050
    CBX-II Integrated voice/data PBX

Santa Clara Systems
    1860 Hartog Dr., San Jose, CA 95131
    PCterminal for PCnet

Science Applications, Inc.
    2109 W. Clinton Ave., Suite 800, Huntsville, AL 35805
    Q-NET; Q-Box; SAID Bus

Scientific-Atlanta, Inc.
    3845 Pleasantdale Rd., Atlanta, GA 30340
    Broadband amplifiers

SDS
    344 Main St., Venice, CA 90291
    SDSNET

SDSystems, Inc.
    Box 28810, Dallas, TX 75228
    MARS/NET

Seel Ltd., 3 Young Square
    Brucefield Industrial Park, Livingston, W Lothian EH54
        9BJ U.K.
    Transring 3000

Seeq Inc.
    1849 Fortune Dr., San Jose, CA 95131
    8001 Ethernet data-link controller chip

Seimac Ltd.
    1378 Bedford Hwy., Bedford, Nova Scotia B4A 1E2
        Canada
    Scientific Data Highway

Seiscor
    P.O. Box 1590, Tulsa, OK 74102
    Panda II voice/data PBX

Sension Scientific Ltd.
    Denton Dr. Industrial Estate, Manchester Rd, Northwich
        CW9 7LU U.K.
    Ethernet products

Siecor FiberLAN
    P.O. Box 12726, Research Triangle Park, NC 27709
    FiberLAN

Siemens
    186 Wood Ave. South, Iselin, NJ 08830
    Ethernet workstations in conjunction with Xerox

Siemens
    5500 Broken Sound Blvd., Boca Raton, FL 33431
    Saturn II & III integrated voice/data PBX

Silicon Graphics Systems
    630 Clyde St., Mountain View, CA 94043
    IRIS (imaging workstation with Ethernet option)

SMT, Inc.
    1145 Linda Vista Dr., #109, San Marcos, CA 92069
    Data aquisition and process control local network for IBM
        PC

SoftCraft, Inc.
    P.O. Box 9802 #590, Austin, TX 78766
    Btrieve/N B-tree file management system for PC local
        networks

SofTech Microsystems
    16885 West Bernardo Dr., San Diego, CA 92127
    Liaison

Software Connections
    2041 Mission College Blvd., Santa Clara, CA 95054
    LAN: DATASTORE, LAN: DATACORE, LAN: Mail
        Monitor, The Classroom

Software Dynamics
    2111 W. Crescent, Suite G, Anaheim, CA 92801
    SDNET (6800/6809 based)

Software Sorcery
    7927 Jones Branch Dr., Suite 400, McLean, VA 22102
    Magus—Electronic mail for Omninet

Southern New England Telco
    Donecor Sys. Div, 367 Orange St., New Haven, CT
        06511
    Sonecor System 2001 voice/data PBX

Spartacus Computers, Inc.
    5 Oak Park Dr., Bedford, MA 01720
    KNET

Standard Data
    1500 N.W. 62 St., Suite 508, Fort Lauderdale, FL 33309
    STANDARD-NET for IBM PC

Standard Engineering
    44800 Industrial Dr., Fremont, CA 94538
    Microlink

Standard Microsystems
    35 Marcus Blvd., Hauppauge, NY 11788
    COM 9026 (Datapoint RIM chip), COM 9032 (trans-
        ceiver), ARCS100 (ARC to S-100)

Star Technologies
    Studebaker, Irvine, CA 92714
    Star*Net (ARCNET for Nova emulation board in IBM
        PC)

Stratus Computer, Inc.
    17-19 Strathmore Rd., Natick, MA 01760
    STRATALINK, Stratus-32

Sun Microsystems
    2550 Garcia Ave., Mountain View, CA 94043
    Sun workstation with Ethernet

Sunol Systems
    1072 Serpentine Ln., Pleasanton, CA 94556
    SUN*MAC (Macintosh), SUN*NET (IBM PC, Apple II,
        others)

Support Systems Intl.
    150 S. Second St. at Ohio, Richmond, VA 94801
    Accessories for local networking products

SWI International Systems
    7741 East Gray Rd., Suite 2, Scottsdale, AZ 85260
    PRO-NET

Sybiotic Computer Systems Ltd.
    Duroma House, 32 Elmwood Rd., Croydon, Surrey CR9
        2TX U.K.
    Symbnet (Apple II, IIc, III, Macintosh)

Sydis, Inc.
    4340 Stevens Creek Blvd., San Jose, CA 95129
    VoiceStation

Symbolics, Inc.
    9600 DeSoto Ave., P.O. Box 705, Chatsworth, CA
        91311
    3600 Lisp-based processing system with Ethernet hard-
        ware

Syntax
6642 S. 193rd Pl., Kent, WA 98032
VAX/VMS Ethernet Server

Syntrex
246 Industrial Way East, Eatontown, NJ 07724
SYNNET

System Development Corp.
2500 Colorado Ave., Santa Monica, CA 90406
MIL/INT (broadband with TCP/IP protocols)

Systems Center, Inc.
2988 Campus Dr., San Mateo, CA 94403
SNA gateway for Omninet

Systems Technology Corp.
727 Airport Blvd., Ann Arbor, MI 48104
ES/4000 (building automation system); 'express bus'

Sytek
1225 Charleston Rd., Mountain View, CA 94043
LocalNet/20

T-Bar, Inc.
141 Danbury Rd., P.O. Box T, Wilton, CT 06897
Virtual Switch Matrix (VSM)

Tandem Computers, Inc.
19333 Vallco Pkwy., Cupertino, CA 95014
Tandem Hyper Link (THL) for HYPERchannel

Tandy Corp.
1800 One Tandy Center, Fort Worth, TX 76102
Network 2 (ARCNET for TRS-80 Model II)

Tangent Technologies
5720 Peachtree Pkwy., # 100, Norcross, GA 30092
ThinkLink

TCL
2066B Walsh Ave., Santa Clara, CA 95050
Plug Compatible Ethernet (PCE) transceiver

TCS Software
3209 Fondren Rd., Houston, TX 77063
QUICK*NET (TCS TOTAL ACCOUNTING SYSTEM
for 3Com EtherSeries)

Technitrol
1952 E. Allegheny Ave., Philadelphia, PA 19134
Manchester encoder/decoder modules

Tecmar
6225 Cochran Rd., Cleveland, OH 44139
Elan

Tektronix, Inc.
P.O. Box 500, D-S 53-077, Beaverton, OR 97077
IEEE-802 related products (under development)

Telco Research Corp.
1818 Division St., Nashville, TN 37203
Local Network Software Tools

Televideo, Inc.
1170 Morse Ave., Sunnyvale, CA 94086
MMMOST

Tellabs, Inc.
4951 Indiana Ave., Lisle, IL 60532
310 Datavoice System

Teltone Corp.
10801 120th NE, Kirkland, WA 98033
DCS-2 Data Carrier System (for PABX systems); transmitter

Texas Instruments
Data Systems Group, Box 402430, H-691, Dallas, TX 75240
EtherSeries for TI Professional

Texas Instruments, Inc.
P.O. Box 1443 M/S 6405, Houston, TX 77001
Token ring VLSI (in conj. with IBM)

Thomas & Betts
920 Rt. 202, Raritan, NJ 08869
Versa-Trak (flat coax)

Thomson-CSF, West Coast Op.
360 N Sepulveda Blvd., Suite 2080, El Segundo, CA 90204
Interfaces to connect SEMS equipment to Ethernet

Tigan Communications, Inc.
4020 Fabian Way, Palo Alto, CA 94303
LAN product developers

TIME Office Computers
99 Mount St., North Sydney NSW 2060 Australia
E-LAN

Timeplex, Inc.
One Communications Plaza, Rochelle Park, NJ 07662
SWITCHING MICROPLEX (distibuted data switching system)

Times Fiber Communications
RF Cable Products Division, Box 384, Wallingford, CT 06492
Ethernet Coax

Toltec
24 Thompson's La., Cambridge CB5 8AQ U.K.
DataRing

Tominy, Inc.
4221 Malsbary Rd., Bldg. One, Cincinnati, OH 45242
DATA BASE-PLUS for IBM PCs on Omninet

Tri-Data Corp.
505 East Middlefield Rd., Mountain View, CA 94043
Netway

Trinity Computing Systems
1020 Holcombe Blvd., Suite 408, Houston, TX 77030
CardioNet

Trompeter Electronics, Inc.
  8963 Comanche Ave., Chatsworth, CA 91311
  Local network passive components (cable, connectors)

TRW
  One Space Park, Redondo Beach, CA 90278
  TRW Concept 2000

U-Microcomputers Ltd.
  Winstanley Industrial Estate, Long Ln., Warrington,
    Cheshire, U.K.
  U-NET for BBC micro

Ungermann-Bass, Inc.
  2560 Mission College Blvd., Santa Clara, CA 95050
  Net/One, CMX

United Technologies, Lexar Div
  31829 West La Tienda Dr., Westlake Village, CA 91362
  Lexar Business Exchange (LBX)

Unlimited Processing, Inc.
  8382 Baymeadows Rd., Suite 8, Jacksonville, FL 32216
  INFORMA (multi-user DB for Microsoft Networks and
    IBM PC Network)

UVEON Computer Systems, Inc.
  300 S. Jackson St., Suite 250, Denver, CO 80209
  Optimum DBMS for PC local networks

Valmet, Inc.
  7 Westchester Plaza, Elmsford, NY 10523
  Dataway (coaxial computer linking system)

Valtec Corp.
  99 Hartwell St., West Boylston, MA 01583
  Fiber optic data transmission links

Vector Graphic, Inc.
  500 N. Ventu Park Rd., Thousand Oaks, CA 91320
  LINC

Versatec
  2710 Walsh Ave., Santa Clara, CA 95051
  Expert Ethernet PCB design workstations

Vertec
  Box 1116, 8079 N. Lake Blvd., Kings Beach, CA 95719
  VAAS (insurance program for Omninet)

ViaNetix
  5766 Central Ave., Boulder, CO 80301
  Vianet

Victor Technologies, Inc.
  380 El Pueblo Rd., Scotts Valley, CA 95066
  Victor Server Network

Victory Computer Systems, Inc.
  2055 Gateway Pl., Suite 300, San Jose, CA 95110
  The FACTOR with Ethernet option

VisiCorp
  2895 Zanker Rd., San Jose, CA 95134
  VisiOn for Ethernet

Vitalink Communications
  1350 Charleston Rd., Mountain View, CA 94043
  TransLAN (satellite link for DECnet)

VLSI Networks, Inc.
  2631 Manhattan Beach Blvd., Redondo Beach, CA
    90278
  1553—NET (IBM PC and S-100)

Wang Laboratories, Inc.
  1 Industrial Way, Lowell, MA 01851
  WangNet

Western Digital Corporation
  2445 McCabe Way, Irvine, CA 92714
  PC-LAN and WD2840 token-passing
  –controller chip

Western Telematic, Inc.
  2435 S. Anne St., Santa Ana, CA 92704
  SS-8

Winsource, Inc.
  5 Northway Lane N., Latham, NY 12101
  WINNET

XCOMP
  3554 Ruffin Rd., San Diego, CA 92123
  X-NET

Xerox Office Systems Div.
  3333 Coyote Hill Rd., Palo Alto, CA 94304
  Ethernet, Star work station, 820, 8000 Network System

Xionics
  68 Oxford St., W1N 9LA, London, W1N 9LA U.K.
  XINET

Xyplex
  Domino Dr., Concord, MA 01742
  The XYPLEX System

Zaisan, Inc.
  13910 Champion Forest Dr., Houston, TX 77069
  ES-1 voice/data workstation

Zeda Computer Intl. Ltd.
  1662 West 820 North, Provo, UT 84601
  INFINET

Zenith Radio
  1000 Milwaukee Ave., Glenview, IL 60025
  Local Area Network Driver (LAND) hybrid module

Zeta Laboratories
  3265 Scott Blvd., Santa Clara, CA 95051
  CATV modems

Zilog, Inc.
  1315 Dell Ave., Campbell, CA 95008
  Second source for AMD Ethernet VLSI

Ztel
  181 Ballavdvale St., Wilmington, MA 01810
  PNX (Private Network Exchange)